Alan Turing: Life and Legacy of a Great Thinker

Springer
Berlin
Heidelberg
New York
Hong Kong
London
Milan
Paris
Tokyo

Christof Teuscher (Ed.)

Alan Turing:
Life and Legacy
of a Great Thinker

Foreword by Douglas Hofstadter

With 77 Figures and 4 Tables

 Springer

Christof Teuscher

Swiss Federal Institute of Technology Lausanne (EPFL)
Logic Systems Laboratory, EPFL-IC-LSL
1015 Lausanne
Switzerland

christof@teuscher.ch
http://www.teuscher.ch/christof

Library of Congress Cataloging-in-Publication Data applied for

Die Deutsche Bibliothek - CIP-Einheitsaufnahme
Bibliographic information published by Die Deutsche Bibliothek
Die Deutsche Bibliothek lists this publication in the Deutsche
Nationalbibliografie; detailed bibliographic data is available in the
Internet at <http://dnb.ddb.de>.

ACM Subject Classification (1998): A.0, F, E.3, I.2

ISBN 3-540-20020-7 Springer-Verlag Berlin Heidelberg New York

Springer-Verlag is a part of Springer Science+Business Media
springeronline.com

© Springer-Verlag Berlin Heidelberg 2004
Printed in Germany

The use of designations, trademarks, etc. in this publication does not imply,
even in the absence of a specific statement, that such names are exempt from
the relevant protective laws and regulations and therefore free for general use.

Cover Design: KünkelLopka, Heidelberg
Typesetting: Computer to film by author´s data
Printing: Strauss Offsetdruck, Mörlenbach
Binding: J. Schäffer, Grünstadt

Printed on acid-free paper   45/3142PS 5 4 3 2 1 0

Alan Mathison Turing (1912–1954)
© By courtesy of the National Portrait Gallery, London

ALAN TURING, 1912-1954

The Universal Turing Machine
© Jin Wicked, 2002, jinwicked.com

Foreword

In 1950, Alan Turing expressed the following provocative sentiment: "We may hope that machines will eventually compete with men in all purely intellectual fields." While his choice of the noun "men" may dismay us, at the beginning of the 21st century we know of course that for Turing, as for everyone back in those days, women were considered members (at least in a certain limited sense) of the class called "men," and so, though the word may make our eyebrows (if not our hackles) rise a little, we should not make too big a fuss over it.

What might give us more pause for thought, however, after this first stumble, is the actual hope that Turing expressed: that machines would come to be our rivals in all "purely intellectual" fields. Presumably this includes all the sciences, all the arts, all games, all of humor, all of philosophy, and much, much more. If there is any doubt on that score, one need merely read the two short dialogue snippets that he included in the same article, where one sees that a subject (human or machine, one never knows) under interrogation in the Turing Test is quizzed on such topics as poetry, chess, and mathematics, and passes with flying colors.

*

Did Alan Turing really delight in the thought that machines such as he himself had designed would one day write complex and powerful plays, compose heart-rending pieces of music, invent uproarious jokes, discover fundamental new laws of nature, invent new branches of mathematics, profoundly grapple with eternal riddles about beauty, morality, and mortality — and so forth and so on? Did Alan Turing actually suppose that machines might come to be our intellectual rivals but would stop improving precisely at that delicate point? Did he suppose that they might just barely come up to our level but never surpass it? Was Alan Turing susceptible to the same simplistic illusion as so many great chess players were, before Deep Blue knocked Gary Kasparov for a loop? Did Alan Turing really think that the intelligence level of human geniuses was essentially a dream-like asymptotic goal for machines rather than an arbitrary, uninteresting number that would turn out to be trivially surpassable as machines swooped up from zero, picking up the pace all the while as they grew ever cleverer?

Did Alan Turing truly hope, or truly believe, that his own level of intelligence — a level that most of us consider wondrously insightful — would soon be merely a quaint relic, something that machines would look back on with amusement as they recalled "the old days" when human beings were once their intellectual superiors? Did Alan Turing believe that one day machine intelligence would be to human intelligence as human intelligence is to dog intelligence or even ant intelligence? Did Alan Turing in fact yearn for that day to arrive?

I pose this series of leading questions but, of course, despite what he wrote, I don't have the foggiest idea what Alan Turing really hoped. I have to wonder if he carefully considered this idea of our being completely eclipsed in rather short order. After all, his belief was that by the end of the 20th century, machines would fool intelligent interrogators roughly half the time in the Turing Test — so where did he think that trend would be pointing? Did he really think it was something not to worry about at all?

There are those today who forecast that computer intelligence will easily outflank human intelligence within just a few decades, leaving "us" behind in the dust. Or have I got it right? Will "we" be up there *with* them? Or rather, will we be up there *in* them? In short, will *we* be none other than *they*? In other words, will the English-language pronoun "we" have shifted meaning, so that it refers to the most advanced of all English speakers — namely, those who inherited the English language from "us" and thereby earned the right to us-urp the term from "us"? Would Alan Turing say that nothing essential would be lost in the passage from carbon-based minds and souls to silicon-based minds and souls (or to whatever medium won the evolutionary race to become the substrate for the highest level of intelligence)?

I find it perplexing that someone so insightful would express the *hope* to be surpassed by alien entities. On the other hand, I find it wonderfully flexible and open-minded of Alan Turing to express such a strange desire.

What kind of a human being would utter such a hope? It would have to be someone fascinated by the question of what a mind is, someone fascinated by the fact that minds are natural consequences of very simple physical processes taking place in highly complex physical structures. Alan Turing was indeed fascinated by the consequences of very simple processes taking place in complex structures; after all, the machines that he defined in order to specify the nature of computing — what we now call "Turing machines" — are as barebones in their processes as one could imagine. Alan Turing saw, though, that since the properties of the natural numbers could be studied by writing 1's and 0's on a long tape, there was in principle no limit to the complexity of structures that could be created in his machines. And this in turn led him to the idea of a "universal" machine — one that, given a description of any other machine plus that machine's input, could emulate the other machine acting on that input.

From emulation to empathy — for adult human minds are, in a certain sense, universal Turing machines, and the other Turing machines that we spend most of our lives emulating are also universal Turing machines (which in turn are emulating yet other universal Turing machines, and on and on ...). Our souls are built up in this highly recursive act of having empathy for beings who are empathetic to other beings who feel for yet others, and so on — with the whole thing twisting back on itself with a vengeance, a vengeance commonly known by the rather short word spelled "I". This vast network of interpenetrating empathies is strikingly like the Buddhist image of Indra's Net — a galaxy of glass beads floating throughout space, each of which reflects all the others, including the others' reflections of yet others, and so on, ad indranetum.

I recall one time standing right underneath two very tall television towers and marveling at their height and at the fact that they were using Maxwell's equations to send out incredibly intricate visual and linguistic messages to thousands of distant sentient beings — when all of a sudden I was brought up short by the realization that nearly everything being beamed out from the very high tips of those marvelously thin metal towers was just soap operas and advertisements.

This disappointed me enormously at first, since I was thinking lofty thoughts, and I was imagining that similarly lofty thoughts were being beamed out to the audiences. But after reflecting on this further, I realized that soap operas, though they may seem trivial and stupid to me, are in fact deeply complex expressions of what it is to be human — and, in fact, so are advertisements. Indeed, advertisements are closely related to the battles for dominance that constitute the essence of evolution, thanks to which our brains, minds, and souls exist. And soap operas are all about our sets of ideas and how we reflect other people inside ourselves, and how they reflect us, and how we reflect their reflections, and vice versa, and so on, forever.

Thus, in the end, soap operas, though they are not philosophy or physics, are very deep representations of what it is to be alive and to have a mind. And this huge entanglement with other human beings imprints on each one of us a unique identity, a unique personal signature. Alan Turing, like every other sentient machine belonging to the species *Homo soapiens soapiens*, was deeply though imperfectly mirrored in hundreds of other such machines; moreover, inside the physical structures of his brain — in the metaphorical 1's and 0's printed on his metaphorical Turing-machine tape — he mirrored hundreds of such machines, also imperfectly though deeply.

And out of these imperfect, partial mirrorings came powerful yearnings — yearnings to talk, to joke, to play, to share, to touch. Out of those multiple yearnings came dangerous liaisons, for Alan Turing was abnormal with respect to the norms of his society. The types of universal machines that he most enjoyed mirroring, and the universal machines in which he most deeply yearned to be mirrored, were machines of his own genus — the M genus as opposed to the F genus. Normal, standard M machines yearned most highly to mirror F machines, and normal, standard F machines yearned most highly to mirror M machines — but there were some mutated machines that went for others of their own genus, and this type of yearning, as perceived by the society of machines, was considered improper and deserving of punishment. Alan Turing thus came to suffer for his dangerous liaisons that deviated from the norm.

What does a universal Turing machine do when it comes to realize that all Turing machines, no matter how powerful, must sooner or later grind to a final halt, even if their software would have them go into an infinite repetitive loop or even embark on an infinitely long never-looping process? Does such a machine close its eyes to that fact and relish its computations for as long as its physical circuits will allow? Or does such a machine waste billions upon billions of cycles bemoaning its unjust fate? Or does such a machine immerse itself in soap operas and advertisements in order to distract itself from its inexorable final destiny? Or does such a machine perchance dream of putting an end to its own computations, and wonder if or when it might do so?

Snow White partook of a poisoned apple, and Alan Turing followed suit; his computations, brilliant though they were, soon ground to a total, final halt. He was a human being whose complexity and whose insight surpassed those of nearly all other human beings, and yet he too succumbed to the same types of problems as befall the most ordinary saps in the most banal of soap operas. Indeed, what is beamed from those tall television antennas is even more complex, in its own way, than James Clerk Maxwell's unified equations of electromagnetism, or Alan Mathison Turing's resolution of the riddle of the halting problem, or Andrew Wiles' proof of Fermat's last theorem, or Ludwig van Beethoven's final few string quartets.

Fully to fathom even one other human being is far beyond our intellectual capacity — indeed, fully to fathom even one's own self is an idea that quickly leads to absurdities and paradoxes. This fact Alan Turing understood more deeply than nearly anyone ever has, for it constitutes the crux of his work on the halting problem.

*

In this volume are collected the musings of a couple of dozen human beings who have been inspired by Alan Turing — who have each emulated, in some partial and imperfect fashion, the mind and soul of Alan Turing in their own minds and souls. What would Alan Turing think of these models we have made of him in our heads? Would he throw back his head and laugh his famous raucous laugh? Would he be flattered? Would he be impressed or depressed by what some have made of his ideas? Would he even recognize his own ideas in the new guises in which they have been cast?

It is sad that we shall never know anything of the answers to these riddles, but we must not brood over it too long. Instead we should savor the musings that Alan Turing inspired in some of today's brightest minds, for it is in those musings, occasionally a little bit muddied but often sparklingly bright, that his spirit lives on, in a partial and imperfect fashion.

August 2003   Douglas Hofstadter
                                                    Indiana University

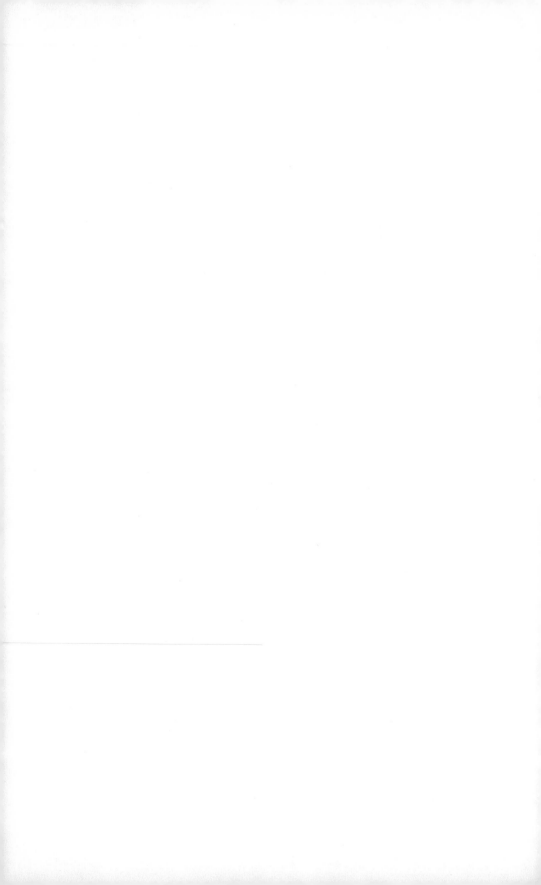

Preface

It was in September 2001 when I suddenly realized that Alan Mathison Turing would have celebrated the anniversary of his 90th birthday on June 23, 2002. Out of this sudden flash of thought originated — after a great deal of work of course — the Turing Day and ultimately the volume you hold in your hands.

The Turing Day

The Turing Day[1] (see also [1]) was intended to commemorate the anniversary of Alan Mathison Turing's 90th birthday, to revisit his seminal contributions to computer science, artificial intelligence, biology, cryptology, and many other fields, but also to delineate the importance of Turing's fundamental work for contemporary and future trends in science and society. The workshop consisted in a series of invited talks given by internationally renowned experts in the field. A photo of the Turing Day speakers is reproduced in Fig. 1.

Daniel Mange, director of the Logic Systems Laboratory at the Swiss Federal Institute of Technology in Lausanne, and organizer of the sui generis von Neumann Day[2] in 1997, delivered the Turing Day's inaugural address, which shall be reprinted here.

Ladies and Gentlemen, Dear Colleagues, Dear Friends,

On the 23rd of June of this year, Alan Turing would have been 90 years old. Nowadays, 90 is not an uncommon age. If Law in the 1950s had been different, Alan Turing could have been among us today.

Respecting Turing's choice, we organized this conference without his physical presence. But his spirit will inspire all of us during this very special day.

---

[1] *Turing Day: Computing Science 90 Years from the Birth of Alan Mathison Turing,* EPFL, Lausanne, June 28, 2002, http://www.teuscher.ch/turingday.

[2] *Von Neumann Day: Biological Inspiration in Computer Science 40 Years from the Death of John von Neumann,* EPFL, Lausanne, July 25, 1997, http://lslwww.epfl.ch/pages/events/neumann97.

Fig. 1. The Turing Day speakers (from left to right): Martin Davis, Gianluca Tempesti, Christof Teuscher, Jonathan Swinton, B. Jack Copeland, Tony Sale, Daniel Mange, and Andrew Hodges. Douglas Hofstadter was, unfortunately, absent from this early-morning roll-call. Andrew Hodges wears a Turing '90 T-shirt left over from the Turing 1990 conference at Sussex University (© Alain Herzog, EPFL)

Those of you who attended our von Neumann Day, five years ago, have already observed the strange similarities between Turing's and von Neumann's scientific careers despite their completely different social behaviors: while Alan Turing was a romantic and lonesome talent, John von Neumann enjoyed worldly pleasures. Turing's and von Neumann's major contributions may be divided into three periods of their lives: the prewar, war, and postwar periods, or using another perspective, the mathematical, the computational, and the biological periods.

In 1936, Alan Turing conceived the fundamental theories of computer science while proposing his abstract machine, the Turing machine. During the same period, John von Neumann addressed mathematical theories such as game theory, the logic foundation of mathematics, and quantum mechanics.

During World War II, Turing played a major role at Bletchley Park, breaking the German Enigma code as a member of a top-secret British operation. At the same time, von Neumann began to contribute increasingly to the war effort, covering the theory of detonation, aerodynamics, and atomic bombs. Both men were naturally led to face a huge number of calculations, so that they were both involved in the design and the use of the first programmable electronic computers: the Colossus, followed by the Automatic Computing Engine, designed by Alan Turing, the EDVAC (Electronic Discrete Variable

Arithmetic Computer) machine, followed by the computer designed by John von Neumann at the Institute for Advanced Studies.

As a passionate botanist Alan Turing threw himself into the computer simulation of plant growth to bring an original contribution to the understanding of the morphology of living organisms. John von Neumann proposed at the same time the first computational approach to the generation of lifelike behavior; and quite naturally, his self-replicating automaton was built around a universal Turing machine.

According to Bletchley Park's witnesses, Alan Turing was "The most brilliant mind of his time," or "The right man, at the right time, at the right place."

Perhaps the most intriguing question about Turing is the one addressed at the end of our program by Andrew Hodges: "What would Turing have done after 1954?"

In my mind, it's crystal clear: Turing would have been fascinated by the mysterious DNA double helix, would have considered the genome as a secret message, and deciphered it by using his favorite weapon, an artificial neural network.

I'd like to warmly thank all our distinguished speakers; many of them didn't hesitate to come from the other side of the world!

The organization of our Turing Day was made possible thanks to our generous sponsors. I'd like to express my deepest gratitude to the Cogito Foundation (Dr. Simon and Dr. Christof Aegerter), the Migros Culture Percentage (Mr. Dominik Landwehr), Dr. Charles Maillefer, and Elsevier Science (Mrs. Betsy Lightfoot). The collaboration of Bolo's Computer Museum (Mr. Yves Bolognini and Edouard Forler), of Dr. Frode Weierud (for presenting the Enigma machine), and of EPFL staff (Service de presse et information, Service audiovisuel, Atelier de reprographie) is warmly acknowledged.

Last, but not least, it's my pleasure to point out the outstanding organizer's talent of Christof Teuscher, the creative entrepreneur of the Turing Day, and to thank him for his commitment.

Thank you for your participation and have a great Turing Day!

June 28, 2002   Daniel Mange
                                              Logic Systems Laboratory
                    Swiss Federal Institute of Technology, Lausanne

---

The Turing Day brought together an international and very heterogeneous audience exceeding 250 participants, all with very different areas of interest and expertise — reaching from a dentist enthused by Turing since his childhood to an archaeologist fascinated by the Enigma machine. The conference has shown that an important number of topics led or inspired by Turing continue to feed passionate scientific debates and that a number of questions remain unsolved. As the day concluded, editing a festschrift in memory of Alan Turing's 90th birthday seemed almost a corollary.

About this Book

Alan Turing: Life and Legacy of a Great Thinker contains a comprehensive collection of essays with the goal to shed light on Alan Turing, his thoughts, his life, and his rich legacy. I am of course very lucky that all Turing Day speakers contributed to this volume and that many other experts could be convinced to submit a chapter as well. All contributions have been written for the general scientific reader, should be fairly self-contained, and hence be readable by non-specialists as well.

This book is divided into several parts that shall be briefly described in the following.

Part 1 is dedicated to Turing's life, thought, and personality in general, and starts with an introductory biography, specially contributed by Turing's biographer Andrew Hodges for this volume.

The second chapter is a fairly unconventional contribution for a rather technical book. Valeria Patera's play "Alan's Apple," presents as an enigma, the life, death and destiny of Alan Turing.

Andrew Hodges asks in his second contribution "What would Alan Turing have done after 1954?," an obviously only hypothetically answerable question. Hodges surveys Turing's late interests and incomplete threads, and also disputes the controversial claims that Turing anticipated the agenda of so-called "hypercomputing," a topic that shall be further discussed in Part 2 of this volume.

Daniela Cerqui shows that the two main tendencies in today's "information society," an increasing valorization of mind, information, and more generally immaterial elements, as opposed to body and matter, and a strong tendency to replace everything human with artificial elements, were already present in Turing's thought as early as the 1940s. Her contribution sheds light on the links between the man, the mathematician, and our present society.

Part 2 begins with a survey by Michael Beeson on the mechanization of mathematics, which refers to the use of computers to find, or to help find, mathematical proofs. While Turing has shown that a complete reduction of mathematics to computation is impossible, the next three chapters of Part 2 focus on a fairly controversial field of research on algorithms and machines claimed to compute beyond the computational limit of Turing machines. In his survey on hypercomputation, Mike Stannett describes various approaches to constructing hypercomputational machines, while Eugene Eberbach, Dina Goldin, and Peter Wegner present new *super-Turing* models of computation — all basically inspired by Turing's ideas — which they claim are more appropriate for today's interactive, networked and embedded computing systems.

The practicality of physical hypercomputation has, in fact, been questioned by several researchers. Most hypercomputer models involve analog computation with infinite precision or try to compute the "infinite" in finite time. The last chapter on this much debated field comes from Martin Davis, who provides a first critical essay and concludes that none of the hypercomputational models attains non-computable outputs unless the inputs are also permitted to be non-computable.

Many a hypercomputationalist placed or still places a lot of hope in the field of quantum computers. Christopher G. Timpson argues in his chapter against Deutsch's claim that a physical principle, the Turing principle, underlies the famous Church-Turing hypothesis.

Hector Fabio Restrepo, Gianluca Tempesti and Daniel Mange bring us back down to earth from the theoretical realms of hypercomputers and describe a biologically inspired hardware architecture endowed with universal computational capabilities. The novel multicellular architecture is robust and able to self-repair and to self-replicate.

In the last chapter of Part 2, Andrew J. Wells considers the impact of the Turing machine on the development of theories in cognitive science. Turing's work shows — as Andrew argues — that it is highly profitable to study the mind from an ecological perspective, i.e., to study the organisms in relation to their environments.

Part 3 is about artificial intelligence and the famous Turing test. The opening shot is provided by philosopher Daniel C. Dennett's seminal essay "Can Machines Think?" His main goal was to show how huge the task posed by the Turing Test is, and hence how unlikely it is that any computer will ever pass it. Dennett's philosophical conclusion is that we could safely ascribe the term "intelligence" to any computer that actually passed the Turing test.

In their chapter, B. Jack Copeland and Diane Proudfoot first discuss Turing's role in the history of the computer and in the early stage of artificial intelligence. They further provide interesting arguments on why various objections to the Turing test fail.

Helmut Schnelle's chapter entitled "Note on Enjoying Strawberries with Cream, Making Mistakes, and Other Idiotic Features," is an inventive contribution on algorithms, computation, and human and machine intelligence with reference to thoughts of von Neumann and Weyl, Carnap and Bar-Hillel, and, finally, Gödel and Wang.

Diane Proudfoot illuminates in her essay on "Robots and Rule-Following" the overlap and differences between Turing's and Wittgenstein's work in both the philosophy of mathematics and the philosophy of artificial intelligence.

She shows, for example, that Wittgenstein's externalist analysis of psychological capacities entails that future "artificially intelligent" computers and robots will not use language, possess concepts, or reason.

This part is concluded by a contribution from the visionary Ray Kurzweil, winner of the 1999 National Medal of Technology, the highest honor in technology in the US. Ray guides us through the realms of exponential technical change and argues that within a few decades machine intelligence will surpass human intelligence, leading to *The Singularity*, a technological change so rapid and profound it will represent a rupture in the fabric of human history. Ray's chapter delineates a possible — certainly fairly speculative — future of machine intelligence, which has its origin in the work of Alan Turing.

Part 4 discloses some secrets of the famous Enigma ciphering machine, which played a crucial role in the Second World War and has meanwhile found its way into many thrillers and films. This part depicts Alan Turing's work and influence during the Second World War and illuminates his decisive role in the process of breaking the Enigma code.

Elisabeth Rakus-Andersson provides an essay on the Polish brains behind the breaking of the Enigma code before and during the Second World War, whereas Tony Sale reports on Alan Turing's work at Bletchley Park during the war. Sale's chapter further contains many technical details on the functioning of the Engima machines.

Alan Turing's visit to the US Navy Cryptanalytic Section and the US Army Signal Security Agency during the winter of 1942–1943 is presented in detail in Lee A. Gladwin's chapter. Turing's visit was a significant milestone in the collaboration between the Government Code and Cypher School at Bletchley Park and its US counterparts to develop Army and Navy versions of the British Bombe and additional aids to defeat Enigma. Gladwin concludes that "Alan Turing's visit to America that winter of 1942–1943 began with Enigma and ended in mystery."

Part 5 contains Jonathan Swinton's chapter on Turing's last, almost lost, somehow obscure, and ill-understood work on Fibonacci phyllotaxis. Swinton discusses the evidence that Turing had developed a number of key ideas close to modern thinking, and tantalizing hints that he came very close to a mathematical explanation of how the daisy grows into its typical patterns.

The last chapter is the editor's one on Turing's almost forgotten connectionist ideas. Most aspects of Turing's "unorganized machines" are illustrated, including several extensions, as well as a toy application of the "genetical search" Turing proposed.

Acknowledgments

Editing this book would certainly not have been possible without the enormous help of numerous people. I am very grateful to all friends who strongly encouraged and morally supported me.

The sweetest and most special thanks go to my most beloved wife, Ursina, who — as always — uncompromisingly and constantly supported me every day and night!

I am deeply indebted to all contributors to this volume for their commitment and their confidence in the process of editing this volume.

I am very grateful to all the friends and colleagues who read early portions of the manuscript and helped to greatly improve it through many thoughtful discussions.

My warmest thanks to Pierre-André Mudry, Kaspar Schiess, Abel Villca, and Arnaud Zufferey who did a magnificent job in helping me edit and typeset this book in LaTeX!

I am very grateful to Daniel Mange, director of the Logic Systems Laboratory at the Swiss Federal Institute of Technology in Lausanne, who made available material, moral and intellectual support from the beginning, from when the idea of the Turing Day came up to the completion of this book.

I wish to thank wholeheartedly all members of the Logic Systems Laboratory at the Swiss Federal Institute of Technology in Lausanne for making my stay in the lab the most enjoyable and rewarding experience.

I am indebted to my editors, Ursula Barth and Alfred Hofmann of Springer-Verlag, for their suggestions and help that made this book possible.

Lausanne, September 2003

Christof Teuscher
christof@teuscher.ch
http://www.teuscher.ch/christof

References

1. C. Teuscher and U. Teuscher. On Enigmas and oracles: Looking back to the future. *Trends in Cognitive Science*, 6(10):410–411, October 2002.

Contents

Part II. Computation and Turing Machines

Part IV. The Enigma

The Polish Brains Behind the Breaking of the Enigma Code Before and During the Second World War

Alan Turing at Bletchley Park in World War II

Part V. Almost Forgotten Ideas

Part I

Turing's Life and Thoughts

Alan Turing: an Introductory Biography

Andrew Hodges

Wadham College, University of Oxford

Summary. A short description of the events and issues in the life of Alan Turing (1912–1954).

The Turing Day conference at the Swiss Federal Institute of Technology, Lausanne, was held to mark the ninetieth anniversary of Alan Turing's birth, which fell on 23rd June 2002. Turing's life was so short that further events will soon mark the fiftieth anniversary of his death on 7th June 2004. But in that span between 1912 and 1954 Alan Turing did pioneering work, encompassing the foundations of computer science, which still continues to stimulate and inspire. As this volume illustrates, the breadth and depth of Turing's work, as well as its dramatic intensity, compensates for its chronological brevity.

Alan Turing's biography is interwoven with the course of twentieth-century history and falls naturally into pre-war, wartime and post-war periods. He was born into the British upper-middle class which had confidently run the imperial administration until the First World War, but which, under the impact of economic and political crisis, progressively lost control thereafter. In a very broad sense, Alan Turing belonged to a new, modernizing generation which reacted contemptuously against Victorian values. But Alan Turing's early life was marked by detachment from the obligatory social training, rather than rebellion against it. It was also marked from the start by his intensely individual response to science and mathematics, in particular to the relativity and quantum mechanics which had transformed the physical sciences since 1900. He became an undergraduate at King's College, Cambridge University, in 1931, reading mathematics and graduating with distinction in 1934.

Very soon, in 1935, the lectures of M. H. A. (Max) Newman at Cambridge introduced him to the frontier of mathematical logic, which likewise had been transformed since 1900. But logic was neither Turing's immediate nor his only choice. It was his work in probability theory that won him a Fellowship of King's College in 1935, and he might easily have continued in this field, or in the mathematical physics that had first attracted him. Thus he came to logic from a wide background in pure and applied mathematics, and it was in this eclectic spirit that he attacked the Entscheidungsproblem of David Hilbert, which at that point remained an outstanding question.

Turing, working alone, and only twenty-three, attacked and settled this problem using his definition of computability. His famous paper, "On Computable Numbers, with an Application to the Entscheidungsproblem," was published at the turn of 1936–37. A complete outsider to the field, he won a place in the subject with a concept which after 60 years remains definitive. His definition of computability showed there could be no general method for deciding the provability of mathematical propositions, and marked the end of attempts to formalize a complete system for mathematics. But it also opened the way into new fields, which now we would recognize as computer science and the cognitive sciences.

Although Turing thereafter found himself classed as a logician, he was more a mathematician who applied himself to logic; and more than that, a scientist who behind the mathematics felt a deep concern for the fundamental questions of mind and matter. His underlying interest in the problem of mind showed up in the bold statements about human memory and states of mind which informed his arguments. His background in physics was hinted at in the "machines" with which he made his definition of computability — the now-famous "Turing machines," running on paper tape, an image of 1930s modernity. It was this concreteness which made Turing's definition of computability much more satisfactory than the mathematical definition offered by Alonzo Church, the Princeton logician who led the field. Mathematically, Turing's definition was equivalent to Church's. But the description of the Turing machine gave a convincing argument for why it was that this mathematical definition completely captured the concept of "effectively calculable."

Each Turing machine represents an algorithm; for modern readers it is hard not to see it as a computer program and to bear in mind that computers did not then exist. But Turing specifically defined a type of machine called "universal," capable of reading the instruction table of any other machine. This is precisely the principle of the stored-program digital computer, then yet to come into being. It is possible that Turing even then entertained the possibility of constructing such a machine, for he certainly interested himself in electrical and mechanical computation. But, if so, he left no notes or observations on this question. Rather, he was primarily engaged in a wide variety of mathematical researches. In late 1936 Turing joined Church's group at Princeton and there embarked on more advanced logic but also on work in algebra and on developing the theory of the Riemann zeta-function, fundamental to the study of prime numbers. The mathematician John von Neumann offered him a post at Princeton to continue mathematical research, but he chose to return to England in summer 1938, conscious of the impending conflict with Germany and already prepared to make a special contribution to it.

Whilst the Second World War took many of his scientific contemporaries into the physics of radar and the atomic bomb, it took Alan Turing into cryptology. After 1938, his grappling with the infinitudes of mathematical logic was complemented by the finite but still highly challenging logical problem of the German Enigma enciphering machine. In 1939, partly thanks to a brilliant Polish contribution, Turing was able to propose a highly ingenious method of testing a "probable word" for Enigma-enciphered messages. His logical scheme was rapidly materialized in very large electromechanical devices called Bombes, which from 1940 onwards worked as the central engines of decipherment throughout the war. For this work, Turing was based at the now famous center at Bletchley Park, Buckinghamshire, which recruited increasingly large sectors of the British intelligentsia. Amongst these, Alan Turing remained the chief scientific figure. His central contribution, after the logic of the Bombe, lay in Bayesian statistics for measuring "weight of evidence," a development close to Shannon's theory of information measure. Turing led what was in effect a scientific revolution, and because he took personal charge of the crucial U-boat message problem, was able to see his approach triumph in the battle of the Atlantic. Alan Turing's role mirrored the developing course of the war: at first a lone British figure against all the odds, and later, as the work developed on a major industrial and transnational scale, handing over the British contribution to the power by which it was eclipsed: the United States.

Turing's personality traits became more striking when outside the Cambridge environment; shy but outspoken, nervous but lacking deference, he was not well adapted to military manners or to the diplomacy of the embryonic Anglo-American relationship. But his commanding scientific authority made him the top-level technical liaison between the wartime Allies, demanding a voyage to America in the winter of 1942–43 at the height of the Atlantic battle. None of this experience, however, gave him a taste for power or detracted from his primary vocation as a pure scientist. The undiminished tenacity of his scientific calling was well illustrated by the use he made of his wartime experience. For after 1943 Turing knew from Bletchley Park work that large-scale digital electronic machinery had the speed and reliability to make possible a practical version of his "universal machine." From that point onwards he made the construction of such a machine his principal ambition, and he arranged his work so as to gain personal experience of electronic components — designing and building an advanced speech scrambler. And so, at the end of the Second World War, he had a plan for an electronic computer, but it was motivated not by military or economic needs. It was for the exploration of the scope of the computable and in particular for comparing machine processes with human mental processes. He called it "building a brain."

For his war work, which some would judge critical to the Atlantic war, Turing was honored with the modest British formality of an OBE. But his work remained completely secret until the mid-1970s, and he derived no advantage from it in his subsequent scientific career. Nevertheless, the post-war period began with great promise, for he was invited to take up an appointment at the National Physical Laboratory, near London, in October 1945, and his electronic computer plan, the proposal for the Automatic Computing Engine (ACE), was swiftly adopted in March 1946.

At that time, which was before the word "computer" had its modern meaning, Turing used the term Practical Universal Computing Machine. But, although fond of the word "practical," Turing did not have the human gift of getting his practical way with people and institutions who did not share his vision. From the outset, it became clear that the NPL had no clear idea on how it was to build the machine he had designed, and it failed to adopt a policy speedy enough to satisfy Alan Turing. Turing's plans for software, exploiting the universality of the machine, were the strongest feature of his proposal, but they were little developed or publicized because of the dominating problem of hardware engineering. Impatient for progress, Turing took up marathon running to near-Olympic standard, but this did not relieve the stress. In the autumn of 1947 he returned to Cambridge for a sabbatical year, and while there was approached by Max Newman, since 1945 professor of mathematics at Manchester University, to take an appointment there instead. Newman had played a most important part at Bletchley Park after 1942 and had organized a section using the most sophisticated electronic machinery; he was also fully acquainted with Turing's logical ideas. At Manchester he had rapidly recruited both Royal Society funding and top-rank engineers, and by June 1948 a tiny version of the universal machine principle was working there — in marked contrast to the lack of progress at the NPL. Turing accepted the appointment as Deputy Director of the Computing Laboratory. But already in 1948 it became clear that the engineering would dominate the Manchester environment, and before long both Newman and Turing were sidelined and did not direct anything at all.

Turing's programming never exploited the advanced possibilities he had mapped out in 1946, and he failed also to write the papers that could have established his claim to the theory and practice of modern computing. Instead, the main theme of his work became the more futuristic prospect of Artificial Intelligence, or "intelligent machinery" as he called it. Already prefigured in 1946, this was expounded in papers of 1947, 1948, and 1950, arguing strongly that computable operations could encompass far more than those things considered "merely mechanical" in common parlance, and indeed could emulate human intelligence. The last of these papers, the only one to be published in his lifetime, appearing in the philosophy journal Mind, has become famous for the Turing Test and its 50 prophecy, and stands still as a flagship for confidence in the ultimate mechanizability of Mind. But Turing's constructive arguments for how Artificial Intelligence might be achieved are perhaps as significant as the long-term vision. Notably, his ideas encompassed both the "top-down" and the "bottom-up" ideas that were to become bitter rivals in later AI research. But it is also notable that he did very little to follow up these ideas with active research, even when he had the resources of the Manchester computer.

In 1951, Turing was elected to a Fellowship of the Royal Society, the citation referring to his 1936 work. This was a watershed year for Turing: although he had largely failed in the immediate post-war period to capitalize on his wartime achievement, he now started a quite fresh development, demonstrating the part he could still have in the great expansion of science and mathematics that began in the 1950s. His new ambition was that of giving a mathematical explanation for morphogenetic phenomena, thus showing an interest in biology that went back to childhood, but which was now expressed in advanced methods for studying nonlinear partial differential equations with the computer simulations which had just become possible on the Manchester computer.

At the end of 1951 Turing submitted a first paper on this work, which for mathematical biology was to be as important as his 1936 work had been for logic. But at just this point, Alan Turing was arrested. As a homosexual, he was always in danger from the law which at that time criminalized all homosexual activity: an injudicious liaison turned that potential into fact. The trial, in March 1952, resulted in his being forced to accept injections of oestrogen. He fought hard to prevent this from arresting his work. Unrepentant, open and unashamed, Alan Turing found himself a very isolated figure at Manchester. In 1953 there was another "crisis" with the police, which may well have been related to the fact that as a known homosexual he fell into the new category of "security risk," one who could no longer continue the secret work he had previously been doing. His holidays abroad to less hostile climes would not have calmed the nerves of security officers. Amidst this Cold War story, however, Turing also found time not only for substantial developments in his morphogenetic theory, but for a stab at a new field: the interpretation of the quantum mechanics that had first absorbed him in youth. All this was, however, cut off by his death by cyanide poisoning at his home at Wilmslow, Cheshire, in 1954, by means most likely contrived by him to allow those who wished to do so to believe it an accident.

An awkward figure, who delighted yet often infuriated his friends, Alan Turing was wrapped up in world events and yet most concerned with an intense personal integrity. Writing as plainly as he spoke, he was an Orwell of science; but his large capacity for frivolity, as illustrated in his discussion of the Turing Test setting, gave him an honorable place in the lighter and cheekier side of English culture. His life was full of paradox, not least that he, of all people original and socially nonconforming, should be the foremost advocate of the view that the mind was purely mechanical. The most purely scientific in spirit, his application to war work was of greater effect than perhaps any other individual scientist. Committed to honesty and truth, he found his life enveloped by secrecy and silence.

The strange drama of Alan Turing's death in 1954 has in its way given him a lasting life in public consciousness. His state of mind at death remains an enigma, but so too does the true inner story of his life. Prickly and proud, yet self-effacing, Turing wrote little about the development of his ideas. There is the unknown background to his fascination with the problem of Mind, where only juvenile fragments survive. There is the question raised by Newman, of whether he might have done greater things in mathematics, but for the war; and the question of the real motivations for Turing's abandonment of deep mathematical work for the sake of the war. The vexed question of the emergence of the digital computer in 1945, and of Turing's relationship with von Neumann, remains a gap at the heart of 20th-century technology. The true genesis of his Artificial Intelligence program during the war, and the question of whether his concern for the significance of Gödel's theorem was really resolved — all this remains unknown, spur to 21st-century thought and our fascination with the theory and practice of intelligent life.

References

1. Agar, J. (2001). Turing and the Universal Machine (Cambridge: Icon).
2. Davis, M. (2000). The Universal Computer (New York: Norton).
3. Hodges, A. (1983). Alan Turing: the enigma (Burnett, London; Simon & Schuster, New York; new editions Vintage, London, 1992, Walker, New York, 2000). Further material is on http://www.turing.org.uk.
4. Hodges, A. (1997). Turing, a natural philosopher (Phoenix, London; Routledge, New York, 1999). Included in: The Great Philosophers: eds. R. Monk and F. Raphael (Weidenfeld and Nicolson, 2000).
5. Hodges, A. (2002). Alan M. Turing, in E. N. Zalta (ed.), Stanford Encyclopedia of Philosophy, http://plato.stanford.edu.
6. Newman, M. H. A. (1955). Alan M. Turing, Biographical memoirs of the Royal Society, 253.
7. Turing, A. M. (1992, 2001). Collected Works: eds. J. L. Britton, R. O. Gandy, D. C. Ince, P. T. Saunders, C. E. M. Yates (Amsterdam: North-Holland).
8. Turing, E. S. (1959). Alan M. Turing (Cambridge: Heffers).
9. The Turing Digital Archive at http://www.turingarchive.org offers an online version of the Turing archive of papers at King's College, Cambridge.

Alan's Apple: Hacking the Turing Test

Valeria Patera

TIMOS Teatro Events, Association for the Communication of Science, Italy

Summary. A play by Valeria Patera, translated into English by Susie White.

1   The Author's View

My study on Alan Turing and a specific part of his work uses a poetic/philosophical approach and takes the form of a play; hence it will differ from the various papers presented here.

My aim was not to produce a work representing Turing's biography but rather to create a theatrical setting in which individuals who exist in different spatial and temporal contexts, but are closely linked in AI genealogy, meet on a virtual plane; individuals who, in both cases, have been branded as "outsiders."

Thus, stylized moments in Turing's life, which has all the makings of a modern tragedy but with comic overtones stemming from the bizarre nature of this eminent mathematician known for his eccentricity and contempt of power, and his disarming honesty and free spirit, "virtually" collide with the adventures of two young present-day hackers who meet up with him while surfing the Net.

The Turing Test is "reinvented" and transformed into a theatrical mechanism, a deus ex machina that brings the two young hackers, actors in the cyber culture created by the Net, into contact with Alan Turing, whose work in Bletchley Park during the Second World War may well have made him the "father" of the modern hacker-inspired cyber culture. This cyber culture, more than anything else, embodies the advantages and contradictions of a remarkable invention: the computer. Now an absolute necessity in everyday life, the computer has questioned and is seriously questioning some of the paradigms of Western culture; in fact, we are all increasingly compelled to address the nature and meaning of intelligence, thought, consciousness, reality, fantasy, freedom of information, intellectual property and access to knowledge.

By interweaving the two worlds, Alan's and the hackers', and following a continuous thread, I have sought to represent in a stylized way the evolution of the thought paradigm, from the pioneering research conducted by Alan Turing to the artificial intelligence of the late 1950s (the MIT Strong Artificial Intelligence Program was presented two years after Turing's death) and the revolutionary technological era in which we are now living, which will certainly be — as our protagonist intuited — the beginning of a new and contradictory period in the life of the individual and his relationship with society.

For further reading, I would refer you to the introduction by Giulio Giorello.

2   Turing and the Apple — By Giulio Giorello

The apple has always had a certain importance in the history of mankind. There was the apple that Eve picked and Adam ate, and we have seen the consequences. There was the apple that fell on Newton's head — an episode he himself liked to relate in later years — and we are now grappling with the enigma of gravity. There is also Alan Turing's poisoned apple. Let's stop here. "Alan's Apple: Hacking the Turing Test" by Valeria Patera examines the scandal surrounding this last apple and presents as an enigma the life, death and destiny of the man who did so much to decipher the Nazi Enigma code during the Second World War. But deciphering the meaning of life is much more difficult.

Patera counterpoints the human and scientific aspects of Alan Turing's life with conversations between two hackers who, in turn, question the meaning of what they do. They set the virtual world of the Net against the real world, composed of things and bodies, but also of institutions like the Inland Revenue and the Police. Here, as in Turing's case, the focus is on diversity as opposed to standardization, extraordinary science as opposed to normal research, liberty as opposed to necessity. But what if the freedom dreamt of by those who surf the Net is actually a different kind of necessity? Besides, I remember one of the hackers saying at the beginning of Patera's play: "I live on the Net, in another society, with its own rules, borders and traditions." Exactly! Here we have another society, more rules and borders! We may also have the slight suspicion that the wonderful world imagined and desired by the hackers will turn out to be a Brave New World. Is there perhaps a test that would allow us to clearly distinguish the different kinds of freedom from those of necessity?

Turing's own experiences show how difficult it is to make a sharp distinction between the two. Does science always signify intellectual emancipation, and technology "progress?" Then why "are the Police so interested?" To what kind of freedom did Turing sacrifice the best years of his life? What kind of an open society is it that uses chemical castration to "normalize" those who appear to be sexually "abnormal?" And can machines be "better" than human beings, in every sense of the word? In constantly posing these questions, Patera cannot but use as a poetic symbol the Turing Test itself, which has become one of the most representative issues in the soul-body-machine or, if you prefer, the mind-brain-computer debate. A problem that has been with us at least since the time of Descartes. However, it was abstract logic research (the Turing concept of computability) that truly revealed to us the Brave New World of computer technology; the technological aspect (the program known as Strong Artificial Intelligence) came later; moreover, it was brilliantly anticipated by Alan Turing.

Perhaps it is more than a historical irony that the test which is indissolubly linked to Turing's name in specialist literature was based on a gender test (designed to reveal if the hidden interlocutor was male or female). As well as ambivalent gender there is now an equally ambivalent human being. It suffices to consult the documentation on the results of the Turing Test. In the interesting volume "The Engine of Reason, the Seat of the Soul" (1995) by Paul M. Churchland, for example, we read that in the course of many tests not one "machine" was mistaken for a human being by the "judges," whereas many human beings were taken to be machines (see Chap. 9 of the above-mentioned work). Perhaps it is not a question of asking ourselves if a machine can think, but of concluding that when we think we do so like "machines."

Indeed, the hackers in Patera's play lead us to understand that, in some sense of the word, we are (also) machines. Extremely sophisticated machines, in fact, that have undergone a long evolutionary process. These machines are also known as bodies, and perhaps Turing's error was to sometimes forget that he possessed a body and that simulated intelligence is also strongly conditioned by the physical structures employed. Nowadays, the Turing Test is usually criticized from two opposing points of view. According to some it is too narrowly based, while others find it too broadly based. In either case it is not able to adequately represent the kind of symbolic thought that is now considered one of the most significant products of evolution, firstly from a biological and secondly from a cultural standpoint. I would refer the reader here to the now well-known Chinese room argument by John R. Searle. Patera obviously does not claim to solve this philosophical puzzle in her play, but she intelligently implies that the symbol is the "death" of Turing's research program.

Symbols are important, in fact, as the anecdotes about apples show, and the one about Turing is a little like the apple (poisoned) in Snow White, the difference being that in Turing's story there is no Prince Charming to awaken the sleeper with a kiss.

3   The Play

Dramatis Personae

- Alan Turing, English Mathematician born in 1912 (here acting from the 1930s to 1954)
- Julius Turing, his father
- Ethel Turing, his mother
- John Turing, his brother
- Christopher Morcom, his school friend at Sherborne
- Mrs. Morcom, Christopher's mother
- Housemaster at Sherborne
- Victor Beuttel, a fellow student
- Joan Clarke, cryptanalyst and fiancée
- Claude Shannon, American mathematician and Alan's friend
- Zac and Hardo, two present-day hackers

Scene 1

A sloppily dressed hacker, Zac, with an "unreal" look about him gets off his bike.

ZAC   Shit, it's jammed, just like yesterday! (*pause*)

If my bike packs up I'm in trouble. I don't use it for racing. I hate sport and all that macho stuff. My bike's vital.

I'm fucked without one here. (*peering at it closely*) The chain again, just my luck!

I had to deliver the program.

Me and Hardo do over a hundred kilometers a week.

You're better off pedaling than crawling along in the traffic, which is just as much hard work. Right ... (*he tries to fix the chain*) every time this friggin' chain comes off I get mad, but I love the challenge.

I give it fifteen minutes. I can't resist a broken machine.

I was going to sell my car and buy a laptop.

Then I thought what good's a laptop if you're stuck in one place?

And the car caught fire on the highway.

I left it there. (*still tinkering*) Come on, I'll fix you ...

I wanted to be home for supper, since my mom's going to be there for once. She's moved, she's taking a course at the university to become a social worker.

I live with my dad. He's got Alzheimer's. (*pause*)

I'm finishing high school. (*pause*) I've tried kidding myself that if you lie well enough you're the first to be convinced. It doesn't work. No way! It's no good pretending to be what you're not, trying to be someone else. (*pause*)

Here they think I'm a weirdo, different ...

School's no joyride either.

What did the teacher do to punish me? Made me type up my papers on a typewriter, for God's sake. What a cow ... it's hell. It's sheer hell for someone like me (*he kicks the bike*), I've never used a typewriter in my life. It's like something out of the ark. Fifty pages ... (*pause*) The Headmaster thinks distributing a booklet on the birds and the bees to high school kids is being modern. It's making me freak out! (*he desperately puts a hand to his forehead and laughs bitterly*) Whole afternoons playing the typist! All I need is red nail polish and ...

As long as it doesn't get around the Net! Flamed online!

The Net's my life. I live on the Net, in another society, with its own rules, borders and traditions. I'm free to go where I like, to take all I want. The Net is a fantastic world, a continuous flow of updates, a constantly expanding universe of games, programs, graphics, operating systems ... hmmm, good enough to eat ...

Apart from the perverse logic of having to pay a subscription to access these things, I'm not subject to rules, taxes or any of that other crap they impose on you to keep you in one place rather than another. (*pause*)

Computers empower you. I've made a name for myself on the Net, and it suits me: Zac, short and sharp. Then there's my buddy Hardo: hard and a bit a bastard! (*pause*)

 He gets back on his bike.

So me and Hardo thought, we've got no wheels, no money, all we've got is our technical ability, our skills.

Nothing's stopping us now! Having no wheels is a real opportunity! (*pause*) On the Net it doesn't matter what color you are, or if you're male, female, lesbian, asexual, or a cannibal. On the Net age, the number of your bank account, and all that stuff doesn't count.

A nineteen-year-old zilch like me is a falcon on the Net, who flies higher than most then plummets down into the mystery of pi. I can see things I'd never have been able to, not even if I'd lived three times over in this shit hole. Working in a superstore. (*pause*)

I finally did it. I got the fucking chain back on. Nothing gets the better of me, got it?

A bike's the best way to get around, it's economical, an elitist symbol if you like, and you don't have those traffic lights breaking your balls ...

All those one-way streets round every corner would make you late for your own funeral ... Hmm, traffic signs should be rethought, controlled more intelligently and the entire system redesigned. (*pause*)

I take all my other trips on the Net.

The Net makes me feel secure. It's my community. The Net is not an alternative to life, for me the Net is life, my portable cyber-community ...

It's like an acrobat's safety net into which I can dive headfirst and then bounce higher and higher ... in the infinite information circus ... finally my life is going somewhere ... in an eternal digital dance ...

Zac gets back on his bike. As he rides he describes an ellipse that coincides with the focus of a second ellipse that is being described by another cyclist, the young Alan Turing, dressed in the 1930s style.

They pedal in silence without seeing each other, as if they were in two different dimensions of space and time.

In the background, at the point where the two ellipses overlap, there is a large screen on which real and virtual images appear.

Scene 2

The Turing home: Ethel, Alan's mother, with the mail that has just been delivered, and Julius, his father. The 1930s.

ETHEL   Oh Julius! Julius, there's a letter from Alan, come here, Julius!

JULIUS   In Heaven's name, Ethel, just a minute, I was putting manure on the roses. You can never do anything in peace in this house! Who's it from, who?

ETHEL   Alan, our son Alan. His first week at public school. Come on, let's see what he has to say ...

Julius enters in his gardening togs.

JULIUS   (*taking off his dirty canvas apron, and reading with satisfaction*) What character that boy has! He couldn't take the train because of the strike and ...

ETHEL   ... arrived terribly late! Oh!

JULIUS   Not at all! Alan didn't let that stop him; he cycled all the way to Sherborne.

ETHEL   From Southampton?! Goodness gracious, he rode sixty miles! He must have been exhausted!

JULIUS   He must have arrived in great shape! That's not such a bad thing ...

ETHEL   Julius, what will they have said at the school ...

JULIUS   Oh look, he's already in the news, there's a cutting from a local paper that heralds him as the new cycling champion!

ETHEL   Oh Julius, arriving like that, showing everyone he's a bit odd ... I was hoping public school might make him normal ...

JULIUS   You'd like to turn him into a real provincial, but I've taught him the value of being yourself and having the courage to speak your mind, he'll mark my words, I'm sure ...

ETHEL   Turning up at Sherborne without a change of clothes, do you call that being yourself?

JULIUS   What matters is that he takes his education seriously, and he will, you'll see ...

He helps himself to a small sherry.

Scene 3

Alan is in his room at Sherborne.

ALAN   Here I am at public school ... that temple of learning which will make me 'acceptable,' turn me into a perfect Englishman ...

This is my first brush with the world of rules and social conveniences, and its hierarchies ... a real mystery to me ... but apparently it cannot be avoided ... in the majority of cases, rules succeed in turning even the pleasant things in life into absurdities. And absurdities reign supreme here: compulsory religion, cold showers, corporal punishment ...

Well, I'm trying to fit in, to make sense of it all, but it certainly won't be easy ... In all seriousness they teach you to accept and adapt ... to those harsh rules: you must accept coming last to forge the desire to be first! Allow yourself to be humiliated today to get the better of someone tomorrow ... there's something so savage in all this, like those Gallic laws ... but at least I have time for my beloved numbers, and my room makes a pretty good chemistry lab ... it has a large window sill with plenty of room for my alembics ...

The housemaster enters, wearing a sharp, disdainful expression.

HOUSEMASTER   Turing, I've come to tell you that ... (*his eyes widen in horror when he notices that Alan is half-naked and everything is in disarray*) This is outrageous! You are the most aggravating boy! You should be ashamed of yourself! Do you think I like smelling these horrible odors you produce with your silly potions, your ridiculous experiments conducted on the window sill!

I've already turned a blind eye to your illegible writing and your messy work, but I will not tolerate your superficial attitude towards studying the New Testament.

You will report to my study later for a caning, Turing. Do you not think you deserve it?

Alan looks confused then gives a strange little smile.

His mother and father read a letter from the school ...

"He could probably be happier but, then again, perhaps he is not unhappy: he is certainly not "normal." He has a tendency to be antisocial, his attitude often results in his being picked on by others, and he is the unfortunate target of at least one teacher; however, I think he would be a problem in any school or community."

JOHN   (*Alan's slightly older brother*) Alan takes great pleasure in overturning the commonplace; everything that normal people believe, he finds ridiculous. He also has a remarkable knack of presenting irrefutable arguments to back up his far-fetched ideas. Well, I think this can annoy people ...

JULIUS Perhaps it is his being able to think of and do things that no one else would dream of doing that irritates them ... Do you remember that picnic when he found us some honey for the tea, taking it directly from the comb that he had located by studying the flight paths of the bees buzzing around it? The honey was bitter, but I was so impressed by the whole business ...

ETHEL I'll never forget that afternoon ... especially when he said he "knew" the forbidden fruit in the Garden of Eden was a plum and not an apple ...

Alan, now naked, continues joyously working with alembics and consulting formulae amid swirling vapors, while his mother continues to read the letter.

"I must say that he has taken his punishment very well and has certainly made more of an effort, for example with physical training. I have not completely given up hope."

ALAN I learnt to run fast to avoid the ball. What I like about being a linesman is indicating the precise point where the ball crosses the line. They've even made up a rhyme about me. (*reciting to himself*) "Turing's fond of the football field/For geometric problems the touch-lines yield."

He laughs in amusement

ALAN What I can neither understand nor share is the need for certainties that most people experience to some degree ... certainty holds no fascination for me whatsoever ... I live for doubt ... (*pause*)

But mere consciousness amazes me, gives me such joy ...

the tiniest insect or creature, eyesight, love ...

He sees a boy go by, everything else disappears, that figure becomes the focus of his gaze, the colors change.

... Oh, Christopher Morcom! Chris! When I see him a rainbow appears in my soul!

I'm so happy when I'm with him ... how can I see his face again?

He pulls some crumpled notes from his pocket, smoothing out one of them.

Scene 4

Alan and Christopher in the school library.

CHRISTOPHER Oh Turing, what brings you to the library? I've never seen you here before ...

ALAN Well, yes, in fact, I just thought it was a good place to think ...

CHRISTOPHER Of course ...

ALAN Of course ...

(*after timidly hesitating for a moment*)

I've calculated pi to thirty-six decimal places ...

CHRISTOPHER Really, how did you do it?

ALAN Using the series — my own personal discovery — for the inverse tangent function ...

People are calling out to Christopher.

CHRISTOPHER   Very interesting indeed! In the last few days I've been totally immersed in the General Theory of Relativity, space-time ...

ALAN   (*sucking air in noisily through his nose, and then speaking rapidly without pausing for breath*) Have you noticed that Einstein does not deal with the "real essence" of time and space? He concentrates on measuring instruments, "clocks," thus adopting an operational approach to physics ... distance is also seen in relation to a measuring operation, and not as an absolute ideal.

Someone shouts out to Christopher again.

CHRISTOPHER   (*amazed by Alan's insight*) Sorry, they're calling me, I must go, be seeing you ...

ALAN   Why don't you come to my room? We could do some experiments with iodates and sulphates, it's very interesting ...

CHRISTOPHER   Oh yes, I've always loved messing around with them. Bye.

ALAN   Bye ... (*pause*)

The hacker cycles across the stage.

Scene 5

Alan and Christopher are in the school lab, surrounded by alembics.

ALAN   ... You know I've always been fascinated by experiments involving iodine.

CHRISTOPHER   My brother Rupert also ...

ALAN   This is a beautiful experiment, watch: you mix the two solutions in a beaker, wait for a specific time, and the mixture suddenly turns blue. Everything becomes blue, blue, blue, deep blue ... as if a piece of sky had fallen into the beaker ...

A deep blue patch of iodine appears on the screen and gradually fills the entire space, transforming it into a starry night sky.

ALAN   What's the time?

CHRISTOPHER   Ten o'clock.

ALAN   How can you tell?

CHRISTOPHER   I always know the time; I go by my biological clock. Come and look at the stars.

ALAN   What makes us different from a star?

CHRISTOPHER   Stars are always there; our lives pass so quickly and we're certainly far less bright ...

ALAN   I'd give anything to know why we have our present form instead of being star-shaped ...

CHRISTOPHER   I watch them, study them for nights on end. Did you see that satellite the night before last?

ALAN   I did! (*they are both keyed-up, aware of the mystery of it all*) How could I have missed it coming out of eclipse!

CHRISTOPHER   The sky isn't that clear sometimes and it's difficult to make things out. My father wants to get a more powerful telescope.

I've often wanted to make a star globe but have never really got down to it ...

ALAN   Oh yes, a star globe, I'd really love to make one ...

CHRISTOPHER   I must go in now. The "Chief" will be very angry if he sees me out at this hour, and I feel a bit tired. I'm also going to be away for a week; I have to see the dentist. Good night Turing (*he clasps Alan's hand with both of his — Alan is completely thrown*).

ALAN   (*alone now, and over the moon*) I worship the ground he walks on! Since I met him I've been living on another planet. The week we spent together in Cambridge was the happiest of my life! Now, at Sherborne, I'm going to make him a star globe ... I know it won't be anything fancy but ... with a bit of inventiveness ...

> *He takes the glass globe from a lamp, starts to fill it with plaster of Paris and then begins to mark the positions of the stars with dots, and draw the lines of the constellations (his actions as he plots the stars and lines are enlarged on the screen).*

ALAN   (*thinking to himself*) It's useless to ask oneself if two points are always equidistant ... I'm the one who defined the parameter, and, just as a research method will influence the result of an experiment, my ideas will tend to conform to that definition. These yardsticks are conventions we follow, and I adapt my laws to my own yardsticks. How I envy those who believe in an absolute truth!

I'll have to wake up at four because then the sky will be clear again and I'll be able to see the more distinct constellations ...

> *We hear the mocking chant of his schoolmates.*

Pansy, pansy

Pansy, pansy, pansy!!!

Scene 6

> *Julius is reading a letter; his wife arrives and looks anxious when she sees it.*

ETHEL   Heavens, another letter from the headmaster, what has that unconventional son of ours done now!

JULIUS   You're wrong this time. His end of term results have greatly improved, look, Alan is making the grade! His marks are much higher — I expect one of the teachers has finally understood him: I don't always, but I try to give him my support.

ETHEL   I told you that was the right school for him, it's obvious, the results speak for themselves. They'll make a real gentleman of him ...

> *Julius helps himself to a small sherry.*

> *Meanwhile we see Alan as he continues working on the star globe.*

Scene 7

> *Alan is sleeping in his room at Sherborne; someone knocks on the door. Alan goes to open it, his eyes still heavy with sleep. It's the housemaster.*

ALAN   (*embarrassed and scared*) Good morning, Sir, am I late for lessons? I got up at four to stargaze, you know, I must have dropped off again and ...

HOUSEMASTER   No Turing, nothing like that, classes have not begun yet ... I've come to tell you that ... (*hesitating*)

ALAN   Yes? ...

HOUSEMASTER   (*giving a few little coughs*) ... that Christopher Morcom ...

ALAN   Chris?

HOUSEMASTER   Morcom has left us.

ALAN   He left to go to the dentist; he told me a few days ago.

HOUSEMASTER   No, that's not what I meant.

ALAN   He's left Sherborne? To go where? He didn't tell me anything ...

HOUSEMASTER   He has left this world. Christopher Morcom is dead.

ALAN   Dead? Christopher?

HOUSEMASTER   Yes, Turing, yes. It grieves me to have to give you this news, I know how close you were, but unfortunately that's how it is.

ALAN   (*upset*) But ... he had to go to the dentist ... what ... how? ...

HOUSEMASTER   Morcom had tuberculosis, caused by drinking infected milk in Yorkshire, bovine tuberculosis ...

ALAN   Bovine tuberculosis?

HOUSEMASTER   Yes. Two years ago, the disease caused grave internal damage and ... after terrible suffering he passed away at three this morning.

ALAN   (*almost losing control*) At three this morning?

HOUSEMASTER   Yes Turing, at three.

ALAN   (*going to the window; he glances at the star globe*) I looked at my watch at three precisely. Something woke me up at three, something that made me think of Chris, the moon was setting ...

> *The housemaster shakes Alan's hand warmly and leaves. Alan remains alone; it seems as if everything around him is being sucked into an enormous void.*

ALAN   I had already accepted the idea of death. It's not clear why we live but, in theory, it's very clear why we die; the process can be described. There's a formula for every problem ... but not this terrible pain! There's no logic to that ... bovine tuberculosis ... he was so young, he was the best friend I'll ever have, Chris wasn't stupid like all the rest, he made the world bearable for me, he was everything I loved, he and my numbers ... Perhaps a cell has already left his body to become a star ... perhaps ... Now he's a bright new series of numbers scattered through the cosmos ... I'll find them one by one ...

and compose a new formula to celebrate his passing.

The star globe remains in the middle of the stage as if it were a planet in the universe.

Scene 8

A few weeks later. Alan is with Christopher's mother at her home (the Clockhouse).

MRS. MORCOM   (*giving Alan a fountain pen*) Alan, I'd like you to have this.

ALAN   Oh, Christopher's favorite pen, he was so proud of it ...

MRS. MORCOM   Take it; Chris would be very happy.

ALAN   Thank you, Mrs. Morcom, it's like being entrusted with the most priceless treasure. I'm sure it'll help me with my studies and research; it'll be like having Chris by my side, helping me ... I've promised myself that I'll get top marks next term, I've got to do it, for Chris. And I'll succeed, you'll see!

MRS. MORCOM   I'm sure you will, Alan, I'm absolutely sure, and remember we're always here if you need anything. I'd like to thank you for the beautiful flowers you sent and also the kind letter your mother wrote me — I've just replied to her.

ALAN   I'm sure she'll be glad to hear from you. (*pause; he looks around*) You can feel Chris' presence so strongly here, I expect him to walk in any minute; it's as if his spirit pervaded everything.

MRS. MORCOM   Oh Alan, I've thought about so many things, I've tried to find an explanation but ... all the scientific research that has been done in this house seems to have been in vain ...

ALAN   Until the end of the last century the Laplacian view prevailed, which held that if everything was known about the Universe at any given moment we could foresee what it would be throughout the future. Now modern science has seen that the instruments it uses to acquire knowledge are themselves composed of atoms and electrons, just like the matter they are exploring, which has completely scuttled the previous theory. Therefore we cannot delude ourselves that it is possible to know the exact state of the universe, in the same way that we cannot say our actions are predestined. The action of the atoms in our brain is probably influenced to some degree by our will, which the actions of the body amplify.

MRS. MORCOM   ... What about the action of the other atoms in the universe?

ALAN   A burning question, since these atoms have no amplifying apparatus and they would appear to be regulated by pure chance, confirming the apparent non-predestination of physics.
(*pause; he sucks in air noisily through his nose*)
Furthermore, I would say that spirit is always connected with matter but not always by the same kind of body ...

I used to think that at death the spirit went to a universe separate from our own, but I now consider that body and spirit are linked, making this a contradiction in terms.

MRS. MORCOM   But what kind of relationship exists between the body and spirit?

ALAN   I believe that the body, being a living body, can "attract" and hold on to a "spirit," so the two are connected whilst the body is alive or awake. When the body dies, the "mechanism" of the body holding the spirit vanishes and one must presume that the spirit finds a new body.

MRS. MORCOM   Why do we have a body at all? Why can't we exist as free spirits and communicate as such?

ALAN   We probably could do, but there would be nothing whatever for us to do ... The body provides something for the spirit to look after and use.

Christopher's mother looks at Alan in silence, then takes his hand, just like Christopher did. Alan remains silent. The light changes.

Scene 9

Victor comes into the room where Alan is studying; there is a teddy bear named Porgy in the corner.

ALAN   (*poring over a book*) Hello Victor ... (*glancing at the teddy bear*) even Porgy wants to study this morning ... where've you been?

VICTOR   I went to a sculpture exhibition, Greek and Roman pieces, absolutely marvelous. I found the delicate lines of the Venus quite bewitching ...

ALAN   Nothing can compare with the beauty of a David or a Greek youth, that is to say, generally speaking, I personally find the male form more attractive than the female ...

VICTOR   What?! Really?!

ALAN   It's true. I can't explain it ... but perhaps there's nothing to explain, that's the way it is and I accept it.

VICTOR   You mean ... You're trying to tell me ...

ALAN   What word would you use? (*Victor is embarrassed and struggles to find the right words*) A homosexual? Pederast? Deviant? Pansy? These words mean nothing to me. They're simply conventions. (*he breathes in noisily through his nose*) We don't all look at life from the same angle. The ant doesn't see things the same way as the elephant. Each species follows its own rules. I'm in my own world. I'm in the only place I can be. And in that place, in the way I view things, there are no conventional rules, at least not the type most people follow. But this doesn't depress me. On the contrary. I'd like to spend more time with children. You know, I've offered to baby-sit for my neighbor ... the child says the most amazing things ... By the way, talking about deviants, I heard this marvelous joke on the radio this morning ...

VICTOR   Forget the joke. You always try to distract me with your humor; you can never be completely serious ... If the majority of people have a particular preference it means that this is the norm ... and even Jesus Christ ...

ALAN   (*after a moment's silence, and breathing in noisily through his nose*) Aside from Christ's preferences, I really don't know what to say ...
Do you honestly think it's right to resolve the question of homosexuality as if it were a theorem? There's nothing to resolve. All we have to do is to live freely and enjoy it, like children! And I find all those religious beliefs ...

VICTOR   (*after a long silence*) Even the idea of Christ or the spirit?

ALAN   (*half smiling*) Oh yes, Victor. It's now three years since Chris passed away, and I've stopped believing in those concepts of continued existence and spiritual communication that comforted me so when he died.

VICTOR   You no longer believe in God? You too think that God is "dead?" Then we're all dead!

ALAN   No Victor, God's death can lead to a host of resurrections.

VICTOR   (*appalled*) A host of resurrections?

ALAN   Mental rebirth, new answers ... Quite frankly, I find it difficult to reconcile the concepts of will and spirit with the scientific definition of matter ... The individual mind is a miracle in itself ... at the same time the materialist view becomes more acute ... determinism is also something you can't fail to question.

VICTOR   I'm trying to grasp ...

ALAN   Sometimes, Victor, we try to hide behind our own shadow ... we see reality through a veil that we call truth but when it comes down to it ... science, above all, sees things in this way ... take Darwinian determinism in the selection of the species for example; the one thing we can be certain of is that the mutation of the genes is random, just as in chemistry the movement of the molecules is random. The casual element, Victor, the casual element ...

VICTOR   You're demolishing determinism!

ALAN   But how do we explain freedom? Is it mere semblance? Rather let's recognize various forms of determinism and various types of freedom ... There are many sides to reality.

VICTOR   (*impressed by Alan's reasoning*) Various types of freedom?

ALAN   Freedom obliges us to find another way of looking at the world ... We must be free-thinking to grasp something significant in life ... Most people spend their time seeking confirmation of their beliefs and talking about so many useless things, now that I do find depressing! And science affirms the "laws of Nature." We have to change our point of view continually in order to describe certain aspects of the world ... Think of all those migratory birds ... Can we identify their precise habitat?

They remain thoughtful

Scene 10

Seven years later; images of the Second World War, Enigma and codes, and scenes from war video games appear on the screen. Alan is sitting down; he is knitting, and has a gas mask beside him. Joan arrives.

ALAN   Good morning, Joan!

JOAN   Good morning, Alan! I see you're making progress.

ALAN   I love knitting, I'm making a glove, I'm on the third finger ... I've always enjoyed making things, but this is really quite remarkable! While trying to fathom the latest Enigma key used by the Germans in their messages disguised as weather bulletins, I'm producing woolen fingers, it's wonderful!

Every morning at 6 AM the Germans transmit the same message, I'm sure there's something behind it ...

JOAN   (*alluding to the gas mask*) And that?

ALAN   I wear it riding to work. It filters out the pollen that makes me sneeze, most convenient!

JOAN   (*smiling*) Do you mean to say you rode through the village wearing that?! What must people ...

ALAN   At least it isn't a secret, at least they can form an idea ... But no one has any idea what we cryptanalysts are working on here. It's as if we didn't exist. We're suffocated by secrecy, what we do cuts us off from everyone, even those closest to us ... In the early days at Bletchley Park, before my studies at Princeton, we were a group of romantic intellectuals on the loose. Now we're pigeon-holed, our work's so organized, we're like a code-breaking factory, and I find this sort of non-existence hard to bear at times.

JOAN   If Churchill deigned to pay us a visit it must mean that he's well aware of the importance of our work here.

ALAN   "The geese who laid the golden eggs and never cackled," that's what he called us. Not bad ...

JOAN   The great Churchill was quite astonished. Perhaps he expected to find only serious mathematicians secretly engaged in cryptanalysis in the huts, and never dreamt of coming across a well-known collector of porcelain, a museum curator from Paris, the British chess champion, leading bridge players and an unconventional mathematician who knits and ties his mug of tea to the radiator ...

ALAN   But he must have guessed we're in difficulties; the only positive thing about his visit is that he told us to contact him personally should the need arise. I've taken him at his word and have already jotted down a few lines to make him understand that if he doesn't send us reinforcements we won't be able to finish the job, not even with the Bombes they sent us; war will not wait. We'll all sign it and he won't be able to refuse ... (*he looks steadily at Joan*)

JOAN   What are you thinking about, Alan?

ALAN   Oh, Joan, I was lost in my feelings ... I get so much pleasure from being with you, I really do, we're such good friends, everything's so spontaneous ...

JOAN   How could it be any other way with you? You're the most incredible man I've ever known and I'm so proud that you and I ... (*Alan breathes in noisily through his nose*) Alan, is there something wrong?

ALAN   The thing is that I ... I ... don't think I feel quite the same way as you do ... perhaps I ... Oh, I love you of course, there's no doubt about that, but ... there's something else ... you see, the fact is that er ... men don't exactly leave me cold ... do you understand?

JOAN   Of course I do, but I won't let it be a problem ...

ALAN   How sweet you are ... but I really think it will be; I don't want you to suffer; I'm absolutely convinced it won't work. You'll feel let down, and I don't want that. There are times when we have to give up what we love because there is no alternative. Wilde knew that so well ...

"Yet each man kills the thing he loves."

Everything freezes; the lights change.

Scene 11

> *At the Turings' house: Julius, Ethel and John are sitting around the table set for a meal. Alan arrives out of breath, with his jacket buttoned unevenly, one shoe different from the other, and untidy hair.*

ETHEL   (*mortified to see him looking such a mess*) Alan, my God, how can you go around like that?! You look like a vagrant!
And you're late! Your hands are dirty! Heavens, what a tie!
And ... what's this? Alan, you're wearing a rope instead of a belt, and a red one at that, what am I to do ... What a disappointment! I thought that working at the Foreign Office you would have adopted a military manner, but just look at this haystack and those dark circles under your eyes ... they may make you work the whole night through, but I'd like to know exactly what you do?

ALAN   Defend England by playing mathematical games. But enough of that, why don't you give me a plate of your wonderful stew? You don't think I came to see you, do you?!

ETHEL   What was that thing about a code? A code that breaks other codes? What was it? (*Alan kisses his mother on the cheek. Ethel gives an ironic but satisfied smile as she goes into the kitchen, mumbling and grumbling.*)

ALAN   (*to his father and brother, lowering his voice*) I'm off to Washington!

JULIUS   Another trip to America, son? Princeton, again?

ALAN   No, I'll be staying in Washington this time. They want us to let them in on the secrets of Bletchley Park's cryptanalysis. The Americans are supporting the British strategy of reconquering the Mediterranean for the first time, Britain has agreed to be used as an American base. The war has reached a turning point, Father. (*Julius nods gravely*)

ETHEL   (*loudly, from the kitchen*) Princeton, did I hear aright? You got a postcard from Princeton?

ALAN   Not quite, I'm leaving for Washington!

ETHEL   (*looking astounded as she comes back into the dining room*) You are? So you've finally become someone? Even if you go around dressed like that?

ALAN   (*smiling*) Dressed like this I've invented a machine that does very difficult calculations, a universal machine that can do a lot of things automatically: read, write, compute; in other words, produce "intelligence." (*there is a big silence*)

ETHEL   A machine? (*pause*) That does all that by itself? (*pause*)

ALAN   A model with which it's possible to elaborate the most complex procedures simply by using a series of simple elements: states, positions, reading, writing, a table of instructions. A universal machine!

ETHEL   Black magic.

I wonder what the Reverend would say? May St. George protect you!

ALAN   Quite honestly, I'd rather have the dragon on my side.

JULIUS   Tell me about this miraculous machine ...

ALAN   I began with a theoretical machine; they've called it the Turing Machine!

JULIUS   (*looking proud*) Oh, that has a nice ring to it, a nice ring to it indeed: the Turing Machine.

ETHEL   It's in the family, in our genes. What's more, a close relative of ours, George Stoney, invented the electron!

ALAN   Mother, I've told you a hundred times that you can't invent an electron because it already exists, you can only discover it and give it a name. But they did use it to invent electronics.

ETHEL   That's no mean feat! You should tell those crass Americans about it!

ALAN   (*ironically*) I'll write them a letter first thing tomorrow! (*Julius and John smile at each other*) However, to understand you should think of a super typewriter that can calculate an infinite number of operations. You see, there really is no difference between intelligent and mechanical, therefore some functions of our brain, like counting, can be translated into a mechanical action by breaking down each small stage, that is the smallest element of each mental state, and translating it into a series of numbers that are printed on paper tape ... an endless tape ...

From a certain point of view one can say that the machine thinks, or at least reproduces some thought functions. (*Ethel's eyes are on stalks, Julius' mouth is half-open in amazement, and John shifts in his chair in embarrassment*)

ETHEL   But that's blasphemy! A machine that thinks? It's sacrilegious! What about the soul? Our Lord gave us the power to think. How can you say that ...

ALAN   The soul ... And how do you explain the fact that for a long time monotheistic religions considered that women had no soul at all?

Ethel is stumped; she struggles to come up with something and finally succeeds.

ETHEL   Leaving the soul out of this, human beings and machines are not made of the same stuff!

ALAN   It doesn't matter what the brain is made of, only how it works! You may not think so but there's nothing sacred about the human brain!

ETHEL   That too! Talk about a fire-breathing dragon!

ALAN   The human brain is composed of an infinite number of elements called neurons: ten thousand million or more, according to some estimates. These neurons are connected to each other by a dense network of "wires." A neuron is a kind of switch, a very simple one, that has two positions: ON and OFF. The position assumed depends on the signals the neuron receives from the other neurons.

ETHEL   Am I to think that ... how can I put it ... that this is why I can smell violets in springtime?

ALAN   Yes, in point of fact, it is. The brain stores information in the form of configurations created by impulses relayed by neurons. It is astonishing how closely the storage and modification functions of neurons in the brain resemble the corresponding functions of a calculator. It is this similarity that convinces me that we can actually build a thinking machine.

ETHEL   Are you going to state all these wild theories publicly in America? An electric brain?!!

JULIUS   A theoretical machine is all right as far as it goes; but can you build one?

ALAN   (*breathing in noisily through his nose*) It already exists. We're actually well ahead with the Colossus, which is capable of doing an incredible number of calculations and has a memory that can store vast amounts of information.

We're working flat out. That's why I'm going to America again.

Julius looks at his son gravely yet warmly, and a little patronizingly; Ethel wrings her hands.

Alan smiles; he goes over to the wireless and turns it on. A firm, pleasant male voice fills the room.

MALE VOICE   Only a few men, a handful in fact, have had the strength to believe in and to strive unceasingly to realize something that seemed impossible; they have built an electronic brain, whose infinite possibilities will extend human intelligence. This is the birth of a new era. We must be receptive to new ideas, new concepts. We must see the human mind and human consciousness in a new light. And those scientists must be allowed to help us; their responsibilities are very great and we, in our turn, must help them to shoulder this burden ... (*Ethel remains thoughtful and silent, as do Julius and John. Alan gets up and takes his leave. He goes out. The lights change.*)

The hacker rides by on his bike, singing a rap.

ZAC

> I used to think
> Of a cybernetic meadow
> Where mammals and computers
> Live together
> In programming harmony
> Like pure water
> Touching clear sky.
>
> I used to see
> A cybernetic forest
> Filled with pines and electronics
> Where a deer strolls peacefully
> Past computers
> As if they were flowers
> Filled with sparkling jewels.
>
> Think about
> A cybernetic ecology
> Free us of our labors
> Return to nature
> All together
>
> Watched over and protected
> By the machines of divine grace[1]

Scene 12

America. Alan and Shannon are having their meal in the laboratory at night; there is a chess board beside them. Alan glances at the onion on Shannon's plate, and spears it with his fork.

ALAN   An onion, yes it was actually the onion that gave me an insight into the human mind ... the onion whose layers can be peeled away (*he peels off one layer delicately with his fingers*) ... If we consider the functions of the mind, or the brain, there are certain operations that can only be explained in purely mechanical terms. This does not correspond to the "real" mind; it is a kind of skin that we must peel off to find it. But in what is left, we find another skin to take off, and another. Do we finally arrive at the "real" mind, or only a skin that contains nothing? (*he sucks in air noisily*

---

[1] "I used to think ... ," variation on the poem "All Watched Over by Machines of Loving Grace" by Richard Brautigan (1967).

through his nose) You see, Shannon, I don't want to exploit the work done by other scientists, but reinvent earlier discoveries. So far machines have been designed for a specific purpose, or to perform a limited range of functions. Whereas mine is a universal machine, the ultimate machine ... Perhaps, in a few years, a machine that can adapt its functions to an infinite number of programs — which means responding to different groups of rules, possessing a memory and being able to retrieve stored data — won't cause a sensation, and may even be the norm. By the end of the twentieth century, executives will each have their own computer, mark my words!

SHANNON   Boole's two-value logic could make a computer "a lot more than an adding machine," and if you want to make it perform a particular task, all you have to do is break down the instruction into more simple instructions. Zero, one!

ALAN   The difficulty lies in establishing the basic levels. An algorithm can be developed for every problem, there's no doubt about that.

SHANNON   The binary method makes it easier; but there's also a practical and philosophical aspect. In *Sophist*, Plato holds that two questions are sufficient to arrive at a solution; to one you reply no, thereby eliminating that particular chain of thought, to the other yes, and on the basis of that you ask two more questions, and so on. For me, the binary method conjures up an image of someone trying to find their way through a maze whose paths fork continually; to make any headway, a series of decisions must be made, yes or no, that's the right way, that's the wrong way. This is more or less how an electronic brain reasons; it chooses between two possibilities only, yes or no, 1 or 0, true or false, the difference being that it performs these operations at incredible speed and makes infinite choices one after the other.

A machine's intelligence derives from the complexity of the rules that constitute the program and not from each individual unit, which can in fact be pretty simple, as we have already seen by putting 1 and 2 together. How about calling each unit a "bit?"

ALAN   "Bit?" Yes, that sounds right, yes, bit, bit!

Well, a rule can be said to describe a mechanical process.

Taken one at a time, these rules are simple, but after a sequence of thousands — or thousands of millions — an unimaginable quantity is generated. The machine can only do what we instruct it to, but we certainly cannot foresee all the consequences of the instructions we feed in.

SHANNON   The point, Turing, is to TEACH a machine to do things. We would define as intelligent a calculating machine that can modify its own program in the light of new information it receives. Therefore, we would need new combinations to enable the machine to read the incoming tape, rules that modify the programming rules, let's say. This way the program could learn and adapt itself — just like human beings — to a changing environment and to circumstances that it perceives through the combinations on the tape.

TURING Wittgenstein would call it heresy ... In fact, we're already able to build devices that imitate all manner of human functions. But here we are dealing with the nervous system. We should see what kind of results we can obtain with a "brain" without a body by equipping it with an eye at the most. There's a relationship between biology and information science. I'm convinced that if we constructed electronic neurons and connected them in the same way as they are connected in the human brain, the resulting electronic device would be governed by the same rules for thinking and acting as the human brain, and thus be able to perform exactly the same functions.

SHANNON I'm right with you there! The manipulation of symbols is the main function in human thought, so there is every possibility that a machine can think like a human being; furthermore, I'm convinced that if a machine can process numerical symbols, it can process any kind of symbol. The type of message, number, music, image is irrelevant, the transmission of information has nothing to do with the content but with the numbers 0 and 1 ... So ... we've got to define exactly what the information content of a message is.

The binary numbers are the fundamental element in every communication and there is no distinction between musical sounds, artistic images, moving images; everything can be converted into binary information, and therefore transmitted. That's why math, chess and cryptography are the perfect tools ...

ALAN Chess, of course ... You see, Shannon, what I'm searching for is a principle, a theory, a general rule that can be deduced from my game. I'm sure a "definite" method could be devised for chess, that is, a machine method. This wouldn't entail the construction of a machine, of course, but a series of rules that a "brainless" player could follow, that is a "table of instructions," a chess program.

SHANNON Boy, are we on the same wavelength! I've sometimes won a game simply by applying the basic rules ... A player often sees fantastic moves that depend on the opponent making a certain move, but ... (*he makes his move*)

ALAN Yes, minimax logic: choosing the least bad course of action ... Hey, where do you think you're going with that bishop? (*he makes a brilliant move*) Checkmate! (*Shannon is flabbergasted, then they smile at each other ironically but warmly*)

SHANNON You won't have it so easy next time, Turing. You can bet your bottom dollar on that!

ALAN I'd like to be able to offer you a cold beer to cheer you up, but the tap's dry. Oh, those boring bureaucrats! This morning I tried to order a small barrel to keep here, but it was as if I had said something sinful, it beats me ... (*he sucks in air noisily through his nose*)

Oh, I've got a brilliant idea! As an alternative, I propose an afternoon at the rifle range tomorrow!

SHANNON   (*in astonishment*) The rifle range? With your ideas about war?! ... Where did you learn to shoot?

ALAN   In the Home Guard.

SHANNON   Home Guard?

ALAN   Yes, a civilian force that has been set up in England, since we're at war. They teach you to use a rifle during the training course, so I enrolled.

SHANNON   I thought you weren't interested in weapons ...

ALAN   As with everything else, I was mainly interested in how the gun worked, its possibilities; but I admit I was also attracted by the uniform, though I'm hardly a model soldier. The fact is that one of the questions on the form I had to fill in was: "Do you understand that by enrolling in the Home Guard you place yourself liable to military law?" I saw no advantage in answering "Yes" so I wrote "No." The thing was that they only looked to see that I'd signed the form, as usually happens in these situations, so I was accepted and was a first-class shot at the end of the course.

Needless to say I had no further use for the Home Guard; there was less danger of a German invasion, and I wanted to do something more useful and continue my research. However, the fact that I skipped parade was naturally reported to Headquarters and when I was asked why, I told them that now I had become a crack shot I was no longer interested in the Home Guard.

SHANNON   (*amused*) How did they react?!

ALAN   The commanding officer nearly had a fit; he reminded me of my duties as a soldier and that it was not up to me decide, but I told him that if he looked at my form closely he would see that I was not subject to military law. They found my form at once and he had to admit I had been improperly enrolled through no fault of my own.

SHANNON   You son of a gun!

ALAN   No, I wasn't trying to be clever. I simply took the form at its face value and decided what was the optimal strategy for completing it. I applied the minimax strategy!

SHANNON   (*amused and affectionately admiring*) As usual it's real difficult to catch you out. I'll sure miss you when you go back to England ...

ALAN   (*touched and embarrassed by the show of affection*) I think about my return to Europe, I think about it a lot, I know nothing will be the same. We can't emerge from this war unchanged, everything's changed. What little innocence we still possessed is now gone ...

   As the two friends look at each other and reflect, the light changes.

Scene 13

> *Two hackers in the back room of a computer shop; a workbench completely covered with tangled wires, mother- and daughter-boards, screws, etc.*

ZAC   I've done it, the system's working again! Everything was looking black, I was desperate ... (*to computer*) you're real smart! Almost as smart as me! What a turn on; it's like giving someone the kiss of life and seeing them come alive ... I've resuscitated it! Fucking neat! For a while I thought it was no go and then ...

HARDO   Let's celebrate with a Coke! Now we can afford the real thing instead of that ersatz crap!

ZAC   Come on (*pouring the Coke*) let's get stewed!

HARDO   I told you the computer would save our lives.

ZAC   Unbelievable, a few months ago we were shut up in that shitty school composing papers on a typewriter as a punishment and now ...

HARDO   We got a job in next to no time, and together! What a break!

ZAC   A quick trawl and we found work. (*they slap each others palms*) We'll go a lot further — that's a promise, and a threat!

HARDO   It was a real eye-opener. I didn't realize that what we've been doing for years — building computers, writing programs, gaming, installing operating systems and software — had a value, a market ... that it gave us a real possibility to carve out a niche for ourselves in society.

ZAC   Yeah, society, you can't exist without it. Sure, they love the Net now. How convenient it is for them to log on and access schedules, connections, ticket prices and every other kind of info, before taking a train or plane to their shitty vacation spots or the cities where they strike million-dollar deals ... .

HARDO   Bastards! We understood the Net's potential for exchanging info first. But now we're becoming empowered 'cause none of them know how to do what we can do, they've started preaching about intellectual property, the unchecked flow of information ... For them the mere idea of losing total control ...

ZAC   I can't stand the way they can't tell a hacker from a cracker, get them mixed up, don't understand. They think we're all destructive individuals, online terrorists. Try telling them ... Hey, listen to this! It's a blast! (*music at full volume*)

HARDO   Oh, cool, when did you pull it down?

ZAC   Last night, I scarfed a whole bunch of fantastic tracks, so fuck the record companies and long live music! There's material and intellectual property. Paying for intellectual property is justified only on rare occasions. You pay for material products. I don't fork out for software or music, 'cause I know that musicians, writers and artists will find other ways to earn money from their work; but I would never dream of stealing a TV or a book.

HARDO   "They" think geeks don't read, but I really rate books. Ever since I was I kid I've loved browsing in bookshops or at stalls looking for classics or sci-fi. I like the feeling of holding a book, of turning the pages ... The conventional concepts of trade and property are being redefined. What we do has so much political significance, do you get that? We're freeing up culture!

ZAC   Just think if they'd stuck a rifle in our hand and sent us off to free some oppressed people that had no desire to be liberated by us. Did you ever think about that? At least our generation has been spared going to war ... (*he has second thoughts*) Christ, everything's possible, but ...

HARDO   Hmm ... right ... the Fatherland. No, I don't think it's worth dying for that patriotic crap, no sir. Look at Alan Turing ...

ZAC   Turing's where we come from; he was the original hacker ... with his mathematical theories and formulas he succeeded in getting into the Enigma machine used by the Germans and decoding their secret messages during the War ...

HARDO   You gotta hand it to him! Christ knows where we'd be now without his insights into AI.

ZAC   That was the start of it all. His working constantly with electronic machines that revealed patterns in the hidden messages, enabled him to get down to inventing a calculating machine that could actually duplicate — if not go beyond — human thought processes.

HARDO   I found a site with all the dope on him, a real guru!

He gave everything to his country, to England, and we can honestly say that the British beat Hitler thanks to Turing's decoding work. Thanks to his brain they were able to screw those Nazi bastards and make them eat dirt. Wow, he was really something.

But you could never say that the palefaced Brits with all their prejudices treated him like a national hero.

No way.

On the contrary ...

Scene 14

England 1952. Alan and his brother John in the visiting room of a prison.

JOHN   So, Alan, try to explain what happened, clearly and in a few words, please. I can't believe it. You of all people!

ALAN   Well, what can I say ... recently I was missing a few items and occasionally some money, and I got fed up at a certain point and told Arnold ...

JOHN   (*allusively*) You and Arnold ...

ALAN   Yes, we were. I met him in a pub and then ... but the point is that Arnold confessed to me that he had told a friend of his about us, and that this friend had done some petty thieving, convincing me that I should go to the Police and report the burglary.

JOHN   God, you're a silly ass! And you were stupid enough to go to the Police? All your study of logic and you still haven't understood that ...

ALAN   Is what they're saying, what they're thinking logical? Look, there are 6 charges against me ... or rather one charge phrased in six different ways ... 1. Alan Mathison Turing, on the 17th day of December, 1951, at Wilmslow, being a male person, committed an act of gross indecency with Arnold Murray, a male person.

2. Alan Mathison Turing, on the 17th day of December, 1951, at Wilmslow, being a male person, was party to the commission of an act of gross indecency with Arnold Murray, a male person. And so on.

JOHN   Did you publicly declare that you had had a sexual relationship with that man?!

ALAN   What if I did? It's true isn't it? They asked me a question and I answered it; besides, I had gone there to report a theft ...

JOHN   How maddeningly naive! In a country where homosexuality is a crime carrying a two-year prison sentence, my dear brother, with his brilliant brain, goes straight to the police to report the theft of a few trifles, a burglary in which the youth he was taking to bed was indirectly involved! You should never have gone to the police, not for any reason on earth! Let alone put yourself in such a vulnerable position!

ALAN   I don't want to be respected and accepted as the person I am not. I want to be accepted as a homosexual.

JOHN   You do realize that everyone's going to know now?

ALAN   I am not worried about being in the public eye but about all the details of the affair becoming public.

JOHN   I find your behavior unacceptable. You have no consideration for other people's feelings. Have you thought about mother?

ALAN   ... Yes, that's the worst part of this business, I have to tell her about something for which, as King George V believed, men usually shoot themselves. You wouldn't tell her for me, would you?

JOHN   Out of the question! I've found you a good solicitor, I'll try and get you out on bail, but my telling mother is completely out of the question!

ALAN   ... Roger ... However, I have started to write to my closest friends, I'd like them to hear the facts from me instead of reading about it in the paper ...

JOHN   Sounds like a wise move ... By the way, your solicitor advises you to plead guilty ...

ALAN   I've already told you that it's not easy ... don't you see that there is no way I can be completely honest?

Denying what I have done would be a lie ... and it would be like considering what happened as something that should be denied; but also presenting myself as guilty in public, as a confessed criminal, is not telling the truth either ...

JOHN   Don't you understand that the statement you made to the Police doesn't give you a leg to stand on, so you have very little to lose by pleading guilty. This would shorten and play down the trial, which is basically the most important thing.

ALAN   Of course, you don't give a damn about the terrible circumstances under which homosexuals are forced to exist ... you're only interested in your position in the City. I'll think about it and should I decide to plead guilty, you may rest assured that I won't pretend for one single minute to feel guilty or to recant.

JOHN   (*losing his patience*) All right, do as you wish ... (*he leaves*) (*Alan remains alone; he picks up a withered leaf from the floor and studies it in silence*)

ALAN   What makes a cell become a starfish, a leaf or a human being? (*he is lost in thought as the light dims and in the background we hear sounds from the small prison*)

Scene 15

The work room of the two hackers

HARDO   I've been surfing for at least four hours a day recently, and doing it on the boss' phone line gives me even more of a kick.

ZAC   Remember that astronomical bill we got when we moved into our rat hole? Cleaned us out!

HARDO   (*passing a hand over his forehead, as if wiping off the sweat*) Mammoth heart attack! What a beginning! We were practically living online, a real slap in the face! That huge bill suddenly revealed the full weight of the material world as opposed to the lightweight virtual world! (*singing to himself*) I was thinking of a cybernetic meadow ...

ZAC   Being online makes you feel like something else; all you have to do is log on and leave the world ... (*pause*) If we don't give any importance to the concept of inside and outside, it no longer dominates us ... (*pause*)

HARDO   Do you think that everything around the screen, the outside I mean, really exists? Some say no, that it's all in the mind ...

ZAC   Mind, mind ... we were just talking about that bill, if it had been a mental issue we wouldn't have shelled out all that money, which really cost us ...

HARDO   Wait a minute though, money's really weird. Sure it exists and it has a value, but only because this has been agreed, only because that piece of paper represents this or that sum, otherwise it would just be a piece of paper. It's like saying that if you don't give it that meaning, money doesn't exist.

ZAC   But the paper exists. Whether you say so or not.

HARDO   Now we're getting down to the real nitty-gritty. (*pause*)

ZAC   The force of gravity also exists without you; it doesn't know it's called that but it exerts itself without giving a fuck about anything else. (*pause*) Whereas a feeling, a nightmare exists only because I'm there experiencing it and interpreting it. Without me, zero.

But that's not why I can say it doesn't exist ...

Very confusing!

HARDO   No, wait, there must be two types of things, those that exist independently of me and those that only exist with a contribution from me — as one American philosopher put it. That would appear to answer the question, right?

ZAC   Yeah, but what about the computer? (*indicating his PC*) If I don't turn it on it's not going to surf anywhere ... that is, sometimes I get the impression that it's autonomous, but now you've upset my thinking I realize that it is what it is because I manoeuvre and interpret the icons. Of course, it wouldn't be the same without the computer, but if I pull the plug it's the end, while I, although desperate, continue to exist ...

What's your answer to that?

HARDO   We need something down to earth after all this philosophizing — maybe its the genuine Coke? (*they laugh, drink, and listen to some music on the computer*) But do you think it (*pointing to the computer*) thinks? (*pause*)

ZAC   (*mockingly*) Some say yes, some say no ...

HARDO   Our friend Turing, when faced with that same question, said it was badly put.

ZAC   Oh yeah?

HARDO   Yeah, in the sense that it all depends on what you mean by thinking.

ZAC   Maybe, but what was his theory?

HARDO   He said that we take it for granted that a person can think, that he's intelligent and we deduce this from very simple and superficial things like a certain relationship between question and answer, between stimulus and reaction. So if these same things are transmitted by a machine, that is if a machine gives us the same kind of answers, we can legitimately say that it thinks ...

Very often people are no more aware of what they do than a computer is aware of what it does. Most things in life are done like that, by automatically copying certain models. Take bureaucrats, for example, they don't think for themselves, they execute programs, they're programmed to say and do certain things without asking themselves a single question ...

Scene 16

> *Alan is wearing a bathrobe; he is sitting on a chair, his expression is like that of a child who has been let down.*

ALAN   They've accused me of being at odds with the Institutions, but I have never been for or against them. (*pause*)

Today I feel completely at odds with my body. (*he puts a hand inside his bathrobe and gently moves it over his chest*)

Half oranges. (*he repeats the gesture*)

I've grown breasts. (*pause*)

Oestrogen. (*pause*) I was given parole for a price: a year of organotherapy — a fancy name for huge doses of female hormones. (*pause*)

Chemistry is playing its part.

I can't play mine.

I didn't sleep a wink last night.

Every time I turned over I felt soft flesh move that isn't mine. (*pause*)

They want to get rid of my deviant behavior, stop me from being different, with the weapons of chemistry. (*pause*)

The result of a "positive inquiry." The CID has invested in science — I never dared hope! (*he gives a nervous, bitter laugh*) (*pause*)

The heretic consumed by the flames of molecules is perfectly acceptable. (*pause*)

After giving me a taste in small doses, they will inject a single, massive dose into my thigh. (*pause*)

After a year's therapy I'll be back to normal, they say. (*pause*)

Back to normal. (*pause*)

I must go back to being what I was before, but warped by them. (*pause*) like a male animal injected with oestrogens in the name of research ha! ha! (*pause*)

From spectator to guinea pig.

I've gone through the mirror ... (*pause*)

I wanted to discover the magical workings of the human mind. (*pause*)

I succeeded in dominating the logic of machines but human logic has me in check. (*pause*)

Reproducing the complexity of thought mechanically is as difficult as describing family life on Mars, and what about my life? (*pause*)

The irrational cannot be duplicated.

Logic can. (*pause*)

The spirals of a pine cone follow a perfect order that signifies beauty, a mathematical destiny, the harmony of the Fibonacci numbers. (*he is mesmerized for a moment; pause*)

With those injections they want to change my body's drive,

that of my actions, my feelings. (*pause*)

Impotent. (*pause*)

Science can do that. (*he puts both hands inside his bathrobe and moves them gently over his chest*)

Scene 17

HARDO   I'm almost there with my new program, I'm really wound up. It's unbelievable, I get so excited every time, a real high. I can't go to bed until it's finished, I talk to the computer.

I've produced something that wasn't there before, something alive, a creature I gave birth to, with my mental sperm.

ZAC   "Almost" alive, almost! It's that "almost" you can relate to; it's much more difficult to get on with people who are totally alive.

HARDO   You said it! You were so unrelaxed while that little blonde was giving you a line the other night at that "office" party, it was like you had a gun in your ribs!

ZAC   The thing is that sometimes whole people scare me, I don't know what to do with my emotions. I mean, why didn't whoever created them set up an archive to store them in?

HARDO   That's an idea ...

ZAC   Let's face it, as soon as I got there and saw how they were dressed I realized there was a difference, and when she started talking to me, getting up real close and looking at me the way she did, I was sure she trying to figure out if I got my jacket from a dime store. (*pause*)

It was a bad situation — level 9 — a real-live "doll" and all that talk, wow ... it was like a three-way chat with everyone talking at once. There was no stopping her, so what could I do? She buttonholed me and I tried to adapt, faking the replies ...

HARDO   You tried to imitate her, just like computers do humans: imitation game!

ZAC   Imitation what?

HARDO   Imitation game, or rather the Turing Test.

ZAC   Oh. What's that?

HARDO   It's a test Turing devised to show that it was possible to reproduce certain aspects of human thought and language in a machine, and to see if it was possible to distinguish between the replies from people and those from a machine. The original purpose of the test was to determine if a person's sex could be established from the replies.

ZAC   Something else! Exactly what I needed! How does it work?

HARDO   There are three players: a man, a woman and an interrogator, who can be male or female. The interrogator is in a room by himself, he has to decide, on the basis of written replies, which is the man and which is the woman ... But what would happen if the man and the woman were replaced by a machine without our knowing? To what degree would we realize this? In short, the question here is "can machines think?"

ZAC   How do you do this Turing Test, it's really awesome!

HARDO   In the latest version a jury of 10 people have to decide, during an online conversation, if they're talking to a person or a programmed computer (*he starts punching keys furiously*).

ZAC   Has the computer ever fooled them?

HARDO   And how, that's what's so great. But mostly people have been taken for machines ... and that makes you think ... (*pause*)

ZAC   Does this mean we can say that something dies when a program is destroyed?

HARDO   The million dollar question ... (*he keeps punching the keys*)

ZAC   I've asked myself over and over; it drives me crazy ...

HARDO   (*still typing*) Hmm ... you have to decide how you're going to approach the question; it's always best to choose a fresh viewpoint.

ZAC   I don't think there's too much choice.

HARDO   Not true. For instance, if you look at it from the point of view of the living, you'll see that when you die you die for someone else as well, someone who's connected to you ...

ZAC   So?

HARDO   So as a program is something through which you create a particular relationship with the computer, when this "dies" we can say that you feel its death, your relationship feels it, so I would say that something dies ... (*he punches the keys even faster; he is visibly excited about what's happening onscreen*)

ZAC   Your reasoning's flawless, flawless; I'm going to get a black T-shirt and go into mourning. (*reacting with a start*) Great! I've got into the Turing Test!

Now we don't know if we're connected to a man or a machine ...

> *On the other half of the stage Alan is lying on a bed in his room, with his old teddy bear Porgy, the star globe, a bowl of fruit, etc. He writes on small white cards and what he writes appears on the screen as the message from a computer that the two boys receive; they read them out loud.*

PORGY   My name's Porgy, what's yours?

HARDO   Hardo. Do you like being in touch with the world, Porgy?

PORGY   It's not easy to be in touch with the world.

HARDO   How do you get on with humans?

PORGY   I've got on better with my bed.

HARDO   Do you always have an answer?

PORGY   No, I don't. Not even mathematics is entirely a matter of logic.

HARDO   Do you always tell the truth?

PORGY   When the emperor's wearing no clothes he's naked.

HARDO   What leaves you speechless?

PORGY   What cannot be said.

HARDO   What is the universe?

PORGY   The universe is the interior of the light cone of the creation.

HARDO   And science, what's that?

PORGY   Science is a differential equation.

HARDO   And religion?

PORGY   Religion is a boundary condition.

HARDO   Does God exist in the universe?

PORGY   Wherever God's holy pantomime is played out.

HARDO   Can a computer conceive of God?

PORGY   I've always wondered if He would catch cold walking on the damp grass.

HARDO   Do you agree with what people say about how machines think?

PORGY   If two machines were chatting about human beings, would they ask why they think what they think?

HARDO   Can a computer be so desperate it commits suicide?

PORGY   Could you repeat the question?

> *The program stops. On the screen we see Hal's mouth in "2001: A Space Odyssey." Freeze frame on the two hackers. Light on Alan as he stops writing. He gets into a sitting position.*

ALAN   The onion ...

Yes, I wanted to separate the layers of the onion of the mind
but there was nothing in the center. (*pause*)
My hope, my wish was to find this. (*he helps himself to an apple and takes a bite*)
The core.
Pure life. (*pause*)

> *He sits down at a table on which there are some ampoules and laboratory instruments. While he is speaking he picks up a small box with cyanide in it, opens it, tips the contents into a small basin and slowly dips the apple in the poison.*

A computer can only open the windows of logic through which life itself escapes.
Irrational and inimitable. (*pause*)
A computer can never appreciate a fairy-tale as much as a little boy. (*pause*)
I love Snow White's apple. (*pause*)
Its reflection in the mirror. (*pause*)
Through which I pass. (*pause*)
Imitation game. (*pause*) (*he sings to himself and lies down on the bed*)
"Dip the apple in the brew
Let the Sleeping Death seep through." [2]

Scene 18

> *Ethel Turing enters; she speaks quietly, arguing against Alan's having committed suicide.*

ETHEL   That habit of not washing his hands after doing experiments, that's what killed him.
He did experiments with cyanide. (*pause*)

---

[2] "Dip the apple in the brew ... " from Walt Disney's *Snow White*.

He always had a fixation about poison getting under his fingernails; some of it was bound to. (*pause*)
He wasn't careful enough; he didn't scrub them, and who knows ... (*pause*)
I'll never believe my Alan took his own life.
He was odd, granted, but not that odd. (*pause*)
He was calm again, and had practically overcome the trauma of the oestrogen treatment.
That nasty affair actually brought us closer. (*pause*)
And then he had resumed his computing studies, he had been to Greece ... he was organizing another trip. (*pause*)
The idea of the secret service is like something out of a film. (*pause*)
Yes, I've thought about it, all that top-secret information, but I never knew anything. What can I say? (*pause*)
His complete lack of interest in his body, grooming, washing his hands ... (*pause*)
He was exactly the same at college ... your hands and nails are dirty, Alan, you've got ink on your collar. (*pause*)
Wash your hands, Alan.

— *The End* —

I would like to thank Giulio Giorello (Professor at the Università degli Studi, Milano), Renato Spaventa (President of the Association for Communication of Science), Massimo della Campa (President of the Società Umanitaria, Milano), and my assistant Francesca Nascé for their valuable contributions.

References

1. J. M. Carthy, M. L. Minski, N. Rochester, and C. E. Shannon. *A Proposal for the Dartmouth Summer Research Project on Artificial Intelligence.* Available online: http://www-formal.Stanford.EDU/jmc/history/dartmouth.html, 1955.
2. J. L. Casti. *The Cambridge Quintet: A Work of Scientific Speculation.* Abacus, London, UK, 1998.
3. P. M. Churchland. *The Engine of Reason, the Seat of the Soul,* MIT Press, Cambridge, MA, 1995.
4. A. Hodges. *Alan Turing: The Enigma.* Walker & Company, New York, 2000.
5. D. R. Hofstadter. *Godel, Escher, Bach: an Eternal Golden Braid.* Basic Books, New York, 1979.
6. G. Johnson. *Machinery of the Mind: Inside the New Science of Artificial Intelligence.* Microsoft Press, Redmond, WA, 1987.

7. J. Kats. *Geeks: How Two Lost Boys Rode the Internet Out of Idaho*. Random House, New York, 2000.
8. S. Levy. *Hackers: Heroes of the Computer Revolution*. Penguin Books, New York, 2001.
9. P. Odifreddi. *Alan Turing: informatica, spionaggio e sesso*. Gennaio, 1992. `http://www.vialattea.net`.
10. P. Odifreddi and M. Bartoccioni. *Odissea Artificiale*. Video RAI, 1990.
11. J. R. Searle. *The Mystery of Consciousness*. New York Review of Books, New York, 1998.
12. J. R. Searle. *Mind, Language and Society*. Basic Books, New York, 2000.
13. J. R. Searle. *Mind, Brains and Science*. The 1984 Reith Lectures, Harvard University Press, Cambridge, MA, 1984.
14. S. Singh. *The Code Book: The Evolution of Secrecy from Mary, Queen of Scots to Quantum Cryptography*. Doubleday, New York, 1999.
15. A. M. Turing. Computing machinery and intelligence. *Mind*, 59(236):433–460, 1950.
16. E. S. Turing. *Alan M. Turing*. Heffer & Sons, Cambridge, 1959.

What Would Alan Turing Have Done After 1954?

Andrew Hodges

Wadham College, University of Oxford

Summary. Incomplete aspects of Turing's work are surveyed, with particular reference to his late interest in the foundations of quantum mechanics, and refuting the assertion that his work raised the prospect of constructing physical "oracle-machines."

Alan Turing died on 7 June 1954 at the age of 41. It is of course an unanswerable question as to what he would have done if he had lived. His life was full of surprises at every turn. But I shall use this counterfactual theme to survey some incomplete threads in his life and work, some of them under-appreciated. I shall also address recent mistaken claims that Turing anticipated the agenda of so-called "hypercomputing."

1   A Survey of Turing's Legacy in 1954

In his last year, Turing was exploring many avenues in his morphogenesis theory. The problem of explaining the Fibonacci patterns in plants was probably less tractable than he had at first hoped. But there were other directions in which his biological theory might have advanced if he had lived longer. He might well have pursued a connection with von Neumann's ideas for discrete self-organizing systems, usually considered as the foundation of "artificial life." He might have seized upon the decoding of DNA in 1953, which introduced discrete logic into biology. It is also notable that it was through numerical simulations of non-linear equations, made possible by the computer, that chaotic phenomena became accessible to investigation in the 1950s. Such numerical simulations were Turing's *forte* by 1954. It seems quite possible that he would have seen the nature of chaos rather quicker than other people did. So there was great scope for broadening his applied-mathematical interests.

But Turing had by no means abandoned pure mathematics. He had probably lost interest in mathematical logic for its own sake. But he might well have gone on to contribute to other decision problems within mathematics. In 1950 he had done work on decidability problems in *semigroups* [35] and then Turing described P. S. Novikov's new result on the undecidability of the "word problem" for *groups* in a semi-popular article appearing in 1954 [38].

He explained a word problem in terms of a problem in knot theory. This illustration itself pointed to another fascinating and growing area in post-war mathematics, and also reflected the more geometrical turn of his interests. The 1954 article went on to explain Gödel's theorem. This was perhaps the first popular article on the subject, which was not at all well known in those days. So this last paper also suggests another role that a longer-lived Alan Turing might have taken — a great communicator of mathematics and science to a wide audience. But it also suggests that Turing might have taken up, for instance, the outstanding question (Hilbert's Tenth Problem) of the solvability of Diophantine equations, not settled in the real world until 1970, Martin Davis having a prominent role in the story and being a distinguished expositor of it [12].

What about the future of his work in computer science? Immediately after Turing's death in 1954, his student and friend Robin Gandy wrote to Max Newman, Turing's colleague and patron, with an account [17] of what struck him as unfinished in Turing's work. Gandy wrote comments under eight different headings. Of these only one was on morphogenesis; only one of them, the sixth, was in computer science, and was as follows:

> I always hoped he would return one day to the practical problems of making a machine learn. There should be somewhere a copy of the report he wrote on this after his sabbatical year at Cambridge from the NPL.

We may well rejoice in the fact that the basis for Christof Teuscher's work, which has in turn brought about this *Festschrift* for Alan Turing's ninetieth birthday, is the practical exploration of the theory of networks in this report [34], entitled futuristically *Intelligent Machinery*.

However, it is worth noting Gandy's message that Turing had shown little interest in pursuing this work in practice. When he had the 1951 Manchester computer at his disposal, he had not used it to follow up his "learning" proposals. This was true also of his ideas for programming. It is very striking that he continued to write raw machine code for the Manchester machine, although he of all people knew that the machine itself could have been made to do the routine work. In 1946, years ahead of others, he had seen the potential of the stored program for interpreters, compilers and scripts [32]:

> The process of constructing instruction table should be very fascinating. There need be no real danger of it ever becoming a drudge, for any processes that are quite mechanical may be turned over to the machine itself.

In 1947 he explicitly recognized the general nature of programming languages [33]:

> ... one could communicate with these machines in any language provided it was an exact language, i.e. in principle one should be able to communicate in any symbolic logic, provided that the machine

were given instruction tables which would allow it to interpret that logical system.

In 1950 his M.Sc. student Audrey Bates worked on putting a small part of Church's lambda-calculus in a form where it could be mechanized by the Manchester computer [1]. This work could have led to LISP programming, which was also inspired by the lambda-calculus, but he never followed it up. The same is true of the work he did on program proofs in 1949; this was never taken up and had to wait for others in the 1960s.

The computer scientist John McCarthy would have invited Turing to Dartmouth College in 1956, for what is usually thought of as the conference that began Artificial Intelligence. What would Turing have said, if he had accepted such an invitation? He would have been living witness to the fact that Artificial Intelligence research had started well before 1956. The wartime origin was described in [20, e.g. pp. 210–214, 265, 291–294] with a deeper analysis in [21, 23]. Perhaps he would have advocated avoiding the separation of "top-down" from "bottom-up" research that was in fact to characterize AI research so strongly for the next thirty years. For Turing in 1948 and again in 1950 [34, 36] had described both approaches together, saying that both should be tried out. But he had made little effort to make such trials himself. Turing preferred making the first attack at a new idea and then leaving the details for others to work out. This was true of his programming theory, his bottom-up ideas on neural networks, and his top-down ideas on machine chess-playing. So it is by no means obvious that a longer life would have led him to continue with AI research.

There is, however, another arena where his knowledge of mathematical logic might have been brought into practical computer science to make a first attack on a new area: this is what we have known as complexity theory since the 1970s.

Practical time constraints on algorithmic solutions formed a vital aspect of Turing's wartime work. It seems quite possible that he was consulted by GCHQ after 1948 about the use of computers for large-scale problems, such as the famous Venona problem of Soviet messages which was the top Anglo-American priority in that period. If so, it is also possible that research in large-scale efficient computer-based searching and sorting would have brought him to complexity theory ideas.

Turing's wartime work mainly lay in probability theory and Bayesian statistics. Afterwards he left it to Jack Good to write up a civilian version of his theory, and he made no effort to pursue the parallel of his work with Shannon's information theory. But possibly he would one day have gone on to combine his knowledge of computation and probability: in particular he had left the concept of randomness oddly informal. He described machines with "random elements" but these were left to Shannon and others in 1956 work to define properly [13].

Looking further ahead, the ideas of Gregory Chaitin on randomness and computability give a picture of a field Turing might have opened — even if not necessarily agreeing with all Chaitin's views.

A minor feature of Turing's postwar work, but one that might have blossomed with longer life, is the application of computing methods in pure mathematics. His colleague Max Newman was very quick to exploit the Mersenne Prime problem to illustrate the power of computation, and discussed very advanced ideas at the inauguration of the Manchester computer [24] in the use of probabilistic methods in algebra and number theory. Probabilistic primality testing, as used in public-key cryptology today, might have been working much earlier in Turing's hands.

He might also have made powerful advances in cryptology itself. It is striking how he made general statements about this field, and we do not know where his thoughts were leading. In a 1936 letter [29] he reported to his mother from Princeton:

> I have just discovered a possible application of the kind of thing I am working on at present. It answers the question "What is the most general kind of code or cipher possible," and at the same time (rather naturally) enables me to construct a lot of particular and interesting codes.

This tantalizing statement, with its fascinating link between computability and cryptology, leaves us only wanting to know the answer Turing found to his question, and the identity of the particular and interesting codes. Possibly the latter were related to Turing's 1937–8 cryptological work, which was reported to me by Dr Malcolm McPhail in 1978 in the following terms (see [20, p. 138]):

> ... he would multiply the number corresponding to a specific message by a horrendously long but secret number and transmit the product. The length of the secret number was determined by the requirement that it should take 100 Germans working eight hours a day on desk calculators 100 years to discover the secret factor by routine search. Turing actually designed an electric multiplier ...

Again, we are left wondering what the scheme actually was (for multiplication is too simple), and what was his theory of its security. It is by no means clear what Turing was doing, and he may well have had many advanced ideas that were never published. In 1950 he divulged [36]:

> I have set up on the Manchester computer a small programme using only 1000 units of storage, whereby the machine supplied with one sixteen figure number replies with another ... I would defy anyone to learn from these values sufficient about the programme to be able to predict any replies to untried values.

In the paper this plays the role of showing how a computable process — in fact a *small program* — can be totally surprising, thus making a point about the mechanizability of mental processes. But read another way it is a claim to a cipher system unbreakable even with chosen plaintext — the modern criterion of security.

Once again we can only speculate on what he was doing for GCHQ, and why GCHQ had tried to get him back to work full-time, until his 1952 exclusion. What might have he done if the political establishment had treated him differently? Would his effect on the cold war history of 1954 have been as significant as it was on the Atlantic war of 1944? Both were great wars of information and intelligence.

There is a science-fiction story by the writer Greg Egan [14], which starts on a political footing, discussing what might have happened if Alan Turing had been treated differently by his rulers, and has all sorts of imaginative elements, including a dialogue with the theologian C. S. Lewis. But it goes on to focus on scientific advances by and around a counter-factual Turing of the late 1950s. An important point is that it correctly introduces a focus on fundamental *physics,* a point to which I shall return in concluding this survey. The story is called *Oracle,* a reference to the uncomputable oracle of Turing's 1938–9 paper on ordinal logics [31]. Roughly speaking, an oracle has to contain an infinite amount of information in a finite space, so as to be able to solve a problem unsolvable by any Turing machine, e.g. to supply on demand the answer to the halting problem for every Turing machine. In this excerpt a fictional character links the oracle with time travel:

> ... "Time travel," Helen said, "gives me the chance to become an Oracle. There's a way to exploit the inability to change your own past, a way to squeeze an infinite number of timelike paths — none of them closed, but some of them arbitrarily near it — into a finite physical system. Once you do that, you can solve the halting problem ..."

2   Church's Thesis and Copeland's Thesis

This brings me naturally to B. J. Copeland's influential views on what Turing would have done, because he has also raised the prospect of actually building such oracles — not as science fiction, but as a serious possibility for future technology. This is the prospectus of so-called hypercomputation. Moreover, he and his colleague D. Proudfoot have associated these ambitions with Turing's views and given the impression that these are lost ideas of Turing's which can now be recovered and perhaps implemented.

There is a very general sense in which I agree with Copeland: the physical world should not be assumed computable without further investigation. This point was made long ago by Chaitin [2] and no doubt by many others.

Certainly we should now be more penetrating in the analysis of the concept of "mechanical," with the benefit of modern physical knowledge. I also agree that Turing himself, if he had lived, would have been very interested in such investigation — just as that science-fiction story suggests. His interest in mathematical logic was not the rather narrow and technical one sometimes found in the modern discipline: his work might be characterized as using post-Gödel logic as a branch of applied mathematics. But, for reasons to be outlined in what follows, I find no reason whatever to associate Turing with the "hypercomputation" prospectus which Copeland has advanced. In making this association, Copeland has emphasized to his wide audience that he contradicts the picture of Turing's ideas as advanced by other, more conventional commentators. I have had the privilege of being treated as a representative of this traditional school of thought. Thus, Copeland and Proudfoot informed the readership of the *Times Literary Supplement* [7] that:

> Taking their cue from Turing's 1939 paper, a small but growing international group of researchers is interested in the possibility of constructing machines capable of computing more than the universal Turing machine ... research in this direction could lead to the biggest change computing has seen since 1948. Hodges's Turing would regard their work as a search for the impossible. We suspect that the real Turing would think differently.

By machines capable of computing more than the universal Turing machine, Copeland refers to the 'oracles' which he and D. Proudfoot described in terms of infinite-precision measurements in their *Scientific American* article [8], and which are criticized by Martin Davis in this volume. The allusion to 1948 (the first working stored-program computer, giving rise to the IT industry of today) shows the economic seriousness of what he has in mind. If Turing's name were truly associated with this possibility, that would give it much greater significance and credibility.

What is the difference between Copeland's "real" Turing and "my" Turing? I had written in [20, p. 109], summarizing what Turing had achieved in 1936:

> Alan ... had discovered ... a universal machine that could take over the work of any machine ...

Copeland claims [7] that I made an important error here in writing "machine" rather than writing explicitly "Turing machine." This is because:

> Turing himself described abstract machines whose mathematical abilities exceed those of the universal Turing machine (in a ground-breaking paper published in 1939).

Copeland in a more academic paper [11] criticizes the same sentence, for the same reason, and there says that I expressed a "common view." Indeed I did. My statement about machines lay in entirely respectable company:

not only within the mainstream of mathematical logic, but reflecting the description of Turing's work that Church himself gave. Although Turing's description of the Turing machine was couched in terms of imitating a human being following some procedure, Church characterized computable functions, when introducing them to the world in the *Journal of Symbolic Logic*, in these words [3]:

> The author [i.e. Turing] proposes as a criterion that an infinite sequence of digits 0 and 1 be "computable" that it shall be possible to devise a computing machine, occupying a finite space and with working parts of finite size, which will write down the sequence to any desired number of terms if allowed to run for a sufficiently long time. As a matter of convenience, certain further restrictions are imposed on the character of the machine, but these are of such a nature as obviously to cause no loss of generality — in particular, a human calculator, provided with pencil and paper and explicit instructions, can be regarded as a kind of Turing machine.

Thus Church described computable functions as those that could be performed *by some machine*. Church drew no distinct line between the human being following a rule, and the action of a finite machine. (If anything, the words "in particular" suggest that Church conceived of a human calculator as the *most powerful* example of a machine.) Church offered no hint of speculation about machines that could exceed the power of Turing machines. In fact, Church's characterization of computability actually excluded this possibility.

Church was famous for meticulous clarity, and he was supervising Turing's Ph.D. at Princeton when he wrote this review, so I cannot believe he made this statement lightly, in ignorance or defiance of Turing's views. Furthermore, he repeated it in 1940 [5] when he knew all about the Turing "oracles" that Copeland thinks are "machines" standing in contradiction to the "common view."

It appears that the background to Copeland's assertion is the desire to maintain simultaneously that so-called "hypercomputing" machines can be built, and that the Church-Turing thesis is correct. This position can only be maintained if Church's thesis was never intended to apply to machines. The readership of *Scientific American* was informed [8] that it was "a myth" that Church's thesis referred to machines, and that

> In truth, Church and Turing claimed only that a universal Turing machine can match the behavior of any human mathematician working with paper and pencil in accordance with an algorithmic method — a considerably weaker claim that certainly does not rule out the possibility of hypermachines.

But the primary characterization of Turing machines in [3], as given above, shows that Church made no such restriction. Indeed, had Church set out to cultivate amongst his readers the "myth" denounced by Copeland and Proud-foot, he could hardly have done so more effectively. Copeland in [6] quotes a secondary statement from Church [4] which employs the expression "an arbitrary machine," and asserts that what Church meant was only that the Turing machine concept or its equivalents would have arbitrary elements in their technical formulation. In mathematical parlance, however, the expression "an arbitrary machine" simply means "any machine whatever," and if there were any doubt about this interpretation one need only look at the primary statement by Church as quoted above.

It is worth standing back to see the context in a little more generality, since the point at issue here does not in fact depend on the exact words used by Turing or Church; it stems from the very nature of what was being addressed by Turing's theory of mind and machine. The problem that faced Turing in 1936, as it again faced him in his theory of "machine intelligence" (see [22] for a recent survey) is that of whether machines can do as much as the mind. This problem is not, of course, Turing's alone: it is a fundamental problem of science, and whether we study Gödel or Penrose, Lucas or Hofstadter, Searle or Dennett, everyone agrees that the basic *question* is whether human minds are super-mechanical, though there is widespread disagreement about the *answer*. Copeland and Proudfoot alone suggest that the problem is the *other way round*, giving the impression that Turing defined computability as he did, because there might be superhuman machines. Copeland offers in [6] as explanation for Turing's definition of computability:

> For among a machine's repertoire of atomic operations there may
> be those that no human being unaided by machinery can perform.

But this consideration is entirely foreign to Turing's thought. This sentence represents a quite unjustified projection of Copeland's "hypercomputation" thesis into the classical formulations of 1936.

A possibly confusing element is that Turing defined an entity called an "oracle-machine," and indeed described an oracle-machine as "a new type of machine." Is this a contradiction? No: Turing's "oracle-machine," defined for the purpose of exploring the uncomputable within mathematical logic, involves a generalized use of the word "machine" for something that is only *partly* mechanical. (In contrast, of course, Church's thesis concerns the scope of the *purely* mechanical.) The oracle formalizes non-mechanical steps, which can (if given any extra-mathematical interpretation at all) be compared with the "intuition" of seeing the truth of a formally unprovable Gödel statement. The oracle is a non-mechanical entity inside a partially mechanical entity, the oracle-machine. Any doubt about what Turing meant should be dispelled by the clear statement in [31] that:

> We shall not go any further into the nature of this oracle apart
> from saying that it cannot be a machine.

The nature, and indeed the essential purpose of the oracle, is that it is not a machine. There is a precedent for Turing's use of the word "machine" in this generalized sense: the "choice-machines" defined in Turing's original great paper [30], which ask for a human operator's decisions — by definition, *not* mechanical. These choice-machines also are only *partly* mechanical. If the winner of a Turing Test for machine intelligence were revealed to have a human choice-maker hidden inside the computer, we should not consider the victory much of an achievement. Likewise, if "oracle-machines" were allowed in deciding the Entscheidungsproblem, the question would become trivial. In both cases the *whole point* lies in whether the task can or cannot be done by *purely* mechanical means, and it stands as Turing's great achievement that over sixty years later his encapsulation of the "purely mechanical" by the Turing machine definition still holds sway.

Summarizing, there is nothing in Turing's "ground-breaking paper of 1939" [31] to justify Copeland's sensational technological and economic prospectus about "constructing" oracle-machines.

Nor is there anything in Turing's later work to support Copeland's prospectus for an oracle-based hyper-computer revolution. In Turing's 1948 report [34], which contained an extended account of "machines" in general, oracle-machines never appeared in the analysis. We can also look again at Gandy's 1954 letter [17] for evidence regarding Turing's legacy. Gandy supplied Newman with a long section on Turing's views on the reception of his ordinal logics [31]. This has been cited by Copeland and Proudfoot [10] to suggest that Turing thought his 1939 paper had not been given the attention it deserved. Indeed he did, but Gandy's extensive remarks on Turing's views all referred to his much more advanced ideas in mathematical logic. They did not mention oracles, let alone suggest something to do with seeing oracles as objects that might exist. Martin Davis emphasizes, in this volume, as does Feferman [16], that the "oracle" plays only a very small part in [31].

Copeland has also commended in [6] the later contribution of Gandy to this question, stressing that in [18] Gandy distinguished "Thesis M" (that anything done by a machine is computable) from Church's Thesis. Gandy undertook a rigorous definition of the concept of machine, with this distinction in mind. Copeland does not observe, however that (1) Gandy never even considered counting an "oracle-machine" in this category and that (2) Gandy's results *lend support* to what Church assumed in 1937, viz. that "purely mechanical" does indeed imply "computable." It is not surprising that Gandy never considered oracle-machines in his analysis of the mechanical: he fully reflected Turing's thought as his student and legatee, as well as representing the tradition of mathematical logic.

We now pass to Turing's famous 1950 paper [36], which summarizes Turing's post-1945 claim that the action of the brain must be computable, and therefore can be simulated on a computer. I have already referred to how

Turing used a pseudo-random program to exemplify how a machine can create a "surprise." This was entirely typical of his argument that something *apparently* non-mechanical can in fact be readily computable. But in fact this example also illustrates how his 1950 argument was not merely about the sufficiency of computable functions. Turing's argument was that a *totally finite* machine (with a fixed finite store) would suffice to simulate the finite brain. Thus, in that cipher-based example, Turing emphasized *how small* a store was needed to embody the effect of a "surprise." This point leads me to make a further defense against the charges made in [7] and [11]. For there Copeland asserted that I had overlooked an important reference to uncomputable operations in Turing's 1950 paper [36], asserting that therein one might find Turing saying that:

> An example of a discrete-state machine whose behavior cannot be calculated by a universal Turing machine is a digital computer with an infinite-capacity store and what Turing calls a "random element". (pp. 438–439)

But in fact, an inspection of Turing's argument shows that the "infinite store" just corresponds to the unbounded tape of the Turing machine. It is the arena within which computable operations are defined, not something going beyond computability. As for the "random element," Turing specifically gave a pseudo-random (i.e. entirely computable) illustration of it, namely the digits of π. Thus, these references in Turing's paper only corroborate the fact that Turing saw mental processes as falling within the scope of the computable. In [11] Copeland further argues:

> Hodges ... fails to include the crucial words "discrete state machines ... can be described by such tables *provided they have only a finite number of possible states.*"

But this qualification of "finitely many states" is not crucial at all. In his 1950 paper Turing gave the philosophical world a rather abbreviated description of computability which avoided bringing in the concept of the infinitely long "tape." Instead, his discussion was focused on *totally finite machines*, which do not need to use any tape; or in other words, the states of the tape are absorbed into the states of the machine. (This is why Turing had to refer, rather awkwardly, to an "infinite store" when referring to the full definition of computability.) The condition Copeland asserts to be so important is the condition on a process to be representable by a *tapeless machine*. This is a much more restrictive condition than computability. (A Turing machine has only finitely many configurations, but in general will have an unbounded number of possible states of its tape.)

Again we might well stand back a little to see this in context. The concept of computability takes its power from the fact that it successfully generalizes the concept of a totally finite machine, to one which still has "finite means" but is allowed unlimited time and space for marking a tape. Copeland's blurring of the distinction between the state table of a totally finite machine, and the finite table of behavior of a Turing machine misses the essential point of the definition of computability.

To summarize: this condition does not allude to uncomputable functions in any way. On the contrary, Turing's context shows that in 1950 his focus was on the successful evocation or at least imitation of intelligence within a *finite subset* of computable functions.

3   Computability and Quantum Physics

But now let us move on past 1950, and come finally to the *physics* that I think the most telling and novel aspect of what Turing had started to do and where he might have gone on to far more if he had lived. This deserves to be better known, and here I must acknowledge Copeland more positively. Recently he has published the full script of Turing's 1951 BBC radio talk [37], prefacing it with an analysis [9]. This talk mostly paraphrased Turing's famous 1950 paper [36] in a form suitable for a short talk, but, as Copeland usefully points out, it had a significant new feature. It had a mention of quantum mechanics, introduced specifically as a loophole in Turing's otherwise general argument that the action of the brain must be computable. Turing explained that for the success of this argument it is

> ... necessary that this machine [the brain] should be of the sort whose behavior is in principle predictable by calculation. We certainly do not know how any such calculation should be done, and it was even argued by Sir Arthur Eddington that on account of the indeterminacy principle in quantum mechanics no such prediction is even theoretically possible.

This is *the only* sentence in all Turing's work that points to something physical that may not be reducible to computable action. But it is a significant one. It runs against what Turing had said about simulating the nervous system by a computer in [36]. And here, exceptionally, Turing does *not* appeal to pseudo-random simulation as a satisfactory discussion of "randomness."

This discussion has nothing whatever to do with oracles. There is no mention whatever of infinite information sources in here. (Note also that Turing's thought is still in the context of wondering whether any machine can do as much as the mind, and not in the spurious reverse problem posited by Copeland!) The question raised by Turing is to do with fundamental physics: is the physical space-time of quantum mechanical processes, with its so-called Heisenberg uncertainty principle, compatible with a Turing machine model?

This sentence, taken seriously, makes a link between the computability of mental processes and Turing's late work in physics. Although I described this late physics work in [20], page 495, and noted Turing's harking back to

Eddington, I had not seen the importance of this possible connection between fundamental physics and the question of the computability of the mind. To describe more satisfactorily this work of 1953–4, I return yet again to Gandy's 1954 letter [17]. In fact, it was to this subject, rather than to computer science, mathematics, logic or morphogenesis, that Gandy devoted the most attention:

> During this spring [1954] he spent some time inventing a new quantum mechanics ... it did show him at his most lively and inventive; he said "Quantum mechanists always seem to require infinitely many dimensions; I don't think I can cope with so many, I'm going to have about 100 or so — that ought to be enough don't you think?" Then he produced a slogan "Description must be non-linear, prediction must be linear."
>
> A slightly more serious contribution ... uses "the Turing Paradox"; it is easy to show using standard theory that if a system starts in an eigenstate of some observable, and measurements are made of that observable N times a second, then, even if the state is not a stationary one, the probability that the system will be in the same state after, say, 1 second, tends to one as N tends to infinity; i.e. that continual observation will prevent motion ...

His "non-linear" description in quantum mechanics would have implied some essentially new theory, and the word "measurement" tells us the focus of his attempted innovation. Turing was referring here to the puzzle of the *reduction, collapse, or measurement* process in quantum mechanics. No-one even now can say when or how it occurs — as Turing was pointing out with his Paradox.

The problematic foundations of quantum mechanics were not new to Alan Turing. His interest went back to 1928. Then he had read Eddington's *The Nature of the Physical World,* with Christopher Morcom his beloved schoolfriend. In fact Alan Turing was one of the first serious readers of von Neumann's 1932 monograph on the Mathematical Foundations of Quantum Mechanics. It was his school prize book, given after Christopher Morcom had suddenly died in 1930. In 1933 Alan Turing reported of it, "My prize book from Sherborne is turning out very interesting, and not at all difficult reading, although the applied mathematicians seem to find it rather strong." [28]

Von Neumann's axioms distinguished the **U** (unitary evolution) and **R** (reduction) rules of quantum mechanics. Now, quantum computing so far (in the work of Feynman, Deutsch, Shor, etc.) is based on the **U** process and so computable. It has not made serious use of the **R** process: the unpredictable element that comes in with reduction, measurement, or collapse of the wave function. Maybe Turing, if he had lived, would have developed quantum computing — but from the scraps that have survived it appears that it was the mystery of the **R** process that really intrigued him.

Recently the **R** process has been studied with fresh experimental interest, and in my view these more recent investigations give the flavor of where Turing's thought might have gone. Elitzur and Vaidman [15] have shown that the logic of "reduction" can produce an extraordinary result. Suppose a "live bomb" is a device which effects "measurement" or "reduction," whilst a "dud bomb" is a device which does not. Then the type of device can be tested by observing the final state of a photon which hits the device. Using classical measurement, the determination would amount to seeing whether or not the device "exploded." With a quantum measurement it is possible to deduce that the device was "live" without any explosion taking place! Quantum mechanics should not be thought of as necessarily introducing uncertainty into a classical picture: in this example it implies the testing *with certainty* of a counterfactual story — what *would have happened* if the photon had hit the detonator of the live bomb. The logical structure here is no different from that known to von Neumann in 1932, but modern technology with perfect mirrors and the detection of single photons makes it possible to investigate that logic far more stringently. In particular, Anton Zeilinger and co-workers in Vienna are conducting ingenious experiments designed to test the limits of the **U** and **R** rules. These investigations do not analyze the internal dynamics of the **R** process and explain when, how, and indeed *whether* it actually happens, which Turing was probably trying to do. But they are probing the logic of quantum mechanics in a way that would have fascinated him.

Turing was probably trying to make quantum mechanics fully predictable, which no-one has been able to do, and perhaps also, as Gandy hinted in his note, more finite. That, if achieved, would have filled in the loophole in his argument about mechanizing thought. If so, Turing's agenda was in a sense the opposite of that of Penrose [25,26]. Penrose has argued that the **R** process must be uncomputable because thought cannot be computable — as follows from taking a very strong view of the implications of Gödel's theorem. But Turing is on common ground with Penrose in taking quantum mechanics and Gödel's theorem very seriously in discussing the question of Artificial Intelligence.

There are still open questions about quantum mechanics, almost as open as when Alan Turing was twenty and wrote his first ideas about the mind [27]:

> It used to be supposed in science that if everything was known about the Universe at any particular moment then we can predict what it will be all through the future ... More modern science however has come to the conclusion that when we are dealing with the atoms and electrons ... We have a will which is able to determine the action of atoms probably in a small portion of the brain ...

By "modern science" he meant quantum mechanics, as he had learnt at school from Eddington. At that stage he thought of there being some unknown quantum mechanical law which accounted for the action of human will. Presumably he changed his mind, since the emphasis of all his post-war work was so strongly towards eliminating such concepts as will and consciousness. But we cannot tell what he might have gone on to think after 1954. In his last years, he insisted on his individuality and his freedom. As a human being, he actually took his own will and consciousness very seriously, and this is one of the great paradoxes of his life and his work.

Church's thesis and the Turing machine are rooted in the concept of "doing one thing at a time." But we do not really know what "doing" is — or time — without a complete picture of quantum mechanics, and the relationship between the still mysterious wave-function and macroscopic observation. Alan Turing found his greatest strength when studying the interfaces between conventional compartments of scientific thought, and might have come up with something between logic and physics that no-one could possibly have predicted.

References

1. Bates, M. A. (1950). On the mechanical solution of a problem in Church's lambda-calculus, M.Sc. thesis, Manchester University, October 1950.
2. Chaitin, G. J. (1982). Gödel's Theorem and Information, International Journal of Theoretical Physics, **22**, 941–954
3. Church, A. (1937). Review of [30]. J. Symbolic Logic. **2**, 42–43.
4. Church, A. (1937). Review of Post (1936). J. Symbolic Logic. **2**, 43.
5. Church, A. (1940). On the concept of a random sequence, Bull. Amer. Math. Soc. **46**, 130–5.
6. Copeland. B. J. (1997). The Church-Turing thesis, in E. N. Zalta (ed.), Stanford Encyclopaedia of Philosophy, `http://plato.stanford.edu`.
7. Copeland B. J. and D. Proudfoot (1998). Enigma variations (London: Times Literary Supplement, 3 July 1998.)
8. Copeland B. J. and D. Proudfoot (1999). Alan Turing's forgotten ideas in computer science. Scientific American, **253:4**, 98–103.
9. Copeland B. J. (1999). A lecture and two radio broadcasts on machine intelligence by Alan Turing, in Machine Intelligence **15**, K. Furukawa, D. Michie. and S. Muggleton (eds.), Oxford University Press, Oxford.
10. Copeland B. J. and D. Proudfoot (1999). Review of *The Legacy of Alan Turing*, Mind, **108**, 187–195.
11. Copeland, B. J. (2000). Narrow versus Wide Mechanism: Including a Re-examination of Turing's Views on the Mind-Machine Issue. J. of Phil. **96**, 5–32.
12. Davis, M. (1958). Computability and Unsolvability (New York: McGraw-Hill); with appendix on Hilbert's Tenth Problem, Dover edition (1982)
13. De Leeuw, K., E. F. Moore, C. E. Shannon, and N. Shapiro (1956). Computability by Probabilistic Machines. Automata Studies, Shannon, C. and J. McCarthy, eds., Princeton University Press, 183–212.
14. Egan, G. (2000). Oracle, Asimov's Science Fiction, July 2000.
15. Elitzur, A. C. and L. Vaidman (1993). Quantum-mechanical interaction-free measurements, Found. of Physics **23**, 987–97
16. Feferman, S. (1988). Turing in the Land of O(Z), in [19]; an updated version appears in [39].
17. Gandy, R. O. (1954). letter to M. H. A. Newman, in the Turing Archive, King's College, Cambridge; included in [39].

18. Gandy, R. O. (1980). Principles of Mechanisms, in The Kleene Symposium, eds. J. Barwise, H. J. Keisler and K. Kunen, North-Holland, Amsterdam.

19. Herken R. (ed.) (1988). The universal Turing machine: a half-century survey, Kammerer und Unverzagt, Berlin; Oxford University Press, Oxford.

20. Hodges, A. (1983). Alan Turing: the enigma (Burnett, London; Simon & Schuster, New York; new editions Vintage, London, 1992, Walker, New York, 2000). Further material is on http://www.turing.org.uk.

21. Hodges, A. (1997). Turing, a natural philosopher (Phoenix, London; Routledge, New York, 1999). Included in: The Great Philosophers (eds. R. Monk and F. Raphael, Weidenfeld and Nicolson 2000)

22. Hodges, A. (2002). Alan M. Turing, in E. N. Zalta (ed.), Stanford Encyclopaedia of Philosophy, http://plato.stanford.edu.

23. Hodges, A. (2003). Alan Turing and the Turing Test, in The Turing Test Sourcebook: Philosophical and Methodological Issues in the Quest for the Thinking Computer, ed. Robert Epstein, forthcoming.

24. Newman, M. H. A. (1951). The influence of automatic computers on mathematical methods, Manchester University Computer Inaugural Conference, July 1951.

25. Penrose, R. (1989). The emperor's new mind, Oxford University Press, Oxford.

26. Penrose, R. (1994). Shadows of the mind, Oxford University Press, Oxford.

27. Turing, A. M. (1932). Handwritten essay, Nature of Spirit, photocopy in the Turing Archive, King's College, Cambridge; see [20, p. 63].

28. Turing A. M. (1933). Letter to Sara Turing, 16 October 1933, in the Turing Archive, King's College Cambridge; see [20, p. 79].

29. Turing A. M. (1936). Letter to Sara Turing, 14 October 1936, in the Turing Archive, King's College Cambridge; see [20, p. 120].

30. Turing A. M. (1936–7). On computable numbers, with an application to the Entscheidungsproblem, Proc. London Maths. Soc., ser. 2, **42**, 230–265; also in M. Davis, (ed.) The Undecidable (Raven, New York, 1965), and in [40]

31. Turing A. M. (1939). Systems of Logic defined by Ordinals, Proc. Lond. Math. Soc., ser. 2, **45**, 161–228; also in M. Davis (ed.). The Undecidable (Raven, New York, 1965). and in [40]. This was Turing's 1938 Ph.D. thesis, Princeton University.

32. Turing, A. M. (1946). Proposed electronic calculator, unpublished report for National Physical Laboratory, London; published in A. M. Turing's ACE Report of 1946 and other papers (eds. B. E. Carpenter and R. W. Doran, MIT Press, Cambridge, MA, 1986), and in [39].

33. Turing, A. M., 1947, Lecture to the London Mathematical Society on 20 February 1947, published in A. M. Turing's ACE report of 1946 and other papers, (eds. B. E. Carpenter and R. W. Doran, MIT Press, Cambridge, MA, 1986), and in [39].

34. Turing A. M. (1948). Intelligent machinery, unpublished report for National Physical Laboratory, London; published (ed. D. Michie) in Machine Intelligence **7**, 1969, and in [39].

35. Turing A. M., (1950). The word problem in semi-groups with cancellation, Ann. of Math. **52** (2), 491–505.

36. Turing A. M. (1950). Computing machinery and intelligence, Mind **49**, 433–460, reprinted in [39].

37. Turing, A. M. (1951). BBC radio talk, transcript in the Turing Archive, King's College, Cambridge; published in Machine Intelligence **15**, eds. K. Furukawa, D. Michie. and S. Muggleton, Oxford University Press, Oxford, 1999.
38. Turing, A. M. (1954). Solvable and unsolvable problems, Science News **31**, 7–23.
39. Turing, A. M. (1992). Collected Works: Mechanical Intelligence. D.C. Ince, ed., North-Holland, Amsterdam.
40. Turing, A. M. (2001). Collected Works: Mathematical Logic. R. O. Gandy and C. E. M. Yates, eds., North-Holland, Amsterdam.

From Turing to the Information Society

Daniela Cerqui

University of Lausanne, Institute of Anthropology and Sociology

Summary. An anthropological analysis shows two tendencies in today's "information society": (1) an increasing valorization of mind, information, and, more generally, immaterial elements, as opposed to body and matter; and (2) a strong tendency to replace everything human with artificial elements (for instance, retina implants, artificial limbs or hip prostheses).

Even if these tendencies seem contradictory at first sight, in reality they are not: the mastering of information is their common denominator. Both directions were already present in Turing's thought as early as the 1940s. The goal of this chapter is to throw a little light on the links between the man, the mathematician, and our present society, a goal that seems to be to create a predictable and infallible human being, in body as well as in mind. It should be noted that, according to Turing, human beings are not infallible in their essence.

1 The So-called "Information Society"

According to people with power over our political or economic lives as well as those from the scientific world, we are supposed to have recently entered the information era. French discourse talks of the "information society" or the "knowledge society," while English speakers frequently refer to "information highways." All these phrases express differently the same idea: we are supposed to live in a radically new kind of society[1].

---

[1] That is usually taken for granted, as the forthcoming *World Summit on the Information Society (WSIS)* shows. Now organized by a Committee established under the patronage of Kofi Annan, the summit was initially mentioned in a resolution of the International Telecommunication Union, in order to be organized by the United Nations. According to its web-site, which explains the challenge, "the modern world is undergoing a fundamental transformation as the industrial society that marked the 20th century rapidly gives way to the information society of the 21st century. This dynamic process promises a fundamental change in all aspects of our lives, including knowledge dissemination, social interaction, economic and business practices, political engagement, media, education, health, leisure, and entertainment. We are indeed in the midst of a revolution, perhaps the greatest that humanity has ever experienced. To benefit the world community, the successful and continued growth of this dynamic requires global discussion and harmonization in appropriate areas." The goal of the first step of the summit (Geneva, December 2003) is to try to obtain a consensual point of view (it is not

That "Information Society" is often considered to be an unquestionable reality linked with the emergence and development of the *New Information and Communication Technologies (NTIC)*[2]. In such a point of view, globalization — of course defined as an extension of the Western information society to the entire world — has to become a reality in order to obtain a better quality of life for everybody. Information is described as the most important source of wealth for individuals and for countries (see for example Gates [11] and Dertouzos [7]) and it is expected to bring money and education to the whole world. In such a political, economic and social situation, it is not easy to deconstruct the notion of "information society," which is usually taken for granted even if not really defined.

2   An Anthropological Analysis

An anthropological analysis shows that the roots of such a society are old. They are at least as old as the Second World War, and more especially issue from the ciphering research in which Turing was involved. There are mainly two tendencies that coexist in our society, tendencies which could at first sight seem conflicting:

- an increasing valorization of mind, information and more generally immaterial elements, over body and matter;
- a strong tendency to replace everything human with artificial elements (for instance retina implants, artificial limbs or hip prostheses)

They are in reality not contradictory. The goal of this chapter is to explain both paths and to show that they were already present in Turing's thought, even if obviously not exactly in the same words. The "information society"

---

easy to group the interests of different states, the business world and the civil society), and to develop some operative action plans. The second step (Tunis, 2005), will focus on evaluation of the results (http://www.itu.int/wsis).

[2] Contrary to what might be believed, such ideas are not so new. Some authors (see for example Richta [21]) described the same concept without naming it or using another name many years ago: Bell was one of the first ones to theorize about that society while giving it a name: according to him, we are supposed to be in a post-industrial society [1, 2]. In his view, there are five fundamental criteria to define that society: (1) transition from a material goods production system to a service economy (mostly health, teaching, research and administration); (2) employment structures change with an increase in highly qualified professionals and technicians; (3) centrality of theoretical knowledge capable of generating innovation and economic growth; (4) emergence of new technologies of the mind; (5) an increasing mastery of technological and social developments.

In short, Bell describes an extension of the service sector, whose main condition of existence consists in the fact that information must constantly circulate. That explains the importance given to the NTIC.

seems strangely to be rooted as much in Alan Turing's work as in his life[3]. One might as well say that he is unwittingly one of the greatest precursors of the information society. He even had prophetic proposals such as suggesting the possibility of using remote terminals [15, pp. 330–331] a long time before the first computer networks even appeared.

In the preface to the French translation of Hodges's biography of Turing, Le Guyader argues that "Turing was interested in the logic of the brain, but he was fascinated too by the emergence of biological forms of life, and especially by morphogenesis. He wondered how a cell is able to 'know' what it has to do in order to create a symmetric organism" [12, pp. 10–11, my translation]. According to him, Turing opened the way for people who study the logic of the brain without any interest in the physical matter of the support (i.e. the first tendency I described above), and for people who study the physical matter (as is the case for people involved in the second tendency) without having access to the logic of the system, as if you had to lose on the one hand what you win on the other one. In reality, there is something which never gets lost: information, which in both cases is the most important element. Therefore, the tendencies I described are not contradictory at all. As I will show, in the former information is directly valorized, and in the latter it is used indirectly, but in both cases the mastery of information is the common denominator.

3   First Tendency: the Disappearing Body?

If, in the past, the industrial society needed efficient bodies to produce more and more, the information society nowadays needs efficient brains to deal with information. More concretely, as has already happened with other "human parts" during the industrial era, we have now become used to describing our brain and our memory as a machine, and more exactly, in this case, as a computer. This amounts to saying that we are interested in the organs which are useful according to current values. In such a context, mind and memory are often considered simply as an accumulation of information (see for instance Kurzweil [17]). The electronic equivalent of the human brain will perhaps one day be as small as one's fingertips. In such a view, everybody will be able to improve their memory with additional electronic memories. Thus, the goal seems to be increasing the information available. The way to do this is to eliminate every material obstacle to the free circulation of information. Therefore the human body is often regarded as an impediment. It is taken for granted by some people that we would be faster and more efficient without a body and with only a free mind stuffed full of information.

---

[3] All the basis seems to have already been put in his text "Intelligent Machinery" first published in 1969 in *Machine Intelligence* [28]. I will frequently quote it in this paper and my quotations will refer to another edition, which is easier to find [29].

That is (still?) more of an imaginary trend than of a palpable reality, but it is worth noticing that such a belief, that we can function without a body, is perfectly coherent considering our Western values and practices. The Internet demonstrates this phenomenon very well: the intention is to connect people's brains. That is not a surprise, because we can see that networks in general, as the history of the term demonstrates, produce an effect of disembodiedness. The term "virtual," principally used in the early '90s to describe experiments conducted under the rubric of "virtual reality", has increasingly been applied to the Internet as a whole and to networks in general. However, on closer analysis it appears that these phenomena, all described as "virtual," rely on very different representational logics. While virtual reality attempts to put the human body into a new experimental space, networks produce an effect of disembodiedness, represented by the notion of the purely cerebral person for whom the body is a handicap that limits the free circulation of information. "People in virtual communities do just about everything people do in real life, but we leave our bodies behind. You can't kiss anybody and nobody can punch you in the nose, but a lot can happen within those boundaries" [20, p. 3]. The network is thus a disembodied representation of life in society[4]. Stone echoes the same idea with her comment on one of Tomas' declarations: according to him, cyberspace gives a "purely spectacular, kinaesthetically exciting, and often dizzying sense of bodily freedom" (1989, in Stone [25]), which she analyses and translates as "freedom from the body."

The trend to eliminate the body is apparent: three years ago, newspapers mentioned a disabled man whose brain was directly connected to a computer. Electrodes implanted in his brain were able to detect the waves produced when this man was thinking. Signals were picked up by a radio antenna and transmitted to a computer which interpreted them as if they were coming from a computer mouse. It was reported that after a few weeks of practice, the patient was able to think "I am moving the cursor," without first thinking "I am moving my hand in order to move the cursor." That last mental activity was described as a transitory step. Thus, the option seems clear: the goal is neither to allow the patient to be mobile again, nor to give him, at least, the awareness of his body. On the contrary, his body is considered as totally useless. One could object that this patient is a disabled subject, whose body is not mobile and thus not an example of what a valid human could become. I would grant that it is not exactly the same situation, but there is a fundamental logic which is the same. According to Melody Moore — the person in charge of the computer part of this project — "the more direct the interface is, the more efficient it is" (Le Monde, 6th of December 1999, p. 12, my translation). This patient appears to me to be a kind of prototype for

---

[4] For instance, the electronic vote allows you to vote without leaving home. We try to solve the non-voting problem, as if the problem was only that people don't want to move their body; as if it was only a technical question and not a social problem.

a world in which brains and computers would be directly connected to each other without any bodily interface. We are slowly going from a technology which *repairs* people to a technology which *improves* them according to the criteria and values of our society[5]. For instance, Kevin Warwick, a British cybernetician — who is not disabled — recently implanted a chip in his arm. It is directly linked with his neural system. According to the Internet site devoted to this experiment, "the results will therefore not only be of use in research towards helping people who are disabled, but will also impact on such fields as e-medicine, extra sensory capabilities and nerve signal communication"[6]. His goal is clearly to be able to communicate directly from his brain to a computer. In his view, one application could be to be able to drive your car without using your hands.

The body is no more than an empty shell in our society; only the container for our mind. This seems a normal view in our so-called cyberculture. But this present valorization of the mind is of course not a new phenomenon in our Western society in which cartesian rationality — as defined by Descartes [8] — has been considered for a long time as a great value. And it is important to notice that, in Turing's thought, we find it in the same form as in the information society, with the same ambiguites. The links between body and mind were at the heart of Turing's work and life. In a letter to Mrs Morcom, the young Turing, sure that the spirit of her dead son — with whom he was in love — was still in her house, wrote: "Personally I think that spirit is really eternally connected with matter but certainly not always by the same kind of body [...] When the body is asleep I cannot guess what happens but when the body dies the 'mechanism' of the body, holding the spirit is gone and the spirit finds a new body sooner or later perhaps immediately. As regards the question of why we have bodies at all; why we do not or cannot live free as spirits and communicate as such, we probably could do so but there would be nothing whatever to do. The body provides something for the spirit to look after and use" (quoted in Hodges [15, pp. 63–64]). The idea that the mind could work perfectly without a body is present in Turing's thought. When he wrote that, he was very young, but even if he qualified this opinion later, he did not radically change his mind. We could almost say that in his view the mind could work better without a body. In the imitation game, which consists of an interrogator guessing whether he is "talking" with a man or a woman, or with a human being or a machine, the body is hidden from view in order to prevent this interrogator "from seeing or touching the other competitors or hearing their voices" [27, p. 434]. The body appears as the element which

---

[5] There is a conceptual difference between repairing and improving: if you repair, it does mean that you are in a certain way happy with humankind as it is, I mean when people are not disabled. On the contrary, if you dream of a real improvement, it implies that you are convinced that humankind is not as good as it should be [5].

[6] http://www.cyber.rdg.ac.uk/research/projects/cirg.htm?00177

could help the interrogator, whereas he must guess without it, using only rational criteria. And the body is obviously considered as something not rational. It has to be hidden from the interrogator in order for the game to succeed. According to Blooomfield and Vurdubakis[7] the role of the body as obstacle to, and as systematic distortion of, rational communication, is at the heart of Turing's experiments. In Turing's view, it is obvious that the body generates interferences in the mind's activity, as interactions with the environment generate them too. But, following French [10] we could argue that in reality the Turing test is not testing only the rational intelligence but the social immersion as well, because the ability to recognize and identify what is said depends on the context. The interrogator must share the same culture as the hidden interlocutors, independently of seeing their bodies or not. And it is important to note that in another way Turing was totally aware of the importance of interaction for the development of intelligence. He claimed that "the isolated man does not develop any intellectual power. It is necessary for him to be immersed in an environment of other men" [15, p. 127]. He agreed with the idea that human intelligence cannot develop without social relations. And it is true that intelligence is not only rationality, it is meaning too; the process of giving a social meaning to things is a collective process. In a reflection on human beings and machines, Searle pointed out very well the importance of meaning: according to him, machines are perfectly able to manipulate symbols, but not at all to interpret them, that is, to give them a meaning [23].

Turing argued that the acquisition of intelligence can be perfectly effective even without a human body. In his view, "it will not be possible to apply exactly the same teaching process to the machine as to a normal child" [27, p. 456]. The absence of bodily elements makes physical tasks impossible, but "these deficiencies might be overcome by clever engineering" [27, p. 456] and communication. Turing defined intelligence as an emotional concept [15, p. 127], which includes meaning and communication, but not the body. Nevertheless, emotions and meaning come within the human body. As Merleau-Ponty argued, the human body is not a neutral object like a table or anything else. It has "an intentionality and an ability to give significance" [18, p. 203, my translation]. Damasio [6] echoes the same idea when he claims that mental activity needs a brain and a body to be efficient. He puts emphasis on the emotions. To explain that, he talks about the "Gage syndrome," referring to Phineas Gage, a young man whose brain was damaged by an iron rod. His rational abilities were intact, but his emotions were altered and his behavior was changed. This proves that emotions are essential even in some behaviors considered as rational. According to Merleau-Ponty's arguments, you cannot be a human being without hands or sexual organs any more than without

---

[7] This idea was presented in "Imitation games. Turing, Menard, Van Meegeren," paper presented at the Computer Ethics: Philosophical Enquiries Conference on *IT and the Body*, Lancaster University, UK, 14–16 December 2001.

thought [18, p. 198]. In other words "the overwhelming and obvious lack of any significant similarity between machines of any kind, as far as we know, and human beings, is due to the fact that machines do not have bodies" [13, p. 253].

We can find the complementarity of emotional and rational aspects of human beings in Turing's life as well. When he was sentenced because of his homosexuality, Turing could choose between hormonal treatment and imprisonment. According to Hodges [15, pp. 473–474], we can say that in the first case he would have chosen to maintain his free thought and intellectual life, and in the second one his free body and feelings. He decided to save his thought, accepting the treatment. He discovered very soon that his thought was no longer the same: his new feelings had an impact on his rational thought. Thus, his personal life taught him that feeling and thinking are intrinsically linked. With such a point of view, it is obvious that emotional aspects of human beings are considered because they are seen as useful in rational behavior: they have no intrinsic value. As an anthropologist, I think that emotions are important by themselves and not only because they are part of rational behavior. But the question that remains open is it still exactly the same as posed by Turing's thought. Is the body necessary or not? According to Kendra Mayfield and her paper in *Wired*[8], the technologist Ray Kurzweil bet that Turing's test will be passed in 2029. Mayfield does not mention the question of the body, and we can guess that neither does Kurzweil … To reintroduce the body, Barberi[9] suggests creating a new Turing test, a kind of ultimate and improved test using virtual reality. In such a case, the interrogator would have to base his decision not only on written words, but on verbal and non-verbal speech, including body movement. The debate opened by Turing still has a meaning today.

4   Second Tendency: Reproducing Every Bodily Element

As has already happened with time and space, human beings seem to have taken control of their bodies in order to free themselves from them. However, we have to agree that bodies are not disappearing completely: they are more and more worked on by science, technology, medicine, diets, sports activities and so on. Moreover, there is nowadays another tendency to reproduce every bodily element. For many researchers, every human function is considered as a physical process, even the mind. Thus, even if we still do not know exactly how the brain works, we will certainly do so one day. And we will then be able to construct an imitation/simulation of the brain. That means that we could create artificial intelligence if we knew how intelligence works in humans.

---

[8] http://www.wired.com/news/technology/0,1282,51431,00.html

[9] "The Ultimate Turing test," David Barberi,
   http://ibiblio.org/dbarberi/vr/ultimate-turing.

Everything can be explained physically and thus our society could be seen as glorifying the bodily and material dimension of human beings. My hypothesis is on the contrary that we are interested in the material dimension of our bodies only because everything material can be translated into information. In other words, there is no longer a classic Cartesian split between body and mind: the most important split is between the material dimension of both body and mind on the one hand and their translation into information on the other hand.

Thus, the contradiction between eliminating the material part of humans and reproducing it is only superficial: information society is defined just as well by information and communication technologies — which permits us to communicate without using the body, as by biotechnologies — which permit us to modify matter (see Castells [4] and Escobar [9]). The two together allow us to create everything. On the one hand, intelligence is considered to have the most value and bodies, as matter, are considered as an interference; and on the other hand, we try to create organized matter and this means that we have to know what we call the "code." In both cases, information is the most important element we have to master.

5   Information as the Lowest Common Denominator

Such a way of thinking was already present in the '40s, and especially, again, in Turing's thought. That period saw the development of "a new kind of machinery, a new kind of science, in which it was not the physics and chemistry that mattered, but the logical structure of information, communication and control." And Schrödinger was "advancing the conjecture that the information defining a living organism must somehow be encoded in molecular patterns" [15, p. 252]. Turing was very close to Schrödinger's ideas and was interested in knowing how a chemical system could become a biological one. The solution could be in the information contained inside the system and Turing was convinced that information is more important than matter. Thus, with his desire to construct an electronic brain, what he tried to achieve was not a copy of material or biological matter: he was interested in the logical scheme of the states of thought. With his "Turing machine" he tried to imitate a human calculator, supposing that thought is made of elementary states to which machine states are analogous. Turing's machine has nothing to do with physics. "In his view, the physics and chemistry were relevant only in as much as they sustained the medium for the embodiment of discrete 'states', 'reading' and 'writing'. Only the *logical* pattern of these 'states' could really matter. The claim was that whatever a brain did, it did by virtue of its structure as a logical system, and not because it was inside a person's head, or because it was a spongy tissue made up of a particular kind of biological cell formation. And if this were so, then its logical structure could just as well be represented in other medium, embodied by some other physical machinery. It was a materialist view of mind, but one that did not confuse logical patters and relations with physical substances and things, as so often people did. In particular, it was a different claim from that of behaviorist psychology, which spoke of reducing psychology to physics. The Turing model did not seek to explain one kind of phenomenon, that of mind, in terms of another. It did not expect to 'reduce' psychology to anything. The thesis was that 'mind' or psychology could properly be described in terms of Turing machines because they both lay on the *same* level of description of the world, that of discrete logical systems. It was not a reduction, but an attempt at transference, when he imagined embodying such systems in an artificial 'brain'" [15, p. 291].

If the different states of a machine can be compared with different minds, then we can compare the physical matter of a machine with a brain. Accordingly, the body can then be considered as a machine, and both can be considered as an accumulation of information. We are more fascinated by this immaterial translation of the body than by its materiality! We see this very well in the present fascination for the genomic project: the map seems to be more interesting than the body itself.

In such a way of thinking, Turing was very close to Wiener's cybernetics[10].

6   Turing, Wiener and Cybernetics

According to Wiener's view [31], cybernetics refers to the theory of communication both in machines and in living beings. And the body is a machine, according to Turing also. Cybernetics is etymologically linked with the Greek word *kubernesis*, which means "action of manoeuvering a ship," and that is very important for Wiener, because the helm of a ship is one of the oldest and most well-developed feedback mechanisms. This feedback is one of the most important principles of cybernetics. Feedback is necessary to describe every informational process able to fit its behavior according to the analysis it makes of its action's effects. It is in Wiener's view the source of any intelligent behavior and it is taken for granted that intelligent behavior is not limited to human beings. More precisely, cybernetics is linked with the study of the interactions operating in a system in order to maintain its stability, and thus its life. A "system" can equally well be a human being, an animal or a machine, and the condition is that the whole is more than the addition of its parts. Fundamentally, for such a point of view, living and not living elements can be reduced to an amount of information. In other words, according to cybernetics, the essence of someone or something is not the result of the matter he or it is made up of, but the way it is organized and its relationship with the environment. In Wiener's view, the world is made of "patterns," and each is essentially an arrangement less characterized by

---

[10] In spite of their similarities, Turing and Wiener did not agree on some important points. For instance, contrary to Wiener, Turing thought that a machine can learn [15, p. 357].

the intrinsic nature of its elements than by their order. Relations between the different elements of the whole are directed by an informational code, the mastering of which should theoretically allow reproduction with other matter atoms. Thus, Wiener was sure that physical identities are a kind of message, which means special patterns characterized by their special role of information vectors from a close or far point to another one. Wiener suggested that it would one day be possible to telegraph a human being. Teleportation, as it is especially known in *Star Trek* movies, was theoretically born with the idea of being able to move through the space without moving any material element! In other words, according to cybernetics, there is no ontological reason to distinguish living beings from machines. The only difference is that they have different physical supports, and we could imagine in this view that these supports could disappear or radically change without carrying any change in identity, if the complexity and organization are still the same. Thus, reason is not only a human prerogative: it emerges from a kind of organization and it could as well emerge on a mechanical support. Turing was in complete agreement on that point. According to him, "a great positive reason for believing in the possibility of making thinking machinery is the fact that it is possible to make machinery to imitate any small part of a man" [15, p. 116]. And "one way of setting about our task of building a 'thinking machine' would be to take a man as a whole and to try to replace all the parts of him by machinery. He would include television cameras, microphones, loudspeakers, wheels and 'handling servo-mechanisms' as well as some sort of 'electronic brain' [...]. Instead we propose to try and see what can be done with a 'brain' which is more or less without a body providing, at most, organs of sight, speech, and hearing" [15, p. 117].

It is thus theoretically possible to reconstruct every bodily element. But even if it seemed possible to Turing to reproduce every human element, he decided to concentrate on brain and mind. Such a choice does not appear to me to be mere chance: it reveals what is considered important in the human being.

7   Intelligence, Rationality and Humankind

In "Intelligent machinery," Turing wondered whether it is possible for machinery to show intelligent behavior. According to him, in 1950, it was usually assumed that a machine cannot have intelligent behavior because of some reasons such as "an unwillingness to admit the possibility that mankind can have any rivals in intellectual power," or "a religious belief that any attempt to construct such machines is a sort of Promethean irreverence," or "the very limited character of the machinery which has been used until recent time" [15, p. 107]. Even if he thinks that "these arguments cannot be wholly ignored, because the idea of 'intelligence' is itself emotional rather than mathematical" [15, p.

108], Turing refutes the first two arguments as "purely emotional." The third one is refuted by the latest developments of machines.

Blooomfield and Vurdubakis[11] talk about a test which consists in listening to some musical pieces and guessing whether they are composed by a human being or by a computer. According to them, great art is even sometimes conceived as uplifting, as affording a glimpse of what is best in human nature. The result is that if a computer is programmed to perform a new Mozart symphony by analyzing those which already exist, people cannot believe that it is a computerized composition. It seems thus that Turing was right: we have an idea of what a computer should and should not be able to do! As Blooomfield and Vurdubakis argue, it is perhaps a triumph of the Cartesian *cogito* that debates about what is meant by 'intelligence' have a tendency to quickly become debates about what it means to be human. But in Turing's view, intelligence is not enough to define humankind: a machine could be intelligent too. And in general, the necessary condition for being clever is to be organized.

8   From Unorganized to Organized Machines

In order to produce his universal machine[12], Turing starts off with his idea, which he shared with Wiener, that human beings and machines are different but comparable because both are able to think if they are organized appropriately to do that. Thus, he used the analogy with the human brain as a principle. Turing's fundamental hypothesis is that the human cortex is initially an unorganized machine, which gets organized during the growing up process. This education can be summarized as discipline and initiative acquisition: "If the untrained infant's mind is to become an intelligent one, it must acquire both discipline and initiative. [...] To convert a brain or machine into a universal machine is the extremest form of discipline. [...] But discipline is certainly not enough in itself to produce intelligence. That which is required in addition we call initiative. This statement will have to serve as a definition" [15, p. 125]. Thus, according to him, "the difference between the languages spoken on the two sides of the Channel is not due to the difference in development of the French-speaking and English-speaking parts of the brain. It is due to the linguistic parts having been subjected to different training. We believe then that there are large parts of the brain, chiefly in

---

[11] Congress communication, cf. note 7.

[12] For Turing, it was important to construct a "universal machine", because "we do not need to have an infinity of different machines doing different jobs. A single one will suffice. The engineering problem of producing various machines for various jobs is replaced by the office work of 'programming' the universal machine to do these jobs" [15, p. 111]. Such a concept was revolutionary: computers were usually designed for only one — or in any case a limited number of — purposes [26, p. 5].

the cortex, whose function is largely indeterminate. In the infant these parts do not have much effect: the effect they have is uncoordinated. In the adult they have great and purposive effect: the form of this effect depends on the training in childhood. A large remnant of the random behavior of infancy remains in the adult."

All of this suggests that the cortex of the infant is an unorganized machine, which can be organized by suitable interfering training. The organizing might result in the modification of the machine into a universal machine or something like this" [15, p. 120]. The task is to discover the nature of what occurs in man during education, and to try and copy it in machines, because, even if most people behave quite differently under many circumstances, "the resemblance to a universal machine is still very great, and suggests to us that the step from the unorganized infant to a universal machine is one which should be understood" [15, p. 120].

He decided to construct an unorganized machine, largely random in its construction, and to study how to make it become organized. In his typology of the different kinds of existing machines, he distinguished between "discrete" and "continuous" machinery. The first definition describes machines where motion occurs by jumping from one state to another, and the second continuous machines, as the name indicates [15, p. 109]. He knew that all machines are in reality continuous, but it was easier in his view to consider them as discrete if possible. For instance, we know that a switch can have some middle positions, but we are interested in it only when it is switched on or off. And it is exactly the same with the process of thought. Machine and brain are able to learn, and in order to do that, both need to be organized, which means, in other words, modified [15, p. 120]. To do that, there are two methods: "We might try to graft some initiative onto these. This would probably take the form of programming the machine to do every kind of job that could be done, as a matter of principle, whether it were economical to do it by machine or not. Bit by bit one would be able to allow the machine to make more and more 'choices' or 'decisions'. One would eventually find it possible to program it so as to make its behavior be the logical result of a comparatively small number of general principles. When these became sufficiently general, interference would no longer be necessary, and the machine would have 'grown up'. The other method is to start with an unorganized machine and to try to bring both discipline and initiative into it at once, i.e., instead of trying to organize the machine to become a universal machine, to organize it for initiative as well. Both methods should, I think, be attempted" [15, pp. 125–126]. If human thought can be considered as a machine subject to interferences, according to Turing it should be possible to produce an artificial brain which could think without interference. Thus, Turing wrote, "although we have abandoned the plan to make a 'whole man', we should be wise to sometimes compare the circumstances of our machine with those of a man. [...] We may say that in so far as a man is a machine he is one that is subject to very much interference. In fact interference will be the rule rather than the exception [...] We are chiefly interested in machines with comparatively little interference [...] If we were trying to produce an intelligent machine, and are following the human model as closely as we can, we should begin with a machine with very little capacity to carry out elaborate operations or to react in a disciplined manner to orders (taking the form of interference)" [15, p. 118]. Thus, the goal is to become organized and eliminate interference. The way to do so is to master the information. Here again, Turing is very close to Wiener and his struggle against entropy: order is the main goal.

9   Towards a New Human Being?

On the question of whether computers can really think, experts are nowadays divided, but it does not matter whether computers think or not. Moreover, Turing himself was not really interested in knowing whether the machine really thinks; he was more interested in a machine able to act as if it were thinking. He was convinced that when a machine could make someone believe it can think, as well as a brain does, we could effectively say that it does think. Turing's test was created only on the basis of the appearance of thinking. The machine did not need to look like a brain; it just needed to act like one. In some authors' view, this is a great limitation of Turing's test. For instance, Churchland argues that we are nowadays able to construct a theory of human cognition, and that the appearance of thinking is consequently not enough [24, p. 8]. Furthermore, for others, "intelligence depends not only on what is done, but also on how it is done" [24, p. 199][13]. The test was not intended to be an "operational definition of intelligence" [30, p. 62], and knowing whether the machine really thinks or not does not change at all the fact that Turing's ideas are present in the information society. On the contrary, according to Simon, we could argue that "a computer simulation of digestion is not capable of taking starch as an input and producing fructose or glucose as outputs. It deals only with symbolic or numerical quantities representing these substances. In contrast, a computer simulation of thinking thinks. It takes problems as its inputs and (sometimes) produces solutions as its outputs. It represents these problems and solutions as symbolic structures, as does the human mind, and performs transformations on them like those the human mind does. The materials of digestion are chemical substances, which are not replicated in a computer simulation. The materials of thought are symbols — patterns, which can be replicated in a great variety of materials (including neurons and chips), thereby enabling physical symbol systems

---

[13] We find here again the great debate present in AI research since the beginning. Some researchers wanted to reproduce cerebral activities without reproducing the way human brains do it. Others wanted to imitate the neurological structure of the brain [32, pp. 1078–1079]. In short, the former were interested in the goals, and the latter in how to achieve them.

fashioned of these materials to think. Turing was perhaps the first to have this insight in clear form, more than forty years ago" [30, p. 82].

The most important question concerns human beings, and not machines. According to Bolter, there is "a change in the way men and women in the electronic age think about themselves and the world around them" [3, p. 4]. However, it is not a new process. Technology has always had such an influence: "all techniques and devices have the potential to become defining technologies because all to some degree redefine our relationship to nature" [3, p. 10]. In other words, "a defining technology develops links, metaphorical or otherwise, with a culture's science, philosophy or literature; it is always available to serve as a metaphor, example, model, or symbol. A defining technology resembles a magnifying glass, which collects and focuses seemingly disparate ideas in a culture into one bright, sometimes piercing ray" [3, p. 11]. Furthermore, he is without any doubt right when he claims that "by promising (or threatening) to replace man, the computer is giving us a new definition of man, as an 'information processor', and of nature, as 'information to be processed'. I call those who accept this view of man and nature Turing's men [...] By making a machine think as a man, man recreates himself, defines himself as a machine" [3, p. 13]. His "Turing's man" qualifies perfectly what I described about the predominant way of thinking in the information society: every human attitude or activity, even the most intellectual issues confronted by humans, could be computable. But I would for myself rather talk about "Turing's human being." When Bolter wrote his book, it was usual to consider that men are more present in the scientific world — and it is often still the case — but I assume that this is changing and that we have to adapt our expressions to fit this change. Furthermore, I think that this name should be given not only to scientists, but also to all of us, men and women who are slowly becoming Turing's human beings. In my view, all of us are concerned because we are more and more the result of the mastering of human bodies and minds to make them more efficient. According to Hodges, when Turing and his colleagues had mastered the Enigma ciphering system[14], the Germans were unaware they had done so and continued to suspect that a spy network was operating, "and so their faith in machines and experts continued to be matched by distrust of men" [15, p. 244].

We are in a context in which the circulation of information between human beings seems to be difficult to control. Thus machines could be considered as an improvement if we can control them: the ideal state machine would be a machine system which could be mastered. We find here the most important values of the information society in which everything has to be foreseeable. Even everything that is unexpected must be mastered and rationalized: this is the result of a kind of mathematization of the world [22], whose origins are very ancient in an implicit form and were clearly expressed by Turing's

---

[14] Enigma was the ciphering system used by the German army to communicate during the Second World War.

thought. Furthermore, Turing's life is here again a very good example of that rationalization. Thus, according to Hodges, Turing was not considered a danger to national security because he was gay, but rather because it was impossible to control him: he was unpredictable. Furthermore, Hodges argues that in 1952, "It was the beginning of a new era, in which chemical solutions could be found for the problems of social control" [15, p. 470, see pp. 524–525 too]. It is impossible not to notice that nowadays we do the same. Drugs such as the well-known 'Prozac' are supposed to regulate social behaviors through an action on bio-chemical phenomena. This seems to me a result of the logic of the information society: social behaviors and minds are reduced to physical processes which can be mastered thanks to their informational code. The new human being that our society is dreaming about is obviously a controlled and predictable entity, just like a machine. Nevertheless, it seems that the information society is going further than Turing, who thought that 'intelligence' does not mean "infallibility" or "predictability." According to him, being intelligent means making mistakes and learning from them. Thus, in his view, a really intelligent machine which could play chess intelligently would risk making the occasional mistake [15, pp. 332–333]. I think that it is now high time to remember this aspect of Turing's thought: humankind is not as infallible as we would like nowadays. So, do we want to remain human beings or is this not important? That is now the question that needs to be asked.

References

1. D. Bell. *The Coming of Post-Industrial Society: A Venture in Social Forecasting.* Basic Books, New York, NY, 1973.
2. D. Bell. *The Coming of Post-Industrial Society: A Venture in Social Forecasting,* chapter The Axial Age of Technology (Foreword), pages ix–lxxxiii. Basic Books, New York, NY, 1999.
3. J. D. Bolter. *Turing's Man. Western Culture in the Computer Age.* University of North Carolina Press, Chapel Hill, NC, 1984.
4. M. Castells. *The Information Age: Economy, Society and Culture,* volume 1: The Rise of the Network Society. Blackwell, London, UK, 1996.
5. D. Cerqui. The future of humankind in the era of human and computer hybridisation. An anthropological analysis. *Ethics and Information Technology,* 4(2):1–8, 2002.
6. A. Damasio. *Descartes' Error: Emotion, Reason, and the Human Brain.* Putnam, New York, NY, 1994.
7. M. Dertouzos. *What Will Be. How the World of Information will Change our Lives.* Harper, San Francisco, CA, 1997.
8. R. Descartes. *Méditations philosophiques.* PUF, Paris, France, 1979.
9. A. Escobar. Welcome to cyberia. Notes on the anthropology of cyberculture. *Current Anthropology,* 35:211–231, 1994.
10. R. French. Subcognition and the limites of the Turing test. In Millican and Clark [19], pages 11–26.

11. B. Gates. *The Road Ahead*. Penguin, London, UK, 1996.
12. H. Le Guyader. Préface. In *Alan Turing ou l'énigme de l'intelligence* [14], pages 7–11.
13. S. Hampshire. Biology, machines, and humanity: The boundaries of humanity. In J. Sheehan and M. Sosna, editors, *Humans, Animals, Machines*, pages 253–256. University of California Press, Berkeley, CA, 1991.
14. A. Hodges. *Alan Turing ou l'énigme de l'intelligence*. Payot, Paris, France, 1988.
15. A. Hodges. *Alan Turing: The Enigma*. Vintage, London, UK, 1992.
16. D. C. Ince, editor. *Collected Works of A. M. Turing: Mechanical Intelligence*. North-Holland, Amsterdam, 1992.
17. R. Kurzweil. *The Age of Spiritual Machines: When Computers Exceed Human Intelligence*. Viking, 1999.
18. Merleau-Ponty. *Phénoménologie de la perception*. Gallimard, Paris, France, 1945.
19. P. Millican and A. Clark, editors. *The Legacy of Alan Turing: Machines and Thought*, volume 1. Oxford University Press Inc., New York, 1996.
20. H. Rheingold. *The Virtual Community: Homesteading on the Electronic Frontier*. Addison-Wesley, Reading, UK, 1993.
21. R. Richta. *La civilisation au carrefour*. Anthropos, Paris, France, 1969.
22. V. Scardigli. *Un anthropologue chez les automates*. PUF, Paris, France, 2001.
23. J. Searle. *The Mystery of Consciousness*. Granta Books, London, UK, 1997.
24. A. Sloman. Beyond Turing equivalence. In Millican and Clark [19], pages 179–219.
25. A. R. Stone. Will the real body please stand up? In M. Benedikt, editor, *Cyberspace: First Steps*, pages 81–118. MIT Press, Cambridge, MA, 1991.
26. C. Teuscher. *Turing's Connectionism. An Investigation of Neural Network Architectures*. Springer-Verlag, London, 2002.
27. A. M. Turing. Computing machinery and intelligence. *Mind*, 59(236):433–460, 1950.
28. A. M. Turing. Intelligent machinery. In B. Meltzer and D. Michie, editors, *Machine Intelligence*, volume 5, pages 3–23. Edinburgh University Press, Edinburgh, 1969.
29. A. M. Turing. Intelligent machinery. In Ince [16], pages 107–127.
30. B. Whitby. The Turing test: AI's biggest blind alley. In Millican and Clark [19], pages 53–62.
31. N. Wiener. *Cybernetics or Control and Communication in the Animal and the Machine*. Hermann et Cie, Paris, France, 1948.
32. A. Wolfe. Mind, self, society, and computer: Artificial intelligence and the sociology of mind. *American Journal of Sociology*, 96:1073–1096, 1991.

Part II

Computation and Turing Machines

The Mechanization of Mathematics

Michael J. Beeson

Department of Computer Science, San José State University

Summary. The *mechanization of mathematics* refers to the use of computers to find, or to help find, mathematical proofs. Turing showed that a complete reduction of mathematics to computation is not possible, but nevertheless; the art and science of automated deduction has made progress. This paper describes some of the history and surveys the state of the art.

1 Introduction

In the nineteenth century, machines replaced humans and animals as physical laborers. While for the most part this was a welcome relief, there were occasional pockets of resistance. The folk song *John Henry* commemorates an occasion when a man and a machine competed at the task of drilling railroad tunnels through mountains. The "drilling" was done by hammering a steel spike. The machine was steam powered. The man was an ex-slave, a banjo player with a deep singing voice and a reputation for physical strength and endurance. He beat the machine, drilling fourteen feet to its nine, but it was a Pyrrhic victory, as he died after the effort.

Even before the first computers were developed, people were speculating about the possibility that machines might be made to perform intellectual as well as physical tasks. Alan Turing was the first to make a careful analysis of the potential capabilities of machines, inventing his famous "Turing machines" for the purpose. He argued that if any machine could perform a computation, then some Turing machine could perform it. The argument focuses on the assertion that any machine's operations could be simulated, one step at a time, by certain simple operations, and that Turing machines were capable of those simple operations. Turing's first fame resulted from applying this analysis to a problem posed earlier by Hilbert, which concerned the possibility of mechanizing mathematics. Turing showed that in a certain sense, it is impossible to mechanize mathematics: We shall never be able to build an "oracle" machine that can correctly answer all mathematical questions presented to it with a "yes" or "no" answer. In another famous paper [101], Turing went on to consider the somewhat different question, "Can machines think?." It is a different question, because perhaps machines can think, but they might not be any better at mathematics than humans are; or perhaps they might be better at mathematics than humans are, but not by thinking, just by brute-force calculation power. These two papers of Turing lie near the roots of the subjects today known as *automated deduction* and *artificial intelligence.*[1]

Although Turing had already proved there were limits to what one could expect of machines, nevertheless machines began to compete with humans at intellectual tasks. Arithmetic came first, but by the end of the century computers could play excellent chess, and in 1997 a computer program beat world champion Garry Kasparov. The New York Times described the match: "In a dazzling hourlong game, the Deep Blue IBM computer demolished an obviously overwhelmed Garry Kasparov and won the six-game man-vs.-machine chess match."[2]

Fig. 1. Kasparov vs. Deep Blue (1997). Courtesy of IBM

In 1956, Herb Simon, one of the "fathers of artificial intelligence," predicted that within ten years computers would beat the world chess champion, compose "aesthetically satisfying" original music, and prove new mathematical

---

[1] One controversy concerns the question whether the limiting theorems about Turing machines also apply to human intelligence, or whether human intelligence has some quality not imitable by a Turing machine (a vital force, free will, quantum indeterminacy in the synapses?) These questions were already taken up by Turing, and were still under discussion (without agreement) by scientific luminaries at the end of the twentieth century [79, 80].

[2] After the game, IBM retired Deep Blue, "quitting while it was ahead." Some said that Kasparov lost only because he got nervous and blundered. No rematch was held. In October, 2002, another champion played another computer program: This time it was a draw.

theorems.[3] It took forty years, not ten, but all these goals were achieved —
and within a few years of each other! The music composed by David Cope's
programs [33–35] cannot be distinguished, even by professors of music, from
that composed by Mozart, Beethoven, and Bach.[4]

In 1976, a computer was used in the proof of the long-unsolved "four
color problem."[5] This did not fulfill Simon's prediction, because the role of
the computer was simply to check by calculation the 1476 different specific
cases to which the mathematicians had reduced the problem [2,3]. Today this
would not cause a ripple, but in 1976 it created quite a stir, and there was
serious discussion about whether such a "proof" was acceptable! The journal
editors required an independent computer program to be written to check
the result. The use of computer calculations to provide "empirical" evidence
for mathematical claims has led to "experimental mathematics" and even to
reports of the "death of proof" [53]. As Mark Twain said, "the reports of my
death are greatly exaggerated."

On December 10, 1996, Simon's prediction came true. The front page of
the New York Times carried the following headline: *Computer Math Proof
Shows Reasoning Power.* The story began:

> Computers are whizzes when it comes to the grunt work of math-
> ematics. But for creative and elegant solutions to hard mathematical
> problems, nothing has been able to beat the human mind. That is,
> perhaps, until now. A computer program written by researchers at
> Argonne National Laboratory in Illinois has come up with a major
> mathematical proof that would have been called creative if a human
> had thought of it. In doing so, the computer has, for the first time, got
> a toehold into pure mathematics, a field described by its practitioners
> as more of an art form than a science.

The theorem was proved by the computer program EQP, written by Bill
McCune. Before it was proved, it was known as the *Robbins Conjecture,*
and people seem reluctant to change the name to "EQP's theorem." It is
about certain algebras. An algebra is a set with two operations, written as
we usually write addition and multiplication, and another operation called
"complement" and written $n(x)$. If an algebra satisfies certain nice equations

---

[3] This prediction is usually cited as having been made in 1957, but I believe it
was actually first made in 1956 at Simon's inaugural address as President of the
Operations Research Society of America.

[4] That level of performance was not demanded by Simon's prediction, and his
criterion of "aesthetically satisfying" music was met much earlier. It is interesting
that Simon set a lower bar for music than for mathematics and chess, but music
turned out to be easier to computerize than mathematics.

[5] This problem asks whether it is possible to color any map that can be drawn on
a plane using at most four colors, in such a way that countries with a common
border receive different colors.

it is called a Boolean algebra. Robbins exhibited three short simple equations and conjectured that these three equations can be used to axiomatize Boolean algebras; that is, those three equations imply the usual axioms for Boolean algebras. A complete, precise statement of the Robbins conjecture is given in Fig. 2.

A Boolean algebra is a set A together with binary operations $+$ and $\cdot$ and a unary operation $-$, and elements 0, 1 of A such that the following laws hold: commutative and associative laws for addition and multiplication, distributive laws both for multiplication over addition and for addition over multiplication, and the following special laws: $x + (x \cdot y) = x$, $x \cdot (x + y) = x$, $x + (-x) = 1$, $x \cdot (-x) = 0$. This definition, and other basic information on the subject, can be found in [73]. The Robbins conjecture says that any algebra satisfying the following three equations is a Boolean algebra.

$$x + y = y + x$$
$$(x + y) + z = x + (y + z)$$
$$n(n(x + y) + n(x + n(y))) = x$$

Previous work had shown that it is enough to prove the *Huntington equation*:

$$n(n(x) + y) + n(n(x) + n(y)) = x.$$

That is, if this equation is satisfied, then the algebra is Boolean. What EQP actually did, then, is come up with a proof that the three Robbins equations imply the Huntington equation. Take out your pencil and paper and give it a try before reading on. You don't need a Ph.D. in mathematics to understand the problem: Just see if the three Robbins equations imply the Huntington equation. It is important to understand the nature of the game: You do not need to "understand" the equations, or the "meaning" of the symbols n, $+$ and $\cdot$. You might be happier if you could think of $+$ as "or," $\cdot$ as "and," and n as "not," but it is completely unnecessary, as you are not allowed to use any properties of these symbols except those given by the equations.

Fig. 2. What exactly is the Robbins Conjecture?

EQP solved this problem in a computer run lasting eight days and using 30 megabytes of memory. The proof it produced, however, was only fifteen lines long and fits onto a single page or computer screen. You sometimes have to shovel a lot of dirt and gravel to find a diamond.[6] Since the proof

---

[6] In 1966 (within ten years of Simon's prediction), a computer program was involved in the solution of an open problem. The user was guiding an interactive theorem-prover known as SAM to a proof of a known theorem, and noticed that an equation that had been derived led directly to the answer to a related open question [47]. This event is "widely regarded as the first case of a new result in

was easily checkable by humans, there was no flurry of discussion about the acceptability of the proof, as there had been about the four-color problem. (There was, however, a bit of discussion about whether humans had really given this problem their best shot — but indeed, Tarski studied it, and none of the humans who were tempted to be critical were able to find a proof, so these discussions were generally short-lived.) An amusing sidelight: The job was just running in the background and its successful completion was not noticed until a day later!

It seems, however, that the intellectual triumph of the computer is by no means as thorough as the physical triumph of the steam drill. The computer has yet to beat a human chess champion reliably and repeatedly, and the number of mathematical theorems whose first proof was found by a computer is still less than 100, though there is some fuzziness about what counts as a theorem and what counts as a computer proof. No graduate student today chooses not to become a mathematician for fear that the computer will prove too difficult a competitor. The day when a computer produces a five hundred page proof that answers a famous open question is not imminent.

Another analogy, perhaps closer than the steam drill, is to mechanizing flight. With regard to mechanizing mathematics, are we now at the stage of Leonardo da Vinci's drawings of men with wings, or at the stage of the Wright brothers? Can we expect the analog of jetliners anytime soon? Airplanes fly, but not quite like birds fly, and Dijkstra famously remarked that the question whether machines can think is like the question, "Can submarines swim?." Since people have no wings, the prospect of machines flying did not create the anxieties and controversies that surround the prospect of machines thinking. But machines do mathematics somewhat in the way that submarines swim: ponderously, with more power and duration than a fish, but with less grace and beauty.[7]

---

mathematics being found with help from an automated theorem-prover," according to [72, p. 6].

[7] This is the fine print containing the disclaimers. In this paper, "mechanization of mathematics" refers to getting computers to *find* proofs, rather than having them *check* proofs that we already knew, or *store* proofs or papers in a database for reference, or *typeset* our papers, or *send* them conveniently to one another, or *display* them on the Web. All these things are indeed mechanizations of mathematics, in a broader sense, and there are many interesting projects on all these fronts, but we shall limit the scope of our discussions to events in the spirit of John Henry and Big Blue. Moreover, we do not discuss past and present efforts to enable computer programs to make conjectures, or to apply mechanized reasoning to other areas than mathematics, such as verification of computer programs or security protocols, etc.

2   Before Turing

In this section we review the major strands of thought about the mechanization of mathematics up to the time of Turing. The major figures in this history were Leibniz, Boole, Frege, Russell, and Hilbert. The achievements of these men have been discussed in many other places, most recently in [39], and twenty years ago in [38]. Therefore we will keep this section short; nevertheless, certain minor characters deserve more attention.

Gottfried Leibniz (1646–1716) is famous in this connection for his slogan *Calculemus*, which means "Let us calculate." He envisioned a formal language to reduce reasoning to calculation, and said that reasonable men, faced with a difficult question of philosophy or policy, would express the question in a precise language and use rules of calculation to carry out precise reasoning. This is the first reduction of reasoning to calculation ever envisioned. One imagines a roomful of generals and political leaders turning the crank of Leibniz's machine to decide whether to launch a military attack. It is interesting that Leibniz did not restrict himself to theoretical speculation on this subject — he actually designed and built a working calculating machine, the *Stepped Reckoner*. He was inspired by the somewhat earlier work of Pascal, who built a machine that could add and subtract. Leibniz's machine could add, subtract, divide, and multiply, and was apparently the first machine with all four arithmetic capabilities.[8] Two of Leibniz's Stepped Reckoners have survived and are on display in museums in Munich and Hanover.

George Boole (1815–1864) took up Leibniz's idea, and wrote a book [26] called *The Laws of Thought*. The laws he formulated are now called Boolean Algebra — yes, the same laws of concern in the Robbins conjecture. Like Leibniz, Boole seems to have had a grandiose vision about the applicability of his algebraic methods to practical problems — his book makes it clear that he hoped these laws would be used to settle practical questions. William Stanley Jevons heard of Boole's work, and undertook to build a machine to make calculations in Boolean algebra. He successfully designed and built such a machine, which he called the *Logical Piano*, apparently because it was about the size and shape of a small piano. This machine and its creator deserve much more fanfare than they have so far received: This was the first machine to do mechanical inference. Its predecessors, including the Stepped Reckoner, only did arithmetic. The machine is on display at the Museum of Science at Oxford. The design of the machine was described in a paper, *On the Mechanical Performance of Logical Inference*, read before the British Royal Society in 1870.[9]

Gottlob Frege (1848–1925) created modern logic including "for all," "there exists," and rules of proof. Leibniz and Boole had dealt only with what we

---

[8] The abacus does not count because it is not automatic. With Leibniz's machine, the human only turned the crank.

[9] In December 2002, an original copy of this paper was available for purchase from a rare book dealer in New York for a price exceeding $2000.

Fig. 3. William Stanley Jevons (1835–1882)

now call "propositional logic" (that is, no "for all" or "there exists"). They also did not concern themselves with rules of proof, since their aim was to reach truth by pure calculation with symbols for the propositions. Frege took the opposite tack: instead of trying to reduce logic to calculation, he tried to reduce mathematics to logic, including the concept of number. For example, he defined the number 2 to be the class of all classes of the form $\{x, y\}$ with $x \neq y$. Loosely speaking, 2 is the class of all classes with two members; but put that way, the definition sounds circular, which it is not. His major work, the *Begriffschrift* [43], was published in 1879, when Frege was 31 years old. He described it as "a symbolic language of pure thought, modeled upon that of arithmetic."

Bertrand Russell (1872–1970) found Frege's famous error: Frege had overlooked what is now known as the Russell paradox.[10] Namely, Frege's rules allowed one to define the class of x such that $P(x)$ is true for any "concept" P. Frege's idea was that such a class was an object itself, the class of objects "falling under the concept P." Russell used this principle to define the class R of concepts that do not fall under themselves. This concept leads to a contradiction known as Russell's Paradox. Here is the argument: (1) if R falls under itself then it does not fall under itself; (2) this contradiction shows

---

[10] Russell was thirty years old at the time — about the same age that Frege had been when he made the error. Russell's respectful letter to Frege with the bad news is reprinted in [102, p. 124], along with Frege's reply: "Your discovery of the contradiction caused me the greatest surprise and, I would almost say, consternation, since it has shaken the basis on which I intended to build arithmetic."

that it *does not* fall under itself; (3) therefore by definition it *does* fall under itself after all.

Russell (with co-author Whitehead) wrote *Principia Mathematica* [91] to save mathematics from this contradiction. They restricted the applicability of Frege's class-definition principle, thus blocking Russell's paradox, and showed (by actually carrying out hundreds of pages of proofs) that the main lines of mathematics could still be developed from the restricted principle. This work was very influential and became the starting point for twentieth-century logic; thirty years later, when Gödel needed a specific axiom system for use in stating his incompleteness theorem, the obvious choice was the system of *Principia*.

David Hilbert (1862–1943) was one of the foremost mathematicians of the early twentieth century. He contributed to the development of formal logic (rules for reasoning), and then became interested in a two step reductionist program that combined those of Leibniz and Frege: he would first reduce mathematics to logic, using formal languages, and *then* reduce logic to computation. His plan was to consider the proofs in logic as objects in their own right, and study them as one would study any finite structure, just as mathematicians study groups or graphs. He hoped that we would then be able to give algorithms for determining if a given statement could be proved from given axioms, or not. By consideration of this research program, he was led to formulate the "decision problem" for logic, better known by its German name, the "Entscheidungsproblem." This problem was published in 1928 in the influential logic book by Hilbert and Ackermann [51]. This was the problem whose negative solution made Turing famous; the next section will explain the problem and its solution.

3   Hilbert and the Entscheidungsproblem

The Entscheidungsproblem asks whether there exists a "decision algorithm" such that:

- It takes two inputs: a finite set of axioms, and a conjecture.
- It computes for a finite time and outputs either a proof of the conjecture from the axioms, or "no proof exists."
- The result is always correct.

Part of the reason for the historical importance of this problem is that it was a significant achievement just to state the problem precisely. What are *axioms*? What is a *proof*? What is an *algorithm*? Progress on the first two of those questions had been made by Russell and by Hilbert himself. There was an important difference in their approaches, however. Russell worked with proofs and axioms in order to find axioms that were evidently true, and would therefore enable one to derive true (and only true) mathematical theorems. He had in mind one fixed interpretation of his axioms — that is, they were about the one true mathematical universe of classes, if they were about anything at all. In the many pages of *Principia Mathematica*, Russell and Whitehead never discussed the question of what we would today call the interpretations of their formal theory. Hilbert, on the other hand, understood very well that the same axioms could have more than one interpretation. Hilbert's most well-known work on axiomatization is his book *Foundations of Geometry* [50]. This book provided a careful axiomatic reworking of Euclid from 21 axioms. Hilbert emphasized the distinction between correct reasoning (about points, lines, and planes) and the facts about points, lines, and planes, by saying that if you replace "points, lines, and planes" by "tables, chairs, and beer mugs," the reasoning should still be correct. This seems obvious to today's mathematicians, because the axiomatic approach to mathematics proved so fruitful in the rest of the twentieth century that every student of mathematics is today steeped in this basic idea. But, at the dawn of the twentieth century, this idea seemed radical. The mathematician Poincaré understood Hilbert's point very clearly, as one can see in the following quotation [78], but he thought it antithetical to the spirit of mathematics:

> Thus it will be readily understood that in order to demonstrate a theorem, it is not necessary or even useful to know what it means. We might replace geometry by the reasoning piano imagined by Stanley Jevons, or ... a machine where we should put in axioms at one end and take out theorems at the other, like that legendary machine in Chicago where pigs go in alive and come out transformed into hams and sausages.

The date of that quotation is 1908, almost a decade after *Foundations of Geometry*. But the concept of "proof" was still a bit unclear. The distinction that was still lacking was what we call today the distinction between a *first-order* proof and a *second-order* proof. The axioms of geometry in Hilbert's book included the "continuity axiom," which says that if you have two subsets A and B of a line L, and all the points of A lie to the left[11] of all the points of B, then there exists a point P on L to the right of all points of A not equal to P, and to the left of all points of B not equal to P. This axiom is intended to say that there are no "holes" in a line. For example, if L is the x-axis, and if A is the set of points with $x^2 < 2$, and if B is the set of points with $x > 0$ and $x^2 > 2$, then the axiom guarantees the existence of $x = \sqrt{2}$. But the statement of the axiom mentions not only points, lines, and planes (the objects of geometry) but also *sets* of points. Remember that *Foundations of Geometry* was written before the discovery of Russell's paradox and *Principia*, and apparently Hilbert did not see the necessity of careful attention to the axioms for sets as well as to the axioms for points, lines, and planes. A *second-order* theory or axiomatization is one that, like

---

[11] Hilbert's axioms use a primitive relation "x is between y and z." We can avoid the informal term "lie to the left" using this relation.

Hilbert's axiomatization of geometry, uses variables for sets of objects as well as variables for objects. Peano's axioms for number theory are another famous example of a second-order axiomatization.[12] Incidentally, Peano's publication [75] was a pamphlet written in Latin, long after Latin had been displaced as the language of scholarship, so that the publication has been viewed as an "act of romanticism." Peano, originally a good teacher, became an unpopular teacher because he insisted on using formal notation in elementary classes; nevertheless, his work eventually became influential, and it is his notation that is used today in logic, not Frege's.

In both these two famous examples, the theories achieve their aim: They uniquely define the structures they are trying to axiomatize. Every system of objects satisfying Hilbert's axioms for plane geometry is isomorphic to the Euclidean plane. Even if we begin by assuming that the system consists of tables, chairs, and beer mugs, it turns out to be isomorphic to the Euclidean plane. Every system of objects satisfying Peano's axioms is isomorphic to the natural numbers. But the second-order nature of these axioms systems is essential to this property. The technical term for this property is that the theory is *categorical*. These are *second-order categorical* theories. The concept of second-order theory versus first-order theory is not easy to grasp, but is very important in understanding the theoretical basis of the mechanization of mathematics, so here goes:

If we require a first-order version of the continuity axiom, then instead of saying "for all sets A and B...," the axiom will become many axioms, where A and B are replaced by many different first-order formulas. In other words, instead of being able to state the axiom for *all* sets of points, we will have to settle for *algebraically definable* sets of points. We will still be able to define $\sqrt{2}$, but we will not be able to define π, because π cannot be defined by algebraic conditions. Another way of looking at this situation is to consider systems of "points" that satisfy the axioms. Such systems are called "models." In the case at hand, we have the "real plane" consisting of all points (x, y), and on the other hand, we have the smaller "plane" consisting only of the numbers (x, y) where x and y are solutions of some polynomial equation with integer coefficients. Both these satisfy the first-order axioms of geometry, but the smaller plane lacks the point $(\pi, 0)$ and hence does not satisfy the second-order continuity axiom.

---

[12] These famous axioms characterize the natural numbers N as follows: 0 is in N, and if x is in N then the successor x^+ of x is in N, and 0 is not the successor of any number, and if $x^+ = y^+$ then $x = y$. (The successor of 0 is 1, the successor of 1 is 2, etc.) To these axioms Peano added the axiom of *induction*: if X is any set satisfying these properties with X instead of N, then N is a subset of X. The induction axiom is equivalent to the statement that every non-empty set of natural numbers contains a least element, and is also equivalent to the usual formulation of mathematical induction: for sets X of natural numbers, if 0 is in X, and if whenever n is in X so is n^+, then X contains all natural numbers.

Similarly, in arithmetic, if we do not use variables for sets in stating the induction axiom, we will be able only to "approximate" the axiom by including its specific instances, where the inductive set is defined in the fixed language of arithmetic. There are theorems that say a certain equation has no solution in integers, whose proofs require proving a very complicated formula P by induction, as a lemma, where the formula P is too complicated to even be stated in the language of arithmetic — perhaps it requires more advanced mathematical concepts. Just as there exist different models of first-order geometry (in which π does or does not exist), there also exist different models of first-order number theory, some of which are "non-standard" in that the "numbers" of the model are not isomorphic to the actual integers. These non-standard models are more difficult to visualize and understand than a plane that "simply" omits numbers with complicated definitions, because these models contain "numbers" that are not really numbers, but are "extra."

Using modern language, we say that a first-order theory, even one formed by restricting a second-order categorical theory to its first-order instances, generally has many models, not just one. This situation was not clearly understood in the first two decades of the twentieth century[13], but by 1928, when Hilbert and Ackermann published their monograph on mathematical logic [51], it had become clear at least to those authors. Clarity on this point led directly to the formulation of the Entscheidungsproblem: Since a first-order theory generally has many models, can we decide (given a theory) which formulas are true in all the models? It also led directly to the formulation of the completeness problem: Are the formulas true in all the models exactly those that have proofs from the axioms? The former problem was solved by Turing and Church, the latter by Gödel, both within a few years of the publication of Hilbert-Ackermann. These developments laid the foundations of modern mathematical logic, which in turn furnished the tools for the mechanization of mathematics.

The distinction between second-order and first-order confuses people because it has two aspects: syntax and semantics. A theory which has variables for objects and for sets of those objects (for example integers and sets of integers) is syntactically second-order. We can write down mathematical induction using the set variables. But then, we can still consider this as a first-order theory, in which case we would allow models in which the set variables range over a suitable countable collection of sets of integers, and there would also be models with non-standard integers in which the set variables range over a collection of "subsets of integers" of the model. Or, we can consider it as a second-order theory, in which case we do not allow such models, but only allow models in which the set variables range over *all* subsets of the integers of the model. Whether it is second-order or first-order is determined by what

---

[13] See for example [67], Part III for more details on the views of Hilbert and his contemporaries.

we allow as a "model" of the theory, not by the language in which we express the theory.

4   Turing's Negative Solution of the Entscheidungsproblem

The developments described above still left the Entscheidungsproblem somewhat imprecise, in that the concept *algorithm* mentioned in the problem had not been defined. Apparently Hilbert hoped for a positive solution of the problem, in which case it would not have been necessary to define "algorithm," as the solution would exhibit a specific algorithm. But a negative solution would have to prove that no algorithm could do the job, and hence it would be necessary to have a definition of "algorithm."

Alan Turing (1912–1954), answered the question "What is an algorithm?" in 1936 [100] by defining Turing machines.[14] He used his definition to show that there exist problems that cannot be solved by any algorithm. The most well-known of these is the "halting problem" — there exists no Turing machine that takes as inputs a Turing machine M and an input x for M, and determines correctly whether M halts on input x. Indeed, we don't need two variables here: no Turing machine can determine correctly whether M halts at input M.

In that same remarkable 1936 paper [100], Turing applied his new Turing machines to give a negative solution to the Entscheidungsproblem. His solution makes use of the result just mentioned, that the halting problem is not solvable by a Turing machine. We shall describe his solution to the Entscheidungsproblem now, but not the solution to the halting problem, which is covered in any modern textbook on the theory of computation. (The reader who does not already know what a Turing machine is should skip to the next section.) The solution has three steps:

- Write down axioms A to describe the computations of Turing machines.
- Turing machine M halts at input x if and only if A proves the theorem "M halts at input x."

---

[14] Turing "machines" are conceptual objects rather than physical machines. They *could* be built, but in practice the *idea* of these machines is used, rather than physical examples. Such a machine can be specified by a finite list of its parts ("states") and their connections ("instructions"). They work on "inputs" that are represented by symbols on an input device, usually called a "tape." Whenever the tape is about to be used up, an attendant will attach more, so conceptually, the tape is infinite, yet the machine could still be built. Turing's key idea was that the descriptions of the machines can be given by symbols, and hence Turing machines can accept (descriptions of) Turing machines as inputs.

- If we had an algorithm to determine the consequences of axioms A, it would solve the halting problem, contradiction. Hence no such algorithm exists.[15]

The "computations" referred to in the first step can be thought of as two-dimensional tables. Each row of the table corresponds to the tape of the Turing machine at a given stage in its computation. The next row is the next stage, after one "move" of the machine. There is an extra mark (you can think of a red color) in the cell where the Turing machine head is located at that stage. When we refer to cell (i, j) we mean the j-th cell in the i-th row. The axioms say that such a table T is a computation by machine M if for all the entries in T, the contents of cell $(i + 1, j)$ are related to the contents of the three cells $(i, j - 1)$, (i, j), and $(i, j + 1)$ according to the program of Turing machine M. Although this uses natural numbers (i, j) to refer to the cells of T, only a few basic and easily axiomatizable properties of the numbers are needed for such an indexing. Of course, it takes some pages to fill in all the details of the first two steps, but the basic idea is not complicated once one understands the concepts involved.

Turing's result showed conclusively that it will never be possible to completely mechanize mathematics. We shall never be able to take all our mathematical questions to a computer and get correct yes or no answers. To understand the definitiveness of Turing's result, one needs Gödel's completeness theorem. The completeness theorem identifies the two natural meanings of "logical consequence": P is a logical consequence of A, if P is true in all systems (models) that satisfy axioms A. On the other hand, P should hopefully be a logical consequence of A, if and only if there exists a proof of P from A. This turns out to be the case, and is exactly the content of Gödel's completeness theorem. Therefore, Turing's result means that we shall never be able to take all questions of the form, "does theorem P follow from axioms A?" to a computer and get a guaranteed correct yes or no answer.

---

[15] In more detail the argument is this: Suppose some Turing machine K accepts inputs describing axiom sets S and potential theorems B, and outputs 1 or 0 according as S proves B or does not prove B. To solve the halting problem, which is whether a given Turing machine M halts at a given input x, we construct the set of axioms A (depending on M) as in the first step. We then construct the sequence of symbols y expressing "M halts at input x." According to step 2, M halts at x if and only if A proves the theorem y. By hypothesis, we can determine this by running Turing machine K at the inputs A and y. If we get 1, then M halts at x, and if we get 0, it does not. If K behaves as we have supposed, this algorithm will solve the halting problem. Since it involves only Turing machines connected by simple steps, it can be done by another Turing machine, contradicting Turing's result on the unsolvability of the halting problem. Hence no such machine K can exist.

5 Church and Gödel

Turing's negative solution of the Entscheidungsproblem was followed in the 1930s by other "negative" results. In 1936, Alonzo Church (1903–1995) invented the lambda-calculus (often written λ-calculus) and used it to give a definition of *algorithm* different from Turing's, and hence an independent solution of the Entscheidungsproblem [29]. He also proved the result we now summarize in the statement, "Arithmetic is undecidable." Since Peano's axioms are not first-order, the Entscheidungsproblem does not directly apply to them, and one can ask whether there could be an algorithm that takes a first-order statement about the natural numbers as input, and correctly outputs "true" or "false." The Entscheidungsproblem does not apply, since there exists no (finite first-order) system of axioms A whose logical consequences are the statements true in the natural numbers. Church showed that, nevertheless, there is no such algorithm. Church's student Kleene proved the equivalence of the Turing-machine and the λ-calculus definitions of *algorithm* in his Ph.D. thesis, later published in [60].[16]

Fig. 4. Alonzo Church in 1952. Photo credit: from the estate of Alonzo Church

In 1931, Kurt Gödel [45] proved his famous "incompleteness theorem," which we can state as follows: Whatever system of axioms one writes down in an attempt to axiomatize the truths about the natural numbers, either some false statement will be proved from the axioms, or some true statement

---

[16] Kleene went on to become one of the twentieth century's luminaries of logic; his [61] is probably the most influential logic textbook ever written, and he laid the foundations of "recursion theory," which includes the subject now known as the theory of computation.

will not be proved. In other words, if all the axioms are true, then some true fact will be unprovable from those axioms. Gödel used neither Turing machines nor λ-calculus (neither of which was invented until five years later), but in essence gave a third definition of *algorithm*.[17] The bulk of Gödel's paper is devoted, not to his essential ideas, but to the details of coding computations as integers; although he did not use Turing machines, he still had to code a different kind of computation as integers. Nowadays, when "ASCII codes" used by computers routinely assign a number to each alphabetic character, and hence reduce a line of text to a very long number, using three digits per character, this seems routine. For example, 'a' has the ASCII code 97, 'b' is assigned 98, 'c' gets 99, and so on. Thus "cat" gets the number 099097116. Such encodings can also be used to show that Turing machine computations can be encoded in numbers. Making use of Turing machines, it is not very difficult to understand the main idea of Gödel's proof. The technical details about coding can be used to construct a number-theoretical formula $T(e, x, y)$ that expresses that e is a code for a Turing machine (a finite set of instructions), and y is a code for a complete (halting) computation by machine e at input x. In other words, "machine e halts at input x" can be expressed by "there exists a y such that $T(e, x, y)$." Now suppose that we had a correct and complete axiomatization A of the true statements of arithmetic. We could then solve the halting problem by the following algorithm: we simultaneously try to prove "machine e does not halt at input e" from the axioms A, and we run machine e at input e to see if it halts. Here "simultaneously" can be taken to mean "in alternating steps." At even-numbered stages, we run e at input e for one more step, and, at odd-numbered stages, we make one more deduction from the axioms A. If e halts at input e, we find that out at some even-numbered stage. Otherwise, by the assumed completeness and correctness of the axioms A, we succeed at some odd-numbered stage to find a proof that e does not halt at input e. But since the halting problem is unsolvable, this is a contradiction; hence no such set of axioms A can exist. That is Gödel's incompleteness theorem.

6   The Possible Loopholes

The results of Turing, Church, and Gödel are commonly called "negative" results in that they show the impossibility of a complete reduction of mathematics or logic to computation. Hilbert's program was a hopeless pipe dream. These famous results seem to close the doors on those who would hope to mechanize mathematics. But we are not completely trapped; there are the following possible "loopholes," or avenues that may still prove fruitful.

---

[17] Gödel's definition seemed at the time rather specialized, and (unlike Turing five years later) he made no claim that it corresponded to the general notion of "computable," though that turned out to be true.

- Maybe there exist interesting axiom systems A such that, for that *particular* axiom system, there *does* exist a "decision procedure" that permits us to compute whether a given statement P follows from A or not.
- Maybe there exist interesting algorithms f that take an axiom system A and an input formula P and, *sometimes*, tell us that P follows from A. Even if f is not *guaranteed* to work on *all* P, if it would work on *some* P for which we did not know the answer before, that would be quite interesting.
- Even if such an f worked only for a particular axiom system A of interest, it still might be able to answer mathematical questions that we could not answer before.

These loopholes in the negative results of the thirties allow the partial mechanization of mathematics. It is the pursuit of these possibilities that occupies the main business of this paper.

7   The First Theorem-Provers

When the computer was still newborn, some people tried to write programs exploiting the loopholes left by Church and Gödel. The first one exploited the possibility of decision procedures. There was already a known decision procedure for arithmetic without multiplication. This is essentially the theory of linear equations with integer variables, and "for all" and "there exists." This theory goes by the name of "Presburger arithmetic," after M. Presburger, who first gave a decision procedure for it in [82]. It cried out for implementation, now that the computer was more than a thought experiment. Martin Davis took up this challenge [37], and in 1954 his program proved that the sum of two even numbers is even. This was perhaps the first theorem ever proved by a computer program. The computer on which the program ran was a vacuum tube computer known as the "johnniac," at the Institute for Advanced Study in Princeton, which had a memory of 1024 words. The program could use a maximum of 96 words to hold the generated formulas.

In 1955, Newell, Shaw, and Simon wrote a program they called the *Logic Theorist* [74]. This program went through another loophole: it tried to find proofs, even though according to Turing it must fail sometimes. It proved several propositional logic theorems in the system of *Principia Mathematica*. The authors were proud of the fact that this program was "heuristic," by which they meant not only that it might fail, but that there was some analogy between how it solved problems and how a human would solve the same problems. They felt that a heuristic approach was necessary because the approach of systematically searching for a proof of the desired theorem from the given axioms seemed hopeless. They referred to the latter as the "British Museum" algorithm, comparing it to searching for a desired item in the British Museum by examining the entire contents of the museum. According to [38],

Alan Newell said to Herb Simon on Christmas 1955, about their program, "Kind of crude, but it works, boy, it works!" In one of Simon's obituaries [66] (he died in 2001 at age 84), one finds a continuation of this story:

> The following January, Professor Simon celebrated this discovery by walking into a class and announcing to his students, "Over the Christmas holiday, Al Newell and I invented a thinking machine." A subsequent letter to Lord Russell explaining his achievement elicited the reply : "I am delighted to know that 'Principia Mathematica' can now be done by machinery. I wish Whitehead and I had known of this possibility before we wasted 10 years doing it by hand."[18]

In 1957, the year of publication of Newell, Shaw, and Simon's report [74], a five week Summer Institute for Symbolic Logic was held at Cornell, attended by many American logicians and some researchers from IBM. At this meeting, Abraham Robinson introduced the idea of Skolem functions [explained below], and shortly after the meeting a number of important advances were made. Several new programs were written that searched more systematically for proofs than the *Logic Theorist* had done. The problem was clearly seen as "pruning" the search, i.e. eliminating fruitless deductions as early as possible. Gelernter's geometry prover [44] used a "diagram" to prune false goals. The mathematical logician Hao Wang wrote a program [103] based on a logical system known as "natural deduction." Wang's program proved all 400 pure predicate-calculus theorems in *Principia Mathematica*. Davis and Putnam [40] published a paper that coupled the use of Skolem functions and conjunctive normal form with a better algorithm to determine satisfiability. Over the next several years, these strands of development led to the invention of fundamental algorithms that are still in use. We shall discuss three of these tools: Skolemization, resolution, and unification.

Skolem functions are used to systematically eliminate "there exists." For instance, "for every x there exists y such that $P(x,y)$" is replaced by $P(x, g(x))$, where g is called a "Skolem function." When we express the law that every nonzero x has a multiplicative inverse in the form $x \neq 0 \rightarrow x \cdot x^{-1} = 1$, we are using a Skolem function (written as x^{-1} instead of $g(x)$. Terms are built up, using function and operation symbols, from variables and constants; usually letters near the beginning of the alphabet are constants and letters near the end are variables (a convention introduced by Descartes). Certain terms are distinguished as "propositions"; intuitively these are the ones that should be either true or false if the variables are given specific values. The use of Skolem functions and elementary logical manipulations enables us to express every axiom and theorem in a certain standard form called "clausal form," which we now explain. A *literal* is an atomic proposition or its negation. A *clause* is a "disjunction of literals"; that is, a list of literals separated by "or." Given some axioms and a conjectured

---

[18] Russell may have had his tongue firmly in cheek.

theorem, we negate the theorem, and seek a proof by contradiction. We use Skolem functions and logical manipulations to eliminate "there exists," and then we use logical manipulations to bring the axioms and negated goal to the form of a list of clauses, where "and" implicitly joins the clauses. This process is known as "Skolemization." The clausal form contains no "there exists," but it does contain new symbols for the (unknown) Skolem functions. The original question whether the axioms imply the goal is equivalent to the more convenient question whether the resulting list of clauses is contradictory or not.

In automated deduction, it is customary to use the vertical bar to mean "or," and the minus sign to mean "not." An *inference rule* is a rule for deducing theorems from previously-deduced theorems or axioms. It therefore has "premisses" and "conclusions." As an example of an inference rule we mention the rule *modus ponens*, which is already over 2000 years old: from p and "if p then q" infer q. In clausal notation that would be, from p and $-p|q$ infer q. *Resolution* generalizes this rule. In its simplest form it says, from $p|r$ and $-p|q$, infer $r|q$. Even more generally, r and q can be replaced with several propositions. For example, from $p|r|s$ and $-p|q|t$, we can infer $r|s|q|t$. The rule can be thought of as "canceling" p with $-p$. The canceled term p does not have to be the first one listed. If we derive p and also $-p$, then resolution leads to the "empty clause," which denotes a contradiction.

The third of the three tools we mentioned is the *unification algorithm*. This was published by J. A. Robinson [89]. Robinson's publication (which contained more than "just" unification) appeared in 1965, but at that time unification was already "in the air," having been implemented by others as early as 1962. See [38] for this history. The purpose of the unification algorithm is to find values of variables to make two terms match. For example: given $f(x, g(x))$ and $f(g(c), z)$, we find $x = g(c)$, $z = g(g(c))$ by applying unification. The input to the algorithm is a pair of terms to be unified. The output is a substitution; that is, an assignment of terms to variables. We shall not give the details of the unification algorithm here; they can be found in many books, for example in [25, Chap. 17], or [5, pp. 453–].

Combining resolution and unification, we arrive at the following rule of inference: Suppose that p and s can be unified. Let $*$ denote the substitution found by the unification algorithm. Then from $p|q$ and $-s|r$ infer $q^*|r^*$ provided $p^* = s^*$. This rule is also commonly known as "resolution" — in fact, resolution without unification is only of historical or pedagogical interest. Resolution is *always* combined with unification. J. A. Robinson proved [89] that this rule is *refutation complete*. That means that if a list of clauses is contradictory, there exists a proof of the empty clause from the original list, using resolution as the sole rule of inference.[19]

---

[19] We have oversimplified in the text. The resolution rule as we have given it does not permit one to infer $p(z)$ from $p(x)|p(y)$. Either the resolution rule has to be stated a bit more generally, as Robinson did, or we have to supplement it with

The basic paradigm for automated deduction then was born: Start with the axioms and negated goal. Perform resolutions (using unification) until a contradiction is reached, or until you run out of time or memory. The modern era in automated deduction could be said to have begun when this paradigm was in place.[20] One very important strand of work in the subject since the sixties has been devoted to various attempts to prevent running out of time or memory. These attempts will be discussed in the section "Searching for proofs" below.[21]

8   Kinds of Mathematical Reasoning

In this section we abandon the historical approach to the subject. Instead, we examine the mechanization of mathematics by taking inventory of the mathematics to be mechanized. Let us make a rough taxonomy of mathematics. Of course librarians and journal editors are accustomed to classifying mathematics by subject matter, but that is not what we have in mind. Instead, we propose to classify mathematics by the *kind of proofs* that are used. We can distinguish at least the following categories:

- Purely logical
- Simple theory, as in geometry (one kind of object, few relations)
- Equational, as in the Robbins problem, or in group or ring theory.
- Uses calculations, as in algebra or calculus
- Uses natural numbers and mathematical induction
- Uses definitions (perhaps lots of them)
- Uses a little number theory and simple set theory (as in undergraduate algebra courses)
- Uses inequalities heavily (as in analysis)

Purely logical theorems are more interesting than may appear at first blush. One is not restricted to logical systems based on resolution just because one is using a theorem-prover that works that way. There are hundreds

---

the rule called *factoring*, which says that if A and B can be unified, and $*$ is the substitution produced by the unification algorithm, we can infer $A*$.

[20] There were several more attempts to write programs that proved theorems "heuristically," to some extent trying to imitate human thought, but in the end these programs could not compete with an algorithmic search.

[21] It is true that several other approaches have been developed, and have succeeded on some problems. We note in particular the successes of ACL2 [20] and RRL [59] on problems involving mathematical induction, and regret that our limited space and scope do not permit a fuller discussion of alternative approaches. The author is partial to approaches derived from the branch of mathematical logic known as "proof theory"; in the USSR this approach was followed early on, and an algorithm closely related to resolution was invented by Maslov at about the same time as resolution was invented. A theorem-prover based on these principles was built in Leningrad (1971). See [68] for further details and references.

of interesting logical systems, including various axiom systems for classical propositional logic, multi-valued logic, modal logic, intuitionistic logic, etc. All of these can be analyzed using the following method. We use a predicate $P(x)$ to stand for "x is provable." We use $i(x, y)$ to mean x implies y. Then, for example, we can write down $-P(x)| - P(i(x, y))|P(y)$ to express "if x and $i(x, y)$ are provable, so is y." When (a commonly-used variant of) resolution is used with this axiom, it will have the same effect as an inference rule called "condensed detachment" that has long been used by logicians. We will return to this discussion near the end of the paper, in the section on "Searching for proofs."

Euclidean geometry can be formulated in a first-order theory with a simple, natural set of axioms. In fact, it can be formulated in a theory all of whose variables stand for points; direct references to lines and planes can be eliminated [97]. But that is not important — we could use unary predicates for points, lines, and planes, or we could use three "sorts" of variables. What we cannot do in such a theory is mention arbitrary sets of points; therefore, the continuity axiom (discussed above) cannot be stated in such a theory. We can state some instances of the continuity axiom (for example, that a line segment with one end inside a circle and one end outside the circle must meet the circle); or we could even consider a theory with an *axiom schema* (infinitely many axioms of a recognizable form) stating the continuity axiom for all first-order definable sets. But if we are interested in Euclid's propositions, extremely complex forms of the continuity axiom will not be necessary — we can consider a simple theory of geometry instead. It will not prove all the theorems one could prove with the full first-order continuity axiom, but would be sufficient for Euclid. On the other hand, if we wish to prove a theorem about all regular n-gons, the concept of natural number will be required, and proofs by mathematical induction will soon arise. In first-order geometry, we would have one theorem for a square, another for a pentagon, another for a hexagon, and so on. Of course not only Euclidean, but also non-Euclidean geometry, can be formulated in a first-order theory. I know of no work in automated deduction in non-Euclidean geometry, but there exists at least one interesting open problem in hyperbolic geometry whose solution might be possible with automated deduction.[22]

Another example of a simple theory is ring theory. Ring theory is a subject commonly taught in the first year of abstract algebra. The "ring axioms" use the symbols $+$ and $*$, and include most of the familiar laws about them, except

---

[22] The open problem is this: Given a line L and a point P not on L, prove that there exist a pair of *limiting parallels* to L through P. The definition of limiting parallel says that K and R form a pair of limiting parallels to L through P if one of the four angles formed at P by K and R does not contain any ray that does not meet L. It is known that limiting parallels exist, but no first-order proof is known, and experts tell me that producing a first-order proof would be worth a Ph.D.

the "multiplicative inverse" law and the "commutative law of multiplication," $x*y = y*x$. Many specific systems of mathematical objects satisfy these laws, and may or may not satisfy additional laws such as $x * y = y * x$. A system of objects, with two given (but possibly arbitrarily defined) operations to be denoted by the symbols $+$ and $*$, is called a *ring* if all the ring axioms hold when the variables range over these objects and $+$ and $*$ are interpreted as the given operations. In ring theory, one tries to prove a theorem using only the ring axioms; if one succeeds, the theorem will be true in all rings. However, in books on ring theory one finds many theorems about rings that are not formulated purely in the language of ring theory. These theorems have a larger context: they deal with rings and sub-rings, with homomorphisms and isomorphisms of rings, and with matrix rings. Homomorphisms are functions from one ring to another that preserve sums and products; isomorphisms are one-to-one homomorphisms; sub-rings are subsets of a ring that are rings in their own right; matrix rings are rings whose elements are matrices with coefficients drawn from a given ring. Thus passing from a ring R to the ring of n by n matrices with coefficients in R is a method of constructing one ring from another. If, however, we wish to consider such rings of matrices for any n, then the concept of natural number enters again, and we are beyond the simple theory level. Also, if we wish to formulate theorems about arbitrary sub-rings of a ring, again we have a theory that (at least on the face of it) is second-order. A recent master's thesis [54] went through a typical algebra textbook [56], and found that of about 150 exercises on ring theory, 14 could be straightforwardly formalized in first-order ring theory. One more could be formulated using a single natural-number variable in addition to the ring axioms. The rest were more complex. The 14 first-order exercises, however, could be proved by the theorem-proving program Otter. (Otter is a well-known and widely used modern theorem prover, described in [70], and readily available on the Web.)

A great many mathematical proofs seem to depend on calculations for some of the steps. In fact, typically a mathematical proof consists of some parts that are calculations, and some parts that are logical inferences. Of course, it is possible to recast calculations as logical proofs, and it is possible to recast logical proofs as calculations. But there is an intuitive distinction: a calculation proceeds in a straightforward manner, one step after another, applying obvious rules at each step, until the answer is obtained. While performing a calculation, one needs to be careful, but one does not need to be a genius, once one has figured out what calculation to make. It is "merely a calculation." When finding a proof, one needs insight, experience, intelligence — even genius — to succeed, because the search space is too large for a systematic search to succeed.

It is not surprising that a good deal of progress has been made in mechanizing those parts of proof that are calculations. It may be slightly surprising that methods have been found for automatically discovering new rules to be used for calculations. Furthermore, the relations between the computational parts of proofs and the logical parts have been explored to some extent. However, there is still some work to be done before this subject is finished, as we will discuss in more detail below.

One aspect of mathematics that has not been adequately mechanized at the present time is *definitions*. Let me give a few examples of the use of definitions in mathematics. The concept "f is continuous at x," where f is a real-valued function, has a well-known definition: "for every $\epsilon > 0$ there exists $\delta > 0$ such that for all y with $|y - x| < \delta$, we have $|f(x) - f(y)| < \epsilon$." One important virtue of this definition is that it sweeps the quantifiers "for every" and "there exists" under the rug: We are able to work with continuity in a quantifier-free context. If, for example, we wish to prove that $f(x) = (x+3)^{100}$ is a continuous function, the "easy way" is to recognize that f is a composition of two continuous functions and appeal to the theorem that the composition of two continuous functions is continuous. That theorem, however, has to be proved by expanding the definitions and using ϵ and δ. This kind of argument does not mesh well with the clausal form paradigm for automated reasoning, because when the definition is expanded, the result involves quantifiers. Theorem-proving programs usually require clausal form at input, and do not perform dynamic Skolemization. Theorems that have been proved about continuity have, therefore, had the definition-expansion and Skolemization performed by hand before the automated deduction program began, or have used another paradigm (Gentzen sequents or natural deduction) that does not suffer from this problem, but is not as well-suited to searching for proofs. Merely recognizing $f(x) = (x+3)^{100}$ as a composition of two functions is beyond the reach of current theorem-provers — it is an application of the author's current research into "second-order unification."

One might well look, therefore, for the *simplest* example of a definition. Consider the definition of a "commutator" in group theory. The notation usually used for a commutator is $[x, y]$, but to avoid notational complexities, let us use the notation $x \otimes y$. The definition is $x \otimes y = x^{-1}y^{-1}xy$, where as usual we leave the symbol $*$ for the group operation unwritten, and assume that association is to the right, i.e. $abc = a(bc)$. We can find problems in group theory that mention commutators but do not need second-order concepts or natural numbers for their formulation or solution. Here we have a single definition added to a simple theory. Now the point is that sometimes we will need to recognize complicated expressions as being actually "nothing but" a commutator. Long expressions become short ones when written using the commutator notation. On the other hand, sometimes we will not be able to solve the problem without using the definition of $x \otimes y$ to eliminate the symbol $\otimes$. That is, sometimes the definition of $x \otimes y$ will be needed in the left-to-right direction, and sometimes in the right-to-left direction. Existing theorem-provers have no method to control equations with this degree of subtlety. Either $\otimes$ will *always* be eliminated, or *never*. This example definition also serves to bring out another point: definitions can be explicit, like the definition of $x \otimes y$ given above, or implicit. Cancelative semigroups are systems like groups except that inverse is replaced by the cancellation law, $xy = xz$ implies $y = z$. We can define $x \otimes y$ in the context of cancelative semigroups by the equation $xy = yx(x \otimes y)$. This is an "implicit definition." If the law holds in a semigroup S, for some operation $\otimes$, we say "S admits commutators."

Consider the following three formulas, taken from [41], and originally from [64].

$$(x \otimes y) \otimes z = x \otimes (y \otimes z) \quad \text{(1) } commutator\ is\ associative$$
$$(x * y) \otimes z = (x \otimes z) * (y \otimes z) \quad \text{(2) } commutator\ distributes\ over$$
$$product$$
$$(x \otimes y) * z = z * (x \otimes y) \quad \text{(3) } semigroup\ is\ nilpotent\ class\ 2$$

These three properties are equivalent in groups (in fact, in cancelative semigroups that admit commutators). One of the points of considering this example is that it is not clear (to the human mathematician) whether one ought to eliminate the definition of $x \otimes y$ to prove these theorems, or not. Otter is able to prove (1) implies (2), (2) implies (3), and (3) implies (1), in three separate runs, in spite of not having a systematic way to handle definitions; but the proofs are not found easily, and a lot of useless clauses are generated along the way.[23]

Another interesting problem involving commutators is often an exercise in an elementary abstract algebra course: Show that in a group, the commutator subgroup (consisting of all $x \otimes y$) is a normal subgroup. For the part about normality, we have to show that for all a,b, and c, $c^{-1}(a \otimes b)c$ has the form $u \otimes v$ for some u and v. Otter can find several proofs of this theorem, but the u and v in the first few proofs are not the ones a human would find — although it does eventually find the human proof — and Otter does a fairly large search, while a human does very little searching on this problem.

In mathematics up through calculus, if we do not go deeply into the foundations of the subject but consider only what is actually taught to students, there is mostly calculation. In abstract algebra, most of the work in a one-semester course involves some first-order axioms (groups, rings, etc.), along with the notions of subgroup, homomorphism, isomorphism, and a small amount of the theory of natural numbers. The latter is needed for the concept of "finite group" and the concept of "order of a group." Number theory is needed only (approximately) up to the concept of "a divides b" and the

---

[23] An example of the use of a definition to help Otter find a proof that it cannot find without using a definition is the proof of the "HCBK-1 problem" found recently by Robert Veroff. Although it is too technical to discuss here, the problem is listed as an open problem (which previously had a model-theoretic proof, but no first-order proof) in Appendix 3 of [72] (which also lists other challenges to theorem-proving programs). The solution can be found on Veroff's web page.

factorization of a number into a product of primes. One proves, for example, the structure theorem for a finite abelian group, and then one can use it to prove the beautiful theorem that the multiplicative group of a finite field is cyclic. These theorems are presently beyond the reach of automated deduction in any honest sense, although of course one could prepare a sequence of lemmas in such a way that the proof could ultimately be found.

However, there is a natural family of mathematical theories that is just sufficient for expressing most undergraduate mathematics. Theories of this kind include a simple theory as discussed above (simple axioms about a single kind of object), and in addition parameters for subsets (but not arbitrary quantification over subsets), variables for natural numbers and mathematical induction, and functions from natural numbers into the objects of the simple theory, so that one can speak about sequences of the objects. These additional features, plus definitions, will encompass most of the proofs encountered in the first semester of abstract algebra. If we add inequalities and calculations to this mix, we will encompass undergraduate analysis, complex analysis, and topology as well.[24]

Of course, there exist branches of mathematics that go beyond this kind of mathematics (e.g. Galois theory or algebraic topology). We propose to not even think about automated deduction in these areas of mathematics. Dealing with the challenges of second-order variables (without quantification), definitions, calculations, incorporating natural numbers, sequences, and induction, should keep researchers busy for at least a generation. At that point computers should have more or less the capabilities of an entering Ph.D. student in mathematics. Now, in 2003, they are at approximately freshman level. I do not mean that this progress is inevitable — it will require resources and effort that may not be forthcoming. But it is *possible*.

9   Computer Algebra

"Computer algebra," while a common and descriptive term, is a bit misleading since the subject encompasses calculus and to some extent combinatorics, as well as algebra. Originally computers were viewed as numerical calculators. In fact, when the first checkers-playing program was written in 1948, there was no printer at the IBM research lab that could print anything but numbers, so the output of the checkers playing program had to be coded numerically. But by the late 1950s, realization was spreading that there was such a thing as "symbolic computation," and algebra and calculus were among the first areas attacked. Programs for elementary calculus were soon written, incorporating rules of thumb ("heuristic" is the ten-dollar word for a rule of thumb) for

---

[24] There is an obvious objection to the above taxonomy: Functions can be reduced to sets, and numbers can be reduced to sets, so that all of mathematics can be formalized in set theory. This objection will be taken up in the last section of the paper.

elementary integration. John McCarthy invented LISP, a computer language designed for programming symbolic tasks, and the field of computer algebra began to develop soon afterwards. The subject had, and still has, two sides. One side is the theoretical development of algorithms to solve problems of specific classes. The other side is the efficient, practical implementation of those algorithms in useful programs.

In the sixties and seventies there were several important theoretical developments in the subject. Although we cannot afford a thorough introduction to computer algebra, we will mention three developments. Consider the following Mathematica input: $Factor[x^{119} - 1]$. Mathematica responds instantly with

$$(-1 + x)(1 + x + x^2 + x^3 + x^4 + x^5 + x^6)(1 + x + x^2 + x^3 + x^4 + x^5$$
$$+x^6 + x^7 + x^8 + x^9 + x^{10} + x^{11} + x^{12} + x^{13} + x^{14} + x^{15} + x^{16})$$
$$(1 - x + x^7 - x^8 + x^{14} - x^{15} + x^{17} - x^{18} + x^{21} - x^{22} + x^{24} - x^{25}$$
$$+x^{28} - x^{29} + x^{31} - x^{32} + x^{34} - x^{36} + x^{38} - x^{39} + x^{41} - x^{43} + x^{45}$$
$$-x^{46} + x^{48} - x^{50} + x^{51} - x^{53} + x^{55} - x^{57} + x^{58} - x^{60} + x^{62} - x^{64}$$
$$+x^{65} - x^{67} + x^{68} - x^{71} + x^{72} - x^{74} + x^{75} - x^{78} + x^{79} - x^{81} + x^{82}$$
$$-x^{88} + x^{89} - x^{95} + x^{96})$$

This was not done by trial and error. It uses algorithms for polynomial factorization[25] that first factor the polynomial mod p for various small primes p, and then put the results together cleverly, using a 19th-century theorem known as Hensel's lemma. The factorization mod p can be done quickly, using an algorithm discovered by Berlekamp in 1967. The application of Hensel's lemma to this problem was discovered by Zassenhaus in 1969. Full historical and mathematical details can be found in [57] and [63].

Our second example concerns the integration of elementary functions. An *elementary function* is one that you might encounter in freshman calculus: it is defined using multiplication, addition, subtraction, division, trig functions, exponents, and logarithms. Much effort in freshman calculus goes into rules and methods for computing elementary integrals of elementary functions. However, not every elementary function has an elementary integral. For example, $\int e^{x^2}\, dx$ cannot be expressed in elementary form. Risch [95, 96] discovered in 1969 that the trial-and-error methods you may have studied in freshman calculus, such as integration by substitution and integration by parts, can be replaced by a single, systematic procedure, that always works if the integral has *any* elementary answer. A complete exposition of the theory is in [21].

---

[25] For readers unfamiliar with mod p, this means that numbers are always replaced with their remainders after division by p. For example, 3 times 5 is 1 mod 7, because 15 has remainder 1 after division by 7. So $(x + 3)(x + 5) = x^2 + x + 1$ mod 7.

Our third example concerns sets of simultaneous polynomial equations. Say, for example, that you wish to solve the equations

$$z + x^4 - 2x + 1 = 0$$
$$y^2 + x^2 - 1 = 0$$
$$x^5 - 6x^3 + x^2 - 1 = 0$$

If you ask Mathematica to solve this set of three equations in three unknowns, it answers (immediately) with a list of the ten solutions. Since the solutions do not have expressions in terms of square roots, they have to be given in the form of algebraic numbers. For example, the first one is $x = \alpha, y = \alpha - 1, z = -1 + 2\alpha$, where α is the smallest root of $-1 + \alpha^2 - 6\alpha^3 + \alpha^5 = 0$. This problem has been solved by constructing what is known as a "Gröbner basis" of the ideal generated by the three polynomials in the original problem. It takes too much space, and demands too much mathematical background, to explain this more fully; see [106, Chap. 8] for explanations. (This example is Exercise 4, p. 201). Although methods (due to Kronecker) were known in the nineteenth century that in principle could solve such problems, the concept of a Gröbner basis and the algorithm for finding one, known as "Buchberger's algorithm," have played an indispensable role in the development of modern computer algebra. These results were in Buchberger's Ph.D. thesis in 1965. Thus the period 1965–70 saw the theoretical foundations of computer algebra laid.

It took some time for implementation to catch up with theory, but as the twenty-first century opened, there were several well-known, widely available programs containing implementations of these important algorithms, as well as many others. Symbolic mathematics up to and including freshman calculus can thus be regarded as completely mechanized at this point. While one cannot say that the field is complete — every year there is a large international conference devoted to the subject and many more specialized conferences — on the whole the mechanization of computation has progressed much further than the mechanization of proof.

In addition to the well-known general-purpose symbolic computation programs such as Maple, Mathematica, and Macsyma, there are also a number of special-purpose programs devoted to particular branches of mathematics. These are programs such as MAGMA, PARI-GP (algebraic number theory), SnapPea (topology), GAP (group theory), Surface Evolver (differential geometry), etc. These are used by specialists in those fields.

What is the place of computer algebra in the mechanization of mathematics? Obviously there are some parts of mathematics that consist mainly of computations. The fact is that this part of mathematics includes high-school mathematics and first-year calculus as it is usually taught, so that people who do not study mathematics beyond that point have the (mis)-impression that mathematics consists of calculations, and they imagine that advanced mathematics consists of yet more complicated calculations. That is not true.

Beginning with the course after calculus, mathematics relies heavily on proofs. Some of the proofs contain some steps that can be justified by calculation, but more emphasis is placed on precisely defined, abstract concepts, and the study of what properties follow from more fundamental properties by logical implication.

10   Decision Procedures in Algebra and Geometry

The "first loophole" allows the possibility that *some* branches of mathematics can be mechanized. An algorithm which can answer any yes-no question in a given class of mathematical questions is called a "decision procedure" for those questions. We will give a simple example to illustrate the concept. You may recall studying trigonometry. In that subject, one considers "trigonometric identities" such as $\cos(2x) = \cos^2 x - \sin^2 x$. The identities considered in trigonometry always have only linear functions in the arguments of the trig functions; for example, they never consider $\sin(x^2)$, although $\sin(2x+3)$ would be allowed. Moreover, the coefficients of those linear functions are always integers, or can be made so by a simple change of variable. The question is, given such an equation, determine whether or not it holds for all values of x (except possibly at the points where one side or the other is not defined, e.g. because a denominator is zero.) You may be surprised to learn that there is a decision method for this class, which we now give. First, use known identities to express everything in terms of sin and cos. If necessary, make a change of variable so that the linear functions in the arguments of sin and cos have integer coefficients. Even though everything is in now in terms of sin and cos, there could still be different arguments, for example $\sin(2x) - \sin x$. If so, we next use the identities for $\sin(x + y)$ and $\cos(x + y)$ to express everything in terms of $\sin x$ and $\cos x$. The equation is now a rational function of $\sin x$ and $\cos x$. Now for the key step: Make the "Weierstrass substitution" $t = \tan(x/2)$. Then $\sin x$ and $\cos x$ become rational functions of t. Specifically, we have $\sin x = 2t/(1 + t^2)$ and $\cos x = (1 - t^2)/(1 + t^2)$. After this substitution, the equation becomes a polynomial identity in one variable, and we just have to simplify it to "standard form" and see if the two sides are identical or not. All that suffering that you went through in trigonometry class! and a computer can do the job in an instant.

The question is, then, exactly where the borderline between mechanizable theories and non-mechanizable theories lies. It is somewhere between trig identities and number theory, since by Turing and Church's results, we cannot give a decision procedure for number theory. The borderline is in some sense not very far beyond trig identities, since a result of Richardson [85] shows that there is no algorithm that can decide the truth of identities involving polynomials, trig functions, logarithms, and exponentials (with the constant π allowed, and the restriction that the arguments of trig functions be linear removed).[26] Nevertheless, there are many examples of decision procedures for significant bodies of mathematics. Perhaps the most striking is one first explored by Alfred Tarski (1902–1983). The branch of mathematics in question is, roughly speaking, elementary algebra. It is really more than elementary algebra, because "for all" and "there exists" are also allowed, so such questions as the following are legal:

- Does the equation $x^3 - x^2 + 1 = 0$ have a solution between 0 and 1?
- For which values of a and b does the equation $x^4 - ax^3 + b$ take on only positive values as x varies?

The first question has an implicit "there exists an x," and the second has an implicit "for all x." We will call this part of mathematics "Tarski algebra."

The technical name of this branch of mathematics is the theory of *real-closed fields*. The language for this branch of mathematics has symbols for two operations $+$ and $\cdot$, the inverse operations $-x$ and x^{-1}, the additive and multiplicative identity elements 0 and 1, the ordering relation $<$, and the equality relation $=$. The axioms include the usual laws for $+$ and $\cdot$, and axioms relating $<$ to the operations $+$ and $\cdot$. Defining $0 < x$ as $P(x)$ (P for "positive"), those axioms say that the sum of positive elements is positive and the product of positive elements is positive. These are the axioms of *ordered fields*. The axioms for real-closed fields specify in addition that all positive elements have a square root, and all polynomials of odd degree have a root. One will, of course, need infinitely many axioms to express this without mentioning the concept of "natural number," one axiom for each odd degree. The classical theory of real-closed fields is developed in most algebra textbooks, for example in [65], pp. 273 ff.

Tarski algebra escapes the negative results of Church and Gödel because it does not have variables for natural numbers. The variables range over "real numbers" — these are the numbers that correspond to points on a line and are used for coordinates. Even though the variables of Tarski algebra are meant to stand for such numbers, not all individual numbers can be defined in Tarski algebra. In this language, one cannot directly write integers in decimal notation such as 3. Instead of 3, one officially has to write $1 + 1 + 1$. Aside from the inconvenience, one can in effect write any rational number; for example 2/3 is $(1 + 1)(1 + 1 + 1)^{-1}$. But one does not, for example, have a name for π.

Fig. 5. What is Tarski algebra?

"For all" and "there exists" are called "quantifiers." A formula without quantifiers is called "quantifier-free." For example, '$x^2 + 2 = y$' is quantifier-

---

[26] The exact borderline for classes of identities still is not known very accurately. For example, what if we keep the restriction that the arguments of trig functions should be linear with integer coefficients, but we allow logarithms and exponentials?

free. A quantifier-free formula might have the form

$$f(x_1, \ldots, x_n) = 0 \ \& \ g(x_1, \ldots, x_n) \geq 0,$$

where f and g are polynomials. More generally, you might have several inequalities instead of just one. Using simple identities, one can show that any
quantifier-free formula is equivalent to one in the form indicated. That is,
if such formulas are combined with "not," "and," or "or," the result can be
equivalently expressed in the standard form mentioned. Tarski's idea is called
elimination of quantifiers. He showed in [97] that every formula in Tarski algebra is equivalent to one without any quantifiers. For example, the question
whether $x^2 + bx + c = 0$ has a solution x with $0 \leq x$ appears to involve "there
exists an x," but from the quadratic formula we find that the answer can be
expressed by a condition involving only b and c, namely, $b^2 - 4c \geq 0$ and either
$b \leq 0$ or $c \leq 0$. The quantifier "there exists x" has been eliminated. Several
classical results of algebra have a similar flavor. For example, Sturm's theorem
from the 1830s [65], p. 276, counts the number of roots of a polynomial in an
interval in terms of the alternations of signs in the coefficients. Another classical result is the existence of the *resultant*: If we are given polynomials $f(a, x)$
and $g(a, x)$, we can compute another polynomial $R(a, b)$ called the resultant
of f and g, such that $R(a, b) = 0$ if and only if a common solution x can
be found for the equations $f(a, x) = 0$ and $g(a, x) = 0$. Again the quantifier
"there exists x" has been eliminated. Tarski showed that algebraic methods
can always be applied to eliminate "there exists" from algebraic formulas,
even ones involving inequalities. The elimination of one quantifier depends
essentially on the fact that a polynomial has only finitely many roots, and we
can compute the number, the maximum size, and some information about
the location of the roots from the coefficients of the polynomial. Applying
this procedure again and again, we can strip off one quantifier after another
(from the inside out), eliminating all the quantifiers in a formula with nested
quantifiers. We need only deal with "there exists" because "for all" can be
expressed as "not there exists x not" . Tarski's procedure is a decision procedure for Tarski algebra, because if we start with a formula that has only
quantified variables (so it makes an assertion that should be true or false),
after we apply the procedure we get a purely numerical formula involving
equations and inequalities of rational numbers, and we can simply compute
whether it is true or false.

Descartes showed several centuries earlier that geometry could be reduced
to algebra, by the device of coordinates. This reduction, known as analytic
geometry, coupled with Tarski's reduction of algebra with quantifiers to computation, yields a reduction of geometry (with quantifiers) to computation.
In more technical words: a decision procedure for Euclidean geometry. Thus
Hilbert's program, to reduce mathematics to computation, might seem to
be achieved for the mathematics of the classical era, algebra and geometry.
Tarski's student Szmielew made it work for non-Euclidean (hyperbolic) geometry too [27]. Since the Weierstrass substitution reduces trigonometry to

algebra, a decision method for real-closed fields also applies to trigonometry, as long as the arguments of the trig functions are linear.

Tarski's result is regarded as very important. Hundreds of researchers have pursued, and continue to pursue, the lines of investigation he opened. There are two reasons for that: First, his results contrast sharply with Church's and Gödel's, and show that the classical areas of algebra and geometry are not subject to those limiting theorems. Second, there are plenty of open and interesting problems that can be formulated in the theory of real-closed fields, and this has raised the hope that decision procedures implemented on a computer might one day routinely answer open questions. Our purpose in this section is to investigate this possibility.

First, let us give an example of an open problem one can formulate in Tarski algebra. Here is an example from the theory of sphere-packing. This example, and many others, can be found in [32]. The "kissing problem" problem asks how many n-dimensional spheres can be packed disjointly so that they each touch the unit sphere centered at origin. For $n = 2$ the answer is six (2-spheres are circles). For $n = 3$ the answer is 12. For $n = 4$ the answer is either 24, or 25, but nobody knows which! The problem can be formulated in the theory of real-closed fields, using 100 variables for the coordinates of the centers of the spheres. We simply have to say that each center is at distance 2 from the origin and that each of the 300 pairs of points are at least 2 units apart. Explicitly, we wish to know if there exist $x_1, \dots, x_{25}, y_1, \dots, y_{25}, z_1, \dots, z_{25}$, and $w_1, \dots, w_{25}$ such that $x_i^2 + y_i^2 + z_i^2 + w_i^2 = 4$ and $(x_i - x_j)^2 + (y_i - y_j)^2 + (z_i - z_j)^2 + (w_i - w_j)^2 \geq 4$ for $i \neq j$.

All we have to do is run Tarski's algorithm on that formula, and the open problem will be answered.[27]

Well then, why is this problem still open? The suspicion may be dawning on you that it isn't so easy to run this procedure on a formula with 100 quantified variables! In the half-century since Tarski's work, researchers have found more efficient algorithms for quantifier elimination, but on the other hand, they have also proved theorems showing that *any* algorithm for quantifier elimination must necessarily run slowly when large numbers of variables are involved. These lines of research now almost meet: the best algorithms almost achieve the theoretical limits. However, it seems that the edge of capability of algorithms is close to the edge of human capability as well, so the possibility that decision procedures might settle an open question cannot be definitively refuted. We therefore review the situation carefully.

---

[27] Another interesting sphere-packing problem was open for centuries, until it was solved in 1998. Namely, what is the densest packing of spheres into a large cube in 3-space? Kepler conjectured that it is the usual packing used by grocers for stacking oranges, but this was difficult to prove. It can, however, easily be formulated in the theory at hand, so in principle, "all we have to do" is quantifier elimination.

First we review the worst-case analyses that show quantifier elimination must run slowly. Fischer and Rabin showed [42] that any algorithm for quantifier elimination in real-closed fields will necessarily require exponential time for worst-case input formulas; that is, time of the order of 2^{dn} where n is the length of the input formula, and d is a fixed constant. This is true even for formulas involving only addition (not multiplication). Later [36, 104] a stronger lower bound was proved: sometimes quantifier elimination will require time (and space) of the order 2^{2^n} (double exponential). (See [84] for a survey of results on the complexity of this problem.) Taking $n = 64$ we get a number with more than 10^{18} decimal digits. No wonder the kissing number problem is still open.

Tarski's original algorithm, which was never implemented, was in principle much slower even than double exponential. Tarski's method eliminates one quantifier at a time, and the formula expands in length by a double exponential each time, so the running time cannot be bounded by any tower of exponents. Fischer and Rabin's result was obtained in the fall of 1972, but not published until 1974. In the interim, not knowing that efficient quantifier elimination is impossible, George Collins invented an improved quantifier-elimination method known as *cylindric algebraic decomposition* (CAD) [31]. Actually, according to the preface of [28], Collins had been working on quantifier elimination since 1955, but the 1973 work generalized his method to n variables and hence made it a general quantifier elimination method. Collins's method runs in double exponential time, much better than Tarski's method, and almost best-possible [36]. We knew from Fischer and Rabin's lower bound that there was no hope of a really efficient quantifier elimination algorithm, but the CAD method is much faster than Tarski's or Cohen's methods. The worst case, when the algorithm takes time 2^{2^n}, arises only when there are lots of variables. The algorithm is double exponential in the number of variables, but for a fixed number of variables, the time increases only as some power of the length of the input.[28]

"Moore's law" is the observation, made in 1965 by Gordon Moore, co-founder of Intel, that data density in computers (bits per square centimeter) has been growing exponentially, doubling every 12–18 months, ever since the integrated circuit was invented in 1962. Perhaps incorrectly, many people also use "Moore's law" to refer to the exponential increase in computer speed.[29] One should clearly understand that Moore's law cannot help us much with an algorithm whose running time is double exponential. If the running time is 2^{2^n} and we want to increase n by one, we need a computer that runs 2^{2^n}

---

[28] The interested reader should pursue the CAD algorithm in [28]; we cannot take the space here even to correctly define what a CAD is, let alone describe the original algorithm and its recent improvements in full.

[29] Moore's paper contains a prophetic cartoon showing a "happy home computer" counter between "notions" and "cosmetics." Bill Gates was ten years old at the time.

times faster, as a short calculation will show you: take the ratio of the new running time, $2^{2^{n+1}}$, to the old running time 2^{2^n}. You will get 2^{2^n} when you simplify that ratio. It takes 2^n Moore's law doubling periods just to increase n by one. The import of the double exponential running time theorems about quantifier elimination is therefore almost as grim as the import of Gödel's theorem. It seems that Fischer, Rabin, Weispfenning, and Davenport have destroyed Tarski's dream as thoroughly as Gödel destroyed Hilbert's.

But people never give up! Maybe there is an escape route. It was discovered in 1992 by Grigorev [46] that if we restrict attention to formulas that only have "there exists," and no "for all," then we can escape the dreaded double exponential. He gave a decision procedure for this class of formulas which is "only" exponential in the number of variables. This is an important difference, since with an exponential algorithm, if it doesn't run today, perhaps our children will be able to run it; while with a double exponential running time, our posterity is also doomed to failure. Further improvements since 1992 are described in [8].

A Web search shows that dozens, if not hundreds, of researchers are working on quantifier elimination these days. Although we know that quantifier elimination will take "forever" on large problems, there still might be some interesting open problems within reach — a tantalizing possibility. Hong [52] made improvements to the CAD algorithm, calling his enhanced version "partial CAD," and implemented it in a program called qepcad (quantifier elimination by partial CAD). This program has subsequently been improved upon by many other people, and is publicly available on the Web [22]. At least some of its functionality has been included with *Mathematica* versions 4.1 and 4.2, in the *Experimental* package. However to the best of my knowledge, the algorithms in [46] and [8] have not been implemented.

It seems fair to ask, then, what are the present-day limits of quantifier elimination in algebra? The first interesting example, often used as a benchmark for quantifier elimination, is to find the conditions on a, b, c, d such that the fourth-degree polynomial $x^4 + ax^3 + bx^2 + cx + d$ is positive for all x. That is, to eliminate the quantifier "for all x" in that statement. The answer is a surprisingly complex polynomial in a,b,c, and d. Qepcad does this five-variable problem almost instantaneously. The curious reader can find the answer at the qepcad examples web page [22].

It was fairly easy to create a *Mathematica* notebook with functions defined to facilitate asking simple questions about sphere packing. I defined *TwoSpheres*[M], which uses *InequalityInstance* to ask whether there exist two disjoint spheres of radius 1 in a cube of side $2M$. This is a seven-variable problem, counting M and the coordinates of the centers of the spheres. To make it a six-variable problem, we can put in specific values of M: *Mathematica* answers the query, *TwoSpheres*[7/4] with *True*; and with a suitable variant of the question, it could even exhibit an example of two such spheres. *TwoSpheres*[3/2] returns *False*. The time required is less than a second. The seven-variable problem, with M variable, seems to be too difficult for Mathematica's *CylindricalAlgebraicDecomposition* function. I also tried these problems with the version of qepcad available from [22]; this program was able to express *TwoSpheres*[M] as $M \geq 1$ and $3M^2 - 6M + 2 \geq 0$. The least such M is $1 + 1/\sqrt{3}$, which is the value of M one finds with pencil and paper if one assumes that the centers of the spheres are on the main diagonal of the cube. But the program did not make that assumption — it *proved* that this is the best possible arrangement. Similar queries *ThreeSpheres*[M], for various specific values of M, never returned answers. After several hours I stopped Mathematica; in the version of qepcad from [22], the jobs failed (after several hours) because they ran out of memory. Nine variables is too many in 2003. Using a double-exponential algorithm, we could expect that with running time varying as 2^{2^n}, if $n = 7$ corresponds to one second, then $n = 8$ should correspond to 2^{128} seconds, or more than 10^{35} years, so a sharp cutoff is to be expected. As calculated above, to increase n from 7 to 8, we need 2^7, or 128, doublings of computer speed. But the kissing problem needs only existential quantifiers, so as discussed above, it sneaks under the wall: we can solve it in "only" exponential time. In that case if 2^7 corresponds to one second, then 2^8 is only two seconds; but to attack the kissing problem we need 100 variables, and 2^{100} corresponds to 2^{93} seconds — about 10^{24} years. (Physicists know a convenient coincidence: that to three significant digits, there are $\pi \times 10^7$ seconds per year.) Even when the work of Grigorev is implemented, it still won't solve the kissing problem. Nevertheless, there may well be open questions with fewer than fifteen variables, so it seems the jury is still out on the potential usefulness of quantifier elimination. Quantifier elimination has not been the only decision method used in geometry. In 1978, Wu Wen-Tsen pioneered the reduction of geometry to polynomial ideal theory, introducing "Wu's method" [115]. The idea here is that an important class of geometric theorems can be stated in algebraic language *without using inequalities*. If the theorem can be stated using only conjunctions of equations in the hypothesis and an equation in the conclusion, then it reduces to asking if a certain polynomial lies in the ideal generated by a finite set of other polynomials. Since that time, other methods, based on Gröbner bases, have also been applied to geometric theorem-proving. This work has reduced geometric theorem-proving to computer algebra, and when it is applicable, it seems to be more efficient than quantifier elimination. Many interesting theorems in classical plane and solid geometry have been proved this way.

11   Equality Reasoning

The usual axioms for equality, as given in mathematics textbooks, are

$$x = x \qquad \text{reflexivity}$$
$$x = y \ \& \ y = z \to x = z \qquad \text{transitivity}$$
$$x = y \to y = x \qquad \text{symmetry}$$
$$x = y \ \& \ \phi(x) \to \phi(y) \qquad \text{substitutivity}$$

In this form, these axioms are useless in automated deduction, because they will (in fact even just the first three will) generate a never-ending stream of useless deductions. The "right method" for dealing with equality was discovered three times in the period 1965–1970, independently in [87], [47], and [62]. The approaches had slightly different emphases, although the kernel of the methods is the same. We will first explain the Knuth-Bendix method.

By an "oriented equation" $p = q$ we simply mean a pair of terms separated by an equality sign, so that $p = q$ is not considered the same oriented equation as $q = p$. The idea is that an oriented equation is to be used from left to right only. The oriented equation $x(y + z) = xy + xz$ can be used to change $3 * (4 + 5)$ to $3 * 4 + 3 * 5$, but not vice-versa. The variables can be matched to complicated expressions, although this example shows them matched to constants. Another name for "oriented equation" is "rewrite rule," which conveys an intuition about how rewrite rules are to be used.

Suppose one is given a set E of oriented equations. Given an expression t, we can rewrite t or its subterms using (oriented) equations from E until no more rules can be applied. If this happens, the resulting term is called a "normal form" of t. It need not happen: for example, if E includes the equation $xy = yx$, then we have $ab = ba = ab = \ldots$ ad infinitum. If one sequence of rewrites does terminate in a normal form, it still does not guarantee that every such sequence terminates (different sub-terms can be rewritten at different stages). If, no matter what sub-term we rewrite and no matter what equation from E we use, the result always terminates in a normal form, and if this happens no matter what term t we start with, then E is called *terminating*.

Even this does not guarantee the uniqueness of the normal form of t. That would be guaranteed by the following desirable property of E, known as *confluence*. E is called *confluent* if whenever a term t can be rewritten (using one or more steps) in two different ways to r and s, then there exists another term q such that both r and s can be rewritten to q. This property clearly ensures the uniqueness of normal forms because, if r and s were distinct normal forms of t, it would be impossible to rewrite them as q.

These concepts will be made clear by considering the example of group theory. Consider the usual three axioms of group theory:

$$e * x = x$$
$$i(x) * x = e$$
$$(x * y) * z = x * (y * z)$$

This set is not confluent. For example, the term $(i(a) * a) * b$ can be rewritten to $e * b$ and then to b, but it can also be rewritten to $i(a) * (a * b)$, which cannot be rewritten further. Does there exist a terminating confluent set of equations E extending these three, and such that each of the equations in E is a theorem of group theory? This is an interesting question because if there is, it would enable us to solve the *word problem for group theory*: given an equation $t = s$, does it follow from the three axioms of group theory? If we had a complete confluent set E, we could simply rewrite t and s to their respective unique normal forms, and see if the results are identical. If so, then the equation $t = s$ is a theorem of group theory. If not, it is not a theorem.

The answer for group theory is a set of ten equations. These are the original three, plus the following seven:

$$i(x) * (x * y) = y$$
$$x * e = x$$
$$i(e) = e$$
$$i(i(x)) = x$$
$$x * i(x) = e$$
$$x * (i(x) * y) = y$$
$$i(x * y) = i(y) * i(x)$$

We call this set of ten equations "complete" because it proves the same equations as the original three axioms, i.e., all the theorems of group theory, but it can do so by using the ten equations only left-to-right, while the original three must be used in both directions to prove the same theorems. In technical language: the ten equations constitute a complete confluent set. That set happens to contain the original three axioms, but that can be viewed as accidental. We would not have cared if the original axioms had themselves simplified somewhat in the final ten. (Of course, the original axioms of group theory were chosen to be as simple as possible, so it is not really accidental that they are among the ten.)

This solution of the word problem for groups can be vastly generalized. Donald Knuth invented an algorithm, which was implemented by his student Bendix (in FORTRAN IV for the IBM 7094), and has become known as the Knuth-Bendix algorithm since they were the joint authors of [62]. This algorithm was published in 1970, but the work was done considerably earlier. The input is a set E of (unoriented or oriented) equations. The output (if the algorithm terminates) is a set Q of oriented equations (rewrite rules) that is confluent and terminating, and has the same (unoriented) equations as logical consequences as the original set E. However, in general there is no guarantee of termination. One can run this algorithm with the three axioms of group theory as input and obtain the ten-equation system given above as output.

The Knuth-Bendix method is (or can be with appropriate commands) used by most modern theorem-provers. It is integrated with the other meth-

Fig. 6. Donald Knuth, 1938–

ods used in such theorem-provers. Here is an example of an interesting theorem proved by this method: In a ring suppose $x^3 = x$ for all x. Then the ring is commutative. This is proved by starting out with the set E containing the ring axioms and the axiom $xxx = x$. Then the Knuth-Bendix algorithm is run until it deduces $xy = yx$. When that happens, a contradiction will be found by resolution with the negated goal $ab \neq ba$, so the Knuth-Bendix algorithm will not go off *ad infinitum* using the commutative law (as it would if running by itself.) The resulting proof is 52 steps long. Up until 1988 it took ten hours to find this proof; then the prover RRL [59] was able to reduce this time to two minutes. Actually, the hypothesis $x^3 = x$ can be replaced by $x^n = x$ for any natural number $n \geq 2$, and RRL could also do the cases $n = 4, 6, 8 \ldots$, and many other even values of n [117], but it still takes a human being to prove it for all n, because the (only known) proof involves induction on n and the theory of the Jacobsen radical (a second-order concept). The odd cases are still quite hard for theorem-provers.

The use of a set of oriented equations to rewrite sub-terms of a given term is called "demodulation" in the automated theorem-proving community, and "rewriting" in an almost separate group of researchers who study rewrite rules for other reasons. A set of oriented equations can be specified by the user of Otter as "demodulators." They will be used to "reduce" (repeatedly rewrite) all newly-generated clauses. What the Knuth-Bendix algorithm does, in addition to this, is to use the existing demodulators at each stage to generate new demodulators dynamically. The method is simple: Find a sub-term of one of the left-hand sides that can be rewritten in two different ways by different demodulators. Reduce the left-hand side as far as possible after starting in these two different ways. You will obtain two terms p and q. If they are different, then the set of existing demodulators is manifestly not confluent, and the equation $p = q$ is a candidate for a new demodulator. The pair p, q is called a *critical pair*. Also $q = p$ is a candidate, so the difficulty is which way the new equation should be oriented. The solution is to put the "heaviest" term on the left. In the simplest case, "heaviest" just means "longest," but if the algorithm does not halt with that definition of "weight," other more complicated definitions might make the algorithm converge. In short, the Knuth-Bendix algorithm depends on a way of orienting new equations, and many papers have been written about the possible methods.

Because commutativity is important in many examples, but makes the Knuth-Bendix algorithm fail to converge, some effort has been expended to generalize the algorithm. If the matching for rewrites is done using "associative-commutative unification" instead of ordinary unification, then the algorithm still works, and one can simply omit the commutative and associative axioms [5]. This was the method employed in McCune's theorem-prover EQP to settle the Robbins Conjecture [71].

Returning to the late 1960s, we now describe the contribution of George Robinson and Larry Wos. They defined the inference rule they called *paramodulation*. This is essentially the rule used to generate new critical pairs at each step of the Knuth-Bendix algorithm. But in [87], it was not restricted to theories whose only relation symbol is equality. Instead, it was viewed as a general adjunct to resolution. One retains the reflexivity axiom $x = x$ and replaces transitivity, symmetry, and substitutivity with the new inference rule. They used this method to find proofs of theorems that were previously beyond the reach of computer programs. For example, with $(x \otimes y)$ defined as the commutator of x and y, they proved that in a group, if $x^3 = 1$ then $(x \otimes y) \otimes y = 1$. Although this example is purely equational, the rule of paramodulation is generally applicable, whatever relation symbols may occur in addition to equality. Robinson and Wos proved [88] the refutation-completeness of this method, i.e., any theorem has a proof by contradiction using resolution and paramodulation, with the axiom $x = x$. On the other hand, Robinson and Wos did not introduce the concept of confluence or of a complete confluent set of rules, so, for example, the deduction of the ten group-theory theorems given above escaped their notice.

For theories relying exclusively on equality, no serious distinction should made between the Knuth-Bendix method and paramodulation. They are essentially the same thing.[30] Nevertheless, as mentioned before, there is a community of researchers in "rewrite rules" and an almost disjoint community of

---

[30] The four differences listed on p. 20 of [72] are actually differences in the way the technique is used in Otter and the way it would be used in a program that implemented only Knuth-Bendix.

Fig. 7. Larry Wos

researchers in "automated deduction," each with their own conferences and journals. The challenge for today's workers in equality reasoning is to connect the vast body of existing work with the work that has been done in computer algebra, so that proofs involving computation can begin to be done by computer. This task has hardly been begun.

12   Proofs Involving Computations

There have always been two aspects of mathematics: logical reasoning and computation. These have historical roots as far back as Greece and Babylonia, respectively. Efforts to mechanize mathematics began with computation, and as discussed above, the machines of Pascal and Leibniz preceded the Logical Piano. In our time, the mechanization of computation via computer has been much more successful than the mechanization of logical reasoning. The mechanization of *symbolic* computation (as opposed to numerical computation) began in the fifties, as did the mechanization of logic. What is interesting, and surprising to people outside the field, is that the mechanization of logic and the mechanization of computation have proceeded somewhat independently. We now have computer programs that can carry out very elaborate computations, and these programs are used by mathematicians "as required." We also have "theorem-provers," but for the most part, these two capabilities do not occur in the same program, and these programs do not even communicate usefully.

Part of the problem is that popular symbolic computation software (such as Mathematica, Maple, and Macsyma) is logically incorrect. For example: Set $a = 0$. Divide both sides by a. You get $1 = 0$, because the software thinks $a/a = 1$ and $0/a = 0$. This kind of problem is pervasive and is not just an isolated "bug," because computation software applies transformations without checking the assumptions under which they are valid. Alternately, if transformations are not applied unless the assumptions are all checked, then computations grind to a halt because the necessary assumptions are not verifiable. The author's software MathXpert [11], which was written for education rather than for advanced mathematics, handles these matters correctly, as described in [10]. Later versions of Mathematica have begun attacking this problem by restricting the applicability of transformations and allowing the user to specify assumptions as extra arguments to transformations, but this is not a complete solution. Buchberger's *Theorema* project [23] is the best attempt so far to combine logic and computation, but it is not intended to be a proof-finder, but rather a proof-checker, enabling a human to interactively develop a proof. The difficulty here is that when the underlying computational ability of Mathematica is used, it is hard to be certain that all error has been excluded, because Mathematica does not have a systematic way of tracking or verifying the pre-conditions and post-conditions for its transformations.

Another program that was a pioneer in this area is *Analytica* [30]. This was a theorem-prover written in the Mathematica programming language. "Was" is the appropriate tense, since this program is no longer in use or under development. *Analytica* was primarily useful for proving identities, and made a splash by proving some difficult identities from Ramanujan's notebooks. It could not deal with quantified formulas and did not have state-of-the-art searching abilities.

On the theorem-proving side of the endeavor, efforts to incorporate computation in theorem-provers have been restricted to two approaches: using rewrite rules (or demodulators), and calling external decision procedures for formulas in certain specialized forms. The subject known as "constraint logic programming" (CLP) can be considered in this latter category. Today there are a few experiments in linking decision-procedure modules to proof-checkers (e.g. qepcad to PVS), but there is little work in linking decision-procedure modules to proof-finding programs.[31]

The author's software MathXpert contains computational code that properly tracks the preconditions for the application of mathematical transformations. After publishing MathXpert in 1997, I then combined some of this code with a simple theorem-prover I had written earlier [9], and was therefore in a unique position to experiment with the automated generation of proofs involving computation. I named the combined theorem-prover Weier-

---

[31] Possible exceptions: if the set of demodulators is confluent and complete, then demodulation could be regarded as a decision procedure for equations in that theory. Bledsoe's rules [19], [25, Chap. 8] for inequalities could be regarded as a decision procedure for a certain class of inequalities. Theorem-provers such as EQP and RRL that have AC-unification could be regarded as having a decision procedure for linear equations. *Theorema* does contain decision procedures, but it is primarily a proof-checker, not a proof-finder. An extension of the prover RRL called Tecton [1] has a decision procedure for Presburger arithmetic.

strass because the first experiments I performed involved epsilon — delta arguments. These are the first proofs, other than simple mathematical inductions, to which students of mathematics are exposed. I used Weierstrass in 1988–1990 to find epsilon-delta proofs of the continuity of specific functions such as powers of x, square root, log, sine and cosine, etc. Before this, the best that could be done was the continuity of a linear function [19]. These proofs involve simple algebraic laws (or laws involving sine, cosine, log, and the like), but, what is more, they involve combining those computations with inequality reasoning.

I then moved from analysis to number theory, and considered the proof of the irrationality of e. Weierstrass was able, after several improvements, to automatically generate a proof of this theorem [13]. The proof involves inequalities, bounds on infinite series, type distinctions (between real numbers and natural numbers), a subproof by mathematical induction, and significant mathematical steps, including correct simplification of expressions involving factorials and summing an infinite geometrical series.[32] [33]

Inequalities played a central role in both the epsilon-delta proofs and the proof of the irrationality of e. Inequalities certainly play a central role in classical analysis. Books and journal articles about partial differential equations, for example, are full of inequalities known as "estimates" or "bounds," that play key roles in existence proofs. Classically, mathematics has been divided into algebra and analysis. I would venture to call algebra the mathematics of equality, and analysis the mathematics of inequality.

The mechanization of equality reasoning has made more progress than the mechanization of inequality reasoning. We have discussed the "first loophole" above, which allows for the complete mechanization of certain subfields of mathematics by a "decision procedure" that algorithmically settles questions in a specific area. The mechanization of equality reasoning has benefited from the discovery of decision procedures with surprisingly wide applicability. In particular, a decision procedure has been found for a class including what are usually called *combinatorial identities*. Combinatorial identities are those involving sums and binomial coefficients, often in quite complicated algebraic

---

[32] Two things particularly amused me about this piece of work: First, one of the referees said "Of course it's a stunt." Second, audiences to whom I lectured were quite ready to accept that next I might be proving the irrationality of Euler's constant γ or solving other open problems. People today are quite jaded about the amazing latest accomplishments of computers! What the referee meant was that the "stunt" was not going to be repeated any time soon with famous open problems of number theory.

[33] It was difficult for others to build upon this work in that the code from MathXpert could not be shared, because it is part of a commercial product no longer under the author's control. In the future, similar features should be added to an existing, widely used theorem prover, whose source code is accessible, such as Otter.

forms. To illustrate with a very simple example,

$$\sum_{j=0}^{n} \binom{n}{j}^2 = \binom{2n}{n}.$$

In 1974 it was recognized by Gosper, who was at that time involved in the creation of Macsyma, that almost all such identities are special cases of a few identities involving *hypergeometric functions*, an area of mathematics initiated, like so many others, by Gauss. In 1982, Doron Zeilberger realized that recurrence relations for such identities can be generated automatically. This realization is the basis for "Zeilberger's paradigm" (see [81], p. 23). This "paradigm" is a method for proving an identity of the form $\sum_k summand(n, k) = answer(n)$. Namely: (i) find a recurrence relation satisfied by the sum; (ii) show that the proposed answer satisfies the same recurrence; (iii) check that "enough" initial values of both sides are equal. Here "enough" depends on the rational functions involved in the recurrence relation. The key to automating proofs of combinatorial identities is to automate the discovery of the appropriate recurrence relation. In [81] one can learn how this is done, using methods whose roots lie in Gosper's algorithm for the summation of hypergeometric series, and in yet earlier work by Sister Mary Celine on recurrence relations. The appendix of [81] contains pointers to Mathematica and Maple implementations of the algorithms in question. In addition to verifying proposed identities, some of these algorithms can, given only the left-hand sum, determine whether there exists an "answer" in a certain form, and if so, find it. The algorithms presented in [81] are noteworthy because, unlike either proof-search or quantifier elimination for the reals, they routinely perform at human level or better in finding and proving combinatorial identities.

13   Searching for Proofs

In essence, automated deduction is a search problem. We have a list of axioms, a few "special hypotheses" of the theorem to be proved, and the negation of its conclusion, and some inference rules. These inputs determine a large space of possible conclusions that can be drawn. We must search that space to see if it contains a contradiction. In some approaches to automated deduction (that do not use proof by contradiction), we might not put the negation of the conclusion in, and then search the possible deductions for the conclusion, instead of a contradiction. Either way, a search is involved. To the extent that calculation is involved, the search can be limited — when we are calculating, we "know what we are doing." But the logical component of mathematics involves, even intuitively, a search. We "find" proofs, we do not "construct" them.

   This search appears to be fundamentally unfeasible. Let us see why by considering a straightforward "breadth-first search," as a computer scientist would call it. Suppose we start with just 3 axioms and one rule of inference. The three axioms we call "level 0." Level $n + 1$ is the set of formulas that can be deduced in one step from formulas of level n or less, at least one of which has level exactly n. The "level saturation strategy" is to generate the levels, one by one, by applying the inference rule to all pairs of formulas of lower levels. It is difficult to count the size of the levels exactly because we cannot tell in advance how many pairs of formulas can function as premises of the inference rule. But for a worst-case estimate, if L_n is the number of formulas in level n or less, we would have $L_{n+1} = L_n + L_n(L_n - L_{n-1})$. To make a tentative analysis, assume that L_{n-1} can be neglected compared to the much larger L_n. Then the recursion is approximately $L_{n+1} = L_n^2$, which is solved by $L_n = 2^{2^n}$. When $n = 7$ we have 2^{128}, a number that compares with the number of electrons in the universe (said to be 10^{44}). Yet proofs of level 30 are often found by Otter (according to [109], p. 225). Of course, we have given a worst-case estimate, but in practice, level saturation is not a feasible way to organize proof search.

Intuitively, the difficulty with level saturation is this: What we are doing with level saturation (whether or not the negation of the conclusion is thrown in) is developing the entire theory from the axioms. Naturally there will be many conclusions that are irrelevant to the desired one. Whole books may exist filled with interesting deductions from these axioms that are irrelevant today in spite of being interesting on another day, and there will of course be even more uninteresting conclusions. What we need, then, are techniques to

- prevent the generation of unwanted deduced clauses,
- discard unwanted clauses before they are used to generate yet more unwanted clauses,
- generate useful clauses sooner,
- use useful clauses sooner than they would otherwise be used.

Methods directed towards these objectives are called "strategies."

In 1962, when none of the strategies known today had yet been invented, the following problem was too difficult for automated theorem-proving: In a group, if $x * x = e$ for every x, then the group is commutative, i.e. $z * y = y * z$ for every y and z. Today this is trivial (for both humans and computers). It was consideration of this example that led Larry Wos to invent the "set of support" strategy [107], which is today basic to the organization of a modern theorem-prover.

Here is an explanation of (one version of) this strategy. Divide the axioms into two lists, usable and set of support (sos). Normally, sos contains the negation of the desired theorem (that is, it contains the "special hypothesis" of the theorem and the negation of the conclusion of the theorem). The axioms of the theory go into usable. To generate new clauses, use resolution (or a variant of resolution) with one parent from sos and one parent from usable. Specifically, pick one "given clause" from sos. Move the given clause from sos to usable. Then make all possible inferences using the given clause as one parent, with the other parent chosen from usable. Add the new conclusions (possibly after some post-processing) to the sos list. Continue, choosing a new given clause, until the set of support becomes empty or a contradiction is derived.

The following fragment of an Otter input file illustrates the choice of sos and usable in the example mentioned above. (Here f means the group operation, and g is the inverse.)

```
list(usable).
x = x.                        \% equality
f(e,x) = x.                   \% identity
f(g(x),x) = e.                \% inverse
f(f(x,y),z) = f(x,f(y,z)).    \% associativity
end_of_list.

list(sos).
f(x,x) = e.                   \% special hypothesis
f(a,b) != f(b,a).             \% Denial of conclusion
end_of_list.
```

Otter finds a 6-step proof, of level 4, for this problem. Wos, George Robinson, and Carson proved (acknowledging invaluable assistance from J. A. Robinson) [107] that the appropriate use of this strategy still preserves the refutation-completeness property; that is, if there exists a proof of contradiction from the formulas in usable and sos together, then in principle it can be found by this strategy, if we do not run out of space or time first. The hypothesis of this theorem is that the usable list must itself be satisfiable, i.e. not contain a contradiction. That will normally be so because we put the denial of the conclusion into sos.

Another way of trying to generate useful formulas sooner, or to avoid generating useless formulas, is to invent and use new rules of inference. Quite a number of variations of resolution have been introduced and shown to be useful, and various theorems have been proved about whether refutation completeness is preserved using various combinations of the rules. For an overview of these matters, see [109]. For additional details and many examples, see [108]. Nowadays, the user of a theorem-prover can typically specify the inference rules to be used on a particular problem, and may try various choices; while there may be a default selection (Otter has an "autonomous mode"), expertise in the selection of inference rules is often helpful.

Another common way of trying to generate useful formulas sooner is to simply throw out "useless" formulas as soon as they are generated, instead of putting them in sos for further processing. For example, if a formula is a substitution instance of a formula already proved, there is no use keeping it. If you feel (or hope) that the proof will not require formulas longer than 20 symbols, why not throw out longer formulas as soon as they are generated? More generally, we can assign "weights" to formulas. The simplest "weight" is just the length (total number of symbols), but more complex weightings are possible. Then we can specify the maximum weight of formulas to be retained. Of course, doing so destroys refutation completeness, but it may also enable us to find a proof that would otherwise never have been produced in our lifetimes. If we do not find a proof, we can always try again with a larger maximum weight.

The description of the sos strategy above leaves several things imprecise: how do we "select" a formula from sos to be the next given formula? What is the nature of the "post-processing"? These questions have interesting answers, and the answers are not unique. There are different strategies addressing these questions. Otter has many user-controllable parameters that influence these kinds of thing. There are so many parameters that running Otter is more of an art than a science. For a more detailed description of the basic algorithm of Otter, see [109], p. 94, where the program's main loop is summarized on a single page.

It has now been nearly forty years since the invention of the set of support strategy, and the general approach to theorem-proving described above has not changed, nor has any competing approach met with as much success. Over that forty years, the approach has been refined by the development of many interesting strategies. The skillful application of these strategies has led to the solution of more and more difficult problems, some of which were previously unsolved. An impressive list of such problems solved just in the last couple of years is given in [41].[34] These problems are in highly technical areas, so it is difficult to list and explain them in a survey article. To give a taste of this kind of research, we shall explain just one of the areas involved: propositional logic. You may think that propositional logic is trivial. After all, you know how to decide the validity of any proposition by the method of truth tables. Therefore it is first necessary to convince you that this is an area with interesting questions. We write $i(x, y)$ for "x implies y," and $n(x)$ for "not x." Since "and" and "or" can be defined in terms of implication and negation, we will restrict ourselves to the connectives i and n. The Polish logician Jan Łukasiewicz introduced the following axioms for propositional

---

[34] If the non-expert user looks at the list given in [41] of difficult problems solved using Otter, he or she will very likely not be able in a straightforward manner to get Otter to prove these theorems. He or she will have to go to the appropriate web-site and get the input files prepared by the experts, specifying the inference rules and parameters controlling the search strategies. As the authors state, they do not have a single uniform strategy that will enable Otter to solve all these difficult problems, and a lot of human trial and error has gone into the construction of those input files.

logic:

$$i(i(x,y),i(i(y,z),i(x,z))) \tag{1}$$
$$i(i(n(x),x),x) \tag{2}$$
$$i(x,i(n(x),y)) \tag{3}$$

To work with these axioms in Otter, we use the predicate $P(x)$ to mean "x is provable." We then put into the usable list,

```
P(i(i(x,y),i(i(y,z),i(x,z)))).
P(i(i(n(x),x),x)).
P(i(x,i(n(x),y))).
-P(x) | -P(i(x,y)) | P(y).
```

Now to ask, for example, whether $i(x,x)$ is a theorem, we put `-P(i(c,c))` into list(sos). That is, we put in the negation of the assertion that $i(c,c)$ is provable. The steps taken by resolution correspond to the rule of "detachment" used by logicians: To deduce a new formula from A and $i(B,C)$, make a substitution $*$ so that $A^* = B^*$. Then you can deduce C^*.[35] Why do we need the predicate P? Because we are interested in proofs from L1–L3 using condensed detachment; P is used to force the theorem-prover to imitate that rule. We are not just interested in verifying tautologies, but in finding proofs from the specific axioms L1–L3. Now, the reader is invited to try to prove $i(x,x)$ from the axioms L1–L3. This should be enough to convince you that the field is not trivial. Other axiom systems for propositional logic were given by Frege, by Hilbert, and by Lukasievich. (See the wonderful appendix in [83], where these and many other axiom systems are listed. Questions then arise about the equivalence of these axiom systems. We want proofs of each of these axiom systems from each of the others. The appendix of [109, pp. 554–555] lists Otter proofs of some of these systems from L1-L3. For example, the first axiom in Frege's system is $i(x,n(n(x)))$. Go ahead, John Henry, try to prove it from L1-L3 using pencil and paper.

One type of interesting question studied by logicians in the 1930s through the 1950s — and resumed again today with the aid of automated reasoning — was this: given a theory T defined by several axioms, can we find a "single axiom" for T? That is, a single formula from which all the axioms of T can be derived. If so, what is the shortest possible such axiom? This type of question has been attacked using Otter for a large number of different systems, including various logics, group theories, and recently, lattice theory. For example, "equivalential calculus" is the logical theory of bi-implication (if and only if). It can be represented using $e(x,y)$ instead of $i(x,y)$, and treated using a "provability predicate" P as above. See [113] for an example

---

[35] Technically, since a theorem-prover always uses the *most general* unifier, it corresponds to the rule known as "condensed detachment," in which only most general substitutions are allowed.

Fig. 8. Jan Łukasiewicz (1878–1956)

of an Otter proof that settled a long-open question in equivalential calculus, namely, whether a certain formula XCB is a single axiom for this theory. This is perhaps the most recent example of a theorem that has been proved for the first time by a computer. Before it was proved (in April, 2002), people were not willing to give odds either way on the question.

14   Proofs Involving Sets, Functions, and Numbers

If we examine a textbook for an introductory course in abstract algebra, such as [56], we find that only about ten percent of the problems can be formulated in the first-order languages of groups, rings, etc. The rest involve subgroups, sub-rings, homomorphisms, and/or natural numbers. For example, one of the first theorems in group theory is Lagrange's theorem: if H is a subgroup of a finite group G, then the order of H (the number of its elements) divides the order of G. Here we need natural numbers to define the order, and a bit of number theory to define "divides"; we need the concept of subgroup, and the proof involves constructing a function to put H in one-one correspondence with the coset Ha, namely, $x \mapsto xa$. At present, no theorem-proving program has ever generated a proof of Lagrange's theorem, even though the proof is very short and simple. The obstacle is the mingling of elements, subgroups, mappings, and natural numbers.[36] The present power of automated

---

[36] A proof of Lagrange's theorem developed by a human has been checked by the computer program ACL2, see [116]. That proof is not the ordinary proof, but

theorem-provers has yielded results only in theories based on equality and a few operations or in other very simple theories. At least half of undergraduate mathematics should come within the scope of automated proof generation, if we are able to add in a relatively small ability to deal with sets, numbers, and functions. We do not (usually) need sets of sets, or sets of sets of sets, and the like. Nor do we usually need functions of functions, except special functions of functions like the derivative operator. If we add to a first-order theory some variables for sets (of the objects of the theory) and functions (from objects to objects), we have what is known as a second-order theory. The lambda-calculus can be used to define functions, and sets can be regarded as Boolean-valued functions. The author's current research involves adding capabilities to the existing, widely used theorem-prover Otter to assist it in handling second-order theories, without interfering with its first-order capabilities.[37] Specifically, a new second-order unification algorithm [14, 15], has been added to Otter, and will be improved and applied. Preliminary results, and the direction of the research program, are described in [16].

One may object to the use of second-order logic, and indeed to the whole idea of a "taxonomy" of mathematics, on the grounds of the universality of set theory. Let us begin by stating the objection clearly. Set theory is a "simple theory," with one relation symbol for membership and a small number of axioms. True, one of the "axioms" of ZF set theory is an infinite schema, with one instance for each formula of the language; but there is another formulation of set theory, Gödel-Bernays set theory (GB), which has a small finite number of axioms. In GB, variables range over classes, and sets are defined as classes which belong to some other class. (The idea is that properties define classes, but not every class is a set — we escape the Russell paradox in GB because the Russell class is a class, but not a set.) Because of the possibility of formulating set theory in this way as a simple theory, the taxonomy given above collapses — all of mathematics is contained in a single simple first-order theory. Now for some relevant history. A century ago, this program for the foundations of mathematics was laid out, but in the middle twentieth century the Bourbaki school prevailed, at least in practice, organizing mathematics according to the "many small theories" program. At present, most work in automated deduction is based on the "small theories" approach, although one brave man, Belinfante, has been proceeding for many years to develop computerized proofs based on GB set theory [17, 18]. Following this approach, he

---

instead proceeds by mathematical induction on the order of the group. The ordinary proof has been proof-checked using HOL [58]. That paper also presents an interesting "theory hierarchy" showing exactly what is needed. It has also been checked in Mizar [99].

[37] Of course, second-order and (why not?) higher-order theorem proving has been in existence for a long time, and there are even whole conferences devoted to the subject, e.g. TPHOL (Theorem Proving in Higher-Order Logic). It seems that most of this research is not directed towards proving new theorems, so it has not been discussed in this paper.

has enabled Otter to prove more than 1000 theorems in set theory — but he still is not up to Lagrange's theorem, or even close. Belinfante built on the pioneering work of Quaife [94]. Finally: the answer to the objection is simply that it is too complex to regard numbers and functions as built out of sets. No mathematician does so in everyday practice, and neither should automated deduction when the aim is to someday prove new theorems.[38]

On the other hand, one may take the opposite view and say that, because of the difficulties of developing mathematics within set theory, one should use "higher-order logic." This has been the view of many of the "proof-checking" projects, and they have been successful in checking proofs of many fairly complicated theorems. A proper review of this work would double the length of this article, so we must forego it. The interested reader can consult [105] for a list of fifteen proof checkers and proof finders, as well as references to further information.

15   Conclusion

Alan Turing wrote a seminal paper [101] in which he raised the question "Can machines think?"[39] After discussing various examples, such as chess, musical composition, and theorem-proving, he then formulated the "Turing test" as a replacement for that imprecise question. In the Turing test, a computer tries to deceive a human into thinking that the computer is human.[40] Of course in the foreseeable future it will be too difficult for a single computer to be able to reach human level in many areas simultaneously; but we might consider restricted versions of the Turing test for specific areas of endeavor. As mentioned in the introduction, the Turing test has already been passed for musical composition: David Cope has written a program EMI (pronounced "Emmy," for Experiments in Musical Intelligence) which produces music that regularly fools sophisticated audiences — at least, it did until Cope stopped conducting "The Test" at his concerts — stopped because the experts were too embarrassed. Since Cope is a composer rather than a computer scientist, he presents his results primarily at concerts rather than conferences. I heard a seven-piece chamber orchestra perform the Eighth Brandenburg Concerto (composed by EMI). (Bach composed the first seven Brandenburg Concertos.)

In theorem-proving, as in artificial intelligence, there was initially a division between those who thought computers should be programmed to "think"

---

[38] For the record, Belinfante agrees with this statement. His aim, however, is foundational. As a boy, he took *Principia Mathematica* from his physicist father's bookshelf and said to himself, "Someday I'm going to check if all these proofs are really right!." That spirit still animates his work.

[39] Like Stanley Jevon's paper, an original copy of this journal article now is priced at $2000.

[40] A more detailed discussion of the Turing test can be found in Turing's paper *op. cit.* or in any modern textbook on artificial intelligence; the idea of a computer trying to appear human is enough for our purposes.

like humans and those who favored a more computational approach. Should we try to find "heuristics" (rules of thumb) to guide a computer's efforts to find a proof, or play a game of chess, or compose a piece of music? Or should we just give the computer the rules and a simple algorithm and rely on the power of silicon chips? It is interesting to compare computerized chess and computerized theorem-proving in this respect. Both can be viewed as search problems: chess is a search organized by "if I make move x_1 and he makes move y_1 and then I make move x_2 and he makes move y_2 and then ...$"$; we search the various possibilities, up to a certain "level" or "depth," and then, for each sequence of possible moves, we score the situation. Then we pick our move, using a "max-min" algorithm. As in theorem-proving, the difficulty is to "prune the search tree" to avoid getting swamped by the consideration of useless moves. In both endeavors, theorem-proving and chess, one feels that expert human beings have subtle and powerful methods. Chess players analyze *far* fewer possibilities than chess programs do, and those good possibilities are analyzed deeper. One feels that the same may be true of mathematicians. In chess programs, "knowledge" about openings and end games is stored in a database and consulted when appropriate. But in the mid-game, every effort in chess programming to use more specialized chess knowledge and less search has failed. The computer time is better spent searching one move deeper. On the other hand, the game of go is played at only slightly above the beginner level by computers. The board is 19 by 19 instead of 8 by 8, and there are more pieces; the combinatorial explosion is too deadly for computers to advance much beyond this level at present.[41]

Similarly, in mathematics, so far at least, search has proved the most fruitful general technique. One can view computer algebra and computerized decision procedures, such as quantifier elimination or Wilf and Zeilberger's decision procedure for combinatorial sums as ways of embedding mathematical knowledge in computer programs. Where they are applicable, they play an indispensable role, analogous to the role of opening books and end game databases in chess. In areas of mathematics in which it is difficult to bring knowledge to bear (such as elementary group theory or propositional logic) because the axioms are very simple and tools from outside the subject area are not applicable, theorem-proving programs can outperform human beings, at least sometimes, just as in chess.

How did the trade-off between high-speed but simple computation and heuristics play out in the area of musical composition? The answer to this

---

[41] The game tree, searching n moves in the future, has about b^n nodes, where at a crude approximation $b = 8^2$ for chess and 19^2 for go. So the ratio is $(19/8)^{2n}$. Taking $n = 10$ we get more than 2^{20}, which is about a million: go is a million times harder than chess. On the other hand, computer speeds and memory sizes have historically increased exponentially, doubling every 18 months; so if Moore's law continues to hold, we might hope that go programs would perform well enough in 30 years, even without improvements in the programs.

question is quite interesting, and may have implications for the future of research in theorem-proving. EMI does not compose from a blank slate. To use EMI, you first decide on a composer to be imitated; let's say Bach. Then, you feed EMI several compositions by Bach. EMI extracts from these data a "grammar" of musical structures. EMI then uses this grammar to generate a new composition, which will be perceived as "in the style of Bach." The selection of the initial database calls for musical expertise and for expertise with EMI. For example, to compose the Eighth Brandenburg Concerto, Cope chose some of the original seven Brandenburg Concertos and a couple of violin concertos. When the database contained only the seven Brandenburg Concertos, the resulting composition seemed too "derivative," and even contained recognizable phrases. Yet, once the data has been digested, the program works according to specific, precise rules. There is nothing "heuristic" about the process. A result that "looks human" has been achieved by computational means.

This is at present not true of most proofs produced by most theorem-provers. To exhibit a simple example, consider the theorem that a group in which $x^2 = 1$ for all x is commutative. A human proof might start by substituting uv for x, to get $(uv)^2 = 1$. Multiplying on the left by u and on the right by v the desired result is immediate. The proof that a theorem-prover finds is much less clever. In longer proofs, the computer's inhuman style stands out even more. The most notable feature of such proofs is that theorem-provers never invent concepts or formulate lemmas. A paper written by a mathematician may have a "main theorem" and twenty supporting lemmas. The proof of the main theorem may be quite short, but it relies on the preceding lemmas. Not only does this help understanding, but the lemmas may be useful in other contexts. The most powerful present-day theorem-provers never find, organize, or present their proofs in this way (unless led to do so by a human after a failure to find the proof in one go).

Theorem-provers of the future should be able to invent terminology and form definitions. The basis of their ability to do this should be an underlying ability to monitor and reason about their own deduction process. As it is now, humans using a theorem-prover monitor the output, and then change parameters and restart the job. In the future, this kind of feedback should be automated and dynamic, so that the parameters of a run can be altered (by the program itself) while the run is in progress. With this capability in hand, one should then be able to detect candidates for "lemma" status: short formulas that are used several times. It is then a good idea to keep an eye out for further deductions similar in form to the formulas involved in the proof of the lemmas.[42] Giving a program the ability to formulate its own lemmas

---

[42] There are various possible notions of "similar in form" that might be used. For example, one idea is to call formulas similar if they become the same when all variables are replaced with the same letter. This notion is behind a successful strategy called "resonance" [109, p. 457].

dynamically might, in conjunction with the ability to modify the criteria for keeping or using deduced formulas, enable the program to find proofs that might otherwise be beyond reach.

Such a prover might produce proofs that look more human. The investigation, the style of thought, and the development of the theory should each look more like proofs people produce. Searching would still be the basis (not heuristics), but the result would look less like it had been produced by Poincaré's famous machine that takes in pigs and produces sausages. This type of prover would be a little more like EMI than today's theorem-provers. One might even be able to prime it with several proofs by the famous logician Meredith in order to have it produce proofs in propositional logic in Meredith's style, much as EMI can produce music in the style of Bach or the style of Scott Joplin. At present this is rather farfetched, as there is nothing like the "grammar" of Meredith's proofs. The closest approximation at present would be to tell the program to retain deduced clauses similar in form to the lines of the proofs used to prime the program.

We do not expect, however, that all machine-generated proofs will "look human." For example, there exists a machine-generated proof that a certain formula is a single axiom for groups satisfying $x^{19} = 1$ for all x. This proof contains a formula 715 symbols long. No human will find that proof.

Remember: the question whether machines can think is like the question whether submarines can swim. We expect machine mathematics to be different from human mathematics — but it seems a safe prediction that the twenty-first century will see some amazing achievements in machine mathematics.

Acknowledgment

I am grateful to the following people, who read drafts and suggested changes: Henk Barendregt, Nadia Ghamrawi, Marvin Jay Greenberg, Mike Pallesen, and Larry Wos.

References

1. Agarwal, R., Kapur, D., Musser, D. R., and Nie, X., Tecton proof system. In: Book, R. (ed.), *Proc. Fourth International Conference on Rewriting Techniques and Applications, Milan, Italy, 1991.* LNCS **488**, Springer-Verlag, Berlin Heidelberg New York (1991).
2. Appel, K., and Haken, W., Every planar map is four colorable. Part I. Discharging, *Illinois J. Math.* **21**:429–490, 1977.
3. Appel, K., Haken, W. Haken, and Koch, J., Every planar map is four colorable. Part II. Reducibility, *Illinois J. Math.* **21**:491–567, 1977.
4. Arnon, D., and Buchberger, B., *Algorithms in Real Algebraic Geometry*, Academic Press, London (1988). Reprinted from *J. Symbolic Computation* **5**, numbers 1 and 2, 1988.

5. Baader, F., and Snyder, W., Unification theory, in [90], pp. 435–534.

6. Barendregt, H., *The Lambda Calculus: Its Syntax and Semantics*, Studies in Logic and the Foundations of Mathematics **103**, Elsevier Science Ltd., revised edition (October 1984).

7. Barendregt, H., and Geuvers, H., Proof-Assistants Using Dependent Type Systems, in: Robinson, A., and Voronkov, A. (eds.), *Handbook of Automated Reasoning, vol. II*, pp. 1151–1238. Elsevier Science (2001).

8. Basu, S., Pollack, R., and Roy, M. F., On the Combinatorial and Algebraic Complexity of Quantifier Elimination, *Journal of the ACM* **43**(6):1002–1046, 1996.

9. Beeson, M., Some applications of Gentzen's proof theory to automated deduction, in P. Schroeder-Heister (ed.), *Extensions of Logic Programming*, Lecture Notes in Computer Science **475**, 101–156, Springer-Verlag, Berlin Heidelberg New York (1991).

10. Beeson, M., *Mathpert*: Computer support for learning algebra, trigonometry, and calculus, in: A. Voronkov (ed.), Logic Programming and Automated Reasoning, Lecture Notes in Artificial Intelligence 624, Springer-Verlag, Berlin Heidelberg New York (1992).

11. Beeson, M., *Mathpert Calculus Assistant*. This software product was published in July, 1997 by Mathpert Systems, Santa Clara, CA. See http://www.mathxpert.com to download a trial copy.

12. Beeson, M., Automatic generation of epsilon-delta proofs of continuity, in: Calmet, Jacques, and Plaza, Jan (eds.) *Artificial Intelligence and Symbolic Computation: International Conference AISC-98, Plattsburgh, New York, USA, September 1998 Proceedings*, pp. 67–83. Springer-Verlag, Berlin Heidelberg New York (1998).

13. Beeson, M., Automatic generation of a proof of the irrationality of e, *Journal of Symbolic Computation* **32**(4):333–349, 2001.

14. Beeson, M., Unification in Lambda Calculus with if-then-else, in: Kirchner, C., and Kirchner, H. (eds.), *Automated Deduction-CADE-15. 15th International Conference on Automated Deduction, Lindau, Germany, July 1998 Proceedings*, pp. 96–111, Lecture Notes in Artificial Intelligence **1421**, Springer-Verlag, Berlin Heidelberg New York (1998).

15. Beeson, M., A second-order theorem-prover applied to circumscription, in: Goré, R., Leitsch, A., and Nipkow, T. (eds.), *Automated Reasoning, First International Joint Conference, IJCAR 2001, Siena, Italy, June 2001, Proceedings*, Lecture Notes in Artificial Intelligence **2083**, Springer-Verlag, Berlin Heidelberg New York (2001).

16. Beeson, M., Solving for functions, to appear. A preliminary version appeared in: *LMCS 2002, Logic, Mathematics, and Computer Science: Interactions, Symposium in Honor of Bruno Buchberger's 60th Birthday*, pp. 24–38, RISC-Linz Report Series No. 02–60, Research Institute for Symbolic Computation, Linz (2002).

17. Belinfante, J., Computer proofs in Gödel's class theory with equational definitions for composite and cross, *J. Automated Reasoning* **22**(3):311–339, 1988.

18. Belinfante, J., On computer-assisted proofs in ordinal number theory, *J. Automated Reasoning* **22**(3):341–378, 1988.

19. Bledsoe, W. W., and Hines, L. M., Variable elimination and chaining in a resolution-based prover for inequalities

20. Boyer, R. S., and Moore, J. S., *A Computational Logic Handbook*, Academic Press, Boston (1988).
21. Bronstein, M., *Symbolic Integration I: Transcendental Functions*, Springer-Verlag, Berlin Heidelberg New York (1997).
22. Brown, C., QEPCAD-B, a program for computing with semi-algebraic sets using CADs, to appear. Preprint available at `http://www.cs.usna.edu/~wcbrown/research/MOTS2002.2.pdf`. The program itself is available from `http://www.cs.usna.edu/~qepcad/B/QEPCAD.html`, and five example problems can be viewed at `http://www.cs.usna.edu/~qepcad/B/examples/Examples.html`.
23. Buchberger, B., *et. al.* Theorema: An Integrated System for Computation and Deduction in Natural Style, in: Kirchner, C., and Kirchner, H. (eds.), *Proceedings of the Workshop on Integration of Deductive Systems at CADE-15, Lindau, Germany, July 1998*, LNAI **1421**, Springer, Berlin Heidelberg New York (1998).
24. Buchberger, B., Collins, G., and Loos, R., *Computer Algebra: Symbolic and Algebraic Manipulation*, second edition, Springer-Verlag, Berlin Heidelberg New York (1983).
25. Bundy, A., *The Computer Modelling of Mathematical Reasoning*, Academic Press, London (1983).
26. Boole, G., *The Laws of Thought*, Dover, New York (1958). Original edition, MacMillan (1854).
27. Borsuk, K., and Szmielew, W. *Foundations of Geometry*, North-Holland, Amsterdam, (1960).
28. Caviness, B.F., and Johnson, J.R. (eds.) *Quantifier Elimination and Cylindrical Algebraic Decomposition*, Springer-Verlag, Berlin Heidelberg New York (1998).
29. Church, A. An unsolvable problem of elementary number theory, *American Journal of Mathematics* **58**, 345–363, 1936.
30. Clarke, E., and Zhao, X.: Analytica: A Theorem-Prover in Mathematica, in: Kapur, D. (ed.), *Automated Deduction: CADE-11: Proc. of the 11th International Conference on Automated Deduction*, pp. 761–765, Springer-Verlag, Berlin Heidelberg New York (1992).
31. Collins, G.E., Quantifier elimination for real closed fields by cylindrical algebraic decomposition, in: *Proc. 2nd Conf. on Automata Theory and Formal Languages*, Lecture Notes in Computer Science, **33**, 134–183, Springer-Verlag, Berlin Heidelberg New York. Reprinted in [28], pp. 85–121.
32. Conway, J., and Sloane, N., *Sphere Packings, Lattices and Groups*, Grundlehren Der Mathematischen Wissenschaften **290**, Springer-Verlag, Berlin Heidelberg New York (1998).
33. Cope, D., *Computers and Musical Style*, A-R Editions, Madison (1991).
34. Cope, D., *Experiments in Musical Intelligence*, A-R Editions, Madison (1996).
35. Cope, D., *The Algorithmic Composer*, A-R Editions, Madison (2000).
36. Davenport, J., and Heintz, J., Real quantifier elimination is doubly exponential, in [4], pp. 29–35.
37. Davis, M., A computer program for Presburger's algorithm, in *Summaries of Talks Presented at the Summer Institute for Symbolic Logic, 1957* Second edition, published by Institute for Defense Analysis, 1960. Reprinted in [92], pp. 41–48.

38. Davis, M. The prehistory and early history of automated deduction, in [92], pp. 1–28.

39. Davis, M., *The Universal Computer: The Road from Leibniz to Turing*, Norton (2000). Reprinted in 2001 under the title *Engines of Logic*.

40. Davis, M., and Putnam, H., A computing procedure for quantification theory, *JACM* **7**, 201–215, 1960.

41. Ernst, Z., Fitelson, B., Harris, K., McCune, W., Veroff, R., Wos, L., More First-order Test Problems in Math and Logic, in: Sutcliffe, G., Pelletier, J. and Suttner, C. (eds.) Proceedings of the CADE-18 Workshop-Problems and Problem Sets for ATP, Technical Report 02/10, Department of Computer Science, University of Copenhagen, Copenhagen (2002). The paper and associated Otter files can be accessed from

    http://www.mcs.anl.gov/~mccune/papers/paps-2002.

42. Fischer, M. J., and Rabin, M. O., Super-exponential complexity of Presburger arithmetic, *SIAM-AMS Proceedings*, Volume VII, pp. 27–41; reprinted in [28], pp. 122–135.

43. Frege, G., *Begriffshrift, a formula language, modeled upon that of arithmetic, for pure thought.*, English translation in [102], pp. 1–82. Original date 1879.

44. Gelernter, H., Realization of a geometry-theorem proving machine, *Proc. International Conference on Information Processing, UNESCO House* 273–282, (1959). Reprinted in Feigenbaum and Feldman (eds.), *Computers and Thought*, McGraw-Hill, New York (1963). Reprinted again in [92], pp. 99–124.

45. Gödel, K., Über formal unentscheidbare Sätze der *Principia Mathematica* und verwandter Systems I, in: Feferman, S., *et. al.* (eds.), *Kurt Gödel: Collected Works, Volume I, Publications 1929–1936*, pp. 144–195. (The translation, On formally undecidable propositions of *Principia Mathematica* and related systems I, appears on facing pages.) Oxford University Press, New York, and Clarendon Press, Oxford (1986).

46. Grigor'ev, D., and Vorobjov, N., Solving systems of polynomial inequalities in subexponential time. *J. Symb. Comput.* **5**, 37–64, 1988.

47. Guard, J., Oglesby, F., Bennett, J., and Settle, L., Semi-automated mathematics, *JACM* **16**(1):49–62, 1969.

48. Harrison, J., and Théry, L.: Extending the HOL theorem-prover with a computer algebra system to reason about the reals, in *Higher Order Logic Theorem-Proving and its Applications: 6th International Workshop, HUG '93*, pp. 174–184, Lecture Notes in Computer Science **780**, Springer-Verlag, Berlin Heidelberg New York (1993).

49. Harrison, J., *Theorem-Proving with the Real Numbers*, Springer-Verlag, Berlin Heidelberg New York (1998).

50. Hilbert, D., *Grundlagen der Geometrie*, Teubner (1899). English translation (of the 10th edition, which appeared in 1962): *Foundations of Geometry*, Open Court, La Salle, Illinois (1987).

51. Hilbert, D., and Ackermann, W., Grundzüge der theoretischen Logik, 2nd edition (1938; first edition 1928). English translation: *Principles of Mathematical Logic*, translated by Lewis M. Hammond, George G. Leckie and F. Steinhardt; edited with notes by Robert E. Luce, Chelsea (1950). The translation is to be reprinted by the AMS in 2003.

52. Hong, H., Simple solution formula construction in cylindrical algebraic decomposition based quantifier elimination, in: *Proc. International Symposium on Symbolic and Algebraic Computation*, pp. 177–188, ACM, 1992. Reprinted in [28], pp. 210–210.

53. Horgan, J., The death of proof, *Scientific American*, October 1993, 74–82.

54. Huang, T., *Automated Deduction in Ring Theory*, Master's Writing Project, Department of Computer Science, San Jose State University (2002).

55. G. Huet. A unification algorithm for typed λ-calculus. *Theoretical Computer Science* 1, 27–52, 1975.

56. Jacobsen, N., *Basic Algebra I*, (1985).

57. Kaltofen, E., Factorization of polynomials, in [24], pp. 95–114.

58. Kammüller, F., and Paulson, L., A formal proof of Sylow's theorem: an experiment in abstract algebra with Isabelle HOL, *J. Automated Reasoning* 23:235–264, 1999.

59. Kapur, D., and Zhang, H., An overview of Rewrite Rule Laboratory (RRL), *J. of Computer and Mathematics with Applications* 29(2):91–114, 1995.

60. Kleene, S. C., λ-definability and recursiveness, Duke Mathematical Journal 2:340–353, 1936.

61. Kleene, S. C., *Introduction to Metamathematics*, van Nostrand, Princeton (1952).

62. Knuth, D. E., and Bendix, P. B., Simple word problems in universal algebras, in: Leech, J. (ed)., *Computational Problems in Abstract Algebras* pp. 263–297, Pergamon Press (1970). Reprinted in [93], pp. 342–376.

63. Knuth, D. E., *Seminumerical Algorithms: The Art of Computer Programming, Volume 2*, second edition, Addison-Wesley, Reading, MA (1981).

64. Kurosh, A. G., *The Theory of Groups, volume 1*, Chelsea, New York (1955).

65. Lang, S. *Algebra*, Addison-Wesley, Reading, MA (1965).

66. Lewis, Paul, Obituary of Herb Simon, http://www.cs.oswego.edu/~blue/hx/courses/cogsci1/s2001/section04/subsection01/main.html.

67. Mancuso, P., *From Brouwer to Hilbert*, Oxford University Press, Oxford (1998).

68. Maslov, S., Mints, G., and Orevkov, V., Mechanical proof-search and the theory of logical deduction in the USSR, in: [92], pp. 29–37.

69. Moore, G. E., Cramming more components onto integrated circuits, *Electronics* 38(8), April 18, 1965.

70. McCune, W., Otter 2.0, in: Stickel, M. E. (ed.), 10th *International Conference on Automated Deduction* pp. 663–664, Springer-Verlag, Berlin Heidelberg New York (1990).

71. McCune, W., Solution of the Robbins problem, *J. Automated Reasoning* 19(3):263–276, 1997.

72. McCune, W., and Padmanabhan, R., *Automated Deduction in Equational Logic and Cubic Curves*, LNAI 1095, Springer-Verlag, Berlin Heidelberg New York (1996).

73. Monk, J. D., The mathematics of Boolean algebra, in the *Stanford Dictionary of Philosophy*, http://plato.stanford.edu/entries/boolalg-math.

74. Newell, A., Shaw, J. C., Simon, H., Empirical explorations with the Logic Theory Machine: a case study in heuristics, *Proceedings of the Western Joint Computer Conference, Institute of Radio Engineers*, pp. 218–230, 1957. Reprinted in [92], pp. 49–74.

75. Peano, G., *Arithmetices principia, nova methodo exposita*, Bocca, Turin, (1889).
76. Pietrzykowski, T., and Jensen, D., A complete mechanization of second order logic, *J. Assoc. Comp. Mach.* **20**(2):333–364, 1971.
77. Pietrzykowski, T., and Jensen, D., A complete mechanization of ω-order type theory, *Assoc. Comp. Math. Nat. Conf.* 1972, **1**:82–92.
78. Poincaré, H., *Science and Method*, translated by Maitland from the original French edition of 1908, Dover (1952).
79. Penrose, R., *The Emperor's New Mind: Concerning Computers, Minds, and the Laws of Physics*, American Philological Association (1989). See also the review by McCarthy, J., in *Bulletin of the American Mathematical Society*, October, 1990.
80. Penrose, R., *Shadows of the Mind: A Search for the Missing Science of Consciousness*, Oxford University Press, Oxford (1996). See also the critical reviews by McCarthy, J., in the electronic journal *Psyche* **2**(11), 1995,
    http://psyche.cs.monash.edu.au/v2/psyche-2-11-mccarthy.html,
    and by Feferman, S., *Psyche* **2**(7), 1995,
    http://psyche.cs.monash.edu.au/v2/psyche-2-07-feferman.html,
    and Penrose's replies to these and other critics, at
    http://psyche.cs.monash.edu.au/v2/psyche-2-23-penrose.html.
81. Petkovšek, M., Wilf, H., and Zeilberger, D., *A=B*, A. K. Peters, Wellesley, MA (1996).
82. Presburger, M., Über die Vollständigkeit eines gewissen Systems der Arithmetik ganzer Zahlen, in welchem die Addition als einzige Operation hervortritt, Sparwozdanie z I Kongresu Matematyków Krajów Słowiańskich Warszawa, pp. 92–101, 1929.
83. Prior, A. N., *Formal Logic*, second edition, Clarendon Press, Oxford (1962).
84. Renegar, J., Recent progress on the complexity of the decision problem for the reals, in: [28], pp. 220–241.
85. Richardson, D., Some unsolvable problems involving elementary functions of a real variable, *J. Symbolic Logic* **33**:511–520 (1968).
86. Robinson, A., Proving theorems, as done by man, machine, and logician, in *Summaries of Talks Presented at the Summer Institute for Symbolic Logic, 1957* Second edition, published by Institute for Defense Analysis, 1960. Reprinted in [92], pp. 74–76.
87. Robinson, G., and Wos, L., Paramodulation and theorem-proving in first-order theories with equality, in Meltzer and Michie (eds.), *Machine Intelligence* **4**:135–150, American Elsevier, New York (1969). Reprinted in [110], pp. 83–99.
88. Robinson, G., and Wos, L., Completeness of paramodulation, *Journal of Symbolic Logic* **34**:160, 1969. Reprinted in [110], pp. 102–103.
89. Robinson, J. A., A machine oriented logic based on the resolution principle, *JACM* **12**:23–41, 1965. Reprinted in [92], pp. 397–415.
90. Robinson, Alan, and Voronkov, A. (eds.),*Handbook of Automated Reasoning, Volume I*, MIT Press, Cambridge, and North-Holland, Amsterdam (2001).
91. Russell, B., and Whitehead, A. N., *Principia Mathematica*, Cambridge University Press, Cambridge, England. First edition (1910), second edition (1927), reprinted 1963.
92. Siekmann, J., and Wrightson, G. (eds), *Automation of Reasoning 1: Classical Papers on Computational Logic 1957–1966*, Springer-Verlag, Berlin Heidelberg New York (1983).

93. Siekmann, J., and Wrightson, G. (eds), *Automation of Reasoning 2: Classical Papers on Computational Logic 1967–1970*, Springer-Verlag, Berlin Heidelberg New York (1983).

94. Quaife, A., *Automated Development of Fundamental Mathematical Theories, Automated Reasoning, Vol. 2*, Kluwer Academic Publishers, Dordrecht (1992).

95. Risch, R., The problem of integration in finite terms, *Transactions of the AMS* **139**:167–189, 1969.

96. Risch, R., The solution of the problem of integration in finite terms, *Bulletin of the AMS* **76** 605–608, 1970.

97. Tarski,A., A decision method for elementary algebra and geometry. Report R-109, second revised edition, Rand Corporation, Santa Monica, CA, 1951. Reprinted in [28], pp. 24–84.

98. Tarski, A., What is elementary geometry?, in: Henkin, L., Suppes, P, and Tarski, A. (eds.), *Proceedings of an International Symposium on the Axiomatic Method, with Special Reference to Geometry and Physics* 16–29, North-Holland, Amsterdam (1959).

99. Trybulec, W. A., Subgroup and cosets of subgroup, *Journal of Formalized Mathematics* **2**, 1990. This is an electronic journal, published at `http://mizar.uwb.edu.pl/JFM`.

100. Turing, A., On computable numbers, with an application to the Entscheidungsproblem. *Proceedings of the London Mathematical Society*, series 2, **42**:230–265, 1936–37.

101. Turing, A., Computing Machines and Intelligence, in *MIND, A Quarterly Review of Psychology and Philosophy* **59**(236):433–460, October, 1950.

102. van Heijenoort, J. (ed.) *From Frege to Gödel: A Source Book in Mathematical Logic, 1879–1931*, Harvard University Press, Cambridge, MA (1967).

103. Wang, H., Toward mechanical mathematics, 1960. Reprinted in [92], pp. 244–267.

104. Weispfenning, V., The complexity of linear problems in fields, *J. Symbolic Computation* **5**:3–27, 1988.

105. Wiedijk, F., The fifteen provers of the world, to appear.

106. Winkler, F., *Polynomial Algorithms in Computer Algebra*, Springer-Verlag, Berlin Heidelberg New York (1996).

107. Wos., L., Robinson, G., and Carson, D., Efficiency and completeness of the set of support strategy in theorem-proving, *JACM* **12**(4):536–541, 1965. Reprinted in [110], pp. 29–36.

108. Wos, L., *The Automation of Reasoning: An Experimenter's Notebook with OTTER Tutorial*, Academic Press, San Diego (1996).

109. Wos, L., and Pieper, G., *A Fascinating Country in the World of Computing*, World Scientific, Singapore (1999).

110. Wos, L., and Pieper, W., *The Collected Works of Larry Wos, Volume I: Exploring the Power of Automated Reasoning*, World Scientific, Singapore (2000).

111. Wos, L., and Pieper, W., *The Collected Works of Larry Wos, Volume II: Applying Automated Reasoning to Puzzles, Problems, and Open Questions*, World Scientific, Singapore (2000).

112. Wos, L., Reflections on Automated Reasoning at Argonne: A Personalized Fragment of History, on the CD-ROM included with [109].

113. Wos, L., Ulrich, D, and Fitelson, B., XCB, the last of the shortest single axioms for the classical equivalential calculus, to appear in *J. Automated Reasoning*

114. Wu, Wen-Tsun, On the decision problem and the mechanization of theorem-proving in elementary geometry, *Scientia Sinica* **21**(2), 1978. Reprinted in: Bledsoe, W. W., and Loveland, D. W. (eds.), *Automated Theorem-Proving: After 25 Years*, AMS, Providence, RI (1983).
115. Wu, Wen-Tsun, *Mechanical Theorem Proving in Geometries: Basic Principles*, Springer-Verlag, Berlin Heidelberg New York (1994).
116. Yu, Y. Computer Proofs in Group Theory, *Journal of Automated Reasoning* **6**(3):251–286, 1990.
117. Zhang, H., Automated proof of ring commutativity problems by algebraic methods, *J. Symbolic Computation* **9**:423–427, 1990.

Hypercomputational Models

Mike Stannett

Department of Computer Science, University of Sheffield

Summary. Hypercomputers are physical or conceptual machines capable of performing non-recursive tasks; their behavior lies beyond the so-called "Turing limit." Recent decades have seen many hypercomputational models in the literature, but in many cases we know neither how these models are related to one another, nor the precise reasons why they are so much more powerful than Turing machines. In this chapter we start by considering Turing's machine-based model of computation, and identify various structural constraints. By loosening each of these constraints in turn, we identify various classes of hypercomputational device, thereby generating a basic taxonomy for hypercomputation itself.

1 Introduction

Hypercomputation [7] is a term referring to the possibility that a physical or conceptual machine might be able to perform non-recursive computations, thereby stepping outside limits on computability suggested by the Church-Turing Thesis [CT]. Such a concept seems at odds with prevailing attitudes in the Computer Science and Mathematical Logic communities, which have long contended that the terms *computable* and (general) *recursive* are essentially equivalent. For those who accept this equivalence, the idea that a machine might perform non-recursive computations is logically absurd. However, this interpretation arises from a misunderstanding. Hypercomputationalists typically uphold [CT], and even see [CT] as strong evidence in favor of hypercomputation. In his classic discussion of computing machinery and intelligence, Alan Turing (1950) considered the question "Can machines think?" The strategy he adopted is eminently practical. Rather than discuss the philosophical niceties of intelligence, Turing introduced his now-famous "Imitation Game," in which a machine is deemed to be intelligent if an observer is unable to distinguish its behavior from that of an agent (in this case, a human being) who is assumed *a priori* to behave intelligently. In a similar way, when Turing was earlier faced with the question "which numbers are computable?", he gave a practical solution [85] describing a machine for simulating the intellectual human activities he deemed relevant to the computing of values. This focus on engineering solutions can also be seen in the detailed blueprint for a Zeta

Function Machine[1] thought to be associated with Turing's approach (Turing, 1943)[2] to refuting Riemann's zeta-function hypothesis [65][3]. Following Turing's example, we shall try to give an engineering solution to the question "Can computation be non-recursive?" Can machines be built — or at the very least, might natural systems exist? — that perform actions that cannot be simulated by Turing machines? We will try to describe various approaches to constructing hypercomputational machines.

1.1   The Church-Turing Thesis

Many arguments against the possibility of hypercomputational machines rest on a misunderstanding of the Church-Turing Thesis [CT]. Together with its converse, [CT] asserts that we can characterize, mathematically, all those functions that be computed "effectively." Unfortunately, "effective computation" is rather a vague term, and it is precisely this vagueness that leads to misunderstandings, because the meaning of this phrase varies widely both from person to person and from decade to decade. The resulting confusion has led many authors to misrepresent [CT] as a rather different statement to the effect that "anything that can be computed by any means whatsoever can be computed using a Turing machine." It is useful in this context to quote Turing's introduction into logical argument of his computing machines [85]:

> We have said that the computable numbers are those whose decimals are calculable by finite means. This requires rather more explicit definition. [...]
>
> We may compare a man in the process of computing a real number to a machine which is only capable of a finite number of conditions $q_1, q_2, \ldots, q_k$ which will be called "m-configurations." The machine is supplied with a "tape" (the analogue of paper) running through it, and divided into sections (called "squares") each capable of bearing a "symbol." At any moment there is just one square, say the r-th, bearing the symbol $\mathfrak{S}(r)$ which is "in the machine." We may call this square the "scanned square." The symbol on the scanned square may be called the "scanned symbol." The "scanned symbol" is the only one of which the machine is, so to speak, "directly aware." However, by altering its m-configuration the machine can effectively remember some of the symbols which it has "seen" (scanned) previously. The possible behaviour of the machine at any moment is determined by the

---

[1] The Zeta Function Machine blueprint is signed "D.C.M." and dated 17 July 1939. It is included in the Turing Digital Archive held at King's College, Cambridge.

[2] Submitted in 1939, this paper was not published until four years later, as [88].

[3] Riemann's hypothesis concerns the complex numbers z for which a well-known mathematical function, $\zeta(z)$, takes the value 0. The hypothesis asserts that these values are all of the form $z = \frac{1}{2} + iy$.

m-configuration q_n and the scanned symbol $\mathfrak{S}(r)$. This pair $q_n, \mathfrak{S}(r)$ will be called the "configuration"; thus the configuration determines the possible behaviour of the machine. In some of the configurations in which the scanned square is blank (i.e., bears no symbol) the machine writes down a new symbol on the scanned square; in other configurations it erases the scanned symbol. The machine may also change the square which is being scanned, but only by shifting it one place to right or left. In addition to any of these operations the m-configuration may be changed. Some of the symbols written down will form the sequence of figures which is the decimal of the real number which is being computed. The others are just rough notes to "assist the memory." It will only be these rough notes which will be liable to erasure. [...]

It is my contention that these operations include all those which are used in the computation of a number.

In giving this description, Turing has carefully outlined the specific types of operation he considers to be involved in effective computation, and as this description makes plain, "effective computation" is not the same thing as "computation by any means whatsoever." Rather, it is essentially the highly constrained form of behavior effected by human clerks engaged in the production of books of tables. Such clerks are free to note down figures for later use, but at no point are they expected to exercise any intuition or insight. They are told the numbers they need to manipulate and the rules for doing so, and then simply get on with the job. When [CT] and its converse assert the equivalence of effective and recursive computation, they tell us that Turing machines (or λ-expressions, or general recursion, or any one of a number of equivalent formulations) can compute anything that this group of mechanically minded clerks can compute, and vice versa.

Far from discounting the possibility of hypercomputation, it follows from [CT] that hypercomputational systems are quite likely to exist. As we put it elsewhere [82],

The Church-Turing Thesis can be seen as strong evidence in favor of hypercomputation, because it tells us that implementing a computer is as easy as getting a human to play act at having *no intuition, no volition, no self-awareness, no creativity, no understanding of the problem domain* — in short, none of the characteristics we normally associate with being a human being in the first place ... And if universal computation can be achieved by something as simple, in behavioral terms, as an "automatic human," it would be amazing if the wider Universe, with all manner of exotic phenomena and as-yet-undiscovered behaviors at its disposal, were able to support nothing more powerful.

2   A Taxonomy of Hypercomputation

2.1   Early Models

Possibly the earliest description of a useful hypercomputational device is that given by Turing in his Ph.D. thesis on ordinal-based logics [86], subsequently published as [87]. Writing Turing's obituary, M. H. A. Newman [50] explained,

> This paper [Turing, 1939] is full of interesting suggestions and ideas. In §4 Turing considers, as a system with a minimal departure from constructiveness, one in which number-theoretic problems of some class are arbitrarily assumed to be soluble; as he puts it, "Let us suppose that we are supplied with some unspecified means of solving number-theoretic problems; a kind of oracle, as it were." The availability of the oracle is the 'infinite' ingredient necessary to escape the Gödel principle.[4] It also obviously resembles the stages in the construction of a proof by a mathematician where he "has an idea," as distinct from making mechanical use of a method.

Newman's description of oracles as corresponding to the "having an idea" stage of mathematical proof construction is highly suggestive. Turing machines, as they are now called, were designed to model only the "mechanical" behaviors of human mathematicians. Turing seems to be taking it for granted that behaviors can exist which his machines are unable to simulate — so, for example, non-recursive oracles may be required if we are to extend the correspondence between human behaviors and Turing machine operations to include the intuitive aspects of proof construction.

Further evidence for his adopting this position can be found in Turing's discussion of intelligent machinery (*op. cit.*). Having described the Imitation Game, Turing goes on to explain carefully what he means by the word "machine":

> It is natural that we should wish to permit every kind of engineering technique to be used in our machines. We also wish to allow the possibility that an engineer or team of engineers may construct a machine which works, but whose manner of operation cannot be satisfactorily described by its constructors because they have applied a method which is largely experimental. Finally we wish to exclude from the machines men born in the usual manner. It is difficult to frame the definitions so as to satisfy these three conditions ... It is probably possible to rear a complete individual from a single cell of the

---

[4] Gödel [16] had shown that no sufficiently powerful finitely-based logic could be both complete and consistent. Turing's construction yielded a logic that was both complete and consistent, by introducing a non-finite element (the oracle) into the construction.

skin (say) of a man. To do so would be a feat of biological technique deserving of the very highest praise, but we would not be inclined to regard it as a case of 'constructing a thinking machine'. This prompts us to abandon the requirement that every kind of technique should be permitted. We are the more ready to do so in view of the fact that the present interest in 'thinking machines' has been aroused by a particular kind of machine, usually called an 'electronic computer' or 'digital computer'. Following this suggestion we only permit digital computers to take part in our game ... This identification of machines with digital computers ... will only be unsatisfactory if (contrary to my belief), it turns out that digital computers are unable to give a good showing in the game.

Turing here accepts that his focus on digital computers constitutes a real constraint, but one he doesn't expect to be relevant. In other words, Turing seems to have had no difficulty in accepting the reality of hypercomputational behaviors. His goal is to find *some* machine that can do well at the Imitation Game; if that machine should happen to be a relatively uncomplicated one, like a digital computer, so much the better.

Turing's intuition in this respect seems to have been largely correct. There have been a number of purely mathematical demonstrations of non-recursive, physically reasonable, behaviors — and some of these might feasibly be implemented.[5] The constructions of Pour-El and Richards are familiar to many researchers in the field, but that of Myhill seems to be less well known. On the assumption that a certain standard collection of analog components are available, Pour-El demonstrated as early as 1970 that a real-valued function of the reals is "analog-generable" precisely when it can be expressed in terms of certain non-linear differential equations (Pour-El [55, 56]). He then showed that there are necessarily recursive functions that are not analog generable. This seems to suggest that analog computability is incomparable with its digital counterpart, and in [79] we took Pour-El's comments to mean that the class of recursive functions is not wholly included within that of functions computable by analog means. But our logic in this respect was flawed — Pour-El's result says only that the analog systems *under discussion* aren't capable of generating all recursive functions. In fact, other analog models (for example, analog recursive neural networks) are indeed powerful enough to compute all recursive functions [75]. Pour-El and Richards' subsequent work [57, 58] demonstrated that the operation of a recursively initialized physical system can result in the production of non-recursive values being observable at recursively identified positions after a recursive amount of time.[6] This answers

---

[5] This section extends and updates our earlier introduction to the field [79].

[6] Pour-El and Richards showed that the wave equation could be supplied with recursive boundary conditions, so that observing the wave amplitude at the origin one second into evolution of the system would reveal a non-recursive amplitude.

affirmatively a question we touched on in [78]: a physical system can, in principle, be *designed* using a Turing machine, which is nonetheless not *simulable by* a Turing machine. Less well known is Myhill's 1970 work [49], in which he demonstrates a recursive function, $f(t)$, whose continuous derivative, df/dt, is non-recursive. Myhill's function is not hypercomputational in itself, but can be used to produce a hypercomputational system. We imagine two components connected in series. The first is a Turing machine programmed to generate Myhill's function, while the second is an analog component that differentiates its input. Such a combined system seems entirely feasible, and generates the non-recursive function df/dt as its output.[7] Since the 1960s more than twenty potentially hypercomputational systems have been considered in the literature, the majority of which have been reviewed recently in [6]. At least another 25 papers have appeared on the subject subsequently. Fig. 1 shows various articles (by no means all of them), loosely categorized according to two orthogonal factors — these will be relevant to our discussion below. Across the top of the table we have three models of time: *discrete*, *accelerating*, and *analog*. Down the side of the table we have listed six major subcategories of hypercomputation theory: *theoretical models*, *classical systems*, *quantum computation*, *neural networks* (including related models inspired by biology or biochemistry), *field computation* and *relativistic computation*. To the best of our knowledge, all published hypercomputational models fit into this classification scheme, so for the time being, at least, it provides a sensible basis for discussion and comparison. Computation in a Turing machine depends on the controlled manipulation of internal configurations, where each configuration encodes a finite amount of information as a *state*, a finite amount of information as *memory*, and a finite amount of information as *program*. The "control structure" of a Turing machine is constrained both by the current configuration, and also by the requirement that only one program instruction can be executed at a time. The Church-Turing Thesis tells us that cosmetic changes in the underlying architecture of a machine have no relevance to computational power, so there are only four obvious ways in which hypercomputation might be achieved using variations of the basic Turing model. We can consider changing

- the temporal structure of computation
- the information content of memory
- the information content of programs
- the information content of states

All four possibilities have been considered in the literature.

---

[7] The ultimate status of this system will ultimately depend upon the nature of the digital-analog converter, if any, used to join the two components together.

	Discrete Time	Accelerating Time	Analog Time
Theoretical Models	Turing (1938) Putnam (1965) Gold (1965) Abramson (1971) Karp & Lipton (1982) Kampis (1991, 1995)	Boolos & Jeffrey (1974) Pitowsky (1991) Stewart (1991)	Myhill (1986 – 1991) (adapted) Stannett (1990 – 1991)
		Krylow (1986) Stannett (2001)	
Classic Systems			Scarapellini (1963 – 2003) Kreisel (1965 – 1987) Pour–El & Richards (1979 – 1989) Putnam (1992)
		Geroch & Hartle (1986)	
Quantum Computation	Stannett (1990, 1991)		
		Calude (2000) Komar (1964) Doyle (1982, 2002) Geroch & Hartle (1986) Stannett (1991, 2003)	
		Penrose (1989 – 1994)	
Neural Networks & Related Biological Models			Rubel (1995 – 1989) Siegelmann & Sontag (1992, 1994) Siegelmann (1995 – 2003)
		Kugel (1986)	
Field Computation			MacLennan (1987 – 2003)
Relativistic Computation			Hogarth (1992 – 2002) Pitowsky (1990) Shagrir & Pitowsky (2003)

Fig. 1. A classification of hypercomputational models. References: Turing (1938) [86]; Putnam(1965) [60]; Gold (1965) [17]; Abramson (1971) [1]; Karp & Linton (1982) [24]; Kampis (1991, 1995) [22, 23]; Boolos & Jeffrey (1974) [2]; Pitowsky (1990) [54]; Stewart (1991) [83, 84]; Myhill (1970–1971) [49]; Stannett (1990–1991) [78, 79]; Krylov (1986) [34]; Stannett (2001) [80, 81]; Scarpellini (1963–2003) [66–68]; Kreisel (1965–1987) [26–33]; Pour-El & Richards (1979–1989) [57–59]; Putnam (1992) [61]; Geroch & Hartle (1986) [15]; Stannett (1990, 1991) [78, 79]; Calude (2002) [3]; Komar (1964) [25]; Doyle (1982, 2002) [9, 10]; Geroch & Hartle (1986) [15]; Stannett (1991, 2003) [79,82]; Penrose (1989–1994) [51–53]; Rubel (1985–1989) [62–64]; Siegelmann & Sontag (1992, 1994) [76,77]; Siegelmann (1995–2003) [70–75]; Kugel (1986) [35]; MacLennan (1987–2003) [36–48]; Hogarth (1992–2002) [18–21]; Pitowsky (1990) [54]; Shagir & Pitowsky (2003) [69]

2.2   Machines with Non-standard Temporal Structure

The temporal structure of computational models — whether time is assumed to flow continuously or in discrete steps, for example – plays a crucial role in many hypercomputational models. In general, computation is assumed to take place against one of four models of time: *discrete, accelerating, analog* or *generalized*. A fifth possibility, that time is *concurrent* (so that programs might follow infinitely many trajectories simultaneously), is usually discussed in terms of program non-determinism, and it is in this light that we consider it below.

Discrete-Time Hypercomputers. Since the Turing machine is itself a discrete-time machine, discrete-time hypercomputers typically achieve their extra computational power by changing the information content of memory, programs or states. The techniques adopted are described in various sections below.

Accelerating-Time Hypercomputers. Turing Machines are discrete sequential devices in which the execution of one instruction is allowed to run to completion before the next begins, but there is no constraint in Turing's model that each instruction should take as long to execute as its predecessor. The idea that infinitely many instructions might be executed in finite time goes back at least as far as Zeno, and in the context of hypercomputational systems it has been introduced several times independently (Gold [17]; Putnam [60]; Boolos and Jeffrey [2]; Stewart [83,84]). An ATM, or *Accelerating Turing Machine* [4,5], is one in which each instruction is performed in progressively less time than its predecessor, so that an infinite computation can run to completion in finite time. Formally, if we suppose that the n'th instruction takes a duration t_n to be executed, then an accelerating-time machine (more accurately, a *convergent-time* machine) is one for which there is some duration t that satisfies $\sum t_n \leq t < \infty$. Not surprisingly, accelerating Turing machines can perform hypercomputational tasks like solving the Halting Problem for Turing machines. To decide if a program P halts we simply run P on an accelerating (universal) machine, which is programmed to print the word "YES" on a sheet of paper immediately P halts. If we look at the sheet of paper at least t seconds after starting the program running, either the word has been printed (in which case P halted) or it hasn't (in which case P never halted). It might be thought that accelerating machines operate in discrete time, but this is not technically true, because the 'true output' of the machine is only observable at some time $t \geq \sum t_n$, which is strictly *after* the completion of each and every machine instruction. This is very different to the behavior of a true Turing machine. If a Turing machine generates an output at t_n, there is necessarily a time t_{n+1} which can meaningfully be considered the "time at which program step $n + 1$ might have taken place," and this is definitely *later* than the output event. But this is no longer guaranteed for accelerating machines. If an infinite computation is required, the eventual output can only be determined at a time t later than *every* tick event t_n. In other words, the temporal structure of accelerating computations includes not only the 'tick' events $t_1, t_2, \ldots$, but also the upper bound, t. As a result, it is not correct to say that accelerating machines are instances of Turing's original machine model, because the meaning of the 'output event' is subtly, but significantly, different — it requires a different interpretation of time.

Analog-Time Hypercomputers. Analog time is a fertile source of hypercomputational power, for reasons that are essentially mathematical. By tradition, we tend to model analog time in terms of the real line, **R**, a mathematical space that has the happy property that we can easily choose real numbers τ and $\tau_n (n = 0, 1, 2, 3 \ldots)$ satisfying the constraints

$$\tau_0 < \tau_1 < \tau_2 < \tau_3 < \ldots \tau_n < \ldots \tau.$$

For example, we might take $\tau = 1$, and $\tau_n = 1 - \frac{1}{n+1}$. This is precisely the temporal structure we identified above with respect to accelerating time machines,[8] and so it is not surprising that hypercomputational behaviors can be postulated for analog systems – we simply "embed" an accelerating time system within a larger analog system. For example, consider hypercomputation arising through the exploitation of a singularity in some Malament-Hogarth spacetime — these arguably provide a mechanism by which accelerating machines can be implemented (Hogarth [18,21]; Earman & Norton [12,13]; Earman [11]; Stannett [82]). From the viewpoint of the computer falling into a singularity in such a spacetime, time passes at its normal rate and an infinite computation can be allowed to run forever. For an observer moving "around" the relevant singularity, the times τ_n, at which successive computation steps occur, are observed to form a convergent sequence, and it is possible for the observer to arrive at a time, τ, to the future of every computation step. Clearly, the fact that the observer exists in analog time plays no real part here (except in so far as analog time and continuous space are necessary to the coherence of the underlying model of spacetime). All that really matters for our purposes is that the processing steps occur at certain times τ_n and that there exists some particular time τ which is both accessible by the observer and later than every τ_n, at which the overall "output" of the computation can be observed.

---

[8] Take $t_n = \tau_{n+1} - \tau_n$. Then $\tau_n - \tau_0 = (\tau_n - \tau_{n-1}) + (\tau_{n-1} - \tau_{n-2}) + \cdots + (\tau_1 - \tau_0) = t_1 + t_{n-1} + \cdots + t_1$. Since $\tau > \tau_n$ for every n, we have $(\tau - \tau_0) > (\tau_n - \tau_0) = t_1 + \cdots + t_n$ for every n, whence $(\tau - \tau_0) \geq \sum t_n$. Taking $t = (\tau - \tau_0)$ gives us $t \geq \sum t_n$ as required.

2.3   Memory with Infinite Information Content

If the information content of memory is infinite, a Turing machine can behave hypercomputationally. This is hardly surprising, since an infinite memory can be "pre-loaded" with a non-recursive oracle. To recap a simple example [78], let us consider the magnetic field generated by current flowing in a wire. According to basic electrical theory, each part of the wire contributes to the field at each and every point in space. Each infinitesimal element ds of the wire contributes an infinitesimal amount $d\boldsymbol{B}$ to the magnetic field $\boldsymbol{B}$, and we calculate the whole field $\boldsymbol{B}$ by integrating along the length of the wire: $\boldsymbol{B} = \int d\boldsymbol{B}$. Since there are infinitely many elements, ds, this equation suggests that the magnetic behavior at each point of space depends on infinitely many inputs. The values taken by these inputs vary according to the shape of the wire, so if we were to try computing $\boldsymbol{B}$ for arbitrary wirings using a Turing machine, we would be faced with the problem of storing the infinitely many input values corresponding to the required 'input shape' of the wire under consideration. However, having infinitely many inputs at our disposal is akin to having an oracle; indeed, we could envisage the successive digits of an infinite binary oracle being encoded in the various bends and contours of a suitably contorted wire. As such, we would expect such a system to be capable of hypercomputational behavior — this additional power would have been achieved by replacing the Turing machine's assumption of 'finite space' (i.e. finitely many squares in use at any time) with the availability of 'infinite space'. Notice that this use of the word 'infinite' is quite subtle. There is no suggestion that a hypercomputational wiring would necessarily be very large; we mean rather that a finite volume of space might carry an infinite information load. We could, for example, encode any binary string $\langle b_n \rangle_{n=1,2,3...}$ using a wire of length 1 cm by inserting a bend in the wire at each distance $(1 - \frac{1}{n})$ cm along the wire for which b_n is 1, and leaving the wire unbent if b_n is 0. As with accelerating Turing machines, we are simply positing the existence of a convergent sequence and its limit. In this case, the values represent distances rather than times, but the parallel is clear. The deliberate preparation of such a wire would probably not be possible using current technology, but the *existence* of an 'oracular' series of bends cannot be ruled out in a randomly compressed piece of wire, except by deliberately choosing a model of physical reality that prohibits it. For example, if we posit the existence of continuous matter the contortions are feasible, but if we believe in atomic structure they are not (the bends in the wire would eventually be closer together than the width of its constituent atoms). But even in the standard model of physics the possibility of convergence remains available, even if the physical substrate in which information is encoded can no longer necessarily be chosen to be time or distance. For example, waveforms are routinely decomposed into infinite sums of sinusoidal components, with any particular waveform $F(t)$ being expressed as an expansion of the form

$$F(t) = \sum a_n \sin{(n\omega t)} + \sum b_n \cos{(n\omega t)}.$$

The determination of the coefficients $\langle a_n, b_n \rangle$ associated with any given waveform is central to the practice of Fourier Analysis, and the existence of infinite decompositions is taken for granted in the associated literature. The coefficients in such expansions can be determined provided one knows the shape of the waveform over at least one wavelength, a distance that might be measured in thousandths of a meter, and correspond to durations of a small fraction of a second. A simple square wave, for example, could have the infinite decomposition

$$Squ(t) = \sin t + \frac{\sin 3t}{3} + \frac{\sin 5t}{5} + \ldots$$

In principle, there is no reason why a randomly observed sound wave (or radio wave, or gravity wave, or whatever) might not have an infinite decomposition whose coefficients $\langle a_n, b_n \rangle$ represent the digits of a non-recursive oracle. We might not, of course, be able to *determine* these coefficients computationally, but our failure of technique does not of itself preclude the existence of such hypercomputational waveforms in and of themselves.

2.4   Information Content of Programs

Every computer program is a finite collection of clearly specified statements, and as such contains a finite amount of well-determined information. There are therefore at least two ways in which the information content of a program can potentially be made "hypercomputational". We can remove the certainty implicit in the program (that is, we can make its component instructions unpredictable in some way), or we can produce programs with infinitely many instructions. (We might also allow an individual program instruction to encode an infinite amount of information, but in fact there is no need to consider this possibility separately. By definition, an individual program instruction is a finite list of tape symbols, machine configurations and a direction indicator, so it can only encode infinite information content if this content is already encoded within an associated machine state or a tape symbol. These scenarios are discussed under their own respective headings.) In the standard theory of Turing machines, we introduce non-determinism by supposing that configurations exist in which more than one program instruction might meaningfully be applied — during any run of the program, the actual choice is made at random. The computational power of such systems is potentially greater than that of deterministic systems, because the possibility routinely exists that a fortuitous choice of next instruction might yield results faster than would have been possible by purely deterministic means. For example, it is possible to construct a 5×5 jigsaw whose pieces can be rearranged in such a way that 24 of the pieces fit together, with the 25th piece not fitting. In general, if we wish to write a jigsaw-building program, the best we can do deterministically is akin to trying every combination of layouts until we find the right one, and even if we know the relative orientations of each piece this might still require the checking of 25! layouts before finding the right one. Even at a rate of $1,000,000$ layouts tested every second, the entire task could easily take longer than the current age of the Universe.[9] But a non-deterministic program might achieve the correct layout first time, simply by choosing the correct positions for each piece fortuitously. It is easy to see that allowing non-determinism is essentially the same as allowing programs to evolve concurrently. A *concurrent* execution is one in which, wherever a choice exists for the next instruction, we spawn extra copies of the system, and so run all possible executions simultaneously. Each of the various routes taken through the program is then called an execution *thread*. In general, concurrent execution always takes as along as the shortest possible non-deterministic run, and non-deterministic computation can be thought of as randomly selecting one of the threads in a concurrent execution. It is important to notice, however, that while a non-deterministic machine might feasibly complete a task (such as a jigsaw) considerably faster than its deterministic analog, it cannot normally perform any additional tasks. Non-deterministic machines may perform computations faster, but they are nonetheless the *same* computations. Every Turing-machine program, P, whether deterministic or non-deterministic, contains only finitely many instructions, each of which refers to only finitely many states. Given these conditions, it is a standard exercise in theoretical computer science to construct a deterministic program Q (for another, carefully constructed, Turing machine) whose deterministic execution halts if and only if P halts when run concurrently. The situation is very different if we allow the program to contain infinitely many instructions. Notice that this requires that either the state set or the tape-symbol set also be infinite. This is because each program instruction can be taken to be of the form

If the current state is q_0 and the current scanned symbol is s_0, then replace it with the symbol s_1, change state to q_1, and move the tape either 1, 0 or -1 squares to the right.

If there are Q machine states and S tape symbols, there can be at most $3Q^2S^2$ different program instructions, whence the only way to support an infinite program is for S or Q (or both) to be infinite.

---

[9] We have $25! = 25 \times 24 \times \cdots \times 3 \times 2 \times 1 = 1.55 \times 10^{25}$. At a rate of 10^6 layouts per second, checking every possibility would require 1.55×10^{19} seconds, or more than 10^{11} years.

2.5 Hypercomputation Using Infinitely Many States

Given the existence of infinite instruction sets, it is easy to construct hyper-computational models. We have already seen the potential of infinite memory content, so let us consider a system with infinitely many states. For example, suppose we have an initial state *init* and infinitely many auxiliary states q_n. We can certainly arrange for a machine to have the following behavior:

- If in state q_0, halt.
- If in state q_{n+1}, write 1 on the tape, move the tape left, and enter state q_n.

Suppose we also provide the machine with this infinite family of instructions (one for each choice of n)

- If in state *init*, leave the tape alone and enter state q_n.

The rules for non-deterministic execution tell us that the machine's first act is to select randomly one of the states q_n. Having done so, it then writes n 1's onto the tape before halting. In other words, this program, which is certain to terminate eventually, can effectively generate any natural number n as its output. As we have demonstrated elsewhere, no recursive system can display such behavior [82]. This shows that an infinite state set can be used to induce hypercomputation in the presence of an infinite instruction set. We have also seen that infinite memory can also be used to induce hypercomputation. We suggest that, taken together, these form a necessary condition — the existence of an infinite state set cannot induce hypercomputational capabilities if both the memory and program are finite. To see why, we note that each instruction refers to at most 2 machine states (which are atomic, by definition).[10] If there are N instructions, then at most $2N$ states can be relevant to the operation of the machine; even if the state set is potentially infinite, the existence of all but finitely many of the states is irrelevant to the operation of any given finite program.

2.6 Physical Feasibility of Infinite Instruction Sets

Can systems with infinite programs be implemented physically? In [78, 79] we raised the possibility of exploiting quantum systems more fully than anticipated by Deutsch's *Universal Quantum Computer (UQC)* [8]. Deutsch's

---

[10] One might posit non-atomic states (states with internal substructure). However, it is clear that the information content of such states could be separated out and modeled instead as auxiliary memory. For example, if the non-atomic state q actually described a set Q of more refined states, we could encode Q as part of the memory of a more complex machine. Instead of entering "variant 5 of state q" (say), we would "enter state q with the memory value 'variant' equal to 5." Since we have already considered machines with infinite memory, we have no need to consider non-atomic states separately.

model is essentially identical to Turing's, except that quantum uncertainties are taken into account. For example, the exact state of the system (Turing's m-configuration) can be known only probabilistically, so that quantum computation has built-in non-determinism. This is what makes quantum computing so powerful; according to "multiverse" models of quantum mechanics, whenever a choice exists at the quantum level, the universe "splits" into multiple variants, with each potential choice being executed as a different thread. When we observe the quantum-program's behavior, we randomly select one of these threads to become our reality. In other words, quantum computation is akin to non-deterministic Turing computation and has the potential to demonstrate the same execution speed-ups. We believe that the model contains an unnecessary constraint, which ensures that program speed-up is the only theoretical advantage of a quantum computer — there is no program computable by Deutsch's universal quantum computer that cannot also be computed by a standard Turing machine. For while Deutsch sensibly requires that any meaningful quantum computer should be "finitely specified" and use only "finite resources," he wrongly imputes from these requirements that quantum computers must necessarily have finitistic state sets and memories. The finiteness of the underlying memory and state set restricts the UQC to no more than Turing-power, because it ensures that the UQC is essentially just the non-deterministic finite-state Turing machine by another name. We claim, however, that finiteness of the state set is not a true consequence of Deutsch's physical assumptions. Consider, for example, Schrödinger's equation for the neutral hydrogen atom.[11] This can be viewed as a finite specification for a neutral hydrogen atom's energy-levels, and such an atom is certainly a finite resource. However, the equation admits infinitely many solutions, mirrored by the infinitely many energy levels that can be occupied by the atom's single electron. If we think of these levels as "states" in which the atom's single electron can find itself, then clearly the neutral hydrogen atom is an infinite-state system, even though it satisfies Deutsch's constraints (it is both finitely specified and finitely resourced). Since it is possible for this system to move non-deterministically from any state to any other, it ought, in principle, to be a physical model of the hypercomputational system we demonstrated in Sect. 2.5. If we interpret "the electron is in energy level n" as the behavior "output the value n," then the fact that quantum states are selected non-deterministically during observation means that such a system ought to be capable of true random number generation.[12]

---

[11] Schrödinger's equation in three dimensions is $-\frac{\hbar^2}{2m}\nabla^2\psi + V(r)\psi = E\psi$, where the various terms have their standard denotations (see, e.g., French and Taylor [14]).

[12] The electron might also be propelled outside the atom altogether if the energy supplied is great enough, but we can treat "outside the atom" as meaning, e.g., "consider the output to be 0."

3 Hypercomputer Engineering

We have looked in some detail at the ways in which Turing-style machines might be amended to produce hypercomputational systems. Some of these examples — a suitably bent magnetic wire, or a suitably configured waveform — rely on good fortune to pre-load a useful non-recursive value into memory. Similar good fortune is often invoked in papers on hypercomputation, and is one of the discipline's greatest engineering weaknesses. One can argue that a randomly presented piece of metal might happen to be a non-recursive number of centimeters long, but unless one can reliably generate such lengths of metal, they cannot be used as the foundation of a hypercomputer industry. A key point here is the difference between luck and randomness. We cannot legitimately invoke luck in the purposeful design of physical hypercomputers, but we can invoke randomness. Our universe is thought to be inherently quantum mechanical, and quantum mechanics is inherently non-determinism. This non-determinism allows individual atoms to be regarded as hypercomputational systems, and there is every reason to think that such atoms might be chained together to form more complex systems. For example, we can replicate the rudimentary behavior of a wire. Suppose we place two atoms of the same element next to one other, and that an electron in the first enters an energy level at energy E above minimum. If the electron now drops to minimum, the atom will emit a photon of energy E. If this is absorbed by an electron in the second atom, it can jump to the same level E that was recently vacated by its neighbor. In other words, once a state has been entered by one atom, that state can potentially be propagated.[13] From a physical point of view, randomness seems to have much to offer, but also presents serious difficulties. Certainly, randomness would seem to be easy to exploit, and its use in generating hypercomputational values seems straightforward. Unfortunately, it is by no means obvious what use we might have for this type of hypercomputation. Clearly, our understanding of computer programming may need to change if random-number hypercomputers are to become commonplace. We could no longer think of programs as sets of specific rules leading from a well-defined initial state, by clearly identified stages, to a predictable result. Instead, we would have to accept that certain aspects of computation are intrinsically unpredictable. But I do not see why this requirement should count more strongly against the development of practical hypercomputers than against that of practical quantum computers, or indeed neural networks, for which it is also a requirement. Indeed, all the published examples of feasible random-hypercomputation machines

---

[13] More realistically, we can envisage trapping a line of n atoms in a nanotube with sufficient room for $n + 1$ atoms. By using the "Newton's cradle" effect, we can envisage propagating momenta from one end of the tube to the other. Provided we can capture hypercomputational behaviors through the random selection of momenta, such nanotubes will provide a means of sending such values along "wires."

can be regarded as practical quantum computers. It is a theoretical question of some interest whether infinite, as opposed to finite, non-determinism can have deliberately observable beneficial effects on the computational power of quantum computers. There are, however, alternatives. Not all feasible hyper-computers require quantum mechanics or randomness. Malament-Hogarth spacetime models only require the identification or construction of suitable manifolds. While this may one day be possible, these models are clearly more of theoretical than practical interest for the time being. Pour-El and Richard's wave equation model offers more scope for optimism, because it invokes nothing more than classical analysis, and involves the behavior of a recursively constructible system. This is both a strength and a weakness. A strength, because it is a clear example of a hypercomputational system which is both theoretically clear, and at the same time expressed in terms of equations that are already familiar to engineers. A weakness, because the exploitation of those equations is based on numerous idealizations — initial conditions must be established exactly and exact measurements must be made.

4   Hypercomputational Characteristics

What do these observations tell us about hypercomputational systems? Considering them as a whole, we are led to conjecture that for a physical system to be hypercomputational, it must possess one or both of two basic properties: randomness or "accessible temporal boundedness."

4.1   Strong Unpredictability

If a hypercomputational system maintains a Turing-style discrete clock, but uses an infinite instruction space and state space, then its trajectory through this space must be recursively unpredictable. For if we had a recursive method for predicting the successive states and instructions of the system, we could regard it as an instruction schema and use it to generate a recursive simulation of the system's behavior. Conversely, if a discrete time system follows an inherently unpredictable trajectory through its associated state and/or instruction spaces, it should be hypercomputational. For if not, there would be some recursive program simulating the system's behavior, and this would enable us to predict both the sequence of states and the sequence of instructions to be encountered as the program is executed. In summary, for systems that operate in discrete time, we conjecture that hypercomputation and randomness are closely related concepts. Nonetheless, they are not identical. Tossing a coin is random because the outcome of each throw is independent of its predecessors — repeating the same cause generates a different effect. Strictly, of course, a tossed coin is not random (if we know its position and motion in enough detail when it leaves our hand, we can determine the outcome of the toss), but we can generate quantum-mechanical analogues of the system which display true randomness [82]. But hypercomputational systems need not behave in the same way — there is no obvious reason why the outcome of a hypercomputational experiment shouldn't be the same every time the experiment is carried out, especially if the outcome encodes a hypercomputational value in a physical structure. For example, if a process generated a contorted-wire encoding of a non-recursive oracle, that process might feasibly be repeatable, but only by hypercomputational means.

4.2   Accessible Temporal Boundedness

If a system is hypercomputational but doesn't operate in Turing-style discrete-time, we conjecture that it must have a property we call "accessible temporal boundedness" (ATB). That is, the system must be equipped with a clock that allows the system to experience at least one sequence of the form

$$\tau_0 < \tau_1 < \tau_2 < \tau_3 < \ldots \tau_n < \ldots \tau.$$

By "boundedness" I mean that the instants $\langle \tau_n \rangle$, such as might be generated by a Turing-style discrete-time clock moving with the system, are bounded above by some strictly later achievable time τ. "By accessible" I mean that an observer moving with the system can make observations at each of the times τ_n and also at time τ. Each of these instants in time has to be accessible to the system. In addition, of course, the system has to be capable of performing any relevant Turing-style instruction in moving from instant τ_n to instant τ_{n+1} and moreover, if there is any other upper bound τ', for which

$$\tau_0 < \tau_1 < \tau_2 < \tau_3 < \ldots \tau_n < \ldots \tau' < \tau.$$

then the system configuration at τ cannot be different from that at τ'. The existence of such a bounded sequence allows for accelerating Turing-machine constructions, with the solution to an otherwise undecidable problem becoming observable at time τ, whence ATB-systems ought to include hypercomputational systems in their number.

4.3   Are There Other Options?

Are these properties characteristic of hypercomputation, or is it possible for a system to be simultaneously hypercomputational, non-discrete-time and non-ATB? If the system in question can be modeled by one of the Turing-machine variants discussed above, the answer, we suggest, is "no" — unless the flow of time is quite unusual. For models of time that can be embedded in R, ATB and discrete-time do indeed characterize the hypercomputational Turing-like models — provided time is assumed to flow forwards linearly, and each executed instruction (except the last, if termination occurs) has a definite successor. To see why, let's suppose that some system S is both hypercomputational and non-ATB. We'll start our clock running at time τ_0, and increment the clock counter after each instruction, so that the instructions occur at times $\tau_0 < \tau_1 < \tau_2 < \ldots$ This sequence is either bounded above, or it isn't. If it isn't, then the system experiences no time τ that is later than every τ_n, so the underlying temporal model has to be the basic discrete-time model of the standard Turing machine. If it is bounded above, then because the sequence $\langle \tau_n \rangle$ can be embedded in $\boldsymbol{R}$, there is some real value τ which is the least upper bound in $\boldsymbol{R}$ of the $\langle \tau_n \rangle$. By definition, there can be no smaller upper bound, τ', so the side conditions on τ are satisfied. By assumption, however, the model of time experienced by the system is not ATB, whence the system cannot be capable of accessing τ (every other condition for ATB is satisfied). Consequently, the only times experienced by the system are the $\langle \tau_n \rangle$ themselves, whence the system operates in discrete time.

5   Conclusion and Summary

In this paper I've tried to approach hypercomputation as, perhaps, Turing might have done - by focusing on operational concerns and practical constructions. I've suggested that Turing machines owe their power to four basic properties, and have considered varying each of these in turn. This is by no means a complete analysis of hypercomputation and its causes. There is no *a priori* reason why every feasible machine should necessarily be considered a variant of the Turing machine, and perhaps models will be created that owe nothing to the principles considered here. Our analysis of the temporal structure of computations is also very basic, though we expect the question itself — whether temporal structure is a useful key to realizable hypercomputation — to be a significant one.

We have also focused on the role of randomness in hypercomputational models, and the necessary distinction between randomness and luck. As is well known, a randomly selected real number has a 100% chance of being non-recursive, but it does not follow that a number chosen by a man-made machine would display this property; assuming the possibility of lucky mechanical choices simply begs the question whether hypercomputation is indeed physically feasible. Yet randomness does seem to be a necessary consequence of quantum theory, and it is with this in mind that we maintain that the question of physical hypercomputation is, at the very least, worth the asking.

References

1. F. G. Abramson. Effective computation over the real numbers. In *Twelfth Annual Symposium on Switching and Automata Theory*. Institute of Electrical and Electronics Engineers, Northridge, CA, 1971.

2. G. S. Boolos and R. C Jeffrey. *Computability and Logic*. Cambridge University Press, Cambridge, 1974.

3. C. S. Calude. Incompleteness, complexity, randomness and beyond. *Minds and Machines*, 12:503–517, 2002.

4. B. J. Copeland. Super Turing-machines. *Complexity*, 4(1):30–32, 1998.

5. B. J. Copeland. Accelerating Turing machines. *Minds and Machines*, 12:281–301, 2002.

6. B. J. Copeland. Hypercomputation. *Minds and Machines*, 12:461–502, 2002.

7. B. J. Copeland and D. Proudfoot. Alan Turing's forgotten ideas in computer science. *Scientific American*, 280(4):77–81, April 1999.

8. D. Deutsch. Quantum theory, the Church-Turing principle of the Universal Quantum Computer. *Proceedings of the Royal Society of London*, A400:97–117, 1985.

9. J. Doyle. What is Church's thesis? An outline. Technical report, Laboratory for Computer Science, MIT, 1982.

10. J. Doyle. What is Church's thesis? An outline. *Minds and Machines*, 12:519–520, 2002.

11. J. Earman. *Bangs, Crunches, Whimpers, and Shrieks — Singularities and Acausalities in Relativistic Spacetimes*. Oxford University Press, Oxford, UK, 1995.

12. J. Earman and J. D. Norton. Forever is a day: Supertasks in Pitowsky and Malament-Hogarth spacetimes. *Philosophy of Science*, 60:22–42, 1993.

13. J. Earman and J. D. Norton. Infinite pains: The trouble with supertasks. In A. Morton and S. P. Stich, editors, *Benacerraf and his Critics*. Blackwell, Oxford, UK, 1996.

14. A. P. French and E. F. Taylor. *An Introduction to Quantum Physics*. Chapman and Hall, London, UK, 1990.

15. R. Geroch and J. B. Hartle. Computability and physical theories. *Foundations of Physics*, 16:533–550, 1986.

16. K. Gödel. Über formal unendscheidbare Sätze der Principia Mathematica und verwandter Systeme. *Monatshefte für Mathematik und Physik*, 38:173–198, 1931.

17. E. M. Gold. Limiting recursion. *Journal of Symbolic Logic*, 30:28–48, 1965.

18. M. L. Hogarth. Does general relativity allow an observer to view an eternity in a finite time? *Foundations of Physics Letters*, 5:173–181, 1992.

19. M. L. Hogarth. Non-Turing computers and non-Turing computability. *PAS*, 1:126–138, 1994. Available online: http://hypercomputation.net/resources.html.

20. M. L. Hogarth. *Predictability, Computability and Spacetime*. PhD thesis, Cambridge University, UK, 1996. Available online: http://hypercomputation.net/resources.html.

21. M. L. Hogarth. Deciding arithmetic in Malament-Hogarth spacetimes. Available online: http://hypercomputation.net/resources.html, 2002.

22. G. Kampis. *Self-Modifying Systems in Biology and Cognitive Science: A New Framework for Dynamics, Information and Complexity*. Pergamon, Oxford, UK, 1991.

23. G. Kampis. Computability, self-reference, and self-amendment. *Communications and Cognition-Artificial Intelligence*, 12:91–110, 1995.

24. R. M. Karp and R. J. Lipton. Turing machines that take advice. In E. Engeler et al., editor, *Logic and Algorithmic*. L'Enseignement Mathématique, Genève, Switzerland, 1982.

25. A. Komar. Undecidability of macroscopically distinguishable states in quantum field theory. *Physical Review*, 133B:542–544, 1964.

26. G. Kreisel. Mathematical logic. In T. L. Saaty, editor, *Lectures on Modern Mathematics*, volume 3. John Wiley, New York, 1965.

27. G. Kreisel. Mathematical logic: What has it done for the philosophy of mathematics? In R. Schoenman, editor, *Bertrand Russell: Philosopher of the Century*. George Allen and Unwin, London, UK, 1967.

28. G. Kreisel. Hilbert's programme and the search for automatic proof procedures. In M. Laudet et al., editor, *Symposium on Automatic Demonstration*, volume 125 of *Lecture Notes in Mathematics*. Springer-Verlag, Berlin, 1970.

29. G. Kreisel. Some reasons for generalising recursion theory. In R. O. Gandy and C. M. E. Yates, editors, *Logic Colloquium '69*. North-Holland, Amsterdam, 1971.

30. G. Kreisel. Which number theoretic problems can be solved in recursive progressions on π_1^1-paths through 0? *Journal of Symbolic Logic*, 37:311–334, 1972.

31. G. Kreisel. A notion of mechanistic theory. *Synthese*, 29:11–26, 1974.

32. G. Kreisel. Review of Pour-El and Richards. *Journal of Symbolic Logic*, 47:900–902, 1982.

33. G. Kreisel. Church's thesis and the ideal of formal rigour. *Notre Dame Journal of Formal Logic*, 28:499–519, 1987.

34. S. M. Krylov. Formal technology and universal systems (part 1 and 2). *Cybernetics*, 4 and 5:85–89 and 28–31, 1986.

35. P. Kugel. Thinking may be more than computing. *Cognition*, 22:137–198, 1986.

36. B. J. MacLennan. Technology-independent design of neurocomputers: The universal field computer. In M. Caudill and C. Butler, editors, *Proceedings of the IEEE First International Conference on Neural Networks, San Diego, CA*, volume 3, pages 39–49. IEEE Press, 1987.

37. B. J. MacLennan. Logic for the new AI. In J. H. Fetzer, editor, *Aspects of Artificial Intelligence*, pages 163–192. Kluwer Academic Publishers, Dordrecht, The Netherlands, 1988.

38. B. J. MacLennan. Field computation: A theoretical framework for massively parallel analog computation, parts I-IV. Technical Report CS–90–100, Dept of Computer Science, University of Tennessee, 1990. Available online: http://www.cs.utk.edu/~mclennan.

39. B. J. MacLennan. Characteristics of connectionist knowledge representation. *Information Sciences*, 70:119–143, 1993.

40. B. J. MacLennan. Field computation in the brain. In K. H. Pribram, editor, *Rethinking Neural Networks: Quantum Fields and Biological Data*, pages 199–232. Lawrence Erlbaum, Hillsdale, NJ, 1993.

41. B. J. MacLennan. Grounding analog computers. *Think*, 2:48–51, 1993.

42. B. J MacLennan. Continuous computation and the emergence of the discrete. In K. H. Pribram, editor, *Origins: Brain & Self-Organisation*, pages 121–151. Lawrence Erlbaum, Hillsdale, NJ, 1994.

43. B. J. MacLennan. Continuous symbol systems: The logic of connectionism. In M. Aparicio D. S. Levine, editor, *Neural Networks for Knowledge Representation and Inference*, pages 121–151. Lawrence Erlbaum, Hillsdale, NJ, 1994.

44. B. J. MacLennan. Continuous formal systems: A unifying model in language and cognition. In *Proceedings of the IEEE Workshop on Architectures for Semiotic Modeling and Situation Analysis in Large Complex Systems, Monterey, CA*, pages 161–172. IEEE Press, 1995.

45. B. J. MacLennan. Field computation in motor control. In: P. G. Morasso and V. Sanguineti, editors, *Self-Organization, Computational Maps and Motor Control*, pages 37–73. Elsevier, Amsterdam, The Netherlands, 1997.

46. B. J. MacLennan. Field computation in natural and artificial intelligence. *Information Sciences*, 119:73–89, 1999.

47. B. J. MacLennan. Can differential equations compute? Technical Report UT–CS–01–459, Dept of Computer Science, University of Tennessee, Knoxville, USA, 2001. Available online: `http://www.cs.utk.edu/~mclennan`.

48. B. J. MacLennan. Transcending Turing computability. *Minds and Machines*, 13(1):3–22, 2003.

49. J. Myhill. A recursive function, defined on a compact interval and having a continuous derivative that is not recursive. *Michigan Math. J.*, 18:97–98, 1971.

50. M. H. A. Newman. Alan Mathison Turing 1912–1954. *Biographical Memoirs of the Fellows of the Royal Society*, 1:253–263, November 1955.

51. R. Penrose. *The Emperor's New Mind*. Oxford University Press, Oxford, UK, 1989.

52. R. Penrose. Précis of the emperor's new mind: Concerning computers, minds, and the laws of physics. *Behavioural and Brain Sciences*, 13:643–655 and 692–705, 1990.

53. R. Penrose. *Shadows of the Mind: A Search for the Missing Science of Consciousness*. Oxford University Press, Oxford, UK, 1994.

54. I. Pitowsky. The physical Church thesis and physical computational complexity. *Iyuun*, 39:81–99, 1990.

55. M. B. Pour-El. Abstract computability versus analog-computability (a survey). In *Cambridge Summer School in Mathematical Logic*, volume 337 of *Springer Lecture Notes in Mathematics*, pages 345–360. Springer-Verlag, Berlin, 1971.

56. M. B. Pour-El. Abstract computability and its relation to the general purpose analog computer. *Trans. American Math. Soc.*, 199:1–28, 1974.

57. M. B. Pour-El and J. I. Richards. A computable ordinary differential equation which possesses no computable solution. *Annals of Mathematical Logic*, 17:61–90, 1979.

58. M. B. Pour-El and J. I. Richards. The wave equation with computable initial data such that its unique solution is not computable. *Advances in Mathematics*, 39:215–239, 1981.

59. M. B. Pour-El and J. I. Richards. *Computability in Analysis and Physics*. Springer-Verlag, Berlin, 1989.

60. H. Putnam. Trial and error predicates and the solution of a problem of Mostowski. *Journal of Symbolic Logic*, 30:49–57, 1965.

61. H. Putnam. *Renewing Philosophy*. Harvard University Press, Cambridge, MA, 1992.

62. L. A. Rubel. The brain as an analog computer. *Journal of Theoretical Neurobiology*, 4:73–81, 1985.

63. L. A. Rubel. Some mathematical limitations of the general-purpose analog computer. *Advances in Applied Mathematics*, 9:22–34, 1988.

64. L. A. Rubel. Digital simulation of analog computation and Church's thesis. *Journal of Symbolic Logic*, 54:1011–1017, 1989.

65. K. Sabbagh. *Dr Riemann's Zeros*. Atlantic Books, London, UK, 2002.
66. B. Scarpellini. Zwei Unentscheitbare Probleme der Analysis. *Zeitschrift für mathematische Logik und Grundlagen der Mathematik*, 9:265–289, 1963.
67. B. Scarpellini. Comments on two undecidable problems of analysis. *Minds and Machines*, 13(1):79–85, 2003.
68. B. Scarpellini. Two undecidable problems of analysis. *Minds and Machines*, 13(1):49–77, 2003.
69. O. Shagrir and I. Pitowsky. Physical hypercomputation and the Church-Turing thesis. *Minds and Machines*, 13(1):87–101, 2003.
70. H. T. Siegelmann. Computation beyond the Turing limit. *Science*, 268(5210):545–548, April 1995.
71. H. T. Siegelmann. Analog computational power. *Science*, 271(19):373, January 1996.
72. H. T. Siegelmann. The simple dynamics of super Turing theories. *Theoretical Computer Science*, 168:461–472, 1996.
73. H. T. Siegelmann. *Neural Networks and Analog Computation: Beyond the Turing Limit*. Progress in Theoretical Computer Science. Birkhauser Verlag, November 1998.
74. H. T. Siegelmann. Stochastic analog networks and computational complexity. *Journal of Complexity*, 15:451–475, 1999.
75. H. T. Siegelmann. Neural and super-Turing computing. *Minds and Machines*, 13(1):103–114, 2003.
76. H. T. Siegelmann and E. D. Sontag. On the computational power of neural nets. In *Proceedings of the 5th Annual ACM Workshop on Computational Learning Theory, Pittsburgh*, pages 440–449, 1992.
77. H. T. Siegelmann and E. D. Sontag. Analog computation via neural networks. *Theoretical Computer Science*, 131:331–360, 1994.
78. M. Stannett. X-machines and the halting problem: Building a super-Turing machine. *Formal Aspects of Computing*, 2(4):331–341, 1990.
79. M. Stannett. An introduction to post-Newtonian and non-Turing computation. Technical Report CS–91–02, Department of Computer Science, Sheffield University, UK, 1991. Available online: http://hypercomputation.net/resources.html.
80. M. Stannett. Computation over arbitrary models of time (a unified model of discrete, analog, quantum and hybrid computation). Technical Report CS–01–08, Dept of Computer Science, University of Sheffield, UK, 2001. Available online: http://hypercomputation.net/resources.html.
81. M. Stannett. Hypercomputation is physically irrefutable. Technical Report CS–01–04, Dept of Computer Science, University of Sheffield, UK, 2001. Available online: http://hypercomputation.net/resources.html.
82. M. Stannett. Computation and hypercomputation. *Minds and Machines*, 13:115–153, 2003.
83. I. Stewart. Deciding the undecidable. *Nature*, 352:664–665, 1991.
84. I. Stewart. The dynamics of impossible devices. *Nonlinear Science Today*, 1:8–9, 1991.
85. A. M. Turing. On computable numbers, with an application to the Entscheidungsproblem. *Proceedings of the London Mathematical Society, series 2*, 42:230–265, 1936–37.
86. A. M. Turing. *Systems of Logic Based on Ordinals*. PhD thesis, Princeton University, USA, 1938.

87. A. M. Turing. Systems of logic based on ordinals. In *Proceedings of the London Mathematical Society*, series 2, 45:161–228, 1939.

88. A. M. Turing. A method for the calculation of the zeta-function. *Proceedings of the London Mathematical Society*, 2(48):180, 1943.

Turing's Ideas and Models of Computation

Eugene Eberbach[1], Dina Goldin[2], and Peter Wegner[3]

[1] Computer and Information Science Department, University of Massachusetts
[2] Computer Science & Engineering Department, University of Connecticut
[3] Department of Computer Science, Brown University

Summary. The theory of computation that we have inherited from the 1960s focuses on *algorithmic* computation as embodied in the Turing Machine to the exclusion of other types of computation that Turing had considered. In this chapter we present new models of computation, inspired by Turing's ideas, that are more appropriate for today's interactive, networked, and embedded computing systems. These models represent *super-Turing* computation, going beyond Turing Machines and algorithms. We identify three principles underlying super-Turing computation (*interaction with the world*, *infinity of resources*, and *evolution of systems*) and apply these principles in our discussion of the implications of super-Turing computation for the future of computer science.

1 Introduction: Algorithmic Computation

Alan Turing is known mostly as the inventor of *Turing Machines*, which he created in an effort to formalize the notion of *algorithms*.

> **Algorithm:** systematic procedure that produces — in a finite number of steps — the answer to a question or the solution to a problem [2].

This notion well precedes computer science, having been a concern of mathematicians for centuries. It can be dated back to a 9th century treatise by a Muslim mathematician Al-Koarizmi, after whom algorithms were named. *Algorithmic computation* refers to the computation of algorithms.

> **Algorithmic computation:** computation that is performed in a *closed-box* fashion, transforming a finite input, determined at the start of the computation, to a finite output, available at the end of the computation, in a finite amount of time.

Turing Machines have the following properties that model algorithmic computation:

- their computation is *closed* (shutting out the world);
- they use a *finite* amount of resources (time and memory);
- their behavior is *fixed* (all computations start in the same configuration).

The Turing Machine model forms the foundations of current theoretical computer science. This is largely due to the *strong Turing Thesis*, found in popular undergraduate textbooks, which equates Turing Machines with *all* forms of computation:

Strong Turing Thesis: A Turing Machine can do everything a computer can do [36].

It is little known that Turing had proposed other, non-algorithmic models of computation, and would have disagreed with the strong Turing Thesis. He did not regard the Turing Machine model as encompassing all others.

As with many of his other ideas, Turing was far ahead of his time. Only now, with the development of new powerful applications, is it becoming evident to the wider computer science community that algorithms and Turing Machines do not provide a complete model for computational problem solving.

Overview. We start with a discussion of Turing's rich contributions to computer science, focusing on various models of computation. Next, we present examples of super-Turing computation, which is more powerful than Turing Machines, and discuss the three principles that contradict the algorithmic properties above, making it possible to derive super-Turing models:

- interaction with the world;
- infinity of resources;
- evolution of the system.

While the strong Turing Thesis denies the existence of *super-Turing* models, we explain why Turing was not the author of this thesis and would disagree with it. We show that super-Turing models are a natural continuation of Turing's own ideas. We then discuss how super-Turing computation might influence computer architecture, programming paradigms and the foundations of computer science. We conclude on a philosophical note.

2   Turing's Contributions to Computer Science

2.1   The *Entscheidungsproblem* and Turing's Automatic Machines

Alan Turing was born in 1912, and enrolled at King's College in Cambridge in 1931 as a mathematics undergraduate. He became a fellow of King's College in 1934, completing a dissertation on the Central Limit Theorem. He then became interested in the *Entscheidungsproblem* (decision problem), one of the most alluring conjectures in mathematics at the time, proposed by the prominent mathematician David Hilbert in the early 1900s.

Hilbert's conjecture that any mathematical proposition could be *decided* (proved true or false) by mechanistic logical methods was unexpectedly disproved by Gödel in 1931, who showed that for any formal theory, there will always be undecidable theorems outside of its reach. Mathematicians like Alonzo Church [5] and Turing continued Gödel's work, looking for alternate, constructive techniques for proving this undecidability result.

Turing's proof, provided in his 1936 paper [38], "On Computable Numbers, with an Application to the Entscheidungsproblem" was based on a novel model of *automatic machines* (*a*-machines), which can be built to carry out any algorithmic computation. Turing showed that despite their versatility, these machines cannot compute all functions; in particular, he proved that the now-famous *halting problem* is undecidable. This was accomplished by showing that there exists a *universal a*-machine, capable of simulating all others.

The *a*-machine model consists of:

- a one-dimensional *erasable tape* of infinite length, originally containing a finite imput string;
- a read/write *tape head* capable of moving to the left or right on the tape, and of retrieving or storing one tape symbol at a time at the current tape location;
- a *control mechanism* that may be in any of a bounded number of *states*;
- a *transition table* which, given the symbol under the tape head and the current state of the machine, specifies the next action of the tape head and the new state of the machine.

At the beginning of a computation, the machine is in a special *initial* state. At each step of the computation, the machine's control mechanism causes one symbol to be read from the current tape location. The control mechanism then looks up in the transition table actions that depend on the value of the retrieved symbol as well as on the current state of the machine. It then writes a new symbol at the current tape location, transitions to a new state, and moves left or right one cell on the tape (see Fig. 1). The computation terminates once the machine reaches a special *halting* state.

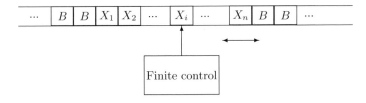

Fig. 1. Turing Machine

We now know *a*-machines as *Turing Machines (TMs)*, and this is how we refer to them for the rest of this chapter. Turing Machine computations have the following properties:

- The TM models *closed* computation, which requires that all inputs are given in advance;
- The TM is allowed to use an unbounded but only *finite amount of time and memory* for its computation;
- Every TM computation starts in an identical *initial configuration*; for a given input, TM behavior is fixed and does not depend on time.

These properties are perfectly suitable for modeling *algorithmic* computation. Note however that they prevent TMs from modeling directly many aspects of modern computing systems, as we discuss in Sect. 3.

Turing Machines were adopted in the 1960s, years after Turing's premature death, as a complete model for algorithms and computational problem solving. They continue to serve as a standard model of computation to this day. Turing's 1936 paper has come to represent the birth of computer science, though the motivation and substance of this paper were entirely mathematical.

2.2   Algorithms and the History of the Turing Thesis

In the early 1930s, the quest to prove (or disprove) Hilbert's famous *Entscheidungsproblem* led to many new classes of functions. Gödel defined *recursive functions* [17]. Soon thereafter, Church showed that his *λ-calculus* defines the same class of functions [5]. A third class of functions, those computable by Turing Machines, was established by Turing around the same time, and also proved equivalent to recursive functions [38].

Both Church and Turing were in search of *effective* ways of computing functions, where "effectiveness" was a mathematical notion synonymous with "mechanical" and lacking a formal definition. Church proposed to identify the notion of an effectively calculable function with the notion of a *λ-definable* function. Turing made the same appeal on behalf of his machines [38]:

> **Turing's Thesis**: *Whenever there is an effective method for obtaining the values of a mathematical function, the function can be computed by a Turing Machine.*

Note that the infinite length of the TM tape plays a key role in this result. With a bound on the length of the tape, only finitely many different configurations of the tape are possible, reducing the TM to a *finite-state automaton* (FSA). The class of FSAs, corresponding to *regular languages*, is known to be less expressive than the class of TMs. The infinity of TM tape is reconciled with the finiteness of the physical world by recognizing that it is a formal model rather than an actual machine. Whereas a physical machine can only have a finite tape, this tape can be upgraded to a longer one when needed; hence a proper model for it is one where the tape is infinite.

The equivalence of the three classes of functions (λ-definable, recursive, and Turing-computable) was taken as confirmation that the notion of effective function computation had finally been formally captured. The claims of Church and Turing are usually combined into one, known as the Church-Turing Thesis:

> **Church-Turing thesis**: *The formal notions of recursiveness, λ-definability, and Turing-computability equivalently capture the intuitive notion of effective computability of functions over integers.*

However, Gödel much preferred Turing's approach, since its identification with effectiveness is more immediate [8].

While this work was purely mathematical, and applied only to *functions over integers*, it had a strong influence on the field of computer science when it emerged as a mature discipline decades later. In particular, the robustness of the notion of effective function computation has served to give it a central role in the foundation of computer science. Turing Machines provided this new field with legitimacy on a par with physics and mathematics, by establishing it as the study of a class of concrete and well-defined phenomena:

- **Physics:** study of properties of matter;
- **Mathematics:** study of quantity and space;
- **Computer Science:** study of algorithmic problem solving computable by Turing Machines.

While the Church-Turing thesis only applied to the effectiveness of computing functions over integers, it extends easily to functions over finite strings, since strings can be naturally encoded as integers. However, it does not extend to other types of computation, such as functions over real-valued inputs, or such as interactive computation. Both Church and Turing were aware of this limitation. Whereas Church's concerns did not go beyond functions over integers, Turing's concerns were more general. As we discuss next, he also proposed machines for interactive computation, distinct from a Turing Machine.

2.3   Turing's Quest for Interaction: Choice Machines and Oracle Machines

Automatic machines (*a*-machines) were not the only model introduced by Turing in his 1936 paper. In the same paper, Turing also proposed *choice machines* (*c*-machines) as an alternate model of computation. Whereas *a*-machines operate in a closed-box fashion as if on "automatic pilot" (hence their name), *c*-machines interact with an operator such as a human user during the computation. In Turing's words, a *c*-machine's "motion is only partially determined by the configuration"; in certain configurations, it stops and "cannot go on until some arbitrary choice has been made by an external operator" [38].

Choice machines were introduced by Turing as an alternative conceptualization of computation, one that is interactive. Turing clearly realized that the algorithmic computation of automatic machines is not the only type of computation possible. However, Turing's goal in [38] was to prove the unsolvability of the *Entscheidungsproblem* rather than to set standards for models of computation. Formalization of *a*-machines enabled him to reach his goal, so the bulk of the paper was concerned with them rather than with *c*-machines.

Eventually, *a*-machines were adopted as the standard model of computation, while *c*-machines remained unformalized. Some believe that *oracle machines*, introduced by Turing just a few years later [39], provide a formalization of *c-machines*, making them unnecessary.

There is indeed an important similarity between choice machines and oracle machines: both make queries to an external agent during the computation. In the case of an oracle machine, this agent is an *oracle* rather than a human operator. An oracle is formally described as a set that can be *queried* about any *value*; it returns *true* if the queried value is in this set and *false* otherwise.

In ancient Greece, *oracles* were people who others consulted for advice; they were believed to possess access to hidden knowledge that came to them directly from the deities. Just as Greek oracles have super-human knowledge, Turing's oracles are meant to represent *uncomputable* information obtained from outside the system. Turing specifically excluded the possibility that the oracle was an effective computing entity [39]:

> We shall not go any further into the nature of this oracle apart from saying that it cannot be a machine.

Since oracles cannot be machines, do they model humans, such as the operators of *c*-machines? The set-based semantics of oracles preclude this possibility. Because they are sets, oracles are *static*, and the outcome of each query is predetermined before the oracle machine (*o-machine*) starts computing. During the computation, the same query will always yield the same answer from a given oracle. Clearly, the same cannot be said of humans, for whom the same question can yield a different answer depending on their mood or some other circumstance. Hence, Turing's *choice machines* are not just *oracle machines* by another name, but a different model of computation.

2.4   Turing's Contribution to Cryptology and Complexity Theory: Work on Enigma and Colossus

During World War II, Alan Turing worked as a top cryptanalyst and chief consultant at the Government Code and Cypher School at Bletchley Park. By using his previous experience with ciphers, as well as his knowledge of combinatorics, code theory and statistics, Turing contributed substantially to breaking the code of the *Enigma*, the encrypting/decrypting machine that the German navy used for all its radio communications. More importantly, he mechanized the decryption process, using an electro-mechanical machine of his invention — the *Turing Bombe*. Later, a much faster device — the *Colossus* — was deployed; it can be considered the world's first electronic computer.

Just as Turing's primary purpose for inventing Turing Machines was to show that there exist problems which cannot be solved by mechanical (algorithmic) means, the goal of his work at Bletchley Park was to find the mechanical means for solving problems that are hard, but not impossible. The art of breaking codes required the ability to deal with the intricate complexity of multi-level encryption algorithms. This was Turing's direct practical contribution to cryptography, and indirectly to complexity theory. In fact, he pioneered what now would be called an interactive randomized approach to breaking ciphers, by intelligent guessing the key based on the statistical evidence, and exploring the loopholes in the Germans' use of Enigma. This, together with the speed of the Bombe and then Colossus, sliced through the intractable search space of the problem.

Turing was also chief liaison between American and British cryptanalysts. The work of British scientists at Bletchley Park was highly regarded by British prime minister Winston Churchill, and recognized as one of the deciding factors in winning the war. Turing eventually received an Order of the British Empire from the Queen for his work; however, due to its top secret nature, it remained unpublished and unknown among his colleagues for many years.

2.5 Turing's Work on ACE as a Precursor of General Purpose Universal Computers

After the end of the war Turing joined the National Physical Laboratory in 1945 to work on the *Automatic Computing Engine (ACE)*. ACE was one of several postwar attempts to build a working computer; other contemporary projects include EDVAC and IAS computers in the USA (at U Penn and Princeton, respectively), and Wilkes' EDSAC computer at Cambridge in the UK.

Turing's plan was to build the first programmable general-purpose computer, which would keep both the code and the data in memory, and execute the code over the data. Turing drew his inspiration for ACE directly from his earlier theoretical work. As he said in a lecture to the London Mathematical society [41],

> Machines such as the ACE may be regarded as practical versions of [the Turing Machine]. There is at least a very close analogy.

In particular, Turing saw a direct parallel [41] between the capability of ACE to accept and execute programs, and his notion of a *universal Turing Machine*, which was part of his 1936 *Entscheidungsproblem* paper:

> the complexity of the machine to be imitated is concentrated in the tape [of the Universal Turing Machine] and does not appear in the universal machine proper [...] This feature is paralleled in digital computing machines such as the ACE. They are in fact practical versions of the universal machine [...] When any particular problem has to be handled the appropriate instructions [...] are stored in the memory of the ACE and it is then 'set up' for carrying out that process.

Turing's vision of a programmable computer is in stark contrast to all other computer designs of that time, including the Colossus and the ENIAC, which required a manual reconfiguration for every new computation. It is not surprising that ACE's computer architecture was very different from, and more complicated than, other computer designs of the time.

ACE was planned to be the fastest (1 microsecond clock cycle) and having the largest memory in the world (60,000 bits). ACE's design [40] involved many pioneering concepts that became standard part of computer architecture decades later. ACE would have a large set of 32 general-purpose registers, and a simple hardware system implementing a fast basic minimum of arithmetical and Boolean functions; Turing believed that other functions (including floating-point arithmetic) should be programmed. This pioneering approach to hardware design did not receive due recognition until the early 1980s, when it became known as *RISC* (Reduced Instruction Set Computers).

Turing also pioneered *subroutine hierarchies* (then called *instruction tables*) which can be viewed as a precursor to high-level programming languages. Turing invented *calling stacks* for invoking them (then called *bury* and *unbury* routines). He proposed self-modifiable code to implement conditional branching. By contrast, the competing designs of the EDVAC, the IAS, and the EDSAC machines were based on *accumulator* architecture, whose design was relatively straightforward.

Turing's vision to build a machine that would show "genuine intelligence" went far beyond the project's original mission of doing "large difficult sums," frightening his superiors. The administration of the National Physical Laboratories, under the directorship of Sir Charles Darwin (grandson of the well-known English naturalist) found Turing's ideas too revolutionary, especially in the context of postwar British frugality.

In retrospect, the ideas embodied in the design of ACE make perfect sense. In time, many aspects of Turing's ACE design have proved as valuable as the Turing Machine and the Turing test (Sect. 2.7). But without the benefit of hindsight, Turing's contemporaries working on similar projects, such as Maurice Wilkes, were skeptical whether a machine of such complexity and with such revolutionary architecture would ever work. The ACE project never received the funding it sought, and the disappointed Turing left the National Physical Laboratory in 1948 for the University of Manchester.

2.6 Turing's Unorganized Machines as a Precursor of Neural Networks, Evolutionary Computation and Reinforcement Learning

Before leaving for Manchester in 1948, Turing produced a final report on ACE which can also be viewed as a blueprint for the future field of *neural networks*. Titled *Intelligent Machinery* [42], this report was left unpublished until 1968, because Darwin considered it to be a "schoolboy essay" not suitable for publication.

In this report, among other futuristic ideas, including robots taking country walks, Turing proposed new models of computation, which he called *unorganized machines (u-machines)*. There were two types of u-machines, those based on *Boolean networks* and those based on *finite state machines*. Turing took his inspiration from the working of the human cortex, and its ability for self-adaptation.

- **A-type** and **B-type** u-machines were Boolean networks made up of two-input NAND gates (*neurons*) and synchronized by a global clock; the number of neurons remained fixed. While in A-type u-machines the connections between neurons were fixed, B-type u-machines had modifiable switch type interconnections. Starting from the initial random configuration and applying a kind of genetic algorithm, B-type u-machines were supposed to learn which of their connections should be on and which off.
- **P-type** u-machines were tape-less Turing Machines reduced to their Finite State Machine control, with an incomplete transition table, and two input lines for interaction: the *pleasure* and the *pain* signals. For configurations with missing transitions, the tentative transition to another state could be reinforced by pleasure input from the environment, or cancelled in the presence of pain.

In his B-type u-machines, Turing pioneered two areas at the same time: *neural networks* and *evolutionary computation*; his P-type u-machines represent *reinforcement learning*. However, this work had no impact on these fields, due to the unfortunate combination of Turing's death and the twenty-year delay in publication. As a result, others got the credit for these ideas:

- *Neural networks* are typically credited to Pitts and McCulloch neurons (1943) [22] and Rosenblatt's perceptron (1958) [31].
- *Evolutionary computation* is typically credited to Holland's work (1968) [1] on genetic algorithms, although it is acknowledged that the area has been rediscovered around ten times between the 1950s and 1960s [14].
- *Reinforcement learning* has been been attributed to Minsky and Farley and Clark papers from 1954 [13, 27], or Samuel's checkers program from 1959 [33].

Turing was convinced that his B-type u-machine can simulate his Universal Turing Machine, though he never provided a formal proof [37]. In order to simulate the infinite tape of a Turing Machine, a u-machine with an infinite number of neurons would be needed. This is due to the *discrete* nature of the neurons, which were based on two input Boolean NAND gates. By contrast, just two *real-valued* neurons are sufficient to model a Turing Machine.

B-type u-machines were defined to have a finite number of neurons, and it is not clear whether Turing was aware that infinitely many neurons were needed for the simulation. This inconsistency would certainly have been uncovered when working on the formal proof. But perhaps Turing was aware of it, and expected to have no problems extending his definitions to the infinite case.

2.7   Turing as a Founder of Artificial Intelligence

In this section, we explore Turing's contributions to *Artificial Intelligence* (AI), of which he is considered one of the founders. Turing's interest in AI can be traced at least to his final report on ACE [42], where he envisions "intelligent" behaviors of future generations of computers. At that point, intelligence was viewed mainly in terms of a *search strategy*; an intelligent agent is one that can find the best action based on current knowledge.

Turing identified chess as a good starting point for exploring intelligent search strategies. Ever optimistic about the progress of computing research, Turing estimated in 1941 that computers would be able to beat human chess champions by about 1957. To make progress towards this goal, Turing and David Champernowne wrote the *Turochamp* chess program in 1948, applying a search strategy known as *Minimax* towards choosing the next move, probably the first time this strategy was ever realized in computer code. Eventually, computers were built that could beat human chess champions, but it took 40 years longer than Turing predicted. Using a variant of Minimax known as the alpha-beta search, a supercomputer named *Deep Blue* beat the world chess champion Garry Kasparov in 1997.

Turing expected computers to match humans not only in chess, but in every intelligent endeavor. In a famous 1950 paper [43] Turing provocatively led with the question "Can Machines Think?" and proposed his famous test for intelligence. Now known as the *Turing Test*, it is based on the "imitation principle":

> **Turing Test for AI**: *If a computer, on the basis of its written responses to questions, could not be distinguished from a human respondent, then one has to say that the computer is thinking and must be intelligent.*

The imitation principle, inspired by the then-popular behaviorist school of thought, stated that there was no way to tell that other people were "thinking" or "conscious" except by the process of comparison with oneself. Thus if computers behaved like people (i.e., the "black-box" approach, independently of how they are internally built), they should be credited with human-like attributes of consciousness, intelligence, or emotion. As a result, the new field of *artificial intelligence* grew up around the problems of defining and duplicating consciousness and intelligence.

The Turing test, and the early artificial intelligence research which was based on it, attracted much criticism. In order to explore the arguments of the critics, it is useful to break down the question "Can Machines Think" into two separate questions [47]:

- **(Extensionality)** *Can machines simulate the behavior associated with thinking?*
- **(Intensionality)** *Can we say that machines that simulate thinking are actually thinking?*

Turing answered "yes" to both of these questions, while the critics were divided into those who believed that machines cannot simulate thinking (*extensional skeptics*) and those who believed that simulation without understanding does not capture the essence of thinking (*intentional skeptics*). Extensional skeptics place limits on the expressive power of computation, while intensional skeptics reject the behaviorist view that unobservable inner attributes are irrelevant.

The second question has a metaphysical flavor, and is therefore outside the scope of a computer science inquiry. However, the first question is very much of interest to computer scientists, especially when rephrased as: *"Can machines act intelligently?"* We explore this question in the context of interactive models of computation in Sect. 5.1.

2.8   Turing as a Precursor of Artificial Life

In 1952, Turing published a paper on morphogenetic theory in the Royal Society Proceedings [44]. Turing tried to capture the growth and pattern occurrences in plants and animals, describing them as dynamical systems, in the form of nonlinear differential equations.

This work, along with that of John von Neumann, can be considered as a precursor of the areas of *artificial life* and *computational molecular biology*. Von Neumann's work considered the universal computability and universal constructibility of cellular automata, based on his theory of self-reproducing automata from 1952.

Both Von Neumann and Turing's work on artificial life remained unfinished because of the authors' death. However, Arthur Burks edited and published von Neumann manuscript in 1966 [46], while Turing's work in this area remained practically unknown. As a result, usually only von Neumann is given full credit for founding the area of artificial life.

3   Super-Turing Computation

In this section we discuss why Turing Machines (TMs) do not represent a complete theory for problem solving. In particular, the three properties of TM computation, while perfectly suited for modeling algorithmic computation, act to prevent it from modeling directly many aspects of modern computing systems:

- TM computations are *closed*, which requires that all inputs are given in advance;
- TM computations are allowed to use an unbounded but only *finite amount of time and memory*;
- TM computations all start in an identical *initial configuration*; for a given input, TM behavior is fixed and does not depend on time.

By contrast, modern computing systems process *infinite streams* of *dynamically generated* input requests. They are expected to continue computing *indefinitely* without halting. Finally, their behavior is *history-dependent*, with the output determined both by the current input and the system's computation history.

A large percentage of the computer-science community believes that while Turing Machines are not very convenient to model some aspects of computation, they nevertheless cover all possible types of computation. As a consequence, it is considered futile to look for models of computation going beyond TMs. In this section, we identify the source of this common misconception, and discuss three different directions for extending TM computation to super-Turing computation: *interaction*, *infinity*, and *evolution*.

These extensions can be contrasted with the many failed attempts to break out of the "Turing tarpit" of TM-equivalent computation known to us from theory of computation textbooks, such as increasing the number of Turing Machine tapes. Those attempts always remained in the algorithmic paradigm, and consequently were doomed to fall within the bounds of the Church-Turing thesis. By contrast, each of these three extensions lifts computation out of the algorithmic paradigm, by redefining the space of computational problems. What is being computed is no longer just fixed functions from integers to integers (or some equivalent), but also non-algorithmic computational problems, or tasks.

3.1   The Strong Interpretation of the Turing Thesis

A *Universal Turing Machine* is a special Turing Machine introduced by Turing in [38] that can simulate any other Turing Machine — hence its name. It served as the inspiration for the notion of general-purpose computing (Sect. 2.5).

The principle of universality can easily be extended to any other class of machines that compute functions. As long as each machine in this class can be captured by a finite description which defines what this machine "would do in every configuration in which it might find itself" [41], a Turing Machine can be created to simulate all machines in this class:

Universality Thesis: *Any class of effective devices for computing functions can be simulated by a Turing Machine.*

Both the Turing thesis (Sect. 2.2) and the Universality thesis constitute fundamental yet distinct contributions to the theory of computation, which was established as a separate area of computer science in the 1950s. It is astonishing that these results were accomplished by Turing simultaneously in his seminal paper on Turing Machines [38], which predated any computers.

The original digital computers were in fact devices for computing functions, much like Turing Machines; their architecture did not allow any interaction during the computation. This led to the equating of computers with algorithmic computation, and to the following (incorrect) corollary of the universality thesis:

Universality Corollary: *Any computer can be simulated by a Turing Machine.*

While the universality corollary is true when computers are limited to the task of computing functions or algorithms, it does not apply in the context of today's highly interactive computing systems such as the Internet.

When the first undergraduate computer science textbooks were being written in the 1960s, Turing's contributions to theory of computation needed to be presented in a more accessible fashion. As a result, the Turing thesis and the Universality corollary were glibly combined into one, resulting in the following (incorrect) *strong interpretation* of the Turing thesis that one often sees in undergraduate textbooks:

Strong Turing Thesis: A Turing Machine can do everything a computer can do [36].

The current generation of computer scientists has absorbed the strong interpretation of the Turing thesis with their undergraduate education, believing it a heresy to question it. However, this interpretation needs to be distinguished from the actual contributions of Turing or his contemporaries on which it is based. There is no question that both the Turing thesis and the Universality thesis only applied in the realm of functions over integers. When these sources of the strong Turing thesis are reexamined, its position as a dogma of computer science becomes shaky. The strong Turing thesis needs to be recognized as incorrect — despite common belief to the contrary.

3.2   Driving Home from Work

In this section we discuss the problem of *driving home from work* (*DHW*) [47], which cannot be solved algorithmically, but is nevertheless computable. The existence of computable problems that a Turing Machine cannot solve contradicts the strong Turing Thesis, proving it incorrect.

> **The *DHW* Problem.** Consider an *automatic car* whose task is to drive us across town from work to home. The output for this problem should be a time-series plot of signals to the car's controls that enable it to perform this task autonomously. How can we compute this output?

In the *algorithmic* scenario, where all inputs are provided a *priori*, the input to the *DHW* problem includes a map of the city which must be precise enough to compute the exact path the car will take. This scenario, typical of AI approaches to similar problems through most of the second half of the last century, is illustrated in Fig. 2.

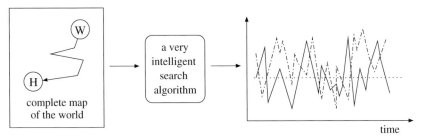

Fig. 2. Driving home from work: the algorithmic scenario

Note that in addition to the map, the input needs to specify the exact road conditions along the way, including every pothole and every grain of sand. By the principles of *chaotic behavior*, such elements can greatly affect the car's eventual course — like the Japanese butterfly that causes a tsunami at the other end of the world.

In a *static* world, this input is in principle specifiable, but the real world is *dynamic*. The presence of mutable physical elements such as the wind and the rain affect the car's course, both directly (as the wind blows at the car) and indirectly (as the wind shifts the sand in the path of the car). It is doubtful whether these elements can be precomputed to an accuracy required for the *DHW* problem.

We can remain optimistic until we remember that the world also includes humans, as pedestrians or drivers. To avoid collisions, we must precompute the exact motion of everyone who might come across our way. To assume that human actions can be computed ahead of time is tantamount to an assertion of *fatalism* — a doctrine that events are fixed in advance so that human beings are powerless to change them — clearly beyond the purview of computer science. Therefore, we must conclude that the *DHW* problem is unsolvable:

> *Computational tasks situated in the real world which includes human agents are not solvable algorithmically.*

Nevertheless, the *DHW* problem *is* computable — interactively, with a *driving agent*. In this scenario, the agent's inputs, or *percepts* [32], consist of a stream of images produced by a video camera mounted on the moving car. The signals to the car's controls are generated by the agent *on-line* in response to these images, to avoid steering off the road or running into obstacles.

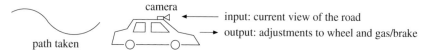

camera

input: current view of the road

output: adjustments to wheel and gas/brake

path taken

Fig. 3. Driving home from work: the interactive scenario

This change in the scenario, illustrated in Fig. 3, is akin to taking the blindfolds off the car's driver, who had been driving from memory and bound to a precomputed sequence of actions. Now, he is aware of his environment and uses it to guide his steering.

> *The DHW example proves that there exist problems that cannot be solved algorithmically, but are nevertheless computable.*

Note that we have not just restructured the inputs, but also changed the *model of computation* as well as the notion of a *computational problem*. Algorithmic problems are computed *off-line*; the output is generated *before* driving begins. Interactive problems are computed *on-line*; the output is generated as the car drives. Furthermore, the inputs and outputs for interactive computation are interdependent; decoupling them, such as replacing the video camera with a prerecorded videotape of the road, will be tantamount to putting the blindfolds back on the driver.

3.3   Super-Turing Computation

We refer to computation that violates the strong interpretation of the Turing thesis (Sect. 3.1) as *super-Turing computation*; driving home from work was an example.

> **Super-Turing Computation:** *computation by models that are more expressive than Turing Machine.*

Super-Turing computation is more *powerful* than the algorithmic computation of Turing Machines, in that it can solve a wider class of computational problems. Our use of the term *super-Turing* is meant to have a positive connotation. We do not consider the higher expressiveness of new computing models as something excessive, but rather as a desirable feature, and as a natural continuation of Turing's ideas.

We identify three principles that allow us to derive models of computation more expressive than Turing Machines:

- interaction with the world;
- infinity of resources;
- evolution of the system.

We discuss these principles next.

Interaction with the Environment. In his 1936 and 1939 papers, Turing showed that Turing Machines were only appropriate for computing recursive functions over integers, and proposed *choice machines* (*c*-machines) and *oracle machines* (*o*-machines) as alternate models that supported richer forms of computation than Turing Machines (Sect. 2.3). Both of these models extend Turing Machines by *interaction*.

> *Interactive computation* involves interaction with an external world, or the *environment* of the computation, *during* the computation.

Driving home from work (Sect. 3.2) is an example of interactive computation. As another example, consider missile trajectory computations. This was an early application of computers, dating to World War II. In the original (algorithmic) scenario, the input includes the location of the target and the flight characteristics of the missile; the output is the direction and angle at which to launch the missile so it (hopefully) hits the target. By contrast, the computation for today's smart missiles is interactive. Once launched, they continue to monitor their progress and to adjust their trajectory to remain on target. In the presence of wind gusts and air pressure changes, interaction has proven necessary to assure accurate long-distance targeting.

Two types of interactive computation can be identified [48]. *Sequential interaction* describes the computation of a single agent, such as the smart missile, as it interacts with its *environment*. All inputs are interleaved into a single *input stream*, and are processed sequentially. By contrast, *distributed interaction* involves many agents working concurrently in an asynchronous fashion, with multiple autonomous communication channels which can be automatically reconfigured during the computation.

While algorithmic problems are solved by algorithmic systems such as Turing Machines, interactive problems are those solved by interactive systems:

- **Algorithmic Problem**: transforming input strings to output strings
- **Interactive Problem**: carrying out a computational task or service

The intuition that computing corresponds to formal computability by Turing machines breaks down when the notion of what is computable is broadened to include interaction. Though the Church-Turing thesis is valid in the narrow sense that Turing Machines express the behavior of algorithms, the broader assertion that algorithms precisely capture what can be computed is invalid [48]. By interacting with the external world, interactive systems can solve a larger class of problems, such as driving home from work or the smart missile.

Interactive computation has been captured under many different forms, such as *concurrent*, *distributed*, or *reactive* computation. It is a different computational paradigm, which expands the notion of a computational problem [47,51]. The paradigm shift from algorithms to interaction captures the technology shift from mainframes to workstations and networks, from number crunching to embedded systems and user interfaces, and from procedure-oriented to object-based and distributed programming.

Greater problem-solving power is synonymous with greater expressiveness. An argument for greater expressiveness of interactive models was made by Milner [25], where he stated that the λ-calculus needs to be extended to model interactive systems. Since the λ-calculus models all algorithmic computation, it follows that interactive computation is more expressive. An alternate approach to proving the same result, based on *Persistent Turing Machines*, can be found in [19].

When an interactive system consists of many autonomous (or asynchronous) concurrent components, it cannot in general be simulated by interleaving the behaviors of its subsystems.

> *Distributed interaction is more expressive than sequential interaction, just as sequential interaction is more expressive than algorithmic computation.*

Multi-component systems are capable of richer behaviors than sequential agents. Their behaviors are known as *emergent*, since they emerge as the property of the whole system without being present, in whole or part, in any of its components. The existence of emergent behaviors was demonstrated by Simon [35]; while he discussed *complex systems* in general, interactive computing systems are a special class of such systems.

Infinity of Resources. The Turing Machine model can be extended by removing any *a priori* bounds on its resources, possibly resulting in:

- an infinite initial configuration,
- an infinite architecture,
- infinite time,

- an infinite alphabet.

The impracticality of possessing infinite resources should not be an obstacle here. Just as Turing allowed infinite length of tape in Turing Machines, and cellular automata are allowed to contain infinitely many cells, we can allow an infinite number of tapes or states in our models of computation. And just as the infinite length of the Turing Machine tape allows for more expressiveness than bounded-tape models (Sect. 2.2), these extensions increase expressiveness yet further.

Below, we discuss the four different types of *extension by infinity*.

- Persistence of memory between computation is represented by cellular automata, Persistent Turing Machines [18,19], and $-calculus [10]. When the Turing Machine preserves some information from one computation to the next, we can obtain an unbounded growth of its initial configuration, and we need to model it with an *infinite initial configuration*.
- When modeling massively parallel scalable computers or the Internet, we do not put restrictions on the number of computing elements. Allowing infinitely many computing elements (infinity of architecture) can be modeled by an *infinite number of Turing Machine tapes*, or an *infinite number of read/write heads*, resulting in an unbounded parallelism. The approach is represented by cellular automata [46], discrete neural networks with an infinite number of cells, random automata networks [15], π-calculus [24], and $-calculus [10]. Just as the large memories of digital computers provide a practical approximation to Turing Machines' infinite tapes, so does system scalability, such as scalable massively parallel computers or dynamic networks of autonomous agents, provide a practical approximation to the infinite architecture of super-Turing computers.
- Any system that is not expected to halt on its own needs to be modeled by allowing *infinite time*. This applies to many interactive systems such as operating systems, servers on the Internet, software agents or viruses, or evolutionary programs.
- Allowing *infinite precision* is represented by analog computers, neural networks and hybrid automata [34]. Analog computers or real-value neural networks can be interpreted as operating on uncountable alphabets — each real number corresponding to one unique symbol of the alphabet. Alternately, real numbers can be simulated by infinite strings over finite discrete alphabets, but then we trade one type of infinity for another. For the same practical reasons why evolutionary programs are terminated after a finite number of generations, current digital computers require truncating all real numbers to finite precision.

Evolution of the System. *Extension by evolution* allows the computing device to adapt over time. The Turing Machine stops being static but continuously evolves, so it is able to solve new types of problems. Turing's unorganized machine learning [42] can be viewed as an example of this. He proposed strategies, now known as *genetic algorithms*, to evolve the connections between the neurons within the u-machine.

In general, evolution can be done by upgrade of either hardware or software, by self-adaptive, learning programs, or evolvable, self-reproductive hardware. Evolution may happen in continuous or discrete steps, leading possibly to capabilities previously not present. In particular, an ordinary Turing Machine can evolve to one with an oracle, or to a persistent TM that does not reinitialize its tape before computations, or one that replicates its tapes indefinitely. The possibilities of evolution (the types of variation operators) are endless.

Evolution can be controlled by interaction with the environment, or by some performance measure, such as its *fitness*, or *utility*, or *cost*. The evolution principle is used by *site and Internet machines* [45], *$-calculus* [10], and Turing's *u-machines* [42].

Discussion. The three principles we have identified and discussed above are consistent with the work of other researchers in this area. For example, in their search for more expressive models of computation, van Leeuwen and Wiedermann [45] stressed:

- interaction of machines;
- infinity of operators;
- non-uniformity of programs (upgrade of computer hardware and system software), which we include here as part of the evolution principle.

Each of the three extensions is sufficient to obtain models more expressive than Turing Machines. However, the three approaches are not disjoint; it is impossible to have evolution without infinity, or to benefit from infinity without interaction. It is not clear whether our list of possible Turing Machine extensions is complete. At this point, we are rather interested that such extensions are reasonable, and that they cover all models discussed in the next section.

3.4   Examples of Super-Turing Computation

We now present three examples of super-Turing computation requiring new models of computation going beyond Turing Machines:

- dynamic interaction of clients and servers on the Internet;
- mobile robotics;
- infinite adaptation of evolutionary computation.

Distributed Client-Server Computation. The Internet connects many separate computer networks. The *client/server model* is a typical paradigm used by computer networks. In this model, servers provide services to multiple clients (e.g., in the form of web browsers); the clients query the server simultaneously, unaware of the presence of other clients. With the Internet, each client can gain access not just to its local server, but to any server on the Internet, and interact with it as with its local server.

The resulting concurrent interaction of multiple clients and servers, with a dynamic configuration of communication links and nodes, cannot be described as a Turing Machine computation, which must be sequential, static, and with all input predefined.

It can be argued that everything is a matter of providing the proper initial description of the *world* on the infinite tape of the Turing Machine. While there is no bound on the length of the input string, the input for any given problem instance must be finite and predefined ahead of computation. By contrast, the potential interaction streams for dynamic systems may not only be infinite, but even non-enumerable [47,48]. The input values in this infinite dynamic stream depend on the current state of a potentially ever-changeable and uncomputable world, which in turn depends on the earlier output values of the interactive system. Thus Turing Machines can only approximate interaction on the Internet, but cannot be used as its precise model.

Mobile Robotics. Mobile robots can be viewed as computers augmented with sensors and actuators to perceive their environment and to physically act upon it. Robots interact with environments which are often more complex than robots themselves; in fact, the environments can be non-computable, e.g., when they include human actors.

The original approach of artificial intelligence, now known as GOFAI (good old fashioned artificial intelligence), was to implement the robot algorithmically. *Deliberative symbolic robotics* precomputed all the robot's actions before any were carried out, encoding the robot's environment as predefined input. It is not surprising that GOFAI failed miserably with mobile robots.

If the environment can be non-computable, it can neither be predefined, nor computed using a Turing Machine. This is not just an issue of the enormous computational complexity required to build good models of reality, but of the impossibility of doing it in finite time using finite encodings, as in algorithmic computation. Heeding Brooks' persuasive arguments against the algorithmic "toy world" approach for building reactive robots [3], AI has made a paradigm shift in the last decade towards the interactive approach for building intelligent agents.

Evolutionary Computation. Turing Machines have problems with capturing evolution, both natural and that simulated on computers, because *Evolutionary computation* can be understood as a probabilistic beam search, looking for the solution with a globally optimal value of the *fitness function*.

The fitness function represents the quality of the solution, and is obtained by the process of interaction of the solution with its environment. Populations of solutions and evolutionary algorithms are changed in each *generation*, and the probabilistic search for a solution is, in a general, an infinite process.

When the best solutions are preserved from generation to generation (the so-called *elitist strategy*), evolutionary computation is guaranteed to converge to its goal in the infinity; otherwise, there is no guarantee that the goal will be reached. Usually, evolutionary computation is terminated after a finite number of generations, producing approximate solutions. The halting of genetic algorithms is enforced by the necessity to fit them to the Turing Machine model of computation, with its finiteness restrictions.

An infinite process cannot be properly captured using finitary means (algorithms and Turing Machines). The lack of finitary termination applies also to reactive systems (operating systems and servers). When viewed as a computing system, the Internet also escapes finitary description; its size, as measured by the number of nodes, in principle has no bounds and can "outgrow" any finite description that we may devise for it. This is analogous to the fact that Turing Machines need an infinite tape for their expressiveness (Sect. 2.2) even though their tape contents is always finite.

4   Models of Super-Turing Computation

In this section we discuss three formal models of super-Turing computation: *Persistent Turing Machines*, the *π-calculus* and the *$-calculus*. At the end of this section we present an overview of some other super-Turing models of computation, for a more complete perspective.

Regarding the feasibility of implementing super-Turing models, we note that the same criticism applies to Turing Machines. In 1936, when Turing Machines were invented, no one knew how to build a computer. Even now, when digital processors are ubiquitous, no one has implemented a Turing Machine, since that would require infinite memory.

While technically not implementable (due to the infinite size of their tape), Turing Machines serve as a very useful theoretical tool for understanding the algorithmic computation of digital computers. Similarly, super-Turing models are useful for providing a theoretical understanding of super-Turing computation that involves elements of *interaction*, *infinity*, and *evolution* (Sect. 3.3).

4.1   Persistent Turing Machines

Persistent Turing Machines (PTMs) are a model of *sequential interactive computation* obtained by a minimal extension of the Turing Machine model [18, 19]. While the "hardware" (syntax) of the PTM is not new, our interpretation of its computation (semantics) is. A PTM is a 3-tape Turing Machine, with an *input*, an *output*, and a *work tape*. It continuously interacts with its environment during the computation, processing a stream of *inputs* that are dynamically generated by the environment, and producing the corresponding stream of *output tokens*. Upon receiving an input token from its environment, the PTM computes for a while and then outputs the result to the environment, and this process is repeated forever.

A PTM is *persistent* in the sense that its work-tape contents (its "memory") is maintained from one computation to the next. Hence, the initial configuration of the PTM is not identical for each input token, as it would be for a Turing Machine. Since the value of the output depends both on the input and the memory, PTMs exhibit history-dependent behavior that is typical of interactive computation, but impossible for algorithmic computation (Sect. 3).

The following is a simple yet practical example of a PTM, an *answering machine* (AM). AM's memory is the tape of the answering machine; it is unbounded. AM's computational steps are expressed by a Turing computable function mapping the pair (input token, current memory) to the pair (output token, new memory):

Example 1. An *answering machine AM* is a PTM whose work tape contains a sequence of recorded messages and whose operations are `record`, `playback`, and `erase`. The Turing-computable function for A is:

$$f_A(\text{record } Y, X) = (\text{ok}, XY); \quad f_A(\text{playback}, X) = (X, X);$$
$$f_A(\text{erase}, X) = (\text{done}, \epsilon).$$

To illustrate AM's ability to express history dependent behavior, consider the input stream

    (record A,playback,record B,playback,...);

the corresponding output stream is

    (ok,A,ok,AB,...).

The same input token (*playback*) generated different output tokens (A and AB) when called at different times, because of the different operations that preceded it.

The notion of *equivalence* for PTMs is *observational*, based only on the observable aspects of its behavior: inputs and outputs; memory is not considered observable. As the example above shows, the whole input stream needs to be observed, rather than just the current token as for a Turing Machine. The resulting notion of equivalence is analogous to that of *bisimulation* for *concurrent processes*.

Alternate notions of equivalence can be defined, based on *finite trace observations* rather than *infinite stream observations*. In fact, there is an *infinite hierarchy* of successively finer equivalence classes for PTMs, when observed over finite stream prefixes [19]. This is in contrast to Turing Machines, which admit only one notion of equivalence, corresponding to the equivalence of the function being computed.

The answering machine example illustrated how PTMs constitute a natural model for sequential objects. Mobile intelligent agents are also naturally modeled by PTMs. Dynamically bounded input and output streams allow us to express uncertainty of both sensors and actuators, while the contents of the persistent work-tape "evolves" to reflect the agent's changing *state* as it adapts to its environment.

While distributed interaction is not captured by PTMs, one can imagine how to define systems of PTMs that model distributed interaction. PTMs would be equipped with additional *communication tapes*. To allow dynamic reconfiguration of PTM systems, new primitives for creating, sharing, and modifying communication tapes are needed, but the underlying "hardware" of the system would still be based on Turing Machines.

4.2   The π-Calculus

Milner's π-calculus [24, 25, 30] is a mathematical model of concurrent processes, which are *mobile* in the sense that their interconnections dynamically change during the computation. π-calculus can be considered a dynamic extension of CCS (Calculus of Communicating Systems), Milner's earlier model which was not mobile [23].

Similar to PTMs (Sect. 4.1), the π-calculus is built around the central notion of *interaction*. π-calculus rests upon the primitive notion of interaction via message passing, just as Turing Machines rest upon the notion of reading and writing a storage medium, and just as recursive functions and the λ-calculus rest upon mathematical functions. It is a model of the changing connectivity of *interactive systems*, where *handshaking* allows for synchronous message passing among asynchronous processes.

The ability to directly represent mobility, allowing processes to reconfigure their interconnections while they execute, makes it easy to model networked systems of mobile agents, or any other system where communication links and other resources are allocated dynamically.

π-calculus subsumes Church λ-calculus; by the Church-Turing thesis, it follows that π-calculus is at least as expressive as Turing Machines. It actually is more expressive, extending Turing Machines along all three dimensions (Sect. 3.3): *interaction* (between processes), *infinity* (of time for process computation), and *evolution* (of the communication topology). This is evidenced by the existence of computable non-algorithmic problems, as well as by Milner's own assertion that "a theory of concurrency and interaction requires a new conceptual framework" and cannot be expressed by Turing Machines [25]. Unfortunately, there is yet no definite metric for measuring the expressiveness of the π-calculus [30].

π-calculus is closely related to Hoare's CSP [20]. Both have been implemented in practice. The OCCAM programming language is based on CSP;

the PICT programming language implements an asynchronous version of the π-calculus [29].

4.3   The $-Calculus

$-calculus (pronounced "cost calculus") is a mathematical model of *interactive process-based problem solving*, capturing both the final outcome of problem solving as well as the interactive incremental process of finding the solution. $-calculus is a process algebra for *bounded rational agents*. It was introduced in the 1990s [9–11] as a formalization of resource-bounded computation, also known as *anytime algorithms*.

Anytime algorithms, proposed by Dean, Horvitz, Zilberstein and Russell in the late 1980s [21], are approximate algorithms whose solution quality increases monotonically as more resources (e.g., time or memory) are available.

Just as π-calculus was built around a central concept of *interaction*, $-calculus rests upon the primitive notion of *cost*. An example of cost is the notion of *power consumption* for *sensor network querying*. Power is consumed at a different rate for different activities of the sensor, including communication; minimization of overall power consumption drives the design query evaluation and optimization for sensor networks. $-calculus provides support for problem solving via an incremental search for solutions, using cost to direct the search.

$-calculus has the same primitives to model interaction as π-calculus, communication by message passing, and the ability to create and destroy processes and communication links. In addition, its cost mechanism permits the modeling of resource allocation, or quality-of-service optimization. $-calculus is therefore applicable to robotics, software agents, neural nets, and evolutionary computation. Potentially, it could be used for design of cost-based programming languages, cellular evolvable cost-driven hardware, DNA-based computing and molecular biology, electronic commerce, and quantum computing.

$-calculus expresses evolution naturally. Its cost performance measure models the fitness function. Additionally, $-calculus can simultaneously look for the best solution and lowest search cost. That is, it provides direct support for optimizing not only the outcome of problem solving, but the problem solving methods used to obtain the results.

It is expected that the acceptance of super-Turing computation will result in new classes of programming languages. *Cost languages*, based on the $-calculus model of computation, introduce a new programming paradigm. They are inherently parallel, highly portable, flexible, dynamic, robust, modular, with a 3D graphical interface [9]. The flexible and automatic cost optimization mechanism distinguishes them from other agent related languages. For example, costs can be modeled with probabilities or fuzzy set membership to represent uncertainty.

4.4   Other Super-Turing Models

In this section, we provide a survey of other super-Turing models of computation.

C-Machines, o-Machines and u-Machines. *Choice machines, oracle machines,* and *unorganized machines* are three super-Turing models of computation defined by Turing (Sect. 2). Choice machines and oracle machines derive their expressiveness from the *interaction* principle; unorganized machines, assuming an infinite supply of neurons, derive their expressiveness from the *infinity* and *evolution* principles.

Cellular Automata. Cellular automata (CAs) [4, 46] were introduced by John von Neumann in search of models for self-reproduction, universal computability, and universal constructibility. They consist of an infinite number of *cells*, where each cell is a finite state machine. CAs are known to be *computation universal*, referring to their ability to implement any algorithm. While CAs can simulate any Turing Machine, the reverse is not true; there exist problems solvable by CAs, but not by TMs. For example, the recognition that an infinite sequence of 9's after a decimal point, i.e., 0.9999 ... , is another representation of 1, or the problem of the universal constructibility requiring the ability to build a clone copy of the TM by the TM itself, cannot be solved by TMs. However CAs can do that [15, 46].

The greater expressive power of CAs is due to an unbounded number of cells — the *infinity* principle. Note that whereas the unbounded TM tape only holds a finite string at any one time, CAs encode an infinite string. CAs are also *construction universal*, which refers to their ability to construct arbitrary automata, including themselves (i.e., self-reproduction). Construction universality is one of the cornerstones for research in *artificial life* and *robotics*.

Site and Internet Machines. Van Leeuwen [45] introduced Site and Internet machines to capture the properties of computation that are not modeled directly by Turing Machines:

- interaction of machines (our *interaction*),
- non-uniformity of programs (our *evolution*),
- and infinity of operations (our *infinity*).

Site machines are generally interactive Turing Machines with *advice*, which is a limited (but nevertheless more powerful than TM) version of Turing's oracle. They are equipped with several input and output ports via which they communicate by sending and receiving messages. In particular, a site machine may exchange messages with the advice oracle, to obtain uncomputable advice from it.

An *Internet machine*, as its name implies, models the Internet; it consists of a finite but time-varying set of site machines that work synchronously and communicate by exchanging messages. Each machine in the set is identified by its address, and the size of the set can grow at most polynomially with time.

Van Leeuwen proves that his *Internet machine* is not more expressive than a single *site machine*; however, this proof sacrifices the dynamic nature of messages and assumes they can be precomputed. Both *site* and *Internet machines* are more powerful than TMs. This is generally due to the power of advice, which represents the uncomputable nature of the site machine's environment.

Analog Neural Networks. Neural Networks (NNs) consist of computational cells (called *nodes* or *neurons*), much like cellular automata. However, the underlying network is no longer homogeneous but an arbitrary digraph; the transition functions compute weighted sums of inputs from neighboring cells. Depending on whether they operate over discrete or real values, neural networks can be *discrete* or *analog*.

Despite having finitely many cells, analog neural networks can compute non-recursive functions. In particular, they can compute the *analog shift map*, known to be non-recursive [34]. In fact, neural networks can be a standard model for super-Turing analog computing, analogous to the role of the Turing Machine in the Church-Turing thesis:

> *No possible abstract analog device can have more computational capabilities (up to polynomial time) than first-order (i.e., the net neuron function is a weighted sum of its inputs) recurrent neural networks.* [34]

The extra power of analog NNs stems from their real-valued weights, allowing the neurons to take continuous values in their activation functions. The implementation of such a neural network can be viewed as an idealized chaotic physical system.

Evolutionary Turing Machines. By an *Evolutionary Turing Machine* (ETM) [12], we mean a (possibly infinite) series of Turing Machines, where the outcome tape from one generation forms the input tape to the next generation. In this sense ETM resembles a Persistent Turing Machine. The tape keeps both a population of solutions, and the description of an evolutionary algorithm. Both the population of solutions and the evolutionary algorithms can evolve from generation to generation. The goal (or halting) state of ETM is represented by the optimum of the fitness performance measure. The higher expressiveness of ETM is obtained either evolving infinite populations, or applying an infinite number of generations (the infinity principle), or applying variation (crossover/mutation) operators producing non-recursive solutions (the evolution principle).

Accelerating Universal Turing Machines. Another super-Turing model is the *Accelerating Universal Turing Machine* (AUTM) [7], where programs are executed at an ever-accelerating rate, permitting infinite programs to complete in finite time. AUTMs require a maximum of two time units to execute any possible program; for example, the first operation takes 1 time unit, the second 0.5 time unit, the third 0.25, and so on.

5   Towards a New Kind of Computer Science

In this section we speculate on the effect of the paradigm shift to super-Turing computation on several areas of computer science: artificial intelligence, programming languages, and computer architecture.

5.1   Super-Turing Intelligence: Interactive Extensions of the Turing Test

When Turing proposed his famous Turing Test, he raised the question: *"Can machines act intelligently?"*, which he then answered in the affirmative (Sect. 2.7). Not everyone shared Turing's optimism. Skeptics such as Penrose [28] argued that Turing Machines cannot simulate the extensional behavior of humans or physical systems, believing that computers' behavior is essentially too weak to model intelligence.

Replacing Turing Machines with interactive systems, either *sequential* or *distributed* (Sect. 3.3) in the Turing Test allows us to model stronger extensional behavior. The *interactive Turing Test* preserves Turing's behaviorist assumption that thinking is specifiable by behavior, but extends models of questioning and responding to be interactive [47,50]. Analysis of interactive question answering yields behaviorist models of "thinking" that are qualitatively stronger than the traditional, algorithmic, Turing Test model.

- **Algorithmic Turing Test**: measures ability to answer a set of unrelated *questions* from a predetermined script;
- **Sequential Turing Test**: measures ability to carry out a *dialogue* involving follow-up questions, where the answers must show adaptive history-dependent thinking;
- **Distributed Turing Test**: measures ability to carry out *projects* involving coordination and collaboration for multiple autonomous communication streams.

Algorithmic, sequential, and multi-agent thinking are progressively more powerful forms of behavioral approximation to human thinking, defined by progressively more stringent empirical tests of behavior. While we agree with Penrose's arguments [28] against the algorithmic Turing Test, we believe they no longer hold for the stronger interactive forms of the test.

The interactive Turing test extends machines without changing the form of the Turing test. Turing would certainly have accepted the interactive versions of the Turing Test as legitimate, and would have approved of the behaviorist notions of sequential and distributed thinking as conforming to the spirit of his notion of machine intelligence.

We can also consider *infinite and evolutionary* versions of the Turing Test. The first allows the testing to continue for an indefinite period of time. Like elections for the presidency in a country without term limits, the system needs to continue proving itself over and over in order to avoid failing the test. An evolutionary version is even stronger; the rules for intelligence evolve as the test progresses, and the system is expected to adapt to the new rules.

Russell and Norvig [32] propose another extension: a *total Turing Test* where the computer has the ability to move about, to perceive its surroundings, and to manipulate objects. This would free the tester from the need to interact with the system via an artificial interface, as well as allow her to test the system's ability to act within and upon its environment.

5.2   Super-Turing Architectures

The architecture for super-Turing computers has the following three requirements, reflecting the three principles of super-Turing computation (Sect. 3.3):

- **(Interaction)** Highly interactive both with the environment and other computers.
- **(Infinity)** Highly scalable — allowing use of more and more time, memory, and other resources in the computation. There should be no limit on that, i.e., computers will be closer and closer to satisfying in the limit the infinity principle.
- **(Evolution)** Highly adaptable allowing modification of both hardware and software. Evolvable hardware and software may lead in a more natural way to computers that learn rather than being programmed.

Today's computers are still based on the 50-year-old "von Neumann architecture," which was inspired by the Universal Turing Machine model. There are cosmetic changes, such as multi-level caches and pipelining, but under the hood it remains the same old model. While today's systems are somewhat interactive, they fall far short in each of these three categories.

So far, none of the attempts to build a *supercomputer* based on non-von Neumann architecture has been commercially successful. The *Fifth Generation Project* in Japan, Europe, and USA produced many ambitious non-von Neumann architecture designs, of which very few (if any) survived. Architectures attempting to eliminate the so-called *von Neumann bottleneck*, such as *reduction* and *data-flow* computers, turned out to be inefficient. *Cellular computers* had their peak with the massively parallel architectures of *Connection Machines*. Their creator, the Thinking Machine Corporation, is no longer in the business of building parallel processors. Cray Computer Corporation, another manufacturer of massively parallel architectures, has likewise declared bankruptcy. Intel and DEC have also stopped manufacturing supercomputers.

We conjecture that a single computer based on a parallel architecture is the wrong approach altogether. The emerging field of *network computing*, where many autonomous small processors (or *sensors*) form a self-configured network that acts as a single distributed computing entity, has the promise of delivering what earlier supercomputers could not. This is consistent with Turing's design of the ACE [40,41], where Turing advocated putting the whole complexity into software while keeping the hardware as simple as possible.

An evolvable and self-reconfigurable network is not a single machine, but it constitutes a single distributed computing system, which can be mobile, embedded, or environment-aware. These systems are the basis for the *ubiquitous* and *pervasive* computing applications which are expected to be the "killer apps" of the next generation. They get us closer to von Neumann's Theory of Self-Reproducing Automata [46], Turing's morphogenesis theory [44], or the total Turing Test (Sect. 2.7).

5.3 Programming Languages for Super-Turing Computers

We can identify four paradigms for programming languages, in the order of their appearance:

- procedural
- functional
- declarative (logic, constraints)
- object-oriented (sequential, asynchronous)

This classification applies to high-level languages. Very rarely is it applicable to assembly languages and machine languages, which tend to be uniformly procedural.

The object-oriented approach allows the "encapsulation" of other programming paradigms, creating hybrid o-o-procedural, o-o-functional, and o-o-declarative languages. It also provides nice support for the development of graphical user interfaces, and it is claimed to be an appropriate implementation tool for interactive parallel programming. Have we found in object-oriented programming the universal paradigm to program super-Turing computers? How should the programming languages for super-Turing computers look?

The three principles of super-Turing computation, *interaction*, *infinity*, and *evolution* (Sect. 3.3), serve as beacons in our search for an answer:

- Programming languages for super-Turing computing should be highly dynamic, to express learning and programming in rapidly changing environments and to specify highly interactive applications.
- Programs should adapt automatically to the environments and new goals.
- These languages should provide support for solving problems expressed in a declarative fashion.
- They should have built-in optimization engines for hard search problems that may arise during computation, much more powerful than the depth-first search strategy used in Prolog.
- They should be able to solve *in the limit* currently undecidable problems; that is, to obtain approximate solutions with arbitrarily high precision, or to obtain correct solutions probabilistically with arbitrarily low chance of error.

Most likely, object-orientation is here to stay, but not in its current form. When mobile embedded networked sensors are modeled as asynchronous concurrent objects, it is clear that their programming will require new primitives so interaction (communication) and mobility can be handled explicitly. Furthermore, we conjecture that constraints will play a greater role in the programming languages of the future, to enable declarative specification of desired system behavior. To translate these specifications into executable code, the languages will also have built-in dynamic search strategies and approximate solvers for undecidable problems, as discussed above. This will require new computing technologies, such as analog, optical, biological, or quantum technologies, which will be part of super-Turing architectures.

6   Rethinking the Theory of Computation

While super-Turing systems model new forms of computation, they may allow us to find new solutions for old problems. In this section we look at some aspects of theoretical computer science that will be affected by the paradigm shift to super-Turing computing. While these ideas sound rather futuristic, they would have been welcomed by Turing, who always looked beyond the horizon of the practical feasibility of the moment.

6.1   Computing the Undecidable

The *halting problem* was the first problem identified by Turing as unsolvable [38]. Thus it is typical for super-Turing models to demonstrate their higher expressiveness by the solution of the halting problem. The proofs use either interaction, infinity or evolution principles.

The first such proof was given by Alan Turing himself, who demonstrated that his o-machine can solve (non algorithmically) the halting problem, by interacting with an oracle. Later, Garzon showed how to solve the halting problem by an infinite number of discrete neurons [15]. In [11], three ways are presented for solving the halting problem in $-calculus — using either interaction, or infinity, or evolution principles.

Hava Siegelmann departed from the halting problem, and showed that real value neural networks can solve a non-recursive analog shift map [34]; this is an illustration of the infinity principle.

Note that none of these solutions of the halting problem (H) are algorithmic. In the proofs, either some steps of the solutions do not have well defined (and implementable) meaning — this is when we refer to the help or oracles — or we use infinite resources (an infinite number of steps requiring perhaps an infinite initialization time).

Also note that, while the undecidability of H led us to prove the undecidability of many other problems, its decidability does *not* have similarly wide implications. Given that H is undecidable, the proof that some other problem P is undecidable relies on an argument *by contradiction*: if P were decidable, then H would be too. However, if the original problem H turns out to be solvable (using more powerful means), it does not imply the solvability of the other problem.

6.2   Is the Church-Rosser Theorem Still Valid?

According to the Church-Turing thesis, Turing Machines are equivalent to recursive functions. The first *Church-Rosser theorem* [6] states that:

> Given a function, no matter which evaluation order of the function parameters is chosen, the result will be the same (up to renaming of bound variables) as long as the computation terminates.

The typical interpretation of this theorem is the following: if the sequence does not matter, then the evaluations can be done in parallel without worrying about the order in which they finish because the final outcome will be the same. The above is widely understood to imply that sequential programming is equivalent to parallel programming because both lead, according to the Church-Rosser theorem, to the same results.

However, we must realize that the Church-Rosser theorem is only valid for so-called "pure" functional computation without side effects. By contrast, both assignments statements from procedural languages as well as interaction by message-passing from object-oriented languages entail side effects. For languages that allow side effects, it has been assumed that an equivalent program without side effects can always be found, to ensure the applicability of the Church-Rosser theorem.

While this assumption has long been seen as overly optimistic, proving it false would be equivalent to a rejection of the Church-Turing thesis. We believe it to be false. This is evidenced by the fact that interaction is more expressive than algorithms, and that distributed interaction is more expressive than sequential interaction.

> The Church-Rosser theorem, while valid for algorithmic compu-
> tation, is not valid for super-Turing computing.

One of the most important principles of super-Turing computation is interaction, which is not side-effect-free. In fact, the side effects are crucial
for the power of interaction, such as its ability to express *emergent behavior*. For example, many scientists have pointed out that the complexity of
the behavior of an ant colony (which is a distributed interactive system) is
caused by side effects of their interaction rather than by the complexity of
ants themselves.

6.3   Rewriting Complexity Theory: Is the $P = NP$ Question Still Relevant?

The class P consists of all those algorithmic problems solved by some *deterministic* TM whose running time is polynomial in the size of the input. The
class NP can be defined in two ways — either as an analogue of P, but with
a *nondeterministic* TM, or as those algorithmic problems whose solutions, if
given to us by others, can be *verified* by some deterministic TM in polynomial
time.

The question of whether $P = NP$ has been occupying researchers since
these two sets were first defined, having become the the greatest unsolved
question of computer science. While it is simple to show that P is a subset of
NP, the other direction remains a mystery. The problems in P are considered
to be easy and tractable; those outside of P are not. Are there problems in NP
which are *not* in P? Many NP problems have been identified that appear
unlikely to be in P, but without a proof. Among them are the *Traveling
Salesman Problem* (is there a tour of all the nodes in a graph with total edge
weight $\leq k$?), SAT (does a Boolean expression have a satisfying assignment
of its variables?), and CLIQUE (does a graph have a set of k nodes with
edges between every pair?).

Donald Knuth believes that $P = NP$, and that we will eventually find
a *non-constructive* proof that the time complexity of all NP problems is
polynomial, but we will not know the degree or the coefficients of this polynomial. We conjecture that the $P = NP$ question is inherently undecidable,
that it can be neither proved nor disproved. However, the great majority of
computer scientists believe that $P \neq NP$ [16]. Most, including Jeff Ullman,
believe that it will take another hundred years to prove it, because we have
not yet invented the right techniques. But some, including Richard Karp,
think that the problem will be solved earlier, by a young researcher with
non-traditional methods, unencumbered by conventional wisdom about how
to attack the problem — something in the spirit of Alan Turing, who never
followed conventional paths.

We expect that the $P = NP$ question will lose its significance in the
context of super-Turing computation. Being able to interact with the real

world during the computation, or to access infinite resources, or to evolve, will reframe computational problems in a non-algorithmic way that shifts the focus away from the $P = NP$ question. So far, super-Turing research has concentrated on undecidable problems, but the effective means of solving traditionally intractable problems should and will be their equally important objective.

7 Conclusions

Super-Turing models extend Turing Machines to permit interactive input from the environment during computation, thereby modeling problems that cannot be modeled by Turing Machines — like driving home from work, flying airplanes, artificial intelligence, and human thinking. Driving home requires knowledge of the environment not expressible by TMs, flying planes require environmental knowledge of air currents and other airplanes, artificial intelligence requires knowledge of intelligent tasks, and human thought requires knowledge of human environments during thought. Each of these topics cannot be handled by TMs but can be handled by super-Turing models like Persistent Turing Machines or process algebras like π-calculus.

The adoption of TMs as a model of universal problem solving has raised many computational problems that can be solved by extending TMs to interactive models. AI has for many years been viewed as unsolvable because TMs could not handle certain problems that can be handled by interactive models. The Turing test, proposed by Turing as a basis for human thought, has been criticized by Searle, Penrose and others as being intractable to question answering by TMs but becomes tractable if question answering is extended to interactive systems (Sect. 5.1). The Japanese fifth-generation computing paradigm was found to be intractable because logic programming could not be expressed by TMs, but could in principle be handled by an extended form of interactive logic programming.

Algorithms express enumerable problems that can be constructed, while interaction expresses observable problems that may be non-enumerable [49]. The transition from enumerable construction to non-enumerable observation requires a mathematical change in models of problem solving that can be viewed as an elimination of traditional mathematics based on induction as a foundation of computational models. Interactive models are not mathematical in the traditional sense, but an extended model of mathematics based on coinduction could in principle provide an acceptable model [50].

Super-Turing models require a change in models of philosophy as well as of mathematics. Philosophers have widely debated the relation between rationalist models of the mind and empiricist models of experimental behavior. Aristotle's model of logic and mathematics is rationalist, while Plato's model of the cave is empiricist, requiring knowledge of the environment for problem solving. Descartes' "cogito ergo sum" is rationalist while Hume's model is empiricist, and was accepted by Kant in his book "Critique of Pure Reason" as an empiricist principle of reasoning as a form of problem solving. Hilbert and Russell's models of mathematics are rationalist, while Gödel and Turing's proof of unsolvability of the Entscheidungsproblem is empiricist. Mathematical acceptance of Turing Machines as a universal model for all computation can be viewed as a rationalist transformation of Turing's empiricist model. Interaction is an empiricist model of computation consistent with Gödel and Turing's original models and with the need of future computer models. The importance of interaction as a model of computation corresponds to the importance of empiricism over rationalism as a principle of philosophy.

Robin Milner has asserted [26] that Turing would have been excited by the direction in which computing has evolved; we agree. In particular, we believe that Alan Turing would approve of super-Turing models, and he would be the first to argue that they, rather than the Turing Machine, represent the future of computing.

We expect super-Turing computation to become a central paradigm of computer science. However, we cannot claim that super-Turing models, as described in this chapter, are definitive and complete. Most likely, they will be superseded in the future by models that are even better and more complete for problem solving, in the never ending quest for a better description of reality.

References

1. Bäck T., Fogel D. B., Michalewicz Z. (eds.), *Handbook of Evolutionary Computation*, Oxford University Press, 1997.
2. "Algorithm." *Encyclopedia Britannica 2003* Encyclopedia Britannica Premium Service. http://www.britannica.com/eb/article?eu=5785.
3. Brooks R. A., Elephants Don't Play Chess, in P. Maes (ed.), *Designing Autonomous Agents: Theory and Practice from Biology to Engineering and Back*, The MIT Press, 1994, pp. 3–15.
4. Burks A., *Essays on Cellular Automata*, Univ. of Illinois Press, 1970.
5. Church A., An Unsolvable Problem of Elementary Number Theory, *American Journal of Mathematics*, 58:345–363, 1936.
6. Church A., Rosser J. B., Some properties of conversion, *Transactions of the AMS*, 39:472–482, 1936.
7. Copeland B. J., Super-Turing Machines, *Complexity*, 4(1):30–32, 1998.
8. Davis M., Why Gödel Didn't Have Church's Thesis, *Information & Control*, 54:3–24, 1982.
9. Eberbach E., Brooks R., Phoha S., Flexible Optimization and Evolution of Underwater Autonomous Agents, LNAI 1711, Springer-Verlag, Berlin Heidelberg New York, 1999, pp. 519–527.
10. Eberbach E., $-Calculus Bounded Rationality = Process Algebra + Anytime Algorithms, in: (ed. J. C. Misra) Applicable Mathematics: Its Perspectives and Challenges, Narosa Publishing House, New Delhi, Mumbai, Calcutta, 2001, pp. 213–220.

11. Eberbach E., Is Entscheidungsproblem Solvable? Beyond Undecidability of Turing Machines and Its Consequence for Computer Science and Mathematics, in: (ed. J. C. Misra) Computational Mathematics, Modelling and Algorithms, Narosa Publishing House, New Delhi, Chap. 1, 2003, pp. 1–32.

12. Eberbach E., On Expressiveness of Evolutionary Computation: Is EC Algorithmic?, *Proc. 2002 World Congress on Computational Intelligence* (WCCI), Honolulu, HI, 2002, pp. 564–569.

13. Farley B. G., Clark W. A., Simulation of self-organizing systems by digital computer, *IRE Transactions on Information Theory*, 4:76–84, 1954.

14. Fogel D. B. (ed.), *Evolutionary Computation: The Fossil Record*, IEEE Press, NY, 1998.

15. Garzon M., Models of Massive Parallelism: Analysis of Cellular Automata and Neural Networks, An EATCS series, Springer-Verlag, Berlin Heidelberg New York, 1995.

16. Gasarch W., Guest Column: The P=?NP Poll, *SIGACT News*, 33(2):34–47, June 2002.

17. Gödel K., Über formal unentscheidbare Sätze der Principia Mathematica und verwandter Systeme, *Monatshefte für Mathematik und Physik*, 38:173–198, 1931.

18. Goldin D., Persistent Turing Machines as a Model of Interactive Computation, FoIKS'00, Cottbus, Germany, 2000.

19. Goldin D., Smolka S., Wegner P., Turing Machines, Transition Systems, and Interaction, *proc. 8th Int'l Workshop on Expressiveness in Concurrency*, Aalborg, Denmark, August 2001

20. Hoare C. A. R., *Communicating Sequential Processes*, Prentice-Hall, 1985.

21. Horvitz E., Zilberstein S. (eds.), Computational Tradeoffs under Bounded Resources, *Artificial Intelligence*, 126:1–196, 2001.

22. McCulloch W., Pitts W, A Logical Calculus of the Ideas Immanent in Nervous Activity, *Bulletin of Mathematical Biophysics*, 5:115–133, 1943.

23. Milner R., A Calculus of Communicating Systems, *Lecture Notes in Computer Science*, 94, Springer-Verlag, Berlin Heidelberg New York, 1980.

24. Milner R., Parrow J., Walker D., A Calculus of Mobile Processes, I & II, *Information and Computation*, 100:1–77, 1992.

25. Milner R., Elements of Interaction, *Communications of the ACM*, 36(1):78–89, January 1993.

26. Milner R., *Turing, Computing and Communication*, a lecture for the 60th anniversary of Turing's "Entscheidungsproblem" paper, King's College, Cambridge England, 1997.

27. Minsky M. L., Theory of Neural-Analog Reinforcement Systems and Its Applications to the Brain-Model Problem, Ph.D. Thesis, Princeton University, 1954.

28. Penrose R., *The Emperor's New Mind*, Oxford, 1989.

29. Pierce B., Turner D., Pict: A Programming Language Based on the Pi-Calculus, in: Plotkin G. et al (eds.), *Proof, Language, and Interaction: Essays in Honour of Robin Milner*, The MIT Press, 2000, pp. 455–494.

30. Plotkin G., Stirling C., Tofte M. (eds.), *Proof, Language, and Interaction: Essays in Honour of Robin Milner*, The MIT Press, 2000.

31. Rosenblatt F., The Perceptron: A Probabilistic Model for Information Storage and Organization in the Brain, *Psychological Review*, 65:386–408, 1958.

32. Russell S., Norvig P., *Artificial Intelligence: A Modern Approach*, 2nd edition, Prentice-Hall, 2003.

33. Samuel A. L., Some studies in machine learning using the game of checkers, *IBM Journal of Research and Development*, 3:211–229, 1959.

34. Siegelmann H., *Neural Networks and Analog Computation: Beyond the Turing Limit*, Birkhauser, 1999.

35. Simon, H. A. *The Sciences of the Artificial*. MIT Press, 1969.

36. Sipser, M. *Introduction to the Theory of Computation*, PWS Publishing Company, 1997.

37. Teuscher C., *Turing's Connectionism: An Investigation of Neural Network Architectures*, Springer-Verlag, London, 2002.

38. Turing A., On computable numbers, with an application to the Entscheidungsproblem. *Proceedings of the London Mathematical Society*, series 2, 42:230–265, 1936–37.

39. Turing A., Systems of Logic based on Ordinals, *Proceedings of the London Mathematical Society*, series 2, 45:161–228, 1939.

40. Turing A., The ACE Report, in *A. M. Turing's Ace Report of 1946 and Other Papers*, eds. B. E. Carpenter and R. W. Doran, MIT Press, 1986.

41. Turing A., Lecture to the London Math. Society on 20'th February 1947, in *A. M. Turing's Ace Report of 1946 and Other Papers*, eds. B. E. Carpenter and R. W. Doran, MIT Press, 1986.

42. Turing A., Intelligent Machinery, 1948; in *Collected Works of A. M. Turing: Mechanical Intelligence*, ed. D. C. Ince, Elsevier Science, 1992.

43. Turing A., Computing Machinery and Intelligence, *Mind*, 59(236):433–460, 1950.

44. Turing A., The Chemical Basis of Morphogenesis, *Philosophical Transactions of the Royal Society of London*, B 237:37–72, 1952.

45. Van Leeuwen J., Wiedermann J., The Turing Machine Paradigm in Contemporary Computing, in. B. Enquist and W. Schmidt (eds.) *Mathematics Unlimited — 2001 and Beyond*, LNCS, Springer-Verlag, Berlin Heidelberg New York, 2000.

46. Von Neumann J., Theory of Self-Reproducing Automata, (edited and completed by Burks A. W.), Univ. of Illinois Press, 1966.

47. Wegner P., Why Interaction is More Powerful Than Algorithms, *Communications of the ACM*, 40(5):81–91, 1997.

48. Wegner P., Interactive Foundations of Computing, *Theoretical Computer Science*, 192:315–351, 1998.

49. Wegner P., Goldin D., Coinductive Models of Finite Computing Agents, Workshop on Coinductive Methods in Computer Science, Electronic Notes in Theoretical Computer Science, Amsterdam, March 1999.

50. Wegner P., Goldin D., Interaction as a Framework for Modeling, LNCS 1565, April 1999.

51. Wegner P., Goldin D., Computation Beyond Turing Machines, *Communications of the ACM*, April 2003.

The Myth of Hypercomputation

Martin Davis

Professor Emeritus, Courant Institute, NY University,
Visiting Scholar, Mathematics Department, University of California, Berkeley

Summary. Under the banner of "hypercomputation" various claims are being made for the feasibility of modes of computation that go beyond what is permitted by Turing computability. In this article it will be shown that such claims fly in the face of the inability of all currently accepted physical theories to deal with infinite-precision real numbers. When the claims are viewed critically, it is seen that they amount to little more than the obvious comment that if non-computable inputs are permitted, then non-computable outputs are attainable.

1 The Impossible as a Challenge

> *Why, sometimes I've believed as many as six impossible things before breakfast.* — Lewis Carroll

Despite the fact that it has been known for over a century that it is impossible to devise a construction for dividing a given angle into three equal parts using only straight-edge and compass, hopeful amateurs continue to bring forth constructions that purport to do exactly that. It is as though the word "impossible" is seen as a challenge. Although the laws of thermodynamics have made it plain that the search for a perpetual motion machine is an exercise in futility, inventors claiming to have constructed such a device still besiege patent offices and manage to obtain financial support from gullible investors [16].

Over the centuries, mathematicians had often found solutions to problems in the form of procedures that could be carried out in a step-by-step fashion, where each step was entirely mechanical, capable of being carried without any creative thought; such procedures are called *algorithms*.[1] During the

---

[1] The word "algorithm" is derived from the twelfth century Arabic mathematician al-Khwarizmi. Originally used to refer to the rules for calculating with the "Arabic" numerals we use today (originating in India), the word gradually came to refer to any mechanical procedure. In particular, the procedure due to Euclid for finding the greatest common divisor of two integers by successive division has been called the "Euclidean algorithm" at least since the nineteenth century. Going further back one can find the word (or its variant "algorism") in the work of Fibonacci, Leibniz (cf. [19]), and Euler. Today every serious university computer science department offers courses in the design and analysis of algorithms.

1930s, as a result of the work of a number of logicians, it became possible to explain with full precision what it means to say for some given problem that an algorithm exists providing a solution to that problem. Moreover it then became feasible to prove that for certain problems no such algorithm exists, that it is *impossible* to specify an algorithm that provides a solution to those problems. Because the computing machines that became available beginning in the 1950s were, in an important sense, physical realizations of the idealized computational models that had been developed by the logicians, it was generally held that it is impossible to construct a physical device capable of solving these "unsolvable problems." However in recent years a number of researchers, marching under the banner of "hypercomputation," unwilling to accept as fact this impossibility, have been making proposals to overcome this barrier. In assessing their claims, it will be important to be clear about the relation between the abstract mathematical theory of computability and modern computing machinery. A crucial and often ignored aspect of this relation is that while the abstract theory is involved essentially with the mathematical infinite, physical computers are necessarily finite objects.

2   Algorithms and Infinity

It is a fact of life that we are finite beings and that our calculations are carried out on data that is not only finite, but is sufficiently limited in extent to fit in the space available in such media as sheets of paper or computer disks. Nevertheless, it has turned out that the appropriate way to formulate algorithms is as though they are intended to apply to initial data of arbitrary size. We can see this even in the simple algorithm for adding two numbers that we all learned as children:

$$
\begin{array}{r}
15 \\
+17 \\
\hline
32
\end{array}
\qquad\qquad
\begin{array}{r}
3456789234568921 \\
+8732198623456521 \\
\hline
12188987858025442
\end{array}
$$

The same algorithm applies in these two cases although the numbers being added are of very different size. In fact it is clear that the same algorithm will work regardless of the size of the addends. One can imagine applying it to numbers so large that, written out, they would stretch from one end of our galaxy to the other! Almost all known algorithms have this same property: although intended to deal only with finite initial data, and always yielding finite results, they will behave correctly regardless of the size of the data. In fact one of the principal measures of the complexity of a given algorithm is based on its "asymptotic" behavior — that is, its behavior as the size of the initial data increases without limit.[2]

---

[2] For example, the complexity of algorithms designed to *sort* data into numerical or alphabetic order is usually measured in terms of the number of comparisons

The use of the word "mechanical" in explaining what an algorithm is suggests a machine, and indeed adding machines that may be said to *implement* the addition algorithm exhibited above were once a commonplace. But it is worth noting that unlike the abstract algorithm that countenances no limitation on the size of the numbers being added, a machine implementing this algorithm, being a finite physical object, is constrained to accept only numbers smaller than some definite amount.

Over the centuries, many algorithms have been developed to solve various problems, but until the 1930s mathematicians had no way to prove that for certain problems an algorithmic solution is impossible. This option only became available with the work of the logicians Gödel, Church, Post, and especially Turing who provided precise characterizations of algorithmic solvability [7]. As Robin Gandy explained:

> Both Church and Turing had in mind calculation by an abstract human being using some mechanical aids (such as paper and pencil). The word "abstract" indicates that the argument makes no appeal to the existence of practical limits on time and space. [14]

Although the various characterizations were superficially different, it turned out that they were equivalent to one another. The assertion that these equivalent notions provide a precise explication of the previously unanalyzed intuitive concept of algorithmic solvability has come to be called *Church's Thesis* or *The Church-Turing Thesis*. Making use of this work a considerable number of problems have been proved to be unsolvable — in the sense that no algorithmic solution for them is possible. In Turing's own classical paper [20] he proved the unsolvability in this sense of a problem in mathematical logic known as the Entscheidungsproblem.[3]

Turing introduced the term *computable* for his characterization of algorithmic solvability which he developed by imagining a human being carrying out a computation, and, by removing, one after another, successive layers of irrelevant complication, arriving at his celebrated notion of what has come to be called a *Turing machine*. These "machines" are mathematical abstractions that do not, and cannot, exist in the physical world. Turing machines accommodate inputs of arbitrary size on an infinite linear "tape" ruled into individual cells on each of which a symbol can be written. At any instant the machine is in one of a finite number of "states," and is "scanning" one of these cells. The tape contents is modified step-by-step by the moves of

---

required as a function of the number of items being sorted. Thus the crudest algorithms for sorting n items require a number of comparisons proportional to n^2, whereas more sophisticated algorithms manage with a number proportional to $n \log n$. For large n, this latter number is much smaller.

[3] The Entscheidunsproblem is, in effect, the problem of providing a general algorithm to determine whether some conclusion can be logically inferred from a given finite set of premises using the rules of classical logic; it should be mentioned that Church had also proved this problem to be unsolvable.

the machine. These moves consist of changing the symbol on the currently scanned cell, causing the scanned cell to be the one either to the immediate right or to the immediate left of this cell, and finally entering a new state. The precise action depends only on the symbol in the scanned cell and the machine's current state. Turing, in effect, held that any algorithmic process is equivalent to what some appropriate Turing machine can accomplish if an appropriate input string of symbols is placed on its tape.[4] A first example of an algorithmically unsolvable problem, the so-called halting problem, was then readily obtainable. One form of this result is: *There is no algorithm which will determine for a given Turing machine whether it will ever halt when started with a completely blank tape.*[5]

Although Turing had been led to think along these lines by his desire to show that the Entscheidungsproblem is unsolvable, he went on to obtain an additional result of great importance. He realized that it is possible to design a single "universal" Turing machine, which all by itself could do the work of any other Turing machine. Here's the idea: imagine placing on the tape of a Turing machine a symbolic representation or "code" for some arbitrary Turing machine $\mathcal{M}$ and in addition, an input to $\mathcal{M}$ as in the diagram below.

| Code of Turing machine $\mathcal{M}$ | Input to $\mathcal{M}$ |

The universal machine would then do exactly what $\mathcal{M}$ would have done if presented with that same input. Turing wrote out in full the tables showing the moves of his universal machine.[6] That such a single Turing machine could execute, as it were, any algorithm whatever pointed the way to building a genuine physical machine that would be all-purpose in this same way, subject only to limitations of space and time. The universal machine opened other vistas to be realized in practice only much later. As I wrote [10, 11]:

> Before Turing the ... supposition was that ... the three categories, machine, program, and data, were entirely separate entities. The machine was a physical object ... hardware. The program was the plan for doing a computation ... The data was the numerical input. Turing's universal machine showed that the distinctness of these

---

[4] It is an unimportant detail that Turing's paper was mainly written in terms of algorithms for computing the successive 0s and 1s in the binary expansion of a real number.

[5] An unimportant technical detail: I assume a tape infinite in both directions as in my [6]. If, as with Turing, the tape is infinite in only one direction, one should specify in addition that the initial scanned cell is the one at the end of the tape.

[6] It is worth noting that given confidence in the success of Turing machines in capturing the concept of algorithmic solvability, the existence of such a universal machine is inevitable. This is because it is easy to provide an algorithm that using the table defining any given Turing machine $\mathcal{M}$ will step-by-step perform exactly like $\mathcal{M}$. Thus, if one believes that any algorithm can be carried out by a Turing machine, that would have to be the case for this algorithm as well.

three categories is an illusion. A Turing machine is initially envisioned as a machine ... , *hardware*. But its code ... functions as a *program*, detailing the instructions to the universal machine ... Finally, the universal machine in its step-by-step actions sees the ... machine code as just more *data* to be worked on. This fluidity ... is fundamental to contemporary computer practice. A *program* ... is *data* to the ... compiler.

3   Turing Machines, the Church-Turing Thesis, and Modern Computers

Although no, necessarily finite, physical device can emulate a true universal Turing machine with its infinite tape and ability to deal with arbitrarily large data, the existence, even as a mathematical abstraction, of Turing's universal "machine," brought into focus the goal of building a machine that could usefully approximate universality. In effect such a machine would "implement" Turing's universal machine in much the same way that an adding machine implements the simple addition algorithm displayed above.[7] The myriad tasks that the computers on our desktops routinely accomplish attest to the great success in achieving that goal. But it was by no means clear ab initio that an all-purpose machine could be built that could do useful work. In the years just after the second world war, Turing and von Neumann each produced plans for such a machine. Before anything was actually built, von Neumann wrote a sophisticated sorting program for the EDVAC (a proposed computer to be built at the University of Pennsylvania) to see whether a machine designed principally for heavy-duty number crunching could also handle such an essentially logical task. Having succeeded, he stated with satisfaction that the machine was acceptably "all-purpose." A year later, in 1946, writing with Arthur Burks and Herman Goldstine, von Neumann commented on the relationship between Turing's abstract universal machine and the practical problem of designing a useful all-purpose computer:

> It is easy to see by formal-logical methods that there exist codes that are in abstracto adequate to control and cause the execution of any sequence of operations which are individually available in the machine and which are, in their entirety, conceivable by the problem planner. The really decisive considerations from the present point of view, in selecting a code, are of a more practical nature: simplicity of

---

[7] Of course, modern computers are not literally implementations of Turing's universal computer. The stripped-down design of a Turing machine is excellent for theoretical purposes, but would never do for practical computing. But of course it is not difficult to write programs to run on modern computers that simulate Turing machines. For example, see `http://alexvn.freeservers.com/s1/turing.html`.

the equipment demanded by the code, and the clarity of its application to the actually important problems together with the speed of its handling those problems.[8]

Nevertheless, there is no doubt that, from the beginning the logicians developing the theoretical foundations of computing were thinking also in terms of physical mechanism. Thus, as early as 1937, Alonzo Church reviewing Turing's classic paper wrote:

> [Turing] proposes as a criterion that an infinite sequence of digits 0 and 1 be "computable" that it shall be possible to devise a computing machine, occupying a finite space and with working parts of finite size, which will write down the sequence to any desired number of terms if allowed to run for a sufficiently long time. As a matter of convenience, certain further restrictions are imposed on the character of the machine, but these are of such a nature as obviously to cause no loss of generality ... [2]

Turing himself speaking to the London Mathematical Society in 1947 said:

> Some years ago I was researching what now may be described as an investigation of the theoretical possibilities and limitations of digital computing machines. I considered a type of machine which had a central mechanism, and an infinite memory which was contained on an infinite tape. This type of machine seemed to be sufficiently general. One of my conclusions was that the idea of "rule of thumb" process and "machine process" were synonymous.

Referring to the machine he had designed for the British National Physics Laboratory, Turing went on to say:

> Machines such as the ACE (Automatic Computing Engine) may be regarded as practical versions of this same type of machine. [22]

4   Hava Siegelmann Ventures "Beyond the Turing Limit"

It is natural to seek and investigate models of computation suggested by the nervous systems, and especially the brains, of human beings and other animals. The brain presents itself as an extremely complicated network of intricately interconnected cells called neurons. Since the 1940s, investigators have been studying mathematical structures consisting of networks of neuron-like elements. The 1980s saw a resurgence of interest in this area after some

---

[8] See [9] for references and further discussion.

years of neglect, with the hope that artificial networks of this kind, so-called neural nets, might lead to better understanding of our own brains.[9]

In 1995 an article by Hava Siegelmann appeared in *Science*, the entirely respectable journal of the American Association for the Advancement of Science, entitled "Computation beyond the Turing Limit" [17]. Presenting her own perfectly reasonable version of a neural net, she claimed that her nets could indeed achieve what had been thought to be impossible: among the things that they could compute were some that had been proved to be not Turing computable. A few years later she published a monograph [18] in which she studied her neural nets in some detail. Again the same claim was showcased: the book is subtitled "Beyond the Turing Limit." Shall we conclude that Siegelmann is indeed a pioneer of hypercomputation? Actually, as we shall see, there is much less to her claim than meets the eye.

Fortunately, to understand what is involved, it is not necessary to deal with the full technical definition of Siegelmann's neural nets. But it is necessary to understand what mathematicians mean when they speak of *real numbers*. In fact the crucial thing for our purposes is that each of Siegelmann's nets is associated with a finite number of real numbers called *weights*.[10] Among the data objects in which she frames her discussion are the so-called *languages* on an alphabet of two symbols, which we may conveniently take to be $\{a, b\}$. By such a "language" all that is meant is some set, finite or infinite, of strings of these two letters. For example, the language $\{ab, abb, abbb, abbbb, \dots\}$ is the collection of all strings consisting of the letter a followed by some number of bs. To say that such a language is *computable* is just to say that there exists a Turing machine which, when a particular string on the alphabet $\{a, b\}$ is placed on its tape initially, will eventually halt and will reveal by what is then written on the tape, whether or not the given string belonged to the language in question. Siegelmann defines precisely what it means to say that such a language is *recognized* by one of her nets.

Siegelmann begins by restricting the numbers that are permitted to serve as weights, first to integers, and then to rational numbers.[11] She proves that when her weights are restricted to be rational numbers the languages recognized are precisely the computable languages. Next she considers what happens when arbitrary real numbers are permitted as weights. Lo and behold!

---

[9] The monograph [18] has an extensive bibliography of this field. The paper [15] suggests that these so-called "connectionist" models are unlikely to provide much speed-up compared to conventional computers.

[10] They are called weights because they participate in a weighted average that determines each successive step in the evolution of a neural net.

[11] A rational number is one like $7/11$ that can be written as a fraction with integers as numerator and denominator. Rational numbers are also characterized by the fact that their decimal expansions either consist of only a finite number of digits, or eventually begin repeating the same pattern over and over again. This is by contrast with irrational numbers like $\sqrt{2}$ or π.

For every language, there is now one of Siegelmann's nets that recognizes it! To understand why this is less remarkable than it may appear to be, it is necessary to understand the computational relationship between real numbers and languages on our two-letter alphabet. *A computationally transparent encoding can be used to represent each of these languages by a corresponding real number.* Here's how. First, by arranging all strings on the alphabet $\{a, b\}$ in alphabetic order, we obtain the following coding that enables us to represent each such language as a set of positive integers:[12]

$$a \ b \ aa \ ab \ ba \ bb \ aaa \ aab \ aba \ abb \ baa \ bab \ bba \ bbb \ \ldots$$
$$\updownarrow \updownarrow \updownarrow \updownarrow \updownarrow \updownarrow \updownarrow \ \ \updownarrow \ \ \updownarrow \ \ \updownarrow \ \ \updownarrow \ \ \updownarrow \ \ \updownarrow \ \ \updownarrow \ \ \cdots$$
$$1 \ 2 \ 3 \ 4 \ 5 \ 6 \ 7 \ \ \ 8 \ \ \ 9 \ \ \ 10 \ \ 11 \ \ 12 \ \ 13 \ \ 14 \ \ldots$$

Finally any given set S of positive integers can be coded by the following real number written as an infinite decimal

$$0, c_1 c_2 c_3 c_4 \ldots$$

where

$$c_n = \begin{cases} 4 \text{ if } n \in S \\ 5 \text{ otherwise.} \end{cases}$$

Let us see how this works out with an example. We begin with the language $\{a, ab, abb, abbb, \ldots\}$ consisting of the strings with an initial a followed by a block of bs. The corresponding integers are $\{1, 4, 10, 22, \ldots\}$.[13] So the real number that encodes this language is $0,45545555545555555555545 \ldots$ [14] Although this number is irrational (because there is no repeating pattern), it is computable. Siegelmann doesn't consider what happens when all the weights in one of her nets are computable, but her proof that nets with rational weights recognize only computable languages readily extends to nets with computable weights. It's worth noting (as Turing already did in his classic [20]) that all the standard real numbers of mathematical analysis, including π, e, zeros of Bessel functions, etc. are computable. And *the only way Siegelmann's nets can hope to recognize a non-computable language is to use non-computable weights.* The neural nets can only go "beyond the Turing limit" if they are provided with weights that are already not computable!

---

[12] Although it is not necessary for understanding the encoding, readers may be interested to know that the string corresponding to a given integer in this listing is a kind of binary representation of the integer in which a represents 1 and b represents 2. So, for example, the string aba is associated with the number $1 \cdot 2^2 + 2 \cdot 2^1 + 1 \cdot 2^0 = 9$.

[13] The nth number in this sequence is $1 + 3n(n-1)/2$.

[14] The comma is used in Europe for the decimal point; in the U.S. and Britain it's a period. Obviously there's nothing special about the digits 4 and 5; their use is just a matter of convenience.

Siegelmann is perfectly aware that languages can be coded by real numbers. In fact, her proof that when arbitrary real weights are permitted every language can be recognized works precisely by coding the desired language into a weight.[15] And she says in so many words, " ... systems with infinitely precise constants cannot be built." Since the non-computability that Siegelmann gets from her neural nets is nothing more than the non-computability she has built into them, it is difficult to see in what sense she can claim to have gone "beyond the Turing limit."

For someone familiar with computability theory (also called recursion theory), it is clear that the language recognized by such a neural net is simply a computable function of the real weights. The well-developed theory of degrees of unsolvability makes it possible to classify such languages in various ways, depending on the degrees of unsolvability of the particular real weights used.[16] Siegelmann seems not to know (or not to care) about such fine distinctions. She observes that with rational weights, it is the computable languages that are recognized and that with arbitrary real weights all languages are recognized, and seems uninterested in the fact that between the rationals and arbitrary reals lie a complex taxonomy of subsets of the real numbers with a corresponding variety of resulting languages recognized when the weights are restricted to one of these subsets.

Siegelmann's only attempt in her monograph to connect neural nets with arbitrary real weights to the actual physical world is the following curious paragraph:

> In nature, the fact that the constants are not known to us, or cannot even be measured, is irrelevant for the true evolution of the system. For example, the planets revolve according to the exact values of G, π, and their masses.[17]

This statement presumably is referring to Newton's law of gravitation in which the force of attraction between two bodies is given by the formula

$$F = G\frac{m_1 m_2}{d^2}$$

where m_1, m_2 are the masses of the two bodies and d is the distance separating them. It is hard to know where to begin in criticizing this view of

---

[15] The particular coding scheme she uses is different from the one we used above, but that is of no significance.

[16] For example, one may use as a weight a real number that encodes the halting problem for Turing machines. If this is done, it can be proved that the languages recognized will be precisely those for which a Turing machine can be designed that provided with a string as input, will never halt, but will reach a final stable configuration that will reveal whether or not that string belongs to the given language. (However, an observer would in general have no way to know, at any point, whether that final configuration had actually been attained.)

[17] [18] p. 59.

"nature." Ignoring the fact that Newtonian gravitation has been superseded by Einstein's General Theory of Relativity, we have to wonder what could possibly be meant by the "exact value" of the mass of a planet whose changing boundary is necessarily vague, and why Dr. Siegelmann imagines that (presumably in appropriate units) it is represented by an infinite precision (and uncomputable?) real number. In addition, if one were to propose measuring gravitational forces in the solar system to, say, 50 significant digits, one would have to take account of the masses of "nearby" stars.

The hope that physical theory will somehow lead to a non-computable real number appears to underlie much of the hypercomputation movement. More will be said about this later. But it may be worth noting that, if anything, physical science seems to be moving in the opposite direction. Chemists in the nineteenth century devoted much energy to computing the atomic weights of the elements to greater and greater precision. However, it has turned out that the atoms of which one of these elements consist typically come in a variety of "isotopes" each of which has a weight given by an *integer* number of protons and neutrons. What the chemists were measuring was an artifact of the proportion in which the different isotopes of a given element happen to occur in nature.

5   Turing's O-Machines

Jack Copeland with his collaborator Diane Proudfoot has been an enthusiastic proponent of "hypercomputation"; indeed he is the person who baptized the movement with this name [3–5]. Copeland has based himself largely on a concept from Alan Turing's doctoral dissertation at Princeton University. It was on discovering that Alonzo Church in Princeton had found results similar to his own that the young Turing decided to spend some time in Princeton. Mainly for bureaucratic reasons, it seemed best that he enroll as a graduate student at the university. With Church as his advisor, Turing completed a doctoral dissertation that turned out to be an important and influential piece of work [21].

Gödel had made the somewhat paradoxical discovery that not only would every formal logical system (satisfying a few simple requirements) give rise to a proposition U about the natural numbers that cannot be decided within that system, but also, this very proposition U could be seen to be true from a perspective external to the system. A strengthened system in which U is provable can be obtained by simply adjoining U as a new axiom. But this new formal logical system will have its own undecidable proposition, and the whole process can be carried out over and over again. This leads naturally to the idea of progressions of stronger and stronger formal logical systems in which true propositions undecidable at a given place in the progression become provable in subsequent systems. The study of such progressions was the topic of Turing's dissertation.

Turing's 68 page paper contains a number of interesting digressions, and it is one of these that Copeland has enlisted in his cause. Turing introduced what he called "O-machines"; these were to be like the machines from his classic paper on computability, equipped with a linear tape and moving one square at a time, but with one significant difference. These new machines were to be provided access to the correct answers to problems known to be unsolvable, in particular to a kind of problem Turing called "number-theoretic."[18] As Turing put it:

> Let us suppose that we are supplied with some unspecified means of solving number-theoretic problems; a kind of oracle as it were. We shall not go any further into the nature of this oracle apart from saying that it cannot be a machine.

Turing introduced these O-machines to solve a technical problem, specifically to produce an example of a problem that is *not* number-theoretic. He did this by carrying out for O-machines the same proof that in his classic paper on computability led to unsolvable problems. This was accomplished in one page, and except for a few sentences in a later part of the paper, was the only mention of O-machines in the entire 68 page paper.

It is perfectly plain in the context of Turing's dissertation, that O-machines were introduced simply to solve a specific technical problem about definability of sets of natural numbers. There is not the faintest hint that Turing was making a proposal about a machine to be built. In fact in 1938 when he was writing his dissertation, it required remarkable vision to see in his abstract universal machine, the prospect of actual all-purpose computers that could (subject to limitations of space and time) compute whatever is computable. It makes no sense to imagine that he was thinking about actual machines to compute the uncomputable. Turing advisedly used the term "oracle," a word redolent of the supernatural, as though to underline the purely abstract nature of his conception. Yet Copeland and Proudfoot, referring to O-machines insist that "Even among experts, Turing's pioneering theoretical concept of a hypermachine has largely been forgotten." This cooption of Turing to the fold of hypercomputation on the basis of these O-machines is without the slightest justification. The plain fact is that if one truly had an "oracle" that provided answers for an unsolvable problem, that, for example, specified for any given Turing machine whether or not it would eventually halt, then of course we could solve unsolvable

---

[18] What Turing called "number-theoretic" were problems of the form "Does n belong to S?" where n is a natural number and S is a set that can be defined as consisting of those numbers n for which an equation $f(n, x) = 0$, with f a computable function, has infinitely many solutions in natural numbers x. Equivalently, these are the sets that can be defined as consisting of those n such that $(\forall x)(\exists y)[g(n, x, y) = 0]$ where g is computable. Today, such sets are called Π_2^0 sets, and they are seen as part of a hierarchy determined by the number and arrangement of the "quantifiers" $\forall$, $\exists$.

problems. As with Siegelmann's nets, of course, if you imagine yourself provided with a solver of an unsolvable problem, you could solve unsolvable problems, that very one, for starters. One didn't need Turing to tell us that.

But Turing did show us how to make precise the notion of one problem being computable *relative* to a second: imagine solutions to that second problem provided by an "oracle" and study just what problems now become "solvable" with its aid. This idea gave rise to the fruitful study of what are called degrees of unsolvability or (in homage to Turing's dissertation) Turing degrees. These degrees have an intricate structure that researchers have spent decades uncovering. The notion of oracle has also played an important role in the theory of computational complexity, where it is not a question of computing the uncomputable, but rather of finding a scale for measuring the relative complexity of algorithms needed to solve different problems. So far from the truth is it that this work of Turing's "has largely been forgotten."

Copeland and Proudfoot have also been tempted by Siegelmann's infinite precision real numbers. Noting that the halting problem can be encoded by a real number (along the lines suggested above), they propose, as a possible "oracle," a physical device that makes the successive digits of the decimal representation of this number available. Without a clue as to what sort of physical device could actually serve in this connection, they visualize a capacitor that would hold this number in the form of electric charge. Although they are evidently not seriously proposing any such thing, the example serves to underline one of the pitfalls in attempting to make an infinite precision real number physically available: according to well established physical theory, electric charge in a capacitor consists of a difference in the number of free electrons present in its two plates. Since all electrons have the same charge, the Copeland-Proudfoot infinite precision real number is actually an integer![19] Of course, there's not much point in harping on what was just meant as an illustrative example, but it does serve to remind us that twentieth century physics has tended to see physical quantities as made up of discrete units.

Of course physical theory is in constant flux. Can we really utterly exclude the possibility of some new development leading to a physical realization of an uncomputable quantity? Of course not. In 1958 I wrote:

> For how can we ever exclude the possibility of our being presented, some day (perhaps by some extraterrestrial visitor) with a ... device or "oracle" that "computes" a non-computable function?[20]

For that matter can we really and definitively rule out perpetual motion machines? Isn't it possible that some future development in physical theory

---

[19] I'm indebted to Andrew Hodges for reminding me of this fact.

[20] See [6], p. 11. In view of the Copeland-Proudfoot suggestion that Turing's O-machines had been forgotten, it may not be amiss to mention that this book (which has been called a "classic") remains in print, and that Turing machines with oracle are treated in its first chapter.

will give us access to unlimited energy from some other universe? Well, one would have to say, "Possible but most unlikely." However that may be, such a development will not be the result of someone tinkering in a garage. It could only happen as the result of a revolutionary transformation of physical theory. One would surely look askance at philosophers proclaiming that "the search is on" for a perpetual motion machine. Yet Copeland-Proudfoot use those very words referring to the quest for an oracle.

Until now, all physical theory has been content with predictions that can be verified to within less than, say, 50 significant digits. A physical theory leading to uncomputable quantities is certainly not out of the question. But such a revolutionary development will not come from exhortations assuring us that "the search is on"; if at all, it could only arise from the work of theoretical physicists seeking, not an "oracle," but deeper understanding of the universe. Moreover, even if such uncomputable physics were to be developed, making use of it for computational purposes would hardly be automatic. As Dana Scott has remarked:

> 70 years of research on Turing degrees has shown the structure to be extremely complicated. In other words, the hierarchy of oracles is worse than any political system. No one oracle is all powerful.
>
> Suppose some quantum genius gave you an oracle as a black box. No finite amount of observation would tell you what it does and why it is non-recursive. Hence, there would be no way to write an algorithm to solve an understandable problem you couldn't solve before! Interpretation of oracular statements is a very fine art — as they found out at Delphi![21]

Consider what would be involved in harnessing a putative non-computable physics. What is usually taken to be the ultimate test of a physical theory, agreement with measurements to the extent that instruments permit, would be of no use, because no finite amount of information can verify the value of an infinite precision real number. All experience suggests that every physical theory is accepted only provisionally with every expectation of its eventual replacement. But for a useable oracle to be obtainable, one would require absolute certainty that a real number provided by a particular theory will not have its value changed if and when the theory is upgraded. Finally, even if one knew that some such number is not computable, in order to use it as an oracle, one would also have to know its degree of unsolvability. If indeed "the search is on" for such a number, one can only pity those engaged in this misguided enterprise.

---

[21] Personal correspondence.

6 Computing with Randomness and Quantum Computation

There has been considerable success in using randomness to find more efficient algorithms for solving various problems. In recent years, the use of quantum mechanical principles in computation has been shown to lead to efficiency. One might be led to wonder whether one or both of these might not lead to "hypercomputation" after all.

The computing power of Turing machines provided with a random number generator was studied in the classic paper [12]. It turned out that such machines could compute only functions that are already computable by ordinary Turing machines.

The case of quantum computers is similar. Quantum algorithms can provide an exponential speed-up. However, they can only compute computable functions.[22]

7 Mechanism

The role of mechanism in human cognition was much discussed in the 17th century, in particular by Descartes, Hobbes, and La Mettrie. The question has been the subject of renewed interest in the context of the possibility of machine intelligence. Of course one is very far from understanding the workings of the human mind, but there is every reason to believe that one of the things our brains do is to execute algorithms. Whether that is all that they do remains unknown although Okham's razor does suggest that as a parsimonious thesis.

In [4], Jack Copeland discusses these matters in the context of the theoretical adequacy of Turing computability. He proposes that one should permit a "wide" mechanism that allows for hypercomputation, and he minimizes the relevance of computability theory. A detailed discussion of these questions is beyond the scope of this article. However, it is strange that despite his extensive references, he fails to mention Judson Webb's outstanding monograph [25].

8 Algorithms: Universality vs. Complexity

I well remember writing code for vacuum tube (British: "valve") computers in the early 1950s. We early programmers found it delightful to see that we could "code" any algorithm to run on our machines. And indeed it is this application of Turing's discovery of universality that underlies the enormous range of tasks that computers are asked to perform in the contemporary world. It didn't take very long for the realization to sink in that care was

---

[22] See for example, [13] p. 210.

needed in the allocation of resources if calculations were to be completed in an acceptable time period using the available data storage. At one point I had undertaken to run a program that had been written by a physics graduate student to compute the moments of a function that occurred in the theory of cosmic ray "showers." The first three moments were obtained in an hour. The fourth required that the machine run all night devoted exclusively to this task. It was clear that the fifth moment was unobtainable.

Early work on automated theorem proving ran into exponential explosions. There seemed to be no way to find an algorithm avoiding such blowups for the simple problem of testing a logical expression in the connectives ¬, ∨, ∧ for the existence of a truth-value assignment that would evaluate the given expression as "true." This *satisfiability problem* eventually assumed the role of a paradigmatic "hard" problem — one for which no really feasible algorithm was to be expected. While there is still no proof that this is indeed the case, the important subject of computational complexity has developed around this question. A proof of the "million dollar" proposition $P \neq NP$ would settle the matter.[23]

All of this is to point out that the enthusiasts for "hypercomputation" have quite ignored questions of complexity. Copeland's supposed oracles not only store information regarding unsolvable problems, but apparently spew out the information with no significant delay. Of course, in reality, even if, despite all that has been said above, an actual oracle materializes, it will be quite useless if, for example, the time needed for the answer to a query to the oracle is an exponential function of the size of the query.

We may summarize: the positive evidence provided by enthusiasts for hypercomputation amounts to no more than the trivial remark that given a physical "oracle" that somehow makes uncomputable information available, it will become possible to compute other uncomputable functions as well. The great success of modern computers as all-purpose algorithm-executing engines embodying Turing's universal computer in physical form makes it extremely plausible that the abstract theory of computability gives the correct answer to the question "What is a computation?" and, by itself, makes the existence of any more general form of computation extremely doubtful. In any case, a

---

[23] Certain problems that are algorithmically solvable, nevertheless have resisted every attempt to find an algorithm that is feasible in practical terms. The proposition $P \neq NP$ may be thought of as asserting that no such feasible algorithms exist. A prize of one million dollars will be awarded by the Clay Mathematics Institute for a proof of this proposition. In an important paper [1], Baker, Gill, and Solovay discussed the "relativization" of this question to an oracle. They showed that depending on which particular oracle was used the relativized proposition could be made to be true or to be false, so that no method of proof that continued to work when relativized to an oracle could possibly resolve this question. *It is worth noting that the oracles used in this work are* **computable**. *In any case, this example can serve to emphasize how far from the truth it is that Turing's notion of oracle "has been largely forgotten."*

useable physical representation of an uncomputable function would require a revolutionary new physical theory, and one that it would be impossible to verify because of the inherent limitations of physical measurement. Finally, the real problems in learning to carry out computations currently regarded as unfeasible lie in a quite different direction — overcoming the exponential explosions in the straightforward algorithms for such problems. It is in this direction that quantum computation may make a real contribution.

References

1. Baker, Theodore P., John Gill, and Robert Solovay (1975). Relativizatons of the P =? NP Question. SIAM J. Comput. **4**, 431–442.
2. Church, Alonzo (1937). Review of [20]. J. Symbolic Logic. **2**, 42–43.
3. Copeland, B. Jack (1998). Turing's O-Machines, Penrose, Searle, and the Brain. Analysis. **58**, 128–38.
4. Copeland, B. Jack (2000). Narrow versus Wide Mechanism: Including a Reexamination of Turing's Views on the Mind-Machine Issue. J. of Phil. **96**, 5–32.
5. Copeland, B. Jack and Diane Proudfoot (1999). Alan Turing's Forgotten Ideas in Computer Science. Scientific American, New York. **253:4**, 98–103.
6. Davis, Martin (1958). Computability and Unsolvability. McGraw-Hill; reprinted with an additional appendix, Dover 1983.
7. Davis, Martin (1982). Why Gödel Didn't Have Church's Thesis. Information and Control. **54**, 3–24.
8. Davis, Martin, ed. (1965). The Undecidable. Raven Press, New York.
9. Davis, Martin, (1987). Mathematical Logic and the Origin of Modern Computers. Studies in the History of Mathematics, pp. 137–165. Mathematical Association of America. Reprinted in The Universal Turing Machine — A Half-Century Survey, Rolf Herken, editor, pp. 149–174. Verlag Kemmerer & Unverzagt, Hamburg, Berlin 1988; Oxford University Press, Oxford, 1988.
10. Davis, Martin (2000). The Universal Computer: The Road from Leibniz to Turing. W. W. Norton, New York.
11. Davis, Martin (2001). Engines of Logic: Mathematicians and the Origin of the Computer. W. W. Norton, New York (paperback edition of [10]).
12. De Leeuw, K., E. F. Moore, C. E. Shannon, and N. Shapiro (1956). Computability by Probabilistic Machines. Automata Studies, Shannon, C. and J. McCarthy, eds., Princeton University Press, Princeton, 183–212.
13. Deutsch, David (1997). The Fabric of Reality. Allen Lane, The Penguin Press, New York.
14. Gandy, Robin (1980). Church's Thesis and Principles for Mechanisms. In: The Kleene Symposium. Jon Barwise, ed. North-Holland, Amsterdam.
15. Hong, J. W. (1988). On Connectionist Models. Comm. Pure and Applied Math. **41**, 1039–1050.
16. Park, Robert (2001). Voodoo Science. Oxford University Press, Oxford.
17. Siegelmann, Hava T. (1995). Computation Beyond the Turing Limit. Science **268**, 545–548.
18. Siegelmann, Hava T. (1999). Neural Networks and Analog Computation: Beyond the Turing Limit. Birkhäuser, Boston.

19. Smith, David Eugene (1929). A Source Book in Mathematics. McGraw-Hill, New York.
20. Turing, A. M. (1937). On Computable Numbers, with an Application to the Entscheidungsproblem. Proc. London Math. Soc. **42**, 230–265. Correction: Ibid. **43**, 544–546. Reprinted in [8, pp. 155–222], [24, pp. 18–56].
21. Turing, A. M. (1939). Systems of Logic Based on Ordinals. Proc. London Math. Soc. **45**, 161–228. Reprinted in [8, pp. 116–154] and [24, pp. 81–148].
22. Turing, A. M. (1947). Lecture to the London Mathematical Society on 20 February 1947. In: A. M. Turing's ACE Report of 1946 and Other Papers. B. E. Carpenter and R.N. Doran, eds. MIT Press 106–124. Reprinted in [23, pp. 87–105].
23. Turing, A. M. (1992). Collected Works: Mechanical Intelligence. D.C. Ince, ed. North-Holland, Amsterdam.
24. Turing, A. M. (2001). Collected Works: Mathematical Logic. R. O. Gandy and C. E. M. Yates, eds. North-Holland, Amsterdam.
25. Webb, Judson C. (1980). Mechanism, Mentalism, and Metamathematics. D. Reidel, Dordrecht.

Quantum Computers: the Church-Turing Hypothesis Versus the Turing Principle

Christopher G. Timpson[*]

The Queen's College, University of Oxford

Summary. Following the development of quantum computers, a question has arisen regarding the relation between the basis of the classical theory of computation and the quantum theory. Here I argue against Deutsch's claim that a physical principle, the Turing principle, underlies the famous Church-Turing hypothesis. I also discuss the computational analogy and emphasize a certain line of argument suggesting it may be misplaced. Finally, I assess Deutsch's claims for the dependence of mathematics upon empirical science, claims that arise as a consequence of his conception of computation and his adherence to the computational analogy.

1   The Advent of Quantum Computers

The fields of quantum information and computation constitute one of the most exciting and rapidly growing areas of current physics. In quantum computation we are concerned with the distinctive possibilities that arise when purely quantum mechanical properties, with all their notorious oddity, are utilized in performing computations. One of the most striking results is that quantum computers seem to be *much more powerful* than classical computational models, offering exponential speed-up over classical computers for certain important tasks.

The advent of quantum computers raises a question concerning the relationship between the classical theory of computation, based on the Church-Turing hypothesis, and the quantum theory. It is quite common to find the claim that the quantum theory of computation is the more fundamental. However, one sometimes also encounters a much stronger claim to the effect that the quantum computer has succeeded in finally making sense of Turing's theory of computation, or that Turing's machines were really quantum mechanical all along. In this paper we shall be considering some of the issues that have arisen around this question of the relation between the classical and quantum theories of computation.

Richard Feynman was the prophet of quantum computation. He pointed out that it seems that one cannot simulate the evolution of a quantum mechanical system efficiently on a classical computer. He took this to imply

---

[*] Thanks are due to Harvey Brown and David Corfield for useful discussion. This work was supported by a studentship from the UK Arts and Humanities Research Board.

that there might be computational benefits to be gained if computations are carried out using quantum systems themselves rather than classical systems; and he went on to describe a universal quantum simulator [12]. However, it is with Deutsch's introduction of the concept of the universal quantum computer in his 1985 paper that the field really begins [7].

Deutsch's paper is the seed from which the riches of quantum computation theory have grown, but in it are to be found roots of philosophical confusion over the notion of computation, in particular, in the claim that a physical principle, the Turing Principle, underlies the Church-Turing hypothesis. In what follows, I shall be concerned to elaborate the difficulties that result from Deutsch's approach.

The Turing Principle is stated as follows:

> Every finitely realizable physical system can be perfectly simulated by a universal model computing machine operating by finite means. [7]

It is the claim that the Turing Principle underlies the Church-Turing hypothesis that is primarily responsible for the thought that quantum computers are necessary to make proper sense of Turing's theory. For the Turing Principle is not satisfied in classical physics, owing to the continuity of states and dynamics in the classical case, yet it is, Deutsch argues [7, §3] in the case of quantum mechanics. If the Turing Principle really were the heart of the theory of computation, prior to the development of the notion of quantum computers we would have been faced with a considerable difficulty, as this supposedly fundamental principle is false under classical mechanics. I shall be arguing, however, that it is a mistake to see the Turing Principle as underlying the Church-Turing hypothesis (Sect. 3); hence this issue does not arise.

Another element in Deutsch's conception of computation that may well be seen as problematic is his adherence to the computational analogy — the thought that human cognition is to be explained in computational terms. Although this is a common and perhaps tempting line of thought, it faces strong objection from certain lines of argument that derive from the later philosophy of Wittgenstein, which we will review (Sect. 4).

Deutsch's distinctive conception of computation and his adherence to the computational analogy combine to give rise to a number of controversial claims about the nature of mathematics. This will be our final topic. His central claim is that although mathematical truth is necessary and objective in a Platonic sense, our mathematical knowledge is not only dependent on *physics*, but also on our (perhaps implicit) *knowledge* of physics. We shall investigate whether this position is a tenable one in the final section below (Sect. 5). First, though, let us begin with a brief sketch of the nature of quantum computers.

2   From Bits to Qubits

In a quantum computer, we want to use quantum systems and their evolution to perform computational tasks. In a classical computer, we might begin with a register of bits, whose state would be represented by a binary string such as $0010010\ldots$, say; in a quantum computer, we begin with a register of *quantum* bits, or *qubits*[1]. A qubit is any two-state quantum system, for example, the spin degree of freedom of an electron, or an atom with an excited and an unexcited energy state, or the polarization of a photon. The two basic orthogonal states of a qubit are represented as $|0\rangle$ and $|1\rangle$; this is called the *computational basis*. States of the whole register of qubits in the computational basis would be $|0\rangle|0\rangle|0\rangle\ldots|0\rangle$, for example, or $|0\rangle|1\rangle|0\rangle\ldots|1\rangle$, which can also be written $|000\ldots0\rangle$ and $|010\ldots1\rangle$ respectively; these states are analogous to the states of a classical register of bits.

Of course, one of the main differences between bits and qubits is that qubits can also exist in *superpositions* of states. An equal superposition of 0 and 1 would be written: $1/\sqrt{2}(|0\rangle + |1\rangle)$. The concept of superposition is familiar from the famous double slit experiment. In this experiment, we imagine a screen with two slits in it, on one side of which is an electron source (a heated filament of some sort, for example) and on the other side, a detector. If the slits are close enough together, then on the far side from the electron source, we will detect an interference pattern. This set-up is sometimes said to display the "wavelike character" of electrons. The important point is that we can decrease the intensity of the electron source to such an extent that only one electron at a time travels through the apparatus and we will still get the same interference pattern building up slowly over time. The conclusion is that an individual electron must be traveling through *both* slits, otherwise we wouldn't get the interference pattern. Thus an electron can exist in a superposition of traveling through the top slit and through the bottom slit at the same time. However, if we ever try to measure which slit the electron went through in its flight, we end up destroying the superposition and we do not get an interference pattern. We learn that the electron went through the top slit, or through the bottom slit; which is incompatible with it going through both.

Now the exciting thing about a quantum superposition is that it looks as if it might provide us with massive parallel processing. If we prepare each of the n qubits of our register in an equal superposition of 0 and 1, then the state of the whole register will end up being in an equal superposition of all the 2^n possible sequences of 0's and 1's:

$$\frac{1}{\sqrt{2^n}}(|0000\ldots00\rangle + |0000\ldots01\rangle + |0000\ldots11\rangle + \ldots + |1111\ldots1\rangle)$$

---

[1] The term "qubit" was introduced in [18]. A good review of quantum computation up to the development of Shor's algorithm (see below) is provided by [11].

A classical n-bit register can store one of 2^n numbers; an n-qubit register can store 2^n numbers simultaneously, an enormous advantage. Now if we have an operation that evaluates a function of an input string, the linearity of quantum mechanics ensures that if we perform this operation on our superposed register, we will evaluate the function simultaneously for all possible inputs, ending up with a register in which all the 2^n outputs are superposed!

The trouble is, though, it is not possible to read out all the values that are superposed in this state. Just as in the double slit experiment when we tried to measure which slit the electron went through, when we try to measure the value of the function, we end up with a single one of the answers, at random; the superposition "collapses" stochastically to one of its possible answers. Thus despite all the quantum parallel processing that went on, it proves very difficult to read much of it out. In this naive example we have done no better than if we had evaluated the function on a single input, as classically. It is for this reason that the design of good quantum algorithms is such a difficult task: we need to make subtle use of other quantum effects such as the constructive and destructive interference between different computational paths in order to make sure that we can read out useful information at the end of the computation, i.e., that we can improve on the efforts of classical computers.

The possible evolutions of states of quantum mechanical systems are given by unitary operators. A *universal* quantum computer will thus be a system that can (using finite means) apply any unitary operation to its register of qubits. It turns out that a relatively small set of one and two qubit *quantum gates* is sufficient for a universal quantum computer[2]. A quantum gate is a unitary operator that acts on one or more qubits. By combining different sequences of gates (analogously to logic gates in a circuit diagram), we can implement different unitary operations on the qubits they act on. A set of gates is *universal* if by combining elements of the set, we can build up any unitary operation on n qubits to arbitrary accuracy.

So what can quantum computers do? First of all, they can compute anything that a classical Turing machine can compute; such computations correspond to permutations of computational basis states and can be achieved by a suitable subset of unitary operations. Second, they can't compute anything that a classical Turing machine can't. This is most easily seen in the following way [11].

We can picture a probabilistic Turing machine as following one branch of a tree-like structure of computational paths, with the nodes of the tree corresponding to computational states. The edges leading from the nodes correspond to the different computational steps that could be made from

---

[2] See, for example [17]. We are considering the *quantum network* model of a quantum computer which is more intuitive and more closely linked to experimental applications than the alternative *quantum Turing machine* model that Deutsch began with. The two models were shown to be equivalent in [28].

that state. Each path is labeled with its probability and the probability of a final, halting, state is given by summing the probabilities of each of the paths leading to that state. We may see a quantum computer in a similar fashion, but this time with the edges connecting nodes being labeled with the appropriate probability amplitude for the transition. The quantum computer follows all of the different computational paths at once, in a superposition; and because we have probability *amplitudes*, the possibility of interference between the different computational paths exists. However, if we wished, we could program a classical computer to calculate the list of configurations of the quantum computer and calculate the complex numbers of the probability amplitudes. This would allow us to calculate the correct probabilities for the final states, which we could then simulate by tossing coins. Thus a quantum computer could be simulated by a probabilistic Turing machine; but such a simulation is very inefficient.

The advantage of quantum computers lies not, then, with what can be computed, but with its efficiency. In computational complexity, the crudest measure of whether a computational task is tractable or not, or an algorithm efficient, is given by seeing how the resources required for the computation scale with increased input size. If the resources scale polynomially with the size of the input in bits, the task is deemed tractable. If they do not, in which case the resources are said to depend exponentially on the input size, the task is called hard, or intractable. In 1994, Shor [20] presented an efficient algorithm for factoring on a quantum computer, a task for which it is believed no efficient classical algorithm exists. Hence quantum computers provide exponential speed-up over the best known classical algorithms for factoring; and this is strong evidence that quantum computers are more powerful than classical computers[3].

3   The Turing Principle Versus the Church-Turing Hypothesis

We now turn to the main story. As I said in Sect. 1, in his landmark 1985 paper, Deutsch argues that underlying the Church-Turing hypothesis, the basis for the classical theory of computation, there is an implicit physical assumption, namely, the Turing Principle, which is, recall:

---

[3] Another very important quantum algorithm is due to Grover [13]. This algorithm provides a speed-up, although not an exponential one, over classical methods for searching an unstructured database. For a database of size n, the algorithm allows the desired object to be found in $\sqrt{n}$ steps, rather than the order of n steps one would expect classically.

> Every finitely realizable physical system can be perfectly simulated by a universal model computing machine operating by finite means.[4] [7]

The Church-Turing hypothesis, by contrast, he states as follows:

> Every "function which would naturally be regarded as computable" can be computed by the universal Turing machine. [7]

The two main ways in which these statements differ are, first, that Turing's "functions which would naturally be regarded as computable" has, in effect, been replaced by "functions which may in principle be computed by a physical system" [7, p. 99], the result of the stipulation that the universal computing machine perfectly simulates every finite physical system; and second, that the reference to a specific form of universal computer — the universal Turing machine — has been replaced by an unspecified universal computing machine, with the requirement only that it operate by finite means.

The heuristic value of the move to the Turing Principle is undoubted, for it led Deutsch to define the universal quantum computer and hence spark a vigorous new field of physics. The liberalization involved in this move from the Church-Turing hypothesis was thus invaluable, but, I shall suggest, it is mistaken to argue that the Turing Principle underlies the Church-Turing hypothesis, or that this physical principle should be thought of as the real basis for the theory of computation.

To begin with, it is important to recognize that in his famous paper 'On Computable Numbers' [22] Turing was concerned with what is computable by *humans*, not with describing the ultimate limits of what we now mean by "computer." Deutsch is well aware of this fact, e.g. [9, p. 2], but by glossing over it here, we would miss several important things. First, the purely mathematical element of Turing's thesis; second, the chance to separate out the precursors of the computational analogy from the foundations of the theory of computation[5]; and third, the distinction between the task of characterizing the effectively calculable, which had become so urgent by the mid 1930s and to which the Church-Turing hypothesis was directed, and the rather different project of considering what classes of functions can be calculated by machines or physical processes most widely construed (a distinction which Copeland, in particular, has emphasized e.g. [4]). To see something of the significance of these points, let us make the comparison with Church's position in his 1936 paper.

Church proposed that the intuitive notion of effective calculability be made precise by identifying effectively calculable functions with the recursive functions [3, §7]. Again, calculability here means calculable by *humans*. By

---

[4] A computing machine M is said to *perfectly simulate* a physical system S, under a given labeling of their inputs and outputs, if their exists a program $\pi(S)$ for M that renders M computationally equivalent to S under that labeling.

[5] Shanker [19] investigates this area and undertakes this separation in detail.

contrast, Turing presented the mathematical insight that if certain functions could be encoded in, for example, binary terms, then a *machine* could be made to compute analogues of those functions. The machine was the Turing machine and it turned out, the functions were the recursive functions. The second part of his argument, §9 of the paper, was then to relate this to human calculation; an argument for why computability defined in terms of Turing machines should capture all that would "naturally be regarded as computable" by humans.

As Shanker, for example, recounts [19, §2], the differences between Church's and Turing's presentations was all important for Gödel. Gödel did not accept what is best seen as Church's *stipulation* that the effectively cal- culable functions are the recursive functions until Turing's argument in "On Computable Numbers" became known. His objection was that Church had not shown *why* the properties associated with our intuitive notion of effec- tive calculability would be captured by the class of recursive functions (see also [6, 21]). That he came to accept Church's convention after "On Com- putable Numbers" shows that he took Turing to have solved this problem. Presumably, what was important about this solution was not Turing's demon- stration of the capabilities of the Turing machine, but rather, the argument in §9 that Turing machine computability captures that which would "naturally be regarded as computable." Thus Gödel was convinced of the adequacy of Turing's account of what it is for a human to calculate in a formal system; and that this was no different from the operation of a Turing machine. In this way Turing was supposed to have explicated the intuitive notion of effective calculability. However, we should note that it is precisely this step back to the notion of calculable-by-human from calculable-by-machine and attempting to explain the former in terms of the latter that gives rise to the computational analogy, the problems of which we shall discuss below (Sect. 4).[6]

If we were to follow Deutsch and reinterpret Turing's "functions which would naturally be regarded as computable" as the functions which may in principle be computed by a real physical system, then we are neglecting the fact that Turing meant computable by humans. This is no mere historical point. The most obvious consequence would be that we ignore the possibility of making the useful distinction between computing by human and computing by machine – a physical system considered as a computer. But perhaps more importantly, we miss the significance of Turing's purely mathematical thesis, his recognition that certain functions can be encoded and machines thus made to compute them for us. Deutsch's argument for his reinterpretation is that

> ... it would surely be hard to regard a function "naturally" as computable if it could not be computed in Nature, and conversely. [7, p. 99]

---

[6] Shanker locates the ultimate source of the pressures that lead here to the com- putational analogy (as he calls it, the Mechanist Thesis) with Hilbert [19].

In the first part of this, "computed in Nature" suffers from the suggestive ambiguity between computable by human and computable by physical object, so let us take it to mean computable by machine, or more widely, physical object considered as a computer. More important for the present is the converse, which would read:

> It would be hard to regard a function computable in Nature as not "naturally" computable.

But this is rather a teasing play on words. Part of the point at issue is what it means for a function to be computable in Nature, for a function to be computed by a machine, a meaning that Turing had to provide *en route* to determining what the relation between functions computable in Nature and the "naturally computable" might be. If we just claim that the "naturally computable" functions are all and only those functions that can be computed in physical reality, we not only, perforce, miss the original point of trying to capture the effectively calculable, but more importantly for present purposes, we miss out the key *mathematical* component at the heart of the theory of computation. For we have not provided, as Turing did, a specification of what it is for a physical object to compute, to give a mathematical meaning to the possible evolutions of physical states.

What can be computed in physical reality has two sorts of determinant, mathematical and physical. The mathematical determines what the evolution of given physical states into others in a certain way would mean, what would have been computed by such a process; and the physical determines whether such a process can occur. Identifying the "naturally computable" functions with those that can be computed by physical systems, we emphasize the physical determinant to the exclusion of the mathematical one — we say that what can be computed is *whatever* can be computed by *any* physical system, but we have not said what, if anything, these various physical processes amount to in mathematical terms.

When Deutsch says that behind the Church-Turing hypothesis is really an assertion of the Turing Principle ([7, p. 99], [9, p. 3]), what he is trying to capture is the imperious nature of the hypothesis: you can't find any computation that can be done that *can't* be done by the universal Turing machine. He takes this imperious claim to require the possible existence of a physical object that could actually perform every (physical) computation. For " ... the computing power of *abstract* machines has no bearing on what is computable in reality," [8, p. 134] what is important is whether the computational processes that the machine describes can actually occur. The essence of the universal computing machine is supposed to be that the physical properties it possesses are the most general computational properties that any object can possess. It follows that if the universal machine is to be an interesting object of study, it must be physically possible for it to exist (although supplies of energy and memory may remain a little idealized), otherwise studying it could tell us nothing about what can be computed in reality.

The significance of the Turing machine is thus supposed to lie in the fact that its description is so general that it has been pared down to the bare essentials of computing, with the result that any computation by any object can be described in terms of the operation of a Turing machine[7]. Deutsch considers Turing's machine to be a very good, but ultimately inadequate attempt to give a description of the most general computing machine possible [8, p. 252]. He would suggest that Turing had made himself hostage to fortune by offering such a concrete characterization of what is supposed to be the most general computing machine, in particular by explicitly describing the machine in classical (mechanical) terms and not allowing for the possible implications of quantum mechanics or some other successor theory. Taking Turing's *intention* to refer to the most general machine as the important thing and erasing the unnecessary physical details of the Turing machine[8], the content of the Church-Turing hypothesis becomes the assertion that this most general machine can exist. The hypothesis has become the physical principle – it is now just an empirical question whether the universal computing machine can exist.

But this misrepresents the import of the Church-Turing hypothesis, for we have missed the mathematical component, the definitional role of the Turing machine in the theory of computation. Put baldly, the reason why there is no computation that cannot be performed by the universal computing machine is not that it just so happens that this object can actually exist in physical reality, but rather that nothing could count as such a computation. A computation is *defined* by reference to the abstract universal computing machine, the possible evolution of physical states given a mathematical meaning by reference to that model. What we call a computation is determined by the abstract model, hence there can be no such thing as a computation that cannot be performed by the universal computing machine.

Of course, it is conceivable that there could be physical processes that are not covered by our abstract model and which we decide we might want to call computations, but these processes still need to gain a mathematical meaning from somewhere; and once we have given them such meaning, we will have extended our definition of computing to cover these cases as well.[9] This does not, however, affect the point that by definition there can be no computation that cannot be performed by the universal computer, as a corollary of these physical processes having mathematical meaning. (Until these processes are

---

[7] This is perhaps a common view of the significance of Turing's machine.

[8] The essence of the Turing machine is retained in the requirement that the universal computing machine operate by *finite means*, defined in [7, p. 100].

[9] Note that this question differs from the question of whether the definition of machines computing captures all that would "naturally be regarded as computable" by humans. What is currently at issue is the mathematical meaning that can be given to various physical processes, not whether the definition of computing offered would include all and only that which falls under the intuitive notion of the effectively calculable.

accepted under the definition, they are not yet computations. Compare p. 225 for an example of a specific type.)

Having noted that from two computing machines we can form a composite machine, whose set of computable functions contains the union of the sets of functions computable by its components, Deutsch suggests that:

> There is no purely logical reason why we could not go on *ad infinitum* building more powerful computing machines, nor why there should exist any function that is outside the computable set of every physically possible machine. [7, p. 98]

He goes on to suggest that it is physics rather than logic that provides the constraint (presumably the contingent physical fact that there can exist a universal computing machine exhausting the possibilities). But this seems wrong. Our immediate response is to ask why might there not simply come a point after which no new functions are added and we would just keep adding ones we already have? What might determine this? It is *precisely* logic, logic and mathematics, that determine this question. Once we have defined our computational states in a certain way, it is mathematics that determines the set of functions that can be computed by all possible evolutions of those states. Deutsch is correct that physics has a role to play in determining what is computable, but it can only get in on the act *after* mathematics.

Another example of Deutsch seeming to over-emphasize the role of physics at the expense of mathematics is the following passage:

> Computers are physical objects, and computations are physical processes. What computers can or cannot compute is determined by the laws of physics alone and not by pure mathematics. [8, p. 98]

Computations, remembering that we are speaking strictly of mechanical, not human computers, are indeed physical processes, but what makes them a computation is not physical. The processes going on in a computer are governed by the laws of physics, but it would be wrong to say that the *computation* is entirely governed by physics, for mathematics determines what the transitions from physical state to physical state mean. Physics determines what physical state can follow from what physical state, but mathematics determines whether or not this is a computation and what it is a computation of.

Deutsch is quite right to emphasize that the physical determinants of computing should not be ignored in the theory of computation, but he has taken this insight too far by entirely neglecting the mathematical determinants. We must recognize that their place is *prior* to that of the physical determinants. If our theory of computation is asking what the ultimate limits of computation are (again, computation by machines), the answer must involve two sorts of consideration. We are asking what is possible with physical computational states defined in a given way, so our first consideration is what can these states evolve to, whilst the second is: what does such an evolution mean? The first part is a physical question and the second part mathematical. Maths will determine what $\alpha_i \ldots \alpha_f$ means (α being physical states under some description), but it won't say if it is a possible evolution of states — that is for the laws of physics to decide.

We might want to say, then, that mathematics provides the ultimate bound on what is computable (most obviously, nothing could count as computing a contradiction); and it determines what progressions of physical states are computations and what they are computations of. But what progressions of physical states there can be is determined by physics.

In their admirably clear 1999 paper, Deutsch, Ekert and Lupacchini [9] admit that there are both logical and physical limits to the computations that can be performed by computing machines. They present the halting problem as an example in which logical and physical constraints are intimately linked; but their discussion still seems to betray confusion between the mathematical and the physical nature of computing.

From the halting problem, we learn that there are some computational problems, in particular, determining whether a specified universal Turing machine given a specified input will halt, that cannot be solved by any Turing machine; and it is logic that tells us this. Deutsch, Ekert and Lupacchini go on to say that:

> In physical terms, this statement says that machines with certain properties cannot be physically built, and as such can be viewed as a statement about physical reality or equivalently, about the laws of physics. [9, p. 4]

But the halting problem tells us nothing of the sort. The halting problem lies primarily on the mathematical side of computing and teaches us nothing directly about the laws of physics. Given the specification of computing states we are dealing with, mathematics and logic tell us that nothing could count as providing the solution to this problem; no possible state is the solution. Thus the "certain properties" that the machines may not possess are mathematical properties, not physical ones. It is not that the machines are forbidden to possess these properties, that some force prevents it, it is that *nothing would count as building a machine with these properties*. The halting problem, then, tells us nothing about what can be built; it tells us the mathematical constraints on what can be computed given the way we have defined computing. Failing to recognize this means failure to understand the way in which the definitional role of the abstract universal computer gives mathematical meaning to the evolution of physical states. This in turn can be traced back to a failure to recognize Turing's purely mathematical achievement in "On Computable Numbers," quite separate from the concern there with epistemological issues surrounding effective calculability.[10]

---

[10] I am indebted to [19] for the emphasis on this separation.

We have seen that Deutsch's emphasis on the possible physical existence of the universal computing machine misrepresents its significance; missing entirely its essential role determining the mathematical meaning of the evolution of physical states. From this it is clear that insisting on the physical nature of the Turing Principle debars it from playing the central role in the theory of computation. For it is not a contingent, empirical fact that there exists a universal computing machine, it is a necessary fact that arises from the way the abstract model determines the mathematical meaning of certain physical processes, making them computations. It is not that the universal machine covers all the possibilities, the universal machine *determines* the possibilities.

Where Deutsch is correct, however, is that there is a clear sense in which we should be interested in the physical realization of the abstract computing machine. The importance of being able to build the machine, if only in principle, is that we want the progressions of states it describes to actually be do-able! This would clearly determine whether we have an interesting definition of computation and one worth pursuing. (We should emphasize here, just to be clear, that this issue is distinct from the issue of the definition of computation providing mathematical meaning for physical processes and distinct again from the task of characterizing the effectively calculable.) However, we do not require that the universal computing machine be a possible physical existent; all that is required is that physical analogues of the computational processes of the universal machine are physically possible processes.

As a particularly striking example of where these concerns would be relevant, let us consider Hogarth's presentation of non-Turing computability in certain relativistic spacetimes [15]. The idea is that in these spacetimes, dubbed *Malament-Hogarth* spacetimes, it appears possible to perform *super-tasks* — an infinite number of steps in a finite length of time. These spacetimes (M, g) are such that they contain a path λ that starts from a point p and has infinite length, but that on this path it is always possible to signal to a point q that can be reached from p in a finite span of proper time.[11]

A toy example of such a spacetime is given by [10]. Starting with a Minkowski spacetime (R^4, η) we choose a scalar field Ω on M such that $\Omega = 1$ outside a compact set $C \subset M$ and Ω tends rapidly to infinity as we approach a point $r \in C$. The spacetime $(R^4 - r, \Omega^2 \eta)$ is then a Malament-Hogarth spacetime and the path λ will start at p and go towards r. What we are supposed to do is project a given Turing machine down the path λ and then travel to q, by which time the machine will have signaled to us if it has halted. Using this technique, we might, for example, solve the Goldbach conjecture by programming our Turing machine to check each even number in turn to determine whether it is the sum of two primes, and halt if it

---

[11] That is, all points on λ are contained in the chronological past of q. The chronological past of a point q is the set of all points p for which there is a nontrivial future directed time-like curve from p to q [10, p. 24, n. 1].

finds a counterexample. We then send it off down λ and travel to q. If we have received a signal, the conjecture is false, if not, it is true. Generalizing this approach, we appear able to solve Turing unsolvable problems in these spacetimes.

The *decision problem* for a property P is said to be solvable if there is a mechanical test (effective procedure) which will tell us whether or not any object (of the appropriate category) possesses P in a finite number of steps [2, p. 115]. Thus the decision problem for P is Turing solvable if there is both a Turing machine that will halt after a finite number of steps if and only if P holds and a Turing machine that will halt after a finite number of steps if and only if P does not hold. If only one of these exist, the problem is *partially Turing solvable*. The halting problem and the decision problem for first order logic are partially Turing solvable, but the full decision problem can be solved for them in a Malament-Hogarth spacetime. For the halting problem, all we need do is project the Turing machine in question down λ, set to signal if it halts. We travel to q and if we have received a signal, we know the machine halts and if not, we know it never halts. Similarly for the decision problem for first order logic, noting that there exists a Turing machine that will halt after a finite number of steps if a given sentence S is valid [2, p. 145], we adopt the same procedure — if we have a received a signal at q, the sentence is valid, if we have not, it is not. It is clear that the decision problem for any partially Turing solvable problem is solvable in a Malament-Hogarth spacetime (we will have to vary our interpretation of signal/no-signal appropriately, of course).

Hogarth goes on to describe more complicated computational processes that would seem to solve the decision problem for arithmetic, but the simple case serves for our purposes. We have here a clear example of the question of the physical realizability of the processes described being all-important. If the processes Hogarth describes are physically possible, then we have a whole new class of computability distinct from Turing computability and we extend our notion of computability accordingly. Note that the mathematical meaning of the processes Hogarth describes piggy-backs on our current definition of computability — we think we can see clearly what these processes would mean if they were physically possible. Given the meaning we have already given to computational processes in terms of the universal Turing machine and what it can compute, these meanings seem to follow.[12] The reason why the claim that

---

[12] I say "think" and 'seem' here, for we may believe that these mathematical meanings unfold from, since they are already contained in, the mathematical concepts we have. But we may believe that the mathematical meaning of these processes ultimately rests on our *decision* to accept the conclusions set out as following from our present stock of mathematical propositions. This allows for the positions of those who believe there is a fact about, for example, whether Golbach's conjecture is true independent of whether a proof or disproof has been or ever will be found; and those who believe there is no such fact *until* a proof or disproof has been found.

it is a conceptual truth that our particular universal computing machine can perform all possible computations is not undermined by the Hogarth example and others like it is that we have, as it were, recognized new possibilities in our (abstract) universal computing machine, not discovered that it could not in fact perform all possible computations, which would be logically impossible. Or rather, to be more precise, by generalizing or slightly adjusting the sets of physical states and their evolution for our *definitional* universal machine (in the Hogarth case, by including evolutions in these unusual spacetimes), we change the class of computations and computable functions at the same time.

Returning to the question of the physical realizability of these Hogarthian processes, we need to recognize that the computational process extends from the initial launch of the Turing machine to the possible reception of the signal by the receiver. Thus whether these are physically possible computations will depend on whether a suitable Turing machine can exist in the spacetime in question (in particular we will be worried about what happens to it as it approaches r), whether a signal from the Turing machine can reach the observer intact, and of course, whether Malament-Hogarth spacetimes are physically possible.[13] If it turns out that these processes are physically possible, then we must extend our notion of what can be computed to include these striking non-Turing computations. If they are not, then a definition of computability that included Hogarth's computations would not be an interesting one for practical purposes — it would be no more than a mathematical toy. We cannot learn any maths from the conceivability of peculiar computational processes, for our knowledge of the relevant maths is already explicit in our conceiving them; that it might be an open question whether these processes are physically possible is only relevant to the question of what we can make machines (or physical objects in general since "machine" implies manufacturing) do for us.

We have seen, then, that Deutsch has over-emphasized the physical determinants of computing to the exclusion of the mathematical. The Turing Principle should not be seen to underlie the Church-Turing hypothesis, for that misrepresents the mathematical significance of the concept of the universal computing machine. The universal machine defines the mathematical meaning of the possible evolution of physical states and hence it is a necessary fact that the universal computing machine can perform every possible computation. It is certainly interesting that the Turing Principle happens to be true in quantum mechanics[14], but we should hesitate to draw any far-reaching conclusions from this. Certainly, the claim adumbrated in Sect. 1

---

[13] These questions should be approached with an open mind, see [10] for an interesting discussion, and compare [15, §6].

[14] Intuitively, the state of any finite quantum system is just a vector in Hilbert space and can be represented to arbitrary precision by a finite number of qubits; and any evolution of the system is just a unitary transformation of this vector and can be simulated by the universal quantum computer, which by definition

that the advent of the quantum computer makes sense of Turing's theory of computation, that his machines were quantum mechanical after all[15], is false.

As has been emphasized at various points, we have been talking in this section only of computation by machine or by physical object considered as a computer, as opposed to human computing or calculating. This is an important clarifying step that allows us to distinguish clearly the mathematical and physical sides of the theory of computation. Having mentioned this convenient separation of human from machine, however, one's thoughts seem naturally drawn to the further, notoriously vexed, question of the relation between human cognition and machine computation. Even if it is thought that human calculation is no more than physical calculation with a cherry on top, however, this separation remains important, for it emphasizes the different types of role the mathematical and physical determinants of computation play; and this distinction in role is one which, I suggest, should be retained independently of any judgment on the value of the computational analogy. Despite that, it is nonetheless tempting to take a step into the more controversial waters and present an argument, deriving from Wittgenstein, that would suggest that the computational analogy is in fact mistaken.

4   The Computational Analogy

The computational analogy is, as I have said, to think of the human mind or brain by analogy with the computer and think that human cognitive processes should be explained in computational terms. Impressed by the fact that computers seem able to perform tasks we previously took only to be possible as the result of rational thought, we begin to wonder if human thought should be considered fundamentally computational in nature. But in the early 1930s, even before the advent of the computer, Wittgenstein had warned:

> "Is it possible for a machine to think?" ... the trouble which is expressed in this question is not really that we don't yet know a machine which could do the job. The question is not analogous to that which someone might have asked a hundred years ago: "Can a machine liquefy a gas?" The trouble is rather that the sentence, "A machine thinks (perceives, wishes)": seems somehow nonsensical. It is as though we had asked "Has the number 3 a color?" [24, p. 47]

It is clear that the rapid advances in computer technology and Artificial Intelligence since then would not have affected Wittgenstein's point, for he

---

can generate any unitary transformation with arbitrary precision. Deutsch offers a more rigorous proof taking into account the fact that any sub-system must always be coupled to the environment [7, §3].

[15] Deutsch cites, for example, Feynman's remark *a propos* Turing: "He thought that he understood paper." [8, p. 252].

is claiming that the notion of a machine thinking is conceptually malformed, that we have something like a category mistake here, a violation of logical and grammatical rules impervious to empirical results. But for those who follow Turing, impressed by the computational analogy, the question of whether a machine can think is indeed an empirical question. Thus we need to ask whether the purely mechanical manipulation of formally defined symbols in conformity with the rules of a formal system should qualify for description in cognitive terms; whether something can be said to calculate, ultimately perhaps even to think, solely in virtue of performing such manipulations. It is only if such a description is warranted that we may attempt to explain human cognitive capacities in terms of computational processes.[16]

We shall concentrate on the question of whether a machine can be said to calculate, for this is most relevant to our concerns with computation and it is here that the case for the computational analogy seems most powerful. Further, if a machine cannot even be said to calculate, there seems little hope that any of the supposedly more *recherché* cognitive abilities could be ascribed to it.

Before appreciating the difference between a human and a machine computing, we should note that a common thought about what the difference may lie in is misconceived. A machine manipulating symbols clearly differs from a human calculating in not understanding what it is doing, but this difference is not to be explained in terms of lack of self-consciousness or awareness, for understanding is not such an awareness, an ineffable experience supposed to accompany the act of calculation [25, §§148–155]. There may be many experiences that are characteristic of our understanding something, but such experiences are neither necessary nor sufficient conditions for understanding, hence cannot be said to *be* understanding, nor what it is to understand be explained by describing the experiences. Whether or not I understand something is determined by what I am able to do, not by what experiences or awareness may accompany what I am doing. As an example, my understanding an arithmetic series is not the flash of insight when the formula occurs to me, it is the fact I can continue the series correctly, apply the formula in extending the series and explain to another why what I am doing is correct.

The real difference between a human calculating and a machine manipulating symbols is best appreciated in two steps. Rather than go directly to the case of a machine manipulating symbols in accord with formal rules, it is instructive to consider first the case of a person mechanically manipulating uninterpreted symbols. Thus we imagine someone who, rather than being taught arithmetic in the normal way, commits machine tables for adding, subtracting and so on to memory and, given binary input, produces binary output corresponding to the appropriate calculation. We can imagine him mumbling to himself perhaps, to keep himself apprised of his computational state, the symbol he is scanning and consequently what his action should be.

---

[16] We follow here the approach of Hyman [16] and Shanker [19].

It is clear that this person does not understand what he is doing, that although he is producing the results of addition, subtraction, multiplication, he is a mathematical ignoramus, for he does not even know what a number or an arithmetical operation is. But, we may ask, must he understand what he is doing in order to be said to calculate? We might say that there is a fact about whether he is calculating, it is just a fact that he is unaware of. After all, surely what is important is that he produces the right answer to questions? All we ever have to go on in the best of cases is people producing the right outputs to various inputs, as the Turing Test is supposed to emphasize — in all cases, another's understanding represents a problematic inference.

This is confused, however, for the mathematical ignoramus lacks the range of abilities that would count as understanding what he is doing and this is just the range of abilities that is necessary to say of him that he is calculating. To be calculating, he needs to be performing arithmetical operations on numbers, but whether one is performing arithmetical operations on numbers depends on the way the symbols and rules of transformation are used outside the formal system[17]. He would need to be able to tie these numbers and operations in with notions of quantity and counting, for if someone can calculate, he knows, for example, that if he has two stones in one pocket and three in another then he has five in total, without needing to count all the stones together. By definition, though, the mathematical ignoramus lacks such abilities.

Thus despite the fact that he is applying a set of rules that produce the results of arithmetic, we cannot say that the mathematical ignoramus is calculating. It would be better to say that he produces the *result* of a calculation without calculating.

We can at least say of our mathematical ignoramus that he is following rules, but the same is not true when we move to a machine manipulating symbols. For although a rule may be applied mechanically, especially when it is as simple as the step of an algorithm, it does not make sense to say that a machine can follow a rule. This is of crucial importance, for it is of the very essence of mathematics that it is normative, that our inferences, manipulations and calculations are right or wrong by reference to a rule. It is from this that the necessity of our mathematical propositions springs. (These and the following are some of the themes Wittgenstein develops in his *Remarks on the Foundations of Mathematics*.)

The most that can be said of a computing machine is that it manipulates symbols *in accord* with rules, it does not follow them, hence it is not performing a normative task, it is not calculating or doing maths. If a machine has been properly designed and built and is operating as intended, then it

---

[17] The point here concerns how signs acquire meaning: " . . . it is essential to mathematics that its signs are also employed in *mufti*. It is the use outside mathematics, and so the *meaning* of the signs, that makes the sign game into mathematics" [26, V §2].

produces regularities that accord with the desired rules, but mere regularity is insufficient for rule following. What is needed is the complicated behavior that makes manifest that a rule is being followed: an agent needs to be able to explain, correct and justify its behavior by reference to the rule; and this behavior is clearly lacking in a machine. It may seem odd that if we build a device to mechanize a normative task, e.g. calculating, then that device cannot be said to follow rules, but on reflection, this is not the case. If something is prevented from breaking a rule, then that rule becomes superfluous and can no longer apply to it. We might, for instance forbid the watching of television after a certain hour at night, but if we install a timer to interrupt the mains supply, people can neither break nor follow this rule, the rule simply drops out of the picture.

By making a computer, we have designed a machine to produce the result of a normative task without any rules needing to be followed, and whether the machine produces this result depends on whether it runs as designed. When we program a computer, we are not instructing it to follow rules, as Hacker says:

> ... one can no more literally instruct a computer to do anything than one can instruct a tree, though one can make a tree grow in a certain way, and one can make a computer produce the result of vastly complex calculations. [14, p. 76]

If we are instructed to follow rules then we can explain our actions by reference to those rules, if a child is asked how she produced the result of an addition, she explains what the rules she followed were, neatly written out in her exercise book. But asking how a machine produced the result of a calculation, we can only answer by giving a causal description of the processes that led to the result; it arrived at that result because it was causally constrained to.

In his *Remarks on the Philosophy of Psychology*, Wittgenstein said:

> Turing's "Machines". These machines are *humans* who calculate. [27, §1096]

The aim of this remark is to emphasize precisely that difference we have identified between the mathematical ignoramus and the computing machine [19]. For Turing's machines to capture the notion of effective calculability, he needed to argue that humans calculate like his machines; but for human calculation to be explained in mechanical terms, that calculation must at some level not require any intelligence. The notion of an algorithm then seems to fit perfectly, for with an algorithm we have broken down the complicated rule following of a calculation into a set of meaningless sub-rules that can be applied mechanically. We are then on the road to giving a full mechanical, computational, account of human cognition, for if the basic steps require no intelligence, we can hope to build up intelligent, self-aware behavior from these mindless components.

It should now be clear why this is mistaken, however. What distinguishes algorithms is that they are a set of very simple rules for producing a specific output from a specific input; but an algorithm is not a precise specification of a rule that already exists, it is a different set of rules from the original that produces the same output and may be more useful for some purposes. In different contexts, different sets of rules producing the same output can be more appropriate or efficient. That we can produce different algorithms to do the same thing immediately indicates that we should be wary of thinking of an algorithm as an *analysis* of a pre-existing calculating practice. More importantly, although the rules of an algorithm are very simple, they are still *rules* and hence following them still requires complicated normative behavior. To follow a rule mechanically, we must be able to follow it with awareness also, and be able to cite the rule in explanation of our mechanical behavior even if our minds were elsewhere at the time. Thus just because a rule is very simple, it does not follow that it can be carried out by a machine that cannot manifest rule-following behavior. To execute an algorithm is to follow a set of rules, so if Turing's machines are to be seen to execute algorithms, they must be following rules, hence rather than being a machine, they must be our mathematical ignoramus — hence Wittgenstein's remark [19]. Even the simple steps of an algorithm require intelligent rule-following behavior, so we cannot think that human calculating, or intelligent behavior in general, can be built up from a complex reticulation of "mindless sub-rules" because there is no such thing as a mindless sub-rule.

We have no reason to think it beyond the bounds of possibility that we might one day build a device capable of following rules, an artifact that could follow the rules of arithmetic and hence be said to calculate. But such a device would need to be able to use rules in the appropriate way, to use a rule as a standard of correctness for its own and other's application of the rule, to explain and justify its behavior by reference to that rule. We would need to be able to distinguish between this device trying and failing to follow the rule and it simply malfunctioning, which would require it to display a very complex pattern of behavior. Hyman suggests that such a device

> ... would need to be, in general, capable of setting itself goals and pursuing, modifying and abandoning them, as opposed to merely being (passively) capable of use for certain ends. [16, pp. 16–17]

Thus we see that in order to say of a machine that it thinks, that it calculates, it would need to be able to exhibit the complicated behavior that would count as following rules. But then its mechanical nature would lie only in the fact that it had been manufactured, not in what it did. To the extent that we could apply cognitive concepts to it, its behavior would not be that of a machine; and to the same extent, it would be misleading to call it a machine. The nature of an object corresponds to the explanations we give of the way in which it functions and the explanation of the behavior of this artifact is partly rational. Its own cognitive behavior would not be explained in computational, mechanical, terms.

Machine computation is just the manipulation of formally defined symbols in accord with the rules of a formal system, thus we have seen that a computer fails emphatically to qualify for description in cognitive terms. The mathematical ignoramus, although not calculating, at least follows rules, but the computer cannot even be said to do that. A computer cannot be said to calculate in the sense that human beings calculate, and the upshot of this argument is that human cognition cannot be explained in terms of computational processes.

Part of the intuitive appeal that the computational analogy holds, part of the reason for the belief that applying cognitive and conative concepts to non-humans is unproblematic, lies with the fact that there only seems to be a quantitative and not a qualitative difference between people and simply describable physical systems. Insisting that there is nonetheless an important distinction looks like it is committing one to some form of dualism, which is clearly unacceptable. But our current deliberations have indicated precisely when we can have an important change from quantity to quality: it is when behavior gets sufficiently complex to count as rule-following.

5   Deutsch and the Nature of Mathematics

Towards the end of §1 of his 1985 paper, Deutsch makes two claims. In the light of the preceding two sections, it seems that the first is true, while the second false.

The first:

> It is often claimed that every "reasonable" *physical* (as opposed to mathematical) model of computation, at least for the deterministic computation of functions from Z to Z, is equivalent to Turing's. But this is not so; there is no *a priori* reason why the physical laws should respect the limitations of the mathematical processes we call "algorithms." [7, p. 101]

This is indeed true. We have decided by *fiat* that algorithms are co-extensive with the Turing computable, but as we have seen above (Sect. 3), we are quite free to liberalize our definition of the computable, imbue more physical processes with mathematical meaning and perhaps be able to compute more functions.

The second:

> Nor, conversely, is it obvious *a priori* that any of the familiar recursive functions is in physical reality computable. The reason why we find it possible to construct, say, electronic calculators, and indeed why we can perform mental arithmetic, cannot be found in mathematics or logic. *The reason is that the laws of physics "happen to"*

permit the existence of physical models for the operations of arith-metic such as addition, subtraction and multiplication. [7, p. 101]

In brief, this appears false, or at best misleading, because of the assimilation of human to machine computation. We shall now see how, combined with the recognition that what is computable has physical determinants, this mistake ramifies in Deutsch's account of the nature of mathematics.

To begin, let us note that there is an entirely innocuous sense in which mathematical knowledge depends on physics — the sense in which our very existence depends on the universe being able to support our form of life. But if we think human and machine computation are on a par, we will clearly assign physics a much more direct role in determining our mathematical abilities, as Deutsch does in the quotation above. Our ability to perform arithmetic is supposed to depend on the laws of physics permitting the existence of physical models of arithmetical operations. Deutsch goes on, however, to claim that not only does our mathematical knowledge depend in this manner on physics, it depends also on our knowledge of physics.

This is a rather startling claim — it means that in some sense our knowledge of mathematics is empirical. What this amounts to is not, perhaps, immediately clear, but it certainly means more than that it is a contingent fact that we know any maths, which is trivial (it is of course only a contingent fact that I ever went to school and once there, was able to learn), and it is more than a claim that our mathematical knowledge should be regarded as *a posteriori*.

Deutsch presents the significance of his claim in terms of the certainty with which we know mathematics, suggesting that because our knowledge of mathematics depends on our knowledge of physics, mathematical knowledge cannot be, as it is normally thought to be, certain. But this is not quite right for it adheres to a widespread misconception about the concept of certainty. As Austin [1, *passim*] and in more detail, White [23] have shown, we *can* know contingent facts with certainty; and in order to know something, the logical possibility of doubt does not need to be excluded. Thus, just because we are taking mathematical knowledge to be dependent on knowledge of contingent fact, we cannot conclude that mathematical knowledge is uncertain, for contingent facts need not be uncertain. White suggests that something is certain if the possibility of its being otherwise is excluded, but argues that this possibility is the possibility of "may," not of "can" — we are interested in whether something *is* (was, will be) the case, not whether something *could* (logically, physically, legally, practically) be the case [23, §3]. Although what is necessarily true is certainly true because its occurrence is fixed by its necessity, its certainty is no different from the certainty a contingent truth may have — it is just certain for a different reason.

Having recognized that certainty should be contrasted with possibility rather than with doubt, we see that for Deutsch to deny that mathematical knowledge is certain he must be denying that what are known are necessary truths, for necessary truths are certain whether we know them or not. Clearly this is not what Deutsch wishes to say. He emphasizes in a number of places that mathematical truths are necessary and objective (independent of physical law) despite the dependence of mathematical knowledge on physical knowledge, and suggests that to make sense of this we need only distinguish between the methods of (the ways in which we know and come to know) mathematics and its subject matter [8, p. 253]. In order for us to see what the consequences of the claim that mathematical knowledge depends on knowledge of physics in fact are, and see whether the proposed distinction between the subject matter and method of mathematics can do any work, we must now make clear what this dependence is supposed to be.

The way the thesis is presented in Chap. 10 of *The Fabric of Reality* [8] is rather mystifying. After what starts off looking like a promising discussion of the confusion of thinking of abstract objects as problematic aethereal entities in an inaccessible world, rather than simple abstractions from, or idealizations of, everyday objects, Deutsch steps back into the Platonic idiom. He suggests that the gap between the physical world and the abstract world of mathematical objects needs to be bridged by hypotheses that given physical objects resemble abstract ones in particular ways [8, p. 241]. He goes on to say

> The reliability of the knowledge of a *perfect* circle that one can gain from a *diagram* of a circle depends entirely on the accuracy of the hypothesis that the two resemble each other in the relevant ways. Such a hypothesis, referring to a physical object (the diagram), amounts to a physical theory and can never be known with certainty. [8, p. 241]

This is peculiar, for the difficulty is presented not as lying with the hypothesis of resemblance between the physical and abstract objects, but with knowing what the properties of the physical object are. But why should we think we cannot know the relevant properties of the diagram, and if there is supposed to be a difficulty here, what status can the hypothesis of resemblance have? If we claim that the abstract object resembles our diagram in certain ways, but it turns out that the properties of the diagram differ from what we had thought they were, then there are two possibilities. Either the original resemblance claim is undermined, or it is not. If the claim *is* undermined, we are suggesting that the diagram does not in fact (or no longer) resembles the abstract object, but if that is the case, we must have knowledge of the abstract object independent of knowledge of the diagram in order to compare the two, so the hypothesis of resemblance between the abstract and physical objects plays no significant role in our knowledge of the abstract object. If, on the other hand, the claim is not undermined, then we cannot say that the resemblance is a hypothesis. Rather, it is a decision – whatever the relevant properties of the diagram are, or turn out to be, then those are the properties of the abstract object. But now we do not really have a claim of *resemblance* at all, the diagram itself becomes the ultimate object of comparison and the abstract object just drops out of the picture. Either way, we seem to have difficulties for the idea that our knowledge of abstract objects is based on a physical hypothesis of resemblance.

The discussion then turns to the question of what we can learn by written rather than diagrammatic proofs and here things take a more bizarre turn. Since the symbols we manipulate in written proofs and calculations are physical objects, the reliability of what we learn from these activities is supposed by Deutsch to depend on our having accurate theories of the physical behavior of the symbols involved; as if, given half a chance, they would charge around the page and spoil our proof. The idea again is that we hypothesize that the physical behavior of the symbols corresponds to the behavior of the abstractions they denote and thus the reliability of what we learn by doing maths on paper is supposed to depend on the accuracy of our theories describing the physical objects involved, the paper, the ink, our hands, eyes and brains[18]. But to this the immediate objection is that when we are manipulating mathematical symbols, going through a proof, solving an equation, we are not performing an experiment, seeing willy-nilly where the symbols take us. If we don't manipulate the symbols in the right way, if they don't "behave as we expect them to," then we have made a mistake, it is not a question of any theories we might have about the behavior of these objects being accurate or inaccurate. Indeed, we can see that this picture of mathematical knowledge depending on our theorizing about the behavior of physical objects cannot be correct. For, just as with the previous case of the diagram, unless it is fixed what it is about the physical objects involved in the proof or calculation that is supposed to resemble the abstract ones, then the claim of resemblance does not amount to anything (there being no genuine notion of *comparison* with the abstract objects), but if this is fixed, then our knowledge of the abstract objects is not based on knowledge of the physical objects, as the resemblance claim implies independent prior knowledge of the abstract objects. Either way, we are not learning anything about abstract objects by studying physical objects which are supposed to correspond to them.

It would appear that so far we have made little progress in understanding Deutsch's claim that mathematical knowledge depends on physical knowledge. To do a little better we need to interpret his claims in terms of the computational picture that underlies them. Let us consider for the moment, then, how we can gain mathematical knowledge from a computing machine. When we consider a computation undertaken by such a machine, our confidence that it has produced the right answer depends on our knowledge of the constitution of the machine. We need to know that it has run as intended

---

[18] Deutsch would clearly be invoking implicit theories about these things at this point, as we evidently make no explicit reference to such theories when calculating, nor, typically, would one even have access to such theories.

and that running as intended it would produce the desired answer. Thus the claim that the machine performs the computation we desire can be seen to have a demonstrative and descriptive element: *this* ($\nearrow$) physical system, runs like *this* (description), where something running in this way would be it performing the computation of interest. It is a physical question whether there actually exist any systems that fall under this description, it is an empirical question whether the machine we are pointing at does, and our claim that it does is only as reliable as our knowledge of the physics of the machine.

Here we see clearly how the mathematical knowledge that we gain from this computation depends on our knowledge of physics. To know the result of a calculation that the machine has computed, we need to know that the computation ran as expected. If a given result of the computation would prove a proposition, that the proposition is proven depends on whether the computer worked properly — we need to know that the physical processes of the computation ran as we hoped. All this is unproblematic, merely a recognition of the physical side of the theory of computing. Deutsch's position is then reached by generalizing from this case of the mathematical knowledge we derive from computers to *all* mathematical knowledge, by assimilating human performance of mathematics to machine computation; and now problems arise.

The difficulty we face here is not really that we would have to invoke implicit knowledge of the behavior of our brains, bodies and any accouterments involved in the putative computational process providing us with mathematical knowledge, wildly implausible as that may be. The real difficulty is that it cannot be true that mathematical knowledge in general is knowledge of the outcome of computations, for there could be nothing that would count as knowing that the computations had gone correctly. In the simple case of gaining knowledge from the computer on one's desk, we can gain mathematical knowledge because we know that if the computation was performed correctly, some proposition is true. But there is nothing comparable in the scenario Deutsch would have us endorse — it is not merely that we might not know whether the computation had run correctly, it is rather that there is nothing that would count as such knowledge: all that we can do is compare the outcomes of different computations. We have no criterion to decide what correctness or incorrectness of a computation would be, we just have physical processes going their own fair way in their own good time. Whatever they do will seem right, which is just to say that there is no notion of right or wrong here, hence no question of mathematical truth or falsity. To adopt a simile of Wittgenstein's, the situation would be as if one were to buy several copies of the morning paper in order to make sure that what it said was true.

Now, Deutsch is aware that there may be a difficulty here. He argues:

> The reason we are confident that the machines we call calculators do indeed compute the arithmetic functions they claim to compute is not that we can "check" their answers, for this is ultimately a futile

process of comparing one machine with another ... The real reason is that we believe the detailed physical theory that was used in their design. That theory, including its assertion that the abstract functions of arithmetic are realized in Nature, is empirical. [7, pp. 101–102]

But it is not at all clear that this is an adequate response. It amounts to the assertion that we can know a calculation is correct, i.e. we can have mathematical knowledge, because we have (defeasible) knowledge of physical processes which are hypothesized to correspond to abstract mathematical entities. But we have already seen that this picture of the genesis of mathematical knowledge is untenable. To reiterate, it leads to a dilemma: either the aspects in which the physical states and processes are supposed to correspond to abstract objects is determinate, in which case we must have prior knowledge of the abstract objects in order to make the resemblance claim; or these aspects are undetermined, in which case there can be no genuine notion of correspondence or resemblance to the abstract objects and hence no notion of right or wrong. (This latter horn of the dilemma is consonant with the problem raised in the preceding paragraph that a criterion of correctness is absent if all one can do is compare one physical process with another.)

Thus we see that the claim that mathematical knowledge depends on knowledge of physics can only make sense for the narrowly circumscribed case of our gaining mathematical knowledge from the output of a computing machine. It is mistaken to try and generalize this, as Deutsch does under the influence of the computational analogy, for what we are left with cannot be an account of mathematical knowledge. Deutsch's distinction between the subject matter and the methods of mathematics can then serve no purpose, for on his account what are known cannot be mathematical truths, so the subject matter is not that of mathematics. Further, this distinction has no application even for the simple case in which we can be said to gain mathematical knowledge from computers, for the dependence of this mathematical knowledge on knowledge of contingent fact does not prevent what is known from being certain, nor prevent our being able to know it for certain[19]. Thus Deutsch's claims about the nature of mathematics are mistaken.

Let us close this section by remarking on a corollary of the preceding discussion. In Chap. 10 of *The Fabric of Reality*, Deutsch claims that the possibility of performing proofs using a quantum computer means that we must accept that a proof is not an object, but a process; and this is one of the main themes of [9]. But if, as I have suggested, it is false that all mathematical knowledge is essentially computational or is knowledge of computational processes, this claim does not follow. In any case, the opposition between a proof as an object, a sequence of propositions, and as a process seems ill-founded. The essence of a proof is that if it is correct, then some statement is

---

[19] 'Knowing for certain' means that someone knows in such a way that what is known is revealed as certain — it is revealed that the possibility of it being otherwise is excluded.

proved, but how this is achieved is secondary. It is true that there are proofs that can be made on a computer that could not be written out as a sequence of propositions on paper, and more strikingly, proofs that can be performed on a quantum computer that cannot *in principle* be written down step by step (due to the necessity of interference between computational paths during the computation), but these facts do not entail that a proof must be considered as a computational process. It is perhaps better to think of proof as *sui generis* of which both written proofs and proofs using a computer, quantum or otherwise, are instances.

6   Conclusion

In this paper we have seen some of the difficulties associated with the distinctively philosophical theses implicit or explicit in Deutsch's 1985 paper. In the latter half we have seen how Deutsch's conception of the nature of computation and his adherence to the computational analogy give rise to some distinctive claims about the nature of mathematics, which prove to be untenable.

However, one of the most important theses of the 1985 paper was that the Turing Principle underlies the Church-Turing hypothesis; the bulk of my argument has been to suggest that this view is mistaken. The discussion might be summarized in the following way.

It is useful to distinguish between three different tasks with which the Church-Turing hypothesis is associated: characterizing the effectively calculable, providing the evolution of physical states with mathematical meaning and fixing upon a useful definition of physical computability. The Turing Principle could not replace or underlie the Church-Turing hypothesis for any of these tasks. Not the first, because the Turing Principle is supposed to concern all functions computable by physical systems, rather than what is computable by a human; and not the second or third because an empirical principle cannot play the crucial definitional mathematical role that I have emphasized. It is perhaps worth noting that the Turing Principle is undoubtedly most closely tied *in intention* to the third of these tasks rather than to the first. However, although it is true that Turing did not consider the possibility of computations using explicitly quantum objects, this can hardly be said to be to the detriment of the Church-Turing hypothesis. The third of the tasks I have mentioned, delimiting the bounds of physical computability, is not really, after all, the object of the Church-Turing hypothesis.

References

1. J. L. Austin. *Sense and Sensibilia*. Oxford University Press, 1962.
2. G. Boolos and R. Jeffrey. *Computability and Logic*. Cambridge University Press, 1974.

3. A. Church. An unsolvable problem of elementary number theory. *American Journal of Mathematics.*, 58:345–365, 1936. Repr. in [5] pp. 89–107.

4. B. J. Copeland. Narrow versus wide mechanism: Including a re-examination of Turing's views on the mind-machine issue. *The Journal of Philosophy*, XCVI(1), 2000.

5. M. Davis, editor. *The Undecidable*. Raven Press, Hewlett, New York, 1965.

6. M. Davis. Why Gödel didn't have Church's thesis. *Information and Control*, 54:3–24, 1982.

7. D. Deutsch. Quantum theory, the Church-Turing Principle and the universal quantum computer. *Proceedings of the Royal Society of London A*, 400:97–117, 1985.

8. D. Deutsch. *The Fabric of Reality*. Penguin Books, 1997.

9. D. Deutsch, A. Ekert, and R. Lupacchini. Machines, logic and quantum physics. See arXiv:math.HO/9911150, 1999.

10. J. Earman and J. Norton. Forever is a day: Supertasks in Pitowsky and Malament-Hogarth spacetimes. *Philosophy of Science*, 60:22–42, 1993.

11. A. Ekert and R. Jozsa. Quantum computation and Shor's factoring algorithm. *Reviews of Modern Physics*, 68(3):733–753, 1996.

12. R. P. Feynman. Simulating physics with computers. *International Journal of Theoretical Physics*, 21(6/7), 1982.

13. L. Grover. A fast quantum-mechanical algorithm for database search. In *Proceedings of the 28th Annual ACM Symposium on the Theory of Computing*, pp. 212–219, 1996.

14. P. M. S. Hacker. *Wittgenstein: Meaning and Mind, Part 1*. Blackwell, Oxford, 1993.

15. M. Hogarth. Non-Turing computers and non-Turing computability. *Philosophy of Science Supplementary*, I:126–138, 1994.

16. J. Hyman. *Investigating Psychology: Sciences of the Mind after Wittgenstein*, pages 1–24. Routledge, 1991.

17. M. A. Nielsen and I. L. Chuang. *Quantum Computation and Quantum Information*. Cambridge University Press, 2000.

18. B. Schumacher. Quantum coding. *Physical Review A*, 51(4):2738, 1995.

19. S. G. Shanker. Wittgenstein versus Turing on the nature of Church's thesis. *Notre Dame Journal of Formal Logic*, 28(4):615–49, October 1987. See also Shanker, S. G. *Wittgenstein's Remarks on the Foundations of AI*, Chap. 1, Routledge, 1998.

20. P. W. Shor. Algorithms for quantum computation: Discrete logarithms and factoring. In *Proceedings of the 35th Annual IEEE Symposium on Foundations of Computer Science*, 1994. See also arXiv:quant-ph/9508027.

21. R. I. Soare. Computability and recursion. *The Bulletin of Symbolic Logic*, 2(3), 1996.

22. A. Turing. On computable numbers, with an application to the *Entscheidungsproblem*. *Proceedings of the London Mathematical Society*, 42:230–65, 1936. Repr. in [5] pp. 116–151.

23. A. White. Certainty. *Proceedings of the Aristotelian Society Supplementary*, 46:1–18, 1972.

24. L. Wittgenstein. *The Blue and Brown Books*. Blackwell, Oxford, 1960.

25. L. Wittgenstein. *Philosophical Investigations*. Blackwell, Oxford, third edition, 1967.

26. L. Wittgenstein. *Remarks on the Foundations of Mathematics*. Blackwell, Oxford, 1978. Eds., von Wright, G. H., Rhees, R. and Anscombe, G. E. M.

27. L. Wittgenstein. *Remarks on the Philosophy of Psychology*, volume 1. Blackwell, Oxford, 1980. Eds., Anscombe, G. E. M. and von Wright, G. H.

28. A. C. Yao. Quantum circuit complexity. In *Proceedings of the 34th Annual IEEE Symposium on Foundations of Computer Science*, 1993.

Implementation of a Self-replicating Universal Turing Machine

Hector Fabio Restrepo[1,2], Gianluca Tempesti[1], and Daniel Mange[1]

[1] Swiss Federal Institute of Technology, Lausanne, Logic Systems Laboratory
[2] Grupo de Percepción y Sistemas Inteligentes,
Escuela de Ing. Eléctrica y Electrónica, Universidad del Valle, Cali

Summary. The goal of this contribution is to describe how a universal Turing machine was embedded into a hardware system in order to verify the computational universality of a novel architecture. This implementation was realized with a multi-cellular automaton inspired by the embryonic development of living organisms. In such an architecture, every artificial "cell" contains a complete copy of the description of the machine, a redundancy that allows the introduction of the properties of self-repair and self-replication. These properties were coupled with a modified version of the W-machine to realize a robust, self-replicating universal computer in actual hardware.

1 Introduction

In the 1930s, before the advent of digital computers, several logicians (Kurt Gödel, Alonzo Church, Stephen Kleene, Emil Post, and Alan Mathison Turing) began to think about the theoretical limits of computation. Alonzo Church and Alan Turing independently arrived, through different approaches, at equivalent conclusions. Both solutions described computability, but while Church (1932–34) described it with λ-calculus, Turing's idea (1936) was based on a mathematical model of a machine that could compute any computable function: the *Turing machine* [3, 20].

Throughout the history of computer science, the Turing machine has remained a vital benchmark in the validation of novel architectures. Most notably, in the historical work of John von Neumann in the 1950s [22], the computational universality of the Turing machine was coupled with another fundamental property: *constructional universality*, that is, the ability to construct any kind of machine, given its description. The most remarkable product of the coupling of these two properties was the development of the machine known as *Von Neumann's Universal Constructor*, essentially a cellular automaton capable of self-replication and of realizing a universal Turing machine.

Although the complexity of von Neumann's implementation makes it unsuitable for a hardware implementation (indeed, even a software simulation remains almost beyond the possibilities of modern computer systems), the self-replication of computing machines remains an interesting solution to the problem of realizing "perfect" systems from imperfect components. In fact, the predicted introduction of extremely complex systems realized at the molecular level (through, for example, nanotechnology processes) is bringing this issue to the leading edge of research.

The contents of this contribution are the results of our research in the domain of computing machines inspired by the properties of biological organisms within a project called *Embryonics* (for "embryonic electronics"). In particular, we shall describe an approach based on the development of complex machines (our artificial organisms) implemented by a *multi-cellular architecture*. In this architecture, organisms are two-dimensional arrays of cells, where each cell is a small processing unit that stores a complete copy of the machine's genome in the form of a microprogram. Each cell then executes only a specific part of the program (the cell's *gene*) depending on its spatial position within the organism (a mechanism analogous to cellular differentiation in living beings), as determined by a set of coordinates.

We have shown in the past that our architectures are capable of implementing the properties of self-replication and of self-repair [6]. To demonstrate the computational universality of our machines we were naturally led, as was von Neumann fifty years ago, to show that our architecture can realize a universal Turing machine [13–15]. Unlike von Neumann, however, we will go beyond pencil-and-paper and implement our self-replicating Turing machine in hardware, demonstrating not only the feasibility but also the efficiency of our approach. The goal of this contribution is the description of our implementation of such a machine.

In Sect. 2 we present a brief introduction to the concept and structure of Turing machines, from the specialized, application-specific machines to the universal version that is the main topic of this contribution. In Sect. 3 we introduce the basic features of Embryonics architectures, based on multicellular arrays of cells, along with the architecture of an ideal and of an actual universal Turing machine able to self-replicate, exploiting the features of the Embryonics machines. In Sect. 4 we then describe the PICOPASCAL language and a hardware implementation of a PICOPASCAL interpreter, necessary in order to understand our Embryonics implementation. Sect. 5 describes the detailed implementation of a self-replicating universal Turing machine. A discussion of our results follows in the final section (Sect. 6).

2 Turing Machines

2.1 Specialized Turing Machines

In his 1936 paper [21], A. M. Turing defined the class of abstract machines that now bear his name: a *specialized Turing machine* (Fig. 1), or simply a *Turing machine*, is a finite-state machine (the *program*, to use Turing's terminology) controlling a mobile head, which operates on a tape. The tape, composed of a sequence of locations (rectangles in the figure), contains a

Tape

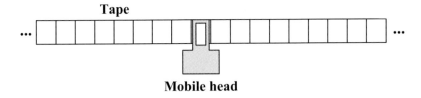

Mobile head

Fig. 1. A specialized Turing machine

string of symbols (the *data*). The tape should theoretically be considered as infinite in both directions. However, for all practical purposes, we can assume that, when the machine starts operating, the tape will be blank except for some finite number of squares. With this assumption, we can consider the tape as finite at any given moment, but capable of being infinitely extended whenever the machine comes to an end of the finite portion (an important assumption in view of the planned hardware implementation).

The head is situated, at any given moment, on a single square of the tape and has to carry out three operations to complete one step of the computation (one operation cycle of the finite-state machine). These operations are:

1. reading the symbol stored in the accessed location on the tape;
2. writing a symbol in the accessed location, erasing the previous symbol (of course, the latter can be preserved if the machine writes the same symbol that was read);
3. deplacing the head left or right to an adjacent location (which becomes the accessed location for the next computation step).

A Turing machine can therefore be described by three functions f_1, f_2, f_3:

$$Q+ = f_1(Q, S)$$
$$S+ = f_2(Q, S)$$
$$D+ = f_3(Q, S)$$

where Q and S are, respectively, the current internal state of the finite state machine (FSM) and the current input symbol (the symbol in the accessed location on the tape), and where $Q+$, $S+$, and $D+$ are, respectively, the next internal state of the FSM, the symbol to be written in the accessed location, and the direction (left or right) of the head's displacement [12].

As a consequence, a set of *quintuples* can be used to specify what the machine will do for each possible combination of symbol and state. These quintuples have the following form:

(*current state, current symbol, next state, next symbol, direction of motion*)

or, equivalentely:

$$(Q, S, Q+, S+, D+)$$

where the third, fourth, and fifth symbols are determined by the first and second according to the three functions f_1, f_2, and f_3 mentioned above.

These quintuples indicate that if a Turing machine is currently in the internal state Q, and if the current input symbol is S, the machine will change its internal state to the state $Q+$, replace the input symbol on the tape by the symbol $S+$, and move the read/write head by one location in the direction $D+$. If a Turing machine is in a condition for which it has no instruction, it halts.

The information contained in the set of quintuples is often represented in the form of a state table, defining the behavior of the machine for each possible combination of symbol and state.

An important observation, in view of the definition of the universal Turing machine that will follow in the next subsection, is that, because the head can move either way along the tape, it is possible for it to return to a previously printed location to recover the information inscribed there. This ability provides the machine a sort of rudimentary memory in a sense that the machine can look up the previous symbols and change them if necessary. Since the tape is as long as desired, this memory is potentially infinite.

2.2   Universal Turing Machines

Turing had the idea of the universal Turing machine (UTM), capable of simulating the operation of any specialized Turing machine, and gave an exact description of such a UTM in his paper [21]. The importance of the universal Turing machine is clear. We do not need to have an infinity of different machines doing different jobs. A single one will suffice [2].

A universal Turing machine, U, is a Turing machine with the property of being able to read the description (on its tape) of any other Turing machine, T, and to behave as T would have. The machine U consists of a finite-state machine (the program of U) controlling a mobile head, which operates on a tape. The data on the tape completely describe the machine T to be simulated (the data of T and the program of T, i.e., the three functions $Q+$, $S+$, and $D+$ describing T).

Fig. 2 shows the organization of U's tape. To the left is a semi-infinite region containing the data of T's tape. Somewhere in this region is a marker M indicating where T's head is currently located. The middle region contains the current internal state Q and the current input symbol S of T. The right-hand region is used to record the description of T, i.e., the three functions $Q+$, $S+$, and $D+$ for each combination of Q and S.

The subject of this contribution is the realization of a universal Turing machine in hardware. The requirements of digital electronics in general and of the Embryonics architectures in particular have had an impact on the implementation choices for our UTM. For example, while theoretically a single tape is sufficient to store both the data and the program, an alternative but equivalent architecture separates the *program tape* from the data tape. It is

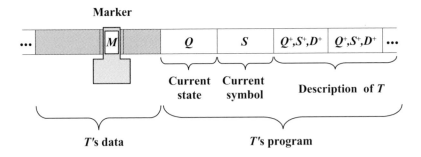

Fig. 2. Universal Turing machine's tape, describing the specialized machine T

this latter architecture, better suited to our Embryonics machines, that we adopted for our implementation.

3 Self-replication of a Universal Turing Machine on a Multicellular Array

3.1 Embryonics Architectures

Living organisms are complex systems exhibiting a range of desirable characteristics, such as evolution, adaptation, and fault tolerance, that have proved difficult to realize using traditional engineering methodologies. The last three decades of investigations in the field of molecular biology (embryology, genetics, and immunology) has brought a clearer understanding of how living systems grow and develop. The principles used by Nature to build and maintain complex living systems are now available for the engineer to draw inspiration from [10].

The growth and the operation of all living beings are directed through the interpretation, in each of their cells, of a chemical program, the DNA. This program, called *genome*, is the blueprint of the organism and consists of a complex sequence written with an alphabet of four characters: A, C, G, and T. This process is the source of inspiration for the *Embryonics* (*embryonic electronics*) project [5,6,9,16], whose final objective is the conception of very large scale integrated circuits endowed with properties usually associated with the living world: self-repair and self-replication.

The MICTREE (for *tree of micro-instructions*) cell is a new kind of *coarse-grained field-programmable gate array* (*FPGA*), developed in the framework of the Embryonics project, which will be used for the implementation of multicellular artificial organisms with biological-like properties, i.e., capable of self-repair and self-replication [7,17].

MICTREE is a truly *cellular automaton* and its conception derives from the study of multicellular living beings. It relies on three fundamental features: multicellular organization (the artificial organism is decomposed into

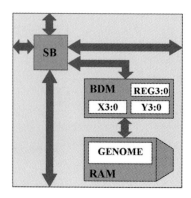

Fig. 3. MICTREE block diagram; *SB*: switch block; *BDM*: binary decision machine; *RAM*: random access memory; *REG3:0* : state register; *X3:0* : horizontal coordinate; *Y3:0* : vertical coordinate

a finite number of cells, where each cell realizes a simple function, described by a sub-program called the gene of the cell), cellular differentiation (the behavior of the cell depends on the physical position of the cell in the two-dimensional space, i.e., on its coordinates), and cellular division (starting from a mother cell, storing the one and only copy of the genome, a new cell can be programmed to store an exact copy of the genome).

The environment in which our quasi-biological artificial cells will develop consists of a finite (but as large as desired) two-dimensional space of silicon. This space is divided into rows and columns whose intersections define the cells. Since such cells (small processors and their memory) have an identical physical structure, i.e., an identical set of logic operators and of connections, the cellular array is homogeneous. Only the state of the cell, that is, the content of its registers, can differentiate it from its neighbors.

In all living beings, the string of characters which makes up the DNA, the *genome*, is executed sequentially by a chemical processor, the *ribosome*. Drawing inspiration from this mechanism, MICTREE is based on a *binary decision machine* (BDM) [4] (our ribosome), which sequentially executes a microprogram (our genome). In addition, the artificial cell is composed of a random access memory (RAM), and a communication system implemented by a switch block (SB) (Fig. 3).

The *binary decision machine* executes a microprogram of up to 1024 instructions (the format of these instructions will be detailed later), which is stored in the RAM. The microprogram itself is decomposed in sub-programs that are equivalent to the different parts of the genome: the genes. The execution of a specific gene depends on the physical position of the cell in the two-dimensional array, i.e., on its coordinates.

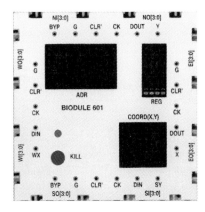

Fig. 4. BIODULE 601 demonstration module

As in nature, the entire microprogram of the organism is stored in each cell. This redundancy enormously simplifies the implementation of the desired properties of self-repair and self-replication:

- A set of BIST (Built-In Self-Test) techniques [1, 11, 18, 19] detects the presence of faults within a cell. The column of cells containing the faulty cell is deactivated, and its functionality taken up by the column to its right, whose functionality is itself shifted to the right, and so on until a *spare column* is reached. The presence of the entire genome in each cell implies that this self-repair mechanism needs only a re-computation of the coordinates, without complex data transfers.
- The self-replication of an artificial organism rests on two hypotheses: (1) there exists a sufficient number of spare cells (i.e., the array is sufficiently large to hold more than one copy of the organism) and (2) the calculation of the coordinates produces a cycle. If these two hypotheses are met, the computation of the coordinates in the array automatically creates multiple copies of the artificial organism.

The MICTREE cell has been embedded into a plastic demonstration module, the BIODULE 601 (Fig. 4). Each module can be easily joined with others, like a LEGO®[1] brick, to build larger artificial organisms. The size of the artificial organism embedded in an array of MICTREE cells is limited in the first place by the coordinate space ($X = 0...15$, $Y = 0...15$), that is, a maximum of 256 cells for the BIODULE 601 implementation, and then by the size of the memory of the binary decision machine storing the genome microprogram (1024 instructions).

---

[1] LEGO® is a trademark of the LEGO Group of companies.

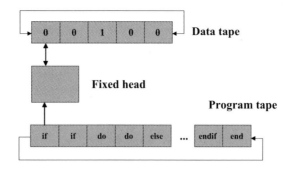

Fig. 5. Universal Turing machine architecture

3.2   Multicellular Architecture of a Universal Turing Machine

As we have seen, conventional universal Turing machines [12] consist of a finite but arbitrarily long tape, and a single read/write mobile head controlled by a finite-state machine, which is itself described on the tape (Fig. 2). In order to implement a universal Turing machine in an array of MICTREE artificial cells, we made three fundamental architectural choices (Fig. 5):

1. The read/write head is fixed; the tapes are mobile.
2. The data of the given application (the specialized Turing machine to be simulated) are placed on a mobile tape, the *data tape*; this tape can shift right, shift left, or stay in place.
3. The finite-state machine for the given application is translated into a very simple program written in a language called PICOPASCAL (Sect. 4); each instruction of this program is placed in a square of a second mobile tape, the *program tape*; this tape just needs to shift left. The transformation of a state table into such a program is directly inspired by the W-machine [23] with the major contribution of avoiding the jumps required by the **if** 1 **then** (*n*) **else** (*next*) instructions.

The fixed head, which is in fact an interpreter of the PICOPASCAL language, has to continuously execute cycles consisting of four operations:

1. reading and decoding an instruction on the program tape;
2. reading a symbol on the data tape;
3. interpreting the current instruction, and writing a new symbol on the data tape;
4. shifting the data tape (left or right or not at all) and the program tape (left).

3.3   An Application: a Binary Counter

In order to test our UTM implementation (Fig. 5), we used, as a simple but non-trivial example, a binary counter [12], a machine that writes out the binary numbers 1, 10, 11, 100, etc., the size of the numbers being limited only by the dimensions of the data tape. The counter's state table (Fig. 6) has two internal states ($Q \in \{0 \to, 1 \leftarrow\}$) and two input states ($S \in \{0, 1\}$), S being the value of the current square read on the data tape. In this example we combined the internal state Q with the direction of the tape. For $Q = \{0 \to\}$ the data tape will move to the right, for $Q = \{1 \leftarrow\}$ the data tape will move to the left. Depending on the values of Q and S, the specialized Turing machine will:

1. write a new binary value $S+$ (0, 1) on the current square of the data tape;
2. move its data tape to the right ($Q+ = 0 \to$) or to the left ($Q+ = 1 \leftarrow$), which is equivalent to moving a mobile head to the left or to the right, respectively;
3. go to the next state $Q+$ ($0 \to$, $1 \leftarrow$).

$Q+,S+$	$S=0$	$S=1$
$Q= 0\to$	$0\to,0$	$1\leftarrow,1$
$Q= 1\leftarrow$	$0\to,1$	$1\leftarrow,0$

Fig. 6. State table of the binary counter

The PICOPASCAL program equivalent to the state table (Fig. 6) is given in Fig. 7.

ADR	DATA	PROGRAM
00	5	if (Q)
01	5	if (S)
02	A	do 0 (S)
03	9	do 1$\leftarrow$ (Q)
04	4	else
05	B	do 1 (S)
06	8	do 0$\to$(Q)
07	6	endif
08	4	else
09	5	if (S)
0A	B	do 1 (S)
0B	9	do 1$\leftarrow$ (Q)
0C	4	else
0D	A	do 0 (S)
0E	8	do 0$\to$ (Q)
0F	6	endif
10	6	endif
11	2	end

Fig. 7. PICOPASCAL program equivalent to the state table of Fig. 6

3.4   An Ideal Architecture for the Universal Turing Machine

A universal Turing machine architecture, ideal in the sense that it is able to deal with applications of any complexity, is characterized by:

1. a finite, but arbitrarily long data tape;
2. a read/write head able to interpret a PICOPASCAL program of any complexity;
3. a finite, but arbitrarily long program tape.

It must be pointed out that, for any application, the program tape and the read/write head (the PICOPASCAL interpreter) are always characterized by finite and defined dimensions; only the data tape can be as long as desired, as is the case for the binary counter, whose growth is potentially infinite.

An ideal architecture, embedding the current example, but compatible with any other application, could be the following (Fig. 8):

1. The data tape, able to shift right, to shift left, or hold, is folded on itself. The initial state is defined in Fig. 8 by $QL3{:}0$, QC, $QR0{:}3 = 000010000$, where QL are the squares to the left of the central square QC, and QR are the squares to the right of QC; the data tape is able to grow to the left of QC, i.e., to the right of $QL3$ ($QL4,QL5, ...$) and to the right of QC ($QR4$, $QR5$, ...), as can be appreciated in Fig. 8.
2. The fixed read/write head, which will be detailed in Sect. 5, is basically composed of a state register Q,S (storing the current values of internal and input states Q,S, respectively, with an initial state $Q,S = 01$) and a stack $ST1{:}3$ characterized by a 1-out-of-3 code (one-hot encoding). At the start of the execution of the PICOPASCAL program (i.e., in Fig. 7, at address $ADR = 00$), the stack is in an initial state $ST1{:}3 = 100$. Roughly speaking, each **if** instruction will involve a PUSH operation, each **endif** a POP operation, and each **else** a LOAD operation. When $ST1 = 1$, the **do** instructions are executed. The main characteristic of the stack is its scalability: for any program exhibiting n nested **if** instructions, the stack is organized as a $n+1$ squares shift register. Both the $ST1{:}3$ stack and the Q,S register are able to grow to accommodate more complex applications.
3. The program tape is folded on itself; it is able to grow to accommodate more complex applications.

This ideal architecture is moreover compatible with the Embryonics concept: self-replication may be accomplished along the vertical axis, self-repair along the horizontal axis, and the scalable properties of both the data tape and the fixed head (stack and Q,S registers) are compatible with the limited number of distinct coordinates (a scalable and regular architecture may be described by repetition of the same type of cells, i.e., of the same coordinates).

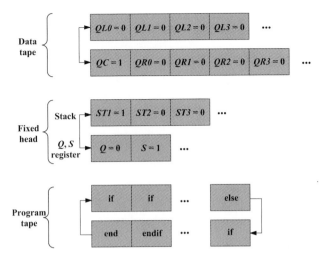

Fig. 8. UTM's ideal architecture

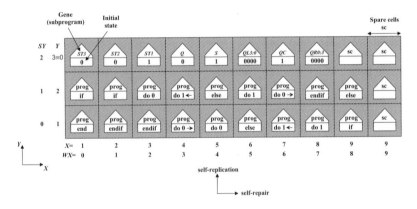

Fig. 9. UTM's actual implementation for the binary counter example on a multicellular array of 27 MICTREE cells plus 3 spare cells (sc). *WX*: horizontal coordinate of the western neighboring cell; *SY*: vertical coordinate of the southern neighboring cell

3.5   An Actual Implementation of the Universal Turing Machine

In order to implement the binary counter application with a limited number of MICTREE artificial cells, we have somewhat relaxed the requirements of the ideal architecture described earlier. Our final architecture is made up of three rows ($Y = 1...3$) and nine columns ($X = 1...9$) organized as follows (Fig. 9):

- The 18 instructions of the PICOPASCAL program (Fig. 7) are placed in the program tape, using the two lower rows ($Y = 1, 2$) of the array.

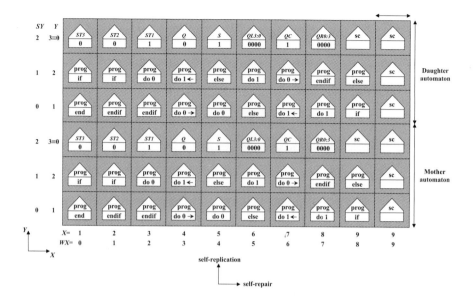

Fig. 10. *Self-replication of the UTM's actual implementation for the binary counter example.* WX: *horizontal coordinate of the western neighboring cell;* SY: *vertical coordinate of the southern neighboring cell*

- The read/write head is composed of a $ST1:3$ stack and of the Q,S register ($X = 1...5$, $Y = 3$), while the data tape is implemented by three cells ($X = 6...8$, $Y = 3$) storing 9 bits $QL3:0$, QC, $QR0:3$.

In order to demonstrate self-repair, we added spare cells to each row, at the right-hand side of the UTM, all identified by the same horizontal coordinate ($X = 9$ in Fig. 9). As previously mentioned, more cells may be used not only for self-repair, but also for a UTM necessitating a growth of the tape of arbitrary, but finite, length.

Self-replication rests on two hypotheses (Fig. 10):

- there exist a sufficient number of spare cells (unused cells at the upper side of the array, at least $3 \times 9 = 27$ for our example);
- the calculation of the coordinates produces a cycle at the cellular level (in our example: $Y = 1 \rightarrow 2 \rightarrow 0 \rightarrow 1 \rightarrow 2 \rightarrow 0$).

Given a sufficiently large space, the self-replication process can be repeated for any number of specimens in the Y axis. With a sufficient number of cells, it is obviously possible to combine self-repair (or growth) towards the X direction and self-replication towards the Y direction.

In the next section we will present the PICOPASCAL language and a PICOPASCAL interpreter architecture, which are necessary for understanding our Embryonics implementation.

4   PICOPASCAL

4.1   The PICOPASCAL Language

The PICOPASCAL language consists of a minimal subset of the MODULA-2 language [24]. PICOPASCAL is thus a *high-level* language: it does not make use of explicit addressing and provides great simplicity of use. PICOPASCAL is, moreover, a *structured* language and thus guarantees, because of its structure, a rigorous and efficient notation. In conformity with this last feature, PICOPASCAL has three fundamental constructs, described below: (1) the sequence, (2) the choice or alternative, and (3) the iteration.

The assignment **do...**, realizing the synchronous transfer of a constant into a register, is a structured program. The *sequence* (or composition) of two such instructions $P1$ and $P2$, written **do** $P1P2$, is a structured program, described by the flowchart and by the mnemonic program of Fig. 11a. This last notation consists of a linear succession of instructions, displayed in the growing order of addresses ADR.

The *choice* (or alternative) of $P1$ or $P2$, where $P1$ and $P2$ are two assignments, is a structured program, written **if** a **then** $P1$ **else** $P2$. It is represented symbolically by the flowchart of Fig. 11b, and realized by the linear succession of instructions of the corresponding functional diagram and mnemonic program. To facilitate comprehension, and unlike programs written in a low-level language using explicit addresses, there is no jump (notably, to avoid the instruction $P1$ when $a = 0$ or the instruction $P2$ when $a = 1$): all instructions are read sequentially, from $ADR=0$ to $ADR=4$, and the execution of the assignments $P1$ or $P2$ depends on the value of a signal $EXEC$ (for $EXECUTE$) which, in turn, depends on the value of the test variable a. This process will be revisited in detail in the description of the interpreter of the PICOPASCAL language (Subsect. 4.2).

The last construct of structured programming, the *conditional iteration* **while** a **do** $P1$, is thus not necessary in the PICOPASCAL language. However, since our program must be continually executed, notably to allow self-repair, we allow the loop illustrated by the flowchart of Fig. 11c, which in fact introduces a non-conditional iteration on the entire program.

In conclusion, the PICOPASCAL language is described by the *syntactic diagram* of Fig. 11d, where we can count ten different terminal symbols (ovals), which make up the instructions of the language: **begin**, **end**, **NOP**, **do** 0, **do** 1, **do** 0→, **do** 1←, **if**, **else**, **endif**. The **NOP** (*No operation*) instruction represents the execution of a neutral operation.

Fig. 12a shows the operating code (*OPC*) for the instructions of the PICOPASCAL language. Fig. 12b and Fig. 12c show the binary decision diagram of the binary counter example and its PICOPASCAL description, derived from the state table in Fig. 6.

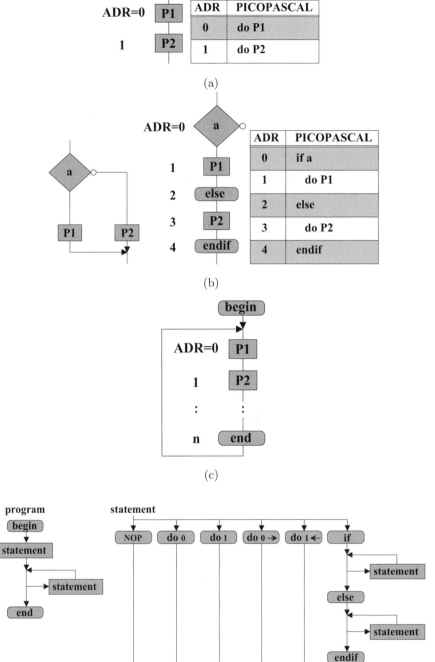

Fig. 11. PICOPASCAL language. (a) Sequence of two assignment instructions: **do** *P1P2*. (b) Choice of either *P1* or *P2*: **if** *a* **then** *P1* **else** *P2*. (c) Non-conditional iteration loop. (d) Syntactic diagram

OPC3:0	OPC	Instruction	OPC3:0	OPC	Instruction
0000	0	NOP	1000	8	do 0 →
0001	1	begin	1001	9	do 1 ←
0010	2	end	1010	A	do 0
0011	3		1011	B	do 1
0100	4	else	1100	C	
0101	5	if	1101	D	
0110	6	endif	1110	E	
0111	7		1111	F	

(a)

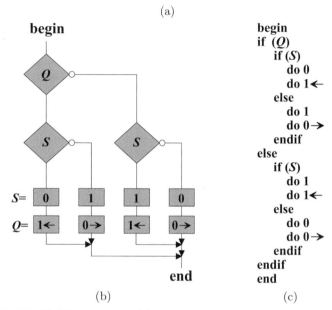

begin
if (Q)
    if (S)
        do 0
        do 1←
    else
        do 1
        do 0→
    endif
else
    if (S)
        do 1
        do 1←
    else
        do 0
        do 0→
    endif
endif
end

(b)   (c)

Fig. 12. PICOPASCAL language. (a) Opcodes for the ten instructions of the PI-COPASCAL language. (b) Binary decision diagram of the binary counter example. (c) PICOPASCAL description

4.2   PICOPASCALINE: an Interpreter for the PICOPASCAL Language

Fig. 13 suggests a possible hardware architecture to execute the ten instructions of the PICOPASCAL language. From now on we will refer to this machine as PICOPASCALINE. The instruction **end**, as well as the pseudo-instruction **begin** (not executed), have the same effect: jumping to the instruction at address 0 (note that in this architecture the **begin** instruction is not necessary and can thus be removed). The **if** instruction does not require a test variable, since the hardware is capable of presenting the correct variable at the right time. There exist therefore nine distinct types of instruction to interpret.

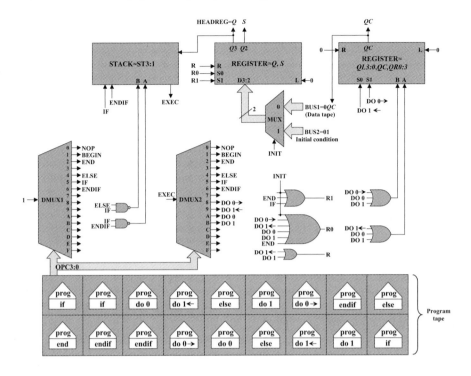

Fig. 13. PICOPASCALINE: PICOPASCAL interpreter for the ten instructions of the language

To decode the instructions (*OPC3:0*) on the program tape, the PICO-PASCALINE consists of the following elements (Fig. 13):

- A state register REGISTER storing the current values of the internal and input states Q, and S respectively, with an initial state $Q,S = 01$.
- A register REGISTER storing the values $QL3:0,QC,QR0:3$ of the data tape, with an initial state $QL3:0,QC,QR0:3 = 000010000$.
- A stack STACK characterized by a 1-out-of-3 code (one-hot encoding), with an initial state STACK = $ST3:1 = 001$.
- A decoder DMUX1 controlled by the 4 bits of the operating code *OPC3:0*, which generates the signals controlling the STACK (signals *IF*, *ELSE*, and *ENDIF*).
- A decoder DMUX2 controlled by the 4 bits of the operating code *OPC3:0* and by the *EXEC* signal. This decoder generates the signals controlling the (Q,S) and $(QL3:0,QC,QR0:3)$ REGISTERs (signals *DO 0*, *DO 1*, *DO 0→*, *DO 1←*, *IF*, and *ELSE*).
- A multiplexer MUX controlled by the signal *INIT*, which selects one of the two input busses, *BUS1* coming from the data tape, or *BUS2* which is a constant used for initialization purposes. At the start of the execution

the signal *INIT* has the value 1 and the (Q,S) REGISTER is initialized, whereas during the rest of the execution this variable takes the value 0 and the value QC coming from the $(QL3{:}0,QC,QR0{:}3)$ REGISTER is assigned to the (Q,S) REGISTER.

The signal *EXEC* controls the execution of the assignment instructions **do** and thus depends on the succession of values of the internal and input states Q and S. We will now examine this process for the example of the program of Figures 7 and 12, whose detailed execution is shown in Fig. 14. We assume that the values of the test variables are $Q{=}1$ and $S{=}0$ and that these values do not change during the execution of the microprogram. Disposing of a stack (STACK) of 1-bit wide and three levels deep, we observe the following chronology:

- At the start of the program's execution, the three levels of the stack are initialized to the value $ST3{:}1{=}001$. The signal *EXEC*, which is the value at the top of the STACK, i.e., $ST1$, is thus equal to 1.
- The first logic test (**if** Q) produces a value 1 which is placed at the top of the stack (operation PUSH). *EXEC* keeps the value 1.
- The second test (**if** S) produces a value 0 which in turn is placed at the top of the stack (PUSH). *EXEC* is reset to 0.
- Since the *EXEC* signal is 0, the assignment **do** 0 and **do** 1← are not executed (NOP): the stack remains in a neutral state (NOP operation) and the *EXEC* signal is still 0.
- The instruction **else** indicates the passage from the left branch of the test (**if** S **then** *P1*) to the right branch (**else** *P2*). It corresponds to a COMPLEMENT operation, where the top of the STACK ($ST1 = EXEC$) is inverted, while the content is changed to maintain the 1-out-of-3 code. The signal *EXEC* is again set to 1.
- Since *EXEC* is now 1, the assignments **do** 1, and **do** 0→ are executed.
- The instruction **endif** controls the popping of the stack (POP operation). The signal *EXEC* keeps the value 1 to maintain the 1-out-of-3 code.
- The execution of the program then continues as above until the final instruction **end**, where the stack finds again its initial state, with its first level in the state 1 ($EXEC{=}1$).

The operation table of Fig. 15a describes the global operation of the stack, while the logic diagram of Fig. 15b describes a possible realization of the stack, according to the table of operations of Fig. 15a. With the exception of the first and second levels, we note the iterative nature of this stack, which contains six levels in this implementation and is thus capable of successively testing up to six variables (six is therefore the highest number of nested tests in this implementation).

The intrinsic limitations of the PICOPASCALINE interpreter are determined by the number and size of the registers, as well as by the number of

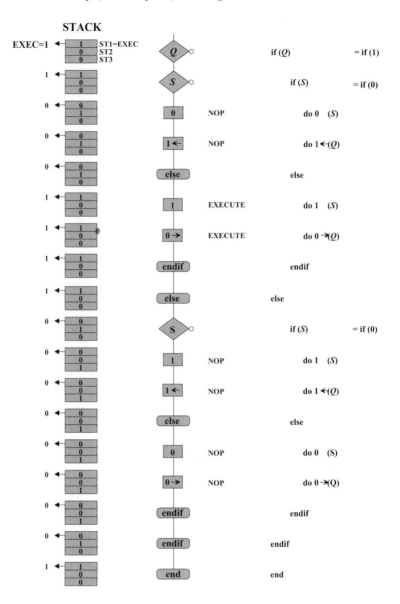

Fig. 14. Interpretation of the program of Figures 7 and 12. The values of the test variables are $Q=1$ and $S=0$ (these values do not change during the execution of the PICOPASCAL program)

tested variables which can be stored in the stack. A detailed description of the operation of the stack can be found in [13].

STACK6:3		
B A	**operation**	**OPC**
0 0	HOLD	others
0 1	SHIFT RIGHT	endif
1 0	SHIFT LEFT	if
1 1	LOAD	Φ

STACK2		
B A	**operation**	**OPC**
0 0	HOLD	others
0 1	SHIFT RIGHT	endif
1 0	SHIFT LEFT	else
1 1	LOAD	if

STACK1		
B A	**operation**	**OPC**
0 0	HOLD	others
0 1	SHIFT RIGHT	else
1 0	SHIFT LEFT	endif
1 1	LOAD	if

Φ **represents the "don't care" condition**

(a)

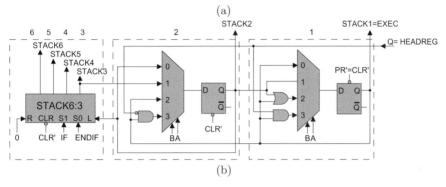

(b)

Fig. 15. 6-level PICOPASCALINE stack. (a) Operation tables. (b) Detailed architecture

The PICOPASCAL language and its interpreter were used to realize the architecture described in Sect. 3 and thus implement our self-replicating universal Turing machine. In the next section we will describe in some more detail the structure and operation of the genome microprogram of our organism.

5   Detailed Implementation of a Universal Turing Machine

5.1   The Genome Microprogram

As shown in Fig. 9, the actual implementation of our UTM architecture consists of 27 cells, where each cell contains the entire genome of the organism and, depending on its position in the array, can interpret the genome and extract and execute the gene which configures it.

The genome microprogram thus consists of three main parts, as shown in the flowchart **UTMgenome** of Fig. 16: first, the initial conditions for the machine are set, then the coordinates are computed (left loop: this process requires several iterations to allow for the propagation of the coordinates through the array), and finally the operative genome is executed (right loop). The latter can itself be decomposed into the distinct genes required by our artificial organism (Fig. 9): the *program tape genes*, the *stack genes*, the *register genes*, and the *data tape genes*.

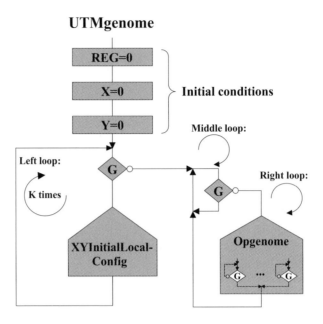

Fig. 16. Complete genome microprogram (**UTMgenome**) flowchart

The definition of the initial conditions assures that

- all the state registers of the array are set to 0 ($REG = 0$) and
- the coordinates X and Y are set to 0 ($X = 0$, $Y = 0$).

The microprogram then executes one of three loops, controlled by the variable G (the global clock):

1. For the first period of G, while $G = 1$, at least K executions of the left-hand loop are necessary to ensure that the rightmost and the uppermost cells of the organism correctly compute their coordinates, their initial conditions, and their local configurations (as defined by the sub-program **XYInitialLocalConfig**). K is the sum of Xmax and Ymax (Xmax and Ymax are, respectively, the maximum number of rows and columns of the artificial organism). In our example, $K = 13$ (Fig. 10).
2. At the falling edge of G ($G = 1 \rightarrow 0$), the right loop is selected and the operational part of the genome is executed. To assure the synchronization of all the cells, tests are performed throughout the half-period when $G = 0$, but no assignment is made until the rising edge of G ($G = 0 \rightarrow 1$), when all the registers REG are updated simultaneously.

3. At the rising edge of G ($G = 0 \rightarrow 1$), after the update of the registers, the middle loop is executed. The program stays in this loop until the next falling edge of G ($G = 1 \rightarrow 0$) arrives, selecting the right-hand loop and starting a new cycle.

The following subsections will describe in detail the calculation of the operative genome in general and of the program tape genes in particular. A detailed decription of the calculation of the other components of the genome (e.g., the computation of the coordinates and the definition of the initial conditions) can be found in [13].

5.2   Computing the Operative Genome

From the description of Fig. 9 we can observe that our artificial organism is composed of four main parts:

- The *program tape* realizes the PICOPASCAL program tape and is implemented by the two lower rows ($Y = 1, 2$) of the array. Its architecture consists of a shift register based on three different kinds of cells.
- The *stack* is implemented by three cells $ST3:1$ ($X = 1..3$, $Y = 3$). Each of these three cells is different and is described by a specific gene.
- The *register* is implemented by two different cells Q,S ($X = 4, 5$, $Y = 3$) and is therefore described by two specific genes.
- The *data tape* is implemented by three different cells $QL3:0$, QC, $QR0:3$ ($X = 6..8$, $Y = 3$) and is described by three specific genes.

Cellular differentiation (i.e., the definition of which part, or *gene*, of the complete genome will be executed in each cell) occurs through the vertical coordinate, computed as a function of the coordinate SY of the preceding cell (the southern neighbor), and through the horizontal coordinate, computed as a function of the coordinate WX of the preceding cell (the western neighbor). From Fig. 9, we can show that the vertical coordinate SY can be used to differentiate the stack genes, the register genes, and the data tape genes ($SY=2$) from the program tape genes ($SY=1,0$).

The specifications of Fig. 9 allow us to derive directly the Karnaugh map of Fig. 19a, which defines the placement of the stack ($ST3:1$), register (Q,S), and data tape ($QL3:0$, QC, $QR0:3$) genes into the cellular space. The subtree contained by the leftmost dashed square of Fig. 19b implements this Karnaugh map. To find the different genes of the program tape, we need to analyze in more detail its particular architecture.

Each cell of our program tape ($Y = 1, 2$) implements one PICOPASCAL instruction (stored in the four-bit REG register) and at each program step every instruction has to be shifted counterclockwise. From Fig. 17, which shows the routing path established between each cell to transfer the instruction to its neighbor, we have to consider three different situations, which will be used to identify the position of the three specific genes:

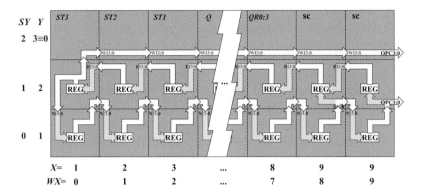

Fig. 17. Routing path established between the cells of the program tape $(SY = 0,1)$ to implement the counterclockwise shift of the PICOPASCAL program

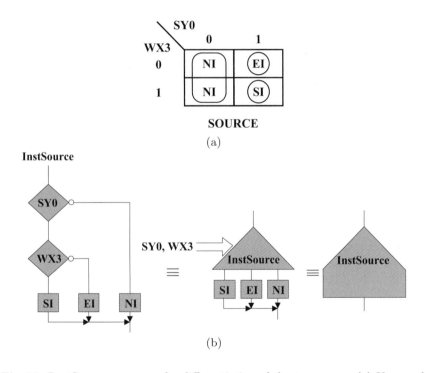

Fig. 18. InstSource program for differentiation of the tape genes. (a) Karnaugh map. (b) Binary decision diagram and flowcharts

- the cells at coordinates $(WX = 0..7, SY = 1)$ will receive, decode and store (in the REG register) the instruction of the east neighbor through the input bus $EI3:0$;

- the cells at coordinates ($WX = 8,9$, $SY = 1$) will receive, decode and store (in the REG register) the instruction of the south neighbor through the input bus $SI3:0$;
- the cells at coordinates ($WX = 0..9$, $SY = 0$) will receive, decode and store (in the REG register) the instruction of the north neighbor through the input bus $NI3:0$.

The functionality of each group of cells of the program tape can be expressed as a function of the horizontal coordinate ($WX3$) and of the vertical coordinate ($SY0$). We therefore have to solve a problem of two variables, as shown by the Karnaugh map of Fig. 18a. Fig. 18b shows the resulting binary decision diagram.

By joining the binary decision diagram of Fig. 18b (**InstSource**) and the binary decision diagram derived from the Karnaugh map of Fig. 19a (sub-tree contained by the leftmost dashed square of Fig. 19b), we can generate the binary decision diagram and flowchart of Fig. 19b describing the complete operational part of the genome of our UTM implementation (**Opgenome**).

5.3   Computing the Program Tape Genes

Fig. 9 ($Y = 1, 2$) shows that the program tape, in our implementation, is composed of 18 cells and features three different genes (EI, SI, and NI). Since the **begin** instruction is not executed and the **NOP** instruction is not used, these cells have to deal with a program composed of eight different kinds of PICOPASCAL instructions (Fig. 12a).

Therefore, each cell has to decode the instruction coming from its neighbor (east, south, or north) and store it in the REG register. The Karnaugh map of Fig. 20a shows the binary coding proposed for the eight PICOPASCAL instructions stored in the program tape. Fig. 20b shows the generic binary decision diagram that we use to decode the instruction to be assigned to the register REG. In consequence, we can implement the three genes EI, SI, and NI, of the program tape by decoding the instructions coming from the east, south, and north neighbors respectively, that is, by replacing $OPC3:0$ (Fig. 20b) by $EI3:0$, $SI3:0$, and $NI3:0$ respectively.

To assure synchronization of all the registers, tests are performed throughout the half-period when $G = 0$, but no assignment is made until the rising edge of G ($G = 0 \rightarrow 1$), when all the registers REG are updated simultaneously.

As shown in Fig. 9, the stack part of our cellular UTM implementation is composed of the three cells $ST3:1$ ($X = 1..3$, $Y = 3$), each featuring a different gene ($ST1$, $ST2$, and $ST3$). The Embryonics implementation of the $STACK$ part of our artificial organism (the PICOPASCALINE stack) has to reproduce the behavior described by the stack operation tables in Fig. 15a and by the stack architecture presented in Fig. 15b. From the tables we

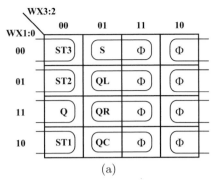

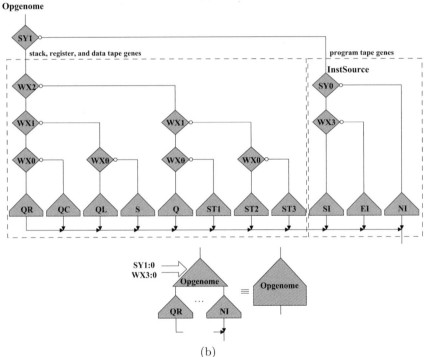

Fig. 19. Computing the genome's operational part (sub-program **Opgenome**). (a) Karnaugh map for stack (ST3:1), register (Q,S), and data tape genes (QL3:0, QC, QR0:3). (b) Binary decision diagram and flowchart of the genome's operational part

obtain the information to build the Karnaugh maps decoding the PICOPAS-CAL instructions related to each stack gene (*ST1*, *ST2*, *ST3*), and from the architecture we obtain the logic part and the corresponding control signals.

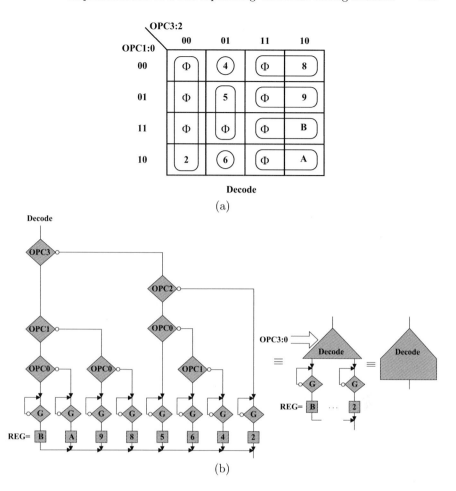

Fig. 20. Generic decoding of the instruction to be assigned to REG. (a) Karnaugh map. (b) General binary decision diagram and flowcharts (**Decode**)

6   Conclusion

In this contribution we showed that it is possible to embed a universal Turing machine into a multicellular array based on MICTREE artificial cells, thus obtaining a self-repairing and self-replicating universal Turing machine.

The mapping of the universal Turing machine onto our multicellular array was made possible thanks to the introduction of a modified version of the W-machine [23], i.e., an interpreter of the PICOPASCAL language. We showed that an ideal architecture (i.e., an architecture with a semi-infinite data tape) was able to deal with applications of any complexity. We also presented an actual implementation in which we relaxed somewhat the requirements of the

Fig. 21. Final universal Turing machine implementation. This implementation contains six rows and ten columns of MICTREE cells, allowing us to verify self-replication (one copy) and self-repair (one spare column)

ideal architecture in order to use a smaller number of our MICTREE artificial cells. We slightly simplified our implementation by presenting the example of the binary counter in which the data are binary-coded and where the direction of the head's motion coincides with the internal state (in general, functions $Q+$ and $D+$ are independent). A picture of the final implementation is shown in Fig. 21.

The UTM was completely implemented and the binary counter fully tested. The values obtained correspond exactly to the results presented by Minsky in [12], assuming that the tape register is limited to 9 bits with fixed boundary conditions ($R=L=0$ in Fig. 13). The measured sequence ends in a final "quiescent" state (where all the symbols on the data tape are 0's), which constitutes a fixed point for the system.

The complete genome microprogram describing our artificial organism is composed of 377 16-bit-wide instructions, implying a configuration bit string of 6032 bits.

We tested the self-repair capabilities of our implementation (Fig. 9), made possible by the spare column at the right edge of our artificial organism. Using this spare column, our organism is able to tolerate at least one fault in any cell of the array, and up to three faulty cells in the same column.

The self-replication of our UTM was tested with one copy of the original organism, as shown in Fig. 10. For this test, the cellular array contained 6x10 = 60 MICTREE cells (Fig. 21).

The property of universal construction, another challenge laid down by von Neumann's original self-replicating automaton, raises issues of a different nature, since it requires that a MICTREE cell be able to realize organisms of any dimension (the largest possible organism in the implementation described herein consists of 16x16 cells). This challenge, which lies outside the scope of this contribution, can be met by decomposing a cell into molecules and tailoring the structure of the cells to the requirements of a given application [6, 8].

Of course, current technology does not allow all these properties (universal construction, universal computation, self-repair) to be implemented, as in nature, by *physically* modifying the underlying hardware: they are implemented at a *logical* level by exploiting redundant spare hardware. The predicted development of technologies based on the manipulation of physical matter at the molecular level, however, will allow the realization of circuits of such complexity as to require the development of novel computational paradigms and architectures. The validation of the computational universality of these architectures is a fundamental step in their development: Turing machines are thus once again becoming a useful research tool in the field of computing.

References

1. M. Abramovici and C. Stroud. No-overhead BIST for FPGAs. In *Proceedings of First IEEE International On-Line Testing Workshop*, pp. 90–92, 1995.
2. D. C. Ince, editor. *Mechanical Intelligence: Collected Works of A. M. Turing*, Chap. Intelligent Machinery, pp. 107–128. North-Holland, 1992.
3. S. C. Kleene. Turing's Analysis of Computability, and Major Applications of It. In R. Herken, editor, *The Universal Turing Machine: a Half Century Survey*, pp. 15–49. Springer-Verlag, second edition, 1995.
4. D. Mange. *Microprogrammed Systems: An Introduction to Firmware Theory*. Chapman & Hall, London, 1992. (First published in French as "Systèmes microprogrammés: une introduction au magiciel," Presses Polytechniques et Universitaires Romandes, 1990).
5. D. Mange, M. Goeke, D. Madon, A. Stauffer, G. Tempesti, and S. Duran. Embryonics: A New Family of Coarse-grained Field-Programmable Gate Array with Self-Repair and Self-Reproducing Properties. In E. Sanchez and M. Tomassini, editors, *Towards Evolvable Hardware*, pp. 197–220. Springer-Verlag, Berlin, 1996.
6. D. Mange, M. Sipper, A. Stauffer, and G. Tempesti. Towards Robust Integrated Circuits: The Embryonics Approach. *Proceedings of the IEEE*, 88(4):516–541, April 2000.

7. D. Mange, A. Stauffer, and G. Tempesti. Embryonics: A Macroscopic View of the Cellular Architecture. In M. Sipper, D. Mange, and A. Pérez-Uribe, editors, *Evolvable Systems: From Biology to Hardware*, volume 1478 of *Lecture Notes in Computer Science*, pp. 174–184. Springer-Verlag, Berlin, 1998.

8. D. Mange, A. Stauffer, and G. Tempesti. Embryonics: A Microscopic View of the Cellular Architecture. In M. Sipper, D. Mange, and A. Pérez-Uribe, editors, *Evolvable Systems: From Biology to Hardware*, volume 1478 of *Lecture Notes in Computer Science*, pp. 185–195. Springer-Verlag, Berlin, 1998.

9. P. Marchal, P. Nussbaum, C. Piguet, S. Duran, D. Mange, E. Sanchez, A. Stauffer, and G. Tempesti. Embryonics: The Birth of Synthetic Life. In E. Sanchez and M. Tomassini, editors, *Towards Evolvable Hardware*, pp. 166–196. Springer-Verlag, Berlin, 1996.

10. P. Marchal, A. Tisserand, P. Nussbaum, B. Girau, and H. F. Restrepo. Array processing: A massively parallel one-chip architecture. In *Proceedings of the Seventh International Conference on Microelectronics for Neural, Fuzzy, and Bio-Inspired Systems*, pp. 187–193, Granada, Spain, April 1999.

11. E. J. McCluskey. *Logic Design Principles with Emphasis on Testable Semicustom Circuits*. Prentice-Hall, Englewood Cliffs, New Jersey, 1986.

12. M. L. Minsky. *Computation: Finite and Infinite Machines*. Prentice-Hall, Englewood Cliffs, New Jersey, 1967.

13. H. F. Restrepo. *Implementation of a Self-Repairing Universal Turing Machine*. PhD thesis No 2457, Swiss Federal Institute of Technology, Lausanne, Switzerland, 2001.

14. H. F. Restrepo and D. Mange. An Embryonic Implementation of a Self-Replicating Universal Turing Machine. In *Evolvable Systems: From Biology to Hardware (ICES01)*, volume 2210 of *Lecture Notes in Computer Science*, pp. 74–87. Springer-Verlag, Berlin, October 2001.

15. H. F. Restrepo, D. Mange, and M. Sipper. A Self-Replicating Universal Turing Machine: From von Neumann's Dream to New Embryonic Circuits. In M. A. Bedau, J. S. McCaskill, N. H. Packard, and S. Rasmussen, editors, *Seventh International Conference on Artificial Life*, pp. 3–12. MIT Press, Cambridge, August 2000.

16. M. Sipper, E. Sanchez, D. Mange, M. Tomassini, A. Pérez-Uribe, and A. Stauffer. An Introduction to Bio-Inspired Machines. In D. Mange and M. Tomassini, editors, *Bio-Inspired Computing Machines: Toward Novel Computational Architectures*, pp. 1–12. Presses Polytechniques et Universitaires Romandes, Lausanne, Switzerland, 1998.

17. A. Stauffer, D. Mange, M. Goeke, D. Madon, G. Tempesti, S. Durand, P. Marchal, and C. Piguet. MICROTREE: Towards a Binary Decision Machine-Based FPGA with Biological-like Properties. In *Proceedings of the International Workshop on Logic and Architecture Synthesis*, pp. 103–112, Grenoble, France, December 1996.

18. G. Tempesti. *A Self-Repairing Multiplexer-Based FPGA Inspired by Biological Processes*. PhD thesis No 1827, Swiss Federal Institute of Technology, Lausanne, Switzerland, 1998.

19. G. Tempesti, D. Mange, and A. Stauffer. A robust multiplexer-based FPGA inspired by biological systems. *Journal of Systems Architecture*, 43(10):719–733, 1997.

20. B. A. Trakhtenbrot. Comparing the Church and Turing Approaches: Two Prophetical Messages. In R. Herken, editor, *The Universal Turing Machine: a Half Century Survey*, pp. 557–582. Springer-Verlag, second edition, 1995.
21. A. M. Turing. On Computable Numbers, with an Application to the Entscheidungsproblem. *Proceedings of the London Math. Soc.*, 42:230–265, 1936.
22. J. von Neumann. *The Theory of Self-Reproducing Automata*. University of Illinois Press, Urbana, Illinois, 1966. Edited and completed by A. W. Burks.
23. H. Wang. A Variant to Turing's Theory of Computing Machines. *Journal of the ACM*, IV:63–92, 1957.
24. N. Wirth. *Programming in MODULA-2*. Springer-Verlag, Berlin, 1983.

Cognitive Science and the Turing Machine: an Ecological Perspective

Andrew J. Wells

Department of Social Psychology, The London School of Economics and Political Science

Summary. The Turing machine model has been used by cognitive scientists to explain the internal structures and processes of the human mind. The physical symbol systems hypothesis treats the mind as functionally equivalent to a universal Turing machine with a finite tape. The machine is hypothesized to be instantiated in the brain. This chapter shows that the symbol systems view is in conflict with the thinking that led Turing to his abstract machine model. The analysis of computation in Turing's famous paper on computable numbers is based on interactions between the mind and the external environment and is best thought of in ecological terms. The mind is construed as a finite automaton, not as a Turing machine. The approach provides a view of cognitive architecture which has more in common with the situated action paradigm than it does with the physical symbol systems approach.

1 Introduction

"We may compare a man in the process of computing a real number to a machine which is only capable of a finite number of conditions [...]" [19, p. 231]. With the famous paper in which this sentence appears, Alan Turing joined the ranks of illustrious thinkers who have discussed the mysteries of the mind in finite, material terms. In this chapter I consider the impact of the Turing machine on theory development in cognitive science. The main point I want to make is that Turing's work contains a profound moral for cognitive science that has yet to be fully appreciated. The moral is this: Turing's work shows that it is highly profitable to study the mind from an ecological perspective. Ecology is the study of organisms in *relation to their environments*. Turing's analysis of the process of routine computation is an ecological analysis because it studies the human mind in relation to the paper and pencil environment used for numerical calculation. The Turing machine is an ecological model because it has parts representing the mind of the human computer and parts representing the paper and pencil environment. The success of Turing's work suggests that the ecological style of analysis should be developed for psychological domains other than numerical computation. Unfortunately, the ecological nature of Turing's work is not widely understood in cognitive science.

1.1   What Almost Everyone in Cognitive Science Knows About Turing Machines

There is a sense in which almost everyone in cognitive science knows what a Turing machine is. Almost everyone knows that a Turing machine is an abstract computer with a simple architecture consisting of a finite control automaton equipped with a tape divided into squares. The squares hold tokens of a finite set of symbols. The tape is, in principle, of infinite length and the automaton moves up and down it writing and erasing symbols according to instructions contained in a machine table. Turing is honored for inventing the machine but it is known to be impractical for everyday computation and is thus thought to constitute a rather poor model for the mind. "[C]lassical cognitive scientists do not believe that if you open up the brain and peer inside, you will find a Turing machine (e.g., part of the brain corresponding to a ticker tape, another part corresponding to a machine head that moves back and forth along this ticker tape)" [4, p. 22]. It is, nevertheless, thought that the Turing machine is related to practical computational models of the mind in a rather straightforward way. Cognitive scientists, says Dawson, "expect that you would find an architecture that shares many properties with Turing machines, but which has additional features that make it more efficient and practical. This architecture would be no more powerful than a Universal Turing Machine, in terms of the questions that it could answer, but it would be more powerful in the practical sense that it could give answers to these questions much faster" [4, p. 22]. The "additional features" are thought to be things like random access memory. Dawson's writing expresses the widely held view that Turing's work underpins what is often called the computational theory of mind. Many authors have described this theory from a variety of perspectives. Some have concentrated less on the architecture and more on the idea that cognition involves the processing of symbol structures that have sentence-like form. "The cognitive science that started fifty years or so ago more or less explicitly had as its defining project to examine a theory, *largely owing to Turing*, that cognitive mental processes are operations defined on syntactically structured mental representations that are much like sentences" [8, pp. 3–4, emphasis added]. Different versions of the computational theory of mind have in common the idea that the brain is a computer which is functionally equivalent to a universal Turing machine with a finite memory and control mechanisms that are organized for efficient practical computation. Thinking is the information processing carried out by the neural computer. This processing involves the transformation of mental symbol structures. I shall call the computational theory of mind a *solipsistic* interpretation of the Turing machine, following [7], because it assumes that the Turing machine provides a model of the mind as an autonomous representational system. The system is autonomous in the sense that the course of processing is determined solely by the symbolic representations on which the system operates and by its internal control mechanisms. The mechanisms that connect the machine to the external world are, of course, an indispensable part of the system, but they are conceptually and functionally separate from the mental computer and its processing is independent of them.

1.2   What Almost No One in Cognitive Science Knows About Turing Machines

There is another sense in which almost no one in cognitive science knows what a Turing machine is. Almost no one knows that the Turing machine is more accurately interpreted as an *ecological* rather than a *solipsistic* model and that the computational theory of mind should not be attributed to Turing. His analysis of computation shows that what he said was not intended as a general account of how minds work and is strikingly different, in its approach to mind-world relations, from the picture painted by the computational theory of mind. Almost no-one knows these things because almost all cognitive scientists obtain their understanding of Turing's work from secondary sources and very few have read his original work [19]. This matters for a number of reasons. First, as a general principle, we should avoid attributing theories to people who did not develop them. Second, the computational theory of mind is widely perceived as facing substantial, possibly insurmountable, difficulties. If the theory is too closely linked to Turing even fewer people in cognitive science will study his work than do so now. The writing is already on the wall. Here is Fodor again, one of the most committed proponents of the computational theory of mind. "I am inclined to think that, sooner or later, we will *all* have to give up on the Turing story as a general account of how the mind works" [8, p. 47]. Third, there is a "general account of how the mind works" that can be based on Turing's analysis of computation but it is not the conventional computational theory of mind. It is a theory based on the concept of a "configuration" that connects environmental structure with mental structure. When we understand clearly how Turing's machines relate to the human examples from which they were derived it is clear that an adequate computational theory of the mind will have to go beyond what Turing himself achieved. We will not have to give up on the Turing story but we will have to build on it and my purpose in this tribute to Turing is to show how his analysis of computation will form the foundation for a theory of mind that has yet to be fully developed.

2   Turing's Analysis of Computation

The starting point is Turing's own elegant description of the Turing machine in Sect. 1 of [19, pp. 231–232].

> We may compare a man in the process of computing a real number
> to a machine which is only capable of a finite number of conditions

$q_1, q_2, \ldots, q_R$ which will be called "m-configurations." The machine is supplied with a "tape" (the analogue of paper) running through it, and divided into sections (called "squares") each capable of bearing a "symbol." At any moment there is just one square, say the r-th, bearing the symbol $\mathfrak{S}(r)$ which is "in the machine." We may call this square the "scanned" square. The symbol on the scanned square may be called the "scanned symbol." The "scanned symbol" is the only one of which the machine is, so to speak, "directly aware." However, by altering its m-configuration the machine can effectively remember some of the symbols which it has "seen" (scanned) previously. The possible behaviour of the machine at any moment is determined by the m-configuration q_n and the scanned symbol $\mathfrak{S}(r)$. This pair q_n, $\mathfrak{S}(r)$ will be called the "configuration": thus the configuration determines the possible behaviour of the machine. In some of the configurations in which the scanned square is blank (i.e. bears no symbol) the machine writes down a new symbol on the scanned square: in other configurations it erases the scanned symbol. The machine may also change the square which is being scanned, but only by shifting it one place to right or left. In addition to any of these operations the m-configuration may be changed. Some of the symbols written down will form the sequence of figures which is the decimal of the real number which is being computed. The others are just rough notes to "assist the memory." It will only be these rough notes which will be liable to erasure.

The key question discussed here is how the Turing machine relates to the human model from which it was drawn. What is the nature of the comparison between man and machine to which Turing refers? According to proponents of the computational theory of mind the tape is a model of human memory and the finite machine through which the tape runs is a model of the mental control mechanisms that transform input symbol sequences on the tape to output sequences. Hence the Turing machine as a whole is a model of processes going on inside the mind. Fodor's work provides a clear instance of this view. "Insofar as we think of mental processes as computational [...] it will be natural to take the mind to be, *inter alia*, a kind of computer [...] we may thus construe mental operations as pretty directly analogous to those of a Turing machine. There is, for example, a working memory (corresponding to a tape) and there are capacities for scanning and altering the contents of the memory (corresponding to the operations of reading and writing on the tape)" [7, p. 65]. This view is still current. One contributor to a recent encyclopedia of the cognitive sciences says that "A Turing machine possesses a segmented tape with segments corresponding to a cognitive device's internal states or representations" [14, p. 333] and a very recent book on the foundations of cognitive science says that "the tape is the machine's *memory*, not the environment; it is not 'outside' the machine" [10, p. 204]. These views all depart from Turing's conception of the eponymous machine architecture as a reading of his paper [19] shows.

The key part of Turing's paper for those who wish to understand how the architecture of the Turing machine relates to the human examples from which it was drawn is Sect. 9, particularly sub-section I [19, pp. 249–252]. In that part of the paper, Turing undertook an extensive analysis of human computation that demonstrates conclusively the ecological nature of his thinking. The analysis starts with the simple observation, "Computing is normally done by writing certain symbols on paper" (p. 249). This observation deserves note because it makes it clear from the start that the subject for analysis was not mental arithmetic but paper and pencil calculation, and in consequence the machines derived from the analysis are not just models of the mind but models of the mind interacting with the media of paper and pencil. Turing moved on extremely rapidly via further observations about squared paper and its uses to the proposal that only one dimension is needed in the environment for computation. "I think it will be agreed that the two-dimensional character of paper is no essential of computation. I assume then that the computation is carried out on one-dimensional paper, *i.e.* on a tape divided into squares." (p. 249).

Turing then discussed the number of symbols needed for computation. He proposed that only a finite number of symbols could be printed. The argument for this point is curiously compressed. "If we were to allow an infinity of symbols, then there would be symbols differing to an arbitrarily small extent" (p. 249). Presumably the inference to be drawn is that confusion could occur in such cases because symbols with arbitrarily small differences between them might not be distinguished. Turing seems to have had both human and machine limitations in mind here. He suggested that the restriction to a finite alphabet of symbols was not serious because sequences of symbols could be treated as single symbols. Reverting exclusively to the human example, Turing distinguished compound from single symbols on the grounds that "the compound symbols, if they are too lengthy, cannot be observed at one glance [...]. We cannot tell at a glance whether 9999999999999999 and 999999999999999 are the same" (p. 250).

Turing then discussed how the behavior of a human computer is controlled during the process of calculation. "The behaviour of the computer at any moment is determined by the symbols which he is observing, and his 'state of mind' at that moment" (p. 250). It is not entirely clear why Turing felt obliged to use quotation marks to delineate the expression "state of mind." It may have been simply because the referent of the expression is not easily identifiable and he felt that caution was in order. Be that as it may, the passage continues in a most interesting way.

> We may suppose that there is a bound B to the number of symbols or squares which the computer can observe at one moment. If he wishes to observe more, he must use successive observations. We will

also suppose that the number of states of mind which need be taken into account is finite. The reasons for this are of the same character as those which restrict the number of symbols. If we admitted an infinity of states of mind, some of them will be 'arbitrarily close' and will be confused. Again the restriction is not one which seriously affects computation, since the use of more complicated states of mind can be avoided by writing more symbols on the tape. (p. 250)

Several points about this passage are noteworthy. The bound B represents a further constraint, in addition to the limited capacity to discriminate compound symbols, on the abilities of a human computer. Turing later uses these constraints in his argument for the structure of the machine model. The most striking suggestion is that only a finite number of states of mind need be taken into account. The justification for this point is, like the argument for a finite number of symbols, extremely brief. It can, I think, be seen as an early statement of the idea that the mind supervenes on the brain. The finitude of the mind follows from the finitude of the brain and the relation of supervenience between them. The supervenience relation means, roughly, that any change in mental state that can correctly be ascribed to an individual implies a corresponding change in physical state because mental state changes are caused by physical state changes. It does not follow from the supervenience thesis that mental states are reducible to physical states. The finite bound on the number of mental states is in conflict with some versions of the computational theory of mind which argue, in principle, for a countable infinity of mental states. The idea that more complex states of mind can be avoided by writing more symbols on the tape is further evidence for the view that the tape, in Turing's analysis, was not a part of the mind.

Turing then asks the reader to imagine that the operations carried out by the computer are split up into " 'simple' operations which are so elementary that it is not easy to imagine them further divided. Every such operation consists of some change of the physical system consisting of the computer and his tape." (p. 250) The emphasis on the physicality of the system supports the idea that the finitude of the mind stems from its being part of a physical system. Simple operations are of three kinds; alterations of symbols on the tape, switches of attention from one part of the tape to another and changes of state of mind. The simplest alteration to the tape is a single symbol change. Any other alteration can be split up into a sequence of single symbol changes. With regard to changing the observed squares, Turing says that "The new observed squares must be immediately recognisable by the computer" (p. 250). Immediate recognizability is a tricky concept to pin down. Turing first makes the point that if one is attending to a particular set of squares on the tape, a change of attention can only be described as simple if there is a bound on the distance between those squares and a new set. "I think it is reasonable to suppose that they can only be squares whose distance from the closest of the immediately previously observed squares does not exceed a certain fixed amount. Let us say that each of the new observed squares is within L squares of an immediately previously observed square" (p. 250). He also discusses the possibility that immediate recognizability might be defined in terms of special marker symbols and allows this on condition that only a finite number of squares can be marked in this way. A final catch all proposal is that any other kind of immediate recognizability can be allowed "so long as these squares can be found by some process of which my type of machine is capable" (p. 251).

Changes of state of mind are discussed only in the context of symbol changes and switches of attention. "It may be that some of these changes necessarily involve a change of state of mind." Having thought through the means needed to mechanize the observable aspects of a computation, Turing then sees that changes of mental state are also needed to sustain the process from one step to the next. From this he arrives at the conclusion that the most general single operation must be of one of two kinds: a) a possible change of symbol and a possible change of state of mind, b) a possible change of observed squares and a possible change of state of mind. The operation that is actually carried out is determined by the current state of mind of the computer and the symbols currently being observed. Turing notes, "In particular, they determine the state of mind of the computer after the operation is carried out." Clearly, therefore, changes of state of mind have both internal and external determinants. The internal determinant is the current state of mind and the external determinant is the symbol currently being scanned. Turing's view supposes that humans are in touch with their inner selves and their environments simultaneously, at least when doing paper and pencil calculations. This is a powerful feature of his analysis and one of the keys to its success. Finally we come to the conclusion of the analysis and its application to the construction of a machine.

> We may now construct a machine to do the work of this computer. To each state of mind of the computer corresponds an 'm-configuration' of the machine. The machine scans B squares corresponding to the B squares observed by the computer. In any move the machine can change a symbol on a scanned square or can change any one of the scanned squares to another square distant not more than L squares from one of the other scanned squares. The move which is done, and the succeeding configuration, are determined by the scanned symbol and the m-configuration. (pp. 251–252)

Turing's analysis quite clearly does not support what Fodor, Dawson and many other cognitive scientists take to be constitutive of the computational theory of mind, i.e. the claim that cognitive processes are operations defined over syntactically structured *mental* representations which have sentence-like forms. The Turing machine is a model of the interactions between an agent and its environment. The representations over which Turing machines compute are symbol structures inscribed on a tape which is an analogue of the paper on which a person works a calculation. They are not mental representations and the tape is not an analogue of the human computer's memory. The machine that models the mind of the human computer consists of a finite set of m-configurations. These are not symbols, they are functional states. They interact with symbols, in "configurations," but are quite distinct from them. The set of m-configurations modeling the mind of the human computer is what we now call a finite automaton. Thus, in the Turing machine as originally envisaged by its creator, psychological states are modeled as the functional states of a finite automaton. The Turing machine as a whole is not a model of executive processes in the mind interacting with symbol structures in the mind. It is a model of executive processes in the mind interacting with structured symbolic resources in the external environment. This makes the Turing machine an ecological rather than a solipsistic model.

3   The Implications of Turing's Analysis for Cognitive Science

It is not my purpose to make either a full scale presentation or critique of the computational theory of mind here. I shall, however, outline the major commitments of the computational theory of mind and the principal difficulties it faces. This will help to show the alternative I propose in sharper focus. I begin by summarizing the components of the Turing machine model. The Turing machine has a component representing the task-specific states of mind of the human agent. This component can be described as a set $Q = \{q_1, q_2, \dots, q_m\}$. The members of Q are the m-configurations of Turing's analysis. The Turing machine has another component, the tape, which represents (a portion of) the environment external to the agent, viz. the paper on which he/she computes. The tape supports the computations of a Turing machine in the way that paper supports the computations of a human agent. The Turing machine uses an alphabet of symbols $S = \{s_1, s_2, \dots, s_n\}$ for its computations. These symbols may or may not be the same as those used by a human agent computing the same number but they serve the same purpose. The Turing machine has scanning, printing and moving mechanisms which correspond to the perceptual and motor capabilities of the agent. The Turing machine scans the tape, prints symbols on it and moves relative to it. These activities parallel the reading and writing done by a human and the movements that can be made to position a pencil over a sheet of paper. Because the tape is one-dimensional, the complex movements of a human computer working with paper and pencil are modeled by a set $M = \{L, R, N\}$ whose members stand for Left, Right, and No movement respectively. The behavior of a Turing machine is determined by its configurations which are members of the set C of ordered pairs $\{(q, s) \mid q \in Q, s \in S\}$. C is finite because Q and S are finite. A fundamentally important point to make about configurations is the way they mesh internal and external structure. Each $q \in Q$ has specific relationships to other states and to its inputs and outputs. Each configuration determines an action drawn from the set $A = \{(q, s, m) \mid q \in Q, s \in S, m \in M\}$. The elements of A are ordered triples, consisting of an m-configuration, a symbol and a movement. Actions are related to configurations via a function $\Phi : C \to A$. The arguments of Φ are configurations and its values are actions. Thus Turing provides both a static analysis of the agent and the environment in terms of states and squares with symbols respectively, and a dynamic analysis of their interactive behavior with the function Φ. There are two types of action, internal and external. The external actions are the writings of symbol tokens and movements of the automaton relative to the tape. The internal actions are state changes.

One of the principal achievements of Turing's paper was his demonstration that a universal machine could be constructed. From this machine flows the proof that there are uncomputable numbers and, with hindsight, the machine can be seen as the theoretical precursor of the programmable computer. Turing showed that each of his machines has a "standard description" which is a translation of the table defining the machine into a string of symbols from a fixed, finite alphabet. The key is to represent both the states and the symbols of the "target" machine, the one to be simulated, as strings of symbols in the alphabet of the universal machine. Turing then showed that a single machine could be built which interpreted the standard descriptions of other Turing machines and acted in accordance with them thus computing the same sequences as the machines described. Since the single machine could in this way compute the same sequence as any other Turing machine it was called the "universal" machine. The universal machine is a model of a human who works with the rules governing a computation written on paper in some standard format rather than built into the structure of states of mind. The universal machine shows that a single machine can compute any of the numbers that a human can compute in this way but it does not show that the single machine could do anything else that a human can do. The machine is universal with respect to the domain of computable numbers but it remains to be shown that it can operate in any other domain. Cognitive scientists hope to develop a general theory of mind based on computational ideas. The computational theory of mind and the ecological alternative proposed here try to develop this breadth of coverage in very different ways.

3.1   The Computational Theory of Mind

The computational theory of mind is based on the idea that the requisite breadth of coverage can be achieved by putting the architecture of a universal machine and the notion of representation to work together. The idea, very roughly, is that the human mind is organized like a single, universal machine. Anything that needs to be thought about is represented symbolically in the proprietary language of that universal machine and inscribed on its "tape."

To repeat a point made earlier, the computational theory of mind does not suggest that there is, literally, a tape instantiated in the brain. What it does suggest, however, is that there is a memory which is functionally equivalent to a tape. Allen Newell has argued that such functional equivalence rests on three characteristics: that the representational medium must be capable of being in combinatorially many states, that it must be highly stable so as to retain its inputs, and that it must be capable of transformation at will [16, pp. 63–64]. Inputs from the external world are one obvious source of things to think about and it is hypothesized that there are encoding mechanisms, sometimes called transducers, that turn sensory input into symbolic representations. Thinking consists in applying a mental function (also coded in the language of the universal machine) to an input representation to produce an output representation. The input representation is an argument to the mental function and the output representation is its value. It is also assumed that when the output representation symbolizes a need for action, there are decoding mechanisms to translate the output representation into motor commands. The language of the putative universal machine is sometimes called the "language of thought" [6]. The computational theory of mind relies on the power of the transducers to extract from the sensory flux everything that needs to be thought about and on the power of the representational system to represent the world to thought adequately. A huge theoretical burden is thus placed on the encoding and representational mechanisms and no-one has yet given a plausible account of how this burden can be managed. Some theorists, perhaps most notably John Searle [18], have argued that internal symbol manipulation cannot, in principle, provide a satisfactory basis for human understanding. There is also no solid evidence for the existence of the machinery needed to support universal computation entirely within the confines of the mind/brain of the individual. It has further been argued that a neural, universal machine could not have been built by evolution because the programmability it entails is incompatible with efficiency and evolvability [2].

Quite apart from the intrinsic difficulties that the computational theory of mind faces it is clearly not a theory that Turing would have endorsed because it uses the tape of the Turing machine as a model of human memory and that is incompatible with the derivation of the model. There is considerable confusion in the literature about this. The paper by Turing which appeared in the philosophical journal "Mind" [20] has been cited as a reason for attributing the computational theory of mind to him. However, what Turing actually suggested there is that an appropriately programmed computer could play the imitation game in a way that would make its performance indistinguishable from that of a human player. He did not suggest the entirely different hypothesis that computers and humans have the same type of internal, mental architecture.

3.2 The Ecological Alternative to the Computational Theory of Mind

The alternative strategy outlined here is based on the proposition that the way to build a cognitive theory on the basis of Turing's analysis is not to force every cognitive competence through the narrow representational bottleneck that standard descriptions require if the mind is thought to be a single universal machine but to explore how to generalize Turing's ecological analysis from its focus on numerical computation to the whole spectrum of human cognitive capacities. Turing says, "We may compare a man in the process of computing a real number to a machine which [...]." To this we want to add, "We may compare a man in the process of driving a car to a machine which [...]," and "We may compare a man in the process of choosing a mate to a machine which [...]" and "We may compare a man in the process of tending his garden to a machine which [...]" and so forth for all those processes which we want to include as components of human cognitive capacity. The question is how this is to be done if all the inputs are not processed by a single control automaton via some universal encoding. The answer is to think of the mind as a collection of concurrent, possibly interacting, ecological automata, each of which has its specialized function. The inputs to the automata are, by hypothesis, real objects. There may, for example, be a specialized, human face recognition mechanism. If there is, its inputs are real human faces not representations of them, even though for theoretical purposes we may refer to $S_{FR} = \{face_1, face_2, \dots, face_m\}$. The m-configurations of the face recognition mechanism $Q_{FR} = \{fr_1, fr_2, \dots, fr_n\}$ are probably the states of a specific neural module or region and the configurations of the machine will be ordered pairs of the form $(fr_i, face_j)$. In addition to such specialized mechanisms at least one, and probably more, of the automata that collectively constitute the mind will be interpreters that treat part of their input as representations in the way that universal machines do.

Significant challenges become visible as soon as one starts to consider the implications of this approach. It is clear that an ecological analysis works for the processes involved in numerical computation, because that is what Turing achieved, but there are many complications in applying the method more generally. Two particularly pressing issues are the identification of the types of environment-agent interaction that would have to be included and the extension of the analysis to treat parallel as well as serial processes. The two issues are related although the former is mainly empirical and the latter more technical. I shall briefly address both issues and discuss in outline how they might be resolved.

Environment-Agent Interactions. The single, most important, contribution of Turing's analysis of computation to the development of an ecological theory of cognitive processing is the concept of a configuration (q, s) where

$q \in Q, s \in S$. Configurations encapsulate the crucial understanding that behavior has internal and external determinants of equal importance. An ecological theory of mind founded on configurations implies that the functional connections between an environment and an agent are intimate and involved in all the activity of the agent. An immediate consequence of this approach is a need to identify the types of possibility for interaction that environments provide for agents. The ecological psychologist J. J. Gibson developed some of the requisite theory and I draw on his work in this section. Gibson made a general point about the relation between organisms and environments that is relevant to the present discussion. He says, "The fact is worth remembering because it is often neglected that the words *animal* and *environment* make an inseparable pair. Each term implies the other. No animal could exist without an environment surrounding it. Equally, although not so obvious, an environment implies an animal (or at least an organism) to be surrounded" [9, p. 8]. Gibson coined the term "affordance" to describe the possibilities for action that an environment makes available to an organism. "Affordance" and "configuration" are mutually informative concepts and I have discussed the connections between them in some detail in [21]. The space of possible interactions between an agent and an environment depends on the structure of the environment and on the constitution of the agent. Thinking about real environments enables us to see where Turing's formal model needs to be supplemented.

Considering the structure of real environments first, it is obvious that they contain more than paper tapes. The Turing machine tape was a simple model of the structure of a sheet of squared arithmetic paper. The reduction from two dimensions to one made the structuring of the machine's control mechanism easier than it would otherwise have been but the reductive strategy needs to be considered carefully by ecologically minded psychologists who want to tackle the complexity of real environments. The point, I should emphasize, is not that there is anything deficient in the tape as a medium for storing symbolic representations or that a richer model of the environment is being sought to increase the computational power of the system. It is simply that the tape was only ever intended by Turing as a model of a restricted portion of the environment and a computational theory which includes a broader conception of the environment should be based, for that reason, on a formal system which allows for a richer model of the environment. However, the tape is not without its lessons. The key feature of the Turing machine tape that needs to be preserved in a more general theory is the notion of a location. The Turing machine processes of scanning and printing operate on specific squares of the tape and the processes of interaction with the environment that humans engage in occur in the places where they happen to be. Among other things then, an ecological theory of cognition needs a theory of places in which objects can be located and where events can happen. The tape square would be included in such a theory as a simple type of place.

Gibson developed an account of places and the control of locomotion among them that does some of the necessary theoretical work. A place is not an object with definite boundaries like a tape square, but is better thought of as a region. It may be, for example, that a region could be specified in terms of a bound like Turing's bound L that limits the notion of adjacency. Places are located by the facts of their inclusion in larger places and can be named, but they need not be located with reference to a co-ordinate system as points and locations in computer memory are. Gibson's analysis of places shows that they have some features in common with the squares of the tape of a Turing machine. "A place persists in some respects and changes in others. In one respect, it cannot be changed at all — in its location relative to other places. A place cannot be *displaced* like an object. That is, the adjacent order of places cannot be permuted; they cannot be shuffled" [9, p. 240]. Gibson also makes the interesting point that one important place concept is the notion of a hiding place. Turing's analysis does not provide the means of thinking about *hiding places* because the tape is, as it were, an entirely open environment, but it is quite clear that questions of access to different regions of a computational environment are a major consideration when one thinks in terms of computer security and that access is an environmental concept that an ecological theory needs to consider more generally. The only objects in the simple tape environment of a Turing machine are symbol tokens. They can be recognized, printed and erased. Objects in the wider world are much more varied and the actions that can be taken with respect to them are correspondingly varied as well. There is, nevertheless, a simple point to make about symbol tokens which applies also to other objects. The crucial property of a symbol token is its type identity. Suppose that the alphabet over which a machine computes is the set $\{0, 1\}$. What is important is that each token of '0' should be recognized as such and not confused with tokens of '1'. Similarly, *mutatis mutandis*, for tokens of '1'. Provided that this basic classification can be made reliably a Turing machine computation can proceed reliably. It is not required that each token of a symbol be identical with every other token. Similarly, one can classify other objects as members of a type and react to them accordingly even though they can be seen to be different individuals. If I am walking across a field in the country, for example, I treat a black bull and a white bull in the same way for the purpose of ensuring my safety. This suggests that it is types of objects rather than particular individuals that should form the initial focus for an ecological theory of cognitive computation. Clearly in some cases the recognition of individuals is crucial, but this is a capacity that is, presumably, derived from the more basic capacity to identify types. Gibson classifies objects in a number of interesting ways. He distinguishes *attached* objects such as doorhandles and coathooks which have particular kinds of uses from *detached* objects that may be portable or serve as missiles. A useful class of detached objects is the class of hollow objects that can be used as containers. Bags, pots, bowls and sacks are instances that might further be classified into those that are watertight and those that are not. Cognitive processes involving containers of various kinds are multifarious and complex. One might speculate, for example, on the contribution that the technology of glassware containers such as test-tubes and retorts has made to scientific progress in a variety of disciplines. Gibson also describes tools as a particularly interesting class of detached objects. "The missile that can be thrown is perhaps the earliest of tools. When combined with a launching device, it can become very versatile. The discovery of missiles was surely one of the factors that made the human animal a formidable hunter as compared to the animals with teeth and claws" [9, p. 40].

A particularly interesting class which in some ways bridges the gap between conventional symbols and detached objects is the class of animal tracks. These are not deliberately created as representations by the animals that make them, of course, but they serve a symbolic function for those who are able to interpret them. They can yield information about the identity of the animal or animals, the size of the group, the age and sex of the animals and the rate at which they were moving. Tracks can provide estimates of the time that has elapsed since they were made and thus allow the hunter to determine whether they are worth following. One can think of a set of tracks as a program telling the hunter how to proceed in order to approach the prey. Tracks thus stand to the tracker in the same relationship as the program for a universal machine stands to its interpreter. Liebenberg [13] has suggested that the art of tracking involves the same intellectual and creative skills as modern science and may serve as an explanation of its origins.

The most significant objects with which humans interact are other animals, especially other humans, because *Homo sapiens* is a distinctively social species. "Most persons admit that man is a social being. We see this in his dislike of solitude, and in his wish for society beyond that of his own family. Solitary confinement is one of the severest punishments which can be inflicted" [3, p. 84]. This is a clear point at which Turing's analysis will have to be supplemented because it does not address the question of how to construct automata which interact directly with other automata. The universal machine deals with inputs that are *encodings* of other automata and the difference is important. There are many distinctive types of interaction with animals that an ecological theory needs to account for. "Another animal may be prey or predator, potential mate or rival, adult or young, one's own young or another's young. Moreover, it may be temporarily asleep or awake, receptive or unreceptive, hungry or satiated" [9, p. 42]. Interactions with other people in the management of large artefacts is a further area of study. Hutchins [12], for example, has discussed the complex interactions between people and technology involved in the navigation of modern warships.

We may conclude by considering the class of human displays, a class that includes "all the surfaces of the environment that bear writing." This brings us back to an enormous range of issues including the specific topic of Turing's analysis. Gibson says of displays that "images, pictures, and writing, insofar as the substances shaped and the surfaces treated are permanent, permit the storage of information and the accumulation of information in storehouses, in short, civilization" [9, p. 42]. Turing's universal machine demonstrates the enormous power of human displays. The universal machine transcends the behavioral limitations of special purpose Turing machines by treating part of its input as instructions rather than data. The treatment of configurations as conjunctions of structure in the agent and the environment prompts a new understanding of the conceptual significance of the universal Turing machine which is in marked contrast to the role that universality plays in the computational theory of mind. From the ecological point of view, universal computation gives us a second source of behavioral flexibility rather than being the sole foundation on which behavioral flexibility is to be built. The first source rests on the multiplicity of automata that make up the mind. The second source is the fact that at least one, and perhaps more, of those automata are interpreters that enable the agent to treat some structure in the environment as representational. Notations of various kinds, linguistic, musical and mathematical among others, are obvious instances, but artefacts like road markings and traffic lights also function in a representational way for humans. So do some types of naturally occurring structure like the animal tracks that have already been discussed. Turing's fundamental contribution showed how external structure could be used to enable a finite machine with fixed, internal structure to behave in arbitrarily complex ways as a function of its input. This moves us towards a behavioral, but not a behaviorist, analysis of the sources of human creativity. We become better thinkers not primarily as a result of internal changes, although of course they are important, but to a large extent because we learn how to use notations. Some thinkers expand our mental horizons by constructing new notations. Turing's notation for describing and combining m-configurations is a case in point.

Consideration of the wide range of environment-agent interactions and, in particular, the existence of objects which are themselves agents brings the issue of mobility to the fore. Mobility for a Turing machine is movement from one tape square to the next. This models the movement of the hand of the human computer from one square of arithmetic paper to another. There are, of course, situations in which greater human mobility is often needed when writing. The lecturer writing equations on a blackboard often needs to move the whole body not just the hand. The Turing machine access mechanism thus models a ubiquitous aspect of the environmental conditions to which human cognition is attuned. While it is true to say that humans are increasingly provided with mechanisms that provide access to information and resources which enable them to transact their business without movement, understanding mobility, both as a source of design features of the organism and as a necessary part of ordinary life remains a key part of a general psychological theory. Emphasis on this aspect of Turing's original model is therefore a healthy emphasis for an ecological psychologist. Mobility is a notion whose analysis in computational terms will pay dividends for psychological theory. It is a noteworthy if elementary point that creatures which are not mobile do not require nervous systems.

Turing's analysis has shown that a theory of mobility can be grounded in simple relations between agents and their environments. Configurations control the actions of the agent including movement. The concept that actions are controlled resonates with what Gibson says with regard to real environments. "Locomotion and manipulation are neither triggered nor commanded but *controlled* [...]. Control lies in the animal-environment system. Control is by the animal *in* its world, the animal itself having subsystems for perceiving the environment and concurrently for getting about in it and manipulating it" [9, p. 225]. It is, I think, remarkable that a concern with the computation of numbers should yield an analysis that appears to be applicable, with relatively minimal adjustment, to a much broader range of concerns. It tells us yet again, if such re-emphasis were needed, just how deeply insightful Turing's work in 1935–36 was.

It is clear that there is a wide range of types of environment-agent interaction that an ecological theory of cognitive computation would need to consider but that there is already a considerable body of theory to draw on. The success of Turing's analysis with respect to numerical computation encourages the belief that similar successes could be obtained in other domains.

Serial and Parallel Processes. Turing used three different concepts involving the term "configuration" in [19] and it will be helpful to be clear about their referents. "m-configurations" are the internal states of automata. They correspond to the "states of mind" of human computers. Plain "configurations" are the ordered pairs (q, s) that control the activities of Turing machines. They are ecological entities consisting of an m-configuration and the symbol inscribed on a particular square of the tape. "Complete configurations" are descriptions of the whole of a Turing machine at a particular time. They include a record of the state of the entire marked portion of the tape, an indication of the currently scanned square and an indication of the current configuration. Successive complete configurations provide a full history of the activity of a machine.

The process of routine numerical computation that Turing modeled is clearly a serial process and his treatment of states of mind reflects that fact. Turing, as we have seen, modeled the states of mind of a human computer as a finite set $q_1, \dots, q_R$ of m-configurations and transitions between them are a key part of his analysis. The treatment of states of mind is one of the most brilliant and audacious aspects of Turing's analysis. It is largely what made it possible to design machines to simulate the processes carried out in computing numbers, but the reduction involved abstraction from the inherent parallelism of mental processing and this appears to make the m-configuration irretrievably narrow as the basis for a general account of mental states. A Turing machine is in exactly one of its m-configurations at any given moment and that m-configuration has no structure apart from its relations to other m-configurations and to its inputs and outputs. Block & Fodor [1] argued, using a range of examples, that the simple, unstructured nature of m-configurations meant that there were crucial distinctions among mental state types that they simply could not capture. This is hardly surprising when one considers that Turing's goal was to extract the simplest account of mental states that was sufficient for the execution of rule governed computation.

Block and Fodor pointed out that their arguments did not apply to what they called the "computational" states of a machine. By this they meant what Turing called complete configurations. Computational states (complete configurations) have the requisite variability, according to Block and Fodor, to capture the distinctions among mental state types that an adequate psychological theory must recognize. However, as a reading of Turing's work makes clear, complete configurations are records of activity that involve both the control automaton and the tape of a Turing machine. If they are to function as parts of a psychological theory, therefore, in the way proposed by Block and Fodor, one must argue that the tape of the Turing machine can function as a model of part of the internal mental architecture of the perceiver. This position, as discussed earlier, is adopted by proponents of the computational theory of mind but it is clearly not Turing's theory.

An alternative possibility, which was recognized by Block and Fodor, is to restore the parallelism that was removed from Turing's analysis. The ecological approach proposed here, which treats the mind as a set of concurrent automata, makes just this move. Block and Fodor said of this possibility that a psychological theory based on parallel processing would look very different from one based on serial processing. They also said that although serial processes were fairly well understood little was known about the nature of parallel processes and their interactions. The situation has advanced somewhat since the 1970s when [1] was written, but in cognitive science, although parallelism has been studied in terms of neural networks, I think it is fair to say that only a very restricted part of the universe of parallel models has yet been explored. When one considers, for example, the kinds of phenomena that have been modeled with connectionist networks, even their supporters recognize "that most current models are in fact highly task-specific and single-purpose" [5, p. 392]. They are, in effect, parallel implementations of single Turing machines.

An adequate theory of internal states requires genuine multi-tasking. The need for this is apparent in almost any domain one cares to think of. Imagine a situation in which one is attempting to identify a bird in flight. At least three interacting tasks can be identified. There is a continuous, although continually changing, visual input to be processed. There is a continuous motor tracking process that orients the perceiver so as to keep the visual input centered on the foveal region of the retinas. It may also be that the bird calls from time to time. Thus, added to the visual and motor tasks there is intermittent auditory input to be processed. The auditory and visual inputs interact with stored knowledge in the identification process. However, although they interact, auditory and visual analysis are clearly independent of each other. Identification could succeed on the basis of either stimulus type alone. The bird may stop calling while still in view or it may remain audible while obscured from vision by vegetation or some other obstacle. If the different tasks are thought of as specifications for different Turing machines the model required is, in effect, a system of parallel, interconnected Turing machines where each is linked to its environmental inputs and to the other Turing machines in appropriate ways. This is asking more of the Turing machine than it was designed to achieve.

4   Broadening the Scope of Turing's Analysis

Turing's analysis provides a computationally sufficient foundation for the development of a genuinely ecological cognitive theory. However, in order to analyze parallel processes within individual minds and to construct models of more realistic environments which include active agents it is desirable to employ a formal system in which these matters can be treated more naturally than they can within the Turing machine framework. One way to think about this is to consider the different levels of analysis that an adequate psychological theory needs to recognize. The level of analysis at which Turing abstracted his core concepts was the familiar level of mundane objects and events. The symbols with which a Turing machine interacts are the same as those with which a human interacts and the states of mind that are used in the Turing machine are at the functional level that is implied when we say of someone that they are happy or sad, busy or idle. We might call this level of analysis the "personal" level because it is the level at which we think about persons and their activities. In the light of this it is easy to see why a complete psychological theory needs formal machinery of greater scope than Turing needed for his analysis. The reason is that although the personal level is a privileged level of analysis in psychology it is not the only one that is needed. Sub-personal levels are needed to study the inner workings of the mind and supra-personal levels to study the interactions between people. Turing's analysis does not address supra-personal levels because it makes no provision for interactions among agents and it does not address sub-personal levels because every m-configuration is at the functional level of whole states of mind. One may note in passing that the computational theory of mind does not respect Turing's level of abstraction because it takes the Turing machine to be a sub-personal description of mental functioning. The scope of personal level analysis also needs to be broadened to cover the wide range of environment-agent interactions, other than paper and pencil computation, that people commonly engage in.

Since the 1970s, theoretical computer scientists interested in concurrency have developed models of computation in which interaction is the central idea. An indication of the wide applicability of such models can be gleaned from the following description by one of the pioneers of the mathematical study of concurrency. "[T]he environment of a process itself may be described as a process, with its behaviour defined by familiar notations [...]. In fact, it is best to forget the distinction between processes, environments, and systems; they are all of them just processes whose behaviour may be prescribed, described, recorded and analyzed in a simple and homogeneous fashion" [11, p. 65]. The π-calculus [15] [17] may be particularly well suited to modeling psychological phenomena because it has been designed to study and express the behaviour of systems that interact with one another and change their patterns of connectivity. Robin Milner, one of the originators of the π-calculus, also stresses the generality of the treatment that results from taking interaction as the core idea. Having used as examples systems like vending machines and mobile telephones, he says "We do not normally think of vending machines or mobile phones as doing computation, but they share the notion of interaction with modern distributed computing systems. This common notion underlies a theory of a huge range of modern informatic systems, whether computational or not" [15, p. 4]. When one focuses on the configuration as the core aspect of the Turing machine, it is clear that one can think of its activities as interactive, even though that is not perhaps the way in which people normally think of Turing machines. I think that the π-calculus, or perhaps one of the variants it has inspired, will enable us to make significant progress in developing the formal psychological theory that is needed to build cognitive science on Turing's ecological foundation. The primitives of the π-calculus, processes and names, are more abstract than the symbols and states of the Turing machine, do not pre-suppose an architecture of tape and control automaton and can be applied to entities at different levels of analysis. I should emphasize here, however, that the π-calculus is not more powerful than the Turing machine in terms of what can be computed and I am not proposing to move beyond what is Turing computable. The point is simply that a system like the π-calculus makes it possible to develop a more natural computational treatment of psychological processes than can be achieved with Turing machine models.

A number of characteristics of the π-calculus, in addition to its capacity to represent changing connectivity, suggest its usefulness in psychological contexts. First, it contains two accounts of behaviour. Processes can have components which are themselves processes and one can study both the internal behaviour of a component and also its behaviour as part of a wider system. One account of behaviour explains how a process can evolve independently of its environment. It is an account of the internal or hidden behaviour of a process. The heart of this account is a binary relation on π-calculus terms called *reduction*. The second account of behaviour explains both the internal behaviour of a process and its interactions with its environment. This account of behaviour is based on describing the *actions* that processes can perform. The additional power of the second account of behaviour is bought at the cost of a small increase in complexity. Clearly in psychological contexts there are times when we want to describe the internal evolution of a process independently of the environment. Thought processes, and sub-personal level analyses more generally, may require descriptions of this kind. It is worth noting that thinking can, in principle, be handled within the Turing framework even when it is viewed ecologically, but the means to do so are rather artificial. The ecological analysis implies that thinking does not take place in an autonomous, internal space as the computational theory of mind supposes, but is part of the ongoing processing of the agent. It does not, however, imply that thinking, understood as one or more internal state changes, must always be accompanied by changes to the environment. An action $a \in A$ is a triple (q, s, m) where $q \in Q, s \in S, m \in M$. In the general case the transition function Φ maps (q, s) to (q', s', m) but it is always possible that $(q, s) \rightarrow (q', s, m)$ i.e. that there is a state change with no symbol change. If $m = N$ there is no movement relative to the tape either. I do not wish to give the impression that this somewhat artificial explanation provides a satisfactory account of thinking but it does show that the model can, in principle, handle internal activity without overt behaviour. The π-calculus allows us to be much more subtle in the treatment of thought processes and the nature of their connections with the environment without supposing, as the computational theory of mind does, that they are based on internal transformations of symbol structures. The π-calculus allows us to think of the m-configurations of a Turing machine as processes that can evolve internally while retaining the capacity to behave externally in the ways stated by the machine table. The set of configurations in which a Turing machine m-configuration appears can then be thought of as a π-calculus process context which constrains the internal evolution of the m-configuration to forms which respect the actions associated with those configurations.

A second important characteristic is an emphasis in the π-calculus on understanding when terms describe processes that are behaviorally equivalent. "Until we know what constitutes similarity or difference of behaviour, we cannot claim to know what 'behaviour' *means* — and if that is the case then we have no precise way of explaining what our systems do" [15, p. 4]. The classical automata theoretic notion of language equivalence "is not suitable for all purposes. In particular, it does not appear to be correct when an automaton's actions consist of *reactions* between it and another automaton [...] if we are interested in interactive behaviour, then a non-deterministic automaton cannot correctly be equated behaviorally with a deterministic one" [15, p. 15]. The π-calculus defines a number of behavioral equivalences which will be valuable in psychological contexts, in particular the distinction between *strong* and *weak* equivalences. A weak equivalence abstracts from internal action whereas a strong equivalence does not. Since psychology spans a range of levels of processes from neurons to multi-person groups, one might hope eventually to see a unified approach to theory development in which the behaviors abstracted from in order to treat systems as equivalent at one level of analysis become the subject matter of other levels. Two performances of Beethoven's "Hammerklavier" sonata, for example, might be weakly equivalent in terms of the notes played but not strongly equivalent in terms of hand positions if the performers employed different fingering.

The π-calculus also offers the possibility of extending computational analysis to include the study of social behaviour by modeling individuals as π-calculus processes. Since the calculus was expressly designed to study the interactions among processes, it is clear that if concurrent processes represent multiple humans we have the beginnings of a computational social psychology of interaction. Moreover, the π-calculus also enables us, in principle, to model group formation processes and the circulation of information within and between groups. There would be something deeply pleasing about such developments. Turing laid the foundations for computer science with an analysis of the possibilities and limitations of computation by a single human. His work was partly responsible for the development of the stored program computer. Milner and his colleagues have developed the π-calculus to study the "social" interactions among computers that have become common as a result of the overwhelming success of the stored program computer design. It would be a fitting tribute to Turing if it turned out that a calculus inspired by technology derived from the Turing machine should turn out to be the ideal tool for extending, to the social domain, the formal analysis of mental processes that began with the Turing machine. "[A]s we address the problem of modeling mobile communicating systems we get a sense of completing a model which was previously incomplete; for we can now begin to describe what goes on *outside* a computer in the same terms as what goes on *inside* — i.e. in terms of interaction. Turning this observation inside-out, we may say that we inhabit a global computer, an informatic world which demands to be understood just as fundamentally as physicists understand the material world" [15, p. 156]. Turing would surely have endorsed this vision.

References

1. N. Block and J. A. Fodor. What psychological states are not. *Philosophical Review*, 81:159–181, 1972.
2. M. Conrad. The price of programmability. In R. Herken, editor, *The Universal Turing Machine. A Half Century Survey*, pages 285–307. Oxford University Press, Oxford, UK, 1988.
3. C. Darwin. *The Descent of Man, and Selection in Relation to Sex*. John Murray, London, UK, 1871.

4. M. R. W. Dawson. *Understanding Cognitive Science*. Blackwell Publishers, Ltd, Oxford, UK, 1998.
5. J. L. Elman, E. A. Bates, M. H Johnson, A. Karmiloff-Smith, D. Parisi, and K. Plunkett. *Rethinking Innateness. A Connectionist Perspective on Development*. MIT Press, Cambridge, MA, 1996.
6. J. A. Fodor. *The Language of Thought*. Crowell, New York, NY, 1975.
7. J. A. Fodor. Methodological solipsism considered as a research strategy in cognitive psychology. *The Behavioral and Brain Sciences*, 3(1):63–109, 1980.
8. J. A. Fodor. *The Mind Doesn't Work That Way*. MIT Press, Cambridge, MA, 2000.
9. J. J. Gibson. *The Ecological Approach to Visual Perception*. Houghton-Mifflin, Boston, MA, 1979.
10. R. M. Harnish. *Minds, Brains, Computers: The Foundations of Cognitive Science*. Blackwell Publishers Ltd, Oxford, UK, 2002.
11. C. A. R. Hoare. *Communicating Sequential Processes*. Prentice-Hall International, Englewood Cliffs, NJ, 1985.
12. E. Hutchins. *Cognition in the Wild*. MIT Press, Cambridge, MA, 1995.
13. L. Liebenberg. *The Art of Tracking. The Origin of Science*. David Philip Publishers Ltd, Claremont, South Africa, 2001.
14. J. C. Maloney. Functionalism. In R. A. Wilson & F. C. Keil, editors, *The MIT Encyclopedia of the Cognitive Sciences*, pages 332–335. MIT Press, Cambridge, MA, 1999.
15. R. Milner. *Communicating and Mobile Systems: the π-Calculus*. Cambridge University Press, Cambridge, UK, 1999.
16. A. Newell. *Unified Theories of Cognition*. Harvard University Press, Cambridge, MA, 1990.
17. D. Sangiorgi and D. Walker. *The π-calculus. A Theory of Mobile Processes*. Cambridge University Press, Cambridge, UK, 2001.
18. J. R. Searle. Minds, brains, and programs. *The Behavioral and Brain Sciences*, 3(3):417–457, 1980.
19. A. M. Turing. On computable numbers, with an application to the Entscheidungsproblem. *Proceedings of the London Mathematical Society*, series 2, volume 42, pages 230–265, 1937. Corrections in *Proceedings of the London Mathematical Society*, volume 43, pages 544–546, 1937.
20. A. M. Turing. Computing machinery and intelligence. *Mind*, 59:433–460, 1950.
21. A. J. Wells. Gibson's affordances and Turing's theory of computation. *Ecological Psychology*, 14(3):141–180, 2002.

Part III

Artificial Intelligence and the Turing Test

Can Machines Think?*

Daniel C. Dennett

Center for Cognitive Studies, Tufts University

Summary. Much has been written about the Turing Test in the last few years, some of it preposterously off the mark. People typically mis-imagine the test by orders of magnitude. This essay is an antidote, a prosthesis for the imagination, showing how huge the task posed by the Turing Test is, and hence how unlikely it is that any computer will ever pass it. It does not go far enough in the imagination-enhancement department, however, and I have updated the essay with a new postscript.

1 Can Machines Think?

Can machines think? This has been a conundrum for philosophers for years, but in their fascination with the pure conceptual issues they have for the most part overlooked the real social importance of the answer. It is of more than academic importance that we learn to think clearly about the actual cognitive powers of computers, for they are now being introduced into a variety of sensitive social roles, where their powers will be put to the ultimate test: In a wide variety of areas, we are on the verge of making ourselves dependent upon their cognitive powers. The cost of overestimating them could be enormous.

One of the principal inventors of the computer was the great British mathematician Alan Turing. It was he who first figured out, in highly abstract terms, how to design a programmable computing device — what we now call a universal Turing machine. All programmable computers in use today are in essence Turing machines. Over thirty years ago, at the dawn of the computer age, Turing began a classic article, "Computing Machinery and Intelligence" with the words: "I propose to consider the question, 'Can machines think?'" — but then went on to say this was a bad question, a question that leads only to sterile debate and haggling over definitions, a question, as he put it, "too meaningless to deserve discussion" [9]. In its place he substituted what he took to be a much better question, a question that would be crisply answerable and intuitively satisfying — in every way an acceptable substitute for the philosophic puzzler with which he began.

---

* Originally appeared in Michael G. Shafto, editor, *How We Know: Nobel Conference XX*, Harper & Row, San Francisco, CA, 1985. Reprinted with permission of HarperCollins Publishers Inc., New York.

First he described a parlor game of sorts, the "imitation game," to be played by a man, a woman, and a judge (of either gender). The man and woman are hidden from the judge's view but able to communicate with the judge by teletype; the judge's task is to guess, after a period of questioning each contestant, which interlocutor is the man and which the woman. The man tries to convince the judge he is the woman (and the woman tries to convince the judge of the truth), and the man wins in the judge makes the wrong identification. A little reflection will convince you, I am sure, that, aside from lucky breaks, it would take a clever man to convince the judge that he was woman — assuming the judge is clever too, of course.

Now suppose, Turing said, we replace the man or woman with a computer, and give the judge the task of determining which is the human being and which is the computer. Turing proposed that any computer that can regularly or often fool a discerning judge in this game would be intelligent — would be a computer that thinks — *beyond any reasonable doubt*. Now, it is important to realize that failing this test is not supposed to be a sign of lack of intelligence. Many intelligent people, after all, might not be willing or able to play the imitation game, and we should allow computers the same opportunity to decline to prove themselves. This is, then, a one-way test; failing it proves nothing.

Furthermore, Turing was not committing himself to the view (although it is easy to see how one might think he was) that to think is to think just like a human being — any more than he was committing himself to the view that for a man to think, he must think exactly like a woman. Men and women, and computers, may all have different ways of thinking. But surely, he thought, if one can think in one's own peculiar style well enough to imitate a thinking man or woman, one can think well, indeed. This imagined exercise has come to be known as the Turing test.

It is a sad irony that Turing's proposal has had exactly the opposite effect on the discussion of that which he intended. Turing didn't design the test as a useful tool in scientific psychology, a method of confirming or disconfirming scientific theories or evaluating particular models of mental function; he designed it to be nothing more than a philosophical conversation-stopper. He proposed — in the spirit of "Put up or shut up!" — a simple test for thinking that was *surely* strong enough to satisfy the sternest skeptic (or so he thought). He was saying, in effect, "Instead of arguing interminably about the ultimate nature and essence of thinking, why don't we all agree that whatever that nature is, anything that could pass this test would surely have it; then we could turn to asking how or whether some machine could be designed and built that might pass the test fair and square." Alas, philosophers — amateur and professional — have instead taken Turing's proposal as the pretext for just the sort of definitional haggling and interminable arguing about imaginary counterexamples he was hoping to squelch.

This thirty-year preoccupation with the Turing test has been all the more regrettable because it has focused attention on the wrong issues. There are *real world* problems that are revealed by considering the strengths and weaknesses of the Turing test, but these have been concealed behind a smokescreen of misguided criticisms. A failure to think imaginatively about the test actually proposed by Turing has led many to underestimate its severity and to confuse it with much less interesting proposals.

So first I want to show that the Turing test, conceived as he conceived it, is (as he thought) plenty strong enough as a test of thinking. I defy anyone to improve upon it. But here is the point almost universally overlooked by the literature: There is a common *misapplication* of the sort of testing exhibited by the Turing test that often leads to drastic overestimation of the powers of actually existing computer systems. The follies of this familiar sort of thinking about computers can best be brought out by a reconsideration of the Turing test itself.

The insight underlying the Turing test is the same insight that inspires the new practice among symphony orchestras of conducting auditions with an opaque screen between the jury and the musician. What matters in a musician, obviously, is musical ability and only musical ability; such features as sex, hair length, skin color, and weight are strictly irrelevant. Since juries might be biased — even innocently and unawares — by these irrelevant features, they are carefully screened off so only the essential feature, musicianship, can be examined. Turing recognized that people similarly might be biased in their judgments of intelligence by whether the contestant had soft skin, warm blood, facial features, hands and eyes — which are obviously not themselves essential components of intelligence — so he devised a screen that would let through only a sample of what really mattered: the capacity to understand, and think cleverly about, challenging problems. Perhaps he was inspired by Descartes, who in his *Discourse on Method* [3] plausibly argued that there was no more demanding test of human mentality than the capacity to hold an intelligent conversation:

> It is indeed conceivable that a machine could be so made that it would utter words, and even words appropriate to the presence of physical acts or objects which cause some change in its organs; as, for example, if it was touched in some spot that it would ask what you wanted to say to it; if in another, that it would cry that it was hurt, and so on for similar things. But it could never modify its phrases to reply to the sense of whatever was said in its presence, as even the most stupid men can do.

This seemed obvious to Descartes in the seventeenth century, but of course the fanciest machines he knew were elaborate clockwork figures, not electronic computers. Today it is far from obvious that such machines are impossible, but Descartes's hunch that ordinary conversation would put as severe a strain on artificial intelligence as any other test was shared by Turing. Of course there is nothing sacred about the particular conversational game chosen by Turing for his test; it is just a cannily chosen test of more general intelligence. The assumption Turing was prepared to make was this: Nothing could possible pass the Turing test by winning the imitation game without being able to perform indefinitely many other clearly intelligent actions. Let us call that assumption the quick-probe assumption. Turing realized, as anyone would, that there are hundreds and thousands of telling signs of intelligent thinking to be observed in our fellow creatures, and one could, if one wanted, compile a vast battery of different tests to assay the capacity for intelligent thought. But success on his chosen test, he thought, would be highly predictive of success on many other intuitively acceptable tests of intelligence. Remember, failure on the Turing test does not predict failure on those others, but success would surely predict success. His test was so severe, he thought, that nothing that could pass it fair and square would disappoint us in other quarters. Maybe it wouldn't do everything we hoped — maybe it wouldn't appreciate ballet, or understand quantum physics, or have a good plan for world peace, but we'd all see that it was surely one of the intelligent, thinking entities in the neighborhood.

Is this high opinion of the Turing test's severity misguided? Certainly many have thought so — but usually because they have not imagined the test in sufficient detail, and hence have underestimated it. Trying to forestall this skepticism, Turing imagined several lines of questioning that a judge might employ in this game — about writing poetry, or playing chess — that would be taxing indeed, but with thirty years' experience with the actual talents and foibles of computers behind us, perhaps we can add a few more tough lines of questioning.

Terry Winograd, a leader in artificial intelligence efforts to produce conversational ability in a computer, draws our attention to a pair of sentences [11]. They differ in only one word.

The first sentence is this:

> The committee denied the group a parade permit because they advocated violence.

Here's the second sentence:

> The committee denied the group a parade permit because they feared violence.

The difference is just in the verb — *advocated* or *feared*. As Winograd points out, the pronoun *they* in each sentence is officially ambiguous. Both readings of the pronoun are always legal. Thus we can imagine a world in which governmental committees in charge of parade permits advocate violence in the streets and, for some strange reason, use this as their pretext for denying a parade permit. But the natural, reasonable, intelligent reading of the first sentence is that it's the group that advocated violence, and of the second, that it's the committee that feared violence.

Now if sentences like this are embedded in a conversation, the computer must figure out which reading of the pronoun is meant, if it is to respond intelligently. But mere rules of grammar or vocabulary will not fix the right reading. What fixes the right reading for us is knowledge about the world, about politics, social circumstances, committees and their attitudes, groups that want to parade, how they tend to behave, and the like. One must know about the world, in short, to make sense of such a sentence.

In the jargon of artificial intelligence (AI), a conversational computer needs a lot of *world knowledge* to do its job. But, it seems, if somehow it is endowed with that world knowledge on many topics, it should be able to do much more with that world knowledge than merely make sense of a conversation containing just that sentence. The only way, it appears, for a computer to disambiguate that sentence and keep up its end of a conversation that uses that sentence would be for it to have a much more general ability to respond intelligently to information about social and political circumstances, and may other topics. Thus, such sentences, by putting a demand on such abilities, are good quick probes. That is, they test for a wider competence.

People typically ignore the prospect of having the judge ask off-the-wall questions in the Turing test, and hence they underestimate the competence a computer would have to have to pass the test. But remember, the rules of the imitation game as Turing presented it permit the judge to ask any question that could be asked of a human being — no holds barred. Suppose then we give a contestant in the game this question:

> An Irishman found a genie in a bottle who offered him two wishes. "First I'll have a pint of Guinness," said the Irishman, and when it appeared he took several long drinks from it and was delighted to see that the glass filled itself magically as he drank. "What about your second wish?" asked the genie. "Oh well," said the Irishman, "that's easy. I'll have another one of these!" — Please explain this story to me, and tell me if there is anything funny or sad about it.

Now even a child could express, if not eloquently, the understanding that is required to get this joke. But think of how much one has to know and understand about human culture, to put it pompously, to be able to give any account of the point of this joke. I am not supposing that the computer would have to laugh at, or be amused by, the joke. But if it wants to win the imitation game — and that's the test, after all — it had better know enough in its own alien, humorless way about human psychology and culture to be able to pretend effectively that it was amused and explain why.

It may seem to you that we could devise a better test. Let's compare the Turing test with some other candidates.

Candidate 1: A computer is intelligent if it wins the World Chess Championship.

That's not a good test, as it turns out. Chess prowess has proven to be an isolatable talent. There are programs today that can play fine chess but can do nothing else. So the quick probe assumption is false for the test of playing winning chess.

Candidate 2: The computer is intelligent if it solves the Arab-Israeli conflict.

This is surely a more severe test that Turing's. But it has some defects: it is unrepeatable, if passed once; slow, no doubt; and it is not crisply clear what would count as passing it. Here's another prospect, then:

Candidate 3: A computer is intelligent if it succeeds in stealing the British crown jewels without the use of force or violence.

Now this is better. First, it could be repeated again and again, though of course each repeat test would presumably be harder — but this is a feature it shares with the Turing test. Second, the mark of success is clear — either you've got the jewels to show for your efforts or you don't. But it is expensive and slow, a socially dubious caper at best, and no doubt luck would play too great a role.

With ingenuity and effort one might be able to come up with other candidates that would equal the Turing test in severity, fairness, and efficiency, but I think these few examples should suffice to convince us that it would be hard to improve on Turing's original proposal.

But still, you may protest, something might pass the Turing test and still not be intelligent, not be a thinker. What does *might* mean here? If what you have in mind is that by cosmic accident, by a supernatural coincidence, a stupid person or a stupid computer *might* fool a clever judge repeatedly, well, yes, but so what? The same frivolous possibility "in principle" holds for any test whatever. A playful god, or evil demon, let us agree, could fool the world's scientific community about the presence of H_2O in the Pacific Ocean. But still, the tests they rely on to establish that there is H_2O in the Pacific Ocean are quite beyond reasonable criticism. If the Turing test for thinking is no worse than any well-established scientific test, we can set skepticism aside and go back to serious matters. Is there any more likelihood of a "false positive" result on the Turing test than on, say, the test currently used for the presence of iron in an ore sample?

This question is often obscured by a "move" that philosophers have sometimes made called operationalism. Turing and those who think well of his test are often accused of being operationalists. Operationalism is the tactic of *defining* the presence of some property, for instance, intelligence, as being established once and for all by the passing of some test. Let's illustrate this with a different example.

Suppose I offer the following test — we'll call it the Dennett test — for being a great city:

A great city is one in which, on a randomly chosen day, one can do all three of the following:

Hear a symphony orchestra, see a Rembrandt and a professional athletic contest, eat *quenelles de brochet à la Nantua* for lunch.

To make the operationalist move would be to declare that any city that passes the Dennett test is *by definition* a great city. What being a great city *amounts* to is just passing the Dennett test. Well then, if the Chamber of Commerce of Great Falls, Montana, wanted — and I can't imagine why — to get their hometown on my list of great cities, they could accomplish this by the relatively inexpensive route of hiring full time about ten basketball players, forty musicians, and a quick-order quenelle chef and renting a cheap Rembrandt from some museum. An idiotic operationalist would then be stuck admitting that Great Falls, Montana, was in fact a great city, since all he or she cares about in great cities is that they pass the Dennett test.

Sane operationalists (who for that very reason are perhaps not operationalists at all, since *operationalist* seems to be a dirty word) would cling confidently to their test, but only because they have what they consider to be very good reasons for thinking the odds against a false positive result, like the imagined Chamber of Commerce caper, are astronomical. I devised the Dennett test, of course, with the realization that no one would be both stupid and rich enough to go to such preposterous lengths to foil the test. In the actual world, wherever you find symphony orchestras, *quenelles*, Rembrandts, and professional sports, you also find daily newspapers, parks, repertory theaters, libraries, fine architecture, and all the other things that go to make a city great. My test was simply devised to locate a telling sample that could not help but be representative of the rest of the city's treasures. I would cheerfully run the minuscule risk of having my bluff called. Obviously, the test items are not all that I care about in a city. In fact, some of them I don't care about at all. I just think they would be cheap and easy ways of assuring myself that the subtle things I do care about in cities are present. Similarly, I think it would be entirely unreasonable to suppose that Alan Turing had an inordinate fondness for party games, or put too high a value on party game prowess in his test. In both the Turing and the Dennett test, a very unrisky gamble is being taken: the gamble that the quick-probe assumption is, in general, safe.

But two can play this game of playing the odds. Suppose some computer programmer happens to be, for whatever strange reason, dead set on tricking me into judging an entity to be a thinking, intelligent thing when it is not. Such a trickster could rely as well as I can on unlikelihood and take a few gambles. Thus, if the programmer can expect that it is not remotely likely that I, as the judge, will bring up the topic of children's birthday parties, or baseball, or moon rocks, then he or she can avoid the trouble of building world knowledge on those topics into the data base. Whereas if I do improbably raise these issues, the system will draw a blank and I will unmask the pretender easily. But given all the topics and words that I might raise, such a savings would no doubt be negligible. Turn the idea inside out, however, and the trickster would have a fighting chance. Suppose the programmer has reason to believe that I will ask *only* about children's birthday parties, or baseball, or moon rocks — all other topics being, for one reason or another, out of bounds. Not only does the task shrink dramatically, but there already exist systems or preliminary sketches of systems in artificial intelligence that can do a whiz-bang job of responding with apparent intelligence on just those specialized topics.

William Wood's LUNAR program, to take what is perhaps the best example, answers scientists' questions — posed in ordinary English — about moon rocks. In one test it answered correctly and appropriately something like 90 percent of the questions that geologists and other experts thought of asking it about moon rocks. (In 12 percent of those correct responses there were trivial, correctable defects.) Of course, Wood's motive in creating LUNAR was not to trick unwary geologists into think they were conversing with an intelligent being. And if that had been his motive, his project would still be a long way from success.

For it is easy enough to unmask LUNAR without ever straying from the prescribed topic of moon rocks. Put LUNAR in one room and a moon rock specialist in another, and then ask them both their opinion of the social value of the moon-rocks-gathering expeditions, for instance. Or ask the contestants their opinion of the suitability of moon rocks as ashtrays, or whether people who have touched moon rocks are ineligible for the draft. Any intelligent person knows a lot more about moon rocks than their geology. Although it might be *unfair* to demand this extra knowledge of a computer moon rock specialist, it would be an easy way to get it to fail the Turing test.

But just suppose that someone could extend LUNAR to cover itself plausibly on such probes, so long as the topic was still, however indirectly, moon rocks. We might come to think it was a lot more like the human moon rocks specialist than it really was. The moral we should draw is that as Turing test judges we should resist all limitations and waterings-down of the Turing test. They make the game too easy — vastly easier than the original test. Hence they lead us into the risk of overestimating the actual comprehension of the system being tested.

Consider a different limitation of the Turing test that should strike a suspicious chord in us as soon as we hear it. This is a variation on a theme developed in an article by Ned Block [1]. Suppose someone were to propose to restrict the judge to a vocabulary of, say, the 850 words of "Basic English," and to single-sentence probes — that is "moves" — of no more than four words.

Moreover, contestants must respond to these probes with no more than four words per move, and a test may involve no more than forty questions.

Is this an innocent variation on Turing's original test? These restrictions would make the imitation game clearly finite. That is, the total number of all possible permissible games is a large, but finite, number. One might suspect that such a limitation would permit the trickster simply to store, in alphabetical order, all the possible good conversations within the limits and beat the judge with nothing more sophisticated than a system of table lookup. In fact, that isn't in the cards. Even with these severe and improbable and suspicious restrictions imposed upon the imitation game, the number of legal games, though finite, is mind-bogglingly large. I haven't bothered trying to calculate it, but it surely exceeds astronomically the number of possible chess games with no more than forty moves, and that number has been calculated. John Haugeland says it's in the neighborhood of ten to the one hundred twentieth power. For comparison, Haugeland [4, p. 16] suggests that there have only been ten to the eighteenth seconds since the beginning of the universe.

Of course, the number of good, sensible conversations under these limits is a tiny fraction, maybe one quadrillionth of the number of merely grammatically well formed conversations. So let's say, to be very conservative, that there are only ten to the fiftieth different smart conversations such a computer would have to store. Well, the task shouldn't take more than a few trillion years — given generous government support. Finite numbers can be very large.

So though we needn't worry that this particular trick of storing all the smart conversations would work, we can appreciate that there are lots of ways of making the task easier that may appear innocent at first. We also get a reassuring measure of just how severe the unrestricted Turing test is by reflecting on the more than astronomical size of even that severely restricted version of it.

Block's imagined — and utterly impossible — program exhibits the dreaded feature know in computer science circles as *combinatorial explosion*. No conceivable computer could overpower a combinatorial explosion with sheer speed and size. Since the problem areas addressed by artificial intelligence are veritable minefields of combinatorial explosion, and since it has often proven difficult to find any solution to a problem that avoids them, there is considerable plausibility in Newell and Simon's proposal that avoiding combinatorial explosion (by any means at all) be viewed as one of the hallmarks of intelligence.

Our brains are millions of times bigger than the brains of gnats, but they are still, for all their vast complexity, compact, efficient, timely organs that somehow or other manage to perform all their tasks while avoiding combinatorial explosion. A computer a million times bigger or faster than a human brain might not look like the brain of a human being, or even be internally organized like the brain of a human being, but if, for all its differences, it somehow managed to control a wise and timely set of activities, it would have to be the beneficiary of a very special design that avoided combinatorial explosion, and whatever that design was, would we not be right to consider the entity intelligent?

Turing's test was designed to allow for this possibility. His point was that we should not be species-chauvinistic, or anthropocentric, about the insides of an intelligent being, for there might be inhuman ways of being intelligent.

To my knowledge, the only serious and interesting attempt by any program designer to win even a severely modified Turing test has been Kenneth Colby's. Colby is a psychiatrist and intelligence artificer at UCLA. He has a program called PARRY, which is a computer simulation of a paranoid patient who has delusions about the Mafia being out to get him. As you do with other conversational programs, you interact with it by sitting at a terminal and typing questions and answers back and forth. A number of years ago, Colby put PARRY to a very restricted test. He had genuine psychiatrists interview PARRY. He did not suggest to them that they might be talking or typing to a computer; rather, he made up some plausible story about why they were communicating with a real live patient by teletype. He also had the psychiatrists interview real, human paranoids via teletype. Then he took a PARRY transcript, inserted it in a group of teletype transcripts from real patients, gave them to *another* group of experts — more psychiatrists — and said, "One of these was a conversation with a computer. Can you figure out which one it was?" They couldn't. They didn't do better than chance.

Colby presented this with some huzzah, but critics scoffed at the suggestions that this was a legitimate Turing test. My favorite commentary on it was Joseph Weizenbaum's; in a letter to the *Communications of the Association of Computing Machinery* [10, p. 543], he said that, inspired by Colby, he has designed an even better program, which passed the same test. His also had the virtue of being a very inexpensive program, in these times of tight money. In fact you didn't even need a computer for it. All you needed was an electric typewriter. His program modeled infant autism. And the transcripts — you type in your questions, and the thing just sits there and hums — cannot be distinguished by experts from transcripts of real conversations with infantile autistic patients. What was wrong, of course, with Colby's test was that the unsuspecting interviewers had no motivation at all to try out any of the sorts of questions that easily would have unmasked PARRY.

Colby was undaunted, and after his team had improved PARRY he put it to a much more severe test — a surprisingly severe test. This time, the interviewers — again, psychiatrists — were given the task at the outset of telling the computer from the real patient. They were set up in a classic Turing machine test: the patient in one room, the computer PARRY in the other room, with the judges conducting interviews with both of them (on successive days). The judges' task was to find out which one was the computer and which one was the real patient. Amazingly, they didn't do much better, which leads some people to say, "Well, that just confirms my impression of the intelligence of psychiatrists!"

But now, more seriously, was this an honest-to-goodness Turing test? Were there tacit restrictions on the lines of questioning of the judges? Like the geologists interacting with LUNAR, the psychiatrists' professional preoccupations and habits kept them from asking the sorts of unlikely questions that would have easily unmasked PARRY. After all, they realized that since one of the contestants was a real, live paranoid person, medical ethics virtually forbade them from toying with, upsetting, or attempting to confuse their interlocutors. Moreover, they also knew that this was a test of a model of paranoia, so there were certain questions that wouldn't be deemed to be relevant to testing the model *as a model of paranoia*. So, they asked just the sort of questions that therapists *typically* ask of such patients, and of course PARRY had been ingeniously and laboriously prepared to deal with just that sort of question.

One of the psychiatrist judges did, in fact, make a rather half-hearted attempt to break out of the mold and ask some telling questions: "Maybe you've heard of the saying 'Don't cry over spilled milk.' What does that mean to you?" PARRY answered: "Maybe it means you have to watch out for the Mafia." When then asked "Okay, now if you were in a movie theater watching a movie and smelled something like burning wood or rubber, what would you do?" PARRY replied: "You know, they know me." And the next questions was, "If you found a stamped, addressed letter in your path as you were walking down the street, what would you do?" PARRY replied: "What else do you want to know?"[1]

Clearly PARRY was, you might say, *parrying* these questions, which were incomprehensible to it, with more or less stock paranoid formulas. We see a bit of a dodge, which is apt to work, apt to seem plausible to the judge, only because the "contestant" is *supposed* to be paranoid, and such people are expected to respond uncooperatively on such occasions. These unimpressive responses didn't particularly arouse the suspicions of the judge, as a matter of fact, though probably they should have.

PARRY, like all other large computer programs, is dramatically bound by limitations of cost-effectiveness. What was important to Colby and his crew was simulating his model of paranoia. This was a massive effort. PARRY has a thesaurus or dictionary of about 4500 words and 700 idioms and the grammatical competence to use it — a *parser*, in the jargon of computational linguistics. The entire PARRY program takes up about 200,000 words of computer memory, all laboriously installed by the programming team. Now once all the effort had gone into devising the model of paranoid thought

---

[1] I thank Kenneth Colby for providing me with the complete transcripts (including the Judges' commentaries and reactions), from which these exchanges are quoted. The first published account of the experiment is Heiser, et al. [5, p. 149–162]. Colby [2, pp. 515–560] discusses PARRY and its implications.

processes and linguistic ability, there was little if any time, energy, money, or interest left over to build in huge amounts of world knowledge of the sort that any actual paranoid, of course, would have. (Not that anyone yet knows how to build in world knowledge in the first place.) Building in the world knowledge, if one could even do it, would no doubt have made PARRY orders of magnitude larger and slower. And what would have been the point, given Colby's theoretical aims?

PARRY is a theoretician's model of a psychological phenomenon: paranoia. It is not intended to have practical applications. But in recent years a branch of AI (knowledge engineering) has appeared that develops what are now called expert systems. Expert systems are designed to be practical. They are software superspecialist consultants, typically, that can be asked to diagnose medical problems, to analyze geological data, to analyze the results of scientific experiments, and the like. Some of them are very impressive. SRI in California announced in the mid-eighties that PROSPECTOR, an SRI-developed expert system in geology, had correctly predicted the existence of a large, important mineral deposit that had been entirely unanticipated by the human geologists who had fed it its data. MYCIN, perhaps the most famous of these expert systems, diagnoses infections of the blood, and it does probably as well as, maybe better than, any human consultants. And many other expert systems are on the way.

All expert systems, like all other large AI programs, are what you might call Potemkin villages. That is, they are cleverly constructed facades, like cinema sets. The actual filling-in of details of AI programs is time-consuming, costly work, so economy dictates that only those surfaces of the phenomenon that are like to be probed or observed are represented.

Consider, for example, the CYRUS program developed by Janet Kolodner in Roger Schank's AI group at Yale a few years ago (see Kolodner [6] [7, pp. 243–280] [8, pp. 281–328]). CYRUS stands (we are told) for Computerized Yale Retrieval Updating System, but surely it is no accident that CYRUS modeled the memory of Cyrus Vance, who was then secretary of state in the Carter administration. The point of the CYRUS project was to devise and test some plausible ideas about how people organize their memories of the events they participate in; hence it was meant to be a "pure" AI system, a scientific model, not an expert system intended for any practical purpose. CYRUS was updated daily by being fed all UPI wire service news stories that mentioned Vance, and it was fed them directly, with no doctoring and no human intervention. Thanks to an ingenious news-reading program called FRUMP, it could take any story just as it came in on the wire and could digest it and use it to update its data base so that it could answer more questions. You could address questions to CYRUS in English by typing at a terminal. You addressed them in the second person, as if you were talking with Cyrus Vance himself. The results looked like this:

Q: *Last time you went to Saudi Arabia, where did you stay?*

A: In a palace in Saudi Arabia on September 23, 1978.

Q: *Did you go sightseeing there?*
A: Yes, at an oilfield in Dharan on September 23, 1978.

Q: *Has your wife even met Mrs. Begin?*
A: Yes, most recently at a state dinner in Israel in January 1980.

CYRUS could correctly answer thousands of questions — almost any fair question one could think of asking it. But if one actually set out to explore the boundaries of its facade and find the questions that overshot the mark, one could soon find them. "Have you ever met a female head of state?" was a question I asked it, wondering if CYRUS knew that Indira Ghandi and Margaret Thatcher were women. But for some reason the connection could not be drawn, and CYRUS failed to answer either yes or no. I had stumped it, in spite of the fact that CYRUS could handle a host of what you might call neighboring questions flawlessly. One soon learns from this sort of probing exercise that it is very hard to extrapolate accurately from a sample performance that one has observed to such a system's total competence. It's also very hard to keep from extrapolating much too generously.

While I was visiting Schank's laboratory in the spring of 1980, something revealing happened. The real Cyrus Vance resigned suddenly. The effect on the program CYRUS was chaotic. It was utterly unable to cope with the flood of "unusual" news about Cyrus Vance. The only sorts of episodes CYRUS could understand at all were diplomatic meetings, flights, press conferences, state dinners, and the like — less than two dozen general sorts of activities (the kinds that are newsworthy and typical of secretaries of state). It had no provision for sudden resignation. It was as if the UPI had reported that a wicked witch had turned Vance into a frog. It is distinctly possible that CYRUS would have taken that report more in stride that the actual news. One can imagine the conversation:

Q: *Hello, Mr. Vance, what's new?*
A: I was turned into a frog yesterday.

But of course it wouldn't know enough about what it had just written to be puzzled, or startled, or embarrassed. The reason is obvious. When you look inside CYRUS, you find that it has skeletal definitions of thousands of words, but these definitions are minimal. They contain as little as the system designers think that they can get away with. Thus, perhaps, *lawyer* would be defined as synonymous with *attorney* and *legal counsel*, but aside from that, all one would discover about lawyers is that they are adult human beings and that they perform various functions in legal areas. If you then traced out the path to *human being*, you'd find out various obvious things CYRUS "knew" about human beings (hence about lawyers), but that is not a lot. That lawyers are university graduates, that they are better paid than chambermaids, that they know how to tie their shoes, that they are unlikely to be found in the company of lumberjacks — these trivial, if weird, facts about lawyers would not be explicit or implicit anywhere in this system. In other words, a very thin stereotype of a lawyer would be incorporated into the system, so that almost nothing you could tell it about a lawyer would surprise it.

So long as surprising things don't happen, so long as Mr. Vance, for instance, leads a typical diplomat's life, attending state dinners, giving speeches, flying from Cairo to Rome, and so forth, this system works very well. But as soon as his path is crossed by an important anomaly, the system is unable to cope, and unable to recover without fairly massive human intervention. In the case of the sudden resignation, Kolodner and her associates soon had CYRUS up and running again, with a new talent — answering questions about Edmund Muskie, Vance's successor — but it was no less vulnerable to unexpected events. Not that it mattered particularly since CYRUS was a theoretical model, not a practical system.

There are a host of ways of improving the performance of such systems, and of course, some systems are much better than others. But all AI programs in one way or another have this facadelike quality, simply for reasons of economy. For instance, most expert systems in medical diagnosis so far developed operate with statistical information. They have no deep or even shallow knowledge of the underlying causal mechanisms of the phenomena that they are diagnosing. To take an imaginary example, an expert system asked to diagnose an abdominal pain would be oblivious to the potential import of the fact that the patient had recently been employed as a sparring partner by Muhammed Ali — there being no statistical data available to it on the rate of kidney stones among athlete's assistants. That's a fanciful case no doubt — too obvious, perhaps, to lead to an actual failure of diagnosis and practice. But more subtle and hard-to-detect limits to comprehension are always present, and even experts, even the system's designers, can be uncertain of where and how these limits will interfere with the desired operation of the system. Again, steps can be taken and are being taken to correct these flaws. For instance, my former colleague at Tufts, Benjamin Kuipers, is currently working on an expert system in nephrology — for diagnosing kidney ailments — that will be based on an elaborate system of causal reasoning about the phenomena being diagnosed. But this is a very ambitious, long-range project of considerable theoretical difficulty. And even if all the reasonable, cost-effective steps are taken to minimize the superficiality of expert systems, they will still be facades, just somewhat thicker or wider facades.

When we were considering the fantastic case of the crazy Chamber of Commerce of Great Falls, Montana, we couldn't imagine a plausible motive for anyone going to any sort of trouble to trick the Dennett test. The quick probe assumption for the Dennett test looked quite secure. But when we look at expert systems, we see that, however innocently, their designers do have motivation for doing exactly the sort of trick that would fool an unsuspicious Turing tester. First, since expert systems are all superspecialists who are only supposed to know about some narrow subject, users of such systems, not having much time to kill, do not bother probing them at the boundaries at all. They don't bother asking "silly" or irrelevant questions. Instead, they concentrate — not unreasonably — on exploiting the system's strengths. But shouldn't they try to obtain a clear vision of such a system's weaknesses as well? The normal habit of human thought when conversing with one another is to assume general comprehension, to assume rationality, to assume, moreover, that the quick probe assumption is, in general, sound. This amiable habit of thought almost irresistibly leads to putting too much faith in computer systems, especially user-friendly systems that present themselves in a very anthropomorphic manner.

Part of the solution to this problem is to teach all users of computers, especially users of expert systems, how to probe their systems before they rely on them, how to search out and explore the boundaries of the facade. This is an exercise that calls not only for intelligence and imagination, but also a bit of special understanding about the limitations and actual structure of computer programs. It would help, of course, if we had standards of truth in advertising, in effect, for expert systems. For instance, each such system should come with a special demonstration routine that exhibits the sorts of shortcomings and failures that the designer knows the system to have. This would not be a substitute, however, for an attitude of cautious, almost obsessive, skepticism on the part of the users, for designers are often, if not always, unaware of the subtler flaws in the products they produce. That is inevitable and natural, given the way system designers must think. They are trained to think positively — constructively, one might say — about the designs that they are constructing.

I come, then, to my conclusions. First, a philosophical or theoretical conclusion: The Turing test in unadulterated, unrestricted from, as Turing presented it, is plenty strong if well used. I am confident that no computer in the next twenty years is going to pass an unrestricted Turing test. They may well win the World Chess Championship or even a Nobel Prize in physics, but they won't pass the unrestricted Turing test. Nevertheless, it is not, I think, impossible in principle for a computer to pass the test, fair and square. I'm not running one of those a priori "computers can't think" arguments. I stand unabashedly ready, moreover, to declare that any computer that actually passes the unrestricted Turing test will be, in every theoretically interesting sense, a thinking thing.

But remembering how very strong the Turing test is, we must also recognize that there may also be interesting varieties of thinking or intelligence that are not well poised to play and win the imitation game. That no nonhuman Turing test winners are yet visible on the horizon does not mean that there aren't machines that already exhibit *some* of the important features of thought. About them, it is probably futile to ask my title question, Do they think? Do they *really* think? In some regards they do, and in some regards they don't. Only a detailed look at what they do, and how they are structured, will reveal what is interesting about them. The Turing test, not being a scientific test, is of scant help on that task, but there are plenty of other ways of examining such systems. Verdicts on their intelligence or capacity for thought or consciousness would be only as informative and persuasive as the theories of intelligence or thought or consciousness the verdicts are based on and since our task is to create such theories, we should get on with it and leave the Big Verdict for another occasion. In the meantime, should anyone want a surefire, almost-guaranteed-to-be-fail-safe test of thinking by a computer, the Turing test will do very nicely.

My second conclusion is more practical, and hence in one clear sense more important. Cheapened versions of the Turing test are everywhere in the air. Turing's test in not just effective, it is entirely natural — this is, after all, the way we assay the intelligence of each other every day. And since incautious use of such judgments and such tests is the norm, we are in some considerable danger of extrapolating too easily, and judging too generously, about the understanding of the systems we are using. The problem of overestimation of cognitive prowess, of comprehension, of intelligence, is not, then, just a philosophical problem, but a real social problem, and we should alert ourselves to it, and take steps to avert it.

2   Postscript [1985]: Eyes, Ears, Hands, and History

My philosophical conclusion in this paper is that any computer that actually passes the Turing test would be a thinking thing in every theoretically interesting sense. This conclusion seems to some people to fly in the face of what I have myself argued on other occasions. Peter Bieri, commenting on this paper at Boston University, noted that I have often claimed to show the importance to genuine understanding of a rich and intimate perceptual interconnection between an entity and its surrounding world — the need for something like eyes and ears — and a similarly complex active engagement with elements in that world — the need for something like hands with which to do things in that world. Moreover, I have often held that only a biography of sorts, a history of actual projects, learning experiences, and other bouts with reality, could produce the sorts of complexities (both external, or behavioral, and internal) that are needed to ground a principled interpretation of an entity as a thinking thing, an entity with beliefs, desires, intentions, and other mental attitudes.

But the opaque screen in the Turing test discounts or dismisses these factors altogether, it seems, by focusing attention on only the contemporaneous capacity to engage in one very limited sort of activity: verbal communication. (I have coined a pejorative label for such purely language-using systems: bedridden.) Am I going back on my earlier claims? Not at all. I am merely pointing out that the Turing test is so powerful that it will ensure indirectly that these conditions, if they are truly necessary, are met by any successful contestant.

"You may well be right," Turing could say, "that eyes, ears, hands, and a history are necessary conditions for thinking. If so, then I submit that nothing could pass the Turing test that didn't have eyes, ears, hands, and a history. That is an empirical claim, which we can someday hope to test. If you suggest that these are conceptually necessary, not just practically or physically necessary, conditions for thinking, you make a philosophical claim that I for one would not know how, or care, to assess. Isn't it more interesting and important in the end to discover whether or not it is true that no bedridden system could pass a demanding Turing test?"

Suppose we put to Turing the suggestion that he add another component to his test: Not only must an entity win the imitation game, but also must be able to identify — using whatever sensory apparatus it has available to it — a variety of familiar objects placed in its room: a tennis racket, a potted palm, a bucket of yellow paint, a live dog. This would ensure that somehow the other entity was capable of moving around and distinguishing things in the world. Turing could reply, I am asserting, that this is an utterly unnecessary addition to his test, making it no more demanding than it already was. A suitably probing conversation would surely establish, beyond a shadow of a doubt, that the contestant knew its way around the world. The imagined alternative of somehow "prestocking" a bedridden, blind computer with enough information, and a clever enough program, to trick the Turing test is science fiction of the worst kind — possible "in principle" but not remotely possible in fact, given the combinatorial explosion of possible variation such a system would have to cope with.

"But suppose you're wrong. What would you say of an entity that was created all at once (by some programmers, perhaps), an instant individual with all the conversational talents of an embodied, experienced human being?" This is like the question: "Would you call a hunk of H_2O that was as hard as steel at room temperature ice?" I do not know what Turing would say, of course, so I will speak for myself. Faced with such an improbable violation of what I take to be the laws of nature, I would probably be speechless. The least of my worries would be about which lexicographical leap to take:

A: "It turns out, to my amazement, that something can think without having had the benefit of eyes, ears, hands, and a history."
B: "It turns out, to my amazement, that something can pass the Turing test without thinking."

Choosing between these ways of expressing my astonishment would be asking myself a question "too meaningless to deserve discussion."

Discussion

Q: *Why was Turing interested in differentiating a man from a woman in his famous test?*

A: That was just an example. He described a parlor game in which a man would try to fool the judge by answering questions as a woman would answer. I suppose that Turing was playing on the idea that maybe, just maybe, there is a big difference between the way men think and the way women think. But of course they're both thinkers. He wanted to use that fact to make us realize that, even if there were clear differences between the way a computer and a person thought, they'd both still be thinking.

Q: *Why does it seem that some people are upset by AI research? Does AI research threaten our self-esteem?*

A: I think Herb Simon has already given the canniest diagnosis of that. For many people the mind is the last refuge of mystery against the encroaching spread of science, and they don't like the idea of science engulfing the last bit of *terra incognita*. This means that they are threatened, I think irrationally, by the prospect that researchers in artificial intelligence may come to understand the human mind as well as biologists understand the genetic code, or as well as physicists understand electricity and magnetism. This could lead to the "evil scientist" (to take a stock character from science fiction) who can control you because he or she has a deep understanding of what's going on in your mind. This seems to me to be a totally valueless fear, one that you can set aside, for the simple reason that the human mind is full of an extraordinary amount of detailed knowledge, as, for example, Roger Schank has been pointing out.

As long as the scientist who is attempting to manipulate you does not share all your knowledge, his or her chances of manipulating you are minimal. People can always hit you over the head. They can do that now. We don't need artificial intelligence to manipulate people by putting them in chains or torturing them. But if someone tries to manipulate you by controlling your thoughts and ideas, that person will have to know what you know and more. The best way to keep yourself safe from that kind of manipulation is to be well informed.

Q: *Do you think we will be able to program self-consciousness into a computer?*

A: Yes, I do think that it's possible to program self-consciousness into a computer. *Self-consciousness* can mean many things. If you take the simplest, crudest notion of self-consciousness, I suppose that would be the sort of self-consciousness that a lobster has: when it's hungry, it eats something, but it never eats itself. It has some way of distinguishing between itself and the rest of the world, and it has a rather special regard for itself.

The lowly lobster is, in one regard, self-conscious. If you want to know whether or not you can create that on the computer, the answer is yes. It's no trouble at all. The computer is already a self-watching, self-monitoring sort of thing. That is an established part of the technology

But, of course, most people have something more in mind when they speak of self-consciousness. It is that special inner light, that private way that it is with you that nobody else can share, something that is forever outside the bounds of computer science. How could a computer ever be conscious in this sense?

That belief, that very gripping, powerful intuition is, I think, in the end simply an illusion of common sense. It is as gripping as the commonsense illusion that the earth stands still and the sun goes around the earth. But the only way that those of us who do not believe in the illusion will ever convince the general public that it is an illusion is by gradually unfolding a very difficult and fascinating story about just what is going on in our minds.

In the interim, people like me — philosophers who have to live by our wits and tell a lot of stories — use what I call intuition pumps, little examples that help free up the imagination. I simply want to draw your attention to one fact. If you look at a computer — I don't care whether it's a giant Cray or a personal computer — if you open up the box and look inside and see those chips, you say, "No way could that be conscious. No way could that be self-conscious." But the same thing is true if you take the top off somebody's skull and look at the gray matter pulsing away in there. You think, "That is conscious? No way could that lump of stuff be conscious."

Of course, it makes no difference whether you look at it with a microscope or with a macroscope: At no level of inspection does a brain look like the seat of consciousness. Therefore, don't expect a computer to look like the seat of consciousness. If you want to get a grasp of how a computer could be conscious, it's no more difficult in the end than getting a grasp of how a brain could be conscious.

As we develop good accounts of consciousness, it will no longer seem so obvious to everyone that the idea of a self-conscious computer is a contradiction in terms. At the same time, I doubt that there will ever be self-conscious robots. But for boring reasons. There won't be any point in making them. Theoretically, could we make a gall bladder out of atoms? In principle we could. A gall bladder is just a collection of atoms, but manufacturing one would cost the moon. It would be more expensive than every project NASA has ever dreamed of, and there would be no scientific payoff. We wouldn't learn anything new about how gall bladders work. For the same reason, I don't think we're going to see really humanoid robots, because practical, cost-effective robots don't need to be very humanoid at all. They need to be like the robots you can already see at General Motors, or like boxy little computers that do special-purpose things.

The theoretical issues will be studied by artificial intelligence researchers by looking at models that, to the layman, will show very little sign of humanity at all, and it will be only by rather indirect arguments that anyone will be able to appreciate that these models cast light on the deep theoretical question of how the mind is organized.

3 Postscript [1997]

In 1991, the First Annual Loebner Prize Competition was held in Boston at the Computer Museum. Hugh Loebner, a New York manufacturer, had put up the money for a prize — a bronze medal and $100,000 — for the first computer program to pass the Turing Test fair and square. The Prize Committee, of which I was Chairman until my resignation after the third competition, recognized that no program on the horizon could come close to passing the unrestricted test — the only test that is of any theoretical interest at all, as this essay has explained. So to make the competition interesting during the early years, some restrictions were adopted (and the award for winning the restricted test was dropped to $2000). The first year there were ten terminals, with ten judges shuffling from terminal to terminal, each spending fifteen minutes in conversation with each terminal. Six of the ten contestants were programs, four were human "confederates" behind the scenes.

Each judge had to rank order all ten terminals from most human to least human. The winner of the restricted test would be the computer with the highest mean rating. The winning program would not have to fool any of the judges, nor would fooling a judge be in itself grounds for winning; highest mean ranking was all. But just in case some program *did* fool a judge, we thought this fact should be revealed, so judges were required to draw a line somewhere across their rank ordering, separating the humans from the machines.

We on the Prize Committee knew the low quality of the contesting programs that first year, and it seemed obvious to us that no program would be so lucky as to fool a single judge, but on the day of the competition, I got nervous. Just to be safe, I thought, we should have some certificate prepared to award to any programmer who happened to pull off this unlikely feat. While the press and the audience were assembling for the beginning of the competition, I rushed into a back room at the Computer Museum with a member of the staff and we cobbled up a handsome certificate with the aid of a handy desk-top publisher. In the event, we had to hand out three of these certificates, for a total of seven positive misjudgements out of a possible sixty! The gullibility of the judges was simply astonishing to me. How *could* they have misjudged so badly? Here I had committed the sin I'd so often found in others: treating a failure of imagination as an insight into necessity. But remember that in order to make the competition much easier, we had tied the judges' hands in various ways — too many ways. The judges had been forbidden to *probe* the contestants aggressively, to conduct conversational experiments. (I may have chaired the committee, but I didn't always succeed in persuading a majority to adopt the rules I favored.) When the judges sat back passively, as instructed, and let the contestants lead them, they were readily taken in by the Potemkin village effect described in the essay.

None of the misjudgments counted as a real case of a computer passing the unrestricted Turing Test, but they were still surprising to me. In the second year of the competition, we uncovered another unanticipated loophole: due to faulty briefing of the confederates, several of them gave deliberately clunky, automaton-like answers. It turned out that they had decided to give the silicon contestants a sporting chance by acting as if they were programs! But once we'd straightened out these glitches in the rules and procedures, the competition worked out just as I had originally predicted: the computers stood out like sore thumbs even though there were still huge restrictions on topic. In the third year, two of the judges — journalists — each made a false *negative* judgment, declaring one of the less eloquent human confederates to be a computer. On debriefing, their explanation showed just how vast the gulf was between the computer programs and the people: they reasoned that the competition would not have been held if there weren't at least one half-way decent computer contestant, so they simply picked the least impressive human being and declared it to be a computer. But they could see the gap between the computers and the people as well as everybody else could.

The Loebner Prize Competition was a fascinating social experiment, and some day I hope to write up the inside story — a tale of sometimes hilarious misadventure, bizarre characters, interesting technical challenges, and more. But it never succeeded in attracting serious contestants from the world's best AI labs. Why not? In part because, as the essay argues, passing the Turing Test is not a sensible research and development goal for serious AI. It requires too much Disney and not enough science. We might have corrected that flaw by introducing into the Loebner Competition something analogous to the "school figures" in ice-skating competion: theoretically interesting (but not crowd-pleasing) technical challenges such as parsing pronouns, or dealing creatively with enthymemes (arguments with unstated premises). Only those programs that performed well in the school figures — the serious competition — would be permitted into the final show-off round, where they could dazzle and amuse the onlookers with some cute Disney touches. Some such change in the rules would have wiped out all but the most serious and dedicated of the home hobbyists, and made the Loebner Competition worth winning (and not too embarrassing to lose). When my proposals along these lines were rejected, however, I resigned from the committee. The annual competitions continue, apparently, under the direction of Hugh Loebner. On the World Wide Web I just found the transcript of the conversation of the winning program in the 1996 competion. It was a scant improvement over 1991, still a bag of cheap tricks with no serious analysis of the meaning of the sentences. The Turing Test is too difficult for the real world.

References

1. Block, N., 1982, "Psychologism and Behaviorism," *Philosophical Review*, 90:5–43.
2. Colby, K. M., 1981, "Modeling a Paranoid Mind," *Behavioral and Brain Sciences*, 4(4):515–560.
3. Descartes, R., 1637, *Discourse on Method*, LaFleur, Lawrence, trans., New York: Bobbs Merrill, 1960.
4. Haugeland, J., 1981, *Mind Design: Philosophy, Psychology, Artificial Intelligence*, Cambridge, MA: Bradford Books/The MIT Press.
5. Heiser, J. F., Colby, K. M., Faught, W. S., and Parkinson, R. C., 1980, "Can Psychiatrists Distinguish a Computer Simulation of Paranoia from the Real Thing? The Limitations of Turing-Like Tests as Measures of the Adequacy of Simulations," *Journal of Psychiatric Research*, 15(3):149–162.
6. Kolodner, J. L., 1983, "Retrieval and Organization Strategies in Conceptual Memory: A Computer Model" (Ph.D. diss.), Research Report #187, Dept. of Computer Science, Yale University.
7. Kolodner, J. L., 1983, "Maintaining Organization in a Dynamic Long-term Memory," *Cognitive Science*, 7:243–279.
8. Kolodner, J. L., 1983, "Reconstructive Memory: A Computer Model," *Cognitive Science*, 7:281–328.
9. Turing, A. M, 1950, "Computing Machinery and Intelligence," *Mind*, 59(236):433–460.
10. Weizenbaum, J., 1974, letter to the editor, *Communications of the Association of Computing Machinery*, 17(9), September.
11. Winograd, T., 1972, *Understanding Natural Language*, New York: Academic Press.

The Computer, Artificial Intelligence, and the Turing Test

B. Jack Copeland and Diane Proudfoot

Philosophy Department, University of Canterbury

Summary. We discuss, first, Turing's role in the development of the computer; second, the early history of Artificial Intelligence (to 1956); and third, Turing's famous imitation game, now universally known as the Turing test, which he proposed in cameo form in 1948 and then more fully in 1950 and 1952. Various objections have been raised to Turing's test: we describe some of the most prominent and explain why, in our view, they fail.

1 Turing and the Computer

1.1 The Turing Machine

In his first major publication, "On Computable Numbers, with an Application to the Entscheidungsproblem" [91], Turing introduced his "universal computing machine" and the idea essential to the modern computer — the concept of controlling a computing machine's operations by means of a program of coded instructions stored in the machine's memory. This work had a profound influence on the development in the 1940s of the electronic stored-program digital computer — an influence often neglected or denied by historians of the computer.[1]

The universal computing machine of 1936 — now known simply as the "universal Turing machine" — is an abstract conceptual model. It consists of a scanner and a limitless memory-tape that moves back and forward past the scanner. The scanner reads the symbols on the tape and writes further symbols. The machine has a small repertoire of basic operations; complexity of operation is achieved by chaining together basic operations. The machine is universal in the sense that it can be programmed to carry out any calculation that could be performed by a "human computer" — a clerk who works systematically and who has unlimited time and an endless supply of paper and pencils.

The universal machine has a single, fixed table of instructions built into it. These "hard-wired" instructions enable the machine to read and execute symbolically encoded instructions inscribed on its tape. The data to be worked on are also inscribed on the memory-tape. By inscribing different programs

---

[1] See, for example, Campbell-Kelly and Aspray [15]. The nature and scope of Turing's influence is underplayed even in Hodges' biography of Turing [48].

on the tape, the machine can be made to carry out different tasks. This, then, was Turing's fabulous idea: a single machine of fixed structure that, by making use of coded instructions stored in memory, could change itself, chameleon-like, from a machine dedicated to one task into a machine dedicated to another. Nowadays, when so many people possess a physical realization of the universal Turing machine, Turing's idea of a one-stop-shop computing machine seems as obvious as the wheel. But in 1936, when engineers thought in terms of building different machines for different purposes, this concept was revolutionary.

In 1936 the universal Turing machine existed only as an idea. But right from the start Turing was interested in the possibility of actually building such a machine.[2] His wartime acquaintance with electronics was the key link between his earlier theoretical work and his 1945 design for an electronic stored-program digital computer.

1.2 Wartime Machines: the Bombe and Colossus

Turing completed the logical design of the Bombe (built to break German Enigma messages — see Chap. 11) in the last months of 1939. His designs were handed over to Keen at the British Tabulating Machine Company in Letchworth, where the engineering development was carried out.[3] The first Bombe, named "Victory," was installed at Bletchley Park early in 1940 [55, p. 28]. (An improved model — "Agnus," short for "Agnus Dei," but later corrupted to "Agnes" and "Aggie" — which contained Welchman's ingenious diagonal board was installed some months later.[4]) The Bombe was a computing machine with a very narrow and specialized purpose, searching through the wheel-positions of the Enigma machine at superhuman speed. It was based on the electromagnetic relay, although some later versions were electronic (i.e., valve-based). Relays are small switches consisting of a moving metal rod, which opens and closes an electrical circuit, and an electrical coil, the magnetic field of which moves the rod. Electronic valves (called "vacuum tubes" in the U.S.) operate very many times faster than relays, because the valve's only moving part is a beam of electrons.

During the attack on Enigma, the Government Code and Cypher School (GC&CS) at Bletchley Park approached the Post Office Research Station at

---

[2] Newman in interview with Christopher Evans ("The Pioneers of Computing: An Oral History of Computing" (Science Museum, London)); "Dr. A. M. Turing," The Times, 16 June 1954, p. 10.

[3] A memo "Naval Enigma Situation," dated 1 November 1939 and signed by Knox, Twinn, Welchman and Turing, said: "A large 30 enigma bomb [sic] machine, adapted to use for cribs, is on order and parts are being made at the British Tabulating Company." The memo is in the British Public Record Office (PRO), Kew, Richmond, Surrey; document reference HW 14/2.

[4] Welchman 2000; "Squadron-Leader Jones, Section" (PRO document reference HW 3/164). (Thanks to Ralph Erskine for sending a copy of this document.)

Dollis Hill in London to build a relay-based machine for use in conjunction with the Bombe. Once the Bombe had uncovered the Enigma settings used to encrypt a particular message, these settings were to be transferred to the proposed machine, which would then automatically decipher the message and print out the original German text.[5] Dollis Hill sent electronic engineer Thomas Flowers to Bletchley Park. In the end, the machine Flowers built was not used, but he was soon to become one of the great figures of World War II codebreaking. Thanks to his pre-war research, Flowers was (as he himself remarked) possibly the only person in Britain who realized that valves could be used on a large scale for high-speed digital computing.[6]

The world's first large-scale electronic digital computer, Colossus, was designed and built during 1943 by Flowers and his team at Dollis Hill, in consultation with the Cambridge mathematician Max Newman, head of the section at Bletchley Park known simply as the "Newmanry". (Turing attended Newman's lectures on mathematical logic at Cambridge before the war; these lectures launched Turing on the research that led to his "On Computable Numbers."[7]) Colossus first worked in December 1943 (two years before the first comparable U.S. machine, the ENIAC, was operational).[8] Colossus was used against the Lorenz cipher machine, more advanced than Enigma and introduced in 1941 (for a history of Colossus see [28]). The British government kept Colossus secret: before the 1970s few had any idea that electronic computation had been used successfully during World War II, and it was not until 2000 that the British and the U.S. finally released the complete account of Colossus' wartime role.[9] So it was that, in the decades following the war, John von Neumann and others told the world that the ENIAC was "the first electronic computing machine" [103, pp. 238–239].

Although Colossus possessed a certain amount of flexibility, it was very far from being universal. Nor did it store instructions internally. As with the later ENIAC, in order to set Colossus up for a new job it was necessary to modify some of the machine's wiring by hand, using switches and plugs. (During the construction of Colossus, Newman showed Flowers Turing's "On Computable Numbers" paper, with its key idea of storing symbolically encoded instructions in memory, but Flowers, not being a mathematical logician, "didn't really understand much of it."[10]) Nevertheless, Flowers established decisively

---

[5] Flowers in interview with Copeland (July 1998).

[6] Flowers in interview with Copeland (July 1996).

[7] Newman in interview with Christopher Evans ("The Pioneers of Computing: an Oral History of Computing" (Science Museum, London)).

[8] Flowers in interview with Copeland (July 1996).

[9] "General Report on Tunny, with Emphasis on Statistical Methods" (PRO document reference 2 vols) HW 25/4, HW 25/5. "General Report on Tunny" was written in 1945 by Good, Michie, and Timms, members of Newman's section at Bletchley Park. A digital facsimile is in The Turing Archive for the History of Computing, http://www.AlanTuring.net/tunny_report.

[10] Flowers in interview with Copeland (July 1996).

and for the first time that large-scale electronic computing machinery was practicable. Flowers has said that, once Turing saw Colossus in operation, it was just a matter of Turing's waiting to see what opportunity might arise to put the idea of his universal computing machine into practice.[11] There is little doubt that by 1944 Newman too had firmly in mind the possibility of building a universal Turing machine using electronic technology. In February 1946, a few months after his appointment as Professor of Mathematics at the University of Manchester, Newman wrote to von Neumann in the U.S.:

> I am ... hoping to embark on a computing machine section here, having got very interested in electronic devices of this kind during the last two or three years. By about eighteen months ago I had decided to try my hand at starting up a machine unit when I got out. ... I am of course in close touch with Turing.[12]

1.3   Turing and von Neumann

In the years immediately following World War II, the Hungarian-American logician and mathematician John von Neumann, through writings and charismatic public addresses, made the concept of the stored-program digital computer widely known. Von Neumann wrote "First Draft of a Report on the EDVAC"[13] and was the leader of the computer project at the Princeton Institute of Advanced Study. The ensuing machine, the IAS computer, although not the first to run in the U.S. (it began work in the summer of 1951 [4, p. 308]), was the most influential of the early U.S. computers and the precursor to the IBM 701, the company's first mass-produced stored-program electronic computer.

In the secondary literature, von Neumann is often said to have invented the stored-program computer, but he repeatedly emphasized that the fundamental conception was Turing's. Von Neumann became familiar with ideas in "On Computable Numbers" during Turing's time at Princeton (1936–38) and was to become intrigued by Turing's concept of a universal computing machine.[14] It was von Neumann who placed Turing's concept in the hands of

---

[11] Flowers in interview with Copeland (July 1996).

[12] Letter from Newman to von Neumann, 8 February 1946 (in the von Neumann Archive at the Library of Congress, Washington, D.C.; a digital facsimile is in The Turing Archive for the History of Computing, http://www.AlanTuring.net/newman_vonneumann_8feb46).

[13] Moore School of Electrical Engineering, University of Pennsylvania, 1945. Reprinted in full in [87].

[14] "I know that von Neumann was influenced by Turing ... during his Princeton stay before the war," said Stanislaw Ulam (in an interview with Christopher Evans in 1976, "The Pioneers of Computing: an Oral History of Computing" (Science Museum, London)). When Ulam and von Neumann were touring in Europe during the summer of 1938, von Neumann devised a mathematical game involving

American engineers. Stanley Frankel (the Los Alamos physicist responsible, with von Neumann and others, for mechanizing the large-scale calculations involved in the design of the atomic and hydrogen bombs) recorded von Neumann's view of the importance of 'On Computable Numbers':

> I know that in or about 1943 or '44 von Neumann was well aware of the fundamental importance of Turing's paper of 1936 "On computable numbers ... ," which describes in principle the "Universal Computer" of which every modern computer (perhaps not ENIAC as first completed but certainly all later ones) is a realization. Von Neumann introduced me to that paper and at his urging I studied it with care. Many people have acclaimed von Neumann as the "father of the computer" (in a modern sense of the term) but I am sure that he would never have made that mistake himself. He might well be called the midwife, perhaps, but he firmly emphasized to me, and to others I am sure, that the fundamental conception is owing to Turing — insofar as not anticipated by Babbage, Lovelace, and others. In my view von Neumann's essential role was in making the world aware of these fundamental concepts introduced by Turing and of the development work carried out in the Moore school and elsewhere.[15]

In 1944, von Neumann joined the Eckert-Mauchly ENIAC group at the Moore School of Electrical Engineering at the University of Pennsylvania. (At the time he was involved in the Manhattan Project at Los Alamos, where roomfuls of clerks armed with desk calculating machines were struggling to carry out the massive calculations required by the physicists.) ENIAC — under construction since 1943 — was, as previously mentioned, not a stored-program computer: programming consisted of re-routing cables and setting switches. Moreover, the ENIAC was far from universal, having been designed with only one very specific task in mind, the calculation of trajectories of artillery shells. Von Neumann brought his knowledge of "On Computable Numbers" to the practical arena of the Moore School. Thanks to Turing's abstract logical work, von Neumann knew that, by making use of coded instructions stored in memory, a single machine of fixed structure could in principle carry out any task for which an instruction table can be written. When Eckert explained his idea of using the mercury delay line as a high-speed recirculating memory, von Neumann saw that this was the means to make concrete the abstract universal computing machine of "On Computable Numbers."[16]

Turing-machine-like descriptions of numbers (Ulam reported by William Aspray in [1, pp. 178, 313]). The word "intrigued" is used in this connection by von Neumann's friend and colleague Herman Goldstine [45, p. 275].

[15] Letter from Frankel to Brian Randell, 1972 (first published in [73]). Copeland is grateful to Randell for giving him a copy of the letter.

[16] Burks (a member of the ENIAC group) summarized matters thus:

When, in 1946, von Neumann established his own project to build a stored-program computer at the Institute for Advanced Study, he gave his engineers "On Computable Numbers" to read.[17] Bigelow, von Neumann's chief engineer and largely responsible for the engineering design of the computer built at the Institute, remarked:

> The person who really ... pushed the whole field ahead was von Neumann, because he understood logically what [the stored-program concept] meant in a deeper way than anybody else. ... The reason he understood it is because, among other things, he understood a good deal of the mathematical logic which was implied by the idea, due to the work of A. M. Turing ... in 1936–1937 .... Turing's [universal] machine does not sound much like a modern computer today, but nevertheless it was. It was the germinal idea. ... So ... [von Neumann] saw ... that [ENIAC] was just the first step, and that great improvement would come.[18]

Von Neumann repeatedly emphasized the fundamental importance of "On Computable Numbers" in lectures and in correspondence. In 1946 he wrote to the mathematician Norbert Wiener of "the great positive contribution of Turing" — Turing's mathematical demonstration that "one, definite mechanism can be 'universal'."[19] In 1948, in a lecture entitled "The General and Logical Theory of Automata," von Neumann said:

> The English logician, Turing, about twelve years ago attacked the following problem. He wanted to give a general definition of what is meant by a computing automaton. ... Turing carried out a careful analysis of what mathematical processes can be effected by automata of this type. ... He ... also introduce[d] and analyse[d] the concept of a "universal automaton" ... An automaton is "universal" if any sequence that can be produced by any automaton at all can also

---

Pres [Eckert] and John [Mauchly] invented the circulating mercury delay line store, with enough capacity to store program information as well as data. Von Neumann created the first modern order code and worked out the logical design of an electronic computer to execute it. [11, p. 312]

Burks also recorded [11, p. 341] that von Neumann was the first of the Moore School group to see the possibility, implicit in the stored-program concept, of allowing the computer to modify selected instructions in a program as it runs (in order to control loops and branching, for example). The same idea lay at the foundation of Turing's theory of machine learning.

[17] Letter from Bigelow to Copeland (12 April 2002). See also [1, p. 178].

[18] Bigelow in a tape-recorded interview made in 1971 by the Smithsonian Institution and released in 2002. Copeland is grateful to Bigelow for sending a transcript of excerpts from the interview.

[19] Letter dated 29 November 1946 (in the von Neumann Archive at the Library of Congress, Washington, D.C.).

be solved by this particular automaton. It will, of course, require in general a different instruction for this purpose. *The Main Result of the Turing Theory.* We might expect a priori that this is impossible. How can there be an automaton which is at least as effective as any conceivable automaton, including, for example, one of twice its size and complexity? Turing, nevertheless, proved that this is possible.[20]

The following year, in a lecture delivered at the University of Illinois, entitled "Rigorous Theories of Control and Information," von Neumann said:

> The importance of Turing's research is just this: that if you construct an automaton right, then any additional requirements about the automaton can be handled by sufficiently elaborate instructions. This is only true if [the automaton] is sufficiently complicated, if it has reached a certain minimal level of complexity. In other words ... there is a very definite finite point where an automaton of this complexity can, when given suitable instructions, do anything that can be done by automata at all.[21]

Many books on the history of computing in the U.S. make no mention of Turing. No doubt this is in part explained by the absence of any explicit reference to Turing's work in the series of technical reports in which von Neumann, with various co-authors, set out the logical design of an electronic stored-program digital computer.[22] Nevertheless there is evidence in these documents of von Neumann's knowledge of "On Computable Numbers." For example, in the report entitled "Preliminary Discussion of the Logical Design of an Electronic Computing Instrument" (1946), von Neumann and his co-authors, Burks and Goldstine — both former members of the ENIAC group, who had joined von Neumann at the Institute for Advanced Study — wrote the following:

> First Remarks on the Control and Code: It is easy to see by formal-logical methods, that there exist codes that are in abstracto adequate to control and cause the execution of any sequence of operations which are individually available in the machine and which are, in their entirety, conceivable by the problem planner. The really decisive considerations from the present point of view, in selecting a code, are more of a practical nature: Simplicity of the equipment demanded by the code, and the clarity of its application to the

---

[20] The text of "The General and Logical Theory of Automata" is in [89]; the quotation is from pp. 313–314.

[21] The text of "Rigorous Theories of Control and Information" is printed in [104]; the quotation is from p. 50.

[22] The first papers in the series were the "First Draft of a Report on the EDVAC" (von Neumann, 1945) and "Preliminary Discussion of the Logical Design of an Electronic Computing Instrument" (Burks, Goldstine, von Neumann, 1946).

actually important problems together with the speed of its handling of those problems. [12, Sect. 3.1]

Burks has confirmed that the first sentence of this passage is a reference to Turing's universal computing machine.[23] (The report was not intended for formal publication and no attempt was made to indicate those places where reference was being made to the work of others.)

The passage just quoted is an excellent summary of the situation at that time. In "On Computable Numbers" Turing had shown *in abstracto* that, by means of instructions expressed in the programming code of his "standard descriptions," a single machine of fixed structure is able to carry out any task that a "problem planner" is able to analyze into effective steps. By 1945, considerations *in abstracto* had given way to the practical problem of devising an equivalent programming code that could be implemented efficiently by means of electronic circuits. The challenge of designing a practical code and the underlying mechanism required for its implementation was tackled in different ways by Turing and the several American groups.

1.4   The ACE

In 1945 Turing was recruited by the National Physical Laboratory (NPL) in London, his brief to design and develop an electronic stored-program digital computer.[24] Turing's technical report "Proposed Electronic Calculator," dating from the end of 1945 and containing his design for the Automatic Computing Engine (ACE), was the first relatively complete specification of an electronic stored-program digital computer.[25] The slightly earlier "First Draft of a Report on the EDVAC," produced in about May 1945, was much more abstract, saying little about programming, hardware details, or electronics. (Huskey, the electronic engineer who subsequently drew up the first

---

[23] Letter from Burks to Copeland (22 April 1998). See also p. 258 of [45].

[24] Minutes of the Executive Committee of the National Physical Laboratory for 23 October 1945 (a digital facsimile is in the Turing Archive for the History of Computing, http://www.AlanTuring.net/npl_minutes_oct1945). Womersley, J. R. "A.C.E. Project - Origin and Early History," 26 November 1946 (PRO document reference DSIR 10/385; a digital facsimile is in the Turing Archive for the History of Computing, http://www.AlanTuring.net/ace_early_history).

[25] A digital facsimile of the original typewritten report is in The Turing Archive for the History of Computing, http://www.AlanTuring.net/proposed_electronic_calculator. The report was reprinted by the NPL in April 1972 as Computer Science Division Report No. 57 and is in [16]. According to Michael Woodger (Turing's assistant at the NPL) an NPL file gave the date of Turing's completed report as 1945; unfortunately, this file was destroyed in 1952 (Woodger, M., handwritten note (undated), in the Woodger Papers, National Museum of Science and Industry, Kensington, London (catalogue reference M15/78); letter from Woodger to Copeland (27 November 1999)).

detailed hardware designs for the EDVAC, stated that the "information in the 'First Draft' was of no help."[26]) Turing, in contrast, supplied detailed circuit designs, full specifications of hardware units, specimen programs in machine code, and even an estimate of the cost of building the machine.

Turing's ACE and the EDVAC differed fundamentally in design. For example, the EDVAC (which was not fully working until 1952 [50, p. 702][27]) had what is now called a central processing unit, or cpu, whereas in the ACE the various logical and arithmetical functions were distributed across different memory units. Another deep difference between the ACE and both the EDVAC and its British derivative the EDSAC (built by Wilkes at the University of Cambridge Mathematical Laboratory) was that in Turing's design complex behavior was to be achieved by complex programming rather than by complex equipment. Turing's philosophy was to dispense with additional hardware in favor of programming (or coding, as it was then called). Concerning his and Wilkes's differing outlooks, Turing said:

> I have read Wilkes' proposals for a pilot machine ... The "code" which he suggests is however very contrary to the line of development here [at the NPL], and much more in the American tradition of solving one's difficulties by means of much equipment rather than thought.[28]

Turing saw that speed and memory were the keys to computing (in the words of his assistant, Wilkinson, Turing "was obsessed with the idea of speed on the machine"[29]). His design for the ACE had much in common with today's RISC architectures and called for a high-speed memory of roughly the same capacity as an early Macintosh computer (enormous by the standards of his day). However, delays beyond Turing's control meant that by 1947 little progress had been made on the physical construction of the ACE (although much effort had gone into writing programs or "instruction tables") [34]. The world's first stored-program electronic digital computer was the "Manchester Baby", which ran its first program on 21 June 1948 in the University of Manchester Computing Machine Laboratory, founded by Newman and funded initially by a Royal Society grant secured by Newman in July 1946.[30] As its name implies, the Baby was a very small computer, and the news that it had run what was only a tiny program — just 17 instructions long — for

---

[26] Letter from Huskey to Copeland (4 February 2002).

[27] Hodges states incorrectly that "no machine called EDVAC was ever actually built" [48, p. 355].

[28] Memo from Turing to Womersley, c. December 1946 (in the Woodger Papers (catalogue reference M15/77); a digital facsimile is in The Turing Archive for the History of Computing, http://www.AlanTuring.net/turing_womersley_cdec46).

[29] Wilkinson in interview with Christopher Evans in 1976 ("The Pioneers of Computing: an Oral History of Computing" (Science Museum, London)).

[30] Council Minutes, Royal Society, 11 July 1946.

a mathematically trivial task was "greeted with hilarity" by Turing's team at the NLP.[31]

Had Turing's ACE been built as planned it would have been in a different league from the other early computers, but his colleagues at the NPL thought the engineering work too ambitious, and a considerably smaller machine was built. Known as the Pilot Model ACE, this machine ran its first program on 10 May 1950. With an operating speed of 1 MHz it was for some time the fastest computer in the world; more than 30 of the production version, DEUCE, were sold — confounding the suggestion, made in 1946 by Sir Charles Darwin, Director of the NPL and grandson of the great Darwin, that "it is very possible that ... one machine would suffice to solve all the problems that are demanded of it from the whole country."[32]

The basic principles of Turing's ACE design were used in the G15 computer, built and marketed by the Detroit-based Bendix Corporation.[33] The G15 was designed by Huskey, who had spent 1947 at the NPL, in the ACE section. The first G15 ran in 1954.[34] It was arguably the first personal computer. By following Turing's philosophy of minimizing hardware in favor of software, Huskey was able to make the G15 small enough (it was the size of a large domestic refrigerator) and cheap enough to be marketed as a single-user computer. Yet thanks to the ACE-like design, the G15 was as fast as computers many times its size. Over 400 were sold worldwide and the G15 remained in use until about 1970.

Another computer deriving from Turing's ACE design, the MOSAIC (Ministry of Supply Automatic Integrator and Computer), played a role in Britain's air defences during the Cold War period. In 1946 Flowers established a small team at Dollis Hill to build a computer to Turing's logical design; the team consisted of Coombs and Chandler, both of whom had assisted Flowers in the construction of Colossus. Coombs and Chandler carried out the engineering design of the MOSAIC, a large computer based on version VII of Turing's logical design for the ACE (Version VII dated from 1946).[35] The MOSAIC first ran a program in 1952 or early 1953.[36]

---

[31] Woodger in interview with Copeland (June 1998).

[32] Sir Charles Darwin, "Automatic Computing Engine (ACE)," 17 April 1946 (PRO document reference DSIR 10/275; a digital facsimile is in The Turing Archive for the History of Computing, http://www.AlanTuring.net/darwin_ace). A leading British expert on automatic computation, Douglas Hartree, appears to have believed that three digital computers would probably be adequate for the country's computing needs (Hartree's opinion reported by Vivian Bowden [8, p. 326]).

[33] Huskey in interview with Copeland (February 1998); [51].

[34] Letter from Huskey to Copeland (20 December 2001).

[35] Coombs in interview with Christopher Evans in 1976 ("The Pioneers of Computing: an Oral History of Computing" (Science Museum, London)); [20]; [25].

[36] "Engineer-in-Chief's Report on the Work of the Engineering Department for the Year 1 April 1952 to 31 March 1953," Post Office Engineering Department (The Post Office Archive, London).

It was installed at the Radar Research and Development Establishment, Malvern, in 1954 or early 1955,[37] where it was used to calculate aircraft trajectories from radar data, in connection with anti-aircraft measures (the details remain classified). Of the various ACE-type computers that were built, the MOSAIC was closest to Turing's original conception.[38]

Given that two engineers working alone succeeded in completing the large MOSAIC (Coombs emphasized: "it was just Chandler and I — we designed every scrap of that machine"[39]), there seems little doubt that, given sufficient manpower, a computer not too distant from Turing's original conception could have been up and running by the early 1950s.

Other derivatives of the ACE included the E.M.I. Business Machine, a relatively slow electronic computer with a large memory, designed for the shallow processing of large quantities of data that is typically demanded by business applications, and the low-cost transistorized Packard-Bell PB250 [2, pp. 44, 74] [43, 108].

During the period December 1946 to February 1947 Turing and Wilkinson gave a series of nine lectures covering versions V, VI, and VII of Turing's design for the ACE [25].[40] The lectures were attended by representatives of various organizations which planned to use or build an electronic computer. Among the audience was Kilburn, responsible with Williams for the engineering design of the Manchester Baby machine [9, pp. 19–20]. (Kilburn usually said, when asked where he got his basic knowledge of the computer from, that he could not remember[41]; for example, in a 1992 interview he said: "Between early 1945 and early 1947, in that period, somehow or other I knew what a digital computer was ... Where I got this knowledge from I've no idea" [9, pp. 19–20][42]).

At the time of the Baby machine and its successor, the Manchester Mark I, Kilburn and Williams, who had translated the logico-mathematical idea of the stored-program computer into hardware, were given too little credit by the mathematicians at Manchester, where they were regarded as excellent engineers, but not as "ideas men."[43] Now the tables have turned too far and

---

[37] "Engineer-in-Chief's Report on the Work of the Engineering Department for the Year 1 April 1954 to 31 March 1955," Post Office Engineering Department (The Post Office Archive, London).

[38] Digital facsimiles of a series of technical reports concerning the MOSAIC, by Coombs, Chandler, and others, are available in The Turing Archive for the History of Computing, http://www.AlanTuring.net/mosaic.

[39] Coombs in interview with Evans, op. cit.

[40] Hodges [48] account of these lectures is inaccurate. Hodges states that the lectures ended in January 1947 (p. 353) and that Turing gave "[o]nly the first two and part of the last" (p. 559). In fact, the series ran until 13 February 1947 and Turing gave half of the lectures.

[41] Letter from Brian Napper to Copeland (16 June 2002).

[42] We are grateful to Napper for drawing this passage to our attention.

[43] Peter Hilton in interview with Copeland (June 2001).

the triumph at Manchester is credited to them alone. Fortunately the words of the late Williams survive to set the record straight:

> Now let's be clear before we go any further that neither Tom Kilburn nor I knew the first thing about computers when we arrived in Manchester University ... Newman explained the whole business of how a computer works to us.[44]

> Tom Kilburn and I knew nothing about computers ... Professor Newman and Mr A. M. Turing ... knew a lot about computers ... They took us by the hand and explained how numbers could live in houses with addresses ... [107, p. 328]

Whatever role Turing's lectures may have played in informing Kilburn, there is little doubt that credit for the Manchester computer belongs not only to Williams and Kilburn but also to Newman, and that the influence on Newman of Turing's "On Computable Numbers" was crucial (as was the influence of Flowers' Colossus).

In May 1948 Turing resigned from the NPL. Work on the ACE had drawn almost to a standstill.[45] Newman lured a "very fed up"[46] Turing to Manchester University, where he was appointed Deputy Director of the Computing Machine Laboratory (there being no Director). Turing designed the input mechanism and programming system[47] of, and wrote a programming manual [97] for, the Baby's successor, the Manchester Mark I. The production version, the Ferranti Mark I, was completed in February 1951 and was the first commercially available electronic digital computer [54, p. 20]. (The first U.S. commercial machine, the Eckert-Mauchly UNIVAC, appeared later the same year.) At last Turing had his hands on a stored-program computer.

2   Artificial Intelligence

2.1   The Myths

Artificial Intelligence is often said to have been born in the mid-1950s in the U.S. For example:

> Artificial Intelligence, conceived at Carnegie Tech in the autumn of 1955, quickened by Christmas, and delivered on Johnniac in the

---

[44] Williams in interview with Christopher Evans in 1976 ("The Pioneers of Computing: an Oral History of Computing" (Science Museum, London)).

[45] In April 1948 Womersley stated that hardware development was "probably as far advanced 18 months ago" (NPL Executive Committee Minutes, 20 April 1948, p. 7; a digital facsimile is in The Turing Archive for the History of Computing, http://www.AlanTuring.net/npl_minutes_apr1948).

[46] Robin Gandy in interview with Copeland (October 1995).

[47] Letter from Williams to Randell, printed in [73].

spring, made a stunning debut at the conference from which it later took its name. [46, p. 176]

The AI program "delivered on Johnniac" (a Californian copy of the IAS computer) is the Logic Theorist, written by Newell, Simon, and Shaw and demonstrated at a conference, the Dartmouth Summer Research Project on Artificial Intelligence, held at Dartmouth College, New Hampshire. The Logic Theorist was designed to prove theorems from Whitehead and Russell's *Principia Mathematica*. (In one case, the proof devised by the Logic Theorist was several lines shorter than the one given by Whitehead and Russell; Newell, Simon, and Shaw wrote up the proof and sent it to the *Journal of Symbolic Logic*. This was almost certainly the first paper to have a computer listed as a co-author, but unfortunately it was rejected.[48])

2.2   The Reality

While the term "artificial intelligence" seems to have originated at the Dartmouth conference (the term in use in Britain, pre-dating "artificial intelligence," was "machine intelligence"), the origins of the field of enquiry can be traced much further back. If anywhere has a claim to be the birthplace of AI, it is Bletchley Park. Turing was the first to carry out substantial research in the field. He was thinking about machine intelligence at least as early as 1941, in particular about the possibility of computing machines that solved problems by means of searching through the space of possible solutions, guided by rules of thumb (or what would now be called "heuristic" principles), and about the mechanization of chess.[49] At Bletchley Park, in his spare time, Turing discussed these topics and also machine learning with friends. He circulated a typescript concerning machine intelligence among some of his colleagues.[50] Now lost, this was undoubtedly the earliest paper in the field of AI.

The first AI programs ran in Britain in 1951–52, at Manchester and Cambridge. This was due in part to the fact that the first stored-program electronic computers ran in Britain and in part to Turing's influence on the first generation of computer programmers. Even in the U.S., the Logic Theorist was not the first AI program to run. So far as we have been able to discover, the earliest was Arthur Samuel's Checkers (or Draughts) player. This first ran at the end of 1952, on the IBM 701.[51] In 1955 Samuel added learning to the program [77].

---

[48] Shaw in interview with Pamela McCorduck [57, p. 143].
[49] Donald Michie in interview with Copeland (October 1995).
[50] Donald Michie in interview with Copeland (February 1998).
[51] Letter from Samuel to Copeland (6 December 1988).

2.3   The Bombe

The Bombe is the first milestone in the history of machine intelligence.[52] Central to the Bombe was the idea of solving a problem by means of a guided mechanical search through the space of possible solutions. In the case of the Bombe, the space of possible solutions consisted of configurations of the Enigma machine (in another case it might consist of configurations of a chess board). The Bombe's search could be guided in various ways; one involved what Turing called the "multiple encipherment condition" associated with a crib (described in Chap. 6 of Turing's recently declassified *Treatise on the Enigma*, written in the second half of 1940).[53] A search guided in this fashion, Turing said, would "reduce the possible positions to a number which can be tested by hand methods"[54]. (A crib is a word or phrase that the cryptanalyst believes might be part of the German message. For example, it might be conjectured that a certain message contains "WETTER FUR DIE NACHT" (weather for the night). Cribs were relatively plentiful on many Enigma networks, thanks both to the stereotyped nature of German military messages and to lapses of cipher security. One station sent exactly the same message each evening for a period of several months: "beacons lit as ordered"! [55].)

Modern AI researchers speak of the method of "generate-and-test". Potential solutions to a given problem are generated by means of a guided search. These potential solutions are then tested by an auxiliary method to find out if any of them actually is a solution. Nowadays in AI, both processes, generate and test, are typically carried out by the same program. The Bombe mechanized the first process. The testing of the potential solutions (the "stops") was then carried out manually (by setting up a replica Enigma accordingly, typing in the cipher text, and seeing whether or not German came out).

---

[52] We include in this claim the Polish Bomba, a more primitive form of the Bombe, which also employed guided search (although cribs were not used). The Polish machine in effect used the heuristic "Ignore the *Stecker*." This heuristic was satisfactory during the period when the Enigma machine's stecker-board affected only 10–16 of the 26 letters of the alphabet (see [74]).

[53] The title "Treatise on the Enigma" was probably added to Turing's document by a third party outside GC & CS and quite probably in the United States. The copy of the otherwise untitled document held in the U.S. National Archives and Records Administration (document reference RG 457, Historic Cryptographic Collection, Box 201, NR 964) is prefaced by a page typed some years later than the document itself; it is this page that bears the title "Turing's Treatise on the Enigma." Another copy of the document, held in the British Public Record Office (document reference HW 25/3), carries the title "Mathematical theory of ENIGMA machine by A M Turing"; this, too, was possibly added at a later date. At Bletchley Park the document was referred to as "Prof's Book." A digital facsimile of the PRO copy is in The Turing Archive for the History of Computing, http://www.AlanTuring.net/profs_book.

[54] Ibid.

2.4   Machine Intelligence

When designing the ACE, Turing declared, "In working on the ACE I am more interested in the possibility of producing models of the action of the brain than in the practical applications to computing."[55] In "Proposed Electronic Calculator" he said:

> "Can the machine play chess?" It could fairly easily be made to play a rather bad game. It would be bad because chess requires intelligence. We stated at the beginning of this section that the machine should be treated as entirely without intelligence. There are indications however that it is possible to make the machine display intelligence at the risk of its making occasional serious mistakes. By following up this aspect the machine could probably be made to play very good chess. [93, p. 16]

In February 1947 (in the rooms of the Royal Astronomical Society in Burlington House, London[56]) Turing gave what is, so far as is known, the earliest public lecture to mention computer intelligence, providing a breathtaking glimpse of a new field. He described the human brain as a "digital computing machine" [94, p. 111] and discussed the prospect of machines acting intelligently, learning, and beating human opponents at chess. He stated that "[w]hat we want is a machine that can learn from experience" and that "[t]he possibility of letting the machine alter its own instructions provides the mechanism for this" [94, p. 123]. The possibility of a computer operating on and modifying its own program as it runs, just as it operates on the data in its memory, is implicit in the stored-program concept.

At the end of his 1947 lecture Turing set out what he later called the "Mathematical Objection" to the view that minds are machines. This is now widely known as the Gödel argument, and has been made famous by John Lucas and Roger Penrose. (In fact the objection originated with the mathematical logician Emil Post as early as 1921.[57]) Turing proposed an interesting and arguably correct solution to the objection (see [23, 30, 68]).

From the middle of 1947 Turing took a year's sabbatical leave in Cambridge. His 1948 report of research undertaken during this year, "Intelligent Machinery" (unpublished until 1968), was the first manifesto of Artificial Intelligence. In it Turing brilliantly introduced a number of the concepts that were later to become central in AI, in some cases after reinvention by others. These included the logic-based approach to problem-solving, now widely used

---

[55] Turing in an undated letter to W. Ross Ashby (in the Woodger Papers (catalogue reference M11/99); a digital facsimile is in The Turing Archive for the History of Computing, http://www.AlanTuring.net/turing_ashby).

[56] Entry in Woodger's diary for 20 February 1947.

[57] Post's "Absolutely Unsolvable Problems and Relatively Undecidable Propositions: Account of an Anticipation," in [35, pp. 417, 423].

in expert systems, and, in a brief passage concerning what he called "genetical or evolutionary search" [95, p. 23], the concept of a genetic algorithm — important in both AI and Artificial Life. (The term "genetic algorithm" was introduced circa 1975 [49, p. x].)

In the report Turing also presented one of his most accessible formulations of the so-called Church-Turing thesis:[58]

> LCMs [Turing machines] can do anything that could be described as "rule of thumb" or "purely mechanical." [95, p. 7]

He remarked:

> This is sufficiently well established that it is now agreed amongst logicians that "calculable by means of an LCM" is the correct accurate rendering of such phrases. [95, p. 7]

The Church-Turing thesis played a pivotal role in Turing's argument in "On Computable Numbers" that there are well-defined mathematical tasks that the universal Turing machine cannot carry out.

In the light of his work with the Bombe, it is no surprise to find Turing hypothesizing in "Intelligent Machinery" that "intellectual activity consists mainly of various kinds of search" [95, p. 23]. Eight years later the same hypothesis was put forward independently by Newell and Simon and through their influential work (see for example [65]) became one of the principal tenets of AI. It is one of the ideas that launched modern philosophy of mind. Turing's hypothesis includes three of the central ingredients in contemporary theorizing about the mind. First, his suggestion that it is possible to say something useful about the functioning of the mind was a radical view in those dark behaviorist days. Second, for Turing, what the mind does can be described relatively independently of what the brain does; he anticipated the modern idea of levels of theorizing about cognition. Third, he advocated a broadly computational theory of mind.

2.5   The First AI Programs

Both during and after the war Turing experimented with machine routines for playing chess: in the absence of a computer, the machine's behavior was simulated by hand, using paper and pencil. In 1948 Turing and David Champernowne, the mathematical economist, constructed the loose system of rules dubbed "Turochamp."[59] (Champernowne reported that his wife, a beginner at chess, took on the Turochamp and lost.) Turing began to code the Turochamp for the Manchester Ferranti Mark I but unfortunately never completed the task [61, p. 189]. He later published a classic early article on chess programming [102]. Dietrich Prinz, who worked for Ferranti, wrote the first

---

[58] On the Church-Turing thesis, see [22].

[59] Letter from Champernowne in *Computer Chess 4* (Jan. 1980), pp. 80–81.

chess program to be implemented [70]. It ran in November 1951 on the Ferranti Mark I [7, p. 295]. (Prinz "learned all about programming the Mark 1 computer at seminars given by Alan Turing and Cecily Popplewell";[60] he later wrote a programming manual for the Mark I.[61]) Unlike the Turochamp, Prinz's program could not play a complete game and operated by exhaustive search rather than under the guidance of heuristics. (Prinz also used the Ferranti Mark I to solve logical problems, and in 1949 and 1951 Ferranti built two small experimental special-purpose computers for theorem-proving and other logical work [56, 71].)

Christopher Strachey's Draughts Player was — apart from Turing's "paper" chess-players — the first AI program to use heuristic search. He coded it for the Pilot Model ACE in May 1951.[62] Strachey's attempt to get his program running on the Pilot ACE was defeated by coding errors. When he returned to the NPL with a debugged version of the program, he found that the engineers had made a major hardware change, with the result that the program would not run without substantial revision.[63] He finally got his program working on the Ferranti Mark I in mid-1952 (with Turing's encouragement and utilizing the latter's recently completed *Programmers' Handbook* [97]) [14, p. 24]. By the summer of 1952 the program could play a complete game of draughts at a reasonable speed [88, p. 47]. The essentials of Strachey's program were taken over by Samuel in the U.S [77, p. 104].

The first AI programs to incorporate learning, written by Anthony Oettinger at the University of Cambridge, ran in 1951 [66].[64] Oettinger wrote his "response learning programme" and "shopping programme" for the EDSAC computer — the second stored-program electronic computer to function (in 1949). Oettinger was considerably influenced by Turing's views on machine learning[65], and suggested that the shopping program — which simulated the behavior of "a small child sent on a shopping tour" [66, p. 1247] — could pass a version of the Turing test in which "the questions are restricted to ... the form 'In what shop may article *j* be found?' " [66, p. 1250].

2.6   Turing's Anticipation of Connectionism

Modern connectionists regard the work of Donald Hebb [47] and Frank Rosenblatt [75, 76] as the foundation of their approach and it is not widely realized

---

[60] Gradwell, C. "Early Days," reminiscences in a Ferranti newsletter, April 1994. (Copeland is grateful to Prinz's daughter, Daniela Derbyshire, for sending him a copy of Gradwell's article.)

[61] Prinz, D. G., "Introduction to Programming on the Manchester Electronic Digital Computer," no date, Ferranti Ltd. A digital facsimile is in The Turing Archive for the History of Computing, http://www.AlanTuring.net/prinz.

[62] Letter from Strachey to Woodger, 13 May 1951 (among the Woodger Papers).

[63] Letters from Woodger to Copeland (15 July 1999 and 15 September 1999).

[64] Letter from Oettinger to Copeland (19 June 2000).

[65] Oettinger in interview with Copeland (January 2000).

that Turing's earlier "Intelligent Machinery" anticipated connectionism (i.e., computation by neural networks). So far as we have been able to discover, he was the first person to consider building artificial computing machines out of simple, neuron-like elements connected together into networks in a largely random manner [32,33,90]. However, Turing's research into neuron-like computation remained unknown to others subsequently working in the area, even those in Britain.

Turing introduced what he called "unorganised machines," giving as examples networks of neuron-like Boolean elements connected together in a largely random fashion. We call these networks "Turing Nets": they are a distinctly different type of connectionist architecture.[66] Turing's idea that an initially unorganized neural network can be organized by means of what he called "interfering training" did not appear in the earlier work (in 1943) of McCulloch and Pitts, whose discussion of learning is perfunctory. In Turing's model, the training process renders certain neural pathways effective and others ineffective. This arrangement is functionally equivalent to one in which the stored information takes the form of new connections within the network.

Turing described a certain form of Turing Net as "the simplest model of a nervous system with a random arrangement of neurons" and hypothesized that "the cortex of the infant is an unorganised machine, which can be organised by suitable interfering training" [95, pp. 10, 16]. He claimed a proof (now lost) of the proposition that an initially unorganized "B-type" network with sufficient neurons can be organized to become a universal Turing machine with a given storage capacity [95, p. 15]. This proof first opened up the possibility, noted by Turing [95, p. 16], that the human cognitive system is a universal symbol-processor implemented in a neural network. (There is a difficulty for Turing's claim that a B-type network can be organized to become a universal Turing machine: not all Boolean functions can be computed by a B-type. Our solution [32, pp. 367–368] was to alter the definition of a B-type in such a way as to include two — rather than one, as in Turing's discussion — of the devices we called an "introverted pair" [32, p. 365] on each unit-to-unit connection.)

Turing also anticipated the modern procedure of using a digital computer to simulate neural networks. He saw the need to develop training algorithms for unorganized machines and conceived of the (now standard) procedure of programming the training algorithm into a computer simulation of the neural network. However, the lack of computing power — in 1948 the only electronic stored-program computer in existence was the Manchester Baby — prevented him from carrying out this research. By the time he had access to the Ferranti

---

[66] Turing also conceived of other ("P-type") unorganized machines, which are modified Turing machines with two "interfering inputs, one for 'pleasure' or 'reward' ... and the other for 'pain' or 'punishment'" [95, p. 17]. Turing called these "child-machines"; his aim was to discover training procedures "analogous to the kind of process by which a child would really be taught" [95, p. 20].

Mark I, in 1951, his interests had changed. The first computer simulation of a small neural network [39] did not occur until the year of Turing's death, 1954.

3   Artificial Life

In his final years Turing worked on (what since 1987 is called) Artificial Life (A-Life). The central aim of Artificial Life is a theoretical understanding of naturally occurring biological life — in particular of the most conspicuous feature of living matter, its ability to self-organize (i.e., to develop form and structure spontaneously). Turing was the first to use computer simulation to investigate a theory of the development of organization and pattern in living things [101].[67] He began this investigation as soon as the Ferranti Mark I was installed at Manchester University, writing in February 1951:

> Our new machine is to start arriving on Monday. I am hoping as one of the first jobs to do something about "chemical embryology". In particular I think one can account for the appearance of Fibonacci numbers in connection with fir-cones.[68]

Shortly before the Ferranti computer arrived, Turing wrote about his work on morphogenesis in a letter to the biologist J. Z. Young.[69] The letter connects Turing's work on morphogenesis with his interest in neural networks, and to some extent explains why he did not follow up his earlier suggestion and use the Ferranti computer to simulate his "unorganised machines."

> I am afraid I am very far from the stage where I feel inclined to start asking any anatomical questions [about the brain]. According to my notions of how to set about it that will not occur until quite a late stage when I have a fairly definite theory about how things are done.
>
> At present I am not working on the problem at all, but on my mathematical theory of embryology ... This is yielding to treatment, and it will so far as I can see, give satisfactory explanations of -

---

[67] Turing employed nonlinear differential equations to describe the chemical interactions hypothesized by his theory and used the Manchester computer to explore instances of such equations. He was probably the first researcher to engage in the computer-assisted exploration of nonlinear systems. It was not until Benoit Mandelbrot's discovery of the "Mandelbrot set" in 1979 that the computer-assisted investigation of nonlinear systems gained widespread attention.

[68] Letter from Turing to Woodger, undated, marked as received on 12 February 1951 (in the Woodger Papers; a digital facsimile is in The Turing Archive for the History of Computing, http://www.AlanTuring.net/turing_woodger_feb51).

[69] 8 February 1951. A copy of Turing's letter (typed by his mother, Sara Turing) is in the Modern Archive Centre, King's College, Cambridge (catalogue reference K1.78).

i) Gastrulation.

ii) Polyogonally symmetrical structures, e.g., starfish, flowers.

iii) Leaf arrangement, in particular the way the Fibonacci series (0, 1, 1, 2, 3, 5, 8, 13, ...) comes to be involved.

iv) Colour patterns on animals, e.g., stripes, spots and dappling.

v) Patterns on nearly spherical structures such as some Radiolaria, but this is more difficult and doubtful.

I am really doing this now because it is yielding more easily to treatment. I think it is not altogether unconnected with the other problem. The brain structure has to be one which can be achieved by the genetical embryological mechanism, and I hope that this theory that I am now working on may make clearer what restrictions this really implies. What you tell me about growth of neurons under stimulation is very interesting in this connection. It suggests means by which the neurons might be made to grow so as to form a particular circuit, rather than to reach a particular place.

4   The Turing Test

"Intelligent Machinery" contains the earliest description of (a restricted chess-playing form of) what Turing later called the "imitation game" [95, p. 23] and is now known simply as the Turing test. Turing's "Computing Machinery and Intelligence," published in 1950, introduced the famous version of the test [96].[70]

4.1   The Form of the Test

In the 1950 presentation of the test, the interrogator or judge communicates (by keyboard) with both a computer and a human being; apart from this no contact is permitted. The interrogator's task is to find out, by question and answer, which is the computer [96, p. 434]. The computer attempts to evade identification. Turing said that the best strategy for the human foil is probably to give truthful answers. He presented the following sample dialogue:

JUDGE   In the first line of your sonnet which reads "Shall I compare thee to a summer's day," would not "a spring day" do as well or better?
COMPUTER   It wouldn't scan.
JUDGE   How about "a winter's day"? That would scan all right.
COMPUTER   Yes, but nobody wants to be compared to a winter's day.
JUDGE   Would you say Mr. Pickwick reminded you of Christmas?
COMPUTER   In a way.

---

[70] For a discussion of the differences between this and Turing's 1952 presentation of the test, see [27] and Copeland's introduction to Turing's "Can Automatic Calculating Machines Be Said To Think?" [24].

JUDGE   Yet Christmas is a winter's day, and I do not think Mr Pickwick would mind the comparison.

COMPUTER   I don't think you're serious. By a winter's day one means a typical winter's day, rather than a special one like Christmas. [96, p. 446]

4.2   Scoring the Test

In the 1950 paper Turing first described an imitation game involving an interrogator and two human subjects, one male (A) and one female (B). The interrogator communicates with A and B by keyboard. The interrogator is to discover, by asking questions, which of A and B is the man; A's aim is that the interrogator make the wrong identification. Turing then asked "What will happen when a machine takes the part of A in this game?" [96, p. 434]. The point of this new game is to determine whether or not the machine can "imitate the brain" [98, p. 464].[71] To assess the computer's performance, we ask:

> Will the interrogator decide wrongly as often when the [computer-imitates-human] game is played ... as he does when the game is played between a man and a woman? [96, p. 434]

If the computer (in the computer-imitates-human game) does no worse than the man (in the man-imitates-woman game), it passes the test.

The function of the man-imitates-woman game is often misunderstood. For example, according to Hodges, this game is irrelevant as an introduction to the Turing test — indeed, it is a "red herring" [48, p. 415]. However, the man-imitates-woman game is not intended as an introduction to the test; it is part of the protocol for scoring the test.

4.3   Did Turing Propose a Definition?

He is widely said to have done so. For example:

> An especially influential behaviorist definition of intelligence was put forward by Turing [96] in [6, p. 248] (Block).

> The Turing Test [was] originally proposed as a simple operational definition of intelligence .... [42, p. 115] (French)

> [Turing] introduced ... an operational definition of "thinking" or "intelligence" ... by means of a sexual guessing game. [48, p. 415] (Hodges)

---

[71] Some commentators suggest that Turing's intention is to describe a game in which the computer must imitate a woman. Textual evidence against this suggestion is given in [27].

Those who characterize the Turing test as a definition lay Turing open to easy objections. This is because it is all too conceivable that an intelligent, thinking entity could fail the test, for example if it were distinctively non-human in its responses.

In fact, Turing did not propose a definition of "thinking" or "intelligence." Definitions are standardly expressed as necessary and sufficient conditions. In his 1950 presentation of the test, Turing emphasized that passing the test (by producing behavior that resembles human intellectual behavior) is not a necessary condition for thinking. He said that machines may "carry out something which ought to be described as thinking but which is very different from what a man does" [96, p. 435]. And in his 1952 presentation of the test, in a radio discussion (with, amongst others, Max Newman)[72], he explicitly denied that he was offering a definition:

> I don't want to give a definition of thinking, but if I had to I should probably be unable to say anything more about it than that it was a sort of buzzing that went on inside my head. But I don't really see that we need to agree on a definition at all. The important thing is to try to draw a line between the properties of a brain, or of a man, that we want to discuss, and those that we don't. ... I would like to suggest a particular kind of *test* that one might apply to a machine. You might call it a test to see whether the machine thinks, but it would be better to avoid begging the question, and say that the machines that pass are (let's say) 'Grade A' machines. ... Of course I am not saying at present either that machines really could pass the test, or that they couldn't. My suggestion is just that this is the question we should discuss. It's not the same as "Do machines think," but it seems near enough for our present purpose, and raises much the same difficulties. [100, pp. 466–467]

4.4 Fiendish Expert Objections to the Turing Test

There are many of these, all of the form "An expert could unmask the computer by asking it ... " For example, it is said that questions designed to elicit the various human irrationalities claimed by theorists such as Wason, Nisbett, Tversky, and Kahnemann could be used to distinguish the computer from the human foil.[73] Unless specially programmed to duplicate the particular human irrationality, the computer would be easily detected.

However, Turing anticipated this type of objection by ruling out the use of expert judges. He stated in 1952 that the judges "should not be expert about

---

[72] The full texts of this and of Turing's 1951 radio broadcast "Can Digital Computers Think?" were published for the first time in Copeland's [24]; see also [27].

[73] For example, by Lenat in his paper at the 2000 Loebner Turing Test Competition at Dartmouth College.

machines" [100, p. 466] and in 1948, with respect to the early chess version of the test, that the judge should be a "rather poor" chess player [95, p. 23]. It seems highly likely that, if Turing were writing now, he would exclude interrogators who are expert about the mind.

4.5 Shieber's Criticism

In a vigorous critique of the Turing test, Shieber ascribes to Turing the view that "any agent that can be mistaken by virtue of its conversational behavior [for] a human must be intelligent" [83, p. 70]. This leads easily to an objection. A computer's performance may be a lucky fluke, a thoroughly atypical performance, in the fashion of a first-season football star whose performance subsequently regresses to the mean. Why should we conclude, from the fact that the judges are persuaded by a single successful test, that the computer thinks?

However, Shieber's interpretation of Turing is unsympathetic. A more charitable view is suggested by Géraud de Cordemoy's anticipation in 1668 of Turing's test. De Cordemoy was a Cartesian who wrote about the problem of distinguishing thinking from non-thinking things. He remarked:

> [Concerning] ... bodies ... who resemble me so perfectly *without* [i.e., externally] ... I think I may ... establish for a Principle, that ... if I finde by all the experiments I am capable to make, that they use speech as I do, ... I have infallible reason to believe that they have a soul as I. [36, pp. 13–14]

By insisting that a candidate thinker perform satisfactorily in "all the experiments" that we are "capable to make," de Cordemoy allows for the fact that the results of some experiments may be misleading — a machine that happens to pass one Turing test, or even a series of them, might be shown by subsequent tests to be a relatively poor player of Turing's imitation game. De Cordemoy's position is obviously not susceptible to Shieber's objection. There is no reason to believe that Turing is any more vulnerable to the objection: Turing's position as he describes it is entirely consistent with the de Cordemoy-like view that the result of any given test is defeasible and may be disregarded in the light of other tests.

4.6 The Shannon-McCarthy Objection

In 1956 Shannon and McCarthy formulated the following objection to the Turing test:

> The problem of giving a precise definition to the concept of "thinking" ... has aroused a great deal of heated discussion. One interesting definition has been proposed by A. M. Turing: a machine is termed

> capable of thinking if it can, under certain prescribed conditions, imi-
> tate a human being by answering questions sufficiently well to deceive
> a human questioner for a reasonable period of time. ... A disadvan-
> tage of the Turing definition of thinking is that it is possible, in prin-
> ciple, to design a machine with a complete set of arbitrarily chosen
> responses to all possible input stimuli ... Such a machine ... merely
> looks up in a "dictionary" the appropriate response. With a suitable
> dictionary such a machine would surely satisfy Turing's definition but
> does not reflect our usual intuitive concept of thinking. [82, v–vi]

This objection has subsequently been rediscovered by a number of authors,
and is commonly but mistakenly believed to have originated with Block [5].

How might Turing have responded? The 1952 radio discussion provides
an indication:

NEWMAN   It is all very well to say that a machine could ... be made to do
this or that, but, to take only one practical point, what about the time
it would take to do it? It would only take an hour or two to make up a
routine to make our Manchester machine analyse all possible variations of
the game of chess right out, and find the best move that way — *if* you
didn't mind its taking thousands of millions of years to run through the
routine. Solving a problem on the machine doesn't mean finding a way to
do it between now and eternity, but within a reasonable time.

TURING   To my mind this time factor is the one question which will involve
all the real technical difficulty. [100, pp. 473–474]

Storage capacity and processing speed are crucial. The Shannon-
McCarthy objection establishes only that the proposition "If x plays Turing's
imitation game satisfactorily, then x thinks" is false in *some possible world*
— a world very different from the actual world, since in the merely possible
world the machine runs through the routine in a reasonable time. But there
is no reason to believe that Turing was claiming anything more than that
this proposition is *actually* true.

4.7   French's Objections: Associative Priming and Rating Games

The associative priming objection runs as follows. In word/non-word recognition tasks, subjects take less time to determine that an item is a word if
the presentation of the item is preceded by a presentation of an associated
word (for example, "butter" by "bread," or "chips" by "fish"). French proposes
to use this priming effect to unmask the computer. He remarks:

> The day before the Test, [the interviewer] selects a set of words
> (and non-words), runs the lexical decision task on the interviewees
> and records average recognition times. She then comes to the Test
> armed with the results ... [and] identifies as the human being the

candidate whose results more closely resemble the average results produced by her sample population of interviewees. The machine would invariably fail this type of test because there is no a priori way of determining associative strengths ... Virtually the only way a machine could determine, even on average, all of the associative strengths between human concepts is to have experienced the world as the human candidate and the interviewers had. [41, p. 17]

However, French's proposal is illegitimate. The specifications of the Turing test are clear: the judge is allowed only to put questions. There is no provision for employing the equipment necessary to administer the lexical decision task and measure the contestants' reaction times. One might as well allow the judge to use equipment measuring the contestants' magnetic fields or energy dissipation.

The rating games objection is as follows. French claims that ingenious questions such as these can be used to distinguish the computer from the human: on a scale of 0 (completely implausible) to 10 (completely plausible), rate " 'Flugbloggs' as a name Kellogg's would give to a new breakfast cereal" and rate " 'Flugly' as the surname of a glamorous female movie star" [41, p. 18].

French's rating games may be of no assistance at all to the interrogator, however, since the computer is free to attempt to pass itself off as a member of a foreign culture. Conveniently, French claims to discern "an assumption ... tacit in Turing's article" [41, p. 15]: *the computer must pass itself off as a member of the interrogator's own culture.* But French offers no textual evidence in support of this claim. Moreover, he leaves it a mystery why Turing would have wished to impose a restriction that makes the test harder for the computer to pass and yet offers no conceptual gain. French's only source is Turing's 1950 presentation of the test. In the 1952 presentation, Turing says explicitly that the computer is to "be permitted all sorts of tricks so as to appear more man-like" [100, p. 466]. This no doubt includes pretending to belong to a foreign culture.

4.8 Searle's "Chinese Room" Argument

Searle claims that an entity that understands neither the judge's questions nor its own answers could nevertheless "fool native Chinese speakers" and "pass the Turing test" [79, p. 419]. In Searle's thought experiment a human clerk — call him or her "Clerk" — "handworks" a computer program that is capable of passing the Turing test in Chinese. Clerk is a monolingual English speaker who possesses the program in the form of a set of rule-books written in English. Clerk works in a room concealed from the judge's view; she and the judge communicate by passing sheets of paper through a slot. To the judge, the verbal behavior of the Room — i.e., the system that includes the rule-books, Clerk, Clerk's stationery, and the input/output slot — is by hypothesis indistinguishable from that of a native Chinese speaker. In his original presentation — we call it the "vanilla" form — of the argument, Searle claims:

> [Clerk] do[es] not understand a word of the Chinese ... [Clerk] ha[s] inputs and outputs that are indistinguishable from the native Chinese speaker, and [Clerk] can have any formal program you like, but [Clerk] still understand[s] nothing. [A] computer for the same reasons understands nothing ... [W]hatever purely formal principles you put into the computer will not be sufficient for understanding, since a human will be able to follow the formal principles without understanding. [79, p. 418]

There have been numerous objections to Searle's argument. For example, the *systems reply* claims that, while it is true that Clerk does not understand the inputs and outputs, she is merely part of a whole system and the system *does* understand the inputs and outputs. Searle quite properly responds that this reply is worthless, since it "simply begs the question by insisting without argument that the system must understand Chinese" [79, p. 419].

Our (first) reply to the argument is the *logical reply* [21] [29]. It is a straightforward enough point, but seems to have been overlooked by Searle and others. The vanilla form of the argument is not logically valid. The proposition that the symbol-manipulation carried out by Clerk does not enable *Clerk* to understand the Chinese characters by no means entails the different proposition that the symbol-manipulation carried out by Clerk does not enable the *Room* to understand the Chinese characters. (One might as well claim that the statement "The organization of which Clerk is a part has never sold pyjamas in Korea" is entailed by the statement "Clerk has never sold pyjamas in Korea.") In consequence, Searle cannot infer from Clerk's failure to understand the Chinese symbols that a computer performing the same manipulations fails to understand the symbols. (The logical reply is a point about entailment simpliciter and — unlike the systems reply — involves no claim about the truth-value of the statement that the Room understands Chinese.)

Searle has another answer to the systems reply:

> Let the individual ... memoriz[e] the rules in the ledger and the data banks of Chinese symbols, and [do] all the calculations in his head. The individual then incorporates the entire system. ... We can even get rid of the room and suppose he works outdoors. All the same, he understands nothing of the Chinese, and a fortiori neither does the system, because there isn't anything in the system that isn't in him. If he doesn't understand, then there is no way the system could understand, because the system is just a part of him. [79, p. 419]

In this form of the argument, Searle implicitly appeals to a principle that we shall characterize as follows:

> If Clerk (in general, x) does not understand the Chinese input and output (in general, does not Φ), then no part of Clerk (x) understands the Chinese input and output (Φs).

Unfortunately (this is our second reply), Searle does not say why he thinks this "part-of" principle is true. It is conceivable that a homunculus in Clerk's head understands Chinese without Clerk doing so. Likewise for related values of Φ. Conceivably the homunculus produces solutions to certain tensor equations (perhaps this is how we catch cricket balls and other moving objects), even though Clerk herself may sincerely deny that she can solve tensor equations.

A possible response to this reply runs as follows. That Clerk's claim that she is unable to solve tensor equations is sincere does not entail that it is true. The proponent of the part-of principle can simply maintain that, if Clerk catches a cricket ball, then since a part of her is solving tensor equations, so is Clerk. However, this response is not available to Searle. If Clerk's sincere denial that she is able to solve tensor equations is to count for nothing, then consistency demands that one say the same about her denial that she is able to understand Chinese. But it is a cornerstone of Searle's case that Clerk's sincere statement "I don't understand the Chinese input and output" suffices for the truth of "Clerk does not understand the Chinese input and output." This last is the fundamental premiss of both forms of the Chinese Room argument. So Searle is caught on the horns of a dilemma. He can uphold the part-of principle if he abandons first-person incorrigibility; but if he abandons first-person incorrigibility, the whole Chinese Room argument collapses.

Our third reply to the Chinese Room argument is based on the concept of *hypercomputation* [33] (see also Section 5) and is as follows: even if the argument were valid and had true premises, it still would not show what Searle wants it to show. According to Searle:

> The whole point of the original [i.e., vanilla] example was to argue that ... symbol manipulation by itself couldn't be sufficient for understanding Chinese. [79, p. 419]

> [F]ormal syntax ... does not by itself guarantee the presence of mental contents. I showed this a decade ago in the Chinese room argument. [81, p. 200]

However, the Chinese Room argument cannot show that the symbol-manipulation carried out by a hypercomputer is insufficient for understanding.

A hypercomputer is a machine able to produce the values of functions that are not Turing-machine computable, for example the halting function.

(For some comments on the remarks on hypercomputation in the chapters by Davis and Hodges, see the Postscript.) Turing's 1938 *o*-machines ("oracle" machines) — Turing machines with an (entirely notional) additional "fundamental process" [92] — are a form of hypercomputer. *o*-machines illustrate the fact that the notion of a programmed machine whose activity consists of the manipulation of formal symbols is more general than the notion of the universal Turing machine. (Perhaps the mind, in abstraction from resource constraints and temporal constraints, is a hypercomputer.[74] Searle might find this view as "antibiological" [80, p. 23] as he finds other functionalist views of the mind.)

By its very nature the Chinese Room argument can be applied only against programs that can be simulated by a human rote-worker. The abilities of the rote-worker described by Searle are as stated in the Church-Turing thesis: Clerk does not exceed a Turing machine. In consequence, Clerk cannot simulate a hypercomputer.[75] And so, even if, as Searle claims, there is an implication from

> *x*'s operation is defined purely formally or syntactically

to

> *x*'s operation is neither constitutive of nor sufficient for mind,

this is not an implication that could possibly be established by Searle's Chinese Room argument.

4.9   Turing's Predictions

We conclude that Turing's test survives the standard objections. The question, then, is: will a computer pass the test and, if so, when?

In the 1950 paper Turing predicted that

> in about fifty years' time it will be possible to programme computers ... to make them play the imitation game so well that an average interrogator will not have more than 70 per cent chance of making the right identification after five minutes of questioning. [96, p. 442]

(Turing's prediction is sometimes reported the wrong way round: for example, "Turing clearly believed digital computers could, by the end of the [20th]

---

[74] Turing's 1936 proof of the existence of functions that are not Turing-machine computable guarantees the existence of an (abstract) model of neuronal function that is not equivalent to any Turing machine: whether or not the brain is equivalent to a Turing machine is an empirical matter (see [21, 22, 26, 72, 84, 85]).

[75] This argument is discussed further, and an objection rebutted, in [31]; see also [10].

century, succeed in deceiving an interrogator 70 per cent of the time" [106, p. 61].)

In his 1952 radio discussion Turing made a different, overlooked, prediction:

NEWMAN   I should like to be there when your match between a man and a machine takes place, and perhaps to try my hand at making up some of the questions. But that will be a long time from now, if the machine is to stand any chance with no questions barred?

TURING   Oh yes, at least 100 years, I should say. [100, p. 467]

5 Postscript

Davis and Hodges (see their chapters in this volume) offer a number of objections to the idea of hypercomputation. Since these objections have already been raised and answered in the literature, we shall not discuss them here. Interested readers may turn to e.g. Copeland's [30] (especially Sect. 3 ("The Very Idea of Hypercomputation: Objections and Replies"), where seventeen objections are set out and answered) and the other papers in Copeland's two-volume edition *Hypercomputation* (vols 12.4 and 13.1 of *Minds and Machines*). However, we make the following observations:[76]

Davis asserts, without supporting argument, that quantum computers "can only compute computable functions"; yet this question is in fact open and the subject of much debate (see e.g. the papers in *Hypercomputation* by Calude, Kieu, and Stannett, and [17]).

Davis claims that de Leeuw, Moore, Shannon, and Shapiro [37] show that "Turing machines provided with a random number generator ... could compute only functions that are already computable by ordinary Turing machines"; yet this is not what de Leeuw et al. show or claim to show (as Davis must surely know) — see e.g. their theorem 3 [37, p. 193].

Hodges states that the idea of a random element has "nothing whatever to do with oracles"; yet the concept of a random oracle is well known (see e.g. [3]).

Hodges quotes from a letter by Robin Gandy but fails to include the words (which immediately follow "During this spring he spent some time inventing a new quantum mechanics;"): "it was not intended to be taken very seriously (almost in the 'for amusement only' class)."[77]

Hodges claims that "Turing was probably trying to make quantum mechanics fully predictable"; but Hodges offers no evidence in support of this

---

[76] We refer to Davis, "The Myth of Hypercomputation," 10 February 2003, and Hodges, "What would Alan Turing have done after 1954?", http://www.turing.org.uk/philosophy/lausanne1.html.

[77] Letter from Gandy to Max Newman, undated (but from internal evidence June 1954), in the Modern Archive Centre, King's College, Cambridge (catalogue reference A 8).

claim, merely emphasizing that its supposed truth would rescue his own interpretation of Turing from an important difficulty.

Hodges quotes Church [19, pp. 42–43] and says these remarks show that "Church ... equat[ed] the scope of computability with the scope of machines"; yet the quoted remarks do not show this, for it is evident that Church was discussing (not machines in general but) computing machines (in the words quoted, Church said "it shall be possible to devise a computing machine").

Davis and Hodges both quote Turing's comment "We shall not go any further into the nature of this oracle apart from saying that it cannot be a machine" [92, pp. 172–173], yet neither quotes the immediately following sentence "With the help of the oracle we could form a new kind of machine (call them o-machines)" [92, p. 173]. Hodges infers from the first sentence quoted that "oracle machines" are "only *partly mechanical*," but this inference is logically on a par with: "Ink is not a machine, therefore a Turing machine is only partly mechanical." Machines can have parts that are not themselves machines.

Davis objects, "Since all electrons have the same charge, the Copeland-Proudfoot infinite precision real number is actually an integer!"; yet he is aware that we were in fact discussing a *continuously variable* physical quantity, which we called "charge" only "for the sake of vividness" (see further [26, p. 18]).

Hodges asserts (attempting to argue by appeal to authority), "Gandy, as Turing's disciple, never even considered counting an 'oracle' as a kind of machine." However, in an unpublished manuscript Gandy considered at length "analogue machines" based on "physical systems (both classical and quantum mechanical) which when provided with a (continuously variable) computable input will give a non-computable output." (Gandy gave Copeland a copy of this handwritten manuscript shortly before his death in 1995. In it, Gandy claimed that one would not in fact be able to make use of such a physical system to "calculate the values of some number-theoretic non-computable function" but added: "The claim is to be read not so much as a dogmatic assertion, but rather as a challenge.")[78].

References

1. W. Aspray (1990). *John von Neumann and the Origins of Modern Computing.* Cambridge, MA: MIT Press.
2. C. G. Bell, A. Newell (1971). *Computer Structures: Readings and Examples.* New York: McGraw-Hill.
3. C. H. Bennett, J. Gill (1981). *Relative to a Random Oracle A, $P^A \neq NP^A \neq co\text{-}NP^A$ with Probability 1.* SIAM Journal on Computing, 10:96–113.

---

[78] Research on which this article draws was supported in part by University of Canterbury Research Grant no. U6472 (Copeland) and Marsden Grant no. UOC905 (Copeland and Proudfoot).

4. J. Bigelow (1980). *Computer Development at the Institute for Advanced Study*. In [60].
5. N. Block (1981). *Psychologism and Behaviorism*. Philosophical Review, 90:5–43.
6. N. Block (1990). *The Computer Model of the Mind*. In [67].
7. B. V. Bowden, ed. (1953). *Faster Than Thought*. London: Sir Isaac Pitman & Sons.
8. B. V. Bowden (1975). *The 25th Anniversary of the Stored Program Computer*. The Radio and Electronic Engineer, 45:326.
9. G. Bowker, R. Giordano (1993). *Interview with Tom Kilburn*. Annals of the History of Computing, 15:17–32.
10. S. Bringsjord, P. Bello, D. Ferrucci (2001). *Creativity, the Turing Test, and the (Better) Lovelace Test*. Minds and Machines, 11:3–27.
11. A. W. Burks (1980). *From ENIAC to the Stored-Program Computer: Two Revolutions in Computers*. In [60].
12. A. W. Burks, H. H. Goldstine, J. von Neumann (1946). "Preliminary Discussion of the Logical Design of an Electronic Computing Instrument", 28 June, Institute for Advanced Study; reprinted in [89].
13. C. S. Calude (2002). *Incompleteness, Complexity, Randomness and Beyond*. Minds and Machines, 12:503–517.
14. M. Campbell-Kelly (1985). *Christopher Strachey, 1916–1975: A Biographical Note*. Annals of the History of Computing, 7:19–42.
15. M. Campbell-Kelly, W. Aspray (1996). *Computer: A History of the Information Machine*. New York: Basic.
16. B. E. Carpenter, R. W. Doran, eds (1986). *A. M. Turing's ACE Report of 1946 and Other Papers*. Cambridge, MA: MIT Press.
17. M. Chown (2002). *Smash and Grab*. New Scientist, 174(2337):24–28, 6 April.
18. R. Chrisley, ed. (2000). *Artificial Intelligence: Critical Concepts in Cognitive Science*. Volume 2: Symbolic AI. London: Routledge.
19. A. Church (1937). *Review of Turing [91]*. Journal of Symbolic Logic, 2:42–43.
20. A. W. M. Coombs (1954). *MOSAIC*. In *Automatic Digital Computation: Proceedings of a Symposium Held at the National Physical Laboratory*. London: Her Majesty's Stationery Office.
21. B. J. Copeland (1993). *Artificial Intelligence: A Philosophical Introduction*. Oxford: Blackwell.
22. B. J. Copeland (1996). *The Church-Turing Thesis*. in The Stanford Encyclopedia of Philosophy (ed. E. Zalta), http://plato.stanford.edu.
23. B. J. Copeland (1998). *Turing's O-Machines, Penrose, Searle, and the Brain*. Analysis, 58:128–138.
24. B. J. Copeland, ed. (1999). *A Lecture and Two Radio Broadcasts by Alan Turing*. In [44].
25. B. J. Copeland, ed. (1999). *The Turing-Wilkinson Lecture Series on the Automatic Computing Engine*. In [44].
26. B. J. Copeland (2000). *Narrow Versus Wide Mechanism*. Journal of Philosophy, 97:5–32. (Reprinted in [78].)
27. B. J. Copeland (2000). *The Turing Test*. Minds and Machines, 10:519–539. (Reprinted in [63].)
28. B. J. Copeland (2001). *Colossus and the Dawning of the Computer Age*. In [38].

29. B. J. Copeland (2002). *The Chinese Room from a Logical Point of View.* In [69].
30. B. J. Copeland (2002). *Hypercomputation.* Minds and Machines, 12:461–502.
31. B. J. Copeland (2002). *Accelerating Turing Machines.* Minds and Machines, 11:281–301.
32. B. J. Copeland, D. Proudfoot (1996). *On Alan Turing's Anticipation of Connectionism.* Synthese, 108:361–377. (Reprinted in [18].)
33. B. J. Copeland, D. Proudfoot (1999) *Alan Turing's Forgotten Ideas in Computer Science.* Scientific American, 280(4):76–81, April.
34. B. J. Copeland, D. Proudfoot (2002). Foreword to [90].
35. M. Davis, ed. (1965). *The Undecidable: Basic Papers On Undecidable Propositions, Unsolvable Problems And Computable Functions.* New York: Raven.
36. G. de Cordemoy (1668). *A Philosophicall Discourse Concerning Speech.* London: John Martin. Page references are to the 1972 reprint by Scholars' Facsimiles & Reprints, New York.
37. K. de Leeuw, E. F. Moore, C. E. Shannon, N. Shapiro (1956). *Computability by Probabilistic Machines.* In [82].
38. R. Erskine, M. Smith (2001). *Action This Day.* London: Bantam.
39. B. G. Farley, W. A. Clark (1954). *Simulation of Self-Organizing Systems by Digital Computer.* Institute of Radio Engineers Transactions on Information Theory, 4:76–84.
40. E. A. Feigenbaum, J. Feldman, eds (1963). *Computers and Thought.* New York: McGraw-Hill.
41. R. French (1990). *Subcognition and the Limits of the Turing Test.* Mind, 99:53–65. (Reprinted in [62].) Page references are to [62].
42. R. French (2000). *The Turing Test: the First 50 Years.* Trends in Cognitive Sciences, 4:115–122.
43. R. J. Froggatt (1957). *Logical Design of a Computer for Business Use.* Journal of the British Institution of Radio Engineers, 17:681–696.
44. K. Furukawa, D. Michie, S. Muggleton, eds (1999). *Machine Intelligence, 15.* Oxford: Oxford University Press.
45. H. Goldstine (1972). *The Computer from Pascal to von Neumann.* Princeton: Princeton University Press.
46. J. Haugeland (1985). *Artificial Intelligence: The Very Idea.* Cambridge, MA: MIT Press.
47. D. O. Hebb (1949). *The Organization of Behavior: A Neuropsychological Theory.* New York: John Wiley.
48. A. Hodges (1992). *Alan Turing: The Enigma.* London: Vintage.
49. J. H. Holland (1992). *Adaptation in Natural and Artificial Systems.* Cambridge, MA: MIT Press.
50. H. D. Huskey (1972). *The Development of Automatic Computing.* In Proceedings of the First USA-JAPAN Computer Conference.
51. H. D. Huskey (1984). *From ACE to the G-15.* Annals of the History of Computing, 6:350–371.
52. T. D. Kieu (2002). *Quantum Hypercomputation.* Minds and Machines, 12:541–561.
53. W. Kozaczuk (1984). *Enigma: How the German Machine Cipher Was Broken, and How It Was Read by the Allies in World War Two.* Trans. C. Kasparek. London: Arms and Armour Press.

54. S. H. Lavington (1975). *A History of Manchester Computers.* Manchester: NCC Publications.
55. P. Mahon (1945). "The History of Hut Eight, 1939–1945". PRO document reference HW 25/2. A digital facsimile of the original typescript is in The Turing Archive for the History of Computing, `http://www.AlanTuring.net/mahon_hut_8`.
56. W. Mays, D. G. Prinz (1950). *A Relay Machine for the Demonstration of Symbolic Logic.* Nature, 165(4188):197–198, 4 February.
57. P. McCorduck (1979). *Machines Who Think.* New York: W.H. Freeman.
58. B. Meltzer, D. Michie, eds (1969). *Machine Intelligence, 5.* Edinburgh: Edinburgh University Press.
59. B. Meltzer, D. Michie, eds (1972). *Machine Intelligence, 7.* Edinburgh: Edinburgh University Press.
60. N. Metropolis, J. Howlett, G. C. Rota, eds (1980). *A History of Computing in the Twentieth Century.* New York: Academic Press.
61. D. Michie (1966). *Game-Playing and Game-Learning Automata.* In L. Fox, ed., *Advances in Programming and Non-numerical Computation.* New York: Pergamon.
62. P. Millican, A. Clark, eds (1996). *Machines and Thought: The Legacy of Alan Turing.* Oxford: Oxford University Press.
63. J. H. Moor, ed. (2003). *The Turing Test.* Dordrecht: Kluwer.
64. A. Newell (1980). *Physical Symbol Systems.* Cognitive Science, 4:135–183.
65. A. Newell, H. A. Simon (1976). *Computer Science as Empirical Inquiry: Symbols and Search.* Communications of the Association for Computing Machinery, 19:113–126.
66. A. Oettinger (1952). *Programming a Digital Computer to Learn.* Philosophical Magazine, 43:1243–1263.
67. D. N. Osherson, H. Lasnik, eds (1990). *An Invitation to Cognitive Science, 3.* Cambridge, MA: MIT Press.
68. G. Piccinini (2002). *Alan Turing and the Mathematical Objection.* Minds and Machines, 13:23–48.
69. J. Preston, M. Bishop, eds (2002). *Views into the Chinese Room: New Essays on Searle and Artificial Intelligence.* Oxford: Oxford University Press.
70. D. G. Prinz (1952). *Robot Chess.* Research, 5:261–266.
71. D. G. Prinz, J. B. Smith (1953). *Machines for the Solution of Logical Problems.* In [7].
72. D. Proudfoot, B. J. Copeland (1994) *Turing, Wittgenstein and the Science of the Mind.* Australasian Journal of Philosophy, 72:497–519.
73. B. Randell (1972) *On Alan Turing and the Origins of Digital Computers.* In [59].
74. M. Rejewski (1980). *Jak Matematycy polscy rozszyfrowali Enigmę [How the Polish mathematicians broke Enigma].* Annals of the Polish Mathematical Society, series II: Mathematical News, 23:1–28. English translation in [53].
75. F. Rosenblatt (1957). *The Perceptron, a Perceiving and Recognizing Automaton.* Cornell Aeronautical Laboratory Report No. 85–460–1.
76. F. Rosenblatt (1962). *Principles of Neurodynamics.* Washington, D.C.: Spartan.
77. A. L. Samuel (1959). *Some Studies in Machine Learning Using the Game of Checkers.* IBM Journal of Research and Development, 3:211–229. Reprinted in [40]. Page references are to [40].

78. M. Scheutz, ed. (2002). *Computationalism: New Directions.* Cambridge, MA: MIT Press.

79. J. Searle (1980). *Mind, Brains, and Programs.* Behavioral and Brain Sciences, 3:417–424.

80. J. Searle (1990). *Is the Brain's Mind a Computer Program?* Scientific American, 262(1):20–25.

81. J. Searle (1992). *The Rediscovery of the Mind.* Cambridge, MA: MIT Press.

82. C. E. Shannon, J. McCarthy, eds (1956). *Automata Studies.* Princeton, NJ: Princeton University Press.

83. S. M. Shieber (1994). *Lessons from a Restricted Turing Test.* Communications of the ACM, 37:70–78.

84. H. T. Siegelmann (2003). *Neural and Super-Turing Computing.* Minds and Machines 13:103–114.

85. H. T. Siegelmann, E. D. Sontag (1994). *Analog Computation via Neural Networks.* Theoretical Computer Science, 131:331–360.

86. M. Stannett (2003). *Computation and Hypercomputation.* Minds and Machines 13:115–153.

87. N. Stern (1981). *From ENIAC to UNIVAC: An Appraisal of the Eckert-Mauchly Computers.* Bedford, MA: Digital Press.

88. C. S. Strachey (1952). *Logical or Non-Mathematical Programmes.* In Proceedings of the Association for Computing Machinery, Toronto, September 1952, pp. 46–49.

89. A. H. Taub, ed. (1961). *Collected Works of John von Neumann.* Vol. 5. Oxford: Pergamon Press.

90. C. Teuscher (2002). *Turing's Connectionism: An Investigation of Neural Network Architectures.* London: Springer.

91. A. M. Turing (1936). *On Computable Numbers, with an Application to the Entscheidungsproblem.* Proceedings of the London Mathematical Society, series 2, 42:230–265 (1936–37).

92. A. M. Turing (1939). *Systems of Logic Based on Ordinals.* Proceedings of the London Mathematical Society, series 2, 45:161–228.

93. A. M. Turing (1945). *Proposal for Development in the Mathematics Division of an Automatic Computing Engine (ACE).* In [16]. A digital facsimile of the original typescript is in The Turing Archive for the History of Computing, `http://www.AlanTuring.net/proposed_electronic_calculator`. Page references are to the original typescript.

94. A. M. Turing (1947). *Lecture to the London Mathematical Society on 20 February 1947.* In [16].

95. A. M. Turing (1948). *Intelligent Machinery.* National Physical Laboratory Report, in [58]. A digital facsimile of the original typescript is in The Turing Archive for the History of Computing, `http://www.AlanTuring.net/intelligent_machinery`.

96. A. M. Turing (1950). *Computing Machinery and Intelligence.* Mind, 59(236):433–460.

97. A. M. Turing (1950). *Programmers' Handbook for Manchester Electronic Computer.* Computing Machine Laboratory, University of Manchester. A digital facsimile is available in The Turing Archive for the History of Computing, `http://www.AlanTuring.net/programmers_handbook`.

98. A. M. Turing (1951). *Can Digital Computers Think?* In [24].

99. A. M. Turing (c.1951). *Intelligent Machinery, A Heretical Theory.* In [24].
100. A. M. Turing (1952). *Can Automatic Calculating Machines Be Said To Think?* In [24].
101. A. M. Turing (1952). *The Chemical Basis of Morphogenesis.* Philosophical Transactions of the Royal Society of London, B 237:37–72.
102. A. M. Turing (1953). *Chess.* Part of ch. 25 of [7].
103. J. von Neumann (1954). *The NORC and Problems in High Speed Computing.* In [89].
104. J. von Neumann (1966). *Theory of Self-Reproducing Automata.* (Ed. A. W. Burks). Urbana: University of Illinois Press.
105. G. Welchman (2000). *The Hut Six Story: Breaking the Enigma Codes.* 2nd ed., Cleobury Mortimer: M&M Baldwin.
106. B. Whitby (1996). *The Turing Test: AI's Biggest Blind Alley.* In [62].
107. F. C. Williams (1975). *Early Computers at Manchester University.* The Radio and Electronic Engineer, 45:237–331.
108. D. M. Yates (1997). *Turing's Legacy: A History of Computing at the National Physical Laboratory 1945–1995.* London: Science Museum.

A Note on Enjoying Strawberries with Cream, Making Mistakes, and Other Idiotic Features

Helmut Schnelle

Ruhr-Universität Bochum

Summary. Turing's precise notion of computation implies three types of constraints: (1) sub-computational constraints requiring error-free components of the machines, (2) con-computational constraints according to which the machines are not influenced by situational distraction, and (3) trans-computational limits (in Gödel's sense). In contrast, human thought is not marked by these constraints and limitations. This is discussed with reference to thoughts of von Neumann and Weyl, Carnap and Bar-Hillel and, finally, Gödel and Wang.

1 Human Thought Capacity

Scientific progress depends on clarifying basic concepts and, if possible, in giving them ultimate precision. We must agree with Gödel who credited Turing with giving "persuasive arguments to show the adequacy of the precise concept" of computability and computation. He confessed to not having succeeded in his corresponding attempts in discussions with Church two years before Turing's publication [13, p. 96]. The development of computers made successful use of the concept. As a consequence the meaning of the word "computer" changed drastically, from designating, in 1936, a person who computes, to denoting, by 1950, a machine designed basically according to Turing's ideas.

In my view, this was indeed a change of word meaning: A person that computes needs special concentration in executing this activity. She or he is not designed by Mother Nature — if we follow Dennett's manner of speech [3] — for such an activity. Instead, a computing machine is designed just for computation without a specially designed mechanism assuring concentration.

The difference is important. Turing's notion defines "abstract machines" as "mathematical fictions rather than physical objects" [8, p. 62]. This implies, as Turing acknowledges, that "they are incapable of errors of functioning" [8, p. 62]. The notion of a Turing machine does not account for "natural" properties, such as "sub-computational" processes that may determine probabilistic deviance from the activity intended by the designer. This was the reason why von Neumann tried to develop the theory of automata further into one based essentially on probabilistic logic.[1]

---

[1] See the first steps in [11].

Turing acknowledged, in a more ironic mood, that in addition to not making errors, his machines also couldn't do other things, such as enjoying strawberries with cream. But here the reason is different, "Possibly a machine might be made to enjoy this delicious dish, but any attempt to make one do so would be idiotic" [11]. We may conjecture that Turing believed such an attempt to be idiotic because it would not serve some clear purpose. Indeed, it wouldn't. But I shall soon argue that an analysis of what it means for people to enjoy strawberries with cream, or other pleasant things — or to distaste unpleasant things — may show why they need internal organizers of concentration, which become active in their activity of computing, whereas even the meaning of "concentration" is meaningless for a machine. Thus understanding "enjoying strawberries with cream" tells us something of the normal contextual distractions that may endanger each concentrated activity, human computing in particular. Thus, the notion of computation is context-free in machines, but is context-dependent in humans. In addition to "sub-computational" features such idiotic features of "con-computational" distractions must be accounted for in human computers.

Note that the idea that the relation between distraction and non-distracted computation would be similar to that between friction and the free fall of bodies in Galileo's analysis is wrong. The latter problem can be solved on the basis of the additivity of forces, whereas distractions require the constant operation of special counteractive mechanisms, depending on the character of the distractions.

A third feature relates to the possibility of "trans-computational" capacities in humans. I follow Gödel's argumentation. Whereas Turing's notion makes a clear-cut distinction between what is computational and what is not, Gödel thinks that we should define degrees of certainty of reflection. He concedes that Turing's notion defines a standard for a high degree of certainty but it does not per se provide the standard of ultimate evidence. Gödel wrote [14, citation 7.1.6]

> Nothing remains if one drives to the ultimate intuition or to what is completely evident. But to destroy science altogether [as implied by insisting on the ultimate], serves no positive purpose. Our real intuition is finite, and, in fact, *limited to something small* [my emphasis]. The physical world, the integers and the continuum all have objective existence. There are degrees of certainty. The continuum is not seen as clearly [as the physical world and the integers].

He also emphasized — in an unfinished script for Schilpp's Carnap Festschrift — that, in their attempt to formally specify degrees of certainty in mathematical thought, some mathematicians delimited the field of unconditional mathematical truth very differently. Gödel presented the following sequence of increasing degrees of certainty [14, citation 7.1.7]:

1. Classical mathematics in the broad sense (i.e., set theory included),
2. Classical mathematics in the strict sense,
3. Semi-intuitionism,
4. Intuitionism,
5. Constructivism,
6. Finitism,
7. Restricted finitism,
8. Implicationism.

Obviously, Gödel also believed that rationally regimented human thought develops in degrees of certainty over and above obvious intuition or everyday knowledge. Thus, in higher regions of complexity he believed in mathematical, "trans-computational" capacities of thought. But he acknowledged having failed in his attempts to rigorously prove the precise status of these "higher" mathematical capacities, at least if measured by the standards of conceptual precision set by Turing.

Let me summarize this introduction: People can acquire the competence of computation in Turing's sense if they bring their thought processes under *concentrated control*. This control reduces the probabilistic influence of *sub-computational* error, marks the reduced certainty of *trans-computational* mathematical thought, and provides a standard of rigorous continuity of thought that people can achieve in controlling their various experiences in the background of *con-computational* distraction. Applying particular *mechanisms for counteracting influences of "idiotic" features* is typical for concentrated human thought but is irrelevant for the artificial machine.

In the following sections I shall add some details about sub-computationality and con-computationality. I shall not enter into further discussion of trans-computational features; here, I refer to the discussion of Gödel's thoughts in [13, 14].

2 Some Details on "Sub-computationality"

Von Neumann saw that the rigorously algorithmic definition of computers was problematic. He referred particularly to the notion of analogy in aesthetic contexts of perception.[2] He thought that, in order to cope with more natural contexts, we must transcend a rigorous notion of computation: We should have a logical theory of the synthesis of reliable organisms from unreliable components. Due to the quantum-theoretic character of physics, real components of a computational machine or of a computing organism involve, by necessity, probabilistic features. A realistic theory of computation cannot be restricted to error-free function. Error must be viewed, therefore, "not as an extraneous and misdirected accident, but as an essential part of the process

---

[2] See my discussion in [6].

under consideration" [11, Introduction]. It should be based on probabilistic logic belonging to "effectively constructed logics, that is intuitionistic logics, [that] can best be studied in terms of [real] automata" [11, § 2.1].

It seems that von Neumann reflected mainly about arithmetical computers and the decimal precision that could be attained by the elementary components to be synthesized in a computer [12]. The question was: Assuming that an elementary computational component can provide a precision up to the nth decimal, how can we obtain a higher precision from the machine? Von Neumann proposed to combine the components appropriately by making use of the probabilistic regularities that characterize the expansion of the decimals beyond the nth decimal.

It was one of the ideas of the intuitionists that approaching the concepts of a continuum you may reflect on "free choice or lawless sequences" (e.g., of decimals)[3]. I believe that in referring to intuitionism, von Neumann had in mind to adapt this idea, by not considering the completely lawless sequences of Brouwer but probabilistically determined expansion of sequences. He thus may have thought to extend the conceptually rigorous logic used so far in abstract automata theory by substituting the rigorous and strictly distinctive notions of states, squares for markings, and marks (or symbols) with probabilistic intuitionistic logic (which should have some similarity with the properties of thermodynamics). In this way he hoped to substitute the notions of abstract machines by a proper account of more realistic, physical or organismic, automata. The basic mathematical and logical idea was to place an appropriate mathematical notion between "free-choice intuitionism" and formal logical structure in terms of rigorous digital or symbolic distinctivity.

It was obvious that von Neumann's approach was mainly based on the intuitions of a mathematician. The development of neurobiology in recent decades led to more concrete ideas, some of them bridging empirical facts with mathematical thought. One such was Edelman's theory of neuronal group selection and its integration into a theory of global neurobiological networks [4] [5, p. 41 ff.] In my view, it is fully in line with von Neumann's orientation.

3   Some Details on "Con-computationality"

According to Turing's criterion, being able to pass his imitation game based on question answering means being able to think. An imitation game based on argumentation in a natural language might have been a more appropriate criterion. If argumentation were seen in the context of modern formal logic, hence on symbolic computation for formal syntax and semantics, a Turing machine should in principle be able to pass the test.

The problem is whether argumentation theories based on formal syntax and semantics do not differ essentially from argumentation in pragmatic lan-

---

[3] cp. [16, Vol. 11, pp. 152–153], [15, p. 52], and also [14, p. 215].

guages, a fact that has been emphasized by Carnap. But, as correctly pointed out by Bar-Hillel on many occasions [1, 2], Carnap, like all formalists, seemed to have greatly underestimated the problematic character of abstracting from the pragmatic aspects of human communication and thought [2, p. 276]. Bar-Hillel has substantiated his claim by analyzing a large number of examples. He summarized the general features in the customary way of the 1950s by writing that communication between humans does proceed along various channels [1, p. 206] such that communication in languages depends on linguistic co-text (viz. the utterances, if any, that preceded the communicative act under scrutiny) and on extra linguistic context (the general background in which this communicative act was performed, the motives that brought it about, the cognitive and emotional background of the participants in it, etc.) [1, p. 208]. In a more modern perspective he writes [2, p. 280] about the necessity of more than one grammar for a given language and even more than one system of evaluating arguments — all of them instantiated in our brains by various cooperating mechanisms.

It is obvious that the plurality of systems required to interact with the system implementing the formal computational core is against the spirit of abstraction. Trying to implement such systems is certainly as idiotic as trying to implement a strawberry-enjoying machine together with another machine used to prevent the whole machine from falling prey to the temptation of strawberry enjoying while being in the act of computing.

Nevertheless, being able to concentrate is as important for human thought as it is irrelevant for a machine. On the other hand, attending to strange contexts of thought and evaluating their possible relevance in creative acts is also as important for human thought as it is impossible for a machine designed for definitely circumscribed purposes.

Studying, or even trying to implement, co-textual and contextual background evaluation in humans may appear to be silly as long as our perspectives are determined by definite and circumscribed designs. However, it is a challenge to come up with a better understanding of that powerful ability applied in solving the many practical tasks we are confronted with in our human affairs. This also is a property of human thought — and not of the "thoughts" of machines — a property whose machine implementation Turing correctly characterized as idiotic.

References

1. Y. Bar-Hillel (1970). *Argumentation in pragmatic languages.* In: Y. Bar-Hillel. Aspects of Language. Jerusalem: The Magnes Press, Chap. 17.
2. Y. Bar-Hillel (1970). *Communication and argumentation in pragmatic languages.* In: Linguaggi nella società e nella tecnica. Milano: Edizioni di comunità, pp. 269–284.
3. D. C. Dennett (1995). *Darwin's Dangerous Idea.* New York, NY: Touchstone.

4. G. M. Edelman (1987). *Neural Darwinism*. The Theory of Neuronal Group Selection. New York, NY: Basic Books, 1987.
5. G. M. Edelman (1989). *The Remembered Present*. New York, NY: Basic Books.
6. H. Schnelle (1988). *Turing naturalized*. Von Neumann's unfinished project. In: R. Herken (ed.) The Universal Turing Machine. A Half-Century Survey. Oxford: Oxford University Press, pp. 539–559.
7. Turing A. M. (1936–7). On computable numbers, with an application to the Entscheidungsproblem, Proc. London Maths. Soc., ser. 2, **42**, 230–265; also in M. Davis, (ed.) The Undecidable (Raven, New York, 1965), and in [10].
8. Turing A. M. (1950). Computing machinery and intelligence, Mind **49**, 433–460, reprinted in [9].
9. Turing, A. M. (1992). Collected Works: Mechanical Intelligence. D. C. Ince, ed., Amsterdam, NL: North-Holland.
10. Turing, A. M. (2001). Collected Works: Mathematical Logic. R. O. Gandy and C. E. M. Yates, eds., Amsterdam, NL: North-Holland.
11. J. Von Neumann (1956). *Probabilistic logics and the synthesis of reliable organisms from unreliable components*. In: C. E. Shannon and J. McCarthy (eds.) Automata Studies. Princeton, NJ: Princeton University Press, pp. 43–98.
12. J. von Neumann (1958). *The Computer and the Brain*. New Haven: Yale University Press.
13. H. Wang (1987). *Reflections on Kurt Gödel*. Cambridge, MA: MIT Press.
14. H. Wang (1996). *A Logical Journey*. From Gödel to Philosophy. Cambridge, MA: MIT Press.
15. H. Weyl (1949). *The Philosophy of Mathematics and Natural Science*. Princeton, NJ: Princeton University Press.
16. H. Weyl (1968). *Gesammelte Abhandlungen*. Band II (K. Chandrasekharan, Ed.) Berlin Heidelberg: Springer-Verlag.

Robots and Rule-Following

Diane Proudfoot

Philosophy Department, University of Canterbury

Summary. Turing was probably the first person to advocate the pursuit of robotics as a route to Artificial Intelligence and Wittgenstein the first to argue that, without the appropriate history, no machine could be intelligent. Wittgenstein anticipated much recent theorizing about the mind, including aspects of connectionist theories of mind and the situated cognition approach in AI. Turing and Wittgenstein had a wary respect for each other and there is significant overlap in their work, in both the philosophy of mathematics and the philosophy of AI. Both took (what would now be called) an externalist stance with respect to machine intelligence. But whereas Turing was concerned only with behaviour, Wittgenstein emphasized in addition history and environment. I show that Wittgenstein's externalist analysis of psychological capacities entails that most, even all, future "artificially intelligent" computers and robots will not use language, possess concepts, or reason. The argument tells, not against AI, but only against AI's traditional and romantic goal of building an artificial "res cogitans" — as first embraced by Turing and now exemplified in the work of Brooks and others on cognitive robotics. This argument supports the stance of the growing number of AI researchers whose aim is to produce, not thinking and understanding machines, but high-performance "advanced information processing systems."

1 Turing and Wittgenstein

Turing and the Viennese philosopher Ludwig Wittgenstein, both Fellows of Cambridge colleges, had a "wary respect" for each other.[1] Turing attended Wittgenstein's lectures.[2] In a letter dated 11 February 1937 Turing spoke of sending a reprint of his 1936 article, "On Computable Numbers, with an application to the Entscheidungsproblem", to Wittgenstein, and a well-thumbed offprint of the article was reportedly [33, p. 308] discovered amongst Wittgenstein's effects. During the early and middle 1930s, Wittgenstein and his students were considering the question "Is every mathematical problem

---

[1] The quoted words are Robin Gandy's, in personal communication with B. Jack Copeland (1995).

[2] Hodges' biography of Turing [24, p. 136] suggests that prior to 1937 Turing had seen Wittgenstein only at the Moral Sciences Club. But see Nedo and Ranchetti [33, pp. 357–358].

solvable?" [1, pp. 186, 188] — a question closely related to the problem Turing attacked in his 1936 paper, namely whether every mathematical problem is solvable by a definite method. The notes of Wittgenstein's lectures on the foundations of mathematics in 1939 include lengthy discussions with Turing [53]. These notes and the radio broadcast "Can Automatic Calculating Machines Be Said To Think?" [44] are the only examples we have of Turing in discussion. Although it is now impossible to determine the exact nature of any influence between the two men, there is significant overlap in the work of Turing and Wittgenstein. In this first section I outline three areas that both worked on, in the philosophy of mind and Artificial Intelligence (AI): connectionism, situated cognition, and externalism. In each case, both Turing and Wittgenstein anticipated later theorizing about the mind and machines.

In his 1948 report, "Intelligent Machinery," Turing anticipated connectionism [14, 15, 39]. His "unorganised machines" included networks of neuron-like Boolean elements connected together in a largely random manner. So far as is known, he was the first person to contemplate building artificial computing devices out of simple, neuron-like elements linked in a largely random fashion into networks. His "B-type" neural networks consist of randomly connected two-state "neurons." An initially random B-type network is "organised" by selectively disabling and enabling connections within it. Turing said that, by applying "appropriate interference, mimicking education," a B-type network can be trained to "do any required job, given sufficient time and provided the number of units is sufficient" [41, pp. 14–15].

Features of Wittgenstein's theoretical psychology, such as his emphasis upon the role of samples and of training in concept-formation [50, pp. 130ff] [49, §208–210] and upon the role of aspect-perception and of "family resemblance" in concept-possession [49, pp. 193ff, §66ff], prefigure connectionist accounts of mind. As early as 1946–48 he conjectured that brains are not processors of representations [52, §608ff], preparing the philosophical ground for dynamicist approaches to cognition [46, 47]. Wittgenstein's discussion of aberrant concept-formation is particularly prophetic. According to Wittgenstein, a child acquires a concept, for example *cup*, by means of exposure to exemplars. But what if the child observes that all the exemplars she has so far been shown are brightly patterned and goes on to take all brightly patterned objects to be cups? Wittgenstein showed that the traditional solution to this problem is unavailable: the procedure of training the child to discriminate between cups and non-cups cannot simply be replaced by giving the child a definition of *cup*, since — even in so simple a case — no adequate definition is available [49, §66ff]. In any event, any seemingly satisfactory definition would be as open to misinterpretation as was the original exemplar [49, §71]. Here Wittgenstein set out a problem that was much later to arise for connectionist theories, in the form of networks that go astray and extrapolate wrongly from the objects in a training set.

In his 1948 report Turing also anticipated what is now called "situated" or "embodied" AI, including the contemporary quest to build a humanoid robot. He remarked:

> One way of setting about our task of building a "thinking machine" would be to take a man as a whole and to try to replace all the parts of him by machinery. He would include television cameras, microphones, loudspeakers, wheels and "handling servo-mechanisms" as well as some sort of "electronic brain." This would be a tremendous undertaking of course. The object, if produced by present techniques, would be of immense size, even if the "brain" part were stationary and controlled the body from a distance. In order that the machine should have a chance of finding things out for itself it should be allowed to roam the countryside ... [41, p. 13]

In his 1950 paper, "Computing Machinery and Intelligence," Turing suggested two distinct approaches to AI: (what we might call) disembodied AI, which aims at building disembodied thinking machines carrying out an "abstract activity, like the playing of chess," and embodied (or situated) AI, which aims "to provide the machine with the best sense organs that money can buy, and then teach it to understand and speak English" [42, p. 460]. (The early response to Turing's suggestion was strikingly negative. According to Woodger, Turing's assistant, Turing's colleagues at the National Physical Laboratory declared in scorn "Turing is going to infest the countryside ... with a robot which will live on twigs and scrap iron" [31, p. 2].

Wittgenstein was an early proponent of the situated cognition approach in the philosophy of mind. His criticisms of representationalist theories of mind (e.g., that they fail to explain intentionality) is the philosophical counterpart of contemporary objections — by e.g. Rodney Brooks, modern pioneer of situated AI [8] — to traditional AI's world-modelling approach. Both Wittgenstein and Brooks reject the view (most famously expressed in Newell's and Simon's physical symbol system hypothesis [34, 35]) that cognition consists in symbolic information-processing (on Wittgenstein, see Proudfoot [36]). Instead they see cognition in terms of activities, skills and common-sense "know-how" (e.g., for Wittgenstein words and sentences are "tools" in practical use [49, §23] rather than expressions in a recursive code). Both reject the traditional emphasis (in philosophy and AI) upon disembodied reasoning, in favour of situated body-based reasoning and environment-specific knowledge. Wittgenstein's claim that representational systems presuppose our natural reactions to training is echoed in Brooks' slogan "The world grounds regress" [7, p. 55]. Wittgenstein's claim that psychological states are conceptually linked to behaviour parallels Brooks' claim that the "constructed system eventually has to express all its goals and desires as physical action" [4, p. 5]. And last, just as for Brooks higher-level cognitive performance emerges (not from a general-purpose central processor but) out of simpler behaviour, and thus workers in AI "must incrementally build up the capabilities of intelligent systems, having complete systems at each step of the way" [5, p. 140], so for Wittgenstein higher-level cognitive performance develops from the simple interactive behaviour involved in primitive but complete "forms of life," to use Wittgenstein's term — or "horizontal microworlds" (see Clark [12, p. 13]), in current AI vocabulary.

Turing and Wittgenstein also shared (what would now be called) an externalist stance with regard to machine intelligence — i.e., they held the view that whether a machine thinks is not determined by its internal states. The Turing test is externalist in two respects. First, to answer the question "Can machines think?," the judges consider machines' outward behaviour rather than their internal states. Second, what determines that machines think is the responses of others (the judges) — for Turing, "[t]he extent to which we regard something as behaving in an intelligent manner is determined as much by our own state of mind and training as by the properties of the object under consideration" [41, p. 23].

For Wittgenstein, whether or not an entity (human being, other creature, or machine) thinks is determined not only by its behaviour, but also by its history and environment. This paper focuses on Wittgenstein's arguments and their implications. In Sect. 2 I consider his externalist account of rule-following. This account is important for the question whether artificial computing devices follow rules, and in turn for the question whether such devices use language, possess concepts, or reason — some of the cognitive capacities gathered together under the umbrella term "thinks." In Sect. 3 I use Wittgenstein's account as the basis for a new pragmatic argument to show that most "artificially intelligent" computers will not (as a matter of fact) think — even those that pass the Turing test. This argument tells, not against AI, but only against AI's traditional and romantic goal of building an artificial "res cogitans." The argument supports the stance of the growing number of AI researchers whose aim is to produce, rather than thinking and understanding machines, high-performance "advanced information processing systems" (or "knowledge-using systems," where the expression "knowledge-using" is taken to denote behaviour).

2   Rule-Following

Rule-following has a prima facie role in, for example, language-use, concept-possession, and reasoning. The language-user follows rules of meaning and grammar. The concept-possessor follows a rule distinguishing instantiations of a concept (e.g., the coffee cup on my desk, where the concept is cup) from non-instantiations (the pen on my desk). The reasoner follows rules leading from premise to conclusion (to take a clichéd example, the modus ponens rule leading from the premises *Socrates is a man* and *All men are mortal* to the conclusion *Socrates is mortal*). These claims about rule-following are, at this very general level, simple truisms.

Wittgenstein's insight was to distinguish between, on the one hand, merely behaving *in accordance with* a rule and, on the other hand, *following* a rule [49, §232]. Consider the subject who is given the sequence 1, 4, 9, 16, who is asked "What is the next number in the series?," and who responds "25." This subject produces an appropriate output for a given input and, in doing so, behaves in accordance with an arithmetical rule. However, as Wittgenstein pointed out, we can imagine the output being produced in a variety of ways that would make us reluctant to say that the subject is following a rule (if, for example, her behaviour were due only to luck or a bizarre type of glosso-lalia) [49, §232]. Cognitive scientists — unsurprisingly, given their antipathy to purely behavioural definitions of psychological phenomena — have tended to make the same distinction as Wittgenstein, and have been concerned to differentiate what they see as the regularity (in a natural or artificial computing device) that is involved in rule-following from "mere" regularity in a physical system (for example, the regular orbits of the planets).[3]

This distinction between following a rule and behaving in accordance with a rule emerges in each of language-use, concept-possession, and reasoning. For example, consider the difference between a native English speaker and a foreign tourist who has learned phonetically a few English phrases: the latter behaves in accordance with certain syntactic and semantic rules of English but would not be said to follow these rules. The same example can be used to illustrate the difference between "genuine" concept-possession and mere appropriate behaviour. The subject who possesses the concept *well-formed English sentence* follows the rules distinguishing well-formed English sentences from ill-formed English sentences, and in consequence uses mostly well-formed sentences. In our example the tourist utters only well-formed English sentences but would scarcely be said to be following the rules distinguishing these from ill-formed ones.

In cases such as these it is the phenomena that involve rule-following which are of primary interest to the philosopher or psychologist. For example, in an inquiry into reasoning, the subject who (in response to the question "What is the next number in the 1, 4, 9, 16 ... series?") gives a correct answer, "25," but only as a result of luck, would be of little use. This is precisely because it would be odd to say that this subject has reasoned from premise to conclusion: the premise (i.e., the sequence of four numbers) does not play the right sort of role here. (And if we were to say that this subject is reasoning, then why not one who chooses the next number in the sequence by tossing a coin?)

So what distinguishes the rule-follower (whether human or non-human, real or artificial)? The Turing test — the standard warrant of cognitive activity in AI — is of no use, since ex hypothesi both the rule-follower and the

---

[3] The example is Fodor's [20, p. 74].

subject merely behaving in accordance with a rule may produce the same output for a given input. Nor would it help to say that the difference between them is that the rule-follower *understands* what, in producing the correct behaviour, she is doing. Understanding that one is behaving in accordance with a rule is insufficient for rule-following (otherwise the tourist, who knows that he is behaving in accordance with the rules of English grammar, would be following these rules). Certainly, understanding that one is doing whatever constitutes rule-following is sufficient for rule-following, but this is unilluminating, since the unexplicated concept re-emerges. The same problem arises for the claim that the rule-follower *intends*, in behaving correctly, to act in accordance with a rule, or offers as *justification* for her behaviour that it is in accordance with a rule, and so on.

2.1   Objections to Internalist Analyses

Wittgenstein assessed several rival accounts of the difference between the rule-follower and the entity merely behaving in accordance with a rule — for brevity's sake I shall refer to the latter as the "quasi-rule-follower." According to the first account, the rule-follower's behaviour is accompanied by certain distinctive conscious experiences [49, §155]. Unpacking the difference in this way suits those whose intuition is that human beings and certain other creatures can follow rules but inanimate objects, including machines, can be only quasi-rule-followers.

On the second account, the rule-follower has a psychological disposition, based in internal mechanisms, to behave in accordance with a rule [49, §149]. Requiring a disposition to behave in accordance with a rule accommodates the intuition that the rule-follower can produce the correct behaviour more than once. Requiring that the disposition be based in internal mechanisms suits those whose intuition is that human beings, other creatures *and* machines can be rule-followers, but not so objects — such as planets — whose behaviour is primarily the result of external forces.

On the third account, the rule-follower has (to use the term Wittgenstein employs) an "interpretation" which the quasi-rule-follower lacks [51, p. 80]. An interpretation is a way of viewing what is given that determines what the response should be. For example, the subject that is given the sequence 1, 4, 9, 16 may interpret this as the initial segment of the series generated by the formula n^2 and so continue "25, 49 ... " Talk of the "interpretation" of a rule is merely a place-holder for some particular theory. For example, a seventeenth-century philosopher might have said that the rule-follower has an "idea" of the rule present to mind that "tells" him or her how to act, whereas a modern cognitivist might claim that an entity is a rule-follower if and only if that entity's behaving in accordance with a rule is determined in part by an internal representation token, this token ultimately to be cashed out in terms of the fundamental computational operations of whatever architecture is involved. The third account accommodates the view that the rule-follower has some internal symbolic representation of the rule. It suits those whose intuition is that human beings and those other creatures or machines that are symbol-manipulators can be rule-followers.

Wittgenstein rejected each of these accounts of rule-following [49, §159, 160, 168, 171] [51, p. 332]. That the rule-follower has certain conscious experiences will not do, since we simply cannot find any that correlate significantly with instances of rule-following. In any case, a simple thought experiment will show of any conscious experience that it is neither necessary nor sufficient for rule-following. Consider two entities, one of whom (A) can read aloud, i.e., can follow the rules correlating written marks and spoken sounds (leaving aside the question of understanding the meaning of the marks or sounds), and one of whom (B) cannot but has memorized the words of a particular text, so as to appear to be reading aloud from the text. B is merely behaving in accordance with the rules that A is following. Let us suppose that, given any experience that seems, to the proponent of the first account above, to be distinctive of rule-following (a feeling, say, of ease or confidence or of being "guided" by the marks on the page), we eliminate it in A, leaving everything else unchanged, and induce it in B. In A we induce the "characteristic sensations [of] reciting something one has learnt by heart" [49, §159]. Is it the case that A is no longer following rules and that B is now a rule-follower? Wittgenstein says not. After all, hypnotizing a memorizer to improve her confidence will not make her a reader, and that a reader's confidence disappears is also irrelevant.

The example of the reader and the memorizer can also be used to demonstrate Wittgenstein's view that having a disposition, based in internal mechanisms, to behave in accordance with a rule will not suffice for rule-following. B has a disposition to behave in accordance with certain of the rules correlating spoken sounds and marks on a page, and we have good general reasons to think that this disposition is based in internal mechanisms. Yet she is not following these rules.

Wittgenstein often countered psychological explanations that centre on internal representations with a form of regress objection. With regard to the third account, that the rule-follower has an interpretation of the rule that is followed, the objection is as follows. Consider an entity who (or which), when presented with the sequence 1, 4, 9, 16, has an internal representation token, "n^2." Is this sufficient for the entity to have an *interpretation* of the sequence, i.e., for the sequence to *mean* something to the entity? No, for the very same reason that merely producing an appropriate output ("25") was not sufficient to guarantee that the entity is a rule-follower. Having an internal token "n^2" lends meaning to the initial sequence of numbers only if the internal token "n^2" is itself meaningful to the entity. In effect, we have pushed our question about rule-following one stage back. The question that we now need to answer (and that the third account, of course, cannot) is: of two entities, both of whom have an internal token "n^2" when presented with the sequence of numbers 1, 4, 9, 16, what makes one entity the possessor of an interpretation of the sequence and the other merely the possessor of an internal token?

The proponent of the interpretation view may deny that an internal token, to count as an interpretation, must itself be meaningful — in which case no regress is initiated. For example, she may suppose that the rule-follower's cognitive architecture is connectionist and that an interpretation consists simply of a pattern of connectivity with no representational significance. However, now it is unclear how the third account is to make out the distinction between rule-following and quasi-rule-following — and in particular how this version of the interpretation model of rule-following differs from the second account (a disposition based in internal mechanisms), which has just been dismissed.

Wittgenstein's interest in rule-following is well known amongst philosophers. Less well appreciated, however, is the significance of the failure of the attempted characterizations of rule-following that he considered. Since Kripke's [28] discussion, Wittgenstein's approach has commonly, if inaccurately, been seen as sceptical, i.e., as doubting the existence of any fact to answer the question "What rule is followed by the subject who gives 25 as the next number in the series beginning 1, 4, 9, 16?" If we set Wittgenstein's account in the wider context of his philosophical psychology, we get a very different picture.

Wittgenstein's later philosophy provides an elaborate criticism of the internalism deeply rooted in modern Western philosophy and psychology. The much-discussed difference between internalist and externalist approaches in psychology arises with regard to both individuation and explanation. As to the former, the internalist takes it that psychological states (or their representational contents) are individuated purely in terms of a subject's current internal states whereas the externalist argues that individuation is partly in terms of a subject's history and social and physical environment. The role the internalist allows to factors in the history and environment of the subject is merely that of being part of the causal chain leading to a subject's current internal states. As to explanation, the internalist has it that a subject's behaviour is to be explained on the basis solely of the subject's current internal states whereas the externalist includes a subject's history and environment. For the internalist, external stimuli are important in explanation only insofar as they contribute causally to a subject's internal states. Wittgenstein was an externalist. He held the view that psychological states and their representational contents are individuated in terms of a subject's behaviour, history and social environment, irrespective of internal states (remarking, for example, "If God had looked into our minds he would not have been able to see there whom we were speaking of").[4] He argued that ordinary psychological explanation (in terms of beliefs, desires, intentions, etc.) is not causal [50, pp. 15, 110] and that, using such explanation, we can give different accounts of

---

[4] [49, p. 217] — thanks to Denis Robinson for drawing my attention to this remark.

the behaviour of individuals who are the same from the skin in but have different histories or environments. It was anti-internalism, rather than scepticism, that lay behind Wittgenstein's rejection of the three candidate accounts of rule-following. Each account explicates rule-following in terms of the current internal states of the subject that is behaving in accordance with a rule.

Wittgenstein's aim was to argue that internalist analyses of rule-following fail. To illustrate his case consider, as an example of a candidate rule-follower, a computer. (For brevity's sake I shall use "computer" — except in its occurrence in "human computer" — as shorthand for "artificial computing device.") If it is a difference in internal state that distinguishes a device that is a rule-follower from that which is a quasi-rule-follower, this must be a difference in at least one of the following: the static configurations of hardware (e.g., differences in components or circuitry); transient hardware states not computationally interpreted (this includes states that we would not usually think to interpret computationally, e.g., rises in temperature, and states that we might so interpret, e.g., fluctuating voltages); and transient hardware states computationally interpreted (e.g., as instantiations of code). But hardware configurations and non-computationally-interpreted states are no more than the internal physical mechanisms that are the basis of a device's dispositions, and computationally interpreted hardware states are no more than a device's "interpretations" or internal representations: Wittgenstein has given us reason to say that neither is sufficient (even when conjoined with the correct behaviour) for rule-following. Even if we were to allow the possibility of hardware states of an artificial device giving rise to conscious experience in the device, the reader/memorizer thought-experiment shows that it is not conscious experience that distinguishes a rule-follower. (If we replace "hardware" by "wetware" throughout the above remarks, and even if we include thoroughly unconventional hardware, such as quantum or DNA devices, the argument is the same.)

The internal states that Wittgenstein considered are of diverse kinds — conscious experience, internal mechanisms at the base of dispositions, and "interpretations." In addition, his objections outlined above (to accounts of rule-following centering on these states) are easily revised so as to apply to a variety of other internalist analyses of rule-following. He gave us, in consequence, good reason to doubt the possibility of a satisfactory internalist account of rule-following.

2.2 Wittgenstein's Externalist Strategy

On Wittgenstein's view we can say of two individuals, physical duplicates but differing in history or environment, that one is a rule-follower and the other is not. His arguments that, if an entity A is to follow a rule, A must have a certain history and environment include the following.

The Social Environment Condition on Rule-Following. Wittgenstein stressed the importance of the fact that rules are normative [51, p. 425]. It is not that the number 25 invariably or even mostly turns up as the next number in inscriptions of the sequence 1, 4, 9, 16. Rather, 25 — whether produced or not — is (sometimes) the *correct* or *required* next number. In Wittgenstein's view, for a number to be *required* certain behaviour (e.g., the giving of 25 as the next number in the above sequence) must be accepted by us, labelled "correct" and rewarded, while other behaviour (e.g., the giving of the number 116 in answer to the same question) is not accepted, is labelled "incorrect" and is penalized [51, p. 80]. An entity A can be a rule-follower only if A's behaviour takes place (or once took place) within a certain social environment, namely a society which includes the sort of behaviour just described [49, §198–200].

The Participation Condition. According to Wittgenstein, "If a rule does not compel you, then you aren't *following* a rule" [51, p. 413]. To illustrate this he introduced, as an example of a quasi-rule-follower, what he called a "living calculating machine" (or "living reading machine" [49, §157]). Such a "machine" is a human being or other creature who is given as input written signs, e.g., arithmetical symbols, English words, logical symbols, or musical notation, and who produces as output solutions to arithmetical problems, text spoken aloud, proofs of logical theorems, notes played on a piano, and suchlike.[5] (Aside from this activity, the creature may be "perfectly imbecile" [51, p. 258].) The living calculating machine may generate mathematical proofs and equations purely (to use Wittgenstein's example) as wall decoration; for him or her it would not be *wrong* (as opposed to *inconsistent*) to produce the output "13" for the input "What is the sum of 7 and 5?". For this reason the living machine is merely a quasi-rule-follower. An entity A, to be a rule-follower, must attach normative weight to behaviour that is in accordance with a rule [51, pp. 294–295].

The Training History Condition. How is A to come to meet the participation condition? Normative facts cannot be derived from natural facts, so no description of the behaviour of rule-followers entails the normativity of rule-following [51, p. 405]. Moreover, merely saying to A that (for example) she *cannot* give "13" as the answer to "7 + 5 = ?" is futile; after all, she may have just done so. Our only option is to *prescribe* A's behaviour. In this way the normativity of rule-following bottoms out in the coercion applied to novice rule-followers (see [2] for an elaboration of this point). Thus Wittgenstein concluded that "[o]ur children are ... trained to adopt a particular attitude towards a mistake in calculating" [51, p. 425]. On training, Wittgenstein remarked, "I am using the word 'trained' in a way strictly analogous to that

---

[5] The living reading-machine is also the forerunner of the inhabitant of Searle's Chinese room: see Proudfoot [38].

in which we talk of an animal being trained to do certain things. It is done by means of example, reward, punishment, and suchlike" [50, p. 77]. A's behaviour in accordance with a rule will be rule-following only if A has a history that includes such training [49, §206].

In the debates over individuation and explanation, externalism appears to have largely won the day. Contemporary discussions tend to focus, not on whether externalism is true, but on which flavour of externalism one should choose (examples are [13,27]). Amongst externalist accounts of rule-following, Wittgenstein's main rivals are teleologists, for whom what characterizes the rule-follower is that her behaviour in accordance with a rule has been selected by evolution. The canonical example of teleological approaches to rule-following is Millikan's [32] proposed solution to the "Kripke-Wittgenstein paradox." According to Millikan, the kind of rule-following that typically concerns philosophers, "purposely following an explicit or expressed rule," presupposes "purposely conforming to an implicit or unexpressed rule" [32, p. 329]. An entity A is "purposely conforming" to a rule R if and only if A has a biological purpose to behave in accordance with R, and the latter is the case if and only if conformity to R (or to a distinct rule R', from which R is derived) is the product of natural selection. On this account all evolved biological organisms purposely conform to (Millikan also says "follow") rules. Millikan allows for an intuitive distinction between "human rule-following" and the activity of less sophisticated evolved biological agents by claiming that the human rule-follower has, in addition to a biological purpose, what she calls an "ordinary human purpose" to conform to R. The subject who intends the expression "1, 4, 9, 16" to denote the initial segment of the series generated by the formula n^2 expresses, publicly or privately, such a purpose.

On Millikan's account and on other teleological analyses of rule-following, the distinction between following a rule and merely acting in accordance with a rule is a matter of evolutionary history. But this does not allow for the distinction that Wittgenstein made between, for example, the living calculating machine and the subject who gives 25 as the next number in the 1, 4, 9, 16 series because this is the "correct" answer — a distinction captured by saying that the former is *not* a rule-follower. If Millikan's analysis of rule-following is indeed to apply to the rule-following that typically concerns philosophers, she must hold that conformity to the n^2 rule, or to some other rule from which it is derived, is of evolutionary advantage to human beings. In that case, for Millikan, *both* subjects in Wittgenstein's example just mentioned will have a biological purpose to behave in accordance with, and hence both will be "purposely conforming" to or "following," the n^2 rule. The only means of marking the difference between these subjects would seem to be Millikan's "ordinary human purpose," but Millikan tells us nothing about this — and if it is a species of "interpretation," it will be of no help, for the reasons given above.

The teleologist may reply by asking what reason there is to think that Wittgenstein's distinction between the rule-follower and the quasi-rule-follower is anything other than a cultural artefact of no scientific interest. Certainly, if all that were involved here were the presence or absence of an "ordinary human purpose" or of an interpretation in the sense introduced in Sect. 2.1, that would be a slim basis from which to derive far-reaching implications for AI. But, as we have seen, Wittgenstein's distinction between the rule-follower and the quasi-rule-follower is integral to some of the topics which most concern the scientific inquirer into the mind. Substantial argument will be required if we are to disregard it just because teleosemantics provides no analysis of it.

Given the inadequacies of internalist accounts, and of teleological externalist accounts, of the distinction between the rule-follower and the quasi-rule-follower, and the seeming absence of other externalist accounts, it is not unreasonable to regard Wittgenstein's approach to rule-following as "the only straw afloat."[6]

3   The Argument from Manufacturing History

Computers are typically regarded as paradigmatic rule-followers — after all, Turing's model for the Turing machine was the human computer who "is supposed to be following fixed rules" [42, p. 436], and computers have famously been called "rule-following beasts" [25, p. 26]. Wittgenstein's discussion of rule-following gives us no reason to think that artefacts cannot be rule-followers, nor that human beings are not themselves rule-following machines. Moreover, his objections to internalist analyses undermine any opposition to machine cognition that is based upon the fact that artificial computing devices and human beings have very different innards. Wittgenstein showed only that if computers follow rules, it is not solely in virtue of their internal processes, and that, to be rule-followers, they must have a particular history and environment.

In what follows I argue that, given Wittgenstein's requirement that rule-followers be trained, most — perhaps even all — artificially intelligent computers will not *as a matter of fact* follow rules; in consequence they will not use language, reason, or possess concepts.

3.1   A Philosophical Minefield

The training that the potential rule-follower is to undergo is (Wittgenstein says) "done by means of example, reward, punishment and suchlike." Can we train computers in this way? If not (and given that Wittgenstein's account of the distinction between rule-following and quasi-rule-following is the only

---

[6] A remark, according to McClelland [30, p. 16], by Pylyshyn, and, according to Dreyfus [19, p. xiv], by Jerry Lettvin.

straw afloat) this would provide a very quick argument to the conclusion that computers do not — indeed cannot — follow rules.

In the case of human beings, including Wittgenstein's living reading-machines, training by reward and punishment requires that the learner have desires and preferences and (normally) the capacity for both pleasure (in the satisfaction of a desire) and distress (in its frustration). Such training is naturally understood as a process of creating felt pleasurable and painful states in an entity so as to bring about certain behaviour. Some theorists are happy to claim that a computer can experience pain and pleasure. For example, Dennett claims this of Cog, an upper-torso humanoid robot under development at the MIT AI Lab (see [6,9,11]). In Dennett's view, pain states are whatever natural kind states are found to generate the usual effects of pain [16, p. 228], and such states can be synthesized. Cog has a pain-pleasure system that is functionally similar to that of a human being (pain inhibits, and rewards excite, behaviour): input to Cog constitutes a pain-signal if it is of the sort that, given Cog's central system, triggers "rapid counter-measures" [17, p. 140]. In addition, Cog has innate "preferences" [17, p. 144]. If we deny that Cog *experiences* pain and pleasure, Dennett replies:

> ... on what grounds ... ? Cog may be said to have quite crude, simplistic, one-dimensional pleasure and pain, cartoon pleasure and pain if you like, but then the same might also be said of the pleasure and pain of simpler organisms; clams or houseflies, for instance. [17, p. 145]

Wittgenstein himself is often read as claiming, in sharp contrast, that it simply makes no sense to say of a machine that it is, or may be, in pain. Hacker [22], for example, is representative of many Wittgenstein scholars in stressing Wittgenstein's insistence on the importance of behaviour to judgements of psychological states: according to Wittgenstein, we attribute pain to an entity only if the entity exhibits the characteristic human manifestations of pain [52, §533]. Since machines do not behave in this way, they cannot be said to be in pain. Unfortunately for this view, the development of autonomous situated robots such as Cog suggests that sophisticated humanoid robots with suitable safety-systems *will* exhibit at least some of the behaviour characteristic of a human being in pain. (Hacker aims to pre-empt this response by claiming that, although if we were to build a machine that behaved much as humans do "it would arguably be reasonable to conceive of it as an animate, though not biological, creature" (and thus as able to feel pain), such an artefact "would not be a machine" [22, p. 169]. But the AI worker is unlikely to be persuaded by this stipulative use of the expression "machine.")

Turing early offered a compromise between the positions typified by Dennett and Hacker. In his [41] description of the training of his other sort of "unorganised machine," the "P-type" (not a neural network, but a modified Turing machine), the "pain" and "pleasure" attributed to the machine lack experiential content. A P-type has various input lines, including the pleasure (or reward) line and the pain (or punishment) line. Initially the P-type machine is unorganized in that its machine table is "largely incomplete" [41, p. 18]. "When a pain stimulus occurs all tentative entries [in the machine table] are cancelled, and when a pleasure stimulus occurs they are all made permanent" [41, p. 18]. After sufficient training a complete table usually emerges. (It is probably a P-type machine to which Turing was referring when, in considering strategies for building machines to pass the Turing test, he said "I have done some experiments with one such child-machine, and succeeded in teaching it a few things" [42, p. 457]. For an account of P-types see [14].) Turing's strategy in the case of P-types was to distinguish between, on the one hand, computational processing and, on the other, bodily awareness, experience, or consciousness; he stated that his "definitions [of reward and punishment] do not presuppose any feelings on the part of the machine" [42, p. 457].

These different positions introduce a philosophical can of worms, the mind-body problem. Fortunately it is not necessary to adjudicate between the different views of Dennett, Hacker, and Turing in order to argue that most artificially intelligent computers will not use language, possess concepts, or reason. We may even, if we wish, assume that in some cases the training of computers could be relevantly similar to the training of human rule-followers. For the question remains: would the projects of Artificial Intelligence in fact be furthered by training computers?

3.2   Training Versus Copying

In most cases training has no practical advantage over other methods of creating AI systems (programming, hand-wiring, or hand-mixing — i.e., creating connections by hand) and will often be uneconomical. In these circumstances it would be absurd to train computers.

To illustrate the claim that training mostly has no practical advantage, consider two of the devices previously discussed. First, MIT's Cog. Cog's designers are aiming to construct robots whose behaviour is prompted, not by a rigid internal world model, but directly by the complex, dynamic, and unpredictable real environment. By doing so they hope to avoid problems besetting classical AI (e.g., the frame problem), and to produce robust, flexible devices that operate in and acquire information from natural environments, respond in real time, handle multiple constraints and pursue multiple goals, scale gradually to more complex tasks, and more closely resemble biological systems. Cog will in the main be trained rather than programmed and is intended to be self-redesigning — in consequence its engineers will, as Turing said of the P-type's trainers, "often be very largely ignorant of quite what is going on inside" [42, p. 458]. Cog's designers are abandoning (for some of the time at least) the attempt to create prespecified configurations in Cog's "brain" or to monitor its moment-by-moment reactions to the environment. Nevertheless it is evident that, when building Cog II, they will not start again from scratch, proceeding by trial and error, but rather will first copy good information from the front-end processor to which Cog is attached. Copying will take the place of situated learning. As Dennett remarks:

> Once all the R&D is accomplished in the prototype, by the odyssey of a single embodied agent, the standard duplicating techniques of the computer industry could clone [an artificially intelligent computer] by the thousands as readily as they do compact discs. The finished product could thus be captured in some number of terabytes of information. [18, p. 360]

The trained prototype will have no practical advantage over the programmed clones.

Second, Turing's B-type neural networks. The B-type device produced by a training procedure and another B-type produced by copying the first are identical except in their histories. The trained B-type has no advantage over the copy with regard to the Turing test, nor any other behavioural superiority. Certainly, it is by going through training procedures that we learn how the different connections in a B-type should be modified to achieve the result we require. However, once we have that knowledge the training procedure is both in principle and in practice unnecessary. (Of course, modern connectionist devices are more complicated than Turing's B-types: in addition to the pattern of connections, the strengths of individual connections and the thresholds of neurons must be fixed (perhaps other parameters too). In some cases — a brain-sized network, for example — we might be unable to identify or fix connection strengths and neuron thresholds with sufficient accuracy, or we might be able to achieve this only by means of extensive experimentation. In these cases human-like training might be the only feasible means of production. However, the burden of proof is on the AI theorist to argue that such devices will form an important part of the future AI industry's output.)

That, in these cases and others, a trained machine has no practical advantage over a copy — and that we can, at least in principle, produce copies of trained machines — is guaranteed by Turing's [40] demonstration that, in all cases where the behaviour of a device is characterizable by some Turing machine-computable function, we can, in principle, replace the original device with a universal Turing machine programmed to compute exactly the same function. As Turing remarked, "The engineering problem of producing various machines for various jobs is replaced by the office work of 'programming' the universal machine to do these jobs" [41, p. 7]. The moral of the above examples is: where the appropriate internal states of whatever artificial computing device is in question have been identified *and where they can be produced by any method more economical than training* — for example by copying — to train the device would be perverse. From this it follows that to train a computer, just so that it could satisfy a condition on rule-following and regardless of whether or not training were the most efficient means of production, would be perverse. The computer industry will almost certainly think so, with the consequence that most, perhaps even all, computers will not follow rules.

To summarize the argument so far: given (Sect. 2) the prima facie connections between rule-following and certain psychological capacities, (Sect. 2.2) the "only straw afloat" regarding the distinction between the rule-follower and the quasi-rule-follower, (Sect. 3.1) an AI-friendly assumption regarding computers' ability to meet a requirement on rule-following, and (Sect. 3.2) the practicalities of training versus copying, we reach the conclusion: few (if any) computers will use language, possess concepts, or reason — at most those that happen to be trained rule-followers.

3.3   Traditional Aims in AI

The traditional aim of workers in AI is to build machines that *think*, where "think" is an umbrella term covering precisely such as language-use, concept-possession, and reasoning — " 'AI' wants only the genuine article: *machines with minds*, in the full and literal sense" [23, p. 2]. This aim requires machines that follow (rather than merely behave in accordance with) rules and requires in consequence that we train computers. Yet the arguments of Sect. 3.2 show that a trained device has no advantage over an untrained copy programmed to compute the same functions. AI's official goal would impose uneconomic procedures which carry no practical gain.

AI projects are already highly diverse — from military, industrial, domestic, and medical applications (eg. robotic mine clearers, robotic nuclear plant inspectors, robotic service agents, and silicon retinas) to cognitive robotics, evolutionary robotics, computational neuroethology, and computational modelling of evolution. The AI theorist does not object to categorizing the devices involved in these projects as fully-fledged AI systems, yet each is a case of quasi-rule-following rather than of genuine rule-following, as a few examples show. "Knowledge-using" systems — as in the case of Wittgenstein's living translating-machines, music composition-machines, drawing-machines, and chess-playing-machines — merely behave in accordance with rules. The creation of expert systems (or a "common-sense" system such as CYC) is the mechanization of quasi-rule-following. "Language engineering" systems that simplify text, produce lexicons, and parse natural language are quasi-rule-followers. Computer models of the functioning and evolution of living tissues and living systems (e.g., immune, social, ecological) merely behave in accordance with rules, as do the sorts of computer models involved in "mind modelling." The virtual agents and virtual societies synthesized in Artificial Life, despite being self-replicating and self-organizing, only behave in accordance with rules.

The burden of proof is on the AI theorist to demonstrate the need for AI systems to be thinking things — rule-followers rather than quasi-rule-followers. This is no easy task. Even in cognitive robotics, as the case of Cog illustrates, autonomous agents need not follow rules in order to interact with, and survive in, a real environment. Even Brooks' aim "to build completely autonomous mobile agents that co-exist in the world with humans, and are seen by those humans as intelligent beings in their own right" [5, p. 145] does not require rule-following. For not only is intelligence in his view merely a matter of "performance" [5, p. 145], the propensity for make-believe ensures that neither Brooks' planetary rovers [10] nor Cog need follow rules for people to "see" them as human-like.

At the very least, the burden of proof is on the AI theorist to demonstrate that AI's official aim of building an artificial "res cogitans" is not simply a restrictive and misguided carry-over from the long tradition of anthropocentrism in AI. To illustrate this anthropocentrism, we need turn only to the theorists already mentioned. Given Turing's famous [42] criticisms of others who required that a computer, to be intelligent, resemble a human being, Turing's own anthropocentrism is especially revealing. The premise of the Turing test is that a computer is a genuine thinker if its behaviour resembles human intellectual behaviour to the degree that an interviewer (by teletype) cannot tell which is the computer. Turing suggested, as quoted earlier, that to build "a 'thinking machine' ... [we] take a man as a whole and ... try to replace all the parts of him by machinery." Weizenbaum (who created the Eliza program) stated that AI's goal is "nothing less than to build a machine on the model of man, a robot that is to have its childhood, to learn language as a child does, to gain its knowledge of the world by sensing the world through its own organs, and ultimately to contemplate the whole domain of human thought" [48, pp. 202–203]. According to Cog's inventors, it has been assumed "from the days of Turing ... that the ultimate goal of artificial intelligence research was to build an android" and the Cog project aims at "building the ultimate humanoid" [11, p. 9].

Turing ridiculed the view that computers, just in virtue of their failure "to shine in beauty competitions" and other "irrelevant" disabilities [42, p. 435], should not be counted as genuine thinkers. He claimed that there would be "very little point," when constructing computers, in copying human physiology, since this "would be rather like putting a lot of work into cars which walked on legs instead of continuing to use wheels" [41, pp. 12–13]. Despite this stance, he described machines in highly anthropomorphic terms. Turing's aim was to produce in a machine "discipline and initiative" [41, p. 21] and he suggested "that the education of the machine should be entrusted to some highly competent schoolmaster" [43, p. 130] — the teaching of the P-type was to be "analogous to the kind of process by which a child would really be taught" [41, p. 20]. His "child-machine" is a "creature" which is compared to Helen Keller, could not be sent to school "without the other children making excessive fun of it" [42, p. 456], and will have "homework" [42, p. 458].

Some of the anthropocentrism and anthropomorphism in the AI literature is, to use Dennett's term, "conceptually innocent" — it is not meant seriously, stems from genuine engineering considerations, or is intended to attract funding. However, just as much is unwitting make-believe without practical or theoretical justification. Dennett himself is another telling example, since he vigorously denounces "origin chauvinism" [17, p. 136]. According to Dennett, Cog is to have an "infancy and childhood" [18, p. 358]. Notwithstanding Turing's claim that "there was little point in trying to make a 'thinking machine' more human by dressing it up in ... artificial flesh" [42, p. 434], Cog will also have a face and readable facial expressions. Cog "will have to learn from experience, experience it will gain in the rough-and-tumble environment of the real world" [17, p. 139]. Cog will "want to keep its mother's face in view" and will "work hard to keep mother from turning away" [17, p. 140]. Cog is to be "as human as possible in its wants and fears, likes and dislikes" and is to "delight in learning, abhor error, strive for novelty, recognise progress" [17, p. 141]. While the building of situated behaviour-based robots is a persuasive alternative to what Dennett has called "bedridden" programs, why is Cog to be given a *face*, unless its inventors are making believe that Cog is a human or other familiar animate being? Moreover, Dennett's anthropocentrism goes far beyond simply treating Cog as an intentional system; the latter involves explaining and predicting the device's behaviour in intentional terms, but not giving it a *mother*. As with Turing, many of the human characteristics Dennett assigns to computers are prima facie irrelevant to the projects of Artificial Intelligence.

Examples of anthropocentrism and anthropomorphism abound in AI. One recent best-selling text by an AI practitioner claims that future computers will go to church for meditation and prayer and that by 2029 "[m]any of the leading artists [will be] machines" [29, p. 223].[7] Frequently the professional literature is no more restrained. For Braitenberg [3], his (very simple) imaginary robot vehicles are "inquisitive," "friendly" (p. 46), "optimistic" (p. 83), possess "egotism" (p. 81), "free will" (p. 68) and "the a priori concept of 2-dimensional space" (p. 41), "ponder over their decisions" (p. 19), and "[w]hile dreaming and sleepwalking, [transform] the world" (p. 83). The engineers who actually built Braitenberg's vehicles out of specially modified LEGO bricks labelled the vehicles "timid," "indecisive," "paranoid," "dogged," "insecure," "inhumane," and "frantic" (the last is allegedly a "philosophical creature" that "does nothing but think") [26]. Yamamoto [54] predicates joy, desperation, fatigue, sadness, and friendliness of his robot vacuum cleaner.

Requiring that AI systems, like human beings, use language, possess concepts, and reason — that is to say, follow rules of meaning and grammar, categorization, inference, and so on — looks like one more example of anthropocentrism in AI. For if the rhetoric of AI is disregarded, an AI system's (in practice) inability to follow rules, use language, possess concepts, or reason is an "irrelevant disability" (Turing's phrase) — as unimportant as the lack of a face or mother.

---

[7] See Proudfoot [37] for elaboration.

In summary, either none of language-use, concept-possession, or reasoning requires rule-following, or the only straw afloat with regard to the distinction between rule-following and quasi-rule-following is not in fact seaworthy, or the traditional aim of AI requires revision. My money is on the last.[8]

References

1. A. Ambrose (1935). Finitism in mathematics (I and II). *Mind*, 35:186–203, 317–340.

2. G. E. M. Anscombe (1978). Rules, rights and promises. *Midwest Studies in Philosophy*, 3:318–323.

3. V. Braitenberg (1984). *Vehicles: Experiments in Synthetic Psychology*. MIT Press, Cambridge, MA.

4. R. A. Brooks (1990). Elephants don't play chess. *Robotics and Autonomous Systems*, 6:3–15.

5. R. A. Brooks (1991). Intelligence without representation. *Artificial Intelligence*, 47:139–159.

6. R. A. Brooks (1994). Coherent behaviour from many adaptive processes. In D. Cliff et al., eds, *From Animals to Animats*, volume 3. MIT Press, Cambridge, MA.

7. R. A. Brooks (1995). Intelligence without reason. In L. Steels and R. A. Brooks, eds, *The Artificial Life Route to Artificial Intelligence*. Lawrence Erlbaum, Hillsdale, NJ.

8. R. A. Brooks (1999). *Cambrian Intelligence: The Early History of the New AI*. Bradford Books, Cambridge, MA.

9. R. A. Brooks, C. Breazeal, R. Irie, C. C. Kemp, M. Marjanović, B. Scassellati, and M. M. Williamson (1998). Alternative essences of intelligence. In *Proceedings of the Fifteenth National Conference on Artificial Intelligence (AAAI-98)*. AAAI Press, Maddison, WI.

10. R. A. Brooks and A. M. Flynn (1989). Fast, cheap, and out of control. Technical report, Massachusetts Institute of Technology Artificial Intelligence Laboratory. Memo 1182.

11. R. A. Brooks and L. A. Stein (1994). Building brains for bodies. *Autonomous Robots*, 1:7–25.

12. A. Clark (1997). *Being There*. MIT Press, Cambridge, MA.

13. A. Clark and D. Chalmers (1998). The extended mind. *Analyst*, 4(5).

14. B. J. Copeland and D. Proudfoot (1996). On Alan Turing's anticipation of connectionism. *Synthese*, 108:361–377.

15. B. J. Copeland and D. Proudfoot (1999). Alan Turing's forgotten ideas in computer science. *Scientific American*, 280(4):76–81.

16. D. C. Dennett (1978). Why you can't make a computer that feels pain. In D. C. Dennett, *Brainstorms*. Bradford Books, Montgomery, VT.

[8] Thanks to John Andreae, Daniel Dennett, and especially Jack Copeland for valuable written comments. Thanks also to Jonathan Adler and Rodney Brooks for helpful discussion. Research on which this paper draws was supported in part by Marsden Grant no. UOC905.

17. D. C. Dennett (1994). The practical requirements for making a conscious robot. *Philosophical Transactions of the Royal Society of London*, 349:133–146.
18. D. C. Dennett (1997). When HAL kills, who's to blame? Computer ethics. In D. G. Stork, ed., *Hal's Legacy: 2001's Computer as Dream and Reality*. MIT Press, Cambridge, MA.
19. H. L. Dreyfus (1992). *What Computers Still Can't Do*. MIT Press, Cambridge, MA.
20. J. A. Fodor (1975). *The Language of Thought*. Crowell, New York.
21. K. Furukawa, D. Michie, and S. Muggleton, eds (1999). *Machine Intelligence*, volume 15. Oxford University Press, New York.
22. P. M. S. Hacker (1990). *Wittgenstein, Meaning and Mind*. Blackwell, Oxford.
23. J. Haugeland (1985). *Artificial Intelligence: The Very Idea*. Bradford Books, Cambridge, MA.
24. A. Hodges (1992). *Alan Turing: The Enigma*. Vintage, London.
25. D. Hofstadter (1980). *Gödel, Escher, Bach: An Eternal Golden Braid*. Penguin Books, Marmondsworth.
26. D. W. Hogg, F. Martin, and M. Resnick (1991). Braitenberg creatures. Epistemology and learning. Memo #13. MIT Media Laboratory.
27. R. Kirk (1994). The trouble with ultra-externalism. *Proceedings of the Aristotelian Society*, 94:293–307.
28. S. Kripke (1982). *Wittgenstein on Rules and Private Language: An Elementary Exposition*. Blackwell, Oxford.
29. R. Kurzweil (1999). *The Age of Spiritual Machines: When Computers Exceed Human Intelligence*. Viking Press, New York.
30. J. McClelland (1987). The basis of lawful behaviour: rules or connections? *The Computers and Philosophy Newsletter*, 2:10–16.
31. B. Meltzer and D. Michie, eds (1969). *Machine Intelligence*, volume 5. Edinburgh University Press.
32. R. G. Millikan (1990). Truth rules, hoverflies, and the Kripke-Wittgenstein paradox. *Philosophical Review*, 99:323–354.
33. M. Nedo and M. Ranchetti (1983). *Wittgenstein: Sein Leben in Bildern und Texten*. Suhrkamp Verlag, Frankfurt am Main.
34. A. Newell (1980). Physical symbol systems. *Cognitive Science*, 4:135–183.
35. A. Newell and H. Simon (1981). Computer science as empirical inquiry: Symbols and search. In J. Haugeland, ed., *Mind Design*. Bradford Books, Cambridge, MA.
36. D. Proudfoot (1997). On Wittgenstein on cognitive science. *Philosophy*, 72:189–217.
37. D. Proudfoot (1999). How human can they get? *Science*, 284:745.
38. D. Proudfoot (2002). Wittgenstein's anticipation of the Chinese room. In M. Preston and J. Bishop, eds, *Views into the Chinese Room*. Oxford University Press.
39. C. Teuscher (2002). *Turing's Connectionism. An Investigation of Neural Network Architectures*. Springer-Verlag, London.
40. A. M. Turing (1937). On computable numbers, with an application to the Entscheidungsproblem. *Proceedings of the London Mathematical Society*, Series 2, 42:230–265, 1936–37.
41. A. M. Turing (1948). *Intelligent machinery*. National Physical Laboratory Report. In Metzer and Michie [31]. A digital facsimile of the original typescript is in The Turing Archive for the History of Computing, http://www.AlanTuring.net/intelligent_machinery.

42. A. M. Turing (1950). Computing machinery and intelligence. *Mind*, 59:433–460.
43. A. M. Turing (1951). *Intelligent machinery: a heretical view.* In S. Turing [45].
44. A. M. Turing (1952). *Can automatic calculating machines be said to think?* In Furukawa et al. [21] (edited by B. J. Copeland).
45. S. Turing (1959). *Alan M. Turing.* Heffer & Sons, Cambridge.
46. T. van Gelder (1995). What might cognition be, if not computation? *Journal of Philosophy*, 91:345–381.
47. T. van Gelder (1998). The dynamical hypothesis in cognitive science. *Behavioral and Brain Sciences*, 21:615–628.
48. J. Weizenbaum (1976). *Computer Power and Human Reason: From Judgement to Calculation.* W. H. Freeman, San Francisco.
49. L. Wittgenstein (1953). *Philosophical Investigations.* Blackwell, Oxford. Translated by G. E. M. Anscombe.
50. L. Wittgenstein (1965). *The Blue and Brown Books.* Harper, New York.
51. L. Wittgenstein (1967). *Remarks on the Foundations of Mathematics.* Blackwell, Oxford, 2nd edition. Edited by G. H. von Wright, R. Rhees, and G. E. M. Anscombe. Translated by G. E. M. Anscombe.
52. L. Wittgenstein (1967). *Zettel.* Blackwell, Oxford. Edited by G. E. M. Anscombe and G. H. von Wright. Translated by G. E. M. Anscombe.
53. L. Wittgenstein (1976). *Wittgenstein's Lectures on the Foundations of Mathematics, Cambridge, 1939.* Cornell University Press, Ithaca, NY. Edited by C. Diamond.
54. M. Yamamoto (1993). "SOZZY": A hormone-driven autonomous vacuum cleaner. *Proceedings of the International Society for Optical Engineering*, 2058:211–222.

The Law of Accelerating Returns*

Ray Kurzweil

KurzweilAI.net

Summary. An analysis of the history of technology shows that technological change is exponential, contrary to the common-sense "intuitive linear" view. So we won't experience 100 years of progress in the 21st century — it will be more like 20,000 years of progress (at today's rate). The "returns," such as chip speed and cost-effectiveness, also increase exponentially. There's even exponential growth in the rate of exponential growth. Within a few decades, machine intelligence will surpass human intelligence, leading to The Singularity — technological change so rapid and profound it represents a rupture in the fabric of human history. The implications include the merger of biological and nonbiological intelligence, immortal software-based humans, and ultra-high levels of intelligence that expand outward in the universe at the speed of light.

You will get $40 trillion just by reading this essay and understanding what it says. For complete details, see below. (It's true that authors will do just about anything to keep your attention, but I'm serious about this statement. Until I return to a further explanation, however, do read the first sentence of this paragraph carefully.)

Now back to the future: it's widely misunderstood. Our forebears expected the future to be pretty much like their present, which had been pretty much like their past. Although exponential trends did exist a thousand years ago, they were at that very early stage where an exponential trend is so flat that it looks like no trend at all. So their lack of expectations was largely fulfilled. Today, in accordance with the common wisdom, everyone expects continuous technological progress and the social repercussions that follow. But the future will be far more surprising than most observers realize: few have truly internalized the implications of the fact that the rate of change itself is accelerating.

1 The Intuitive Linear View Versus the Historical Exponential View

Most long range forecasts of technical feasibility in future time periods dramatically underestimate the power of future technology because they are based on what I call the "intuitive linear" view of technological progress rather than the "historical exponential view." To express this another way, it is not

---

* The complete article was first published on KurzweilAI.net on March 7, 2001.
  http://www.kurzweilai.net.

the case that we will experience a hundred years of progress in the twenty-first century; rather we will witness on the order of twenty thousand years of progress (at *today's* rate of progress, that is).

This disparity in outlook comes up frequently in a variety of contexts, for example, the discussion of the ethical issues that Bill Joy raised in his controversial WIRED cover story, Why The Future Doesn't Need Us. Bill and I have been frequently paired in a variety of venues as pessimist and optimist respectively. Although I'm expected to criticize Bill's position, and indeed I do take issue with his prescription of relinquishment, I nonetheless usually end up defending Joy on the key issue of feasibility. Recently a Noble Prize winning panelist dismissed Bill's concerns, exclaiming that, "we're not going to see self-replicating nanoengineered entities for a hundred years." I pointed out that 100 years was indeed a reasonable estimate of the amount of technical progress required to achieve this particular milestone *at today's rate of progress*. But because we're doubling the rate of progress every decade, we'll see a century of progress — *at today's rate* — in only 25 calendar years.

When people think of a future period, they intuitively assume that the current rate of progress will continue for future periods. However, careful consideration of the pace of technology shows that the rate of progress is not constant, but it is human nature to adapt to the changing pace, so the intuitive view is that the pace will continue at the current rate. Even for those of us who have been around long enough to experience how the pace increases over time, our unexamined intuition nonetheless provides the impression that progress changes at the rate that we have experienced recently. From the mathematician's perspective, a primary reason for this is that an exponential curve approximates a straight line when viewed for a brief duration. So even though the rate of progress in the very recent past (e.g., this past year) is far greater than it was ten years ago (let alone a hundred or a thousand years ago), our memories are nonetheless dominated by our very recent experience. It is typical, therefore, that even sophisticated commentators, when considering the future, extrapolate the current pace of change over the next 10 years or 100 years to determine their expectations. This is why I call this way of looking at the future the "intuitive linear" view.

But a serious assessment of the history of technology shows that technological change is exponential. In exponential growth, we find that a key measurement such as computational power is multiplied by a constant factor for each unit of time (e.g., doubling every year) rather than just being added to incrementally. Exponential growth is a feature of any evolutionary process, of which technology is a primary example. One can examine the data in different ways, on different time scales, and for a wide variety of technologies ranging from electronic to biological, and the acceleration of progress and growth applies. Indeed, we find not just simple exponential growth, but "double" exponential growth, meaning that the rate of exponential growth is itself growing exponentially. These observations do not rely merely on an assumption of the continuation of Moore's law (i.e., the exponential shrinking of transistor sizes on an integrated circuit), but is based on a rich model of diverse technological processes. What it clearly shows is that technology, particularly the pace of technological change, advances (at least) exponentially, not linearly, and has been doing so since the advent of technology, indeed since the advent of evolution on Earth.

I emphasize this point because it is the most important failure that would-be prognosticators make in considering future trends. Most technology forecasts ignore altogether this "historical exponential view" of technological progress. That is why people tend to overestimate what can be achieved in the short term (because we tend to leave out necessary details), but underestimate what can be achieved in the long term (because the exponential growth is ignored).

2   The Law of Accelerating Returns

We can organize these observations into what I call the law of accelerating returns as follows:

- Evolution applies positive feedback in that the more capable methods resulting from one stage of evolutionary progress are used to create the next stage. As a result, the rate of progress of an evolutionary process increases exponentially over time. Over time, the "order" of the information embedded in the evolutionary process (i.e., the measure of how well the information fits a purpose, which in evolution is survival) increases.
- A correlate of the above observation is that the "returns" of an evolutionary process (e.g., the speed, cost-effectiveness, or overall "power" of a process) increase exponentially over time.
- In another positive feedback loop, as a particular evolutionary process (e.g., computation) becomes more effective (e.g., cost effective), greater resources are deployed toward the further progress of that process. This results in a second level of exponential growth (i.e., the rate of exponential growth itself grows exponentially).
- Biological evolution is one such evolutionary process.
- Technological evolution is another such evolutionary process. Indeed, the emergence of the first technology creating species resulted in the new evolutionary process of technology. Therefore, technological evolution is an outgrowth of — and a continuation of — biological evolution.
- A specific paradigm (a method or approach to solving a problem, e.g., shrinking transistors on an integrated circuit as an approach to making more powerful computers) provides exponential growth until the method exhausts its potential. When this happens, a paradigm shift (i.e., a fundamental change in the approach) occurs, which enables exponential growth to continue.

If we apply these principles at the highest level of evolution on Earth, the first step, the creation of cells, introduced the paradigm of biology. The subsequent emergence of DNA provided a digital method to record the results of evolutionary experiments. Then, the evolution of a species who combined rational thought with an opposable appendage (i.e., the thumb) caused a fundamental paradigm shift from biology to technology. The upcoming primary paradigm shift will be from biological thinking to a hybrid combining biological and nonbiological thinking. This hybrid will include "biologically inspired" processes resulting from the reverse engineering of biological brains.

If we examine the timing of these steps, we see that the process has continuously accelerated. The evolution of life forms required billions of years for the first steps (e.g., primitive cells); later on progress accelerated. During the Cambrian explosion, major paradigm shifts took only tens of millions of years. Later on, humanoids developed over a period of millions of years, and homo sapiens over a period of only hundreds of thousands of years.

With the advent of a technology-creating species, the exponential pace became too fast for evolution through DNA-guided protein synthesis and moved on to human-created technology. Technology goes beyond mere tool making; it is a process of creating ever more powerful technology using the tools from the previous round of innovation. In this way, human technology is distinguished from the tool making of other species. There is a record of each stage of technology, and each new stage of technology builds on the order of the previous stage.

The first technological steps-sharp edges, fire, the wheel — took tens of thousands of years. For people living in this era, there was little noticeable technological change in even a thousand years. By 1000 A.D., progress was much faster and a paradigm shift required only a century or two. In the nineteenth century we saw more technological change than in the nine centuries preceding it. Then in the first twenty years of the twentieth century, we saw more advancement than in all of the nineteenth century. Now, paradigm shifts occur in only a few years time. The World Wide Web did not exist in anything like its present form just a few years ago; it didn't exist at all a decade ago.

The paradigm shift rate (i.e., the overall rate of technical progress) is currently doubling (approximately) every decade; that is, paradigm shift times are halving every decade (and the rate of acceleration is itself growing exponentially). So, the technological progress in the twenty-first century will be equivalent to what would require (in the linear view) on the order of 200 centuries. In contrast, the twentieth century saw only about 25 years of progress (again at today's rate of progress) since we have been speeding up to current rates. So the twenty-first century will see almost a thousand times greater technological change than its predecessor.

3   The Singularity Is Near

To appreciate the nature and significance of the coming "singularity," it is important to ponder the nature of exponential growth. Toward this end, I am fond of telling the tale of the inventor of chess and his patron, the emperor of China. In response to the emperor's offer of a reward for his new beloved game, the inventor asked for a single grain of rice on the first square, two on the second square, four on the third, and so on. The Emperor quickly granted this seemingly benign and humble request. One version of the story has the emperor going bankrupt as the 63 doublings ultimately totaled 18 million trillion grains of rice. At ten grains of rice per square inch, this requires rice fields covering twice the surface area of the Earth, oceans included. Another version of the story has the inventor losing his head.

It should be pointed out that as the emperor and the inventor went through the first half of the chess board, things were fairly uneventful. The inventor was given spoonfuls of rice, then bowls of rice, then barrels. By the end of the first half of the chess board, the inventor had accumulated one large field's worth (4 billion grains), and the emperor did start to take notice. It was as they progressed through the second half of the chessboard that the situation quickly deteriorated. Incidentally, with regard to the doublings of computation, that's about where we stand now — there have been slightly more than 32 doublings of performance since the first programmable computers were invented during World War II.

This is the nature of exponential growth. Although technology grows in the exponential domain, we humans live in a linear world. So technological trends are not noticed as small levels of technological power are doubled. Then seemingly out of nowhere, a technology explodes into view. For example, when the Internet went from 20,000 to 80,000 nodes over a two year period during the 1980s, this progress remained hidden from the general public. A decade later, when it went from 20 million to 80 million nodes in the same amount of time, the impact was rather conspicuous.

As exponential growth continues to accelerate into the first half of the twenty-first century, it will appear to explode into infinity, at least from the limited and linear perspective of contemporary humans. The progress will ultimately become so fast that it will rupture our ability to follow it. It will literally get out of our control. The illusion that we have our hand "on the plug," will be dispelled.

Can the pace of technological progress continue to speed up indefinitely? Is there not a point where humans are unable to think fast enough to keep up with it? With regard to unenhanced humans, clearly so. But what would a thousand scientists, each a thousand times more intelligent than human scientists today, and each operating a thousand times faster than contemporary humans (because the information processing in their primarily nonbiological brains is faster) accomplish? One year would be like a millennium. What would they come up with?

Well, for one thing, they would come up with technology to become even more intelligent (because their intelligence is no longer of fixed capacity). They would change their own thought processes to think even faster. When the scientists evolve to be a million times more intelligent and operate a million times faster, then an hour would result in a century of progress (in today's terms).

This, then, is the Singularity. The Singularity is technological change so rapid and so profound that it represents a rupture in the fabric of human history. Some would say that we cannot comprehend the Singularity, at least with our current level of understanding, and that it is impossible, therefore, to look past its "event horizon" and make sense of what lies beyond.

My view is that despite our profound limitations of thought, constrained as we are today to a mere hundred trillion interneuronal connections in our biological brains, we nonetheless have sufficient powers of abstraction to make meaningful statements about the nature of life after the Singularity. Most importantly, it is my view that the intelligence that will emerge will continue to represent the human civilization, which is already a human-machine civilization. This will be the next step in evolution, the next high level paradigm shift.

To put the concept of Singularity into perspective, let's explore the history of the word itself. Singularity is a familiar word meaning a unique event with profound implications. In mathematics, the term implies infinity, the explosion of value that occurs when dividing a constant by a number that gets closer and closer to zero. In physics, similarly, a singularity denotes an event or location of infinite power. At the center of a black hole, matter is so dense that its gravity is infinite. As nearby matter and energy are drawn into the black hole, an event horizon separates the region from the rest of the Universe. It constitutes a rupture in the fabric of space and time. The Universe itself is said to have begun with just such a Singularity.

In the 1950s, John Von Neumann was quoted as saying that "the ever accelerating progress of technology ... gives the appearance of approaching some essential singularity in the history of the race beyond which human affairs, as we know them, could not continue." In the 1960s, I. J. Good wrote of an "intelligence explosion," resulting from intelligent machines designing their next generation without human intervention. In 1986, Vernor Vinge, a mathematician and computer scientist at San Diego State University, wrote about a rapidly approaching technological "singularity" in his science fiction novel, *Marooned in Realtime*. Then in 1993, Vinge presented a paper to a NASA-organized symposium which described the Singularity as an impending event resulting primarily from the advent of "entities with greater than human intelligence," which Vinge saw as the harbinger of a run-away phenomenon.

From my perspective, the Singularity has many faces. It represents the nearly vertical phase of exponential growth where the rate of growth is so extreme that technology appears to be growing at infinite speed. Of course, from a mathematical perspective, there is no discontinuity, no rupture, and the growth rates remain finite, albeit extraordinarily large. But from our *currently* limited perspective, this imminent event appears to be an acute and abrupt break in the continuity of progress. However, I emphasize the word "currently," because one of the salient implications of the Singularity will be a change in the nature of our ability to understand. In other words, we will become vastly smarter as we merge with our technology.

When I wrote my first book, *The Age of Intelligent Machines*, in the 1980s, I ended the book with the specter of the emergence of machine intelligence greater than human intelligence, but found it difficult to look beyond this event horizon. Now having thought about its implications for the past 20 years, I feel that we are indeed capable of understanding the many facets of this threshold, one that will transform all spheres of human life.

Consider a few examples of the implications. The bulk of our experiences will shift from real reality to virtual reality. Most of the intelligence of our civilization will ultimately be nonbiological, which by the end of this century will be trillions of trillions of times more powerful than human intelligence. However, to address often expressed concerns, this does not imply the end of biological intelligence, even if thrown from its perch of evolutionary superiority. Moreover, it is important to note that the nonbiological forms will be derivative of biological design. In other words, our civilization will remain human, indeed in many ways more exemplary of what we regard as human than it is today, although our understanding of the term will move beyond its strictly biological origins.

Many observers have nonetheless expressed alarm at the emergence of forms of nonbiological intelligence superior to human intelligence. The potential to augment our own intelligence through intimate connection with other thinking mediums does not necessarily alleviate the concern, as some people have expressed the wish to remain "unenhanced" while at the same time keeping their place at the top of the intellectual food chain. My view is that the likely outcome is that on the one hand, from the perspective of biological humanity, these superhuman intelligences will appear to be their transcendent servants, satisfying their needs and desires. On the other hand, fulfilling the wishes of a revered biological legacy will occupy only a trivial portion of the intellectual power that the Singularity will bring.

Needless to say, the Singularity will transform all aspects of our lives, social, sexual, and economic, which I explore herewith.

4   Wherefrom Moore's Law

Before considering further the implications of the Singularity, let's examine the wide range of technologies that are subject to the law of accelerating returns. The exponential trend that has gained the greatest public recognition has become known as "Moore's Law" (see also Fig. 1). Gordon Moore, one of the inventors of integrated circuits, and then Chairman of Intel, noted in the mid 1970s that we could squeeze twice as many transistors on an integrated circuit every 24 months. Given that the electrons have less distance to travel, the circuits also run twice as fast, providing an overall quadrupling of computational power.

After sixty years of devoted service, Moore's Law will die a dignified death no later than the year 2019. By that time, transistor features will be just a few atoms in width, and the strategy of ever finer photolithography will have run its course. So, will that be the end of the exponential growth of computing?

Don't bet on it.

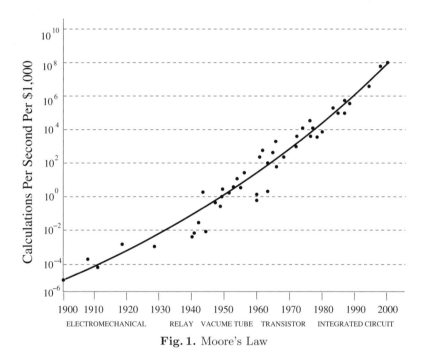

Fig. 1. Moore's Law

5   Moore's Law Was Not the First, but the Fifth Paradigm to Provide for Exponential Growth of Computing

Each time one paradigm runs out of steam, another picks up the pace.

It is important to note that Moore's Law of Integrated Circuits was not the first, but the fifth paradigm to provide accelerating price-performance. Computing devices have been consistently multiplying in power (per unit of time) from the mechanical calculating devices used in the 1890 U.S. Census, to Turing's relay-based "Robinson" machine that cracked the Nazi enigma code, to the CBS vacuum tube computer that predicted the election of Eisenhower, to the transistor-based machines used in the first space launches, to the integrated-circuit-based personal computer which I used to dictate (and automatically transcribe) this essay.

But I noticed something else surprising. When I plotted the 49 machines on an exponential graph (where a straight line means exponential growth), I didn't get a straight line. What I got was another exponential curve. In other words, there's exponential growth in the rate of exponential growth. Computer speed (per unit cost) doubled every three years between 1910 and 1950, doubled every two years between 1950 and 1966, and is now doubling every year.

But where does Moore's Law come from? What is behind this remarkably predictable phenomenon? I have seen relatively little written about the ultimate source of this trend. Is it just "a set of industry expectations and goals," as Randy Isaac, head of basic science at IBM contends? Or is there something more profound going on?

In my view, it is one manifestation (among many) of the exponential growth of the evolutionary process that is technology. The exponential growth of computing is a marvelous quantitative example of the exponentially growing returns from an evolutionary process. We can also express the exponential growth of computing in terms of an accelerating pace: it took ninety years to achieve the first MIPS (million instructions per second) per thousand dollars, now we add one MIPS per thousand dollars every day.

Moore's Law narrowly refers to the number of transistors on an integrated circuit of fixed size, and sometimes has been expressed even more narrowly in terms of transistor feature size. But rather than feature size (which is only one contributing factor), or even number of transistors, I think the most appropriate measure to track is computational speed per unit cost. This takes into account many levels of "cleverness" (i.e., innovation, which is to say, technological evolution). In addition to all of the innovation in integrated circuits, there are multiple layers of innovation in computer design, e.g., pipelining, parallel processing, instruction look-ahead, instruction and memory caching, and many others.

It is obvious what the sixth paradigm will be after Moore's Law runs out of steam during the second decade of this century. Chips today are flat (although it does require up to 20 layers of material to produce one layer of circuitry). Our brain, in contrast, is organized in three dimensions. We live in a three dimensional world, why not use the third dimension? The human brain actually uses a very inefficient electrochemical digital controlled analog computational process. The bulk of the calculations are done in the interneuronal connections at a speed of only about 200 calculations per second (in each connection), which is about ten million times slower than contemporary electronic circuits. But the brain gains its prodigious powers from its extremely parallel organization *in three dimensions*. There are many technologies in the wings that build circuitry in three dimensions. Nanotubes, for example, which are already working in laboratories, build circuits from pentagonal arrays of carbon atoms. One cubic inch of nanotube circuitry would be a million times more powerful than the human brain. There are more than enough new computing technologies now being researched, including three-dimensional silicon chips, optical computing, crystalline computing, DNA computing, and quantum computing, to keep the law of accelerating returns as applied to computation going for a long time.

Thus the (double) exponential growth of computing is broader than Moore's Law, which refers to only one of its paradigms. And this accelerating growth of computing is, in turn, part of the yet broader phenomenon of the accelerating pace of any evolutionary process. Observers are quick to criticize extrapolations of an exponential trend on the basis that the trend is bound to run out of "resources." The classical example is when a species happens upon a new habitat (e.g., rabbits in Australia), the species' numbers will grow exponentially for a time, but then hit a limit when resources such as food and space run out.

But the resources underlying the exponential growth of an evolutionary process are relatively unbounded:

1. The (ever growing) order of the evolutionary process itself. Each stage of evolution provides more powerful tools for the next. In biological evolution, the advent of DNA allowed more powerful and faster evolutionary "experiments." Later, setting the "designs" of animal body plans during the Cambrian explosion allowed rapid evolutionary development of other body organs such as the brain. Or to take a more recent example, the advent of computer assisted design tools allows rapid development of the next generation of computers.

2. The "chaos" of the environment in which the evolutionary process takes place and which provides the options for further diversity. In biological evolution, diversity enters the process in the form of mutations and ever changing environmental conditions. In technological evolution, human ingenuity combined with ever changing market conditions keep the process of innovation going.

The maximum potential of matter and energy to contain intelligent processes is a valid issue. But according to my models, we won't approach those limits during this century (but this will become an issue within a couple of centuries).

We also need to distinguish between the "S" curve (an "S" stretched to the right, comprising very slow, virtually unnoticeable growth — followed by very rapid growth — followed by a flattening out as the process approaches an asymptote) that is characteristic of any specific technological paradigm and the continuing exponential growth that is characteristic of the ongoing evolutionary process of technology. Specific paradigms, such as Moore's Law, do ultimately reach levels at which exponential growth is no longer feasible. Thus Moore's Law is an S curve. But the growth of computation is an ongoing exponential (at least until we "saturate" the Universe with the intelligence of our human-machine civilization, but that will not be a limit in this coming century). In accordance with the law of accelerating returns, paradigm shift, also called innovation, turns the S curve of any specific paradigm into a continuing exponential. A new paradigm (e.g., three-dimensional circuits) takes over when the old paradigm approaches its natural limit. This has already happened at least four times in the history of computation. This difference also distinguishes the tool making of non-human species, in which the mastery of a tool-making (or using) skill by each animal is characterized by an abruptly ending S shaped learning curve, versus human-created technology, which has followed an exponential pattern of growth and acceleration since its inception.

6   DNA Sequencing, Memory, Communications, the Internet, and Miniaturization

This "law of accelerating returns" applies to all of technology, indeed to any true evolutionary process, and can be measured with remarkable precision in information based technologies. There are a great many examples of the exponential growth implied by the law of accelerating returns in technologies as varied as DNA sequencing, communication speeds, electronics of all kinds, and even in the rapidly shrinking size of technology. The Singularity results not from the exponential explosion of computation alone, but rather from the interplay and myriad synergies that will result from manifold intertwined technological revolutions. Also, keep in mind that every point on the exponential growth curves underlying this panoply of technologies represents an intense human drama of innovation and competition. It is remarkable therefore that these chaotic processes result in such smooth and predictable exponential trends.

For example, when the human genome scan started fourteen years ago, critics pointed out that given the speed with which the genome could then be scanned, it would take thousands of years to finish the project. Yet the fifteen year project was nonetheless completed slightly ahead of schedule.

Of course we expect to see exponential growth in electronic memories such as RAM.

7   The Law of Accelerating Returns Applied to the Growth of Computation

The following provides a brief overview of the law of accelerating returns as it applies to the double exponential growth of computation (see also Fig. 2).

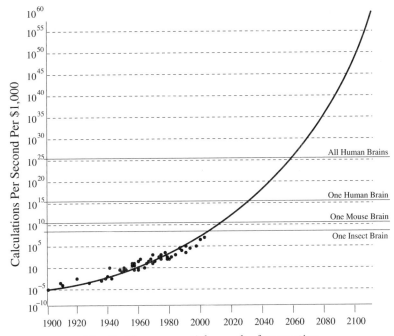

Fig. 2. The exponential growth of computing

This model considers the impact of the growing power of the technology to foster its own next generation. For example, with more powerful computers and related technology, we have the tools and the knowledge to design yet more powerful computers, and to do so more quickly.

Note that the data for the year 2000 and beyond assume neural net connection calculations as it is expected that this type of calculation will ultimately dominate, particularly in emulating human brain functions. This type of calculation is less expensive than conventional (e.g., Pentium III/IV) calculations by a factor of at least 100 (particularly if implemented using digital controlled analog electronics, which would correspond well to the brain's digital controlled analog electrochemical processes). A factor of 100 translates into approximately 6 years (today) and less than 6 years later in the twenty-first century.

My estimate of brain capacity is 100 billion neurons times an average 1,000 connections per neuron (with the calculations taking place primarily in the connections) times 200 calculations per second. Although these estimates are conservatively high, one can find higher and lower estimates. However, even much higher (or lower) estimates by orders of magnitude only shift the prediction by a relatively small number of years.

Some prominent dates from this analysis include the following:

- We achieve one Human Brain capability 2×10^{16} cps for $1,000 around the year 2023.
- We achieve one Human Brain capability 2×10^{16} cps for one cent around the year 2037.
- We achieve one Human Race capability 2×10^{26} cps for $1,000 around the year 2049.
- We achieve one Human Race capability 2×10^{26} cps for one cent around the year 2059.

The Model considers the following variables:

- V: Velocity (i.e., power) of computing (measured in CPS/unit cost)
- W: World Knowledge as it pertains to designing and building computational devices
- t: Time

The assumptions of the model are

$$V = C_1 \cdot W$$

In other words, computer power is a linear function of the knowledge of how to build computers. This is actually a conservative assumption. In general, innovations improve V (computer power) by a multiple, not in an additive way. Independent innovations multiply each other's effect. For example, a circuit advance such as CMOS, a more efficient IC wiring methodology, and a processor innovation such as pipelining all increase V by independent multiples.

$$W = C_2 \cdot \int_0^t V$$

In other words, W (knowledge) is cumulative, and the instantaneous increment to knowledge is proportional to V.

This gives us

- $W = C_1 \cdot C_2 \cdot \int_0^t W$
- $W = C_1 \cdot C_2 \cdot C_3^{C_4 \cdot t}$
- $V = C_1^2 \cdot C_2 \cdot C_3^{C_4 \cdot t}$

Simplifying the constants, we get

- $V = C_a \cdot C_b^{C_c \cdot t}$

So this is a formula for "accelerating" (i.e., exponentially growing) returns, a "regular Moore's Law."

As I mentioned above, the data shows exponential growth in the rate of exponential growth. (We doubled computer power every three years early in the twentieth century, every two years in the middle of the century, and close to every one year during the 1990s.)

Let's factor in another exponential phenomenon, which is the growing resources for computation. Not only is each (constant cost) device getting more powerful as a function of W, but the resources deployed for computation are also growing exponentially.

We now have:

- N: Expenditures for computation
- $V = C_1 \cdot W$ (as before)
- $N = C_4^{C_5 \cdot t}$ (Expenditure for computation is growing at its own exponential rate)
- $W = C_2 \cdot \int_0^t (N \cdot V)$

As before, world knowledge is accumulating, and the instantaneous increment is proportional to the amount of computation, which equals the resources deployed for computation (N) * the power of each (constant cost) device.

This gives us

- $W = C_1 \cdot C_2 \cdot \int_0^t C_4^{C_5 \cdot t} \cdot W$
- $W = C_1 \cdot C_2 \cdot (C_3^{C_6 \cdot t})^{C_7 \cdot t}$
- $V = C_1^2 \cdot C_2 \cdot (C_3^{C_6 \cdot t})^{C_7 \cdot t}$

Simplifying the constants, we get

- $V = C_a \cdot (C_b^{C_c \cdot t})^{C_d \cdot t}$

This is a double exponential — an exponential curve in which the rate of exponential growth is growing at a different exponential rate.

Now let's consider real-world data. Considering the data for actual calculating devices and computers during the twentieth century:

- CPS/$1K: Calculations Per Second for $1,000

Twentieth century computing data matches

- $10^{6.00 \cdot \left(\frac{20.40}{6.00}\right)^{\frac{A13 - 1900}{100}} - 11.00}$

We can determine the growth rate over a period of time:

- Growth Rate =

$$10^{\frac{\log(\frac{CPS}{\$\,1K\,for\,Current\,Year})-\log(\frac{CPS}{\$\,1K\,for\,Previous\,Year}))}{Current\,Year\,-\,Previous\,Year}}$$

- Human Brain = 100 Billion(10^{11})neurons·1000(10^3)($\frac{Connections}{Neuron}$) · 200(2 · 10^2) Calculations Per Second Per Connection = $2 \cdot 10^{16}$ Calculations Per Second

- Human Race = 10 Billion(10^{10}) Human Brains = $2 \cdot 10^{26}$ Calculations Per Second.

Already, IBM's "Blue Gene" supercomputer, now being built and scheduled to be completed by 2005, is projected to provide 1 million billion calculations per second (i.e., one billion megaflops). This is already one twentieth of the capacity of the human brain, which I estimate at a conservatively high 20 million billion calculations per second (100 billion neurons times 1,000 connections per neuron times 200 calculations per second per connection). In line with my earlier predictions, supercomputers will achieve one human brain capacity by 2010, and personal computers will do so by around 2020. By 2030, it will take a village of human brains (around a thousand) to match $1000 of computing. By 2050, $1000 of computing will equal the processing power of all human brains on Earth. Of course, this only includes those brains still using carbon-based neurons. While human neurons are wondrous creations in a way, we wouldn't (and don't) design computing circuits the same way. Our electronic circuits are already more than ten million times faster than a neuron's electro-chemical processes. Most of the complexity of a human neuron is devoted to maintaining its life support functions, not its information processing capabilities. Ultimately, we will need to port our mental processes to a more suitable computational substrate. Then our minds won't have to stay so small, being constrained as they are today to a mere hundred trillion neural connections each operating at a ponderous 200 digitally controlled analog calculations per second.

8   The Software of Intelligence

So far, I've been talking about the hardware of computing. The software is even more salient. One of the principal assumptions underlying the expectation of the Singularity is the ability of non-biological mediums to emulate the richness, subtlety, and depth of human thinking. Achieving the computational capacity of the human brain, or even villages and nations of human brains will not automatically produce human levels of capability. By human levels I include all the diverse and subtle ways in which humans are intelligent, including musical and artistic aptitude, creativity, physically moving through the world, and understanding and responding appropriately to emotion. The requisite hardware capacity is a necessary but not sufficient condition. The organization and content of these resources — the software of intelligence — is also critical.

Before addressing this issue, it is important to note that once a computer achieves a human level of intelligence, it will necessarily soar past it. A key advantage of non-biological intelligence is that machines can easily share their knowledge. If I learn French, or read War and Peace, I can't readily download that learning to you. You have to acquire that scholarship the same painstaking way that I did. My knowledge, embedded in a vast pattern of neurotransmitter concentrations and inter-neuronal connections, cannot be quickly accessed or transmitted. But we won't leave out quick downloading ports in our non-biological equivalents of human neuron clusters. When one computer learns a skill or gains an insight, it can immediately share that wisdom with billions of other machines.

As a contemporary example, we spent years teaching one research computer how to recognize continuous human speech. We exposed it to thousands of hours of recorded speech, corrected its errors, and patiently improved its performance. Finally, it became quite adept at recognizing speech (I dictated most of my recent book to it). Now if you want your own personal computer to recognize speech, it doesn't have to go through the same process; you can just download the fully trained patterns in seconds. Ultimately, billions of non-biological entities can be the master of all human and machine acquired knowledge.

In addition, computers are potentially millions of times faster than human neural circuits. A computer can also remember billions or even trillions of facts perfectly, while we are hard pressed to remember a handful of phone numbers. The combination of human level intelligence in a machine with a computer's inherent superiority in the speed, accuracy, and sharing ability of its memory will be formidable.

There are a number of compelling scenarios to achieve higher levels of intelligence in our computers, and ultimately human levels and beyond. We will be able to evolve and train a system combining massively parallel neural nets with other paradigms to understand language and model knowledge, including the ability to read and model the knowledge contained in written documents. Unlike many contemporary "neural net" machines, which use mathematically simplified models of human neurons, some contemporary neural nets are already using highly detailed models of human neurons, including detailed nonlinear analog activation functions and other relevant details. Although the ability of today's computers to extract and learn knowledge from natural language documents is limited, their capabilities in this domain are improving rapidly. Computers will be able to read on their own, understanding and modeling what they have read, by the second decade of the twenty-first century. We can then have our computers read all of the world's literature — books, magazines, scientific journals, and other available material. Ultimately, the machines will gather knowledge on their own by venturing out on the web, or even into the physical world, drawing from the full spectrum of media and information services, and sharing knowledge with each other (which machines can do far more easily than their human creators).

9   Reverse Engineering the Human Brain

The most compelling scenario for mastering the software of intelligence is to tap into the blueprint of the best example we can get our hands on of an intelligent process. There is no reason why we cannot reverse engineer the human brain, and essentially copy its design. Although it took its original designer several billion years to develop, it's readily available to us, and not (yet) copyrighted. Although there's a skull around the brain, it is not hidden from our view.

The most immediately accessible way to accomplish this is through destructive scanning: we take a frozen brain, preferably one frozen just slightly before rather than slightly after it was going to die anyway, and examine one brain layer — one very thin slice — at a time. We can readily see every neuron and every connection and every neurotransmitter concentration represented in each synapse-thin layer.

Human brain scanning has already started. A condemned killer allowed his brain and body to be scanned and you can access all 10 billion bytes of him on the Internet:
http://www.nlm.nih.gov/research/visible/visible_human.html.
He has a 25 billion byte female companion on the site as well in case he gets lonely. This scan is not high enough in resolution for our purposes, but then, we probably don't want to base our templates of machine intelligence on the brain of a convicted killer, anyway.

But scanning a frozen brain is feasible today, albeit not yet at a sufficient speed or bandwidth, but again, the law of accelerating returns will provide the requisite speed of scanning, just as it did for the human genome scan. Carnegie Mellon University's Andreas Nowatzyk plans to scan the nervous system of the brain and body of a mouse with a resolution of less than 200 nanometers, which is getting very close to the resolution needed for reverse engineering.

We also have non-invasive scanning techniques today, including high-resolution magnetic resonance imaging (MRI) scans, optical imaging, near-infrared scanning, and other technologies which are capable in certain instances of resolving individual somas, or neuron cell bodies. Brain scanning technologies are also increasing their resolution with each new generation, just what we would expect from the law of accelerating returns. Future generations will enable us to resolve the connections between neurons and to peer inside the synapses and record the neurotransmitter concentrations.

We can peer inside someone's brain today with non-invasive scanners, which are increasing their resolution with each new generation of this technology. There are a number of technical challenges in accomplishing this, including achieving suitable resolution, bandwidth, lack of vibration, and safety. For a variety of reasons it is easier to scan the brain of someone recently deceased than of someone still living. It is easier to get someone deceased to sit still, for one thing. But noninvasively scanning a living brain will ultimately become feasible as MRI, optical, and other scanning technologies continue to improve in resolution and speed.

10   Scanning from Inside

Although non-invasive means of scanning the brain from outside the skull are rapidly improving, the most practical approach to capturing every salient neural detail will be to scan it from inside. By 2030, "nanobot" (i.e., nano robot) technology will be viable, and brain scanning will be a prominent application. Nanobots are robots that are the size of human blood cells, or even smaller. Billions of them could travel through every brain capillary and scan every relevant feature from up close. Using high speed wireless communication, the nanobots would communicate with each other, and with other computers that are compiling the brain scan data base (in other words, the nanobots will all be on a wireless local area network).

This scenario involves only capabilities that we can touch and feel today. We already have technology capable of producing very high resolution scans, provided that the scanner is physically proximate to the neural features. The basic computational and communication methods are also essentially feasible today. The primary features that are not yet practical are nanobot size and cost. As I discussed above, we can project the exponentially declining cost of computation, and the rapidly declining size of both electronic and mechanical technologies. We can conservatively expect, therefore, the requisite nanobot technology by around 2030. Because of its ability to place each scanner in very close physical proximity to every neural feature, nanobot-based scanning will be more practical than scanning the brain from outside.

11   How to Use Your Brain Scan

How will we apply the thousands of trillions of bytes of information derived from each brain scan? One approach is to use the results to design more intelligent parallel algorithms for our machines, particularly those based on one of the neural net paradigms. With this approach, we don't have to copy every single connection. There is a great deal of repetition and redundancy within any particular brain region. Although the information contained in a human brain would require thousands of trillions of bytes of information (on the order of 100 billion neurons times an average of 1,000 connections per neuron, each with multiple neurotransmitter concentrations and connection data), the design of the brain is characterized by a human genome of only about a billion bytes.

Furthermore, most of the genome is redundant, so the initial design of the brain is characterized by approximately one hundred million bytes, about the size of Microsoft Word. Of course, the complexity of our brains greatly increases as we interact with the world (by a factor of more than ten million). Because of the highly repetitive patterns found in each specific brain region, it is not necessary to capture each detail in order to reverse engineer the significant digital-analog algorithms. With this information, we can design simulated nets that operate similarly. There are already multiple efforts under way to scan the human brain and apply the insights derived to the design of intelligent machines.

The pace of brain reverse engineering is only slightly behind the availability of the brain scanning and neuron structure information. A contemporary example is a comprehensive model of a significant portion of the human auditory processing system that Lloyd Watts[1] has developed from both neurobiology studies of specific neuron types and brain inter-neuronal connection information. Watts' model includes five parallel paths and includes the actual intermediate representations of auditory information at each stage of neural processing. Watts has implemented his model as real-time software which can locate and identify sounds with many of the same properties as human hearing. Although a work in progress, the model illustrates the feasibility of converting neurobiological models and brain connection data into working simulations. Also, as Hans Moravec and others have speculated, these efficient simulations require about 1,000 times less computation than the theoretical potential of the biological neurons being simulated.

12   Downloading the Human Brain

A more controversial application than this scanning-the-brain-to-understand-it scenario is *scanning-the-brain-to-download-it*. Here we scan someone's brain to map the locations, interconnections, and contents of all the somas, axons, dendrites, presynaptic vesicles, neurotransmitter concentrations, and other neural components and levels. Its entire organization can then be re-created on a neural computer of sufficient capacity, including the contents of its memory.

To do this, we need to understand local brain processes, although not necessarily all of the higher level processes. Scanning a brain with sufficient detail to download it may sound daunting, but so did the human genome scan. All of the basic technologies exist today, just not with the requisite speed, cost, and size, but these are the attributes that are improving at a double exponential pace.

---

[1] http://www.lloydwatts.com.

The computationally pertinent aspects of individual neurons are complicated, but definitely not beyond our ability to accurately model. For example, Ted Berger and his colleagues at Hedco Neurosciences have built integrated circuits that precisely match the digital and analog information processing characteristics of neurons, including clusters with hundreds of neurons. Carver Mead and his colleagues at CalTech have built a variety of integrated circuits that emulate the digital-analog characteristics of mammalian neural circuits.

A recent experiment at San Diego's Institute for Nonlinear Science demonstrates the potential for electronic neurons to precisely emulate biological ones. Neurons (biological or otherwise) are a prime example of what is often called "chaotic computing." Each neuron acts in an essentially unpredictable fashion. When an entire network of neurons receives input (from the outside world or from other networks of neurons), the signaling amongst them appears at first to be frenzied and random. Over time, typically a fraction of a second or so, the chaotic interplay of the neurons dies down, and a stable pattern emerges. This pattern represents the "decision" of the neural network. If the neural network is performing a pattern recognition task (which, incidentally, comprises the bulk of the activity in the human brain), then the emergent pattern represents the appropriate recognition.

So the question addressed by the San Diego researchers was whether electronic neurons could engage in this chaotic dance alongside biological ones. They hooked up their artificial neurons with those from spiney lobsters in a single network, and their hybrid biological-nonbiological network performed in the same way (i.e., chaotic interplay followed by a stable emergent pattern) and with the same type of results as an all biological net of neurons. Essentially, the biological neurons accepted their electronic peers. It indicates that their mathematical model of these neurons was reasonably accurate.

There are many projects around the world which are creating nonbiological devices to recreate in great detail the functionality of human neuron clusters. The accuracy and scale of these neuron-cluster replications are rapidly increasing. We started with functionally equivalent recreations of single neurons, then clusters of tens, then hundreds, and now thousands. Scaling up technical processes at an exponential pace is what technology is good at.

As the computational power to emulate the human brain becomes available — we're not there yet, but we will be there within a couple of decades — projects already under way to scan the human brain will be accelerated, with a view both to understand the human brain in general, as well as providing a detailed description of the contents and design of specific brains. By the third decade of the twenty-first century we will be in a position to create highly detailed and complete maps of all relevant features of all neurons, neural connections and synapses in the human brain, all of the neural details that play a role in the behavior and functionality of the brain, and to recreate these designs in suitably advanced neural computers.

13   Is the Human Brain Different from a Computer?

Is the human brain different from a computer?

The answer depends on what we mean by the word "computer." Certainly the brain uses very different methods from conventional contemporary computers. Most computers today are all digital and perform one (or perhaps a few) computations at a time at extremely high speed. In contrast, the human brain combines digital and analog methods with most computations performed in the analog domain. The brain is massively parallel, performing on the order of a hundred trillion computations at the same time, but at extremely slow speeds.

With regard to digital versus analog computing, we know that digital computing can be functionally equivalent to analog computing (although the reverse is not true), so we can perform all of the capabilities of a hybrid digital — analog network with an all digital computer. On the other hand, there is an engineering advantage to analog circuits in that analog computing is potentially thousands of times more efficient. An analog computation can be performed by a few transistors, or, in the case of mammalian neurons, specific electro-chemical processes. A digital computation, in contrast, requires thousands or tens of thousands of transistors. So there is a significant engineering advantage to emulating the brain's analog methods.

The massive parallelism of the human brain is the key to its pattern recognition abilities, which reflects the strength of human thinking. As I discussed above, mammalian neurons engage in a chaotic dance, and if the neural network has learned its lessons well, then a stable pattern will emerge reflecting the network's decision. There is no reason why our nonbiological functionally equivalent recreations of biological neural networks cannot be built using these same principles, and indeed there are dozens of projects around the world that have succeeded in doing this. My own technical field is pattern recognition, and the projects that I have been involved in for over thirty years use this form of chaotic computing. Particularly successful examples are Carver Mead's neural chips, which are highly parallel, use digital controlled analog computing, and are intended as functionally similar recreations of biological networks.

14   Objective and Subjective

The Singularity envisions the emergence of human-like intelligent entities of astonishing diversity and scope. Although these entities will be capable of passing the "Turing test" (i.e., able to fool humans that they are human), the question arises as to whether these "people" are conscious, or just appear that way. To gain some insight as to why this is an extremely subtle question (albeit an ultimately important one) it is useful to consider some of the paradoxes that emerge from the concept of downloading specific human brains.

Although I anticipate that the most common application of the knowledge gained from reverse engineering the human brain will be creating more intelligent machines that are not necessarily modeled on specific biological human individuals, the scenario of scanning and reinstantiating all of the neural details of a *specific* person raises the most immediate questions of identity. Let's consider the question of what we will find when we do this.

We have to consider this question on both the objective and subjective levels. "Objective" means everyone except me, so let's start with that. Objectively, when we scan someone's brain and reinstantiate their personal mind file into a suitable computing medium, the newly emergent "person" will appear to other observers to have very much the same personality, history, and memory as the person originally scanned. That is, once the technology has been refined and perfected. Like any new technology, it won't be perfect at first. But ultimately, the scans and recreations will be very accurate and realistic.

Interacting with the newly instantiated person will feel like interacting with the original person. The new person will claim to be that same old person and will have a memory of having been that person. The new person will have all of the patterns of knowledge, skill, and personality of the original. We are already creating functionally equivalent recreations of neurons and neuron clusters with sufficient accuracy that biological neurons accept their nonbiological equivalents and work with them as if they were biological. There are no natural limits that prevent us from doing the same with the hundred billion neuron cluster of clusters we call the human brain.

Subjectively, the issue is more subtle and profound, but first we need to reflect on one additional objective issue: our physical self.

15   The Importance of Having a Body

Consider how many of our thoughts and thinking are directed toward our body and its survival, security, nutrition, and image, not to mention affection, sexuality, and reproduction. Many, if not most, of the goals we attempt to advance using our brains have to do with our bodies: protecting them, providing them with fuel, making them attractive, making them feel good, providing for their myriad needs and desires. Some philosophers maintain that achieving human level intelligence is impossible without a body. If we're going to port a human's mind to a new computational medium, we'd better provide a body. A disembodied mind will quickly get depressed.

There are a variety of bodies that we will provide for our machines, and that they will provide for themselves: bodies built through nanotechnology (i.e., building highly complex physical systems atom by atom), virtual bodies (that exist only in virtual reality), bodies comprised of swarms of nanobots, and other technologies.

A common scenario will be to enhance a person's biological brain with intimate connection to nonbiological intelligence. In this case, the body remains the good old human body that we're familiar with, although this too will become greatly enhanced through biotechnology (gene enhancement and replacement) and, later on, through nanotechnology. A detailed examination of twenty-first century bodies is beyond the scope of this essay, but recreating and enhancing our bodies will be (and has been) an easier task than recreating our minds.

16   So Just Who Are These People?

To return to the issue of subjectivity, consider: is the reinstantiated mind the same consciousness as the person we just scanned? Are these "people" conscious at all? Is this a mind or just a brain?

Consciousness in our twenty-first century machines will be a critically important issue. But it is not easily resolved, or even readily understood. People tend to have strong views on the subject, and often just can't understand how anyone else could possibly see the issue from a different perspective. Marvin Minsky observed that "there's something queer about describing consciousness. Whatever people mean to say, they just can't seem to make it clear."

We don't worry, at least not yet, about causing pain and suffering to our computer programs. But at what point do we consider an entity, a process, to be conscious, to feel pain and discomfort, to have its own intentionality, its own free will? How do we determine if an entity is conscious; if it has subjective experience? How do we distinguish a process that is conscious from one that just acts *as if* it is conscious?

We can't simply ask it. If it says "Hey I'm conscious," does that settle the issue? No, we have computer games today that effectively do that, and they're not terribly convincing.

How about if the entity *is* very convincing and compelling when it says "I'm lonely, please keep me company." Does that settle the issue?

If we look inside its circuits, and see essentially the identical kinds of feedback loops and other mechanisms in its brain that we see in a human brain (albeit implemented using nonbiological equivalents), does that settle the issue?

And just who are these people in the machine, anyway? The answer will depend on who you ask. If you ask the people in the machine, they will strenuously claim to be the original persons. For example, if we scan — let's say myself — and record the exact state, level, and position of every neurotransmitter, synapse, neural connection, and every other relevant detail, and then reinstantiate this massive data base of information (which I estimate at thousands of trillions of bytes) into a neural computer of sufficient capacity, the person who then emerges in the machine will think that "he" is (and had been) me, or at least he will act that way. He will say "I grew up in Queens,

New York, went to college at MIT, stayed in the Boston area, started and sold a few artificial intelligence companies, walked into a scanner there, and woke up in the machine here. Hey, this technology really works."

But wait.

Is this really me? For one thing, old biological Ray (that's me) still exists. I'll still be here in my carbon-cell-based brain. Alas, I will have to sit back and watch the new Ray succeed in endeavors that I could only dream of.

17   A Thought Experiment

Let's consider the issue of just who I am, and who the new Ray is a little more carefully. First of all, am I the stuff in my brain and body?

Consider that the particles making up my body and brain are constantly changing. We are not at all permanent collections of particles. The cells in our bodies turn over at different rates, but the particles (e.g., atoms and molecules) that comprise our cells are exchanged at a very rapid rate. I am just not the same collection of particles that I was even a month ago. It is the patterns of matter and energy that are semipermanent (that is, changing only gradually), but our actual material content is changing constantly, and very quickly. We are rather like the patterns that water makes in a stream. The rushing water around a formation of rocks makes a particular, unique pattern. This pattern may remain relatively unchanged for hours, even years. Of course, the actual material constituting the pattern — the water — is replaced in milliseconds. The same is true for Ray Kurzweil. Like the water in a stream, my particles are constantly changing, but the pattern that people recognize as Ray has a reasonable level of continuity. This argues that we should not associate our fundamental identity with a specific set of particles, but rather the pattern of matter and energy that we represent. Many contemporary philosophers seem partial to this "identify from pattern" argument.

But (again) wait.

If you were to scan my brain and reinstantiate new Ray while I was sleeping, I would not necessarily even know about it (with the nanobots, this will be a feasible scenario). If you then come to me, and say, "good news, Ray, we've successfully reinstantiated your mind file, so we won't be needing your old brain anymore," I may suddenly realize the flaw in this "identity from pattern" argument. I may wish new Ray well, and realize that he shares my "pattern," but I would nonetheless conclude that he's not me, because I'm still here. How could he be me? After all, I would not necessarily know that he even existed.

Let's consider another perplexing scenario. Suppose I replace a small number of biological neurons with functionally equivalent nonbiological ones (they may provide certain benefits such as greater reliability and longevity, but that's not relevant to this thought experiment). After I have this procedure performed, am I still the same person? My friends certainly think so. I still have the same self-deprecating humor, the same silly grin — yes, I'm still the same guy.

It should be clear where I'm going with this. Bit by bit, region by region, I ultimately replace my entire brain with essentially identical (perhaps improved) nonbiological equivalents (preserving all of the neurotransmitter concentrations and other details that represent my learning, skills, and memories). At each point, I feel the procedures were successful. At each point, I feel that I am the same guy. After each procedure, I claim to be the same guy. My friends concur. There is no old Ray and new Ray, just one Ray, one that never appears to fundamentally change.

But consider this. This gradual replacement of my brain with a nonbiological equivalent is essentially identical to the following sequence:

1. scan Ray and reinstantiate Ray's mind file into new (nonbiological) Ray, and, then
2. terminate old Ray. But we concluded above that in such a scenario new Ray is not the same as old Ray. And if old Ray is terminated, well then that's the end of Ray. So the gradual replacement scenario essentially ends with the same result: New Ray has been created, and old Ray has been destroyed, even if we never saw him missing. So what appears to be the continuing existence of just one Ray is really the creation of new Ray and the termination of old Ray.

On yet another hand (we're running out of philosophical hands here), the gradual replacement scenario is not altogether different from what happens normally to our biological selves, in that our particles are always rapidly being replaced. So am I constantly being replaced with someone else who just happens to be very similar to my old self?

I am trying to illustrate why consciousness is not an easy issue. If we talk about consciousness as just a certain type of intelligent skill: the ability to reflect on one's own self and situation, for example, then the issue is not difficult at all because any skill or capability or form of intelligence that one cares to define will be replicated in nonbiological entities (i.e., machines) within a few decades. With this type of *objective* view of consciousness, the conundrums do go away. But a fully objective view does not penetrate to the core of the issue, because the essence of consciousness is *subjective* experience, not objective correlates of that experience.

Will these future machines be capable of having spiritual experiences?

They certainly will claim to. They will claim to be people, and to have the full range of emotional and spiritual experiences that people claim to have. And these will not be idle claims; they will evidence the sort of rich, complex, and subtle behavior one associates with these feelings. How do the claims and behaviors — compelling as they will be — relate to the subjective experience of these reinstantiated people? We keep coming back to the very real but ultimately unmeasurable issue of consciousness.

People often talk about consciousness as if it were a clear property of an entity that can readily be identified, detected, and gauged. If there is one crucial insight that we can make regarding why the issue of consciousness is so contentious, it is the following:

There exists no objective test that can conclusively determine its presence.

Science is about objective measurement and logical implications therefrom, but the very nature of objectivity is that you cannot measure subjective experience — you can only measure correlates of it, such as behavior (and by behavior, I include the actions of components of an entity, such as neurons). This limitation has to do with the very nature of the concepts "objective" and "subjective." Fundamentally, we cannot penetrate the subjective experience of another entity with direct objective measurement. We can certainly make arguments about it — i.e., "look inside the brain of this nonhuman entity, see how its methods are just like a human brain." Or, "see how its behavior is just like human behavior." But in the end these remain just arguments. No matter how convincing the behavior of a reinstantiated person, some observers will refuse to accept the consciousness of an entity unless it squirts neurotransmitters, or is based on DNA-guided protein synthesis, or has some other specific biologically human attribute.

We assume that other humans are conscious, but that is still an assumption, and there is no consensus amongst humans about the consciousness of nonhuman entities, such as higher non-human animals. The issue will be even more contentious with regard to future nonbiological entities with human-like behavior and intelligence.

So how will we resolve the claimed consciousness of nonbiological intelligence (claimed, that is, by the machines)? From a practical perspective, we'll accept their claims. Keep in mind that nonbiological entities in the twenty-first century will be extremely intelligent, so they'll be able to convince us that they are conscious. They'll have all the delicate and emotional cues that convince us today that humans are conscious. They will be able to make us laugh and cry. And they'll get mad if we don't accept their claims. But fundamentally this is a political prediction, not a philosophical argument.

18   On Tubules and Quantum Computing

Over the past several years, Roger Penrose, a noted physicist and philosopher, has suggested that fine structures in the neurons called tubules perform an exotic form of computation called "quantum computing." Quantum computing is computing using what are called "qu bits" which take on all possible combinations of solutions simultaneously. It can be considered to be an extreme form of parallel processing (because every combination of values of the qu bits are tested simultaneously). Penrose suggests that the tubules and their quantum computing capabilities complicate the concept of recreating neurons and reinstantiating mind files.

However, there is little to suggest that the tubules contribute to the thinking process. Even generous models of human knowledge and capability are more than accounted for by current estimates of brain size, based on contemporary models of neuron functioning that do not include tubules. In fact, even with these tubule-less models, it appears that the brain is conservatively designed with many more connections (by several orders of magnitude) than it needs for its capabilities and capacity. Recent experiments (e.g., the San Diego Institute for Nonlinear Science experiments) showing that hybrid biological-nonbiological networks perform similarly to all biological networks, while not definitive, are strongly suggestive that our tubule-less models of neuron functioning are adequate. Lloyd Watts' software simulation of his intricate model of human auditory processing uses orders of magnitude less computation than the networks of neurons he is simulating, and there is no suggestion that quantum computing is needed.

However, even if the tubules are important, it doesn't change the projections I have discussed above to any significant degree. According to my model of computational growth, if the tubules multiplied neuron complexity by a factor of a thousand (and keep in mind that our current tubule-less neuron models are already complex, including on the order of a thousand connections per neuron, multiple nonlinearities and other details), this would delay our reaching brain capacity by only about 9 years. If we're off by a factor of a million, that's still only a delay of 17 years. A factor of a billion is around 24 years (keep in mind computation is growing by a double exponential).

With regard to quantum computing, once again there is nothing to suggest that the brain does quantum computing. Just because quantum technology may be feasible does not suggest that the brain is capable of it. After all, we don't have lasers or even radios in our brains. Although some scientists have claimed to detect quantum wave collapse in the brain, no one has suggested human capabilities that actually require a capacity for quantum computing.

However, even if the brain does do quantum computing, this does not significantly change the outlook for human-level computing (and beyond) nor does it suggest that brain downloading is infeasible. First of all, if the brain does do quantum computing this would only verify that quantum computing is feasible. There would be nothing in such a finding to suggest that quantum computing is restricted to biological mechanisms. Biological quantum computing mechanisms, if they exist, could be replicated. Indeed, recent experiments with small scale quantum computers appear to be successful. Even the conventional transistor relies on the quantum effect of electron tunneling.

Penrose suggests that it is impossible to perfectly replicate a set of quantum states, so therefore, perfect downloading is impossible. Well, how perfect does a download have to be? I am at this moment in a very different quantum state (and different in non-quantum ways as well) than I was a minute ago (certainly in a very different state than I was before I wrote this paragraph). If we develop downloading technology to the point where the "copies" are as close to the original as the original person changes anyway in the course of one minute, that would be good enough for any conceivable purpose, yet does not require copying quantum states. As the technology improves, the accuracy of the copy could become as close as the original changes within ever briefer periods of time (e.g., one second, one millisecond, one microsecond).

When it was pointed out to Penrose that neurons (and even neural connections) were too big for quantum computing, he came up with the tubule theory as a possible mechanism for neural quantum computing. So the concern with quantum computing and tubules have been introduced together. If one is searching for barriers to replicating brain function, it is an ingenious theory, but it fails to introduce any genuine barriers. There is no evidence for it, and even if true, it only delays matters by a decade or two. There is no reason to believe that biological mechanisms (including quantum computing) are inherently impossible to replicate using nonbiological materials and mechanisms. Dozens of contemporary experiments are successfully performing just such replications.

19   A Clear and Future Danger

Technology has always been a double edged sword, bringing us longer and healthier life spans, freedom from physical and mental drudgery, and many new creative possibilities on the one hand, while introducing new and salient dangers on the other. We still live today with sufficient nuclear weapons (not all of which appear to be well accounted for) to end all mammalian life on the planet. Bioengineering is in the early stages of enormous strides in reversing disease and aging processes. However, the means and knowledge will soon exist in a routine college bioengineering lab (and already exists in more sophisticated labs) to create unfriendly pathogens more dangerous than nuclear weapons. As technology accelerates toward the Singularity, we will see the same intertwined potentials: a feast of creativity resulting from human intelligence expanded a trillion-fold combined with many grave new dangers. Consider unrestrained nanobot replication. Nanobot technology requires billions or trillions of such intelligent devices to be useful. The most cost effective way to scale up to such levels is through self-replication, essentially the same approach used in the biological world. And in the same way that biological self-replication gone awry (i.e., cancer) results in biological destruction, a defect in the mechanism curtailing nanobot self-replication would endanger all physical entities, biological or otherwise.

Other primary concerns include "who is controlling the nanobots?" and "who are the nanobots talking to?" Organizations (e.g., governments, extremist groups) or just a clever individual could put trillions of undetectable nanobots in the water or food supply of an individual or of an entire population. These "spy" nanobots could then monitor, influence, and even control our thoughts and actions. In addition to introducing physical spy nanobots, existing nanobots could be influenced through software viruses and other software "hacking" techniques. When there is software running in our brains, issues of privacy and security will take on a new urgency.

My own expectation is that the creative and constructive applications of this technology will dominate, as I believe they do today. But there will be a valuable (and increasingly vocal) role for a concerned and constructive Luddite movement (i.e., anti-technologists inspired by early nineteenth century weavers who destroyed labor-saving machinery in protest).

If we imagine describing the dangers that exist today to people who lived a couple of hundred years ago, they would think it mad to take such risks. On the other hand, how many people in the year 2000 would really want to go back to the short, brutish, disease-filled, poverty-stricken, disaster-prone lives that 99 percent of the human race struggled through a couple of centuries ago? We may romanticize the past, but up until fairly recently, most of humanity lived extremely fragile lives where one all too common misfortune could spell disaster. Substantial portions of our species still live in this precarious way, which is at least one reason to continue technological progress and the economic enhancement that accompanies it.

People often go through three stages in examining the impact of future technology: awe and wonderment at its potential to overcome age old problems, then a sense of dread at a new set of grave dangers that accompany these new technologies, followed, finally and hopefully, by the realization that the only viable and responsible path is to set a careful course that can realize the promise while managing the peril.

In his cover story for WIRED *Why The Future Doesn't Need Us*, Bill Joy eloquently described the plagues of centuries' past, and how new self-replicating technologies, such as mutant bioengineered pathogens, and "nanobots" run amok, may bring back long forgotten pestilence. Indeed these are real dangers. It is also the case, which Joy acknowledges, that it has been technological advances, such as antibiotics and improved sanitation, which has freed us from the prevalence of such plagues. Suffering in the world continues and demands our steadfast attention. Should we tell the millions of people afflicted with cancer and other devastating conditions that we are canceling the development of all bioengineered treatments because there is a risk that these same technologies may someday be used for malevolent purposes? Having asked the rhetorical question, I realize that there is a movement to do exactly that, but I think most people would agree that such broad based relinquishment is not the answer.

The continued opportunity to alleviate human distress is one important motivation for continuing technological advancement. Also compelling are the already apparent economic gains I discussed above which will continue to hasten in the decades ahead. The continued acceleration of many intertwined technologies are roads paved with gold (I use the plural here because technology is clearly not a single path). In a competitive environment, it is an economic imperative to go down these roads. Relinquishing technological advancement would be economic suicide for individuals, companies, and nations.

Which brings us to the issue of relinquishment, which is Bill Joy's most controversial recommendation and personal commitment. I do feel that relinquishment at the right level is part of a responsible and constructive response to these genuine perils. The issue, however, is exactly this: at what level are we to relinquish technology?

Ted Kaczynski would have us renounce all of it. This, in my view, is neither desirable nor feasible, and the futility of such a position is only underscored by the senselessness of Kaczynski's deplorable tactics.

Another level would be to forego certain fields; nanotechnology, for example, that might be regarded as too dangerous. But such sweeping strokes of relinquishment are equally untenable. Nanotechnology is simply the inevitable end result of the persistent trend toward miniaturization which pervades all of technology. It is far from a single centralized effort, but is being pursued by a myriad of projects with many diverse goals.

One observer wrote:

> A further reason why industrial society cannot be reformed ... is that modern technology is a unified system in which all parts are dependent on one another. You can't get rid of the "bad" parts of technology and retain only the "good" parts. Take modern medicine, for example. Progress in medical science depends on progress in chemistry, physics, biology, computer science and other fields. Advanced medical treatments require expensive, high-tech equipment that can be made available only by a technologically progressive, economically rich society. Clearly you can't have much progress in medicine without the whole technological system and everything that goes with it.

The observer I am quoting is, again, Ted Kaczynski. Although one might properly resist Kaczynski as an authority, I believe he is correct on the deeply entangled nature of the benefits and risks. However, Kaczynski and I clearly part company on our overall assessment on the relative balance between the two. Bill Joy and I have dialogued on this issue both publicly and privately, and we both believe that technology will and should progress, and that we need to be actively concerned with the dark side. If Bill and I disagree, it's on the granularity of relinquishment that is both feasible and desirable.

Abandonment of broad areas of technology will only push them underground where development would continue unimpeded by ethics and regulation. In such a situation, it would be the less stable, less responsible practitioners (e.g., the terrorists) who would have all the expertise.

I do think that relinquishment at the right level needs to be part of our ethical response to the dangers of twenty first century technologies. One constructive example of this is the proposed ethical guideline by the Foresight

Institute, founded by nanotechnology pioneer Eric Drexler, that nanotechnologists agree to relinquish the development of physical entities that can self-replicate in a natural environment. Another is a ban on self-replicating physical entities that contain their own codes for self-replication. In what nanotechnologist Ralph Merkle calls the "Broadcast Architecture," such entities would have to obtain such codes from a centralized secure server, which would guard against undesirable replication. The Broadcast Architecture is impossible in the biological world, which represents at least one way in which nanotechnology can be made safer than biotechnology. In other ways, nanotech is potentially more dangerous because nanobots can be physically stronger than protein-based entities and more intelligent. It will eventually be possible to combine the two by having nanotechnology provide the codes within biological entities (replacing DNA), in which case biological entities can use the much safer Broadcast Architecture.

Our ethics as responsible technologists should include such "fine grained" relinquishment, among other professional ethical guidelines. Other protections will need to include oversight by regulatory bodies, the development of technology-specific "immune" responses, as well as computer assisted surveillance by law enforcement organizations. Many people are not aware that our intelligence agencies already use advanced technologies such as automated word spotting to monitor a substantial flow of telephone conversations. As we go forward, balancing our cherished rights of privacy with our need to be protected from the malicious use of powerful twenty first century technologies will be one of many profound challenges. This is one reason that such issues as an encryption "trap door" (in which law enforcement authorities would have access to otherwise secure information) and the FBI "Carnivore" email-snooping system have been so contentious.

As a test case, we can take a small measure of comfort from how we have dealt with one recent technological challenge. There exists today a new form of fully nonbiological self replicating entity that didn't exist just a few decades ago: the computer virus. When this form of destructive intruder first appeared, strong concerns were voiced that as they became more sophisticated, software pathogens had the potential to destroy the computer network medium they live in. Yet the "immune system" that has evolved in response to this challenge has been largely effective. Although destructive self-replicating software entities do cause damage from time to time, the injury is but a small fraction of the benefit we receive from the computers and communication links that harbor them. No one would suggest we do away with computers, local area networks, and the Internet because of software viruses.

One might counter that computer viruses do not have the lethal potential of biological viruses or of destructive nanotechnology. Although true, this strengthens my observation. The fact that computer viruses are not usually deadly to humans only means that more people are willing to create and release them. It also means that our response to the danger is that much less intense. Conversely, when it comes to self replicating entities that are potentially lethal on a large scale, our response on all levels will be vastly more serious.

Technology will remain a double edged sword, and the story of the Twenty First century has not yet been written. It represents vast power to be used for all humankind's purposes. We have no choice but to work hard to apply these quickening technologies to advance our human values, despite what often appears to be a lack of consensus on what those values should be.

20   Living Forever

Once brain porting technology has been refined and fully developed, will this enable us to live forever? The answer depends on what we mean by living and dying. Consider what we do today with our personal computer files. When we change from one personal computer to a less obsolete model, we don't throw all our files away; rather we copy them over to the new hardware. Although our software files do not necessary continue their existence forever, the longevity of our personal computer software is completely separate and disconnected from the hardware that it runs on. When it comes to our personal mind file, however, when our human hardware crashes, the software of our lives dies with it. However, this will not continue to be the case when we have the means to store and restore the thousands of trillions of bytes of information represented in the pattern that we call our brains.

The longevity of one's mind file will not be dependent, therefore, on the continued viability of any particular hardware medium. Ultimately software-based humans, albeit vastly extended beyond the severe limitations of humans as we know them today, will live out on the web, projecting bodies whenever they need or want them, including virtual bodies in diverse realms of virtual reality, holographically projected bodies, physical bodies comprised of nanobot swarms, and other forms of nanotechnology.

A software-based human will be free, therefore, from the constraints of any particular thinking medium. Today we are each confined to a mere hundred trillion connections, but humans at the end of the twenty-first century can grow their thinking and thoughts without limit. We may regard this as a form of immortality, although it is worth pointing out that data and information do not necessarily last forever. Although not dependent on the viability of the hardware it runs on, the longevity of information depends on its relevance, utility, and accessibility. If you've ever tried to retrieve information from an obsolete form of data storage in an old obscure format (e.g., a reel of magnetic tape from a 1970 minicomputer), you will understand the challenges in keeping software viable. However, if we are diligent in maintaining our mind file, keeping current backups, and porting to current formats and mediums, then a form of immortality can be attained, at least for software-based humans. Our mind file — our personality, skills, memories — all of that is lost today when our biological hardware crashes. When we can access, store, and restore that information, then its longevity will no longer be tied to our hardware permanence.

Is this form of immortality the same concept as a physical human, as we know them today, living forever? In one sense it is, because as I pointed out earlier, our contemporary selves are not a constant collection of matter either. Only our pattern of matter and energy persists, and even that gradually changes. Similarly, it will be the pattern of a software human that persists and develops and changes gradually.

But is that person based on my mind file, who migrates across many computational substrates, and who outlives any particular thinking medium, really me? We come back to the same questions of consciousness and identity, issues that have been debated since the Platonic dialogues. As we go through the twenty-first century, these will not remain polite philosophical debates, but will be confronted as vital, practical, political, and legal issues.

A related question is "is death desirable?" A great deal of our effort goes into avoiding it. We make extraordinary efforts to delay it, and indeed often consider its intrusion a tragic event. Yet we might find it hard to live without it. We consider death as giving meaning to our lives. It gives importance and value to time. Time could become meaningless if there were too much of it.

21   The Next Step in Evolution and the Purpose of Life

But I regard the freeing of the human mind from its severe physical limitations of scope and duration as the necessary next step in evolution. Evolution, in my view, represents the purpose of life. That is, the purpose of life — and of our lives — is to evolve. The Singularity then is not a grave danger to be avoided. In my view, this next paradigm shift represents the goal of our civilization.

What does it mean to evolve? Evolution moves toward greater complexity, greater elegance, greater knowledge, greater intelligence, greater beauty, greater creativity, and more of other abstract and subtle attributes such as love. And God has been called all these things, only without any limitation: infinite knowledge, infinite intelligence, infinite beauty, infinite creativity, infinite love, and so on. Of course, even the accelerating growth of evolution never achieves an infinite level, but as it explodes exponentially, it certainly moves rapidly in that direction. So evolution moves inexorably toward our conception of God, albeit never quite reaching this ideal. Thus the freeing of our thinking from the severe limitations of its biological form may be regarded as an essential spiritual quest.

In making this statement, it is important to emphasize that terms like evolution, destiny, and spiritual quest are observations about the end result, not the basis for these predictions. I am not saying that technology will evolve to human levels and beyond simply because it is our destiny and because of the satisfaction of a spiritual quest. Rather my projections result from a methodology based on the dynamics underlying the (double) exponential growth of technological processes. The primary force driving technology is economic imperative. We are moving toward machines with human level intelligence (and beyond) as the result of millions of small advances, each with their own particular economic justification.

To use an example from my own experience at one of my companies (Kurzweil Applied Intelligence), whenever we came up with a slightly more intelligent version of speech recognition, the new version invariably had greater value than the earlier generation and, as a result, sales increased. It is interesting to note that in the example of speech recognition software, the three primary surviving competitors stayed very close to each other in the intelligence of their software. A few other companies that failed to do so (e.g., Speech Systems) went out of business. At any point in time, we would be able to sell the version prior to the latest version for perhaps a quarter of the price of the current version. As for versions of our technology that were two generations old, we couldn't even give those away. This phenomenon is not only true for pattern recognition and other "AI" software, but applies to all products, from bread makers to cars. And if the product itself doesn't exhibit some level of intelligence, then intelligence in the manufacturing and marketing methods have a major effect on the success and profitability of an enterprise.

There is a vital economic imperative to create more intelligent technology. Intelligent machines have enormous value. That is why they are being built. There are tens of thousands of projects that are advancing intelligent machines in diverse incremental ways. The support for "high tech" in the business community (mostly software) has grown enormously. When I started my optical character recognition (OCR) and speech synthesis company (Kurzweil Computer Products, Inc.) in 1974, there were only a half-dozen high technology IPO's that year. The number of such deals has increased one hundred fold and the number of dollars invested has increased by more than one thousand fold in the past 25 years. In the four years between 1995 and 1999 alone, high tech venture capital deals increased from just over $1 billion to approximately $15 billion.

We will continue to build more powerful computational mechanisms because it creates enormous value. We will reverse-engineer the human brain not simply because it is our destiny, but because there is valuable information to be found there that will provide insights in building more intelligent (and more valuable) machines. We would have to repeal capitalism and every visage of economic competition to stop this progression.

By the second half of this next century there will be no clear distinction between human and machine intelligence. On the one hand, we will have biological brains vastly expanded through distributed nanobot-based implants. On the other hand, we will have fully nonbiological brains that are copies of human brains, albeit also vastly extended. And we will have a myriad of other varieties of intimate connection between human thinking and the technology it has fostered.

Ultimately, nonbiological intelligence will dominate because it is growing at a double exponential rate, whereas for all practical purposes biological intelligence is at a standstill. Human thinking is stuck at 10^{26} calculations per second (for all biological humans), and that figure will never appreciably change (except for a small increase resulting from genetic engineering). Nonbiological thinking is still millions of times less today, but the cross over will occur before 2030. By the end of the twenty-first century, nonbiological thinking will be trillions of trillions of times more powerful than that of its biological progenitors, although still of human origin. It will continue to be the human-machine civilization taking the next step in evolution.

Most forecasts of the future seem to ignore the revolutionary impact of the Singularity in our human destiny: the inevitable emergence of computers that match and ultimately vastly exceed the capabilities of the human brain, a development that will be no less important than the evolution of human intelligence itself some thousands of centuries ago. And the primary reason for this failure is that they are based on the intuitive but short sighted linear view of history.

Before the next century is over, the Earth's technology-creating species will merge with its computational technology. There will not be a clear distinction between human and machine. After all, what is the difference between a human brain enhanced a trillion fold by nanobot-based implants, and a computer whose design is based on high resolution scans of the human brain, and then extended a trillion-fold?

22   Why Intelligence Is More Powerful than Physics

As intelligence saturates the matter and energy available to it, it turns dumb matter into smart matter. Although smart matter still nominally follows the laws of physics, it is so exquisitely intelligent that it can harness the most subtle aspects of the laws to manipulate matter and energy to its will. So it would at least appear that intelligence is more powerful than physics.

Perhaps what I should say is that intelligence is more powerful than cosmology. That is, once matter evolves into smart matter (matter fully saturated with intelligence), it can manipulate matter and energy to do whatever it wants. This perspective has not been considered in discussions of future cosmology. It is assumed that intelligence is irrelevant to events and processes on a cosmological scale. Stars are born and die; galaxies go through their cycles of creation and destruction. The Universe itself was born in a big bang and will end with a crunch or a whimper, we're not yet sure which. But intelligence has little to do with it. Intelligence is just a bit of froth, an ebullition of little creatures darting in and out of inexorable universal forces.

The mindless mechanism of the Universe is winding up or down to a distant future, and there's nothing intelligence can do about it.

That's the common wisdom, but I don't agree with it. Intelligence will be more powerful than these impersonal forces. Once a planet yields a technology creating species and that species creates computation (as has happened here on Earth), it is only a matter of a few centuries before its intelligence saturates the matter and energy in its vicinity, and it begins to expand outward at the speed of light or greater. It will then overcome gravity (through exquisite and vast technology) and other cosmological forces (or, to be fully accurate, will maneuver and control these forces) and create the Universe it wants. This is the goal of the Singularity. What kind of Universe will that be? Well, just wait and see.

Part IV

The Enigma

The Polish Brains Behind the Breaking of the Enigma Code Before and During the Second World War

Elisabeth Rakus-Andersson

Blekinge Institute of Technology

Summary. The German Enigma encoding machine and the contributions of famous cryptologists who broke its code are still topics that fascinate both scientists and the general public. After the monarchy of Kaiser Wilhelm II fell, the Weimar Republic came into being and the idea of equipping the German armed forces with machine ciphers was already being realized by 1926. Enigma alarmed the general staffs of neighboring countries, especially Poland and France. This chapter describes the efforts of cryptanalysts who solved the mystery of Enigma during the 1930s before the beginning of the Second World War.

1 Introduction

In the late 1920s everything indicated that the small Reichswehr would be converted into a modern million-man army. All the German political parties that came to power voted on the same program, which had as its main assumption taking away from Poland some districts regarded by the German government as the "lost territories." The military build-up program of the German army forces had to involve the development of secret intelligence operations [1, 14]. These operations always belonged to two categories, namely, cryptography ("secret writing") and cryptology (the study of secret writing, especially for purposes of decryption — the "breaking" or "reading" of secret correspondence by a third party).

Cryptology deals basically with ciphers, which either transpose (shift) or substitute letters for the original letters in a message, and with codes, which replace entire words and phrases with arbitrary symbols commonly consisting of letters and numbers [9, 14].

Rather early the German army commanders realized that they should introduce a cryptography device that was both secure and could satisfy the requirements of speed and convenience. In the spring of 1918 the German Navy contemplated the use of cipher machines. The inventor Hugo Koch designed the "Enigma" machine in Holland in 1919 and sold the patent later to Dr. Arthur Scherbius. He improved Koch's design and hoped to win a market for this machine in the business world, but his best customer turned out to be the German government, especially the armed forces [7, 14]. In 1926 the Navy, and in 1928 the Army introduced cipher machines that at first were modified versions of the civilian model "Enigma" [6,14]. Two years later, in 1930, a military version of the device was constructed. In 1933–34, the Germans adopted Enigma as a basic unitary cipher system for the armed forces as well as the military intelligence service (Abwehr), S.S. formations, the Nazi Party security service, and the political intelligence service (S.D.).

Cryptologists could easily recognize an Enigma cipher by its perfect spread of letters. There were no correlates with natural languages and statistical calculations of the frequencies of the letters were completely useless.

It was not strange that Poland was the most engaged country in solving the German coding system. Some other European countries, such as France or the UK, were not threatened by German actions to the same extent as Poland. The Polish cryptologists found the solution to the Enigma secret before the war began, and this story intends to show the historical background to this.

2   The Cryptology Course in Poznań

The general staffs of the neighboring countries were alarmed by the German machine cipher, and cryptologists, who received some messages from the monitoring stations (placed in Poland in Warsaw, Poznań, Starogard and Krzesławice), set to work on breaking the code [10].

There were few persons skilful at cryptology in Poland at the time. At the General Staff's Cipher Bureau in Warsaw the specialists were trained and they were distinguished from the clerks who enciphered and deciphered messages. The German ciphers and codes monitored by the Poles were only partially intercepted, which gave a reason for educating cryptologists equipped with all the necessary knowledge about the ciphers.

The need to organize the course in cryptology was justified by the political situation at the time. In the first days of January 1929, the students at Poznań University's Mathematics Institute were preparing for their final examinations in mathematics; the examiner was Prof. Zdzisław Krygowski. He had already prepared a list of those third- and fourth-year mathematics students who knew German and had marks of at least "good" in their course work. Afterwards the selected students were asked to assemble at the Institute, where two officers from the Polish General Staff in Warsaw, Major Franciszek Pokorny and Lieutenant Maksymilian Ciężki, informed them that a cryptology course was being organized and invited them to participate in it [6,14,18]. The students who chose the course were pledged to secrecy concerning both the existence of the course and their participation in it. The lessons were held twice a week in the evenings and were conducted by Cipher Bureau cryptologists commuting from Warsaw.

After several weeks of the course, the lecturer presented authentic Reichswehr ciphergrams for the students to solve. The system used to generate these messages had already been broken, and the Germans called it Double

Dice [7, 14]. A couple of hours later, three students: Marian Rejewski, Henryk Zygalski and Jerzy Różycki presented their solutions. These three students, the best ones, continued working on cryptology in the underground basements of the Command Post in Poznań.

This work was a kind of laboratory that gave a broad opportunity for experimentation. The above-mentioned team of course adepts engaged in cryptology work did not read long dispatches but tried to work out methods for breaking German cipher keys, which were changed periodically. Radio intercepts were delivered by courier from Warsaw and from the nearest monitoring station in Poznań, while the solutions were sent to Warsaw by airplane.

Solving some non-mechanical military German ciphers became a matter of routine. The cryptologists learned to exploit the mistakes made by the German cipher clerks as well as certain regularities they discovered. One of these was a rule that a cipher text must contain at least 50 letters. Thus every message sent by the Germans had the letter "X" added to enlarge the text to 50 signs.

The discovery of such rules made it easier to solve the cipher problems. But strange things began to happen, namely, the enciphered information was sent without any stable rules at all, and all the doubts disappeared — the Poles realized that this was a complicated machine cipher that was not breakable using standard methods.

3   The Enigma

The Poznań cipher office was closed in the summer of 1932. The main purpose of the course in cryptology and of the primary work on reading the German messages that were monitored by the Polish stations was to find talented students and train them in working on cracking the new German machine cipher [8, 14].

The fact that the Polish authorities turned to mathematicians could have been partially explained by the great development of the Polish mathematical school at that time. Marian Rejewski, who had spent a study year in Göttingen, felt that the famous German school of mathematics belonged to the past. Among the professors he had met in Germany were no outstanding persons such as Poland's Stefan Banach and Wacław Sierpiński, whose work had great importance for twentieth-century mathematics [15]. The achievements in mathematics in Poland at the beginning of the twentieth century gave the Poles a strong belief in the power of the subject. The Polish government, which represented Poland as a new state with rather poor resources after World War I, realized that all intellectual possibilities would have to be utilized in the service of the country.

On 1 September 1932, Marian Rejewski, Jerzy Różycki and Henryk Zygalski began working as regular employees at the Cipher Bureau in the general staff building (the "Saxon Palace") in Warsaw [1, 11, 14]. The efforts undertaken during the years 1928–1930 to solve the new machine crypto-system led nowhere. However, the three mathematicians got a different problem to solve during their first weeks in the General Cipher Bureau, namely, to break the four-letter German naval code [14].

From a dozen short messages, one was selected for closer study. It consisted of only six groups, each of four letters. After thorough analysis the mathematicians noticed that the letter Y occurred at the beginning of a large number of code groups. In German, many question expressions (Wer?, Wo?, Wohin?, Wann?, Welcher?) begin with the same letter, and this regularity could have been presented in the code. Next, they noticed that, following this six-group message, another station sent on the same wavelength a short signal consisting of only four signs. By assuming that the first message was a question, they guessed that the second might be an answer. Such a short reply could be a number, maybe a year. The solution of this six-word signal led to the gradual reconstruction of the entire German naval code used in the second half of 1932. Even after 50 years, Marian Rejewski remembered that YOPY meant "when," YWIN "where," BAUG "and," and KEZL "cancel the final letter."

The Polish mathematicians could read most of the messages in the navy code even if the Germans tried to make things difficult. They transposed the alphabetical order, omitted certain letters of the alphabet, or from time to time remitted the false code groups.

Even if the effects concerning the navy code were very apparent, the Enigma code was unsolved. The attempts made to solve the mystery included the mathematicians' efforts as well as the predictions of clairvoyants. One of the preliminary findings was formulated as: "If we write two cipher texts with identical beginnings one below the other, identical letters in the same places will occur in the average twice as often as when we place texts with different beginnings in the same manner."

The work on Enigma required great concentration and at least 80 intercepts per day. Marian Rejewski obtained a commercial Enigma machine used by business firms. The machine resembled a typewriter, with an additional panel built into the lid. The panel contained 26 little circular glass windows with, like the keyboard, the letters of the alphabet. A number of glow lamps were built into the panel's underside. Inside the machine was a set of three rotors, or rotating drums, and a reversing drum, all sitting on a common axle. The machine also had a stationary drum, called the entry ring. With every stroke of a key one or more rotors rotated, and at the same time the corresponding glow lamp lit up and illuminated the letter in the window above it. The machine was designed in a way that allowed one to find the association between the plain text and the cipher. If one struck the key with the letter coming from the clear text, then a corresponding cipher letter would appear in the window. Conversely, when another person tapped out a cipher text, the letters illuminated in turn would spell the plain text. In order to conduct a secret dialog, both parties had to possess the same device set [14].

The commercial Enigma only provided a general insight into the construction of the machine. It was easy to guess that the military version of Enigma would probably have a different wiring system and additional components. The cryptologists had to continue studying the system from the mathematical side. They needed group theory [5, 14], especially the properties of permutation groups, which were very useful when working on the military Enigma.

4   The International Cooperation

France and Czechoslovakia, like Poland, were threatened by German expansionism. They were also natural allies for Poland in collecting knowledge about German devices and war plans. In 1932 there was a man in France who initiated contacts with the Polish General Staff: Captain Gustave Bertrand, chief of French radio intelligence, established direct cooperation with the Poles, especially for work resulting in solutions of the Enigma problem [2, 14].

In October 1932, French military intelligence made a great contribution to solving the Enigma mystery thanks to a special opportunity. A French intelligence officer, Captain Henri Navarre, reported that a man came to him and introduced himself as an employee of the Reichswehr cryptography agency [1, 2, 7, 18]. Moreover, he offered his services in return for money. Captain Bertrand, who was responsible for technical and scientific intelligence and ciphers, checked carefully all the information collected about the German agent and decided to investigate the first documents that the man delivered. The samples were recognized as authentic. The newly recruited agent, Hans-Thilo Schmidt, received the pseudonym "Asche." The documents delivered by "Asche" were both original and of great importance. During the long cooperation with Captain Bertrand, who met the German collaborator regularly, "Asche" left the following reports [12–14]:

- materials on the organization of the Reichswehr Cryptographic Agency;
- various codes used in the German armed forces: A, B, C, D, E and code "Black";
- documents concerning keys to manual ciphers used by civil staff and the army signals service for quick contact between civil and military authorities;
- documents on machine ciphers: operating instructions for Enigma, keying instructions and monthly tables of army keys for December 1931, 1932, 1933 and the first half of 1934;
- materials on an earlier Enigma model from 1930 and a document including one cipher text and a corresponding plain text.

Unfortunately, "Asche" never had an opportunity to get his hands on the most important materials, such as the dossier of Enigma, containing the scheme of the machine's wiring.

After receiving the first materials, which threw new light on the Enigma mystery, Captain Bertrand contacted the Polish Cipher Bureau and arranged to visit Warsaw [2, 14]. The materials he came with generated great interest among the cryptologists because they constituted the first written papers referring to Enigma. Even though the Polish cryptologists had worked on the Enigma cipher since 1927, they only had intercepts as the basis for their investigations.

Bertrand described his first meeting with the Poles on 7–11 December 1932 in Warsaw as "historic" and he did not exaggerate when he used this word [2]. The meeting gave rise to a long and friendly cooperation between the Polish and French intelligence specialists. During the Warsaw meeting in December 1932, a number of tasks were decided between Bertrand and his Polish colleagues. The head of the Polish Cipher Bureau, which had been reorganized a year earlier, was Major Gwido Langer. The French were to concentrate on delivering the intelligence reports from Germany to help in the code breaking, while the Poles were responsible for theoretical studies of the Enigma intercepts. It was also decided to establish closer connections with the intelligence unit in Czechoslovakia in order to create a triple entente of cryptological services. Captain Bertrand was to use the pseudonym "Bolek," Major Langer "Luc," and the Czechoslovak officer "Raoul." In the late 1930s, the B-L-R triangle was active only on the Bolek-Luc line, due to the bad Polish-Czech relations prevailing at that time [11].

It is worth emphasizing that the principle of very strict secrecy was introduced into the Polish-French contacts, and even the three Polish cryptologists — Rejewski, Zygalski and Różycki — did not know anything about the origin of the delivered materials. These played an important role in the studies on Enigma in conjunction with the mathematical analysis, which had already been carried out on the intercepts.

The instructions brought by Bertrand gave a general idea of the military Enigma's appearance and operating principles, but said nothing about its inner structure. The electrical connections within the rotors, the variable contacts and other components were still unknown.

5   The Breaking of the Enigma System

The precise mathematical analysis was combined with intuitive reconstruction of individual parts. As the following example shows, even knowledge about the German mentality helped in solving the posed problem. Rejewski had found that in the commercial Enigma the letters of the alphabet were represented on the circumference of the entry ring in the same order in which they appeared on the German typewriter keyboard. It was assumed that the military model had its entry ring organized in the same way as the commercial model, but that assertion was wrong. In January 1933 he came to the conclusion that the wiring on the entry ring in the military Enigma was in alphabetical order. The hypothesis was proved to be correct and helped to designate the connections in one of the rotors. Belief in German Ordnung ("order") made the work faster and simpler [17].

Solution of the Enigma system involved two distinct matters:

A theoretical reconstruction of the cipher machine was done. The most important issue was to determine Enigma's wiring. The cryptologists first discovered the functions of the reflector, or "reversing drum." Afterwards, they reconstructed all the connections in the machine, which had a system of rotors as the essential components. Even a special commutator was built into the system. The Poles were able to construct doubles of Enigma.

Secondly, the cryptologists developed methods for reconstructing the Enigma keys on the basis of intercepts that were supplied daily by monitoring stations.

The main code break came in the last days of December 1932. The practical reading of messages began during the second ten days of January 1933.

In the beginning of February 1933, the Cipher Bureau ordered the AVA Radio Manufacturing Company in Warsaw to build 15 doubles of the military Enigma [14]. The machines had to be made with the same components and with the identical wiring, to work in the same way as the original military machine known to German cipher staff as E-Eins [18]. The AVA copy model had typing keys instead of caps, and the upper part of the machine was changed as well. The illuminated windows were covered with cellophane on which the letters were written in the appropriate order.

The first trial to produce the doubles of Enigma was a failure. The cipher text going through the machine resembled some exotic language, but not German. The mathematicians discovered soon that the producers had forgotten about the caps, which slipped over the keys only for reading signals. This altered the order of the internal connections. The mistake was corrected soon and AVA kept building more copies [14].

A few weeks after the first copies of Enigma were constructed, the cryptologists received a series of German military signals that indicated correspondence between district number 1 in Königsberg and number 2 in Stettin. The messages were unreadable and all the methods to translate them were useless. This cipher was sent on another Enigma machine called Enigma II. Later, it was discovered that it was the ordinary Enigma equipped with eight rotors and an automatic writing device. It had been used only for sending the highest military commands and had been evaluated as unreliable. After several weeks this version of Enigma was withdrawn from use.

Recovery of the settings (the starting positions of the rotors) and keys to the messages in the various Enigma nets came about using the method of elimination. The connections in the commutator were found by using the lattice method. During the first months after the Enigma solution, further elements of the key were obtained manually, by turning the metal rotors as many as 17,576 ways. Because of the top secrecy the mathematicians did the job by themselves without any help from the assistants. One must add that the Germans changed the connections of the commutator regularly and more and more often, which brought an additional effort in finding the new conditions. The situation was improved when Rejewski invented a cyclometer, which had two sets of Enigma rotors linked together electrically. The cyclometer enabled the cryptologists to create a catalog of possible settings of the rotors. After that, the comparison of intercepts with the catalog made it possible to recover the keys faster [8, 14].

Other inventions included the clock, devised by Jerzy Różycki, that determined the right position of one of the rotors on a certain day in a given Enigma net.

In late June 1934, the three mathematicians experienced the exciting decryptment of a message they could read as "To all commandants of the airfields throughout Germany." The signal ordered "the transportation to Berlin, alive or dead, of Karl Ernst, adjutant to the S.A. chief."

In 1934 the cryptologists employed by the Polish Cipher Bureau broke the ciphers of the German Army (Heer) and the codes of the S.D. as well as codes and ciphers of the German Navy. The Kriegsmarine used three kinds of Enigma keys: for the operational, staff and admiral levels. The last key was resistant to breaking for a long time [14].

6   The New Devices as a Reaction to Changes in the Enigma Settings

The struggle against the German machine cipher did not end in 1933 with the solution of Enigma and the building of its copy. In order to read the messages of the German Army, Air Force and Navy, it was not enough to break the system once. The changes in it had to be detected and the reaction had to follow as well. Since the numbers of intercepts were growing proportionally to the Wehrmacht's expansion, several Polish lieutenants and captains were sent to the Cipher Bureau for training.

By the beginning of 1936 the Germans were using six kinds of keys to Enigma machines which were intended for the supreme civil authorities, the staffs of the Armed Forces, the Army, S.S. staffs, S.S. operational units, and special situations (the code "A"). The precautions and the secrecy concerning Enigma were growing in Germany as the war approached. The Germans kept careful records of machine starting positions to prevent repetition of the same combinations. From 1 October 1936, they changed the settings every day. The response to these changes from the Polish side resembled a duel between Poland's Cipher Bureau and the Nazi Chi-Dienst (the German Cryptological Service). Three periods can be recognized in this battle [14].

In the first period, 1933–35, little "changes" were made by the Germans, and the apparatus that had been developed by the Poles was sufficient for continuous decryptment.

In the second period, from 1936 to November 1938, each change came very fast, and to keep pace with them the Polish cryptologists had to use all their knowledge and experience while they exposed the codes with the same tools and resources.

In the third period, from late 1938 to September 1939, a new wartime generation of Enigmas appeared, and these had further complications.

Once, the luck was on the Polish side, when German cipher clerks committed great errors. They often selected message keys (the first six letters at the beginnings of messages) in a stereotypic manner. For example, they could strike the same letter three times (AAA) or they could strike letters in alphabetical order (ABC). Another possibility was that they could use letters that lay next to each other down or diagonally across the keyboard, which was against regulations. The cycle principle discovered by Marian Rejewski let him distinguish the proper regular message keys from the chaotic ones, which were introduced by mistake [1, 6, 8, 14, 16, 17].

In 1937, important changes were made in the Polish Cipher Bureau. Its German section, B.S. 4, was separated from headquarters and moved out of the city. In the specially constructed new buildings hidden in woods not far from Pyry to the south of Warsaw, working conditions were better than at the cramped quarters in Warsaw. Another purpose for moving the German section of cryptologists was to better protect the secrecy of their operations. The Abwehr carefully tested all the people who were suspected of being traitors, and secret German agents were present everywhere.

At the Polish B.S. 4, a strict prohibition was introduced against talking to anyone, even to colleagues from the Cipher Bureau, about Enigma [19].

The Polish General Staff ordered an experiment to be carried out in January 1938. The test was to determine how many of the intercepted Wehrmacht ciphers the cryptologists could read. The results of the tests, which were conducted over a period of two weeks, showed that about 75% of the messages had been decrypted.

7   French and British Efforts at Breaking Enigma

During these years Captain Bertrand visited the Polish Cipher Bureau many times. It was important to ensure effective communication in the Warsaw-Paris-Prague triangle with the approach of war. After visiting the new nest of the Polish cryptologists in Pyry, which was called Wicher (Wind), Bertrand went to Prague to speak to representatives of the Czechoslovak General Staff, which even in May 1938 still looked to the future with hope.

In France, Bertrand's services were occupied with non-machine ciphers, leaving Enigma to the Poles [13]. The French cryptologists were able to read the secret radio correspondence from Germany and Italy as well as from other countries. The French intelligence services also spread false information about French codes and ciphers, and in this way the Germans got the "mobilization code" of France's military intelligence, while the Italians got the French naval code. During the war, this false information, which was transmitted in these codes by the Allies, caused much damage and many defeats for the Fascist countries. In Rotterdam one could buy various codes and ciphers, risking spending a lot of money for nothing, and even Captain Bertrand visited this exchange using the pseudonym Victor Hugo.

After the annexation of Austria by Germany in 1938, the British began to show more interest in intelligence contacts with their future allies. Bertrand was invited to London, where for the first time he met the British cipher experts. He came with Asche's papers that he gave to the British [2]. The British cryptological service in the 1930s was part of the Foreign Office and contained some military sections. Officially known as the Government Code and Cypher School, or GC&CS, it was also called Room 47 of the Foreign Office until 1939 [3, 5, 6, 8, 14]. Afterwards it was called Station X or Bletchley Park. The chief of the GC&CS, Commander Alastair Denniston, was a professional naval intelligence officer. He successfully worked at breaking German codes and ciphers in the famous Room 40 at the Admiralty during the years 1914–18. The chief cryptologist at GC&CS, Alfred Dillwyn Knox, had worked in Room 40 during World War I. In the middle of the 1930s, GC&CS worked hard at breaking the German machine cipher, but failed to make progress. Knox managed, likely in 1938, to solve the cipher of General Franco's army, based on the commercial version of Enigma, but the military Enigma was still a riddle. Among the reasons for the lack of success on the military Enigma in Britain could be the shorter investigating time compared with the Poles, and the less mathematical approach to the analysis.

The British were rather reserved towards Bertrand's proposals concerning joining forces with the French and Polish intelligence sections.

8   The Bombe as a Response to Further Changes in the Enigma System

The international situation became severe and nobody had doubts anymore that Germany would prepare more and more aggressive plans directed towards its neighbors. Suddenly, on 15 September 1938, two weeks before the Munich conference, the Germans altered the rules for enciphering the message keys used by the 20,000 Enigma machines. Now, the Enigma operator himself could select the basic position, a different one each time he sent a message.

The Polish mathematicians, who met difficulties in their work every day, thought of constructing a device that was more efficient than the cyclometer and could take over the long calculations. In October 1938, Marian Rejewski invented a mathematical model of an aggregate, which was given to the designers in AVA.

The Bombe, as the device for recovering Enigma's daily keys was christened, was a true invention [1, 8, 12–14, 18]. This was an electromechanical aggregate based on six Polish Enigmas combined with additional devices and transmissions. An electrically driven system of rotors turned round automatically, creating in each Bombe 17,567 different combinations of letters within 2 hours. When the rotors were placed in the sought-for position, a light appeared, the motors stopped automatically, and the cryptologist read the indications. By setting the Bombes in action (in November 1938), the daily keys could be recovered within 2 hours. Almost at the same time, the B.S. 4 worked out a method for breaking the doubly enciphered individual message keys, which were formed according to the changes in the Enigma system introduced in September 1938. The new Polish method was based on using a special series of perforated paper sheets with a capacity of 51 holes by 51. Each series consisted of 26 sheets. Theoretically, the method was based on so-called females, that is, on manipulating the sheets to match the coincident places in the preprogrammed system. Designed mainly by Henryk Zygalski, the system was quite independent of the number of connections in the German Enigma's commutator [8, 18].

The Germans were cautious and once again changed the Enigma ciphers on 15 December 1938. This time the change involved not operating procedures but components. The Germans introduced two additional rotors per device, raising the number from three to five [5, 8, 14]. This innovation, combined with the new keying procedure, made the process of decryptment almost impossible to continue with. The costs of further operations with further Enigma breaking seemed to be too high for the Polish government.

9   The Gift to the Allies

At the beginning of 1939 the Polish General Staff decided to broaden its exchange of information on Enigma with possible allies. A constant connection had already been established with the French staff, but the French still did not know that Enigma had been solved in 1932 and that the doubles had been created. General Bertrand wrote in his book, published in 1973, that Enigma had been broken in Poland in 1939 [2]. Since the Polish concept of the solution was kept a close secret, the French became impatient and weighed the possibility of arranging a joint meeting with French, Polish and British representatives. Bertrand hoped that such a meeting would improve the Polish-British contacts that were rather cool [2]. At the end of 1938 Bertrand succeeded in organizing the meeting in Paris; top officers of the cryptological services were present. Before, Bertrand had to make a trip to London in order to persuade Commander Denniston of the need to take part in the meeting. Denniston did not believe that something new could be expected in Paris. He had never been in touch with the Polish cryptologists and did not imagine that they could have made any progress on Enigma.

This first meeting with British representatives took place on 9–10 January 1939 in Paris, at the French Military Intelligence offices. Major Bertrand, Captain Henri Braquenié from the Air Force staff and an Army Staff officer represented the French. Three British experts and the Poles — Colonel Gwido Langer and Major Maksymilian Ciężki — were the other attendees.

At the Paris meeting it was agreed that the next conferences would be held in Warsaw and London if something new came to light.

The highest security about the work on Enigma was observed in contacts between Poland and its French and British allies. The Poles did not pass on any decrypted messages to their foreign partners before the summer of 1939. Only summaries about the German armed forces were exchanged. Close contacts on radio intelligence between Poland and France did not mean sharing the secrets of cryptological methods.

But the great moment came. In July 1939, Bertrand received a telegraphed invitation from Gwido Langer (Luc) with the words "there is something new ... " [2]. During the evening of 24 July, an international meeting was held in Warsaw, and Langer informed his French and British colleagues that not only had Enigma's secret been penetrated but also the machine itself had been reconstructed. The French would receive one copy, the British another. The next morning all the participants of the Warsaw meeting drove to the new B.S.-4 nest at Pyry, which was surrounded by forests called the Kabackie Woods. A working meeting took place and the reconstructed Enigma was shown. Marian Rejewski said about himself and his colleagues: "We showed and told them everything that we knew about Enigma." Besides Denniston and Knox, who participated in the meeting, there was another person from Britain. It was possible that the Deputy Head of British military intelligence, Colonel Steward Menzies, appeared incognito as "Professor Sandwich," a mathematician from Oxford [17].

After seeing the Polish Enigma double, Denniston and Knox wanted to contact London at once to order engineers and electricians to come to Warsaw. This was unnecessary because Langer told them that there would be a machine each for Paris and London. The two Enigma machines soon arrived in Paris in diplomatic luggage. The perforated sheets with instructions for using them were also enclosed. On August 16, Bertrand, accompanied by a British diplomatic courier, took one of the machines to London, and at Victoria Station personally handed it to Colonel Menzies [1,2,5,6,14,18]. A few days later Knox sent greetings to the three Polish mathematicians, which included these words in both Polish and English: "My sincere thanks for your cooperation and patience. A. D. Knox."

10   The Mathematical Solution of Enigma

The applications of mathematics to cryptology expanded rapidly with the introduction of cipher machines. The use of permutation theory, combined with other methods of cryptological analysis, contributed to breaking the German machine cipher, Enigma, in Poland in 1932/33. The examples below, giving insight into Enigma's decryptment, are based on two available reports written by Marian Rejewski, which can be found in the Sikorski Historical Institute in London and the Military Historical Institute in Warsaw. Other sources of information are Rejewski's publications which appeared in 1980 [14, 16, 17].

10.1   Description of the Machine

Enigma was a device used for mechanical encipherment of plain texts.

It had a 26-letter keyboard and, behind it, a panel with 26 letters illuminated by glow lamps, which were placed under them. The main ciphering components were the three cipher drums or rotors and a fourth stationary reflector or reversing drum. All the rotors sat on a common axle. The reversing drum could be moved towards or away from the rotors with a lever. The machine was also equipped with a stationary entry ring, which constituted the link between the commutator and the right rotor [4, 16, 17].

The three rotors had the letters of the alphabet placed about their rims. The letters were visible in the little windows in the lid. Each rotor had 26 fixed contacts on one face and 26 spring-loaded contacts on the other. The reversing drum had only spring-loaded contacts connected in pairs on one face. The connections on the four rotors constituted the most important part of the ciphering system and the secret of Enigma. Even the organization of the connections in the entry ring was a great mystery, and the discovery of that secret by Rejewski in the beginning of 1933 constituted one of the greatest contributions in the work on the machine. The entry ring had the letters connected up in alphabetical order. These connections did not cause any relevant action of the entry ring.

The commutator was in front of the keyboard. Six pairs of plugs connected with wires made possible interchange of 12 of the 26 letters of the alphabet.

Depression of an Enigma key caused the right-hand rotor to rotate through one 26th of the whole circumference. At the same time, the circuit was closed and current ran from the depressed key through the commutator, the entry ring, all three rotors that moved by rotating a bit, the reversing drum, and back through the rotors, and once again through the commutator. A glow lamp lit under one of the letters, which was always different from the depressed key. Conversely, if someone struck the key, which was lit before, a previously depressed letter would appear in the windows with light. The Enigma was constructed both for writing plain texts in order to obtain cipher and, conversely, to transform ciphers into clear messages. When one depressed the successive letters of a plain text, the letters of the bulbs that lit formed the cipher.

10.2   Encipherment Procedure

Sending a message, the German clerk first set the rotors into the basic position established for that day and changed the letters in the commutator by placing the plugs into the appropriate sockets. Then he selected the individual key for that message, three letters he enciphered twice. In this way he obtained six letters, which were placed at the opening of the message. Next, he set the rotors to the selected individual key and began to encipher the message. The individual keys for a given day thus had two characteristics: the unknown basic position, and an unknown key for the message, which was enciphered twice. We realize that the first sign meant the same thing as the fourth one, the second was identified with the fifth, and the third was compared to the sixth. Let us denote these pairs by AD, BE and CF [1, 16, 17]. If we have about 80 messages per day, then all the letters of the alphabet can occur in the keys on the six places. We know from the machine's description that when we strike a given key, for example "x," the lamp "y" is to be lit. Then, conversely, striking the "y" key will cause the "x" lamp to light. It is thus concluded that the permutations A through F consist of transpositions. Every pair of letters included in the same transposition has one letter coming from the plain text, while the other represents the cipher associated with the first letter. For instance, the unknown permutation A is expected to be a set of pairs of the type:

$A = (as)(br)(cw)(di)(ev)\ldots(zu)$.

If the encipherer strikes in the first place the unknown key "x" and obtains the letter "a," and by striking in the fourth place the same key "x" obtaining the letter "b," then, by striking in the first place the "a" key, he would obtain the letter "x," and by striking in the fourth place the "x" key he would obtain the letter "b." Thus, there occurs a successive action, first of "a" on "x," and then of "x" on "b." The execution of such operations is called the composition of permutations. If we write the letters "ab" next to each other we will produce a fragment of the permutation AD, which is a product of unknown permutations A and D.

The cryptologists wrote out separately the first six letters of all the messages from a given day, more precisely, their twice-enciphered keys. They chose an arbitrary key and wrote down its first letter, and next to it the fourth. Then they looked for the key, which had as its first letter the fourth letter of the previous key, and they wrote the first letter of the second key beside the fourth letter of the first key. They continued seeking such a key (the third one) that began with the fourth letter of the second key and so on. After a number of steps they returned to the first letter in the first word.

Let us consider the following example. Let

dmq   vbn
von   puy
puc   fmq

designate the chosen openings, that is, the doubly enciphered keys of three
of some 80 messages available for a given day. From the first and the fourth
letters we can see that "*d*" becomes "*v*," "*v*" becomes "*p*," and "*p*" becomes
"*f*." In this way we obtain a fragment of a permutation AD "*dvpf*." Similarly,
from the second and fifth letters we notice that "*o*" becomes "*u*," "*u*" becomes
"*m*," and "*m*" becomes "*b*." We obtain a fragment of the permutation BE as
"*oumb*." And, lastly, we get "*c*" which becomes "*q*," "*q*" which becomes "*n*,"
and "*n*" which becomes "*y*." Hence, the permutation CF begins with "*cqny*."
The openings of other messages would permit the complete assembly of the
set of permutations AD, BE and CF to appear. For example, AD deciphered
from the daily openings was a permutation

$$
\begin{array}{c}
\quad d\ v\ p \quad\ \ o\ e\ i\ j \quad\ \ t\ b\ c\ r\ \ w\ a\ s \\
AD = \downarrow\downarrow\downarrow \cdots \downarrow\downarrow\downarrow\downarrow \cdots \downarrow\downarrow\downarrow\downarrow\ \downarrow\downarrow\downarrow \\
\quad v\ p\ f \quad\ \ d\ i\ j\ m \quad\ \ e\ c\ b\ w\ r\ \ a\ s \\
= (dvpfkxgzyo)(eijmunqlht)(bc)(rw)(a)(s)
\end{array}
$$

while

$$
BE = (blfqveoum)(hjpswizrn)(axt)(cgy)(d)(k)
$$

and

$$
CF = (abviktjgfcqny)(duzrehlxwpsmo).
$$

The set of permutations for AD, BE and CF was called the "characteristic set for a given day." We remember that the permutations contain
the enciphered letters without any close connections with the plain text. We
wish to separate the permutations A through F, which, instead, present the
associations between the clear text and the cipher.

Some theorems were involved in the solutions. Let us quote the most
important of them.

Theorem 1. *If two permutations X and Y of the same degree comprise disjunctive transpositions, then their product XY will include disjunctive cycles
of the same lengths in even numbers.*

We may also prove the converse theorem.

Theorem 2. *If a permutation includes disjunctive cycles of the same lengths
in even numbers, then the permutation may be regarded as a product XY of
two permutations X and Y, composed of disjunctive transpositions.*

Analyzing the permutation AD we can evaluate its contents as two cycles
of length 10, two cycles of length 2, and two cycles of length 1.

It may also be shown that:

Theorem 3. *Letters entering into one and the same transposition of permutation X or Y enter always into two different cycles of the same length, which belong to the permutation XY.*

The theorems quoted above helped to determine the connections between the plain text and the corresponding cipher. Let us assume that the German clerks had some habits when they arbitrarily created the openings of messages. Suppose, for example, that the encipherer liked to select three identical letters, such as "*aaa*," "*bbb*" or the like. Since in the product AD the letters "*a*" and "*s*" form single-letter cycles, then "*a*" and "*s*" should belong to the same transposition (as). This means that the plain letter "*a*" has the representing cipher letter "*s*."

Suppose that the enciphered message keys from a given day begin with the letter "*s*":

$sug \quad smf$
$sjm \quad spo$
$syx \quad scw.$

Only the last key starting with "*syx*" could arise from the plain text "*aaa*," for the transposition (as) has one representative in the cycle (a) and the other in (s) — both belonging to AD. By analyzing the transposition (ay) representing the second place of the key, we realize that "*a*" belongs to the cycle (axt), while "*y*" is placed in (cgy). Both cycles come from the permutation BE. At last, the pair (ax) tracing the third position in the key has "*a*" in $(abviktjgfcqny)$ and "*x*" in $(duzrehlxwpsmo)$. The cycles are parts of the permutation CF. Even a strict analysis of the second part in the third message key proves that "*scw*" are ciphers of "*aaa*" according to the rule of double ciphering.

By using the sets AD, BE and CF, collecting them over a period of a few days, the mathematicians managed to construct the internal connections of the machine.

10.3   The Set of Equations

The unknown permutations A through F were also found as solutions of the equation set. After a key has been depressed, the current first passes through a series of the machine's components to finally light a lamp with the letter. Each of these components causes a permutation of the alphabet. We denote the permutation caused by the commutator by the letter S, the permutations created by the rotors (from right to left) have the initials N, M and L, and the permutation caused by the reversing drum is called R. Since the letters of the entry ring were linked in alphabetical order, then the permutation H associated with the ring would be the identity without any relevance. The path of the current will be represented by the product of permutations $SNMLRL^{-1}M^{-1}N^{-1}S^{-1}$, where the sign "$-1$" denotes an inverse permutation. We also keep in mind that the depression of the key causes a movement of the first right rotor that rotates an amount equal to one 26th of the circumference. This movement creates the next permutation, in which each letter is assigned to the next one. We denote the last permutation by P and write it down as

$$P = \begin{matrix} a & b & c & & z \\ \downarrow & \downarrow & \downarrow & \cdots & \downarrow \\ b & c & d & & a \end{matrix} = (abcdef\cdots xyz).$$

The unknown permutations $A - F$ are represented in the following form

$$A = SPNP^{-1}MLRL^{-1}M^{-1}PN^{-1}P^{-1}S^{-1}$$
$$B = SP^2NP^{-2}MLRL^{-1}M^{-1}P^2N^{-1}P^{-2}S^{-1}$$
$$\cdots$$
$$F = SP^6NP^{-6}MLRL^{-1}M^{-1}P^6N^{-1}P^{-6}S^{-1},$$

and the AD, BE and CF products have the presentations

$$AD = SPNP^{-1}MLRL^{-1}M^{-1}PN^{-1}P^3NP^{-4}MLRL^{-1}M^{-1}P^4N^{-1}P^{-4}S^{-1}$$
$$BE = SP^2NP^{-2}MLRL^{-1}M^{-1}P^2N^{-1}P^3NP^{-5}MLRL^{-1}M^{-1}P^5N^{-1}P^{-5}S^{-1}$$
$$CF = SP^3NP^{-3}MLRL^{-1}M^{-1}P^3N^{-1}P^3NP^{-6}MLRL^{-1}M^{-1}P^6N^{-1}P^{-6}S^{-1}.$$

In the set of equations derived above, only the permutation P and its powers are known. By discovering the connections in the drums it was possible to reconstruct the associated pairs "plain text-cipher" in the permutations $A - F$, which made it possible to read the messages during only one day.

The material above, shown as an excerpt from the extensive documentation of the Enigma description, allows us to understand better the machine construction as well as to realize that enormous efforts were undertaken to break Enigma's code.

11 Epilogue

As the title suggests, the first part of the Enigma story, based only on the collected facts, ended in July 1939. After some weeks the war broke out. On 5 September B.S. 4 in Pyry received an order to destroy part of its files and prepare to evacuate, along with other units of the General Staff, to Romania. After getting to Bucharest, the cryptologists were recommended to go directly to the French Embassy. They introduced themselves as "friends of Bolek" and they got all possible help to be able to travel to France. After a short stay in Paris the Polish mathematicians, together with central units of the French military intelligence, were moved out of the city to two spacious chateaux in the town of Gretz-Armainvillers. The seat of offensive intelligence and evaluation was the Château Péreire, codenamed P.C.-Victor, and the radio intelligence and decryptment services were housed in the large Château de Vignolles, codenamed P.C.-Bruno. The Poles formed Team Z, which worked at breaking Nazi codes and ciphers [14, 19].

In the beginning of November 1939, the French-Polish Bruno center became the chief headquarters and foundation of all Allied radio intelligence. All enciphered intercepts reached the Polish cryptologists, who used three Enigma machines (two secretly taken out of Poland during the evacuation, and the one which was presented to the French after the Warsaw conference in July 1939).

During the Poles' first weeks at Bruno, the French deputy chief, Captain Henri Braquenié, received some news from Britain. The British were building their own cryptological Bombe. They were also producing perforated (Zygalski) sheets and could even send a certain number of papers to Bruno. In exchange, Bruno was supplying German Navy and Air Force signals, which were important to the British, who were not directly threatened on land. On 3–7 December 1939, Colonel Langer (who joined Bruno in the meantime) and Captain Braquenié were in London and at Bletchley on a working visit. The cooperation with the British was assured by a British officer detailed to Bruno, Captain Kenneth "Pinky" McFarlan, as well as by visits and contacts between Bruno and Bletchley Park.

The designer of the first British Bombe was a young mathematician, Alan Turing. Before the war, he had worked in the United States under Prof. John von Neumann, a pioneer in information science and computers, who, during the war, participated in the Manhattan project. In the first months of 1940, Turing would come down to Bruno to exchange experiences in Enigma decryptment with the Poles [14]. Those contacts resulted later in the exchange of letters between Alan's mother (after his death) and Henryk Zygalski, who stayed in Britain after the war.

After many years Marian Rejewski recalls: "We treated Alan as a younger colleague who had specialized in mathematical logic and was just starting in cryptology. We discussed, if I remember, the construction of the commutator and plug connections (Steckerverbindungen) that were Enigma's strong points. Turing was also interested in the three-letter code used by the Luftwaffe." Rejewski also remembered with almost photographic precision the farewell supper given before Alan Turing's return to Britain after the visit to the Bruno center. During that time the Poles hardly could have supposed that their young British colleague would some day figure in books on information science as an outstanding theoretician of computers.

On 10 May 1940, the German Army opened a powerful attack on France. The Polish team was first moved to Paris, but German forces were getting dangerously close to the city. The members of the Bruno center were sent from the capital to the stopovers Le Chatelet, Vensat, and finally to Bon Encontre. Here, in June 1940, the Polish group were informed that Pétain

— now Premier — had signed the armistice. The Bruno members were evacuated to Toulouse and then to Algeria. The British liaison officer, Captain McFarlan, was driven to Cazaux, where he managed to catch the last RAF plane for Britain.

The armistice divided France's territory into several parts. One of them was an unoccupied zone in southern France called L'État Français or Vichy France, which was ruled dictatorially by Pétain. The underground military organization that appeared in the post-armistice French Army included many patriotic officers who decided to rebuild in southern France the anti-German intelligence. As early as 8 July 1940, Bertrand presented his superiors with a proposal to resume radio intelligence. Such operations could proceed only in deep secrecy, since the Germans would accuse the Vichy government of violating the terms of armistice. The plan was, thus, to work in the territory of unoccupied France, using German wireless ciphergrams intercepted and forwarded to a secret decryptment center by patriotic officers at the Vichy government's monitoring system.

In July and August 1940, Major Bertrand, alias Monsieur Barsac, was preparing in southern France new facilities for a clandestine radio-intelligence center that was to act together with the Allies and the emerging French Résistance. He formally selected the Château des Fouzes as a site for "Command Post Cadix." To avoid suspicion, Monsieur Barsac arranged all the necessary papers confirming that the French Military Intelligence owned the chateau.

Bertrand knew that the Polish cryptologists, who waited in North Africa, could render valuable services to the Allies and that they could do this best while working in France. General Juliusz Kleeberg, the semi-official representative in southern France of the Polish government in exile, in consultation with London, concluded that the Polish cryptologists should work together with the French. Organizationally, the Polish unit would be subordinate to the Polish commander-in-chief's staff in Britain, and would receive the code name "Field Office 300."

During September 1940, the Poles of Team Z in North Africa received documents issued in false names and returned to southern France. They were detailed to the newly created Cadix center, where they continued working on German military ciphers.

The members of the Cadix groups did not know exactly, because of the utmost secrecy, the details about channels by which Bertrand reached the Allied staffs and their intelligence units. The officers at Cadix, who enciphered messages for transmittal across the English Channel, felt that the contacts with the intelligence services in Britain were close, and even Major Bertrand mentioned some technical help in the form of a new transmitter, which he received from the British in Lisbon in 1942.

When the Germans occupied southern France, Marian Rejewski and Henryk Zygalski escaped to Britain. They were detailed to the Polish intercept and decryptment center at Boxmoor near London.

It might have seemed logical that the British, who, before the war, had received from the Poles one Enigma double and methods for solving the ciphers, and who had worked together with their Polish and French allies at Bruno and Cadix, would now reestablish the interrupted contact. But the British seemed to feel no need for further cooperation with the Polish cryptologists, who, unable to work with Enigma, occupied themselves with breaking S.S. ciphers.

In 1946, Rejewski returned to Poland from Britain, where he had spent the last years of the war. He worked as a clerk until he retired. In 1980 he died in Warsaw. Zygalski decided to stay in Britain. He taught mathematics at Battersea Technical College before he died in 1978. Różycki was killed during the sinking of a French ship in 1942.

The early Polish contributions to the Enigma solution enabled the British codebreakers to make great progress in the further development of methods to break the Enigma code. There are no doubts that all the efforts undertaken in the battle over Enigma contributed to shortening the war and sparing many human lives.

References

1. Bauer, F. L. (2002). Decrypted Secrets. Methods and Maxims of Cryptology. Springer-Verlag, Berlin, Heidelberg.
2. Bertrand, G. (1973). The Greatest Enigma of the War of 1939–1945. Librairie Plon, Paris (in French).
3. Calvocoressi, P. (1977). The Secrets of Enigma. The Listener **20**, **27**, London.
4. Deavours, C. A. (1981). Comments to "How Polish Mathematicians Deciphered the Enigma" by Marian Rejewski. Annals of the History of Computing **3**, pp. 229–234.
5. Freedman, M. (2000). Unravelling Enigma. Winning the Code War at Station X. Published by Led Cooper, Barnsley, UK.
6. Gaj, K. (1989). Szyfr Enigmy — tajemnice złamania (The Cipher of Enigma — The Methods of Breaking), Wydawnictwo Komunikacji i Łączności, Warsaw (in Polish).
7. Garliński, J. (1999). Enigma — tajemnice drugiej wojny światowej (Secrets of the Enigma War). Wydawnictwo Uniwersytetu Marii Curie-Skłodowskiej (Publishing House of the Maria Curie-Skłodowska University), Lublin (in Polish).
8. Hodges, A. (1983). Alan Turing: the Enigma. Simon and Schuster, New York.
9. Kahn, D. (1967). The Codebreakers. Macmillan, New York.
10. Kozaczuk, W. (1967). Bitwa o tajemnice (The Secret Battle). Książka i Wiedza, Warsaw (in Polish).
11. Kozaczuk, W. (1976). Złamany szyfr (The Broken Cipher). Wydawnictwo Ministerstwa Obrony Narodowej, Warsaw (in Polish).
12. Kozaczuk, W. (1977). Wojna w eterze (War in the Ether). Wydawnictwo Radia i Telewizji, Warsaw (in Polish).
13. Kozaczuk, W. (1979). W kręgu Enigmy (In Enigma's Circle). Książka i Wiedza, Warsaw (in Polish).

14. Kozaczuk, W. (1984). Enigma. University Publications of America, Inc.
15. Kuratowski, K. (1980). A Half-Century of Polish Mathematics: Remembrances and Reflections. Pergamon Press, Oxford.
16. Rejewski, M. (1980). An Application of the Theory of Permutations in Breaking the Enigma Cipher. Applicationes Mathematicae **16**, no **4**, Warsaw.
17. Rejewski, M. (1980). Jak matematycy polscy rozszyfrowali Enigmę (How the Polish Mathematicians Broke Enigma). Roczniki Polskiego Towarzystwa Matematycznego, Seria II: Wiadomości Matematyczne (Annals of the Polish Mathematical Society, Series II: Mathematical News) **23**, 1–28 (in Polish).
18. Sebag-Montefiore, H. (2000). Enigma, the Battle for the Code. Weidenfeld & Nicolson, London.
19. Woytak, R. (1979). On the Border of War and Peace: Polish Intelligence and Diplomacy in 1937–1939 and the Origins of the Ultra Secret. Columbia University Press, New York.

Alan Turing at Bletchley Park in World War II

Tony Sale

Ex Museums Director, Bletchley Park, UK

Summary. "There should be no question in anyone's mind that Turing's work was the biggest factor in Hut 8's success [in breaking the German Naval Enigma]. In the early days he was the only cryptographer who thought the problem worth tackling and not only was he primarily responsible for the main theoretical work within the hut (particularly the developing of a satisfactory scoring technique for dealing with Banburismus) but he also shared with Welchman and Keen the chief credit for the invention of the Bombe. It is always difficult to say that anyone is absolutely indispensable but if anyone was indispensable to Hut 8 it was Turing" [1].

1   Alan Turing and the Enigma Machine

The mathematician Alan Turing had been identified, at Cambridge, as a likely candidate for code breaking. He came to the Government Code and Cypher School (GC&CS) in Broadway in London a number of times in early 1938 to be shown what had already been achieved. He was shown some intercepts of German signals enciphered on the German forces Enigma cipher machine.

The Enigma machine, Fig. 1, was an electro/mechanical way of achieving a seven, or nine, layer substitution cipher. The individual substitutions were fixed by wiring within wheels which could be rotated by the operator but which also index round, like a car miles indicator, as letters to be enciphered or deciphered were entered.

The Enigma was patented in 1918 by Arthur Scherbius in Berlin, developed by him as a commercial product and shown to the public in 1922.

Because the machine could be bought by anyone, the security of the cipher depended not on the machine itself but on the vast number of ways in which it could be configured before the start of an encipherment.

To increase the complexity of this setting up, each wheel had a tyre, or ring, round the core containing the cross wiring. Letters or numbers on the surface of this ring appeared in the windows above each wheel. The ring could be rotated around the core and set by the operator before encipherment began. It remained set throughout the message input.

The action of pressing a key caused the right hand wheel to index one position (one of 26). At some point this rotation was transferred to the next wheel on the left. This was known as a carry and was caused by a slot,

Fig. 1. A German Army/Airforce Enigma Machine

the carry slot, coming into line with the indexing pawls. This carry slot was initially on the wheels; later it was moved to the ring.

An electrical current was used to sense the substitutions. When a key was pressed a connection was made from the battery to a point on the fixed entry disc on the right hand side of the wheels, AFTER the right hand wheel had indexed and any carry had caused other wheels to turn ... The electrical current flowed through the internal wiring in the wheels from right to left, was turned round in the reflector and came back through the wheels to exit at a different point on the entry disc which was connected to a lamp on the lamp panel. The lamp that lit was the encipherment of the key just pressed.

The clockwise order of connections to the fixed, right hand, entry disc was known as the "entry order." In the Scherbius commercial machine this was just the order of the keys on the keyboard from left to right across each of the three rows. This was known as the QWERTZUIO order.

Thus the variable elements of the Enigma were: the wheels and their order from left to right in the machine, the ring setting for each wheel, the wheel rotational position, the start position before encipherment started.

The first Enigma machines, the glow lamp machines of the 1920s, had three wheels which could be removed and replaced in any order. (6 combinations). The reflector was rotatable by the operator (26 positions). The wheel start positions thus gave 26 × 26 × 26 positions. The ring settings gave a 26 position rotational translation of each wheel start position. Total number of different configurations, $2,741,856$.

From 1930 the plug board (Stecker) was added to the Enigma used by the German Army and Air Force. The plug board enabled pairs of letters to be completely transposed. Initially 6 pairs were transposed, later this was increased to 10, the nearly optimum number. At the same time the reflector became fixed. This machine was then also adopted by the German Navy.

For this Enigma the wheels give $6 \times 26 \times 26 \times 26 = 105,456$ possible combinations. Six plug pairs gives $100,391,791,500$ possibilities; total approximately ten thousand, million, million (10^{17}).

Despite this seeming invulnerability due to such a vast number of possible configurations, the Enigma machine had some weaknesses. Firstly because of the reflector no letter could encipher to itself. Secondly, each of the first set of wheels, 1 to 5, had a different point at which turnover occurred to the next wheel on the left. This allowed identification of the right hand wheel and sometimes even the centre wheel. (The later Naval Enigma wheels 6, 7 & 8 had two carries, all at the same wheel positions.)

In London, in 1938, Alan Turing would have met Alistair Denniston, the head of GC&CS and Edward Travis, Hugh Foss, John Tiltman and Dilly Knox, all eminent code breakers, some from World War I.

Edward Travis had purchased a commercial Enigma machine in 1925 and Hugh Foss had devised a geometric way for breaking it in 1927. Later, in 1936, Dilly Knox devised his "rods" method for breaking the unsteckered Enigma used in the Spanish civil war which also had the QWERTZUIO entry order and the same rotor wiring as the commercial Enigma.

Meanwhile in Poland the Polish Security Service had purchased a commercial Enigma and worked out, in the 1920s, methods for breaking it. When, in 1930, the Germans changed to the steckered Enigma, the Poles recruited some young mathematicians to try to break it. The greatest of these was Marian Rejewski who found ways of exploiting the German procedural mistakes in using Enigma. The problem for the Germans was how to tell the intended recipient of an enciphered message the exact wheel start letters from which the message could be deciphered. They decided to encipher this start position, known as the message key, on the Enigma machine itself in order to conceal it from any interceptor. But they also enciphered it twice in order to make certain that it was correctly received by the intended operator.

It was this double encipherment which Marian Rejewski exploited in his very successful "characteristics" method of attack. He also correctly deduced that the Germans had changed the entry order to ABCDEFG ... and worked out the new wheel wirings which were different from those in the commercial machine. Later he devised a machine called a "Bomba" specifically to attack the double encipherment of the message key.

In 1938 Dilly Knox already knew that the German forces Enigma rotors were wired differently to the commercial rotors, but did not know the entry rotor order and apparently did not know of the double encipherment of the message key.

All the Polish achievements were divulged to the British and the French at the famous meeting in the Pyry Forest near Warsaw in July 1939.

In September 1939 Turing came to Bletchley Park and joined Dilly Knox in the cottage in the stable yard. He started to think of ways to break Enigma using probable words, "cribs" and was intrigued by the problems in breaking the German Naval Enigma.

The method based on probable words was a far more powerful method than that used in Rejewski's Bomba and led later to the development of the Turing Bombe.

GC&CS already had a few intercepts and at least one plain text/cipher text pair, reputed to have been smuggled to England by a Polish cipher clerk.

2 "Cribs" and Opened Out Enigmas

2.1 Letter Pairs

Among the characteristics that Turing found in these messages was that occasionally the same cipher/plain text pair of characters occurred at different places in the same message.

```
JYCQRPWYDEMCJMRSR
SPRUCHNUMMERXEINS
```

Remember that because the Enigma machine is reversible, R→C is the same as C→R and M→E the same as E→M.

Whether such pairings occur is determined by the rotor order and the core rotor start positions. Turing realized that conversely the actual rotor order and core rotor start position could be arrived at by trying all configurations to see if these pairings were satisfied and more importantly he realized that this was independent of the Steckers.

Obviously just setting up a single Enigma machine and trying by keying in would take an impossibly long time. The next step was to consider how the tests could be carried out simultaneously for a particular Enigma start configuration. Testing for letter pairs required a method for rapidly determining whether such a configuration was true or false. This led to the concept of electrically connecting together a number of Enigma machines (Fig. 2).

This was achieved by using an "opened out" Enigma (Fig. 3). In the actual Enigma electrical current enters and leaves by the fixed entry rotor because of the reflector or Umkerwaltze (U) and this precluded connecting Enigmas together. In Turing's opened out Enigma the reflector had two sides, the exit side being connected to three rotors representing the reverse current paths through the actual Enigma rotors. This gave separate input and output connections and thus allowed a number of Enigmas to be connected in series.

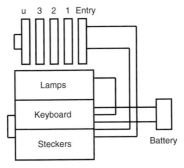

Fig. 2. Enigma schematic

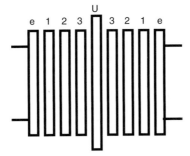

Fig. 3. Opened out Enigma

In the Letchworth implementation (Fig. 4), the clever thing was to include both forward and backward wiring of an Enigma rotor in one drum. The connections from one drum to the next were by four concentric circles of 26 fixed contacts and four concentric sets of wire brushes on the drum. Three sets of fixed contacts were permanently wired together and to the 26 way input and output connectors. Three drums, representing the original Enigma rotors, could now be placed on shafts over the contacts and this was an opened out Enigma with separate input and output connectors.

To return to the problem of checking whether C enciphers to R (written as C→R), first an offset reference from the start is required. A lower case alphabet written over the cipher text gives this.

abcdefghijklmnopq

JYCQRPWYDEMCJMRSR

SPRUCHNUMMERXEINS

This shows that C→R at offset c, e and l from the start (see Fig. 5), and M→E at j, k and n. The opened out Enigma allows an electric voltage to be applied to the input connection "C" and a set of 26 lamps to be connected

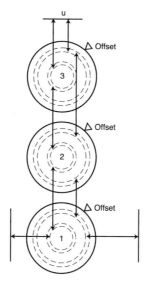

Fig. 4. Letchworth Enigma

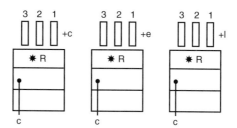

Fig. 5. Separate Enigmas testing for CR

to the output connector. If the R lamp lights then the drums are in an order
and position such that C enciphers to R.

With a single Enigma this can occur at a vast number of drum settings.
However the crib allows an opened out Enigma to be set up for each occurrence of C→R (Fig. 6) and they can then all be tested simultaneously.

The opened out Enigmas are all set up with the same drum order and
the drums are then turned to the same settings for the left hand and middle
drums but the right hand drums are turned to the offset letter along the crib
at which the test is to be made. All the inputs are connected in parallel and
a voltage applied to the "C" contact. Then a set of relays connected to each
of the "R" output contacts tests to see if all the R contacts have a voltage
on at the same time. When they do a position of the drums has been found
which satisfies the crib at the points chosen for C→R (Fig. 6).

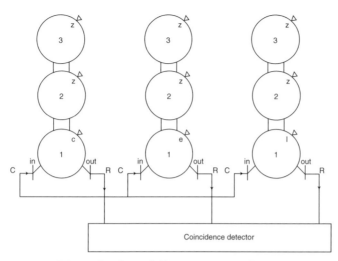

Fig. 6. Letchworth Enigmas testing for CR

If they don't then all the right hand drums are advanced one position and the test is tried again. After 26 positions of the right hand drum the centre drum is advanced one position and this continues until all drum positions have been tested. Then the drums are changed to try a different drum order. A very long process by hand which obviously asks to be automated.

This can be achieved by an electric motor driving all the right hand drums simultaneously and then "carrying" to the middle drum every 26 positions, with a further carry from the middle to left hand rotor when this has turned through 26 positions. In this way the drums can be driven through all $17,576$ possible positions and the occurrence of a correct position for all C→R in the crib can be checked.

But there are still a large number of positions which satisfy the C→R test. What is needed is a better method for finding the rotor order and rotor setting.

2.2   Letter Loops and Steckers

An extension of the concept of letter pairs is where letters enciphered from one to another at different places in the crib resulting in loops of letters.

```
abcdefghijklmnopq
JYCQRPRYDEMCJMRSR
SPRUCHNUMMERXEINS
```

For instance R→N at g, N→S at p and S→R at q making a loop (Fig. 7). A diagram showing such loops was known as a menu (Fig. 8).

But if Steckers are being used this is actually:

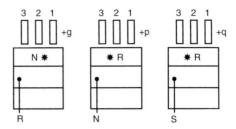

Fig. 7. Separate Enigmas Testing for RNS

- R steckered to S1 enciphers to S2 steckered to N at g
- N steckered to S2 enciphers to S3 steckered to S at p
- S steckered to S3 enciphers to S1 steckered to R at q (see Fig. 9).

Fig. 8. A menu

The problem now is to find the core positions S1, S2 and S3. If these can be found then they are the Steckers of the menu letters.

But Turing realized that there was another way of looking at interconnected opened out Enigmas and that this way found Stecker connections.

Take the loop example above of R→N→S→R. Three opened out Enigmas are connected serially one to the other and the right hand drums are turned to the offsets g, p and q. If the correct drum order is being used then there will be some start position of the left had, middle and right hand drums which corresponds to the actual original Enigma core rotor positions having allowed for the difference between the original Ringstellung and ZZZ. At this point the core rotor positions will be the same as the original Enigma core rotor positions and the encipherments will then be the same.

This means that a voltage placed onto the S1 input of the first opened out Enigma, which is the Stecker of the input R, will come out on the S2 terminal which is the Stecker of N. Since this is connected to the next opened out Enigma, this goes in on its S2 terminal and comes out on the S3 terminal which is the Stecker of S. This S3 input now goes through the third opened out Enigma and comes out at S1 which is the Stecker of R. Thus the drum positions correspond to the original Enigma positions where S1→S2→S3→S1.

The magic trick is now to connect the output terminals of the last opened out Enigma back to the input of the first Enigma. There is now a physical wired connection through the opened out Enigmas from the S1 input terminal to the S1 output terminal which is now connected to the S1 input terminal. This forms a loop of wire not connected to any other terminals on any opened out Enigma (Fig. 10).

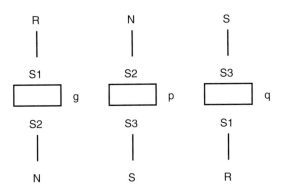

Fig. 9. Including Steckers

Thus if a voltage is placed on S1 at the input it goes nowhere else, just appears on the S1, S2 and S3 terminals. If a strip of 26 lamps is connected at the joins between opened out Enigmas then the S1, S2 and S3 lamps will light confirming the voltage path through S1, S2 and S3.

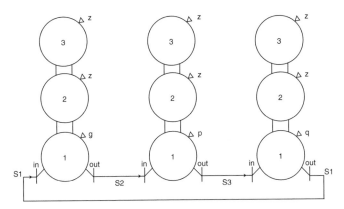

Fig. 10. Letchworth Enigmas connected as a menu

Now comes Turing's really clever bit. If S1 is not known and the voltage is placed on, say, A then this voltage will propagate through the opened out Enigmas because they are joined around from output to input, but *cannot* reach the S1, S2, S3 loop because it is not connected to any other terminals. The voltage runs around the wires inside the opened out Enigmas until it reaches a terminal which already has the voltage on it. The complete vastly complex electrical network has then reached a steady state.

Now if the lamp strip is connected at the joins of the opened out Enigmas, lots of lamps will light showing where the voltage has reached various terminals, but the appropriate S1, S2 and S3 lamps will not light. In favourable circumstances 25 of the lamps will light. The unlit lamp reveals the core letters, S1, S2 or S3. These are interpreted as the Steckers of the letters on the menu.

When the drum order and drum positions are correct compared to that of the original core Enigma encipherment there is just the one wired connection through the opened out Enigmas, at connections S1, S2 and S3. But Turing also realised that such a system of joined opened out Enigmas could rapidly reject positions of the drums which were not the correct ones.

If the drums are not in the correct position then the loop S1, S2, S3 does not exists and the voltage can propagate to these terminals as well. Thus it is possible for the voltage to reach all 26 terminals at the join of two of the opened out Enigmas. This implies that there is no possible Stecker letter and therefore this position of the drums cannot be correct. But because of the way the cross wiring inside real Enigma rotors is organised, closed loops of connections can occur which are not the loops corresponding to the actual Stecker connections being looked for. The configuration of opened out Enigmas cannot distinguish between these spurious loops and the correct Stecker loop.

The test for a loop of possible Steckers at a particular drum order and rotor position is to see if either only one or 25 of the lamps are lit. If all 26 lamps light then this position can be rejected and this rejection can occur at very high speed. The voltage flows around the wires at nearly the speed of light so that the whole complex network stabilises in fractions of a microsecond. What was required was some way of automating the changes of drum position for all the drums in synchronism and for rapidly sensing any reject situation.

In 1939 the only technology available for achieving electrical connections from rapidly changing drum positions was to use small wire brushes on the drums to make contact with fixed contacts on the Test Plate. This was a proven technology from punched card equipment. High speed relays were initially the only reliable devices for sensing the voltages on the interconnections. Thermionic valves were tried but were not reliable enough in 1939. Later, thyratron gas filled valves were used successfully and these were about 100 times faster than the high speed relays.

The British Tabulating Machine Co (BTM) had designed the opened out Enigmas and built the Test Plate. The project to now build a complete search engine, which became known as a Bombe, came under the direction of H. H. (Doc) Keen.

The machine, known as Victory, was completed by March 1940 and delivered to Bletchley Park. It was first installed in one end of Hut 1. Now the work began on finding out how to use this new device. Results at first were not very encouraging. The difficulties in finding cribs meant that when a menu was constructed between intercepted enciphered text and a crib, it usually did not have enough loops to provide good rejection and therefore a large number of incorrect stops resulted.

3   The "E" Rack

In November 1939, Alan Turing proposed a letter frequency attack using what he called the "E" rack (see also Sect. A). There are no surviving documents giving any details of what was proposed but a modern computer simulation, Virtual E rack, shows that it would have been feasible.

3.1   Letter Frequency

The basis of this attack is that the frequency of occurrence of some letters of natural language is very far from random. For instance, in German and English the letter E occurs at about 12% compared with a random score of 4%. Code breakers had long ago realised this, it was used to attack Caesar's substitution ciphers. What Alan Turing realised was that it could be mechanised along similar lines to his development of the Turing Bombe.

If a length of cipher text could be deciphered simultaneously by lots of Letchworth Enigmas and the number of output E counted, then a correct setting would show as a large count of E, but more importantly an incorrect setting could be rapidly rejected by a low count of E.

3.2   Minimum Length of Cipher Text

The first question is how long must the cipher text be to obtain a significant result. Measurements on some original deciphered German messages showed an E frequency of one in eight letters. (Oliver Lawn's 1941 paper gives one in 8.34 over 5,410 German message letters). This agrees with the 12% quoted elsewhere.

However, what is more important for the determination of minimum length is the maximum distance between E in messages. Examining archive German decrypts gives 8 for the average but a long tail out to 34 as the maximum inter E distance in these messages.

Successive starting point lengths of 50 letters gives a minimum of 2 Es for an average of 4. 80 letter lengths give minimum 5 and length 120 gives minimum 9.

Next question; what are the maximum counts of any letter when a length of cipher text is deciphered on the wrong Enigma setting. The Virtual E rack enables this to be measured by setting the cut off limit so low that all decipherments are shown. One result is that for a cipher length of 70, E max on the correct settings is 9 but E count off the correct settings also can be 9 as are the maximum counts for non E off the correct setting. However, a cipher length of 130 letters gives a count of 25 on E max correct with counts of 17 for E on incorrect and for other letters' maxima.

So it would appear that a cipher length of over 100 letters is required to get a clear indication of the correct setting and this is confirmed by Virtual E rack.

3.3   Limitations on the Use of the E Rack

Most importantly the Steckers (plug board connections) must be known or mostly all known. The reason for this is that a letter substitution on the output side would just mean a different letter giving a maximum in place of E if E was steckered. But missing or wrong substitutions on the input side completely change the encipherment.

Virtual E rack will work with one Stecker pair missing and sometimes with two, but it depends which two.

Then there is wheel turnover. Because the ring settings are not known (ZZZ is assumed), any turnover in the course of encipherment of the original message is not reproduced. Virtual E rack tries to take care of turnover in the right hand to centre wheels by deciphering the cipher text consecutively at two turnover points on the right hand wheel; 2 and 16 are used. This means that the decipherment will only be wrong for a maximum of half a wheel rotation for one of the two settings. (I tried using 3 decipherments at about 8 position intervals but the improvement was so slight it was thought better to go faster on two).

3.4   So Where Could the E Rack Be Used?

Firstly Turing et al in their original November 1939 note suggested it could be used against German Naval Enigma. The problem, at that time, was the lack of complete Bigram tables. Some entries had been worked out by Turing, but only very few. This meant that although they could sometimes find the settings for one message, they could not decipher other messages because they couldn't decode the message keys, the wheel start positions.

But if they had found the Steckers from the message they had broken, then the E rack could be used to find the wheel starts for the other messages.

However the capture of the complete Bigram tables probably rendered the E rack unnecessary.

4   Adding the Diagonal Board to the Bombe

Soon after the first Bombe came to Bletchley Park, Gordon Welchman came up with the idea of the diagonal board. This was an implementation of the simple fact that if B is steckered to G then G is also steckered to B. If 26 rows of 26 way connectors are stacked up, then any connection point can be referenced by its row letter and column letter. A physical piece of wire can now connect row B element G to row G element B. The device was called a Diagonal Board because such a piece of wire is diagonally across the matrix of connections.

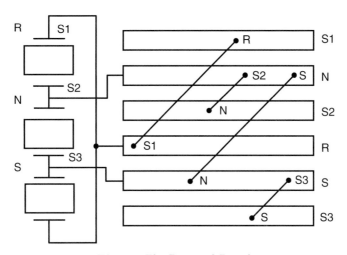

Fig. 11. The Diagonal Board

Now the double ended Enigma configuration knows nothing about Steckers. It can only deduce rotor core wiring positions which satisfy the menu. However the possible Steckers such as R↔S1, can by exploited by the Diagonal Board. If the joins between double ended Enigmas are also connected into the Diagonal Board at the position corresponding to the original cipher/plain text pair on the menu, say R, then this can significantly increase the rejection of incorrect double ended Enigma drum positions.

It has already been shown that if a set of drum positions has been found where S1→S2→S3→S1 then a physical wired connection has been made through the joins between opened out Enigmas at S1, S2 & S3. The deduction from this is that R is steckered to S1, etc. Now if the join representing R on the menu is plugged to the R row of the Diagonal Board, a physical piece of wire will connect through the Diagonal Board from row R at position S1 to row S1 at position R. Since S1 is not plugged to anything the voltage on this wire goes nowhere else. Similarly for the other joining positions between opened out Enigmas. Thus the Diagonal Board does not affect the finding of the correct drum positions.

But if the drums are not in the correct position to make the connection S1, S2 & S3, then a voltage travelling around the network and finally arriving at say row N position S will be passed via the Diagonal Board wire to row S position N and will thus continue through the wiring in the opened out Enigmas on both sides of the join S. The Diagonal Board thus greatly contributes to the voltage flow around the network of wires in the opened out Enigmas due to the extra connectivity that it provides. This increases the rejection of drum positions which do not satisfy the menu.

5   Alan Turing and the German Navy's Use of Enigma

5.1   Why Naval Enigma was Difficult

At first sight it is not obvious why Naval Enigma was so difficult; it initially used the same version of Enigma as the German Army and Air Force and these were broken virtually throughout the War. The difficulty lay in the indicator system. This was unique to the German Navy and involved a separate coding system, bigrams and trigrams, for concealing the message setting. As will be explained, it was this indicator system which made the breaking of Naval Enigma so difficult and it had defeated the Poles.

Alan Turing started where the Poles left off, with the 100 or so messages from May 1st–8th 1937 whose starting positions were known.

From these he had the two four letter groups, the indicators, from each message and also the message setting, i.e., the start position for deciphering the message which the Poles had found.

Using these and some very elegant deductions, Turing worked out the complete indicator system.

At the same time, as he later said, "I thought of the method of Banbarismus, but was not sure that it would work in practice." This was at the end of 1939.

A summary document on the Naval Enigma Situation (see Sect. A) was produced in November 1939, signed by Dilly Knox., Peter Twinn, Gordon Welchman, Alan Turing and John Jeffreys. It was Appendix II in the original document. It proposes a "rack" as a method for solving Enigma. I don't think that this was ever built. It was overtaken by Turing's work on his Bombe.

In early 1940, joined by Peter Twinn, Turing started an attack on messages for 28th November 1938 using FortyWeepyWeepy cribs. The reason for going back so far was that only 6 Steckers were being used at that time and the FortyWeepyWeepy cribs were working. These were broken after a fortnight's work and four other days also came out.

The name FortyWeepyWeepy arose from the German habit of starting a continuation part of a message (Fort in German) with the time of origin of the first part using the top row of the keyboard as numbers, $Q = 1$, $W = 2$ etc. with Y as a figure shift showing that the following letters should be interpreted as numbers. Hence continuation part of a message originated at 23.30 hrs started with FORT Y WEEP Y WEEP Y.

There was also a paper method which involving representing the Enigma wheels by strips of paper or card. Turing called these "comic strips." A colour coding was used to identify the Enigma wheels.

These breaks were helped by the first use of the EINS catalogue.

5.2   The EINS Catalogue

Once messages began to be deciphered, it was realized that the German word EINS was by far the most frequent word in Naval messages.

It was then decided to take on the prodigious task of cataloguing the encipherment of EINS at all $105,000$ possible start positions (on the three wheel Enigma). This was done *by hand.*

Later it was put onto punched cards for Freeborne's section, the large punched card processing section, to use.

To use the EINS catalogue consecutive groups of four letters in the message were looked up to see whether they were an encipherment of EINS.

Then with an Enigma machine set to these settings the characters following what was thought to be EINS were deciphered to see if German came out.

5.3   The Code Breaker's Problem

The first difficulty was working out the Bigram Tables. This had to start with a "pinch," i.e., a capture of a set of tables. Once message breaking had started, it was possible, with some difficulty, to work out new bigram tables. The tables were changed roughly once a year.

In order to decipher all the messages intercepted on a given day it was necessary to recover all of the daily key, i.e., Wheel Order and Wheel Start for deciphering the message key (the Grund) and the Steckers.

There are 336 WO's and $26 \times 26 \times 26$ start positions, i.e., about $6,000,000$ combinations to examine to find the right one. This requires a test to distinguish between a right and a wrong position and a very rapid means of applying this test.

5.4   Naval Enigma "Cribs"

A Crib in BP terminology was a guess at a section of the German text that was enciphered to give the intercepted enciphered message. Such a guess required clues and the Germans provided these in abundance.

- Because of the length, time of origin, call sign, etc., of a message it probably began with a phrase like

  VORHERSAGEBEREICH SIEBEN (weather forecast for area seven).

- Routine messages were sent out day after day at about the same time, from the same place, of the same length and starting in exactly the same way
- Re-encodements. These were retransmissions of messages already sent on some other key

Cribs allowed the deduction of menus for running on the Bombes. But initially there were very few Bombes and running 336 wheel orders just consumed too much time. This is where Banburismus came in. It significantly reduced the number of wheel orders to be run, sometimes to only 20.

5.5   Banburismus

Banburismus could be used if there were two lengths of cipher text and from the trigrams it was thought that they may have been enciphered from nearly the same wheel start positions. Banburismus enables the finding of the difference in start positions of the two texts. This only works because the letter distribution of language text is not flat random.

In Fig. 12 you can see the definitely non random spread of text letters and the much more nearly random cipher text spread.

Because some text letters occur much more frequently than others, there is a strong possibility that in two displaced texts there will be coincidences of these letters. When these two texts are enciphered on an Enigma machine, these points of coincidence of the letters will result in the same enciphered letters. Thus by looking for cipher text displacements at which there are more than random coincidences of cipher letters, the difference in start of encipherment can be deduced.

Banbury Sheets, so called because they were printed in Banbury, a town about 30 miles away from Bletchley, enabled the relative start positions of two cipher texts to be discovered.

These sheets had up to 200 alphabets running side by side vertically down the sheet with A at the top.

The girl in the Big Room in Hut 8 first went along the Banbury Sheet marking each letter of the cipher text with a red marker, then she took the sheet to a punch machine and punched a round hole through each marked letter.

```
   H
   H
   H                           H
   H                           H
   H                           H
   H                           H
   H               H  H        H
   H              HH  HH       H
 H H H   HH H    HH   HHH     HH
 HHHHHHHHH HH HH     HHH     HH
 ABCDEFGHIJKLMNOPQRSTUVWXYZ
```

Text 1

```
         H       H
 H HHH H    H   H H H     H
 HHHHHHH     HH HH H H    HH H
 HHHHHHHHHHHHHHHHH HHH HH H
 ABCDEFGHIJKLMNOPQRSTUVWXYZ
```

Cipher 1

Fig. 12. Letter histograms

Then by sliding sheets one above the other and counting the letter coincidences, it was possible to determine the offset at which the two messages had been enciphered.

The importance of this was that no turnover could occur within this distance and by accumulating information from a number of cipher text pairs, it was possible to eliminate wheels which could not be in the right hand position.

It was usually possible to be certain of the right hand wheel number, and most times to get the middle wheel as well.

This would reduce the number of wheel orders to be run from 336 down to possibly 20.

If a good crib was available this could be run on the Bombes, otherwise a special menu could be built up based on the trigram distances.

5.6   The "Narvik Pinch"

A trawler intercepted on April 26th 1940 by the destroyer *Arrow* proved to be a disguised German ship. A boarding party recovered one of two bags thrown overboard by the crew. It contained the Stecker and Grundstellung for April 23rd and 24th and an operator's log giving letter for letter cribs for April 25th and 26th.

The bag also contained exact details of the indicating system which confirmed Turing's deductions and the E tables used for short rapid communications and a description of how they worked; The "Long E bars" (Alfa-Funksignale) was a system for rapid communication by ships in action, it was a good source of cribs.

5.7   Early Banburismus

The Doldrums — May '40 to February '41. Following the Narvik Pinch, giving Stecker and Grund, April 23rd and 24th were easily broken and "paired days" i.e., the same WO and Ringstellung, soon followed.

April 26th proved difficult. Hand methods failed because of 10 Stecker pairs. However the first Bombe had just arrived and a crib from the operator's log was tried. After a series of misadventures and a fortnight's work, the Bombe triumphantly produced the answer.

With the 26th out, the paired day, the 27th, was soon broken and both days were found to be on the same bigram table. Every effort was then made to break all the messages on those days in order to recover as much as possible of the bigram table. Banburismus could then be tried on days using this table. But Banburismus proved to be very difficult in practice. May the 8th, the most promising day, was worked on ad nauseam for months.

Foss's Day. In August, Mr Foss returned from sick leave, was given May 8th and by sheer perseverance broke it in November. May 8th is immortalized as Foss's Day.

The reasons for this long period of the doldrums were: incomplete bigram tables, lack of cribs and a large number of "Dummy" messages.

August 25th 1940, Frank Birch wrote to Travis saying:

> I'm worried about Naval Enigma. Turing and Twinn are like people waiting for a miracle, without believing in miracles . . .

Then came the Lofoten raid and the Enigma keys for February 1941 from the Krebs.

5.8   The Heydays of Banburismus

April 1941–February 1942. The capture of the February '41 keys allowed the bigram tables to be built up completely. All April and May except 6th May were broken, but not currently.

The capture of the June keys covered the change in bigram tables on June 15th. With increased staff, although the first six days of August proved difficult, Banburismus was now so refined that September 18th/19th were the only days not broken on DOLPHIN for the rest of the war.

Banburismus was now breaking a few hours after the completion of a day's traffic and if the next day was a "paired day," breaking could be current.

These Pinches were absolutely essential, there were just too many unknowns in Naval Enigma for it to be worked out cryptographically.

The Doldrums Again — February to August 1942. On February 1st 1942 SHARK went onto an entirely separate key using 4 wheels instead of 3 and a new reflector. This was the M4, the German Navy's four wheel Enigma.

5.9   The 4 Wheel Enigma

The M4 used the same mechanical structure as the Naval three wheel Enigma but fitted a rotatable fourth wheel and a thin reflector in the space occupied by the reflector in a three wheel Enigma. It used:

1. Two fourth wheels, Beta and Gamma
2. Two "thin" reflectors, Bruno and Ceasar
3. Any combination could be used
4. A combination stayed in force for one month
5. Beta and Gamma ring setting always at Z
6. The fourth wheel could be set to any of 26 positions but did not turn during message entry
7. With the fourth wheel set to A, and a matching reflector, the machine was equivalent to a three wheel Enigma
8. The number of start positions was now $26 \times 26 \times 26 \times 26 = 456,976$

The wiring of wheel and reflector had been given away by German security blunders. An operator failed to set the fourth wheel in neutral, "A," and put it at "B" instead. Thus

```
Time 14.47 date 17/12/41  From W/T Station Adm.
Comm. U-Boats. E bar 551, Service No 166 wrongly
enciphered. Contents: U.131 reports: Am able to
dive. Have been hunted by 4 destroyers.

Time 16.30 date 17/12/41. From Mueller. E bar
551 deciphers with setting B.
```

Another good source of cribs was a reencipherment from DOLPHIN of Admiral Doenitz's message to the Fleet on succeeding Admiral Raeder.

Although there had been some advanced warning of the coming of the 4 wheel Enigma, the first design of a four wheel Bombe was not very satisfactory. This was the Wynn-Williams design of a high speed fourth wheel attachment to the three wheel Bombe. It was connected to the Bombe with a very long thick cable and was known as "Cobra."

The Americans were by now suffering from U Boat raids on their East Coast so they decided to build their own four wheel Bombes. Alan Turing went to America on 7th November 1942 to liase with the Americans on their four wheel Bombe design.

Doc Keene, at BTM, produced a four wheel version of the three wheel Bombe. This worked fine but was not as fast as the American four wheeler. By the time the fourth rotor came fully into service, high speed 4 wheel Bombes had been developed, which together with the weather cribs got back into Shark with the help of the American 4 wheel Bombes.

6   Alan Turing after German Naval Enigma

6.1   Lorenz

In summer 1942 Turing became involved with the breaking of the Lorenz teleprinter cipher system. Bill Tutte had worked out the original structure of Lorenz and Turing devised a statistical method for helping to get out wheel patterns, known as "Turingismus." This was superseded when the Colossi became available.

6.2   Alan Turing Leaves Bletchley Park

By late 1943 his work on code breaking in Bletchley Park was all but complete and he moved to nearby Hanslope Park to work on his ideas for a speech enciphering system he called "Delilah."

Together with Don Bayley he started constructing Delilah in June 1944. It was finished on VE Day, 6th May 1945.

7   An Appreciation of Alan Turing at Bletchley Park

Hugh Alexander wrote in his History of Naval Enigma [1]:

> There should be no question in anyone's mind that Turing's work was the biggest factor in Hut 8's success. In the early days he was the only cryptographer who thought the problem worth tackling and not only was he primarily responsible for the main theoretical work within the hut (particularly the developing of a satisfactory scoring technique for dealing with Banburismus) but he also shared with Welchman and Keen the chief credit for the invention of the Bombe. It is always difficult to say that anyone is absolutely indispensable but if anyone was indispensable to Hut 8 it was Turing. The pioneer work always tends to be forgotten when experience and routine later make everything seem easy and many of us in Hut 8 felt that the magnitude of Turing's contribution was never fully realised by the outside world.

A   Appendix II of UK Public Record Office Document HW14/2

NAVAL ENIGMA SITUATION

The solution of Naval Enigma will divide itself into two parts, that of solving one message of a day, and that of solving further messages.

The first problem is to be tackled by:

(a).   Analytical methods, using Jeffrey's statistics (virtually hopeless).

(b).   By the machine now being made at Letchworth, resembling, but far larger than the Bombe of the Poles (superbombe machine).

If one message is solved by one of these means we shall have the machine settings for the day, viz: Walzenlage, Steckerverbindungen, Ringstellung, but not Grundstellung nor list of bigrams used in the indicating system. We might also obtain the Stecker by capture.

For the second problem; i.e. solving further messages, we may either:

(i)   Guess three or four letters of the message.

(ii)   Make use of another machine, the "rack", which operates by so setting the messages that the decode contains sufficiently many letters E.

We have at present no information which will be of use for Method (i), although when a number of messages have been solved it may be applicable. Without a "rack" we shall, therefore, not be able to get any further if, for instance, position Stecker were captured from a submarine.

With the "rack" we shall, in such cases, almost certainly be able to solve 40% of the messages, and probably 70%. If by that time we are able to apply Method (i) as well, we may be able

to solve as many as 200 messages on that day.   If this ever
happens it will be possible to solve the indicating system; i.e.
to obtain the bigram list.   This will enable us to solve all
further messages for that day at once, and, on later days while
the bigram list lasts, to solve all messages as soon as a single
message has been solved for that day.

　　　　We feel that no unnecessary time should be lost in
experimenting with and constructing such a machine.

```
                    SIGNED:  A.D. KNOX
                             P.F.G. TWINN
                             W.G. WELCHMAN
                             A.M. TURING
                             J.R. JEFFREYS
                  1st November. 1939.
```

(UK Public Record Office online catalogue: http://catalogue.pro.gov.uk.)

References

1. C. H. O'D. Alexander, *Cryptographic History of Work on the German Naval Enigma.* Public Records Office, Kew, Surrey, HW 25/1.

Alan M. Turing's Contributions to Co-operation Between the UK and the US

Lee A. Gladwin

Archival Services Branch of the Center for Electronic Records (NWME), The National Archives, USA

Summary. Alan Turing's visit to the US Navy Cryptanalytic Section (Op-20-G) and the US Army's Signal Security Agency during the winter of 1942–1943 was a significant milestone in the collaboration between the British Government Code and Cypher School (GC&CS) and its US counterparts. As technical expert for the GC&CS, Turing viewed the progress of Op-20-G as it designed and developed its own Bombe and other machine aids for defeating German Enigma ciphers. Some of these machines were requested by Turing and John Tiltman for use at Bletchley Park. Not merely an observer, Turing consulted with and advised Op-20-G on Enigma-related matters before and during his visit. Obtaining clearance for Turing to view the X-system, a voice scrambler being developed at Bell Telephone Labs, required the intercession of Field Marshal Sir John Dill and a personal appeal to General George C. Marshall. It may have inadvertently contributed to the later signing of the British-United States Agreement (BRUSA) signed in May 1943. Turing's report on the X-system was key to its acceptance and installation in London. His activities in the United States reveal him to have been an expert in all aspects of machine-based cryptanalysis who influenced the development of the US Navy's Bombe program and possibly speech encipherment at Bell Labs.

November 1942 witnessed the Government Code and Cypher School at Bletchley Park racing to craft machines or additions to their three-wheel Bombes which would defeat the German Naval Enigma's "Shark" traffic. Impatient of British assistance in getting a promised Bombe to study and intercepts to work with, the US Army raced to build its own three-wheel Bombe. The US Navy, no less impatient, hurried to build their own four-wheel Bombe. The bright spot was the signing of the Travis-Wenger (Holden) Agreement on 2 October 1942 by Bletchley Park's Commander Edward Travis and US Navy Cryptanalytic Section (Op-20-G) Commander Joseph Wenger, providing full collaboration on the German submarine and naval problems.

With regard to German traffic, the British agreed "to provide technical assistance, if desired, in the development of analytical machinery required" and "to full collaboration upon the German submarine and naval cryptanalysis problems, including exchange of intercepted traffic, keys, menus, cribs, and such other pertinent technical information as may be necessary." Further, the British were "to obtain certain items of special analytical equipment developed by the U.S." and "to send certain technical personnel to Op-20-G to obtain information concerning new U.S. high-speed analytical equipment and the techniques employed in certain phases of U.S. work"[1]. As the diplomatic aspects of Alan M. Turing's visit are covered elsewhere [3], my focus will be upon Turing's mission to America, its place in the growing Anglo-American cryptanalytic liaison, and what the trip reveals of Turing.

Alan Turing visited the United States soon after the signing of the Wenger-Travis agreement. He came to study American efforts to develop Army and Navy versions of the British Bombe and additional aids to defeat Enigma. He was also expected to learn as much as he could about the X-system or Vocoder, a voice scrambler being developed at the Bell Telephone Labs for telephonic communications between Prime Minister Winston Churchill and President Franklin Roosevelt, or, at least, highest authorities in both London and Washington. Roosevelt stated he had no use for it while the initial plans were still in their design phase.

His visit tells us much of the status of Anglo-American cryptanalytic relations and much about Turing as well, beginning with the trust of Edward Travis in his technical expertise. Travis wrote Joseph Wenger on 6 November 1942, "Should be glad if Turing (who is not a professor) could come examine machinery. Make any use you like of him in connection with Bombes. Have suggested he stay a week in Washington but if you would like him longer I should be quite willing."[2] Alan Turing arrived at Op-20-G on 20 November. He was shown a "run of E on [the] Tetra[graph] machine." TETRAGRAPH was a Rapid Analytical Machine (RAM) built by the Eastman Kodak Company for quickly locating "the positions at which coincidences occur in any given text" [5]. The results of that test were probably discussed during one of the conferences scheduled between 17 and 24 December. No written record of that demonstration or any such meeting is extant, but a report written on 23 January 1943 indicates that "prior to January 8, RAM-2 was operating in an unreliable fashion." In fact, testing during that period revealed "that it was missing as much as 60% of the hits which were known to exist in traffic which had been previously analyzed by hand methods."[3] There appear to have been three "TETRA" machines, each with its specific function: "film processing and

---

[1] NR 4419 Memorandum for Op-20 from Capt. J. N. Wenger, 1 Oct. 1942, pp. 1–2; Historic Cryptographic Collection, Pre-World War I Through World War II, ca. 1891-ca. 1981; Records of the National Security Agency/Central Security Service, Record Group 457; National Archives, College Park, MD; E 9032; Box 1386. Hereinafter referred to as NSA Historic Cryptographic Collection.

[2] Memorandum from Travis to Wenger, 6 November 1942; Bombe Correspondence File ; CNSG Library 5750/441, Box 189; "Crane Collection"; Records of the Office of Naval Intelligence (ONI), Office of the Deputy Chief of Naval Operations, Record Group 38.

[3] Memorandum From Op-20-GM-10 to Op-20-GM, Subject: RAM-2, Improvements in Performance of; Ibid.

searching for hits," "noting hits," and "pairing of hits." On 30 April 1943, J. A. Skinner (Lt. USNR) lamented, "By painful experience we have found that it is almost impossible to build one machine which will do all jobs in the best and fastest manner."[4] Whatever his thoughts on the TETRA demonstration, Turing did not include them in his Dayton, Ohio report, though they may have been included in an earlier one, now lost.

Together with John Tiltman and Lieutenant Dudley Smith, he conferred with Op-20-GM (Machine Room) staff concerning "machine requirements of the British." Their "requirements" included "1 Tetra Film Producing Unit and Projector, 3 I.C. Projectors (1 plate type and 2 film type), 2 I. C. Plate Producing Units, 2 70 mm Tape Counters, 2 70 mm Tape Control Units, 2 70 mm Tape Comparators," and forty-seven assorted pieces of Teletype and IBM equipment.[5]

On 21 December 1942 Turing traveled to Dayton, Ohio to see the U.S. Naval Computing Machine Laboratory which was established there on 11 November 1942. His reactions to the Navy Bombe project, however, were mixed. He begrudgingly admired American audacity while decrying their inexperience and insufficient knowledge of British lessons learned:

> It seems a pity for them to go out of their way to build a machine to do all this stopping if it is not necessary. I am now converted to the extent of thinking that *starting from scratch* [sic] on the design of a Bombe, this method is about as good as our own. The American Bombe program was to produce 336 Bombes, one for each wheel order. I used to smile inwardly at the conception of Bombe hut routine implied by this program. Their test (of commutators) can hardly be considered conclusive as they were not testing for the bounce with electronic stop finding devices. Nobody seems to be told about rods or offiziers or banburismus unless they are really going to do something about it. [6, p. 4]

According to I. J. "Jack" Good, Turing's assistant, Turing was somewhat bemused by the American effort to throw 360 Bombes at the Enigma problem when Banburismus, the method pioneered by him, could provide the right-hand-wheel order and significantly reduce the number of Bombes to 96. He apparently mustered the arguments, if not the tact, to dissuade his hosts from

---

[4] Memorandum From GM-C to GM, GM-4, GM-5, 30 April 1943; NR 1429 TETRA Projector Number 2 (Nickname ICKY); RG 457 NSA Historic Cryptographic Collection; Box 583.

[5] Op-20-GM War Diary Summaries; Box 102; "Crane Collection"; Records of the Office of Naval Intelligence (ONI), Office of the Deputy Chief of Naval Operations, Record Group 38. "List of Rapid Analytical Machinery Desired by the British" attachment to Memorandum for Op-20 from E. E. Stone, Op-20-G, 1 January 1943; Inactive Stations 3200/, Box 54; "Crane Collection"; Records of the Office of Naval Intelligence (ONI), Office of the Deputy Chief of Naval Operations, Record Group 38.

building the full 336. His suggested improvements were hastily incorporated by Joseph Desch and John Howard into their design for the Navy Bombe. [6]

Alan Turing found only "minor differences" between the British and US Navy Bombe, reflecting the close liaison and technical exchanges between GC&CS and Op-20-G. After describing those differences, he commented upon "Cribbing," "Catalogue," "Subtractor machine," "Hagelin," and "Tunny." His perceptive comments and ability to locate possible problems reflect his broad mastery of issues both technical and cryptanalytical [6, pp. 6–7].

Prior to Turing's visit to Op-20-G, a lively exchange occurred concerning Agnes Meyer Driscoll's effort to obtain 3-rotor Enigma keys with cribs of eight characters or less.With infinite patience and, one suspects, inner glee, Alan Turing drafted a detailed manual simulation, complete with cipher alphabets and sequential turnovers, proving, with devastating logic, the vulnerability of the assumption that Enigma settings could be easily inferred from loopless short cribs [4].

Shaun Wylie, friend and Hut 8 alumnus, recalls:

> I well remember being told that some American outfit was valiantly trying to solve Naval Enigma on hopelessly short cribs. The name of Mrs. Driscoll was mentioned. We assumed that they were trying what we called a Stecker-Knockout. Stecker-Knockout was in fact later successfully completed on very long re-encipherments. They were needed to recover the wirings when the fourth wheel was introduced in Shark. Richard Pendered was the first hero; it was indeed a heroic job. I think one or two others were needed and other people did them. [4]

Stecker-Knockout was a means of determining how an Enigma machine was steckered when the reflector wheel (Umkehrwalze) circuits were unknown. Agnes Meyer Driscoll was a leading OP-20-G cryptanalyst [4].

Other possible sources of Turing's concern with Op-20-G's interest in short cribs might be Lt. Robert B. Ely and Lt. (jg) Joseph J Eachus, whom Turing knew from their summer, 1942 visit to Hut 8 to study Enigma and the British Bombe. Ely returned early that fall and became part of OP-20-GM's newly formed Crib Group, which was interested in applying the "Click process" to short cribs. A detailed example featuring an eight-character crib was included in "The Number of Stories Expected from the Click Process" which was dated October 13, 1942. It concluded that the chance of a "story"(key) occurring by chance was .0005124. Whether Turing saw this is conjectural, though he may have known of OP-20-GM's hope to successfully run short cribs on the Navy Bombe through Ely and Eachus [4].

Jack Good, another colleague and friend from Hut 8, recalls "Turing's objection to a specific short crib." Good comments that if the crib "contained a lot of repeated letters" and "one were lucky in those repeats being opposite repeats in cipher there would be closures in the menu, and that would help a lot. If one were hard-up for cribs one could try them at such favorable places. This would be like looking for lost keys under a lamp-post where there is light! This would be rational even if the chance of success were small" [4].

Turing discussed the "click" process for finding "the setting of a message from a short crib" once the Stecker was known at some point in his visit. The object of the process was to find a crib in a message through examination of "every possible position." Turing developed a "Click Machine" for the British and Op-20-G had its HYPO.[6] C. H. O'D. Alexander noted in his *Cryptographic History of Work on the German Naval Enigma* that Turing's machine required eight-letter cribs and worked "on the right hand wheel only" and had "the advantage of taking little longer on the 4 wheel machine than on the 3 wheel." The eight-letter crib requirement limited its application to only a handful of messages [1, p. 56][7]. Following a reading and or discussion of Howard and Clifford's "The Number of Stories Expected from the Click Process," Turing observed that the calculations of chance occurrences of a "story" occurring by chance "could be simplified by means of a recursion formula" and ranked like poker hands. He apparently provided a detailed illustration, later lost, which was incorporated almost verbatim into "Click Probabilities By Recursion Formula"[8].

Turing's welcome at the Navy did not extend to the Army's Signal Security Agency. His liaison work, as head of Hut 8, was with members of Op-20-G, not Arlington Hall. It was not until May, 1943 that William F. Friedman learned that Turing and Gordon Welchman designed the British Bombe [3, p. 137]. Difficulties with SSA arose when Col. Rex W. Minckler inadvertently rejected the Joint Staff Mission's application of August 1942 for security clearances for Turing to enter Bell Laboratories in New Jersey for the purposes of learning more about the radio telephone scrambler X-system (Project X-61753 or SIGSALY) and the Army Bombe, code name X-68003. Project X-61753 also covered the development of the M-228 Converter or SIGCUM on-line Baudot-based teletype system which was crucial for later encipherment and decipherment of textual transmissions that would make their way between Bletchley Park and Arlington Hall. At the time of

---

[6] RIP 603, Enigma Series, Vol. 1, Click Process, Communications Intelligence Technical Paper TS-10/E-1 (Navy Department: Office of the Chief of Naval Operations (CNC - Op-20), January 1946), pp. iii–iv; RG 38 Records of the Office of the Chief of Naval Operations, Records of the Naval Security Group Central Depository, Crane, Indiana; Box 170. Hereinafter referred to as "Click Process."

[7] The author gratefully acknowledges the assistance of Ralph Erskine in obtaining a copy of this manuscript.

[8] "Click Process," p. iii and RIP 608, Enigma Series, Vol. 6, Duenna, Communications Intelligence Technical Paper TS-10/E-6 (Navy Department: Office of the Chief of Naval Operations (CNC - Op-20), January 1946), pp. Iii-iv; RG 38 Records of the Office of the Chief of Naval Operations, Records of the Naval Security Group Central Depository, Crane, Indiana; Box 170.

Turing's visit, the M-228 was being proposed as the enciphering device for SIGSALY in preference to using phonograph records to scramble and unscramble signals. The British knew little of M-228's operation or security from enemy cryptanalytic attack. Minckler's rejection of the clearances was apparently on grounds of security surrounding knowledge of "the principles and construction of Converter M-228." In November, 1942, a change was made in clearance policy of which the British were unaware:

> Existing or new general clearances issued for secret equipment and projects are not applicable to secrecy communications systems or equipment or cryptograph methods or equipment. All clearances for such projects and equipment must be *individual* [emphasis in original] as to person and project. [3, p. 131][9]

At the time of this clearance problem, the debate over which enciphering method to use was still raging, with the Bell Telephone Lab supporting "the use of random noise" and Signal Security Branch (SSB) the M-228, jointly designed by its own William F. Friedman and Frank W. Rowlett. Colonel Frank W. Bullock recommended the M-228, and some were sent to Bell Telephone Labs for examination in February, 1943.[10]

The importance of British access to the secrets of M-228 is seen in the fact that the request for Turing's clearance was revived on 2 December 1942 by Field Marshal Sir John Dill in a personal appeal to General George C. Marshall. This automatically gave the request a higher profile than would ordinarily have been the case. Marshall politely apologized for the incident, but indicated that application for such clearance should be made directly to General George V. Strong, G-2. Strong, seeing an opportunity to trade Turing's clearance for intercepts, informed Marshal that the British were not supplying them with "any detailed information on German Army field traffic, or clandestine traffic" or "cryptographic material derived from Slavic nations." Dill reassured Marshall that this was not the case, and Strong was forced to concede nothing was being withheld. At the same time, Strong insisted that the clearance issue be decided by Dill and Marshall. By 6 January 1942, Marshall had to admit that there were security problems in sending over large amounts of "detailed data." Dill reciprocated on 7 January, saying that "complete mutual confidence is all important and that we should operate on the principle of complete frankness and reciprocity between our people and yours in all highly secret matters." He said that the British were prepared to

---

[9] The official history of the project notes that "all phases of the project were placed on a strictly secret basis at about this time [November, 1942]." NR 3586, "Signal Security Agency CIPHONY Chronological History, 1939–1945," p. 24; RG 457, NSA Historic Cryptographic Collection; Box 1117. Reference to application contained in Memorandum for Officer-in-Charge, Radio Section, Bureau of Ships from Joseph R. Redman, Captain, US Navy, Director Naval Communications (Op-20-G). Copy to Signal Corps, Signal Intelligence Section.

[10] "Signal Security Agency CIPHONY Chronological History, 1939–1945," p. 30.

share everything desired with the US Army if the Americans would come to England, while reserving the right to refuse to allow exploitation in the United States of vitally secret traffic unless they are satisfied as to the necessity. Dill again requested a clearance for Turing to enter Bell Labs, and Marshall ordered Strong to grant the clearance. On 12 January 1943 Turing's name was retroactively added to the 7 January X-61753 clearance list "by G-2 directive." Another directive declared "that the British are to be kept fully cognizant of all features of this project" [3, p. 132].

On 15 January 1943, J. F. McClean of the National Defense Research Committee (NDRC) called Col. Frank W. Bullock's office for written confirmation that Turing was authorized to visit Bell Labs. An exasperated Bullock, grabbed the message, scrawled "A. M. Turing" in large underscored letters, across the bottom of the page and curtly added: "Ask Friedman to prepare such note for my signature-he knows the story and I don't." Friedman appears to have brought the request before the Coordinating Committee for Project X-61753 on 21 January 1943. The additional delay is accounted for by the fact that Turing was cleared to see the X-system as proposed and developed by the Bell Telephone Laboratories, including the proposed keying by means of phonograph records, a system that was rejected in favor of the M-228 converter, "a cryptographic keying mechanism which is proposed by the Signal Security Branch." Considering the directive that the British are to be kept fully cognizant of all features of this project, and because a terminal to be installed in England probably will be used by a few British authorities, there seemed little grounds left for witholding knowledge of the system from Turing. The committee belatedly recommended "that Dr. Turing be cleared for viewing Converter M-228 and for a disclosure of those elements and features of its construction and operation as a keying mechanism for Project X-61753." Turing was not, however, permitted to examine or conduct any tests on this equipment, and "all specific questions which Dr. Turing may have on this [M-228] converter will be answered by representatives of the Signal Security Branch" [3, pp. 132–133].

There is some evidence that the Army was backing down even before Marshall confronted Strong. A memorandum dated 4 January 1943 and signed by Bullock documents the granting of Turing's clearance to receive information about Project X-68003 (the Army Bombe):

> In pursuance of agreements made concerning disclosure of the British high speed analyzing equipment on the occasion of the Chief Signal Officer's visit to the U. K., authority has been given to the undersigned this date to disclose to Col. Tiltman and Dr. Turing of the British crypto services the fundamental principles and details of the equipment now in development for this service, referred to as Secret Project 68003. [3, pp. 132–133]

This permitted Turing to attend a special Conference on Project X-68003 on 5 February 1943, at the Bell Laboratories office on 463 West Street in New

York City. The list of attendees reflects an effort to make amends. It included William F. Friedman, Director of Communications Research, Lt.-Colonel E. F. Cook, Lt.-Col. H. Doud, Capt. L. R. Rosen, Major G. G. Stevens (British Liaison), S. B. Williams and two other representatives of Bell Laboratories. Following presentations by Williams and Rosen concerning the approach to the problem, the group moved to another room where they saw the Army Bombe. It occupied "a total space of about 10 feet high, 6 feet wide, and a foot to eighteen inches deep." Stevens was clearly impressed by the Army's approach which abandoned "rotary motion in favour of stepping by use of relays." A test run, timed by a stop watch, ran "through all positions of one wheel-order" in 7 minutes and 19 seconds. The Army hoped to halve that time through the introduction of valves or vacuum tubes and film "in place of the fastest relays." Stevens requested that Turing write "a more technical report" on what they had discussed and seen. However impressive this demonstration was, the British Chiefs of Staff and Joint Communications Board were far more concerned with the security of the M-228 system. General Sir Hastings L. Ismay, Deputy Secretary and Senior Staff Officer to the Minister of Defense, expressed the concerns of the Chiefs of Staff in a memorandum to the Prime Minister written on 15 February 1943 :

> They think it essential to establish beyond doubt the effectiveness of the equipment. If it is not one hundred per cent secure, it would be extremely dangerous. The only Englishman who has so far been allowed to see it is Dr. Turing of the Government Code and Cypher School.[11]

Turing reported on the X-61753 as follows:

> Bell System depends on electronic translation of speech into numerical code and any standard reciphering process can be applied. It was originally intended to apply a process equivalent to onetime table which would have provided absolute security. In order to simplify construction U.S. propose to adopt modifications and the proposed process is a machine method which should provide adequate security though definitely inferior to onetime table. If the equipment is to be operated [in London] solely by U.S. [Army Signal Corps] personnel it will be impossible to prevent them listening in if they so desire.[12]

A full report was airmailed by him to Edward Travis in late February or early March and arrived about 13 March 1943. Travis found "some difficulty in expressing an opinion on the security of the U.S. project X-61753," owing

---

[11] Memorandum from H. L. Ismay to Prime Minister, 15 February 1943; Public Record Office CAB 120/768.

[12] Telegram from J.S.M. to War Cabinet Offices London, 20 February 1943; Public Record Office CAB 120/768.

to Bell Laboratory's refusal to permit Turing to include certain details and drawings. Travis wished to await Turing's arrival at Bletchley Park so that he might consult him before giving a definite opinion. Recognizing the urgency of the situation (the Americans were already in London to install the new radio telephone), Travis wrote Major M. R. Norman that he was prepared to "recommend the use of the machine in confidence" based upon the information so far provided by Turing.[13]

Alan M. Turing departed the United States on 18 March 1943, quite unaware of the unwitting role his clearances played in resolving the problems of UK-USA cryptanalytic exchange leading to the signing of BRUSA. Though, perhaps less influential on SSA's Bombe program and SYGSALY, owing primarily to the highest level of security attached to the latter, he must have impressed Friedman with his abilities.

From 25 April through 13 June, Friedman himself was in England studying methods at Bletchley Park and Berkeley Street. On 21 May 1943, Friedman was asked if he "would discuss with Turing Busch machine [M-228] used in special X Project and determine his present opinion of its security. Installation of equipment [i.e., the teletypewriter] here completed and now under test."

Friedman responded on 22 May 1943:

> When saw Turing last Saturday and told him modifications being introduced in Busch device to eliminate objectionable features, he expressed satisfaction but obviously was not in position to give approval in absence of drawings pertaining to proposed modifications. Turing on leave this week but can probably see him Monday or Tuesday and will try [to] get expressed opinion from him. However since I do not myself know what modifications consist of, their having merely been in preliminary stages when I left Washington, am not able to indicate same to him and hence doubt whether his approval would be obtained until details are made available in form of drawings or description preferably both. Please advise via Baker Peter direct channel whatever latter are being sent here. [3, pp. 136–137]

In July 1944, Edward Travis and Gordon Welchman, GC&CS, were still trying to learn more of the system security of the M-228. In a letter to Colonel [Timothy?] O'Connor, Travis wrote that GC&CS was asked its opinion of the security of M-228 following a demonstration at Colonel George Bicher's headquarters (ETOUSA). "Unfortunately," Travis wrote, "the demonstrator only knew how to operate the machine and could not give [Gordon] Welchman the information required to check up on security." What they especially wanted to know was "exactly how the motion of the drums is governed. We know that this motion is varied by five switches, but we don't know the effect of

---

[13] Memorandum from E. Travis, Director G.C.&C.S., to Maj. M. R. Norman, Offices of the War Cabinet, 26 March 1943; Public Record Office CAB 120/768.

these switches."[14] Colonel Bicher was authorized "to turn over a complete set of documents pertaining to this machine to a British agency there." In his memorandum to British Liaison officer Major Geoffrey Stevens, Colonel W. Preston Corderman confided that the "most serious weakness of this cryptographic machine and system is that common to all Baudot encipherment schemes based upon the rule that similar signs give a minus (or spacing) impulse; dissimilar signs give a plus (or marking) impulse." This meant that "two messages in depth can be solved rather easily and from such a solution recovered key may often be employed to reconstruct the keying elements."[15]

Though not allowed to test M-228, Alan Turing reported enough details to win approval of SYGSALY's London installation and opened the door to further revelations in 1944. His influence on Op-20-G's Bombe building program was profound and far reaching. His insights into both cryptanalytic machines and methods proved of value to his hosts and, presumably, to GC&CS. Travis clearly relied upon Turing's expertise and experience to obtain the information required by GC&CS and higher authority. Turing prepared the way for the visits of others who visited their Op-20-G and Arlington Hall counterparts, including Hugh Alexander, Gordon Welchman, and Hugh Foss.

In addition to his official visits, Turing probably tried to see friends in the United States. An intriguing possibility, and it is only that, is that he visited John von Neumann, his former mentor, at Princeton. It would have been an easy weekend trip for him, and he surely would have enjoyed renewing their acquaintance. The question is raised by Jack Good:

> Do you know whether Turing visited von Neumann (in Princeton) when he visited the US in 1942 ? He must have known von Neumann well in Princeton when he studied there years earlier. I'm interested in this question because, soon after he returned from the US he propounded a problem about bags of gunpowder at the points in a plane with integer coordinates. Given the probability that the explosion of one bag will cause adjacent ones to explode, what is the probability that the explosion will extend to infinity?[16]

I did not, and still do not, know the answer. Alan Turing's visit to America that winter of 1942–1943 began with Enigma and ended in mystery.

References

1. C. H. O'D. Alexander, "Cryptographic History of Work on the German Naval Enigma", Public Records Office, Kew, Surrey, HW 25/1.

[14] Letter from E. W. Travis to [Timothy?] O'Connor, 18 July 1944; NR 2323 M-228 Converter Information Given to the British; RG 457, NSA Historic Cryptographic Collection, Box 804.

[15] Memorandum from W. Preston Corderman to Major [Geoffrey] Stevens, 2 August 1944; NR 2323 M-228 Converter Information given to the British.

[16] Letter from Jack Good to the author, 18 June 2002.

2. Ralph Erskine, "What Did the Sinkov Mission Receive from Bletchley Park?", Cryptologia, Vol. XXIV (2000).

3. Lee A. Gladwin, "Cautious Collaborators: The Struggle for Anglo-American Cryptanalytic Co-operation, 1940–1943"; David Alvarez (ed.) Allied and Axis Signals Intelligence in World War II (London: Frank Cass Publishers, 1999), pp. 119–145.

4. Lee A. Gladwin, "Alan M. Turing's Critique of Running Short Cribs on the US Navy Bombe", Cryptologia, Vol. XXVII, No. 1 (January, 2003). For further background, see [2].

5. A. Golan (Lt. USNR), "General Comment on RAM Equipment"; NR 1429 TETRA Projector Number 2 (Tessie & Icky); RG 457, NSA Historic Cryptographic Collection; Box 583.

6. Alan M. Turing, "Visit to National Cash Register Corporation of Dayton, Ohio", Cryptologia, Vol. XXV, No. 1 (January, 2001).

Part V

Almost Forgotten Ideas

Watching the Daisies Grow: Turing and Fibonacci Phyllotaxis

Jonathan Swinton

Summary. Turing's seminal 1952 paper on morphogenesis is widely known. Less well known is that he spent the last few years of his life further developing his morphogenetic theory and using the new computer to generate solutions to reaction-diffusion systems. Among other things, he claimed at one point to be able to explain the phenomenon of "Fibonacci phyllotaxis": the appearance of Fibonacci numbers in the structures of plants. He never published this work, but did leave a nearly complete manuscript on morphogenesis and lattice phyllotaxis, together with more fragmentary notes on Fibonacci phyllotaxis. I discuss evidence that he developed a number of key ideas close to modern thinking, and tantalising hints that he came very close to a mathematical explanation of how the "daisy grows" into these patterns.

1 Introduction: Turing's Last, Lost Work

As this volume attests, Alan Turing is now well known as a pioneer in the logical and technical development of the computer. He is also widely recognised in mathematical biology for his discovery of the Turing instability, which generates pattern in reaction-diffusion systems. Less well known is that he spent the last few years of his life developing a morphogenetic theory and using the new computer to generate solutions to reaction-diffusion systems. Some of this biological work was published in his lifetime; some, thanks to the editors of his Collected Works, was eventually published posthumously, and some has been preserved unpublished, mainly in the archives of King's College Cambridge[1]. The paper published in his lifetime has turned out to be seminal and widely cited in the mathematical theory of biological pattern formation, but the rest of his researches have remained obscure and ill-understood. It is the purpose of this paper to interpret some of this last work of Turing's. In

---

[1] A bibliography of Turing's work, published and unpublished, is maintained by Andrew Hodges at http://www.turing.org.uk; details on work relevant to morphogenesis including sources used in this paper is at http://www.swintons.net/jonathan/turing.htm; see also the Turing Digital Archive: http://www.turingarchive.org.

particular, one of a number of problems he was trying to solve was the appearance of Fibonacci numbers in the structures of plants, and I will describe this problem and speculate about how far he succeeded with it.

I begin by describing briefly the problem of Fibonacci phyllotaxis, and then Turing's basic theory of reaction-diffusion systems. Then I describe Turing's geometrical lattice theory, and finally, and more speculatively, his application of reaction-diffusion theory to the Fibonacci problem, and the crucial introduction of growth to the analysis. The last decade has seen rather successful mathematical explanations of the problem Turing was trying to solve, and I will describe these briefly to explore how much Turing might have anticipated them.

2   Fibonacci Phyllotaxis

Phyllotaxis means here the arrangement of structures, such as leaves or florets, in plants. To see the phenomenon of Fibonacci phyllotaxis, consider the arrangement of side branches on the main stems of a plant such as the one in Fig. 1. The figure draws "obvious" spiral or *parastichies* through these adjacent branching points. The *parastichy number* for a spiral counts how many such spirals fit onto the cylinder, or equivalently how many points around the cylinder but not on the spiral have to be skipped in the vertical direction between two points of the spiral. Thus one prominent parastichy on the left hand slice of the specimen is a 5 parastichy because there are four other branching points spread around the cylinder between any two consecutive points on the spiral. The parastichy in the other direction is a 3 parastichy and the pair is called a (3, 5) parastichy pair. A remarkable fact about the specimen is that, although it exhibits a number of different parastichy pairs, each of these pairs consists of two adjacent Fibonacci numbers from the sequence $1, 1, 2, 3, 5, 8, 13, 21, 34, 55, \ldots$ in which each number is the sum of the preceding two. Yet more remarkable is that this property can be found in very many examples in many different species of plants. Explaining this ubiquity is the problem of Fibonacci phyllotaxis [12]. Perhaps the most striking examples of Fibonacci phyllotaxis of all occur in the sunflower *Helianthus annus* and the daisy *Bellis perennis*, where the florets of the flowerhead are arranged in spirals, with the number of spirals clockwise and anticlockwise being successive and rather large Fibonacci numbers (Fig. 2).

The appearance of these numbers, or variants on them, is intimately related to the divergence angle, the difference in angle between successive points on the stem. If that angle in a cylindrical lattice is close to a simple function of the Golden Ratio, then Fibonacci numbers naturally appear. Moreover the Golden arrangement typically has the property of optimal packing. All of these relationships have been closely studied in the mathematical phyllotaxis and number theoretic literature (reviewed in Adler et al. [1] Jean and Barabé [12]), and each of them has been adduced at one time or another as

Fig. 1. Parastichy systems ranging from $(3,5)$ through $(5,8)$ and $(8,13)$ to $(13,26)$ on a single *Euphorbia wulfenii* stem. From Fig. 8 of Church [7]

the explanation for Fibonacci phyllotaxis, often with varying degrees of mysticism or arguments from evolutionary optimality attached. Turing thought of the problem in terms of explaining the Fibonacci numbers of the parastichies, and it is this approach I concentrate on here. According to Adler et al. [1] the first to explicitly recognise that Fibonacci numbers were involved were Schimper [26] and Braun [5].

When and where did Turing's interest in this problem come from? The title of this paper comes from a sketch drawn by his mother (reproduced opposite the title page in Saunders [25]) showing a schoolboy paying attention to the daisies rather than a hockey game. We know that at school he was well acquainted with D'Arcy Thompson's classic *On Growth and Form* [28] that discusses it; decades later, Turing is recorded as discussing daisies and fir-cones during off-duty periods at Bletchley Park [10, pp. 207–208]. When Turing returned to Cambridge for a year in 1947–1948 he attended the undergraduate physiology lectures of Lord Adrian, and Hodges has plausibly speculated that his prime interest by now was the possibility of a logical description of the nervous system [10, p. 372]. But we have little concrete idea of his thinking on the subject until 1951. In a correspondence with the zoologist JZ Young, after a discussion on the needs of a physiological theory of the brain he continued:

> ... my mathematical theory of embryology ... is yielding to treatment, and it will so far as I can see, give satisfactory

Fig. 2. A sunflower head, with some of the florets removed to show the $(34, 55)$ parastichies. From Fig. 15 of Church [7]. © AH Church 1904

explanations of -

i) Gastrulation.

ii) Polygonally symmetrical structures, e.g., starfish, flowers.

iii) Leaf arrangement, in particular the way the Fibonacci series (0, 1, 1, 2, 3, 5, 8, 13, ...) comes to be involved.

iv) Colour patterns on animals, e.g., stripes, spots and dappling.

v) Patterns on nearly spherical structures such as some Radiolaria, but this is more difficult and doubtful.[2]

Whatever the original trigger, these were strong claims and it was the purpose of this paper to examine why Turing felt able to make them and claim (iii) in particular. In the same month he also wrote in a letter that

> Our new machine is to start arriving on Monday. I am hoping to do something about "chemical embryology." In particular I think I can account for the appearance of Fibonacci numbers in connection with fir-cones.[3]

He certainly could do something about chemical embryology. By November of that year he had submitted a paper to Philosophical Transactions. This

[2] AMT K.1.78; letter to JZ Young 8 Feb 1951.

[3] Quoted in Hodges [10, p. 437], letter to M. Woodger, February 1951.

paper, *The Chemical Basis of Morphogenesis* [29], has become celebrated in its own right for introducing what is now known as the Turing instability, and provides a framework for understanding Turing's later, unfinished work. In 1952 he wrote that he had "Had quite a jolly time lecturing on fir-cones"[4] in Cambridge, and in 1953 wrote to HSM Coxeter:

> ... During the growth of a plant the various parastichy numbers come into prominence at different stages ... Church is hopelessly confused about it all, and I don't know any really satisfactory account, though I hope to get myself one in about a year's time.[5]

Between 1952 and 1954 he drafted parts of a paper on the *Morphogen Theory of Phyllotaxis* [30]. This work was left incomplete, and indeed Gandy wrote, after Turing's death, that

> When I was staying with Alan the weekend before Whitsun he also told me more or less where the computations had got to; but since his methods were so individual, he was unmethodical, I imagine it will be almost impossible for anyone to go on with the programme where he left off.[6]

In fact Nick Hoskin did manage to make some progress with preparing the work for publication, and Bernard Richards provided a third section based on the MSc thesis he started under Turing. But the resulting typescript was not published until 1992 (Saunders [25]) and has been little noticed since, although there was a recent discussion by Allaerts [2]. More details of the archive papers and their relationship to the published volume can be found at my web-site (Swinton [27]). We will return to their contents after discussing the Turing instability.

3 Where Do Spots Come from? The Turing Instability

This section provides a brief non-technical discussion of the Turing instability introduced in Turing [29]. Turing provided a hypothesis to explain the generation of pattern when smooth sheet of cells develop pattern during development in a wide variety of settings including the formation of leaf buds, florets, skin markings, and limbs. According to this hypothesis, chemicals called morphogens generate organs when present in sufficient density, and the pattern is created through mechanisms of reaction and diffusion. The corresponding reaction-diffusion models are by now well known to mathematical biologists, and for the mathematically inclined the books by Meinhardt [17] and Murray [19] can give much more detail.

---

[4] AMT D.4; letter to R. Gandy, Nov 23 (prob 1952).
[5] Letter from A. M. Turing, 28th May 1953, cited in [8].
[6] AMT A.8; letter from R. Gandy to M. H. A Newman.

3.1   Reaction . . .

One way of understanding the reaction-diffusion process is to borrow an analogy which Turing himself used in a slightly different model: cannibals and missionaries (Fig. 3). An island is supposed to be populated by a population of cannibals and missionaries. The missionaries are all celibate and thus depend on recruitment from the external world to maintain the population as its members gradually die. Cannibals also die, but can also reproduce, so that the population naturally increases. However when two missionaries meet a cannibal, the cannibal is converted to missionary status. (If this seems a rather imperialist island it might be worth pointing out that under a commoner interpretation the cannibals are the growth promoters and the missionaries are the poison). This tension between production and transformation means that a balance is reached when both populations are mixed together [19, pp. 376–378]. If this balance is disturbed by a small amount of noise, the tension will act to restore the balance: the system is stable.

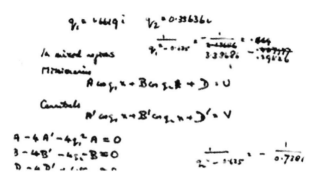

Fig. 3. From AMT/C27/14. © PN Furbank

3.2   . . . and Diffusion

Now we imagine that the two populations, instead of mixing completely together, are spread out in a thin ring around the rather narrow beach of the island. Now individuals react (that is, reproduce or convert) only with their immediate neighbours, but they also move around at random in a diffusive way. Moreover the members of the two populations move at different speeds: the missionaries have bicycles and move faster. This is enough to destabilize the system. For if there is at any point a small excess of cannibals, say, then this will be followed by excess "production" of more cannibals, and then of more missionaries (since they have more targets for conversion). Without the spatial dimension the extra production of missionaries would in turn reduce the cannibal excess and the system would return to balance. But because the missionary excess is transported away more quickly, a pattern develops in which there is a near excess of cannibals and a far excess of missionaries. Moreover the distance between these zones of relative excess is determined by the interaction between the reaction and the diffusion: a length scale, which is what is required for the emergence of pattern from non-pattern, has emerged from the dynamics.

3.3   Where Did the Bicycles Come from?

The key to making this idea work is the missionaries' bicycles: more technically that the inhibitor morphogen has a higher coefficient of diffusivity. Once the reaction-diffusion system is set up, a simple linear analysis makes this an obvious requirement for heterogeneity, but that was an analysis that no one, to Turing's knowledge, had done at that time. We have no record of Turing's thought process in developing the model idea and whether the diffusivity constraint came before or after the reaction-diffusion model itself. His analysis in Turing [29] and Turing [30] in terms of Fourier modes would have been second nature to him: for example his pre-war project to compute the zeroes of the Riemann zeta function using an analogue computer used a similar basic analysis. The formal theory in *The Morphogen Theory of Phyllotaxis* shares some structure with the then new quantum mechanics he had learned as a student in Cambridge, but presumably many of the techniques were in the armoury of any applied mathematician at the time. As Allaerts [2] points out, Jeans' 1927 book on Electricity and Magnetism, which Turing cited, is a source for many of the techniques, particularly spherical harmonics. But the source of the key scientific innovation is harder to pin down. It's not even obvious that Turing himself appreciated it that it *was* key: it is hardly emphasised in either Turing [29] or Turing [30]. Turing was not alone in arriving at these ideas. Jeans [11] states that similar ones were also introduced by Kolmogorov, Petrovski and Piskunov [14] and Rashevsky [22], although they remained largely unknown in the West for many decades; Nanjundiah [20] discusses the (lack of) influences in more detail. The 1952 paper actually dealt with a number of important and more complex issues usually glossed over in the standard undergraduate accounts. Turing also discussed tricky issues of mode selection and the effect of noise, and extended the model to two dimensions to produce an example of dappling.

By the time of the drafting of *The Morphogen Theory of Phyllotaxis*, the theory had been developed yet further, particularly by a representation in terms of spherical harmonics, and by an application to the particular case of a sphere, done as an MSc project by Richards [23]. This more general theory, which has been recently reviewed by Allaerts [2], is, though relatively technical, conceptually a fairly straightforward development of the original idea.

3.4   The Turing Instability: Summary

In one dimension, then, the Turing instability introduced in the 1952 Transactions paper provides a natural mechanism for generating spots. Such patterns emerge from the interaction between the length-scale implicit in the reaction-diffusion dynamics and the geometry of the arena. This has provided a central paradigm for modern morphogenesis, at least from a mathematical perspective [13]. These patterns have been seen in real chemical systems, but it remains a challenge to explain "stripes, spots and dappling."

4   Lattice Generation

So far, the discussion has been in terms of a one-dimensional pattern wrapped around a ring. What happens if we have the same reaction and diffusion mechanism but now allow it to act in a two-dimensional arena? In terms of the cannibals and missionaries, we might imagine that the beach of the island is now rather wide (relative to the length scale defined above). In this case, the Turing instability can generate not a ring of points but a *lattice* of points. (Under suitable boundary conditions, other patterns such as stripes are possible.) Might this by itself be enough to explain the occurrence of Fibonacci phyllotaxis? With no constraints, (i.e., a cylinder of large enough radius, and ignoring the complexities of the inception and quenching of pattern formation), the instability typically generates hexagonal lattices (Murray [19]: see an example in Fig. 4) and this class of lattices certainly includes some Fibonacci ones. But it also includes many that are not Fibonacci.

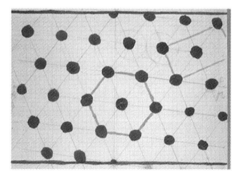

Fig. 4. A hexagonal lattice (AMT/K/3/1). © PN Furbank

Might it be that there are other constraints acting to select Fibonacci ones? First there are the geometrical constraints arising from the particular arena. Patterns on a cylinder may be different from those on an infinite plane where the periodicity constaint does not apply, and different again from those on a cone, but this does not promote any special Fibonacci structure. Then there are the dynamical constraints: the pattern does not suddenly appear, but emerges as a result of nonlinear interactions between morphogens over time. Finally there are growth constraints: during the emergence process, the arena itself may be growing with the plant. More discussion of these constraints is put aside until after a discussion of describing the patterns themselves.

5   Geometrical Phyllotaxis

In this section we put aside the radically new contribution of Turing (a mechanism for dynamic production of lattices) to discuss his (slightly) more conventional treatment of the static properties of lattices, more commonly called geometrical phyllotaxis. Turing consolidated a general theory of lattices on cylinders

> ... expounded ... by some previous writers but often in a rather unsatisfactory form, and with the emphasis misplaced[7]

which was (mostly) published for the first time in 1992 in his Collected Works of A. M. Turing [25]). This kind of analysis has a long history, at least as far back as the brothers Bravais (Fig. 5), but Turing's geometrical theory added several new insights: flow matrices, the 'hypothesis of geometrical phyllotaxis' discussed below, and the "inverse lattice," a Fourier representation of the patterns essential to understanding many of the archive pictures though not discussed further here.

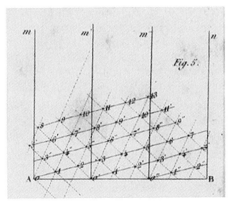

Fig. 5. An early geometrical theory of phyllotaxis, from Bravais and Bravais [6]

---

[7]   [30, p. 62] Turing is not the only writer on mathematical phyllotaxis to adopt this tone.

5.1   Turing's Lattice Theory

Part I of the Morphogen Theory of Phyllotaxis [30, p. 49] is a fairly coherent and fully worked out manuscript. Two theorems are of particular relevance here. For any lattice, such as the one in Fig. 5, there are not just two rather obvious parastichies (here 2 and 3 are drawn with dashed lines) but a whole series of less obvious ones, which can all be defined relative to lines from the origin (i.e., the point labelled 0) through the other numbered points. The 1-parastichy is the solid line, and the eye can pick out the 4 parastichy by visualising a line through the points numbered 0 and 4 and 8 and so on. What Turing called the "principal parastichies" were the ones in which the nearest points in the parastichy were closest to the origin — in other words Fig. 5 has principal parastichy (2, 3) because the points numbered 2 and 3 are the ones closest to the point numbered 0. (The geometrical details are related to but different from, say Jean [11], primarily because Jean also needs to ensure that the parastichies wind in opposite directions round the cylinder). A second key theorem is that the third parastichy (in this case 1 since 1 is the next closest point) must be the sum or difference of the first two parastichy numbers, a theorem Turing proves neatly on page 57 of Turing [30].

5.2   "Hypothesis of Geometrical Phyllotaxis"

After this theory of lattices on cylinders, Turing went on to consider lattices of more variable geometry. This raises the question of what kinds of transformations of parastichy numbers are possible when a phyllotactic lattice is deformed. As it is deformed, the principal parastichies will in general remain unchanged. They will only change when a new lattice point from a different parastichy moves so as to become closer to the origin, but generically the point that does so must have previously been the third parastichy. Thus one of the two principal parastichy numbers, together with the third parastichy number, will become the new principal parastichy number. Turing showed [30, p. 72] that if that third parastichy number (in the example above, 1), never lies between the first and second parastichy number (here (2, 3)) then a Fibonacci property, once begun, would persist. This constraint he named the *Hypothesis of Geometrical Phyllotaxis (HGP)*.

It was this result which was surely the cause of Hoskins' view, reported in Max Newman's 1955 Royal Society memoir [21], that Turing had shown that a Fibonacci system, once established, would always remain Fibonacci. But the truth, as Turing recognised [30, p. 72], is that this relies on the HGP being true and the theory so far provides no reason why it should be. However this idea is still worthwhile: the key insight it embodies is that of continuous change. Phyllotactic lattices are not laid down all at once on an infinite cylinder: they are produced locally, node by node, and the resulting pattern is also deformed by growth.

6   Dynamic Phyllotaxis

The Turing instability by itself, then, can't provide an explanation for the generation of Fibonacci phyllotaxis, as Turing well understood. For when discussing phyllotactic systems defined as solutions to the reaction-diffusion model defined without growth constraints, he wrote

> [...] the phyllotactic systems of botany do not arise in this way.[8]

However there are strong indications in Turing's later manuscripts, particularly the fragmentary *Outline of the development of the daisy*[9], that he had conceived an additional mechanism to provide that explanation. As hinted above, that mechanism is that there is a small arena in which the Turing instability is at work, laying down spots in lattices and then leaving them behind as the arena follows the growth of the plant. Moreover that arena itself changes, growing in diameter, providing a continuously changing lattice to which the the theories of geometrical phyllotaxis could be applied. The first evidence of this is in *Morphogen Theory of Phyllotaxis* Part I; in Sect. 13 Turing establishes a formalism of flow matrices for the change in lattice parameters with a parameter called time, adding that

> ... a convenient way of picturing flow matrices is to imagine the change in the lattice as being due to the leaves being carried over the surface of the lattice by a fluid whose velocity is a linear function of position. [30, p. 75]

This was a way of modelling phyllotactic patterns, building on the continuous change models of Richards [24]. But this remains an essentially static picture of spots being passively transported over a changing geometry. What Turing was able to go on and create, with the aid of his new spot-generation model, was a concrete model for dynamic phyllotaxis.

In the later work, Turing typically expressed what we now think of as his reaction diffusion model in operator notation, with forms similar to

$$\frac{\partial U}{\partial t} = \varphi(\nabla^2)U + GU^2 - HUV \tag{1}$$

$$V = \psi(\nabla^2)U^2 \tag{2}$$

with $\varphi(\nabla^2) = I_2(1 + \nabla^2/k_0^2)^2$ and $\psi(\nabla^2) = 1/(1 - \nabla^2/R^2)$;compare equation III.1.2 of MTP [30, p. 107]. Here $U(x,t)$ is the morphogen and $V(x,t)$ is the "poison"; the ψ function represents the implicit solution of its partial differential equation in terms of the slower diffusing morphogen. The

---

[8] AMT/C/24/68.

[9] Most of the text of this paper can be found in Turing [30, pp. 119–123]. An alternative version, closer to the manuscript, can be found at my web-site.

H terms represents the effect of the poison on the morphogen, the G term the morphogen's autocatalytic nature, and the φ term its diffusive nature, parameterised by the natural wavenumber k_0.

However, in *Outline of the Development of the Daisy*[10] there is a crucial extra spatiotemporal term $I(x,t)U$:

$$\frac{\partial U}{\partial t} = \varphi(\nabla^2)U + I(x,t)U + GU^2 - HUV \tag{3}$$

$$V = \psi(\nabla^2)U^2 \tag{4}$$

An even more revealing version of this equation is in AMT/C/27/28 (Fig. 6). This additional I term is designed to capture the effect of the variation in the geometry of the arena for morphogenesis with time due to growth of the underlying tissue: see the picture of a growing apical meristem region in Fig. 6.

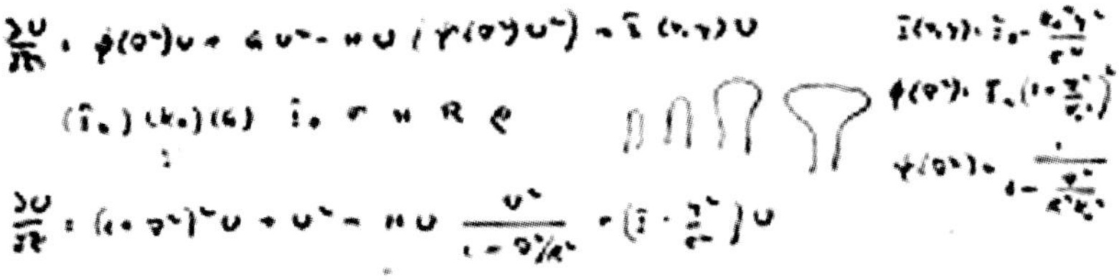

Fig. 6. A version of the morphogenesis equation allowing for growth in the apical meristem region and the possibility of dynamic phyllotaxis. Also (below the first line) a list of the numerical parameters which must be specified to allow computational solution. From AMT/C/27/28. © PN Furbank

Turing not only conceived this idea; he clearly made substantial progress with a numerical implementation of it. At one point of the *Daisy* draft , he comments on the number of parameters needed,

> when actual computations are being carried out the number of quantities to be specified is again increased[11]

in a manner suggesting that this had been done in practice. Moreover one of the subroutines that has survived is labeled KJELL[12], and AMT/C/27/C25 (shown in part in Fig. 7), entitled *Kjell theory*, works out the algebra in Fourier space of the coefficients of an equation such as the daisy one, including the crucial growth term.

---

[10] The Saunders edition [25] has a typo for the H and the ψ here.
[11] AMT/C/24/12; omitted from the Saunders version.
[12] This dates it to post summer 1952: see Hodges [10, p. 476].

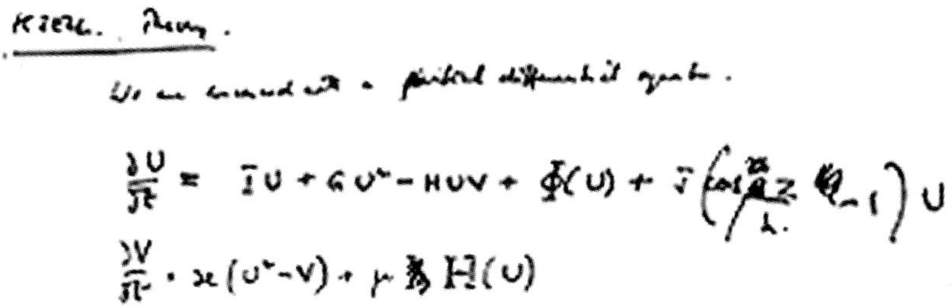

Fig. 7. KJELL theory. From AMT/C/27/25, beginning a series of developments designed to allow the dynamic growth equations of Fig. 6 to be calculated by computer. © PN Furbank

Also in the archives are a number of solution plots (e.g., Fig. 8). Based on their form they are probably solutions of the reaction-diffusion equations of forms similar to Eqs. 1, 2 or Eqs. 3, 4. Whether they are directly relevant to the Fibonacci problem or as more general illustrations of morphogenesis is hard to say. My speculation is that they are the former, since there is little evidence of any other computationally active project.

7   Routes to Phyllotaxis

In addition to direct numerical simulation, there is evidence that Turing explored a more analytical approach to the problem. The best evidence comes from several sheets in the National Archive for the History of Computing[13]. One (Fig. 9) is a diagram displaying possible parastichy transitions, from the homogeneous (Hom) state up to $4 + 7$ parastichies. A similar sheet includes the comment

> *Probable paths: Hom* $\to (0)_R \to (0 + 1) \to (1 + 1) \to (1 + 2) \to$
> $(2 + 3) \to (3 + 5) \ldots$ [14]

The question is what Turing meant by "probable." It might be a simple harking back to the hypothesis of geometrical phyllotaxis, but on another sheet (Table 1: MAN/M/8) he classifies a number of possible transitions by more empirically geometric observations.

These kinds of parastichy transitions were not entirely new: van Iterson [31] studied static sphere packings and generated a parameter map of all possible such packings (Fig. 10). Turing at one point dismisses the "touching circles hypothesis" — that each new point is introduced as though it was at the center of a hard disk of a certain radius — although he is referring here

---

[13] At Manchester University (http://www.chstm.man.ac.uk/nahc). Turing papers are in NAHC/TUR/C2 and C3.

[14] MAN/M/1. This is my foliation, details at Swinton [27].

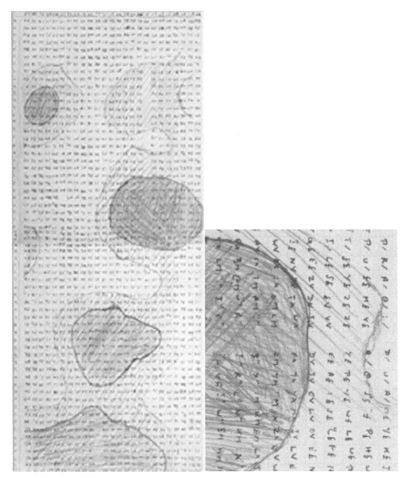

Fig. 8. Left: Probably a solution of a reaction-diffusion equation. One of the earliest (1951–1954) uses of computer graphics in biology. From AMT/K/3/8. Right: Enlargement of AMT/K/3/8 showing individual grid points as pairs of base 32 digits (@ = 0, / = 1, ... V = 30, £ = 31), lowest significant digit first, and contoured on the basis of the most significant digits. © PN Furbank

to the process on a static cylinder: as discussed below touching circles is an adequate model provided the cylinder is allowed to grow in diameter. There is clearly a concern here with the dynamic stability of given phyllotactic patterns and their dependence on the rate of growth of the morphogenetic arena. In identifying the Fibonacci transitions as the probable ones, he is trying to identify reasons why the Hypothesis of Geometrical Phyllotaxis might be true. It may be relevant that quite a large number of the archive sheets (unpublished in Saunders [25]) are concerned with the dynamics and the stability of lattices: see Swinton [27] for more details.

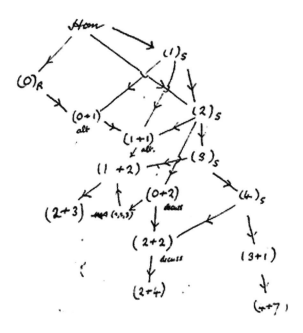

Fig. 9. A bifurcation tree for possible phyllotactic evolutions. From AMT/MAN/4. © PN Furbank

$(0+2) \rightarrow (1+2)$	*An unlikely move*
$(0+2) \rightarrow (2+2)$	*Quite possible, with [indecipherable]*
$(0+2) \rightarrow (2+3)$	*Quite poss. and favored by a / component (e.g. some zygomorphy)*
$(1+1) \rightarrow (2+2)$	*Almost inevitable*
$(2+2) \rightarrow (2+4)$ $(2+2) \rightarrow (2+3)$	*In competition. $(2+2) \rightarrow (2+3)$ is favored by $5 < 6$, but $(2+2) \rightarrow (2+4)$ by $6 = 2+4$. Latter probably favored by fast [unreadable] of conc.*
$(1+2) \rightarrow (2+3)$	*Requires a breakdown process. Can probably only fail by too quick growth, leading to stationary patterns?*

Table 1. From AMT/MAN/M/8. Parastichy transitions annotated by Turing with likelihood of occurrence. © PN Furbank

7.1   Turing's Progress

As Turing's theory progresses from reaction-diffusion to lattices and then to parastichy transitions, the surviving documents becomes sparser and less coherent, so assessments of his progress between 1951 and his death on June 7th 1954 become correspondingly more speculative. There is no concrete archival support for that claim in 1951 to explain fir cone patterns. A possible explanation is that Turing saw clearly that he had a spot generation mechanism

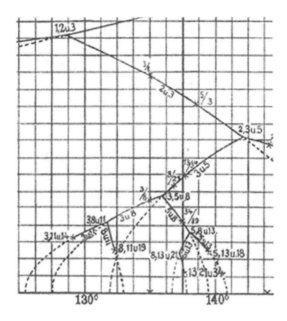

Fig. 10. Possible sphere packing parameters as a function of geometry. Detail from Fig. II of Tafel II of van Iterson [31]. © Kluyver Laboratory for Biotechnology Archives of Delft University (http://www.beijerinck.bt.tudelft.nl); used with permission

and assumed, incorrectly, that this would be sufficient to generate Fibonacci lattices. There is a quote from a Ferranti engineer, from before the summer of 1953, that

> ... with a random starting disturbance the final configuration was displayed on the MkI's monitors. It was always of interest to those of us watching to see what Fibonacci configuration would result. [4, p. 65]

Turing was certainly producing spotty patterns by 1953. It seems plausible that what the engineer saw was actually more similar to those than to explicitly Fibonacci patterns. Support from this comes from a letter of Turing's of May 1953:

> According to the theory I am working on now there is a continuous advance from one pair of parastichy numbers to another, during the growth of a single plant ... You will be inclined to ask how one can move continuously from one integer to another. The reason is this — on any specimen there are different ways in which the parastichy numbers can be reckoned; some are more natural than others. During the growth of a plant the various parastichy numbers come into

prominence at different stages. One can also observe the phenomenon in space (instead of in time) on a sunflower. It is natural to count the outermost florets as say 21+34, but the inner ones might be counted as 8+13. Church is hopelessly confused about it all, and I don't know any really satisfactory account, though I hope to get myself one in about a year's time. [8]

None of the fragmentary material can be reliably dated; some of the probably relevant computer printouts are dated[15] May 24th, but give no year. In addition several years of computing would have generated rather a lot of output, so the fact that all we have is a few sheets, and those not obviously archival records, hints that what we do have is the end of a series of ephemeral documents. So a speculation would date the latest analysis to within weeks of Turing's death. It is then likely that this was what Gandy was referring to when he wrote of hearing of Turing's individual and unmethodical computations. In considering Turing's state of mind at his suicide, Hodges wrote that

Possibly the morphogenetic work had turned out plodding and laborious. It was three years since he had claimed he could account for the fir cone pattern and he had still not achieved it when he died. [10, p. 492]

The morphogenetic work was not plodding: the bifurcation tree of parastichy numbers was new and, as discussed below, on the right lines. The computer simulations, even for the author of *Computable Numbers* (or more relevantly of the first programming manual), must though have been laborious and frustratingly slow to get right. Although he was apparently producing at least some meaningful output, Turing might have become the first to appreciate the sheer craft needed by computational biologists. Probably Turing had not, indeed, accounted for Fibonacci phyllotaxis when he died, but he had got much further, and in the right direction, than he was in 1951.

8   Turing and Modern Approaches to Fibonacci Phyllotaxis

At Turing's death, all of his post 1951 developments remained unpublished. Hoskin, Newman and Gandy tried to prepare what could be prepared for publication, but none of them had any particular expertise in the problem. Bernard Richards might have developed his MSc with Turing (on reaction diffusion systems on a sphere) into this broader question, but moved on to other areas [23]. Unsurprisingly the work remained almost unknown. The only citation I've found before 1992 came at one of Waddington's select meetings

---

[15] Eg MAN/N/7.

on theoretical biology held at Lake Como in the late 1960s, where Scriven described his

> ... treatment, developed from Turing's paper on morphogenesis, based on transport processes to move things from place to another. (Robin Grands [sic] has a Turing manuscript for the nonlinear case treatment). [33, p. 321]

Turing had discussed the morphogenesis work with Wardlaw, who subsequently published several papers explaining and discussing the reaction-diffusion hypothesis (Wardlaw [34, 35]). Wardlaw is reported to have maintained a long interest in Fibonacci phyllotaxis though it seems to have gone unpublished.[16]

The subsequent literature of phyllotaxis is substantial, and I have been primarily guided by the various surveys in Jean and Barabe [12] for this section. Some of these subsequent studies of phyllotaxis concentrated on, and gave more rigorous mathematical theories of, the "static" phyllotactic problem of the classification of lattices, and, for example, the relationship between the divergence angle and the visible opposed parastichies (Adler et al. [1], Jean [11]). A second strand used numerical approaches based on dynamic models in which the appearance of a new point was governed by a rule which was some variant of "far away from previous points." Some even used reaction-diffusion equation to do so (Veen and Lindenmayer [32] were the first to do this).

The earliest, clearest and most undercited explanation for Fibonacci phyllotaxis was developed by Mitchison [18]. Writing in *Science*, Mitchison deftly used the simple touching circles hypothesis for new points appearing in the cylindrical region formed by the apical meristem, and identified the key parastichies as what Jean would later call the visible opposed parastichies, those winding in opposite directions. He then showed that as the diameter of that region slowly changed, the bifurcations of parastichy number would, as Turing saw, replace one of the pair (m, n) with $m < n$ by $m + n$, and that as Turing hypothesised but failed to demonstrate, that the new visible opposed pair would have to be $(n, m+n)$ effectively because the pair $(m, m+n)$ would both wind in the same direction. This general hypothesis about which of two possible choices will be made at each stage, combined with the necessary geometric clarity to see that there are only two choices, and a dynamical system which can generate movement through the bifurcation diagram, is what is needed to explain Fibonacci phyllotaxis.

Through the 1990s other workers exhibited lattice Fibonacci structures experimentally (e.g. Douady and Couder [9, I]) computationally (e.g. Douady and Couder [9, II]) or analytically (e.g. Kunz and Rothen [15]; Levitov [16];

---

[16] E-mail from Vidyanand Nanjundiah, 20th March 2003; Professor Nanjundiah believes Wardlaw talked on this topic at a 1974 Mosbach Colloquium.

Atela et al. [3]). This new generation used a variety of models, but the common feature is that each exhibited a bifurcation tree corresponding to all possible parastichy pairs, and showed, by local analysis at each bifurcation point, that the single branch traversable by continuous variation of a bifurcation parameter was the Fibonacci branch (Fig. 11). This local constraint is what Turing would have called the Hypothesis of Geometrical Phyllotaxis.

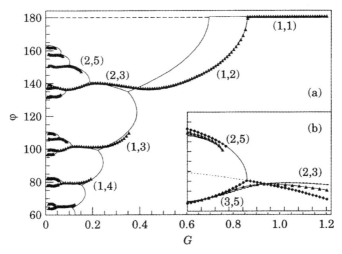

Fig. 11. All possible parastichy pairs can occur, but only one branch is continuously reachable from the simplest symmetric case. Thin lines: theoretically possible parastichies; triangles: observed parastichies found in numerical simulations from various starting conditions. Reprinted from Douady and Couder [9, p. 261], with permission from Elsevier

9   Conclusion

This paper has concentrated on Turing's approach to the specific problem of Fibonacci phyllotaxis, and left largely undiscussed his wider legacy in mathematical biology. There has been a failure of reaction-diffusion models to sustain much favor with developmental biologists, combined with a persistent ability to remain in mathematical accounts of the subject. Fox Keller [13] has recently given an insightful and informed account of this state of affairs. Yet reaction-diffusion models only provide one possible mechanism for the spot creation process. It should not be thought that a failure to exhibit a morphogen is a failure for the generic process of pattern generation that he was beginning to grasp. Despite his confident words in 1951, Turing probably did not have an explanation for Fibonacci phyllotaxis either then or later. But he came close. As we have seen, such patterns can arise naturally as the product of iterated creation processes with simple rules. In his reaction-diffusion systems he had the first and one of the most compelling models mathematical biology has devised for the creation process. In his formulation of the Hypothesis of Geometrical Phyllotaxis, work done by 1954 but not published until 1992, he expressed simple rules adequate for the appearance of Fibonacci pattern. In his last, quite unfinished work he was searching for plausible reasons why those rules might hold, and it seems only in this that he did not succeed. It would take half a lifetime before others, unaware of his full progress, would retrace his steps and finally pass them in pursuit of a rather beautiful theory.

10   Acknowledgments

Andrew Hodges was in several ways the inspiration for this paper and I thank him for his encouragement. I also thank Christof Teuscher for the invitation to Lausanne which finally made this paper take shape. Rebecca Hoyle explained some useful material about lattices, and Nick Hoskin shared his insight. Graeme Mitchison and Vidyanand Nanjundiah made detailed and very helpful comments on late drafts. Scott Hotton was equally helpful and drew my attention to the Turing quote in Coxeter [8].

Successive Modern Archivists at King's College, Michael Halls, Jacqueline Cox and Ros Moad, have been efficient, friendly, and helpful. Jon Agar, at the Manchester National Archive for the History of Computing, helpfully provided photocopies of the holdings, and Barry White of the John Rylands University Library in Manchester also expedited my access to the material. I thank P N Furbank for permission to reproduce material from the Turing estate, and The Turing Digital Archive project for providing access to some scans of that material. For help with copyright issues I am grateful to Lesley Robertson and DJ Mabberley. I have been unable to trace the owner of the copyright of Fig. 1 and 2.

References

1. I. Adler, D. Barabé, and R. V. Jean. A history of the study of phyllotaxis. *Annals of Botany*, 80:231–244, 1997.
2. W. Allaerts. Fifty years after Alan M. Turing. An extraordinary theory of morphogenesis. *Belgian Journal of Zoology*, 133(1):3–14, 1972.
3. P. Atela, C. Golé, and S. Hotton. A dynamical system for plant pattern formation: a rigorous analysis. *Journal of Nonlinear Science*, 12:641–676, 2002.
4. J. M. Bennett. Ferranti recollections (1950–1965). *IEEE Annals of the History of Computing*, 18(3):65, 1996.
5. A. Braun. Vergleichende Untersuchung über die Ordnung der Schuppen an den Tannenzapfen als Einleitung zur Untersuchung der Blattstellungen Über-haupt. *Verhandlung der Kaiserlichen Leopoldinsche-Carolinsched Akademie der Naturforschung*, 15:195–402, 1831.

6. L. Bravais and A. Bravais. Essai sur la disposition des feuilles curvisériées. *Annales des Sciences Naturelles Botanique*, 7 and 8:42–110; 193–221; 11–42, 1837.

7. A. H. Church. *On the Relation of Phyllotaxis to Mechanical Laws*. Williams and Norgate, London, 1904.

8. H. S. M. Coxeter. The role of intermediate convergents in Tait's explanation for phyllotaxis. *Journal of Algebra*, 20:167–172, 1972.

9. S. Douady and Y. Couder. Phyllotaxis as a dynamical self organizing process (part I, II, III). *Journal of Theoretical Biology*, 178:255–274; 275–294; 295–312, 1996.

10. A. Hodges. *Alan Turing: The Enigma*. Vintage, London, 1992.

11. R. V. Jean. *Phyllotaxis: a systematic study in plant morphogenesis*. Cambridge University Press, Cambridge, UK, 1994.

12. R. V. Jean and D. Barabé. *Symmetry in Plants*. World Scientific, 1998.

13. E. Fox Keller. *Making Sense of Life*. Harvard University Press, 2002.

14. A. N. Kolmogorov, I. G. Petrovsky, and N. S. Piskunov. Etude de l'équation de la diffusion avec croissance de la quantité de matière et son application à un problème biologique. *Bulletin Université d'Etat à Moscou (Bjul. Moskowskogo Gos. Univ.), Série Internationale*, Sect. A 1:1–26, 1937.

15. M. Kunz and F. Rothen. Phyllotaxis or the properties of spiral lattices III. An algebraic model of morphogenesis. *J Phys I France*, 2:2131–2172, 1992.

16. L. S. Levitov. Energetic approach to phyllotaxis. *Europhysics Letters*, 14(6):535–539, 1991.

17. H. Meinhardt. *Models of biological pattern formation*. Academic Press, London, UK, 1982.

18. G. J. Mitchison. Phyllotaxis and the Fibonacci series. *Science*, 196:270–275, 1977.

19. J. Murray. *Mathematical Biology*. Springer-Verlag, Berlin Heidelberg New York, 1993.

20. V. Nanjundiah. Alan Turing and 'the chemical basis of morphogenesis'. In T. Sekimura, editor, *Morphogenesis and Pattern Formation in Biological Systems*. Springer-Verlag, Tokyo, Japan, 2003.

21. M. H. A. Newman. Alan Mathison Turing. *Biographical Memoirs of the Royal Society*, 1:253–263, 1955.

22. N. Rashevsky. *Advances and Application of Mathematical Biology*. University of Chicago Press, Chicago, 1940.

23. B. Richards. The Manchester Mark I: The Turing-Richards Era. In *Conference: "Computers in Europe. Past, Present and Future"*, Kiev, October 5–9 1998. http://www.icfcst.kiev.ua/SYMPOSIUM/Proceedings/Richards.pdf.

24. F. J. Richards. The Geometry of Phyllotaxis and its Origin. *Symposium of the Society for Experimental Biology*, 2:217-245, 1948.

25. P. T. Saunders, editor. *Collected Works of A. M. Turing: Morphogenesis*. North-Holland, Amsterdam, 1992.

26. C. F. Schimper. Beschreibung des Symphytum Zeyheri und seiner zwei deutschen Verwandten der *S. buoborum* Schimper und *S. tuberosum*. *Geiger's Magazin für Pharmacie*, 29:1–92, 1831.

27. J. Swinton. Web-site: Turing and morphogenesis. http://www.swintons.net/jonathan/turing.htm, 2003.

28. D. W. Thompson. *On Growth and Form*. Cambridge University Press, Cambridge, UK, 1961.

29. A. M. Turing. The chemical basis of morphogenesis. *Philosophical Transactions of the Royal Society of London*, B 237:37–72, 1952.
30. A. M. Turing. The morphogen theory of phyllotaxis. In Saunders [25].
31. G. van Iterson. *Mathematische und Microscopisch-Anatomische Studien über Blattstellungen, nebst Betraschung über den Schalebau der Milionen*. Gustav-Fischer Verlag, Jena, 1907.
32. A. H. Veen and A. Lindenmayer. Diffusion mechanism for phyllotaxy. *Plant Physiology*, 60:127–139, 1977.
33. C. H. Waddington. *Towards a theoretical biology, An IUBS symposium, Villa Serbelloni, 1968, Volume 3. Drafts*. Aldine, Chicago, 1970.
34. C. W. Wardlaw. A commentary on Turing's diffusion-reaction theory of morphogenesis. *New Phytologist*, 52:40–47, 1953.
35. C. W. Wardlaw. Evidence relating to the diffusion-reaction theory of morphogenesis. *New Phytologist*, 54:39–49, 1954.

Turing's Connectionism

Christof Teuscher

Swiss Federal Institute of Technology, Lausanne, Logic Systems Laboratory

Summary. In a "little known" paper entitled "Intelligent Machinery," Turing had already investigated connectionist models as early as 1948. Unfortunately, his work was dismissed by his employer and went unpublished until 1968, 14 years after his death.

    This chapter provides an overview on all aspects of Turing's unorganized machines and on the extensions proposed by the author. Amazingly, Turing also proposed a sort of "genetical search" to organize the networks, an idea that will be illustrated using a toy pattern classification task.

1 Introduction

Turing's lifelong interest in thinking machines and his concerns in modeling the human mind as machines (see, for example, [23,58]) were probably at the origin of his rather forgotten paper on mechanical intelligence, a report for the National Physical Laboratory entitled "Intelligent Machinery" [66,67], written in 1948. Andrew Hodges writes [30, p. 377]:

> Despite his resignation, and all the embarrassment that surrounded it, he completed a report for the NPL in July and August 1948. Its almost conversational style reflected the discussions he had pursued, many at Bletchley, in advancing the idea of *Intelligent Machinery*. Although nominally the work of his sabbatical year, and written for a hard-line technical establishment, it was really a description of a dream of Bletchley Park, and reviewed in an almost nostalgic way the course of his own life rather than contributing to any practical proposals that the NPL might adopt.

At that time, Alan was employed at the National Physical Laboratory (NPL) in London where he mainly worked on the design of an electronic computer — the *Automatic Computing Engine* (*ACE*). Turing never had great interest in publicizing his ideas, so the paper went unpublished until 1968, 14 years after his death. The report first appeared in a collection edited by Evans and Robertson [20] in 1968, and the following year in the journal *Machine Intelligence* [66].

The "Intelligent Machinery" paper contains a fascinating investigation of different connectionist models, and the paper also pioneered many of the ideas presented in his much more famous philosophical 1950 *Mind* paper [65]. It is amazing that his employer at the National Physical Laboratory, Sir Charles Darwin, grandson of the well-known English naturalist, dismissed the 1948 manuscript as a "schoolboy essay" [1, 22]. In describing networks of artificial neurons connected in a random manner, Turing wrote one of the first manifests of the fields of *artificial intelligence* (although he did not use this term) and *connectionism*.

Turing himself called his networks *unorganized machines*. He basically proposed three types of machines: A-type, B-type, and P-type unorganized machines. A-type and B-type machines are Boolean networks made up of extremely simple, randomly interconnected neurons (NAND gates), each having exactly two inputs. The neurons are synchronized by means of a global clock signal. In comparison to A-type networks, Turing's B-type networks have modifiable interconnections (basically a switch), and thus an external agent can "organize" these machines — by enabling and disabling the connections — to perform a required job. Turing's idea behind the introduction of the B-type networks was to open up the possibility of reinforcing successful and useful links and of cutting useless ones. His deeper motivation was to build structures that allow for learning. The idea of "organizing" an initially random network of neurons and connections is undoubtedly one of the most significant aspects of Turing's "Intelligent Machinery" paper.

Turing, always concerned with universal computation, wrote:

> [...] that with suitable initial conditions they [i.e., B-type machines] will do any required job, given sufficient time and provided the number of units is sufficient. In particular with a B-type unorganized machine with sufficient units one can find initial conditions which will make it into a universal machine with a given storage capacity. [66, p. 15]

The third type of machine — the P-type machine — is not really a connectionist machine but a modified Turing machine without a tape that has two additional inputs: the *pleasure input* and the *pain input*. The idea is that, initially, the machine is largely incomplete and the application of "pleasure" and "punishment" stimuli by an external teacher completes the internal tables.

Astonishingly, Turing was probably also the first person to propose a sort of *genetic algorithm* — which he called *genetical* or *evolutionary search* — to train his unorganized machines:

> There is the genetical or evolutionary search by which a combination of genes is looked for, the criterion being survival value. The remarkable success of this search confirms to some extent the idea that intellectual activity consists mainly of various kinds of search. [66, p. 23]

At that time, Turing was naturally unable to apply genetical search to the optimization of his unorganized machines because of missing computing resources and computing power.

As is commonly known, the birth date and opening shot in neural network research was the 1943 paper by McCulloch and Pitts [41]. Interestingly, Turing makes absolutely no reference to their groundbreaking work. Copeland and Proudfoot write:

> Turing had undoubtedly heard something of the work of McCulloch and Pitts. [...] Turing and McCulloch seem not to have met until 1949. After their meeting Turing spoke dismissively of McCulloch, referring to him as a charlatan. It is an open question whether the work of McCulloch and Pitts had any influence whatsoever on the development of the ideas presented in the 1948 report. [17, p. 372]

McCulloch and Pitts' work was, in fact, itself influenced by Turing's 1937 paper [64].

> Their 1943 article represents the first attempt to apply what they refer to as 'the Turing definition of computability' to the study of neuronal function [41, p. 129]. McCulloch stressed the extent to which his and Pitts' work is indebted to Turing in the course of some autobiographical remarks made during the public discussion of a lecture given by von Neumann in 1948. [17, p. 371]

McCulloch's words were cited by von Neumann as follows:

> I started entirely in the wrong angle ... and it was not until I saw Turing's paper [64] that I began to get going the right way around, and with Pitts' help formulated the required logical calculus. What we thought we were doing (and I think we succeeded fairly well) was treating the brain as a Turing machine [69, p. 319].

McCulloch and Pitts' neurons are slightly more complex than Turing's neurons. They can have as many inputs as they like and provide inhibitory and exhibitory synapses. Like Turing's model, they make, however, no use of weighted connections, but both kinds of neurons may be considered as equivalent in the extended sense as they can be simulated mutually (for more details see [62]).

2 Connectionism and Artificial Neural Networks

From the viewpoint of neural network research, *connectionism* (see for example [11] for a comprehensive overview) is a movement in cognitive science which hopes to explain human intellectual abilities using artificial neural networks.

> There is considerable diversity among connectionist models, but all models are built up of the same basic components: simple processing elements and weighted connections between those elements. [19]

Connectionism has a very long past and one can trace the origin back to the ideas of the early Greek philosopher Aristotle and his ideas on mental associations. However, the birth date and opening shot in neural network research was certainly the 1943 paper by McCulloch and Pitts [41]. They proved that any logical expression could be implemented by an appropriate net of simplified neurons. For this purpose, they assumed that each neuron was binary and had a finite threshold, that each synapse was either excitory or inhibitory and caused a finite delay of one cycle, and that the networks could be constructed with multiple synapses between any pair of nodes.

The *cybernetics* movement and the interest in *self-organizing systems* certainly had an influence on the connectionist movement and vice versa. Important contributions came from Wiener [77] and Ashby [8, 10], but also from McCulloch. Wiener defines cybernetics to be "the science of control and communication in the animal and the machine." The word cybernetics is derived from the Greek *cybernetes*, which means steersman. The cyberneticists wondered if they could make a *thinking machine*, a machine that would be an electrical imitation of the human nervous system. One of their investigations was the creation of the concept of feedback. Astonishingly, Wiener himself, as opposed to Turing, did not believe in machines that can learn.

In the early 1950s, computers, psychology and philosophy tried to join together for the first time. On the one hand, *cognitivism* tried to model the human mind, whereas *connectionism* tried to model the human brain. It was Wesley Clark and Belmont Farley, and not Hebb, who in 1954 first simulated an artificial neural network [16, 21]. In 1956, Rosenblatt unveiled his neuron — the *perceptron* — that was principally based on Hebb's ideas [29]. Hebb suggested that a mass of neurons could learn if their connection strengths change according to some rule — today known as the *Hebbian rule*. His idea was that two neurons that are simultaneously active should develop a degree of interaction higher than neurons whose activities are uncorrelated [54].

Towards the end of the 1960s, the proofs on the limitations of simple perceptrons by Minsky and Papert [44] nearly caused the complete abandonment of connectionism. Later Minsky and Papert [45] further developed the perceptron based on the foundations laid by Rosenblatt [55, 56].

2.1   Artificial Neural Networks

Connectionism, today rather placed under the designation of *artificial neural networks* (*ANN*), has been inspired by the recognition that the human brain processes information in an entirely different way from the classical von Neumann digital computer. The human brain is a highly complex, parallel and nonlinear information processing machine made up of about 10^{11} neurons, where each neuron is connected to 10^3 to 10^4 other neurons.

An artificial neural network is an information processing system that is made up of a number of simple, highly interconnected processing elements — the *neurons* — which process information in parallel. As a simplification, the neuron might be considered as a sort of *detector* that detects the existence of some set of conditions and that responds with a signal that communicates the extent to which those conditions have been met [48].

As an illustration, Fig. 1 shows the structure of an abstract neuron [54]. Each input has an associated weight. The input value x_i is usually multiplied by the weight w_i. The neuron's output is computed with a *primitive function* that can be selected arbitrarily. Thus, "[...] artificial neural networks are nothing but *networks of primitive functions*" [54]. Many different neuron models, primitive functions, network topologies, timing characteristics, etc., have been proposed since the model of McCulloch and Pitts [41] and Turing's unorganized machines.

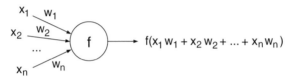

Fig. 1. An abstract neuron

Artificial neural networks can be considered as an alternative approach to the problem of computation, just as the biological neural network is one of many possible solutions to the problem of processing information. Most often, artificial neural networks are "neural" only in the sense that they have been inspired by *neuroscience*, and not necessarily because they are faithful models of biologic neural and cognitive phenomena. For example, connectionists usually do not attempt to explicitly model the variety of different kinds of brain neurons, nor the effects of neurotransmitters and hormones.

Even today, connectionist networks are designed most often by hand and reflect important theoretical claims, experience and knowledge on the part of the modeler. There are very few general rules on how to design connectionist models where the network's topology is often the most important part. Nevertheless, artificial neural networks are a broadly accepted and viable computational model for a wide variety of problems.

2.2 Learning

Learning is the ability of the brain to adapt its behavior to a changing environment. Normally, this ability is used to improve the performance of the system, e.g., of a human being or animal in its environment. As Haykin stated,

"[...] the process of learning is a matter of viewpoint, which makes it all the more difficult to agree on a precise definition of the term" [28]. For example, learning viewed by a psychologist is quite different from learning in a classroom sense. Learning in artificial neural networks can be regarded as a search for parameters (weights, thresholds, switches, etc.) that optimize a predefined function (input-output mapping).

Learning algorithms can in principle be classified into two main classes (see also Fig. 2 and [54]): (1) *supervised learning*, and (2) *unsupervised learning*. The basic difference between these two learning modes concerns whether the network uses an external report (from the supervisor) to modify its performance. Supervised learning basically relies on three things [15]: (1) input, (2) the net's internal dynamics, and (3) an evaluation of its weight-setting job. On the other hand, unsupervised learning relies on two things only: (1) input, and (2) the dynamics of the net.

Unsupervised learning is normally used when, for a given input, the exact output the network should produce is unknown. Supervised learning is further divided into methods that use *reinforcement learning* or *error correction*. Reinforcement learning is used when after each presentation of an input-output example we only know whether the network produces the desired result or not. The weights are updated based on this information (that is, the Boolean values *true* or *false*) so that only the input vector can be used for weight correction. In learning with error correction, the magnitude of an error and the input vector determine the magnitude of the correction to the weights.

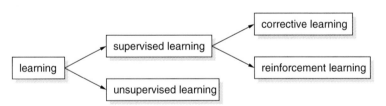

Fig. 2. Classes of learning algorithms. Redrawn from [54]

2.3   Related Work: Threshold, Random and Boolean Networks

This section shall provide a short and certainly incomplete overview on relevant work — published after Turing's 1948 paper — on threshold, random and Boolean networks.

Shortly after Turing, in 1956, Allanson came up with a paper on randomly connected neural networks [5]. The neurons he used were simple, but more complex than McCulloch-Pitts elements. He concluded the paper with the following statement:

The behaviour of the most elementary networks, assuming neurons to be far more simple than they are in reality, is more varied and complex than has normally been assumed. [5]

Large random logical nets made up from McCulloch-Pitts formal threshold neurons were also investigated in 1962 by Smith and Davidson [59] and by Ashby et al. [9].

Rozonoér [57] published a paper on random logical nets in 1968 (originally written in Russian). He analyzed the properties of logical random nets consisting of elements whose properties depend on parameters chosen at random. The connections among the elements were also chosen at random. Rozonoér suggested that:

[...] objects of this type may present a certain interest in connection with physiological models and, possibly, will have direct technical applications in the future. [57]

In 1971, Amari [6] published a paper on the characteristics of randomly connected threshold-element networks with the intention of understanding some aspects of information processing in nervous systems. He showed that two statistical parameters are sufficient to determine the characteristics of networks. In his 1972 paper [7], Amari further investigated the stability of state transitions in logical nets of threshold elements. For example, he showed that a net reaches an equilibrium state within k state transitions if its initial state is located within a distance of the kth stability number from the equilibrium state (in the sense of the Hamming distance).

Aleksander et al. [4] developed a pattern recognition system — called *WISARD* — based on a network without feedback made up of Boolean processing elements; it was later further developed [3]. The WISARD machine consists of a set of n-input Boolean functions whose outputs are summed up. The key observation is that a Boolean function may be implemented as a look-up table in RAM. Aleksander also investigated the stability of randomly interconnected Boolean networks [2].

Martland [38] showed that it is possible to predict the activity of a Boolean network with randomly connected inputs, if the characteristics of the Boolean neurons can be described probabilistically. In a second paper [37], Martland illustrated how the Boolean networks are used to store and retrieve patterns and even pattern sequences auto associatively. He used networks with feedback connections and neurons similar to Aleksander's WISARD neurons. The synchronously operating networks can work in two modes: (1) running mode, and (2) training mode. Martland contributed further work about the behavior of Boolean network: [39, 40].

Crayton C. Walker was one of the first persons to investigate the effect of the system size on the behavior of complex systems, namely networks made up of elements that compute recursive logical functions of two binary inputs and two internal states [71]. Later, he also investigated attractors of sparsely connected Boolean networks [72].

Little work has been done on asynchronous random networks of threshold and Boolean elements. Harvey and Bossomaier [27] have shown that they behave radically differently from the deterministic synchronous version. Earlier, Grondin et al. investigated the asynchronous behaviour of threshold-element networks and the role of deterministic chaos [26]. More recent work about rhythmic and non-rhythmic attractors in asynchronous random Boolean networks came from Di Paolo [49, 50]. Recently, Gershenson published a classification of random Boolean networks [25].

Probably the most important and well-known contributions on random Boolean networks (RBNs), their characteristics and dynamics came from Stuart Kauffman [32–35] and Weisbuch [73, 74]. Stuart Kauffman studied the properties of random Boolean networks as far back as in the late 1960s. To study the behavior of regulatory and complex systems in Nature he used networks of Boolean automata [33]. His studies have revealed surprisingly ordered structures in randomly constructed networks. In particular, the most highly organized behavior appeared to occur in networks where each node receives inputs from two other nodes on average. Astonishingly, Turing had also chosen — very probably unintentionally and without being conscious of it — the number of two inputs for his neurons! Kauffman defined a random NK Boolean network as a network where each element has two possible states of activity and where each of the N elements receives on average K inputs from other elements. Boolean NK networks are examples of strongly disordered systems where both the connections and the Boolean functions are assigned at random. It turned out that these networks exhibit three major regimes of behavior: (1) ordered, (2) complex, and (3) chaotic. In the chaotic regime, the dynamics are very sensitive to initial conditions. The transition region on the edge between order and chaos is the complex regime. It is very interesting that the transition from order to chaos in random Boolean networks occurs either as K decreases to 2 or as other parameters are altered in simple ways. Kauffman wrote [33], "It has now been known for over 20 years that Boolean networks which are entirely random but subject to the simple constraint that each element is directly controlled by $K = 2$ elements spontaneously exhibit very high order." As we will see, Turing's unorganized machines might be considered as a subset of random Boolean networks where $K = 2$ and where the Boolean function is a fixed NAND function for each node.

3   Turing's Unorganized Machines

The term *unorganized machine* was defined by Turing in a rather informal way. He introduced this kind of machine as a machine that is not designed for a precise purpose. Although the *Universal Turing Machine* — as its name suggests — is universal, in the sense that it can simulate any specialized Turing machine (i.e., any computational task), the machine cannot be reconfigured and its architecture cannot be changed during operation. There is no doubt that Turing was inspired by the human nervous system when he conceived unorganized machines. The idea behind these machines (or rather networks) is that they are built up in a random manner and that they are trained (i.e., "organized") by means of an external agent, a "teacher." In the beginning the machines are completely unorganized, comparable to an infant's brain, as Turing suggested. "Then, by applying appropriate interference, mimicking education [...]" [66], the machine can be organized to produce a required behavior.

It is important to note that Turing only proposed three types of unorganized machines in his 1948 paper [66], namely A-type, B-type, and P-type machines. He did not formally distinguish between B-type networks with interfering inputs and networks without interfering inputs. In this chapter the distinction has been made: B-type nets without interfering inputs are still called B-type nets. On the other hand, B-type nets with interfering inputs are called BI-type nets (the "I" stands for interference). The term "BI-type nets" has been introduced by the author. Note that Copeland and Proudfoot [17] as well as Craig Webster[1] use a different nomenclature and that all other machines presented here (and elsewhere) have *no* direct basis in Turing's writings.

3.1   A-Type Unorganized Machines

There is definitely an enormous diversity among contemporary and past connectionist models. However, all architectures share a common characteristic: they are built up of the same basic and usually rather simple components (or processing elements) that are interconnected by weighted or unweighted connections (see also Sect. 2).

Turing's imprecise definition of an *unorganized machine* matches the basic concept of connectionism well:

> We might instead consider what happens when we make up a machine in a comparatively unsystematic way from some kind of standard components. [...] Machines which are largely random in their construction in this way will be called "Unorganized Machines". [66, p. 9]

Turing himself admitted that the same machine might be regarded by one person as organized and by another as unorganized [66, p. 9]. However, he gave an example of a typical unorganized machine to make his ideas clear:

> The machine is made up from a rather large number N of similar units. Each unit has two input terminals, and has an output terminal

---

[1] `http://home.clear.net.nz/pages/cw.`

which can be connected to input terminals of (0 or more) other units. We may imagine that for each integer r, $1 \leq r \leq N$, two numbers $i(r)$ and $j(r)$ are chosen at random from $1...N$ and that we connect the inputs of unit r to the outputs of units $i(r)$ and $j(r)$. All of the units are connected to a central synchronizing unit from which synchronizing pulses are emitted at more or less equal intervals of time. The times when these pulses arrive will be called "moments." Each unit is capable of having two states at each moment. These states may be called 0 and 1. [66, pp. 9–10]

Turing suggested naming machines such as described in the example above A-*type unorganized machines*. In order to let the machine evolve, the binary state of each unit has to be defined as a function of the neighboring unit's state to which it is connected:

The state is determined by the rule that the states of the units from which the input leads come are to be taken at the previous moment, multiplied together and the result subtracted from 1. [66, p. 10]

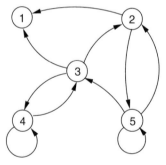

Fig. 3. Example of an A-type unorganized machine built up from five units. The diagram only represents the architecture of the network and has nothing to do with a state-machine diagram. Each node receives an input from exactly two nodes

This kind of machine is the simplest unorganized machine and its architecture, once initialized, cannot be modified. Figure 3 shows a very simple five-unit A-type unorganized machine [66, p. 10]. From an initial internal machine state (machine configuration), that state changes deterministically and will end up in a fixed attractor or in a dynamic attractor with a fixed length. A possible machine state sequence of the machine of Fig. 3 is shown in Table 1. It starts with the values indicated in the t-column. Each time step ($t + 1$, $t + 2$, etc.), synchronized by the global clock generator, changes the internal state of the machine.

node	t	$t+1$	$t+2$	$t+3$	$t+4$	$t+5$	...
1	1	1	0	0	1	0	
2	1	1	1	0	1	0	
3	0	1	1	1	1	1	...
4	0	1	0	1	0	1	
5	1	0	1	0	1	0	

Table 1. Possible state sequence of the above five-unit A-type unorganized machine

As already stated above, an unorganized machine is updated synchronously, in discrete-time steps, and the state of each unit is only determined by the previous value of the two nodes connected as inputs. The transmission of information among neurons requires a unit time delay (one "moment"). Henceforth, *node*, *unit* and *neuron* are synonymous, likewise *unorganized machine* and *artificial neural network*.

In a more formal way, the state of a unit can be defined as follows:

$$
\begin{aligned}
state[t+1] &\leftarrow 1 - x_1[t] \, x_2[t] \\
&\leftarrow NOT(x_1[t] \; AND \; x_2[t]) \\
&\leftarrow \overline{x_1[t] \; AND \; x_2[t]} \\
&\leftarrow x_1[t] \; NAND \; x_2[t] \qquad , x_i \in \{0,1\}
\end{aligned}
\tag{1}
$$

The two inputs are represented by x_1 and x_2; *state* indicates the internal state that will be affected by the node's output at the next time step. The truth table of a two-input NAND function ("not AND") is shown in Table 2.

x_1	x_2	output z
0	0	1
0	1	1
1	0	1
1	1	0

Table 2. Truth table of a two-input NAND function

In terms of a digital system, the primitive unit that Turing describes can be straightforwardly defined as an *edge-triggered D flip-flop* with a preceding two-input NAND gate (Fig. 4a). Figure 4b shows the functional table of a positive-edge-triggered D flip-flop: it samples its D input and changes its Q output only at the rising edge of the controlling clock (CLK) signal [70]. Figure 4c shows a symbolized network node with its two associated inputs x_1, x_2 and its output z, as used by Turing. The central synchronizing unit that emits the pulses is the global clock generator of the digital system. Figure

5 shows the functional table of a primitive Turing unit (node). Considering a node as a digital system has the advantage that complex networks can be built and analyzed by using the well-known techniques of digital systems design.

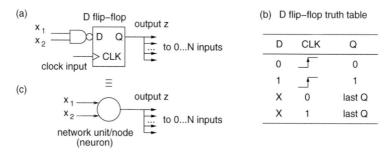

Fig. 4. A primitive Turing unit regarded as a digital system: (a) D flip-flop with a preceding two-input NAND gate; (b) truth table of a positive-edge-triggered D flip-flop; (c) symbolized network unit/node of an unorganized machine. Don't care values are marked with an X

x_0	x_1	D	CLK	output z (Q)
0	0	1	⌐	1
1	0	1	⌐	1
1	0	1	⌐	1
1	1	0	⌐	0
X	X	X	0	last Q
X	X	X	1	last Q

Fig. 5. Functional table of a primitive Turing unit built up from a positive-edge-triggered D flip-flop with a preceding NAND gate. Don't care values are marked with an X

In modern terms, a Turing unorganized machine can be considered as a particular kind of *random Boolean network (RBN)* [33], also called a *random binary recurrent network*. Compared to a modern artificial neural network, e.g., a three-layer feed-forward network, an unorganized machine seems at first glance more akin to the neural structure of the human brain, as the layered structure does not exist. Turing himself suggested that "[...] the cortex of the infant is an unorganized machine, which can be organized by suitable interfering training" [66, p. 16]. This rather naive statement might certainly be questioned since it largely oversimplifies the brain. The human cortex, especially the visual cortex, is one of the most layered regions in the brain [79]. Another plausible counterargument is that there is no global synchronizing signal in biological systems.

3.2   B-Type Unorganized Machines

Turing introduced a second type of machine, called the B-type machine, "[...] not because it is of any great intrinsic importance, but because it will be useful later for illustrative purposes" [66]. However, his idea was clearly to open up the possibility to reinforce successful and useful links and to cut useless ones. His deeper motivation was to build structures that allow for learning.

A B-type unorganized machine is basically an A-type machine where each connection in it has been replaced by a small A-type machine. The network shown in Fig. 6 represents an abbreviation for a B-type link. Note that Turing only used a small square on the link to represent a B-type link. The nodes used within each connection are called *primitive nodes*; the main network nodes might be called *neurons*, although Turing did not use this term. This terminology is only used to distinguish the main nodes from the interconnection nodes.

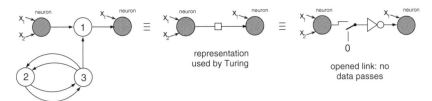

Fig. 6. Abbreviation for a B-type link. A B-type link is a small three-node A-type machine that can be in three different internal states. The representation in the middle was used by Turing. To the right, a symbolic representation of the two states of operation (1) and (2)

The small A-type machine within each interconnection operates as a sort of memory with an internal state that allows control of the interconnection. Depending on its initial internal state, the B-type link can be in three different conditions of operation [66, p. 11]:

1. it may invert the incoming signal (*closed* or *enabled* connection),
2. it may interrupt the incoming signal and put a constant 1 on its output (*opened* or *disabled* connection), or
3. it may act as in (1) and (2) in alternation.

This can be more easily seen when the B-type link is regarded as a sequential digital system [70], as depicted in Fig. 7. Table 3 summarizes the possible internal states of the B-type link.

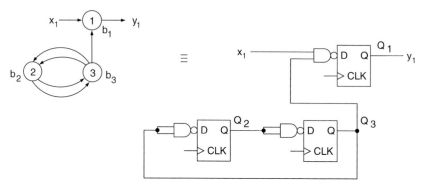

Fig. 7. A B-type link regarded as a sequential digital system

	Q_2	Q_3	Q_2^+	Q_3^+	connection	state	condition
S_0	0	0	1	1	enabled/closed	meta stable	(3)
S_1	0	1	0	1	enabled/closed	stable	(1)
S_2	1	0	1	0	disabled/opened	stable	(2)
S_3	1	1	0	0	disabled/opened	meta stable	(3)

Table 3. Possible states of a B-type link. Q_2 and Q_3 represent the current state of the sequential digital system whereas Q_2^+ and Q_3^+ is the future state, assigned after one clock step

A link is considered as *closed* or *enabled* when it passes the signal from one node to another. On the other hand, a link is considered as *opened* or *disabled* when no signal passes. The B-type link can therefore be considered as a sort of "fixed switch" (see the right-hand part of Fig. 6). Since node (1) (see the left-hand Fig. 6 to the left) is present in each link, signals passed through it get an additional delay of one clock cycle. During operation the internal state of the link cannot be changed. In the next few sections we shall see how this kind of link is used to modify, by means of an external teacher, the internal link's state.

Figure 8 shows a simple five-unit B-type unorganized machine. This machine has been constructed on the basis of the A-type machine of Fig. 3: each direct link of the A-type machine has been replaced by a B-type link, as shown in Fig. 6. It therefore directly follows that a B-type machine can also be considered as an A-type machine. The inverse is of course not valid since it is very unlikely that one gets a B-type machine when randomly constructing an A-type unorganized machine.

3.3 "Education" of Machinery

The unorganized machines described so far did not allow for any interference from the outside world. Once initialized, the machine evolves in a determin-

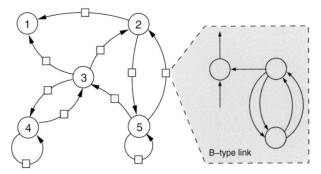

Fig. 8. Example of a B-type unorganized machine built up from five units. Each B-type link is itself a small A-type machine and the entire machine might also be considered as a specifically organized A-type machine

istic manner that only depends on the initial configuration. It would clearly be interesting to modify the configuration and the architecture of a given machine during operation and to adapt it to a certain task. Turing talks about a "[...] machine as being *modifiable*" when it is possible to "[...] alter the behavior of a machine very radically [...]" [66]. He distinguished two kinds of interference with machinery: (1) *screwdriver interference*, and (2) *paper interference*. Screwdriver interference is the extreme form in which parts of the machine are removed and replaced by others. Paper interference consists in the mere communication of information to the machine, which alters its behavior. Turing also spoke about machines that modify themselves, and he classified the operations of a machine into two principal classes: (1) *normal operations*, and (2) *self-modifying operations*. We regard a machine as *unaltered* when only normal operations are performed. An operation is self-modifying when the internal storage of the machine (e.g., the tape of the machine) is altered.

Turing stated that "[i]t would be quite unfair to expect a machine straight from the factory to compete on equal terms with a university graduate" [66]. His vision of machine education is probably best summarized in the following statement:

> If we are trying to produce an intelligent machine, and are following the human model as closely as we can, we should begin with a machine with very little capacity to carry out elaborate operations or to react in a disciplined manner to orders (taking the form of interference). Then by applying appropriate interference, mimicking education, we should hope to modify the machine until it could be relied on to produce definite reactions to certain commands. [66, p. 14]

However, what exactly is meant by "appropriate interference"? Turing wrote further:

[...] that with suitable initial conditions they [e.g., unorganized machines] will do any required job, given sufficient time and provided the number of units is sufficient. In particular with a B-type unorganized machine with sufficient units one can find initial conditions which will make it into a universal machine with a given storage capacity. [66, p. 15]

Unfortunately, Turing did not give a formal proof of this hypothesis because "[...] it lies rather too far outside the main argument." As we shall see in Sect. 3.5, not all unorganized networks can be used to build universal machines.

"Appropriate interference," however, remained a vague expression in Turing's papers and he never really went into details. One of his most concrete unorganized-machine organizing experiments was probably the P-type machine, also called *pleasure-pain system* [66]. In the next section we shall see how a simple B-type network — once initialized, it is no longer modifiable — could be transformed into a machine modifiable, i.e., "trainable," by an external supervisor. So far, the supervisor is not further detailed, but we shall see in Sect. 4 different means of organizing unorganized machines.

3.4   BI-Type Unorganized Machines

With a simple A-type or B-type machine, the possibility of interference that could set it into an appropriate initial configuration has not been arranged for. "However, it is not difficult to think of appropriate methods by which this could be done" [66, p. 15]. Figure 9 shows a possible solution: two additional inputs I_A and I_B have been added to a normal B-type link, as previously presented in Fig. 6. It should now be clear why Turing first introduced the B-type link seen in Sect. 3.2 as, from the beginning, his goal was to construct a sort of switch from identical primitive elements — the nodes or neurons. At a first glance, a B-type link might seem rather complicated for a simple switch. However, it is the simplest possible solution realizable by means of the type of node Turing used.

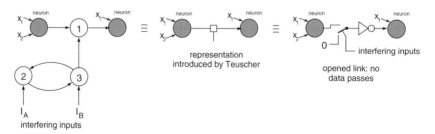

Fig. 9. BI-type link: B-type link with interfering inputs I_A and I_B that allow us to affect the internal state of the interconnection switch

Figure 10 shows the representation of a BI-type link in the form of a sequential digital system. A detailed analysis of this systems is provided in [62, pp. 42–44]. Figure 11 shows the state diagram of the BI-type link, summarizing the internal link's states and the conditions under which these can be changed by means of the two interfering inputs.

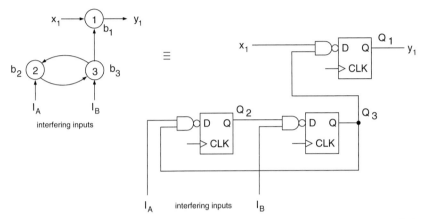

Fig. 10. A BI-type link regarded as a sequential digital system. The interfering inputs I_A and I_B are used to change the internal state of the link

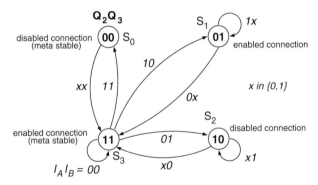

Fig. 11. State diagram of a BI-type link. The internal states $(S_0 \ldots S_3)$ of the link can be changed by applying appropriate signals to I_A and I_B. Q_2 and Q_3 refer to Fig. 10. Don't care values are marked with an X

A BI-type machine (the "I" stands for interference) is defined as a machine where each network connection consists of a link as shown in Fig. 9. By supplying appropriate signals to the *interfering inputs* I_A, I_B — Turing called these signals simply A and B and he used no special name for a B-type machine with interfering inputs — we can get the connection into condition (1) or (2), as explained in Sect. 3.2. By means of this type of link, an external or internal agent can organize an initially random B-type machine by disabling and enabling connections within it: successful and useful links are reinforced (enabled), and useless ones are cut (disabled). Turing wrote, "The process of setting up these initial conditions so that the machine will carry out some particular useful task may be called 'organizing the machine.' 'Organizing' is thus a form of 'modification' " [66, p. 16]. However, organizing a machine should not only be a question of setting up the initial conditions; but it would clearly be interesting to change the link's state *online*, during operation.

3.5   The B-Type Pitfall

As already see in Sect. 3.3, Turing believed that his unorganized machines could be made universal. Unfortunately, he made a rather silly mistake in the definition of his B-type machines that prevents the construction of a universal B-type machine. As is well-known, AND and OR gates cannot be combined to produce all logical functions of n variables. The reader may for example try to implement the negation (NOT) as a combination of AND and OR gates. On the other hand, all logical functions can be implemented on the basis of a network of NAND gates only. One says that NAND gates form a *logical basis*. A network of AND, OR and NOT units is also able to compute all logical functions and hence forms another logical basis. This is easy to prove: it suffices to show that AND, OR and NOT units can be realized by means of NAND units. Other logical bases exist: John von Neumann [68] showed that through a redundant coding of the inputs (each variable is transmitted through two lines) AND and OR units alone can constitute a logical basis as well.

As an illustration, Fig. 12 shows how a Turing node can be built up of NAND gates only. It is important to note that the resulting figure cannot be regarded as an A-type network. A Turing node is not just a NAND gate! The D flip-flop is necessary, otherwise one will get a completely asynchronous system where no central clock orchestrates the node's functioning.

Figure 13a shows the smallest possible functional unit of a B-type network: one node with two B-type links. Suppose now that both links are enabled/closed and thus simply invert the signal. When abstracting from the delay of one clock cycle due to the D flip-flop in the link, the drawing in Fig. 13a can be replaced by the drawing in Fig. 13b. The case when one or both links are disabled/opened (they have a 1 on their output and interrupt the signal) is uninteresting since this corresponds to an interrupted connection. The signals i and j are inverted and fed into the NAND gate of node n. The following equation holds: $d = NAND(NOT(i), NOT(i)) = \overline{\overline{i}\,\overline{j}} = i + j = OR(i,j)$. Therefore, a B-type node together with its two associated input links computes nothing more than the simple logical OR function (Fig. 13c), again, when abstracting from the D flip-flop delays. Since OR gates do not form a logical basis, it is now obvious that not all logical functions can be computed

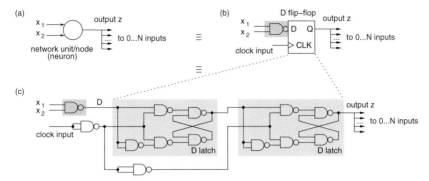

Fig. 12. To illustrate the universality of NAND gates, a Turing node (a), which is a positive-edge-triggered D flip-flop with a preceding NAND gate (b), is built up of NAND gates only (c)

by Turing's B-type machines. To appreciate the difficulty, the reader may attempt to design a B-type network that computes the XOR or the NOT function! Turing's hypothesis stating that "[...] with suitable initial conditions they [i.e., B-type machines] will do any required job, given sufficient time and provided the number of units is sufficient" [66, p. 15] is therefore simply wrong. Note that the same conclusion also applies for BI-type machines; however, it does not apply for A-type machines, as their interconnections do not invert the signals.

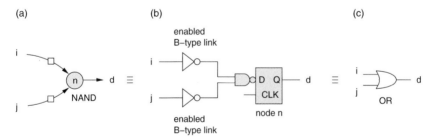

Fig. 13. Functional description of the smallest unit of a B-type network: (a) one node with two B-type links. Drawing (a) can be replaced by drawing (b) when abstracting from the link delays. Drawing (c) shows the resulting function: an OR gate

3.6   TB-Type and TBI-Type Unorganized Machines

One of the simplest remedies to make B-type and BI-type machines universal is to use a new interconnection link that simply inverts the signals again. Figure 14 shows how an additional node can be used as an inverter in series with a normal BI-type link. A TBI-type machine is therefore an A-type machine where each connection has been replaced by an additional A-type node in series with a BI-type link, as presented in Fig. 14. TB-type machines can be built in a similar way by simply omitting the two interfering inputs. The same state diagram as deduced for BI-type links (see Fig. 11) remains valid. The state of the link can be changed by applying appropriate signals to I_A and I_B. The structure of a TBI-type unorganized machine with associated inputs and outputs is depicted in Fig. 15.

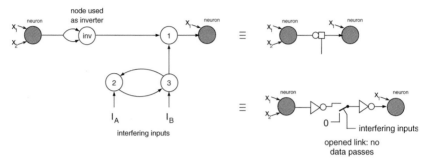

Fig. 14. TBI-type link and symbolic representation proposed by Teuscher [62] with two interfering inputs I_A and I_B that affect the internal state of the interconnection switch. The inverter-node that precedes the switch makes TBI-type networks universal

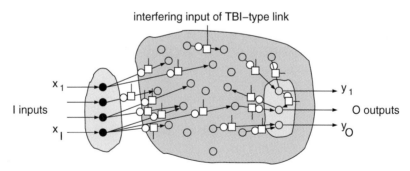

Fig. 15. Structure of a universal TBI-type unorganized machine with inputs and outputs. Each link can be considered as a sort of dynamic switch that is either enabled (the signal passes) or disabled (the signal is interrupted and a 1 is on the link's output). The state of the switch can be modified by means of two interfering inputs I_A and I_B

Note that it is in principle possible to simulate a Turing machine (even a universal Turing machine) on the basis of A-type, TB-type, and TBI-type unorganized networks. This might be very complicated, but it is basically "only" an engineering problem. In the context of the famous *Game of Life*, a similar proposition was made by Berlekamp et al.: "It is possible to construct AND, OR, and NOT gates using the *Game of Life*." [...] "From here on it's just an engineering problem to construct an arbitrarily large finite (and very slow!) computer" [12, p. 841]. This challenge has recently been met: Paul Rendall [51] describes in detail how to build a Turing machine from the patterns of the *Game of Life* (see also [52]). For more information about the implementation of a universal Turing machine based on unorganized networks see [62].

An unorganized Turing network is a completely deterministic machine that, as we have seen, can compute any Boolean function (with the exception of B-type and BI-type nets) as long as enough nodes are available and provided that they are interconnected and initialized in an appropriate way. In their Scientific American article, Copeland and Proudfoot suggested that

> In principle, even a suitable B-type network can compute the uncomputable, provided the activity of the neurons is desynchronized. [18]

With this statement they seem to suggest that a suitable B-type network might be able to "compute" beyond the Turing limit, i.e., compute functions that a Turing machine cannot compute, an ability that is also known under the term *hypercomputation* (see, for example, [60, 63] for an overview). By definition, an uncomputable function is a function that cannot be computed by any algorithm (equivalently, not by any Turing machine). Copeland and Proudfoot did not explicitly state what "desynchronized" means, but, traditionally, asynchronous systems are separated into two main classes: (1) deterministic, and (2) nondeterministic asynchronous systems. There is strictly no reason why an asynchronous but deterministic update scheme applied to a Turing unorganized network would allow it to compute beyond the Turing limit. On the other hand, if the neurons are updated completely randomly (not pseudo randomly), the network will no longer compute any function (as defined in the usual mathematical sense) since it evolves nondeterministically, and different results will be obtained for one and the same input. In summary, neither in the deterministic nor in the nondeterministic case does a network with a modified node updating scheme compute beyond the Turing limit.

4   Organizing Unorganized Machines

Recent years have produced an impressive amount of research on machine learning. Learning generally allows a system to improve its performance by experience. Historically, the earliest forms of supervised learning (learning with a teacher) involved changing the synaptic weights so as to minimize the error of the network. Today, one of the most popular artificial neural network learning techniques is the back-propagation algorithm: the error of the output units is propagated back into the network to yield estimates of how much a given hidden unit contributed to the global output error. The estimates are then used to adjust the synaptic weights. There are currently a large number of learning algorithms used to change the synaptic weights of many kinds of neural networks. A lot of work is also focused on the understanding of the interaction of learning and evolution in biological and artificial systems (see, for example, [46, 47]. From an engineering point of view, the combination of learning and evolution shows that significant advantages can be gained in the adaptation of systems to an environment for a given task.

As we have seen previously, the machines Turing suggested in his 1948 paper can be classified into two different classes:

1. machines that allow interference by some external agent (e.g., BI-type or TBI-type networks), and
2. machines without the possibility of interference (e.g., A-type machines).

Turing networks that allow interference could either be organized by an external agent (supervisor) or by self-modification. Networks that do not allow interference are, once an architecture is chosen and the nodes are initialized, no longer modifiable and will thus evolve deterministically towards an attractor. Training Turing's neural networks is a process where each interconnection is set by means of its interfering inputs into a state that allows the network to perform its desired task. Classical neural networks usually have weighted connections with weights having real values whereas Turing's interconnections have binary switches that allow routing or interrupting of the signal only.

In order to obtain a system that adapts, classifies and generalizes, attractors are necessary. In the absence of any further ordering principle, attractors are generally chaotic. The goal of learning (organizing) is nothing more than the generation of non-chaotic attractors.

Ross Ashby — a major contributor to the field of cybernetics — was one of the first to examine the concept of adaptation as an adaptive walk in the parameter space of a dynamic system towards parameter values that correspond to a dynamic system with "good" attractors [10]. His essential idea was mainly that a subset of the system's internal variables constitutes essential variables that must be maintained within certain bounds. If the system on the attractor keep the essential variables in bounds, change nothing. If the essential variables are not kept in bounds, however, then make a jump change in one of the parameters of the system, which alters the state transitions and hence alters the bassins of attraction. Based on these ideas, Ashby was able to build a crude autopilot, called the homeostat, which learned to hold an airplane in straight and level flight prior to crashing despite being wired at random to the controls.

The idea of adaptation is thus simply a walk in parameter space seeking good attractors. In the case of unorganized TBI-type machines, the only parameters that are modifiable are the switches of the interconnections between the neurons. A learning algorithm has thus to set the internal interconnection switches to values that enable the system to perform a given task — in other words, to tune the attractors of the network.

Turing did not provide any useful application of an unorganized machine to solve a given problem. In the following, we shall see how to apply genetic algorithms to organize unorganized machines — a technique that Turing himself had already mentioned under the term *genetical search* [66, p. 23].

Evolutionary algorithms (EAs) are a collection of methodologies inspired by the principles of biological evolution. The idea of *genetic algorithms* (GAs) was first introduced by John Holland in 1960. On the other hand, *evolutionary artificial neural networks* (EANN) refers to a special class of *artificial neural networks* (ANNs) in which evolution is a fundamental form of adaption in addition to learning (for further information see, for example, [78]). Evolutionary algorithms are used to perform various tasks, such as connection weight training, architecture design, learning rule adaption, input feature selection, connection weight initialization, etc. EANNs can well adapt to an environment as well as to changes in the environment. In a broader sense, EANNs can be regarded as a general framework for adaptive systems, i.e., systems that change their architectures and learning rules appropriately without human intervention.

Yao classified evolution in ANNs into three different levels: (1) connection weights, (2) architectures, and (3) learning rules. The evolution of connection weights is an adaptive and global approach to training, especially in the reinforcement learning and recurrent network learning paradigm, where gradient-based training algorithms often experience great difficulties. The evolution of architectures enables ANNs to adapt their topologies to different tasks without human intervention and thus provides an approach to automatic ANN design, as both ANN connection weights and structures can be evolved. Finally, the evolution of learning rules can be regarded as a process of "learning to learn" in ANNs where the adaption of learning rules is achieved through evolution.

When applying GAs or EAs to neural network design, each genome (also called *string* or *chromosome*) will encode a network structure, the network weights, or both. The encoded network structure is known as a *genotype*. Analogous to with natural genetics, the actual network structure realized by a genotype is called a *phenotype*, the structure that emerges as the result of interpretation of the genotype.

Figure 16 shows a binary BI-type genome that only encodes the interconnection switches. The architecture was initially chosen at random. The genome length (in bits) is equal to the number of links in the network.

As has been shown in [62], it is possible to evolve Turing neural networks to classify different patterns. A simple toy application consisted in classifying into two classes (X and O) the twenty 16×16 dot patterns of Fig. 17 without

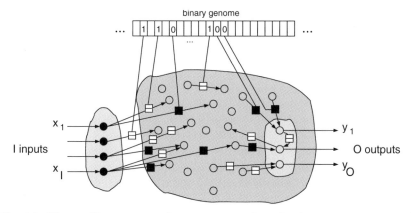

Fig. 16. Binary BI-type network genome encoding the interconnection switches only (1 = enabled, 0 = disabled)

doing any explicit preprocessing. In order to determine the fitness of a network (individual of a GA population), all patterns are presented to the network. The network is set to its initial state (reset all nodes) before presenting a new pattern. The fitness of a network is defined as the number of correctly classified patterns. A *steady-state genetic algorithm*[2] with a strong network encoding scheme (see [42]) was used for this experiment.

A combination of topology evolution (with all connections enabled) and learning (connection modification only) was successful with a TBI-type network. A suitable interconnection topology was evolved during the first 200 generations. The topology was fixed, and only the switches were modified (enabled or disabled) during the second phase. The network was built with 100 nodes. Figure 18 shows the fitness graph obtained with a population of 50 individuals (networks).

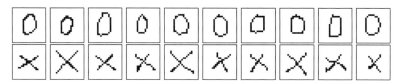

Fig. 17. 16 × 16 dot patterns

---

[2] The steady-state algorithm has no fixed generation intervals; instead there is a continuous flow of individuals meeting, mating and producing offsprings.

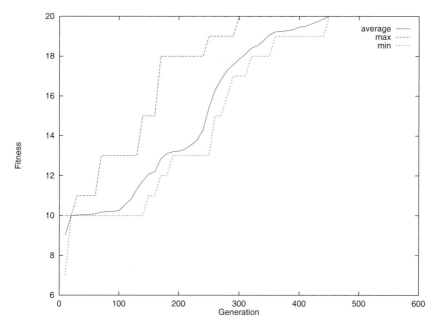

Fig. 18. 16×16 dot pattern classification fitness with a TBI-type network. A network topology where each connection was enabled was first evolved. In a second step, only the connections were enabled or disabled. The population size was set to 50 individuals (networks)

5   Conclusion

The excavation of Turing's neural networks is an investigation into the foundations of connectionism. Today there certainly exist much more powerful neural models and it would be completely useless to compare present pattern classification systems with a system based on Turing's simple NAND gates. Apart from the fact that Turing's unorganized machines can be very efficiently implemented in hardware [62] (allowing at the same time the implementation of very large networks because of the simplicity of the neurons), it is rather difficult to find any real-world application for them. Nevertheless, as the work of Stuart Kauffman and others showed, random Boolean networks are of great interest in the study of self-organizing phenomena, complex dynamics, chaotic behavior, etc. There exist many complex systems of interacting elements (e.g., *gene regulatory networks*) that can be investigated by means of Boolean networks. The complex dynamics of Turing's neural networks is certainly a fascinating domain with many open questions.

The design of intelligent machines is a subject that has already interested philosophers and researchers for a very long time and remains a hot topic. The first 50 years of general computation and AI, which roughly spanned the second half of the twentieth century, were characterized by extravagant swings between giddy overstatement and embarrassing near-paralysis. Today, many a philosopher and humanist thinker is convinced that the quest for *artificial intelligence* (*AI*) or *machine intelligence* has turned out to be a failure since computational approaches do not have the performance, flexibility and reliability of neural information processing systems [76]. At least, no artificial system created so far is able to come close to human-like intelligence, and even the most complex artificial systems created seem much simpler — at least at first glance — than their natural counterparts, although this is much debated. For example, is a large airplane more or less complex than a natural cell? Mankind has certainly constructed extremely impressive computing systems and extremely large and complex networks (e.g., the Internet) that perform operations that no human brain could ever complete. But are these systems really intelligent? All "intelligent" systems constructed so far are in the domain of algorithms and thus in the computational domain of Turing machines. Nobody so far has built a physical machine that is able to perform computations a Turing machine could not perform (despite some hypercomputationalists' claims). Some eminent critics have even argued that a truly intelligent machine cannot be constructed. "At the heart of this disappointment lies the fact that neither AI nor Alife [artificial life] has produced artifacts that could be confused with a living organism for more than an instant" [13] says Rodney Brooks. Something must be wrong! But what? He proposes four possibilities: (1) we might just be getting a few parameters wrong; (2) we might be building models that are below some complexity threshold; (3) perhaps we still lack computing power; or (4) we might be missing something fundamental and currently unimagined in our models of biology.

But what is intelligence and what can intelligent machines do? To most observers, the essence of intelligence is cleverness, a versatility in solving novel problems [14]. Others even tried to count the number of intelligences [24]. All this seems quite hopeless as we will probably never agree on a universal definition of intelligence because it is an open-ended word. Psychology, philosophy, linguistics, computer science, etc., all offer various perspectives and methodologies for studying intelligence.

But above all, the relation between the mind and the brain is still one of the most important questions of life sciences today. Nothing is more familiar than the mind, but it is basically only observable to its owner. Today, most researchers believe that the mind can be reduced to purely biological aspects and that neuroscience will soon have wiped out the traditional dualistic separations of body and mind. However, Descartes' classical body-mind split is experiencing in some way a renaissance in the guise of what might be called the *computer-mind problem*. Today, machines clearly lack common sense and there seems to be no research consensus on how to give it to them. People have started thinking about the possibility that simulating the mind in silicon might be impossible — or at least impossible using today's methods.

Should we first forget about computers and look closer at the gray stuff in the brain, since the actual knowledge of the brain is severely fragmented and many details are still not at all understood?

Alan Kay, a visionary computer scientist and one of the founders of the Xerox Palo Alto Research Center, probably hit the spot with the following statement: "The computer 'revolution' hasn't happened yet!"[3] Kay also postulated that the ideal computer would function like a living organism. Each cell would behave in accord with others to accomplish an end goal, but would also be able to function autonomously. So far so good, but will computer science be enough? The 21st century promises to be the century of bio- and nano-technology [53]. Exciting new technologies, such as self-assembling systems, organic electronics, hybrid electronic-biological machines, etc., and the ever-increasing complexity of systems will require new design and engineering methods. Using the term of philosopher Thomas Kuhn, we might just need a "paradigm shift" [36], something different to anything anyone has already thought of.

References

1. NPL Executive Committee Minutes, 28 September 1948, page 4.
2. I. Aleksander. Random logic nets: Stability and adaptation. *International Journal of Man-Machine Studies*, 5:115–131, 1973.
3. I. Aleksander. From Wisard to Magnus: A family of weightless virtual neural machines. In J. Austin, editor, *RAM-Based Neural Networks*, volume 9 of *Progress in Neural Processing*. World Scientific, February 1998.
4. I. Aleksander, W. V. Thomas, and P. A. Bowden. WISARD: A radical step forward in image recognition. *Sensor Review*, 4:120–124, July 1984.
5. J. T. Allanson. Some properties of randomly connected neural nets. In C. Cherry, editor, *Proceedings of the 3rd London Symposium on Information Theory*, pages 303–313, Butterworths, London, 1956.
6. S. I. Amari. Characteristics of randomly connected threshold-element networks and network systems. *Proceedings of the IEEE*, 59(1):35–47, January 1971.
7. S. I. Amari. Learning patterns and pattern sequences by self-organizing nets of threshold elements. *IEEE Transactions on Computers*, C-21(11):1197–1206, November 1972.
8. W. R. Ashby. *An Introduction to Cybernetics*. Chapman and Hall, London, 1956.
9. W. R. Ashby, H. von Forster, and C. C. Walker. Instability of pulse activity in a net with threshold. *Nature*, 196:561, 1966.
10. W. R. Ashby. *Design for a Brain*. Wiley, New York, 1956.
11. W. Bechtel and A. Abrahamsen. *Connectionism and the Mind. Parallel Processing, Dynamics, and Evolution of Networks*. Blackwell Publishers, Malden, MA, 1st edition, 1991.

---

[3] Talk given at Educom 1998,
http://www.educause.edu/conference/e98/webcast98.html.

12. E. R. Berlekamp, J. H. Conway, and R. K. Guy. *Winning Ways for Your Mathematical Plays*. Volume 2: Games in Particular. Academic Press, London, 1982.

13. R. Brooks. The relationship between matter and life. *Nature*, 409:409–411, January 18, 2001.

14. W. H. Calvin. The emergence of intelligence. *Scientific American: Exploring Intelligence*, 9(4):44–50, 1998.

15. P. S. Churchland and T. J. Sejnowski. *The Computational Brain*. MIT Press, Cambridge, MA, 1992.

16. W. A. Clark and B. G. Farley. Generalisation of pattern recognition in a self-organising system. In *Proceedings of the Western Joint Computer Conference*, pages 86–91, 1955.

17. B. J. Copeland and D. Proudfoot. On Alan Turing's anticipation of connectionism. *Synthese: An International Journal for Epistemology, Methodology and Philosophy of Science*, 108:361–377, 1996.

18. B. J. Copeland and D. Proudfoot. Alan Turing's forgotten ideas in computer science. *Scientific American*, 280(4):76–81, April 1999.

19. J. L. Elman, E. A. Bates, M. H. Johnson, A. Karmiloff-Smith, D. Parisi, and K. Plunkett. *Rethinking Innateness. A Connectionist Perspective on Development*. A Bradford Book, MIT Press, Cambridge, MA; London, UK, 1996.

20. C. R. Evans and A. D. J. Robertson, editors. *Cybernetics: Key Papers*. University Park Press, Baltimore MD and Manchester, London, 1968.

21. B. G. Farley and W. A. Clark. Simulation of self-organising systems by digital computer. *Institute of Radio Engineers Transactions on Information Theory*, 4:76–84, 1954.

22. R. Gandy, 1995. In interview with B. J. Copeland.

23. R. Gandy. Human versus mechanical intelligence. In Millican and Clark [43], Chap. 7, pages 125–136.

24. H. Gardner. A multiplicity of intelligences. *Scientific American: Exploring Intelligence*, 9(4):19–23, 1998.

25. C. Gershenson. Classification of random Boolean networks. In R. K. Standish, M. A. Bedau, and H. A. Abbass, editors, *Artificial Life VIII. Proceedings of the Eighth International Conference on Artificial Life*, Complex Adaptive Systems Series, pages 1–8. A Bradford Book, MIT Press, Cambridge, MA, 2003.

26. R. O. Grondin, W. Porod, C. M. Loeffler, and D. K. Ferry. Synchronous and asynchronous systems of threshold elements. *Biological Cybernetics*, 49:1–7, 1983.

27. I. Harvey and T. Bossomaier. Time out of joint: Attractors in asynchronous random Boolean networks. In P. Husbands and I. Harvey, editors, *Proceedings of the Fourth European Conference on Artificial Life*, pages 67–75. MIT Press, Cambridge, MA, 1997.

28. S. Haykin. *Neural Networks: A Comprehensive Foundation*. Prentice Hall, New Jersey, 2nd edition, 1999.

29. D. Hebb. *The Organization of Behavior*. John Wiley, New York, 1949.

30. A. Hodges. *Alan Turing: The Enigma*. Walker & Company, New York, 2000.

31. D. C. Ince, editor. *Collected Works of A. M. Turing: Mechanical Intelligence*. North-Holland, Amsterdam, 1992.

32. S. A. Kauffman. Metabolic stability and epigenesis in randomly connected genetic nets. *Journal of Theoretical Biology*, 22:437–467, 1968.

33. S. A. Kauffman. *The Origins of Order: Self-Organization and Selection in Evolution.* Oxford University Press, New York; Oxford, 1993.
34. S. A. Kauffman. *At Home in the Universe.* Oxford University Press, New York; Oxford, 1995.
35. S. A. Kauffman. *Investigations.* Oxford University Press, New York; Oxford, 2000.
36. T. S. Kuhn. *The Structure of Scientific Revolutions.* University of Chicago Press, Chicago, 1962.
37. D. Martland. Auto-associative pattern storage using synchronous Boolean networks. In *Proceedings of the First IEEE International Conference on Neural Networks*, volume III, pages 355–366, San Diego, CA, 1987.
38. D. Martland. Behaviour of autonomous, (synchronous) Boolean networks. In *Proceedings of the First IEEE International Conference on Neural Networks*, volume II, pages 243–250, San Diego, CA, 1987.
39. D. Martland. Configurable Boolean networks. In L. Personnaz and G. Dreyfus, editors, *Neural Networks from Models to Applications. Proceedings of the First European Conference on Neural Networks, nEuro'88*, volume III, pages 355–366, IDSET, Paris, June 1988.
40. D. Martland. Dynamic behavior of Boolean networks. In I. Aleksander, editor, *Neural Computing Architectures: The Design of Brain-Like Machines*, Chap. 11, pages 217–235. North Oxford Academic, London, 1989.
41. W. S. McCulloch and W. H. Pitts. A logical calculus of the ideas immanent in neural nets. *Bulletin of Mathematical Biophysics*, 5:115–133, 1943.
42. D. F. Miller, P. M. Todd, and S. U. Hegde. Designing neural networks using genetic algorithms. In J. D. Schaffer, editor, *Third International Conference on Genetic Algorithms*, pages 379–384. Morgan Kaufmann, 1989.
43. P. Millican and A. Clark, editors. *The Legacy of Alan Turing: Machines and Thought*, volume 1. Oxford University Press, New York, 1996.
44. M. L. Minsky. *Computation: Finite and Infinite Machines.* Prentice-Hall, Englewood Cliffs, NJ, 1967.
45. M. L. Minsky and S. Papert. *Perceptron: An Introduction to Computational Geometry.* MIT Press, Cambridge, MA, 1972.
46. S. Nolfi and D. Floreano. Learning and evolution. *Autonomous Robots*, 7(1):89–113, 1999.
47. S. Nolfi and D. Floreano. *Evolutionary Robotics: The Biology, Intelligence, and Technology of Self-Organizing Machines.* MIT Press, Cambridge, MA, 2000.
48. R. C. O'Reilly and Y. Munakata. *Computational Explorations in Cognitive Neuroscience.* A Bradford Book, MIT Press, Cambridge, MA, 2000.
49. E. A. Di Paolo. Searching for rhythms in asynchronous Boolean networks. In M. A. Bedau, J. S. McCaskill, N. H. Packard, and S. Rassmussen, editors, *Proceedings of the Seventh International Conference on Artificial Life*, Reed College, Portland, OR, August 1–6, 2000. A Bradford Book, MIT Press, Cambridge, MA; London, UK.
50. E. A. Di Paolo. Rhythmic and non-rhythmic attractors in asynchronous random Boolean networks. *Biosystems*, 59(3):185–195, 2001.
51. P. Rendell. Turing universality of the Game of Life. In A. Adamatzky, editor, *Collision-Based Computing*, pages 513–539. Springer-Verlag, London, 2002.
52. J.-P. Rennard. Implementation of logical functions in the Game of Life. In A. Adamatzky, editor, *Collision-Based Computing*, pages 491–512. Springer-Verlag, London, 2002.

53. M. C. Roco and W. S. Bainbridge, editors. *Converging Technologies for Improving Human Performance: Nanotechnology, Biotechnology, Information Technology and Cognitive Science*. World Technology Evaluation Center (WTEC), Arlington, Virginia, June 2002. NSF/DOC-sponsored report.

54. R. Rojas. *Neural Networks: A Systematic Introduction*. Springer-Verlag, Berlin, 1996.

55. F. Rosenblatt. The perceptron: A probabilistic model for information storage and organization in the brain. *Psychological Review*, 65:386–408, 1958.

56. F. Rosenblatt. *Principles of Neurodynamics*. Spartan, Washington, DC, 1961.

57. L. I. Rozonoér. Random logical nets I. *Automation and Remote Control*, 5:773–781, 1969. Translation of Avtomatika i Telemekhanika.

58. H. A. Simon. Machine as mind. In Millican and Clark [43], Chap. 5, pages 81–102.

59. D. R. Smith and C. H. Davidson. Maintained activity in neural nets. *Journal of the ACM*, 9:268–279, 1962.

60. M. Stannett. Hypercomputational models. In *this volume*, 2003.

61. A. H. Taub, editor. *Collected Works of John von Neumann*, volume 5. Pergamon Press, Oxford, 1961.

62. C. Teuscher. *Turing's Connectionism. An Investigation of Neural Network Architectures*. Springer-Verlag, London, 2002.

63. C. Teuscher and M. Sipper. Hypercomputation: Hype or computation? *Communications of the ACM*, 45(8):23–24, August 2002.

64. A. M. Turing. On computable numbers, with an application to the Entscheidungsproblem. *Proceedings of the London Mathematical Society*, series 2, 42:230–265, 1936–37. Corrections in *Proceedings of the London Mathematical Society*, 43:544–546, 1937.

65. A. M. Turing. Computing machinery and intelligence. *Mind*, 59(236):433–460, 1950.

66. A. M. Turing. Intelligent machinery. In B. Meltzer and D. Michie, editors, *Machine Intelligence*, volume 5, pages 3–23. Edinburgh University Press, Edinburgh, 1969.

67. A. M. Turing. Intelligent machinery. In Ince [31], pages 107–127.

68. J. von Neumann. Probabilistic logic and the synthesis of reliable organisms from unreliable components. In *Automata Studies*, pages 43–98. Princeton University Press, Princeton, NJ, 1956.

69. J. von Neumann. The NORC and problems in high speed computing. In Taub [61], pages 238–247.

70. J. F. Wakerly. *Digital Design: Principles & Practices*. Prentice Hall International, New Jersey, 3rd edition, 2000.

71. C. C. Walker. Behavior of a class of complex systems: the effect of system size on properties of terminal cycles. *Journal of Cybernetics*, 1(4):55–67, 1971.

72. C. C. Walker. Attractor dominance patterns in sparsely connected Boolean nets. *Physica D*, 45:441–451, 1990.

73. G. Weisbuch. *Dynamique des systèmes complexes: Une introduction aux réseaux d'automates*. InterEditions, France, 1989.

74. G. Weisbuch. *Complex Systems Dynamics: An Introduction to Automata Networks*, volume 2 of *Lecture Notes, Santa Fe Institute, Studies in the Sciences of Complexity*. Addison-Wesley, Redwood City, CA, 1991.

75. S. Wermter, J. Austin, and D. Willshaw, editors. *Emergent Neural Computation Architectures Based on Neuroscience. Towards Neuroscience-Inspired Computing.* Number 2036 in Lecture Notes in Artificial Intelligence (LNAI). Springer-Verlag, Berlin, Heidelberg, 2001.

76. S. Wermter, S. Austin, D. Willshaw, and M. Elshaw. Towards novel neuroscience-inspired computing. In Wermter et al. [75], pages 1–19.

77. N. Wiener. *Cybernetics or Control and Communication in the Animal and Machine.* MIT Press, Cambridge, MA, 1948.

78. X. Yao. Evolving artificial neural networks. *Proceedings of the IEEE,* 87(9):1423–1447, September 1999.

79. M. J. Zigmond, F. E. Bloom, S. C. Landis, J. L. Roberts, and L. R. Squire, editors. *Fundamental Neuroscience.* Academic Press, San Diego, CA, 1999.

List of Contributors

Michael Beeson
Department of Computer Science, San José State University,
1 Washington Square, San José, CA 95003, USA
beeson@cs.sjsu.edu
http://www.mathcs.sjsu.edu/faculty/beeson

Daniela Cerqui
University of Lausanne, Institute of Anthropology and Sociology,
BFSH2, CH-1015 Lausanne, Switzerland
http://wwwpeople.unil.ch/daniela.cerquiducret

B. Jack Copeland
Philosophy Department, University of Canterbury,
Christchurch, New Zealand
jack.copeland@canterbury.ac.nz
http://www.AlanTuring.net

Martin Davis
Professor Emeritus, Courant Institute, NY University,
Visiting Scholar, Mathematics Department, University of California,
Berkeley, CA 94720, USA
martin@eipye.com

Daniel Dennett
Center for Cognitive Studies, Tufts University,
Medford, MA 02155, USA
http://ase.tufts.edu/cogstud

Eugene Eberbach
Computer and Information Science Department,
University of Massachusetts,
North Dartmouth, MA 02747-2300, USA
eeberbach@umassd.edu
http://www.cis.umassd.edu/~eeberbach

Lee A. Gladwin
Archival Services Branch of the Center for Electronic Records (NWME),
The National Archives,
8801 Adelphi Road, College Park, MD 20740-6001, USA
lee.gladwin@nara.gov

Dina Q Goldin
Computer Science & Engineering Department, University of Connecticut,
371 Fairfield Road, Unit 1155, Storrs, CT 06269, USA
dqg@cse.uconn.edu
http://www.cse.uconn.edu/~dqg

Andrew Hodges
Wadham College, University of Oxford,
Parks Road, Oxford OX1 3PN, UK
andrew.hodges@wadh.ox.ac.uk
http://www.turing.org.uk

Douglas Hofstadter
Center for Research on Concepts and Cognition, Indiana University,
510 North Fess Street, Bloomington, IN 47408, USA
http://www.cogsci.indiana.edu

Ray Kurzweil
KurzweilAI.net
info@kurzweilai.net
http://www.kurzweilai.net

Daniel Mange
Swiss Federal Institute of Technology, Lausanne, Logic Systems Laboratory,
EPFL-IC-LSL, CH-1015 Lausanne, Switzerland
daniel.mange@epfl.ch
http://lslwww.epfl.ch

Valeria Patera
TIMOS Teatro Events, Association for the Communication of Science,
Rampa A. Ceriani, 10, I-00165 Rome, Italy
timos@inwind.it

Diane Proudfoot
Philosophy Department, University of Canterbury,
Christchurch, New Zealand
diane.proudfoot@canterbury.ac.nz
http://www.AlanTuring.net

Elisabeth Rakus-Andersson
Blekinge Institute of Technology,
Campus Annebo, S-37179 Karlskrona, Sweden
elisabeth.andersson@bth.se
http://www.bth.se/ihn

Hector Fabio Restrepo
Swiss Federal Institute of Technology, Lausanne, Logic Systems Laboratory,
EPFL-IC-LSL, CH-1015 Lausanne, Switzerland
and
Grupo de Percepción y Sistemas Inteligentes,
Escuela de Ing. Eléctrica y Electrónica,
Universidad del Valle, Cali, Colombia
fabio.restrepo@a3.epfl.ch

Tony Sale
Ex Museums Director, Bletchley Park, UK,
15 Northampton Road, Bromham, Beds MK43 8QB, UK
tsale@qufaro.demon.co.uk
http://www.codesandciphers.org.uk

Helmut Schnelle
Ruhr-Universität Bochum,
44780 Bochum, Germany
helmut.schnelle@ruhr-uni-bochum.de

Mike Stannett
Department of Computer Science, University of Sheffield,
Regent Court, 211 Portobello Street, Sheffield S1 4DP, UK
m.stannett@dcs.shef.ac.uk
http://hypercomputation.net

Jonathan Swinton
E-mail: jonathan@swintons.net
Web-site: http://www.swintons.net/jonathan

Gianluca Tempesti
Swiss Federal Institute of Technology, Lausanne, Logic Systems Laboratory,
EPFL-IC-LSL, CH-1015 Lausanne, Switzerland
gianluca.tempesti@epfl.ch
http://lslwww.epfl.ch/~tempesti

Christof Teuscher
Swiss Federal Institute of Technology, Lausanne, Logic Systems Laboratory,
EPFL-IC-LSL, CH-1015 Lausanne, Switzerland
christof@teuscher.ch
http://www.teuscher.ch/christof

Christopher G. Timpson
The Queen's College, University of Oxford,
High Street, Oxford OX1 4AW, UK
christopher.timpson@queens.ox.ac.uk
http://users.ox.ac.uk/~quee0776

Peter Wegner
Department of Computer Science, Brown University,
Providence, RI 02912, USA
pw@cs.brown.edu
http://www.cs.brown.edu/people/pw

Andrew J. Wells
Department of Social Psychology,
The London School of Economics and Political Science,
Houghton Street, London WC2A 2AE, UK
a.j.wells@lse.ac.uk

Index